Y0-AWK-668

My Awakening

DAVID DUKE

MY AWAKENING

A PATH TO RACIAL UNDERSTANDING

DAVID DUKE

In a time of universal deceit, telling the truth is a revolutionary act
— *George Orwell*

FREE SPEECH PRESS

Free Speech Press
Covington, LA 70434

© 1998 by David Duke. All Rights Reserved. Printed in the United States of America. No part of this book may be reproduced or transmitted by any means, electronic or mechanical, without permission from the publisher. For information:
Free Speech Press P.O. Box 88 Covington, LA 70434. (504) 626-7714

Representative Duke Internet address: www.duke.org

First Edition

Printed in the United States of America

Duke, David

Back of book jacket photo used with the permission of Harry Benson.

Library of Congress Catalog Card Number: 98-86509

ISBN #1-892796-00-7

I dedicate this work to my friend, William Shockley — scientist, inventor, activist and Nobel Prizewinner. Dr. Shockley invented the transistor, laid the foundation of Silicon Valley and thus ushered in the electronic, computer and information age. He not only fought bravely for the truth, his scientific work made its dissemination inevitable. He not only crusaded for our heritage, he gave it the means to victory. Future generations will someday realize his vital role in the struggle for the survival of our people and the securing of our freedom.

TABLE OF CONTENTS

FOREWORD BY GLAYDE WHITNEY
AUTHOR'S PREFACE

PART I: AN AMERICAN SON

1. AN AMERICAN SON 1
2. SANCTUARY IN BOOKS AND NATURE 12
3. SON OF THE SOUTH 22
4. TRANSFORMATION 25

PART II: RACE AND REALITY

5. RACE AND REASON 37
6. A QUESTION OF INTELLIGENCE 45
7. HEREDITY OR ENVIRONMENT? 50
8. RACE AND INTELLIGENCE 58
9. THE ROOTS OF RACIAL DIFFERENCE 71
10. THE EVOLUTION OF RACE 80
11. RACE HISTORY 112
12. RACE AND SOCIETY 131
13. THE RISING TIDE OF COLOR 173
14. SEX AND SOCIETY 191

PART III: THE JEWISH QUESTION

15. THE JEWISH QUESTION 217
16. JEWISH SUPREMACISM 237
17. RACE, CHRISTIANITY AND JUDAISM 256
18. JEWS, COMMUNISM AND CIVIL RIGHTS 274
19. WHO RUNS THE MEDIA? 293

20. JEWISH INFLUENCE IN POLITICS	314
21. THE ROOTS OF ANTI-SEMITISM	327
22. ISRAEL: JEWISH SUPREMACY IN ACTION	367
23. A HOLOCAUST INQUIRY	396
24. THE JEWISH ROLE IN IMMIGRATION	440
25. JEWISH EVOLUTIONARY STRATEGY	450

PART IV: THE FIGHT FOR THE TRUTH

26. MY BEGINNING ACTIVISM	473
27. A LSU "WHITE TIGER"	487
28. AROUND THE WORLD	506
29. MY INDIAN ODYSSEY: A GHOST HAUNTS ME STILL	515
30. A TASTE OF ISRAEL	526
31. GREECE: A CELEBRATION OF LIFE	535
32. TO EUROPE AND HOME	545
33. IN THE BELLY OF THE BEAST	557
34. THE KNIGHTS OF THE KU KLUX KLAN	571
35. THE KLAN RISES	577
36. THE GRAND DRAGON AND THE JEWISH PSYCHE	598
37. DISILLUSIONMENT AND NEW DIRECTIONS	604
38. POLITICAL VICTORY	609
39. AN ARYAN VISION	637
40. WHAT WE MUST DO NOW	669

REFERENCES (ENDNOTES)   675

INDEX   706

Foreword
By Glayde Whitney

Over two hundred years ago, one of the most influential of the social critics that made the Enlightenment was Francois Marie Arouet. Even though Voltaire deemed it prudent to write anonymously under a pen name, still he was imprisoned for eleven months and spent years in exile. One of his most famous quotations became a central pillar of American freedom. It was in 1770 that Voltaire wrote, "Monsieur l'Abbe, I detest what you write, but I would give my life to make it possible for you to continue to write."

Now over two hundred and twenty five years later, with the great good fortune to be living in the "Land of the Free", under the protection of the First Amendment's guarantee of freedom of speech, and with the further umbrella of academic tenure – an institution whose only purpose is to make possible the speaking of truth to power – it is still with great trepidation that I pen this preface.

David Duke has the distinction of being the only American politician to be smeared more viciously than Patrick Buchanan. With the entire establishment against him: press, church and state, he won public office as a state representative. In a bid for Governor, he defeated in the first primary, the sitting republican Governor, and then lined up against a dubious democrat character with a reputation for graft and corruption. Vastly outspent, one of the prime slogans against Duke that appeared on bumper stickers throughout the state was "Vote for the Crook – It's Important." The crook won. Corruption was preferable to political apostasy. Even so, Duke won a landslide of more than 60 percent of European-American voters in each of two statewide races.

Duke has endured an intense and unrelenting smear campaign for decades. Once you read this book you will know why he has been attacked by those of immense power. He challenges all the sacred cows of modern life, and he does so with intelligence and emotion.

Voltaire and David Duke are warriors in a conflict that is as old as civilization. The Harvard biologist, historian and philosopher of science Ernst Mayr suggested that as human populations evolve from savagery to civilization their approach to knowledge takes one or another of two paths. One approach leads to modern rationality, including the values of post-Enlightenment free societies and the questing after truth that forms the basis of modern science. The other approach leads to totalitarianism based in dogmatic authority. The direction toward freedom, traceable back to the philosophies of ancient Greece, is unique to Western European Civilization.

The direction toward rationality and science traces to the first recorded Western philosopher, Thales of Miletus (c.636 – c. 546 BC). Thales maintained that to gain knowledge and understanding one should start with naturalistic observation, that is, descriptions of events as they exist in the real world. We should then seek natural explanations for natural phenomenon. A third major position was that it is acceptable, even encouraged, to question existing explanations, to entertain diverse viewpoints, to have the freedom to use criticism in order to improve knowledge and theories. These three principles, which trace to the beginnings of recorded Western thought, capture the essence of modern freedom and science. Alas, from Thales' time down to the David Duke of today, this approach has been a minority position under constant attack.

The road to dogma starts with assertions of knowledge based in authority. Marxian economics, Boasian egalitarianism, and Freudian psychoanalytic theory equally well illustrate dogmatic belief systems. Not only are criticism and questioning not encouraged, they are condemned. The questioner is shunned, outcast, outlawed and labeled a heretic, hater and evil sinner. David Duke is a questioner.

It is clear from David Duke's autobiography that he was an intelligent, indeed a precocious child, and much of a free-thinker from the beginning. An impartial clinical psychologist might detect elements of an oppositional personality in his self-description. An essential feature of such a child is a provocative opposition to authority figures. When told how things are, such a child asks "why" a bit more than is usual. If bright enough, the child might take great delight in checking the facts for himself. Rare is the student that digs in the library for the original sources. DSM-3, a now somewhat dated psychiatric diagnostic manual says, "The most striking feature is the persistence of the oppositional attitude even when it is destructive to the interests and well-being of the child or adolescent." Seekers of truth, shifters of paradigms, innovators in civilization, have shared such traits, and have often failed to outgrow them, whether they be Socrates, Thomas Aquinas, Martin Luther, Galileo Galilei, Isaac Newton, William Shockley or David Duke.

It is easy to imagine how a brilliant child from a traditional Christian background, but with oppositional tendencies, might be profoundly affected by growing up in a southern city through the turmoil of the civil rights movement. Starting from an unquestioning acceptance of Christian and American ideals [and still a believer in both, I should add] as learned from home, church, school, and media: equality for all, loving brotherhood of all men, turn-the-other-cheek, the sermon-on-the-mount, and do unto others. Imagine the life-wrenching shock for such a precocious child who relates intellectually, as well as with deep emotion, to the inscription on the Jefferson Monument, "*Nothing is more certainly written in the book of fate than that these people [Negroes] are to be free.*", but then uncovers for himself the full context of the quote, the next sentence from which was taken the inscription: "*Nor is it less certain that the two races, equally free, cannot live in the same government.*" But David Duke tells this tale of his awakening much better than I can paraphrase.

David Duke's awakening is presented here in three interconnected major themes of his discoveries of honest truths that are politically incorrect. One of his honest truths is that from a thorough immersion in modern science he became convinced that racial egalitarianism is the scientific equivalent of the flat-Earth theory. He rejects the smear of "racist" while maintaining that the true data are very different from those that most of us have been led to believe. A second of his sets of honest truths is that a powerful and cohesive self-serving group has promoted a dishonest and hypocritical version of egalitarianism that is inimical to the interests of Western Christian Civilization. He rejects the smear of "anti-Semite" while maintaining that the true data are very different from those that most of us have encountered through the mass media.

In a style to be expected from a sincere oppositional who is truth-telling as best he can, David Duke's ultimate challenge to his reader not to take his word for it, but to check it out for yourself. Toward that end he provides on the order of a thousand references and footnotes. The gauntlet is clearly thrown down. Here is the evidence, here are the sources: *Check it out for yourself.*

It is a powerful approach. It is the approach of Western Civilization traceable right back to Thales. No amount of dogmatic name-calling, no smear, no hate-speech laws, no internet filters, no criminalization of history, not even total quarantine and book-banning, can stand against a simple guide to where the truth is to be found. If read by his fellow citizens David Duke's story of his own *awakening* might *awaken* them as well, and in so doing rattle civilization to its very core.

How is it that I came to write this preface to a book written by a man that I have never met in person? David Duke tells us how he dreamed to become a scientist and instead, growing in the turbulent urban south, he was diverted into a life of politics. I, on the other hand, had the fortune, good or bad, to be born in Montana and raised in Minnesota. I was fully adult before I had many real encounters with racial or ethnic diversity and have never been into politics. Fascinated since childhood by animal diversity, and also an avid birdwatcher, I trained toward a scientific career at the interface of evolution, genetics, and psychology. Raised in Minnesota I became a Hubert Humphrey liberal – and remain one to this day. Equality of opportunity for each individual, equal treatment before the law, in an orderly society with rule-of-law, these are ideals I treasure.

The social disruptions of the middle and late 1960s that formed David Duke were never a real part of my personal experience. At Alamogordo New Mexico, just down the road from the Trinity Site and on the edge of the White Sands Missile Range, we were helping to reach for the Moon. Research preparatory for the Apollo Missions was a heady assignment for a young scientist. By the time I returned to civilian life and to a position as a faculty member at a state university, the worst of the troubled times were over.

One of my favorite senior colleagues, a mentor at my new university, cautioned that although I was into behavior genetics, it would be prudent to avoid that "human business." He said that being at a southern university I would have no credibility, and that none of us needed the flak. He had once published a scholarly paper dealing with the tested intelligence of black and white school children – and had been savaged by vicious *ad hominem* attacks and personal threats. Those were hassles that I did not need, especially since there were so many other intellectually challenging research opportunities. It was easy to climb into the ivory tower of basic research.

Over the years I did my research and followed that of others, raised a family and had little or no interest in politics. Still, there were discussions of some pretty silly things. Like blatant racial discrimination under the label of "affirmative action." Embarrassingly unprepared and incapable people being cajoled into situations for which they were unsuitable while competent potentials were being turned away. As time went on, the public rhetoric became ever more distant from the scientific realities. The technical questions had always been why -- what were the reasons for the large intellectual gap between blacks and whites? As the hard scientific data came in, it became more certain that genetic differences (heredity) played a large role in the discrepancy. But in public it became politically incorrect to even acknowledge that there was a difference.

It was disturbing that some of my respected scientific colleagues seemed to be less than candid. The private discussions at scientific meetings became weirdly disjointed from public pronouncements. Simply, scientists lied by omission and by commission. Some had a frankly elitist attitude, that "the masses" could not be trusted with the truth. The famous Richard Lewontin is quoted as having written "Sometimes even scientists tell conscious lies to make a point." He should know. Honesty had always been to me the first and the highest of scientific requirements. But some of my colleagues in science had a different agenda.

Completely separately from David Duke, my inquiries led to essentially the same places and some of the same conclusions, that he spells out in this book.

My own "awakening" involved a second major wake-up call on that most forbidden of subjects. It resulted from a close friendship with an extended family, Americans of Christian Lebanese ancestry. Through long talks with "Uncle Mike", a kindly physician who was the family patriarch, I learned of the naked aggression of Israel against the Palestinian people. Slowly, my eyes were opened to an international racism that was at least as pernicious as that alleged against David Duke. At the same time, I discovered that Duke's "racism" was not born of hatred, but of science and of history.

At the present time in Western science, I believe that an important distinction must be acknowledged between individuals and Judaism as a group endeavor. As individuals, scientists of Jewish ancestry cover the entire spectrum of interpretations and approaches to race and heredity. To mention just two individuals, the late Richard Herrnstein was a co-author of *The Bell Curve*, (1994), while Michael Levin, author of *Why Race Matters*, (1997), has withstood much wraith for his truth telling. From personal experience in academia, it is sometimes hard to believe that Jews constitute only 2% or 3% of the general population. Individuals of Jewish ancestry are vastly overrepresented in the ranks of highly successful scientists. They are among my best students and closest friends.

Organized Jewry, on the other hand, dogmatically attempts to keep the general population from awareness of the findings of modern science. The Anti-Defamation League [ADL] of B'nai B'rith [BB] was founded in 1913 from its father organization the B'nai B'rith. The B'nai B'rith promoted socialist and egalitarian revolution. It was founded in the decade of *The Communist Manifesto* amid widespread unrest throughout Europe. From that time Jewish chauvinism, communism and Zionism were all intertwined.

The confounding and confusion of Semitism and socialism that occurred at the beginning continues to the present day. Anti-liberalism is apparently often confused with anti-Semitism within the present-day Jewish community. To illustrate, in the newsletter *Details* for July 1997, published by "The Jewish Policy Center", Rabbi Daniel Lapin explained why he thought anti-Semitism and Jewish liberalism are intertwined: "They realize that liberalism...is largely responsible for the fact that life in America has become more squalid, more expensive and more dangerous over the past 30 years. Thus, many decent Americans are disturbed by Jewish support for liberalism and liberal causes. Though virtually all Americans are too decent to let this blossom into full-fledged anti-Semitism, there is always that threat. We can 'tweak the lion's tail' only so long."(p.1-2).

Early on, Jewish intellectual leaders boasted of the racial distinctiveness and superiority of the Jewish people. Only later did the strange strategy evolve that Jewish distinctiveness could only be preserved by eliminating distinctiveness among non-Jews. Franz Boas and other Jewish intellectuals believed that the Jewish people would only be safe with the elimination of all vestiges of racism among the Gentiles. From there, it was a short step to using other groups in furtherance of the Jewish agenda, such as founding the NAACP, and adopting cryptic "behind the scenes" financing and control of Black and Gentile front organizations. David Duke provides many of the references, in the Jewish triumphalist literature.

The Anti-Defamation League may have been founded to counter bigotry, sadly it has transformed into one of the most bigoted of organizations. Wielding the two mega-smears of "racist" and "anti-Semitic" it attacks whomsoever it dislikes. Just as Peter Brimelow (in *Alien Nation*) pointed out that the new definition of "racist" is anyone who is winning an argument with a liberal," so an "anti-Semite" has become anyone out of favor with the ADL.

One of the most chilling documents that I have encountered in many years is *B'NAI B'RITH Reports and Analyses* (available on the Internet at bnaibrith.org). It goes on for page after page listing legislative initiatives in many countries to criminalize- *whatever they dislike*! Much of what Voltaire and the American First Amendment is dedicated to, as well as Thales' approach to civilization, are completely alien to this mindset. Dislike a book (there are quite a few titles that are disliked), criminalize its distribution. Go to jail for possession. Speech – say something insensitive or unpopular, go to jail and pay a fine. Newspaper-shut it down, go to jail, pay a fine, for possession or distribution. Question a "sacred truth" of History –don't you dare, go to jail, pay a fine, lose your passport, no visa. Distasteful symbols, flags, jewelry – go to jail, etc. etc. What they have not yet managed to have outlawed, they say they are now "monitoring." And these same people are avidly pushing for federalization of newly invented crimes and "hate offenses" in the United States. The activities listed in this document, if nothing else, would induce me to heartily recommend the book written by David Duke.

As we approach the beginning of the third millennium from the birth of Jesus, western society is poised on a cusp. We are toying with a path that leads to another Dark Age; a possible millennium of censorship, speech codes and hate thought laws. Blasphemers, free thinkers and honest people could be suppressed. Thought-crime and hate-speech law advocates are substituting ideological suppression for honest science. We could fall into another totalitarian Dark Age, or rational freedom could prevail. The balance of past history does not encourage blind optimism. Alternatively, the path from ancient Greek philosophy to freedom and modern science, which is unique to Western Christian Civilization, could lead to a greater Golden Age.

As a scientist who specializes in the field of Behavioral Genetics, I must tell you that I have gone over David Duke's considerable data on genetics and race and find it in line with the latest scientific discoveries and knowledge in this area. His grasp of this area of research is quite remarkable for having a degree in History rather a doctorate in the biological disciplines. As to the meaning he poses for the racial truth he tells, politics is his realm, not mine. But, it is fascinating to see how his political life has been an outgrowth of an intimate relationship with the natural world as a child, and then later his study of it in scientific books and extracts.

As I read this book and prepared for this preface, one word kept coming to my mind: *powerful*. Indeed, even though I know that contributing this preface could lead to some discomfort from those who hate free speech, it seemed to me that this book was more than just a book. It is a painstakingly documented, academically excellent work of socio-biological-political history that has the potential to raise tremendous controversy and change the very course of history. *My Awakening* has the prospect of becoming to the race issue, what *Wealth of Nations* is to capitalism or *Das Kapital* is to Marxism. Moreover, David Duke's notoriety gives this book the chance to be read. It will not easily be hidden away.

What of politics, and what of David Duke? About the path of politics from the cusp on which we are perched, I cannot say. Scientists have never been particularly adept at politics. History could come to treat David Duke in many different ways. Perhaps he will be remembered as a Moses-like prophet who upon awakening them, led his people out of bondage. Perhaps he will be remembered not at all: down George Orwell's memory hole as civilization sinks into another Dark Age. Perhaps he will be remembered as a John-the-Baptist, a wee bit too early, one who awakened his people and paved the way for the future.

"Stand Up and Tell the Truth," a line from this book, could just as well be the title of this remarkable autobiography from a remarkable man. He has had the courage to live it and to write it, to lay down on paper the results of a lifetime of study, reflection and activism. We can only hope that many of his fellow citizens will have the courage to read and discuss it.

Glayde Whitney
Tallahassee
August 1998

Glayde Whitney is a past president of the Behavior Genetics Association

Author's Preface

My Awakening is a thesis in autobiographical form. It is the story of my path to racial understanding that began when I was a young man in the middle 1960s. Most of my fundamental understanding was in place by the end of that decade, but my racial knowledge has grown much deeper over the last 30 years. Since the 1960s, much new scientific and political material has become available. In recounting my path to understanding, I am not trying to give the reader the impression that all the materials or studies I cite were available in the 1960s. I weave into this narrative contemporary data and documentation so the reader has the benefit of the latest information. Also, for reasons of coherence and organization, Part II and III focus on one primary area of discovery at a time, while in life, the acquisition of knowledge is not so neatly compartmentalized.

Also, I would be remiss not to say that when I write "I learned" or "I discovered" — I take no credit for original research, for my education on these subjects came from innumerable authors and their books and articles. I am in debt to them as well as to my many supporters and friends who have educated me with the insights and knowledge acquired in their own awakening. I assemble, organize, analyze and comment on materials collected by scholars and writers from ancient times to the present.

This book may well challenge many currently held beliefs by the reader. That is why I include many direct quotations from major authorities rather than merely allude to them. They speak far more powerfully than my own commentary, so I indent them and place them in bold type. In regard to the ever-controversial Jewish issue, I purposely and primarily use quotes and documents from Jewish sources. I encourage you to review them carefully, for they will amaze you.

In recounting my awakening on matters of race, I offer you a view of the real world which has been obscured by the media. May it constitute a scientific and natural basis for the survival of our people.

David Duke

PART I
AN AMERICAN SON

Chapter 1:
An American Son

I was born in the nation our European forefathers built.

As a young man, I came to love that heritage so much that I devoted my life to preserving it.

After twenty-five years of activism, I was elected to the Louisiana House of Representatives following the most controversial campaign for a state legislative seat in American history.

I had just been sworn in. As I approached my desk on the house floor, two legislative pages delivered postal bins overflowing with mail. They held over 6,000 letters from well-wishers from all over the United States and the world. A postcard sat conspicuously atop a short stack of mail on my desk. It bore a cancellation stamp from New York City. Somehow, it made its way to my desk at the Louisiana Capitol addressed only: DUKE — LOUISIANA.

The hand-written note on the back simply said,
> THANK YOU FOR SPEAKING FOR EVERY
> POLITICALLY-INCORRECT EUROPEAN AMERICAN.

The huge media coverage heaped upon me came not from the minor importance of a state house seat, but because the press was in horror that a man who dared to promote the preservation and rights of the European American could be elected to public office. In reality it wasn't even my Klan past that bothered them, it was my *present agenda*. Senator Robert Byrd of West Virginia also was a former Klansman, but he became a liberal Democrat — so his past became just a footnote — mine became a headline. I knew I would never find redemption in the media, because I would not recant my views on race. However, I knew that thousands of people voted for me because I said out loud what they felt in their hearts. I also knew that a lot of goodwill toward me came because I arrived at my legislative seat much like the postcard I had just read — against tremendous odds.

As the stir in the chamber subsided, I pondered the long road that led me to become America's most notorious "racist" and its best known state legislator. I thought about my implausible story when my phone light blinked. It was the capitol switchboard operator asking if I would take a call from Mrs. Cindy Reed, from Gentilly Woods (the New Orleans neighborhood where I grew up). Suddenly, I realized that she was the family friend who often baby-sat me. Cindy told me that she was proud of me, and we talked for a few moments reminiscing about the old neighborhood, and then she said something that especially touched me. She commented, "Pinky always used to say you'd be president someday."

Pinky, I thought, *She's been gone a long time.* Pinky was my family's Black housekeeper who seemed like part of our family. She cared for me as if I were her own son, prepared many of my meals, mended my wounds, and listened to my dreams. I was 11 years old when she died, and thinking about her now warmed my heart.

So how did it happen, that despite my childhood love for Pinky, I became a spokesman today for what the postcard sender had called the "politically-incorrect European American?" As my life and thoughts unfold in this book, you will find out why. I will lay bare the formative parts of my life — the experiences that stand out in my memories, and the search for truth that led to *my awakening*.

In telling my story I will challenge the vital premises of the establishment and roast some sacred cows. I will anger those who worship fashion rather than independent thought. Hopefully, a few of the more open-minded will pause to think. In this book I offer an eye-opening view of the world today, a revolutionary view to be sure. I also offer my evolutionary vision of the *new* world that shall be created *tomorrow*.

My Beginning

Aware of the power of heredity and genetics that shape us, the story of an individual life cannot truly begin with his birth — or even his conception. The genes that made me and every other European American were forged during the ice ages and passed down for thousands of unbroken generations. There is no room for ego, for every trait, every sinew, every chromosome, every gene and every molecule, both good and bad in me, has been bequeathed to me from thousands of forebears who had each struggled successfully for life. Each generation survived at least long enough to pass their genes to the next. Ultimately, over eons of time, my forefathers and foremothers passed on their heritage to my own mother and father. Although discouraged by her doctor, my mother fought hard to give me life, determined to add another life to that unbroken chain.

Mother often told me the circumstances of my birth. After difficulty bearing my sister, Dotti, and after two subsequent miscarriages, her doctor insisted that she could have no more children. He said that if by some misfortune she were to become pregnant that the baby could never survive to term. My mother would not listen to Doctor Wilson. She already had a five-year-old daughter, Dotti; now she wanted a son, and my Father hoped for one as well to carry on the Duke name. They kept trying.

When my parents were both 38-years-old, their perseverance was rewarded when Mother became pregnant. Mother knew this was her last chance to have another child, and she followed a regimen of special diets, short exercise and bed rest, while my grandmother helped her and prayed devoutly. My mother often told me that Grandmother called the unborn child her "prayer baby" and was sure I would grow up to be a preacher. But she had no idea what kind of preacher destiny had in mind. After almost six months in bed, many prayers and much difficulty, Mother gave birth to me by Cesarean section at 11:36 a.m. on July 1, 1950, at St. John's Hospital in Tulsa, Oklahoma.

It interests me how so many people place importance on the date of their birth and read their horoscopes religiously. Long before people understood genetics, they supposed that the arrangement of the sun, moon, and stars at the moment of birth determined the destiny of the child. If the planets do have an impact, I think it occurs at the instant of conception rather than at the time of birth. Just as the moon and heavens determine the tide, perhaps they could influence the meeting of egg and sperm. Ultimately, of course, it is not the positions of the stars that are important but what two sets of genes come together at conception. Every day science shows us that the abilities and even the behavior of that new life are greatly influenced by the genetic code it carries. Our genetic makeup combined with our life experiences make us who we are.

When I consider the selection that occurs over the thousands of generations leading up to each birth, I realize how precious genealogy is — and how fragile. If just one of my direct antecedents, over thousands of generations back, would have chosen a different spouse or simply made love at a different moment in time, my genetic code

With my mother and my sister Dotti

4 My Awakening

Visiting Buckingham Palace

Our family's Christmas card: 1954

would be different making me an entirely different person. It interests me that our sex-obsessed society dwells on the act itself, failing to understand that it is the choice of mate that is truly important, for that choice influences not only the quality of one's own life, but the character of generations to come.

I was born very near the geographic center of America, of parents who had been born in the Kansas of the north and the Missouri of the south. My roots reach deep into the very genesis of America. My father's grandmother, Maria Hedger, had William Bradford as an ancestor, a leader of the Plymouth Settlement. As I grew up in the suburbs of New Orleans, where my family lived from the time I was five, I was reluctant to divulge the Yankee part of my heritage to my friends. My schoolmates and I identified with everything Southern (as I still do). I couldn't admit to having had a family member, even a remote ancestor, who hailed from the state of Massachusetts. That was just too far north.

Other than the illustrious personality of William Bradford, my early antecedents were undistinguished folk who tilled the Earth. My mother's folk were farmers and ranchers. Their families farmed the soil from Plymouth, across the Midwest, and down into Missouri and

Kansas. Another branch of the family came to America from Scotland in the early 1800s. They, too, cultivated the Earth.

As I got older, it became obvious to my parents that I was not a preacher. I was too quiet for the pulpit. So Father encouraged me to read. Starting when I was three-and-a-half, he insisted that I sit and read for at least one hour every day. I rebelled at first. But once the habit took hold, I excitedly devoured my books. Some of my earliest recollections are of sitting in my little red rocking chair in our house at Kawlaan 6 in Den Hague, Netherlands, reading the poems and stories of *Aesop's Fables*. Often I would get so involved in the story that I would remain in my rocker until Mother called me to come, "right this minute," to the dinner table.

Father held a job as a petroleum engineer with Shell Oil Company, and when I was four years old, Shell transferred him and his little family to Den Hague. There I attended a Dutch kindergarten. Father and Mother recall that after a month in the Dutch-speaking school, when asked if I had understood the lessons, I announced to my parents, "They speak English here." At that young age the Dutch language came so easily that I could slip in and out of Dutch and English. My parents sometimes had to ask me to repeat myself in English, and I thought it fun knowing more Dutch than they did.

In the 1950s, Holland was a travel poster — a land of bicycles and festivals and wooden clogs, with windmills and tulips everywhere. The canals and the wooden barges punctuate my memories, as does

With the family in the Swiss Alps

Our Dutch Housekeeper Ellen

6 MY AWAKENING

the man with his three-wheeled bicycle who traveled the streets selling bread and milk and tasty fresh cheese calling in a deep voice: "Brood!" "Melken!" In keeping with the spirit of the place, Mother bought me a pair of wooden shoes, which I wore around our small yard until my toes ached and I kicked them off in favor of bare feet.

My parents hired a Dutch housekeeper named Ellen, a diligent and caring woman whom I loved dearly. She would take me on long walks during which she would tell me, in broken English or simplified Dutch, the legends and stories that the Dutch shared with their children.

On practically every weekend, and sometimes on longer trips, my family would pile into our Nash Rambler automobile and head for adventures somewhere in Europe. My father and I climbed the tower of Pisa in Italy, castles in Scotland, and we walked on glaciers in Austria and Switzerland. We even went into the Russian Zone in Vienna. I recall riding a little red train up to the village of Zermatt and marveling at the Matterhorn. Along the way, while seeing rock-filled chalky streams that looked like flowing milk, my father, a petroleum engineer, explained the rock formations and the effects of glaciers and erosion.

In an old castle ruin in Scotland we climbed some rusty iron stairs that gave way, scraping and breaking my nose (for the first time), and leading to the wound showing up again and again in my childhood photos taken in Europe.

We visited the Gross Glockner, a huge, high-elevation glacier in Austria. On some trails you could — very carefully — make your way beneath the surface of the glacier into beautiful caverns of blue ice. My father told me how our prehistoric ancestors once lived on the

Inspecting a Soviet tank in the Austrian Russian Zone

great glaciers that covered most of Europe during the ice ages.

In 1955, our family returned to the United States on the *R.M.S. Queen Mary*. We settled in New Orleans, where my father worked for Shell as a petroleum engineer. Development of the vast oil reserves off the Louisiana coast had just begun. We lived in a two-story home in a recently built suburb called Gentilly Woods, a neighborhood that epitomized the traditional image of mid-'50s middle-class. When the TV program *Leave it to Beaver* aired, my family would always comment how it looked like *our* neighborhood.

Most people have memories of an early teacher who had an especially powerful impact on their lives. Mine was my second-grade teacher, Mrs. Zena Strole, at William C. Claiborne School. Mrs. Strole helped me overcome pronunciation problems that I had developed, partly from the residual Dutch sounds in my speech. Other than my father and mother, she was the first person who would discuss with me, sometimes long after class, the world, politics and science. She was the first teacher who put to good use the copious reading my father had encouraged at home. Mrs. Strole was a strict disciplinarian, but at the end of the school day she always bestowed a big, embarrassing bear hug on each student.

All the way from American kindergarten through sixth grade, I never saw any drugs at the William C. Claiborne School. I saw no pornography, nor alcohol. None of my fellow students, envious of a classmate's sneakers or jacket, gunned him down in the corridor. In fact, I witnessed no violence other than the occasional wrestling matches and fistfights among the boys, and no one ever used a weapon in those altercations. (In fact, for fear of being called a sissy, in those years boys would not even kick at their combatant.) Stealing and cheating were rare. When they did happen, the offender never

On the deck of the Queen Mary

A serious second grader.

bragged about it. The most serious offenses at school were chewing gum or being out of class without a pass.

We were, of course, mischievous. My friends and I read *Tom Sawyer* and *Huckleberry Finn* and reenacted adventures from these books. We found our fantasies in the pages of Sir Walter Scott, filled with courageous knights in battles for freedom. We loved John Wayne, westerns, war movies, and Steve Reeves, the Hollywood Hercules.

All of my neighborhood friends and I watched Walt Disney's television series: *Davy Crockett*. I idolized and identified with this frontiersman and statesman, perhaps partially because I had the same first name. I had my very own coonskin cap, as did millions of other children, and believed that I could stare down a bear, if only I were brave enough — just by grinning at the beast. I knew only a little of Crockett's political battles at this time and never dreamed of forging my own political career. But I considered the last stand of Davy Crockett and his comrades at the Alamo the most heroic episode in American history.

We were young. We played war and loved hunting fishing and camping. For us, Davy Crockett embodied the epitome of those skills as a legend of the great American frontier. I had devout Christian beliefs, and found in him a Christ-like ideal of self-sacrifice. For two years, I could hardly be found outdoors — even in the heat of an August afternoon in south Louisiana — without my coonskin cap. In later years, I imitated his woodsmanship in the bayou country and cypress forests near my home.

The mythos of the frontier — and the frontiersman such as Davy Crockett, the settling the West, battling the elements, subduing the hostiles, and building a great nation from the wilderness — has animated Americans for two hundred years. In the 1950s and early 1960s, it inspired us. In the last three decades, I believe, that mythos has changed. Thanksgiving, traditionally a holiday commemorating the struggle of our Pilgrim forefathers to create this nation and settle its land, is no longer treated by many as a day of thanksgiving for our triumph in that struggle. Increasingly it has become an occasion for fuzzy multicultural hobnobbing between Americans of European descent and Indians. The establishment has subsumed the entire White and Indian conflict into a paean to diversity and a guilt trip for the White American.

It is a clear sign that we have forgotten our heritage when we permit one of our most important holidays to become deformed in pursuit of political correctness. The establishment has dictated that most Americans know at least something of the battle at Wounded Knee, a firefight that erupted during negotiations between the U.S. Cavalry and an Indian band in the Dakotas, leaving dozens of Indians dead, including women and children. But nowadays, few Americans are even aware of the Ft. Mims Massacre[1] in which 250 Whites, mostly women and children, died at the hands of marauding Indians.[2] It was the worst massacre in American history on either side of the conflict. Books, movies, and television often portray our American heroes of the Indian Wars as savage war criminals and depict the Indians as morally superior, peace-loving people brutalized by unspeakably-evil Whites.

There is much to honor in the character of the American Indian: their understanding of Nature and their indomitable spirit against overwhelming odds. It is only right that Indian children should learn pride in the heritage and accomplishments of their ancestors. I honor the Indians for standing up for their heritage and defending it with their lives. But does not the same hold true for young European-Americans? Should our children not learn and understand what their own forefathers achieved?

European Americans brought Christianity to these shores and fought for principles that have made us the freest nation on Earth. Our people introduced medicine and law and great architecture and prosperity and security. They brought Western Classical civilization to this continent — its philosophies, histories, poetry, plays and music to this land. It was our scientists, inventors and craftsmen who gave us the technology that ultimately accomplished man's most dramatic achievement, reaching the moon. Our great-grandfathers and great-grandmothers went through untold sacrifices and hardships to build this nation. The telling of their story is our proud American mythos, and at the heart of it is the frontier.

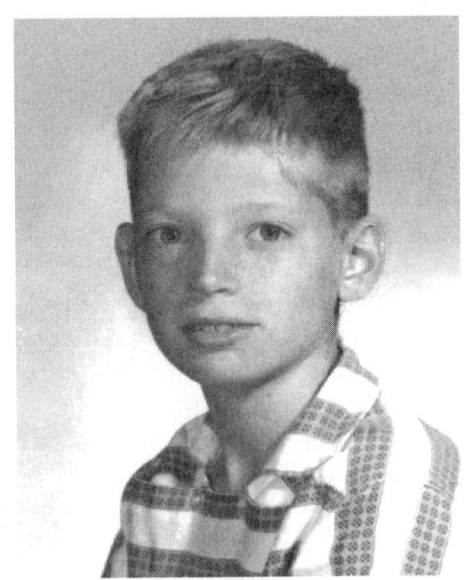

At six   **At ten**

10   MY AWAKENING

We are all taught that it was honorable for the Indians to defend *their* land and heritage from the massive immigration of those who would change it. But, strangely, that same media teaches us that it is immoral for *us* to defend *our* land and heritage today.

Most Americans are descendants of the men and women who settled that frontier, from the backwoods of Maine to the white beaches of west Florida, to the bayous of south Louisiana, to the bluegrass of Kentucky, and ultimately to the rocky coast of California and the mountains of Alaska. If our children lose sight of where they came from and where they are headed in the new American reality, they will discover themselves strangers in the nation their forefathers built.

When I was in grade school, my friends and I knew we were the sons of the frontier, inheritors of the spirit of Davy Crockett and Daniel Boone, of George Washington and Thomas Jefferson, of Teddy Roosevelt, and also of Jefferson Davis and Robert E. Lee. And we, in our own small ways, were fighters as they were.

We welcomed the prospect of hurricanes, fires and catastrophes of all sorts; not from any nihilism or bitterness, but because we wanted excitement, adventure. It was our desire to face a great test. We wanted to have the opportunity to be heroic.

My friends and I chose sides, as if preparing for a baseball or football game, and became instant, temporary enemies in the game of war. We would form armies on each side of the train tracks or a large drainage work called People's Canal. From our respective sides we

Fort Mims: the worst massacre in American history

would lob the heavy artillery — granite railroad rocks — at the opposing forces. We loved combat movies and stories of soldiering and guns. We loved pictures of fighter planes, submarines and battleships — and built models of British spitfires and German Messerschmitts as well as aircraft carriers and B-52s. We also loved fireworks and we frequently experimented with different formulas of gunpowder and made crude homemade rockets that seldom worked as we hoped. One of my friends blew off three fingers of his left hand making a homemade device.

We were spirited and we were proud. We knew what honor meant, and we held on to ours tenaciously. Inspired by our myths, we were often wild and fearless. We read stories about American fighting men who were captured by the enemy and then tortured to make them talk. If the same thing were to happen to us one day, we knew we would never talk. Name, rank and serial number — nothing more. The young men of Gentilly Woods wanted the opportunity to be heroic. We longed to face a great test. We wanted to take risks, to make sacrifices for a righteous cause, to be courageous as our heroes had been.

Sometimes we took our bravado and lust for adventure too far. My best friend, Richard Smith, and I once played chicken on our bicycles. We solemnly shook hands, then retreated to the dead end of Mirabeau Street and readied our bikes. We faced one another, with grim looks on our faces, then gave one another a wave of the hand and took off, pumping our pedals with all the strength we could muster. We rode our machines as fast as we could toward each other, looking fierce as we could. Either of us could have steered his bicycle off the pavement and into the safety of a neighbor's yard. But our honor would not permit it.

I still recall the fleeting images of flashing spokes and the glint of a handlebar; the last-second look of astonishment in Richard's eyes. And then, flying over the handlebars and rolling on gray asphalt. The street bit into my skinny shoulders and scraped my arms along with every knuckle of my backbone.

Limping home from such adventures, sometimes bloodied and with my clothes torn but my honor preserved, I had been for a short few minutes a knight jousting much as I had seen in the movies. I was a character out of the novels of Sir Walter Scott — the conquering hero returning home to a warm hearth and loving kin, who ministered his wounds. Often I returned home from such adventures to find that my dear mother was unable to mend my clothes or clean my wounds. She couldn't ease my troubles, for she had already, with alcohol, anesthetized her own.

Chapter 2:

Sanctuary in Books and Nature

In the summer of 1956 my father traveled from New Orleans to Kansas City. There he was to meet my mother's sister and her husband, Mildred and Wally Hatcher, who were scheduled to arrive on a United Airlines flight from Los Angeles. The flight was late. He inquired at the ticket counter and was told that there was some sort of problem. The ticket personnel would say no more. Father paced the corridors of the airport, and finally, after waiting for hours with the other anxious relatives of the plane's passengers, he went out to his car and switched on the radio. A news flash reported that my aunt and uncle's plane had collided with another passenger plane over the Grand Canyon in the worst civilian air disaster in history. The tragedy ultimately changed Mother and the rest of my family in profound ways.

My mother, Alice Maxine Crick, had grown up pampered and protected in Independence, Missouri. Her father, Thomas Crick, an inventor, turned stove manufacturer, had built one of the largest companies in the Kansas City area. Mother always seemed a little frail and thin after a youthful bout with scarlet fever. During her illness Mother's sisters, Mildred and Madeline, stayed with her, caring for her, wiping away the fevered sweat, and saying prayers by the bed. As Mother recovered, the two girls played hands of cards with her, and invariably Mother almost always won. It was a skill that remained with her until she had a stroke three years before her death.

After her death in 1993, I found one of Mother's high-school yearbooks. Her classmates had filled it with beautifully written original poems and erudite inscriptions. They were all in a crisp, fine penmanship. I compared her yearbook to one of my own yearbooks and wondered about the so-called progress education has made in this century. I also found a photograph of the young Maxine Crick. She was uncharacteristically serious-looking, almost studious, with her hair flowing in a golden wave around a perfect face and her large eyes looking deep blue even in the black-and-white snapshot. She was already tall enough, at five-foot-ten, that she seemed almost too thin. But the photographer had captured on

Maxine Crick

film something about her that matched a description of her I had found in the yearbook: She was indeed "angelic."

In 1932 a young man who was working his way through college with a job at Central Drugstore took an interest in Alice Maxine Crick. She, in turn, admired the aproned young man who filled prescriptions, cleaned the floors and made sodas. When he donned his Army Reserve officer's uniform, he looked the part of a man moving up in the world. The young man's name was David Hedger Duke.

My father's mother, Florence Hedger, who had been a chemistry professor at Kansas University and co-author of textbooks in that discipline (long before the days of women's liberation) had died when my father was 12. His father grew up on a farm eight miles straight west of the University of Kansas in Lawrence. There he met and romanced Professor Hedger, whom he married in 1910. Ernest M. Duke had left college his senior year to support his father's family as well as his own new family. He worked for the U.S. Postal Service.

My father held jobs consistently from grade school onward to help support his family. Because the Duke house was small, Father had to sleep beneath layers of quilts on an unheated back porch. Winter mornings in Kansas City can sometimes hit zero. Every morning he would rise at 4 a.m. and deliver *The Kansas City Star*, finish in time for school at 8 a.m., and then delivered the *Star's* evening edition right after school — all on foot.

Father worked his way through junior college and college at KU, always carrying a full-time job. He and Maxine married after his graduation in 1936. Afterward, he went to work for Shell Oil as a petroleum engineer. He was on active duty during the Second World War from 1940 until 1946 and then went on inactive duty as a full colonel. He remained in active reserves through the '60s.

Although years and miles had separated Mother's sisters, it seemed letters filled with pictures of their husbands and children were always in our mailbox. Father would always protest Mother's long telephone conversations and would scold her about the bill. Every month, just the same, the phone bill came high.

I cannot recall the details of how Mother first received the news of Aunt Mildred and Uncle Wally's deaths in the Grand Canyon crash. But I faintly remember the black-and-white images on TV and the heavy black headlines in the pages of the New Orleans newspaper, which lay about the house like shrouds. I remember the sound of Mother's

Col. David H. Duke

sobbing, and our always affectionate dog, Friskey, trying to lick the streaks of tears from Mother's drawn face and from the clenched hands that collected the glistening droplets. To my sister and me it seemed like the end of the world — the end not only for Aunt Mildred and Uncle Wally but for us too. For three days and nights we cried together: a little girl, a little boy, and their distraught mother draped out across a bed in anguish.

Dotti and I did not cry only for our aunt and uncle and our orphaned cousins. We hurt for our mother. We cried with her, just as we had laughed when she laughed. Her tears were as contagious as her laughter, and the sadness we saw in each other just gave it an inertia of its own.

Every time the television repeated the news, the words seared us, telling us again that the disaster was real and not just some awful nightmare on a humid summer night in New Orleans.

Order returned to the household when Father got home from Kansas City. During his absence, Dotti and I had slept in Mother's arms or on the carpet at the foot of her bed. Dotti and I were made to return to our own beds. In my room during the nights that followed, it occurred to me that I was blessed where my cousins were cursed. Death had taken their mother and father but had spared mine. I was at home, safe in my room, in the home occupied by my mother and father and sister.

But then Mother left. She packed her things and departed for a few weeks' stay in California, where she was to look after my cousins. Father, even with his military bearing and heavy job responsibilities, quickly adapted to Mother's roles. He woke Dotti and me in the morning, fed us a good breakfast — usually oatmeal because it "sticks to the ribs" — and made sure we got dressed appropriately and left for school on time.

David and Maxine Duke

In California, while caring for and trying to comfort Mildred's distraught children, Mother went on grieving as she had in those first few days after hearing the news. She sought solace in alcohol and by the time she returned to Louisiana two months later, she was an alcoholic. It all happened as quickly as that. I was too young to understand that Mother suffered from a drinking problem even before the crash and that Aunt Mildred's death had simply tipped it beyond control.

Upon her return from California, Mother seldom got up in the morning to cook us breakfast and get us off to school. She had been an excellent golfer and still sometimes went to the golf course but spent more time in the clubhouse playing cards and drinking than trying for birdies.

Mother's condition continued to deteriorate. She withdrew more and more from the lives of my father and Dotti and me. Often, when I tried to tell her about my latest adventures — or just to talk to her after coming home from school — I found her incoherent, her speech slurred and her movements spastic. Because I had been ashamed after one of my visiting friends saw her intoxicated, I seldom brought friends into our house thereafter. I became determined to battle the disease. One evening I prayed for hours, kneeling by my bed in the quiet of my upstairs room, tearfully asking God to make Mother well. I would sometimes search for her hidden bourbon bottles and grimly pour them down the kitchen drain. I reacted to the drama in my home by growing up faster than most of my friends.

Father kept his patience through it all. He loved Mother as deeply as Dotti and I, and her condition wounded him terribly. It seemed that hardly a day went by without his pleading with her to stop drinking. Sometimes he got her to promise to stop, but inevitably, within a few days or sometimes after a few weeks, he would return home from work to find her alone in the bedroom, quietly drinking bourbon and Coca-Cola.

Father coped with Mother's drinking as he dealt with every other hardship in his life. He immersed himself in work. He arose about 4:30 a.m. and worked at home for a couple of hours, then — just as he had during Mother's absence in California — every day he made Dotti and me breakfast and sent us off to school. Then he would go off to work at Shell. After work he would don his construction clothes and go out to supervise his small construction company's home-building. Back at home in the late evenings, he would work on engineering projects for Shell or on the blueprints for another home.

Often Father would take me with him to construction sites after I got home from school, and we would work side-by-side on carpentry, plumbing, wiring, roofing and painting. He had learned some of these trades from his father, who in turn had learned them from his father. Some of the tools Father and I used were my grandfather's and great-grandfather's and I still have them to this day. The knowledge of how to use them had also been passed down, and even then I was thankful for the inheritance.

16   MY AWAKENING

I was in awe of my father. It seemed that he could do anything, and he just about could. He designed the houses he built, right down to the most minute intricacies specified on the blueprints, and he could build a house from the ground up using his own mind and muscle.

Father paid me a dollar an hour for my labors, which I thought was a fortune in those times. But he gave me such a generous salary on the condition that I saved at least half of it. By the time I was 12, I could plane a door, skillfully drive a nail at just the right angle, and caulk, prime, or paint a window frame as well as any skilled adult laborer. I also had a good bankroll for a 12-year-old, and every penny of it I had earned.

Just as Mother withdrew from her family into the depths of alcoholism, and as Father found his relief from the circumstances at home by withdrawing into his work, I withdrew too. I found my sanctuary in books and my chemistry set. Inspired by the movie *Swiss Family Robinson*, I built a crude tree house in a backyard willow, with old pieces of driftwood for foot- and handholds. Here I could devour books and *National Geographic, Science Digest, Popular Mechanics,* and *Scientific American* — my favorite magazines.

As I grew a little older I found my greatest sanctuary in the lush swampland and bayou country along Lake Ponchartrain in New Orleans East. Two or three afternoons a week over a period of three years I rode my bike a few short miles and entered a biologist's dream. Amphibians, reptiles, and small mammals such as nutria, rabbits, squirrels, wild pigs, fish, and thousands of insects and birds, as well as varied flora filled these nearby swamps and cypress forests.

Soon I was collecting and caging creatures of every kind. I kept them in the backyard or garage — water turtles, box turtles, chameleons, toads, baby squirrels, snakes, tadpoles and frogs and every sort of strange insect.

I learned to distinguish which species of insect and other creatures I could safely pick up and those that had a painful bite or sting. I knew which snakes were venomous and could tell which of the nonvenomous ones had a dangerous bite. I knew which snakes would wrap themselves around my arms, almost in an embrace, but never bite, even when provoked.

A Blue runner once twisted in my hand and bit me so hard between my thumb and forefinger that it drew streams of blood. I wiped the blood on my T-shirt and wore this red badge proudly as I rode my bike home late that afternoon. Over the years, I became quite an expert on being bitten. I was unceremoniously bitten by a crow I had captured, by a young squirrel, and once even by a bat that I had found with a broken wing. I knew about the dangers of rabies, but I never told my parents about the bites because I feared the rabies vaccine series more than the disease. Once a furry, humpbacked caterpillar stung me so badly that I returned home in searing pain, made a great deal worse to me by the sight of red streaks that ran up under the skin of my forearm. But before I had gone to bed that evening — after a trip to the doctor — I was planning my next excursion into the swamps.

The swamp, with its forbidding stagnant waters and algae, its lush undergrowth, venomous snakes, wild boar and ravenous mosquitoes kept out all but the most hardy of human trespassers. But my friends and I craved the hardships and frankly, the danger. We thrived on them. No matter how the gnats, flies, mosquitoes, brambles, or poison ivy and oak struck at our flesh, we would not be kept from our muddy wonderland. We just brushed the insects away or smashed them into our skin. Bumps and rashes and frequent itching were just the price of admission, an entrance fee that we quickly forgot.

Perhaps the love of Nature that I developed as a child was an expression of the genes of my forefathers who lived many generations by farming. Every farmer knows not only the tilled soil, but also the natural life beyond the plowed fields and barnyards. On long summer days I rode my bicycle to the swamps and forests around New Orleans. Here I loved the bright sun, the humid breeze across the swampland, the shade of the live oak trees that gave me respite on the hottest days. Under their moss-draped branches, I rested on mats of naturally woven grass thicker and softer than the plushest carpet. From there I gazed up wide-eyed at the needle-like rays of sunlight that pierced the green canopy of leaves and shot beams of energy into the shade. Here, far away from the noise of the city, I heard the calls of frogs and birds and always listened for the faintest murmurs of life, and I would find such in the reeds and ivy. In the brackish waters of Lake Ponchartrain, I could dive four yards downward to the cool, squishy mud at the bottom and then blast upward, flying to the surface world of sky and air.

With only crooked sticks and bare hands, my friends and I would capture water moccasins and rattlers, as well as a number of other reptiles, which we could sell to the snake farm in nearby Slidell. Twice I encountered wild pigs that came hurtling at me, razor-sharp tusks leading their way. Both times I escaped into algae-covered pools. I am firmly convinced that facing such dangers I was not so much brave, but simply accustomed to the risk. We were no braver than the boar that charged us. We were in the swamp and the forest because it answered the natural longings inside of us to be there. I had no thought of the threat to my life any more than that wild pig had. Never was I more alive than in those days of long ago.

My friends and I would ride down a break in the muck and shoulder-high weeds called Dead Man's Road (so called because on it the police had once found a body that was never identified). We would hide our bikes in the bushes just off the overgrown path and walk a half-mile back into the mire, trees, and brush, alternating open and algae-covered stagnant water, and brown sand banks or grassy dry areas. No one — not even the hunters who would sometimes come down the muddy road in search of rabbit, squirrel, wild pig or gator — would venture even ten yards from Dead Man's Road. The foliage was too thick; the water and mud too deep. But they were not too deep for us.

I once worked for a month hollowing a canoe out of an old log, and I remember my disappointment the day I put her in the water and she turned over to a perfectly balanced upside-down float. Defeated, I filled her with water and unceremoniously scuttled her, but I couldn't even succeed in doing that for all she did was float off — upside down. A month later I found an abandoned Indian-style canoe and patched her up. She floated upright, thankfully, and for the next two years, whenever I wanted, she carried me faithfully and swiftly to the most remote places of the swamp.

After many months I knew every piece of solid ground, the depth of every stagnant pool. I knew where I could find mud or sand or thick stands of trees and exactly where I could find algae-free water. I learned all the things that I could eat and where to look for them. Hearts of palm, fish, wild onions and strawberries, radishes, raspberries — all of them were there for the taking, and I ravenously helped myself to this wild banquet.

And the fish! Never have I eaten better-tasting fish. The fishing was wonderful in the almost inaccessible bayous and ponds. All I needed was a cane pole — or even a broken branch — and some fishing line, some dry wood for a cork, and a fishhook or two. The bait was always easy to find. I could *whoosh* out of the shallow, warm, muddy water all the minnows, tadpoles, frogs, or tiny fish I needed. Or I could turn over the rich black soil and uncover more earthworms than needed for a hundred hooks.

I would clean the fish and impale them on a stick over a small fire and sear them to perfection. As for water, in a couple of choice spots I kept a couple of old Clorox bottles cut in half, with screen wire over them to keep out mosquitoes and their larvae. In rainy South Louisiana, the bottles stayed full of the finest distilled water to quench my thirst: a gift from Heaven.

Only twice do I remember seeing anyone other than my friends in these remote areas. Once an old Cajun in a carved cypress pirogue saw me trudging through the mud and said nothing to me as he, with unbroken strokes, paddled silently on through the reeds and out of sight. And once, when my friend and I returned to Dead Man's Road from an afternoon in the swamp, there stood my companion's father. Angry, he was muddied to his knees from searching for the son he thought lost in the swamp. My friend's father could not understand why we were back in what he called "that God-forsaken place." It struck me as odd then that anyone would call the place I loved "God-forsaken." To me the swamps and cypress woods of New Orleans East spoke God's Word as eloquently as the Bible itself.

During this period I read Rachel Carson's *Silent Spring*[3], the book that popularized environmental thinking in the 1960s. From the first few words I read, the ideas of ecological preservation became as real to me as the Nature I played and swam in almost every day. I also devotedly read the fascinating books by Theodore Roosevelt on his great safaris in the wilds of Africa and the Amazon. They gave me my first understanding that the science and the Nature I so loved had a relationship to government and society as a whole, for people could respect or destroy the natural world. Politics might have more importance than it seemed to me on first thought; still I found it boring compared to the life I found in Nature and the science that explained its secrets.

We also had definite ideas of the behavior of men and women. For us it was taboo to cry. No matter how it hurt, a man was not supposed to cry. Perhaps the only exception to that was a funeral. At the age of 11, when a car ran over my dog, Friskey, I gathered her broken body up off the street and felt death closely for the first time. In fact, although she only weighed 12 pounds, she had no rigidity beneath her coat, and I found to my horror when I went to pick her up that her insides just slipped about like a liquid in a plastic sack. Somehow I got her back to the house and laid her down in the back yard. For half my young life, Friskey was with me constantly. She slept at the foot of my bed, followed me to the ball fields and even into the swamp with a loyalty seldom found in humans. I was as devoted to her as she was to me, and now I knew that those were the last moments I would ever see her or pet her slick coat.

It hurt to think that she would never run by my side or explore with me again the swamps near my home. As I laid her still warm body in a bed of dark green clover, I thought about the times that she had consoled me with her bright eyes and wagging tail when I was down, and how with her sharp pointed ears she could hear my voice calling from almost anywhere in the neighborhood, and she always came running at my call.

As I dug the damp grave my sweat poured out, and I wasn't sure whether it was tears or just sweat that stung my eyes. Later that night, an ache welled up in my chest that hurt worse than anything I had ever felt. I turned my head to my pillow and cried. Even then, I was determined to be a man about it, so I willed myself not to make a single sob, not a noise. I gritted my teeth and buried my head deeper into the pillows, fighting the tears. But still they streamed and dampened my pillow.

I understood that a man could feel great pain and hardship, but it was something that except in extraordinary circumstances he did not show in public. There were, however, a few times in the most private moments of my youth when my emotions would spill out on my sleeves or on my pillow. The death of Friskey was one of those rare times.

In fact, in those times my friends and I viewed it as quite weird for men even to hug one another, save instances such as a funeral where men would use a hug to comfort the bereaved. Yet, even then such physical contact was awkward. At a friend's grandfather's funeral I noticed how when men hugged, even in grief, they often did so like dancers out of step. Of course, my mother wanted the hugs and kisses that all mothers require, and I obliged her, but with the onset of puberty my father seldom hugged me, nor did I want such girlish displays of affection. We shook hands, but those firm handshakes expressed the love of father and son in a complete way that I still remember with pleasure.

Mother gave Father and Dotti and me her love and her concern as well as moments of anguish. But most of all I recall her loving and sensitive spirit, her playfulness and laughter. Sometimes I think that her acute sensitivity and idealism were factors in her withdrawal into alcoholism. When life turned out to be not so idyllic, she found refuge in drink.

Today, when critics claim that my political opinions are the result of the wrong kind of upbringing, an unhappy childhood, a dysfunctional family burdened by alcoholism, I think that, on the contrary, Mother made me care about the important things of life more than I would have otherwise. Her alcoholism, for instance, is what led me to my first social consciousness.

On the brink of my teenage years I contemplated the injury that alcohol had inflicted on my family. Because I personally felt its tragedy, I realized that behind its grim statistics of tremendous societal damage were real families suffering like my own. How many millions of marriages has it ruined, careers smashed, auto deaths and disfigurements caused? How many robberies, murders and rapes has it encouraged? How many millions of assaults has it initiated? How many millions have faced loss of health or an agonizing death from the substance? I thought about how the movie industry glamorized drinking and made it fashionable. In the movies, all the beautiful and successful people come in from a hard day and mix a martini or pour a scotch on the rocks. The lesson is clear: If one faces depression, have a drink. If one is elated, have a drink. If one needs to calm down, have a drink.

Yet, in spite of Mother's affliction, I too was swept along with the peer pressure. I remember the first time I drank too much at a party and how sick I felt afterward. A couple of days later, my friends and I, trying to appear grown up, began to brag about getting drunk. I realized then that I had let myself be controlled by fashion rather than doing what was right. Even before I became a teenager, I realized that the only real victory over alcohol abuse could come not by laws — but by a mass media and government that promoted an entirely different value system, one that made a higher ethic of a bright mind and healthy body more fashionable than getting high on alcohol or any drug.

Mother lived the last few years of her life with my sister's family in Oregon. Due in great part to Dotti's care and dedication; Mother eventually conquered her drinking problem. I visited her shortly after my election to the Louisiana House of Representatives in 1990, and she was pleased about my victory. She was bedridden, and I sat beside her on the bed while we talked.

I wanted her to know that I held not the slightest resentment toward her for the sad times she sometimes brought me as a child. In fact, I told her, I was *grateful* to her. Not only had she given me half my genes, but during my boyhood she had given me a precious gift: In her own challenges and frailty she had made me care more intensely about life and family, more so than if there had been no struggle at home. And in my search for sanctuary from those problems, I discovered the beauty in Nature and my love of science and books. She had given me more than she ever thought, and I was thankful. I thank God that I could let her know my feelings in the twilight of her life.

The last time I saw Mother was a few weeks before her death in 1993. A terrible stroke had partially paralyzed her, and she couldn't talk well. But she could smile and write messages on an erasable board. Although her sickness had weakened her body, she still had that same beautiful light in her eyes that caused a high-school admirer to write in the yearbook of her angelic beauty. A few weeks later she was buried at a national cemetery on a hillside in full view of snow-capped Mt. Hood.

Chapter 3:

Son of the South

There is always romance in a lost love — or a lost cause. Most boys growing up in the South in the 1950s and '60s were infatuated with the Confederacy. We celebrated Robert E. Lee's birthday. We rooted for the South in every "Civil War" movie, and we embraced the ideal of honor and chivalry that Robert E. Lee, Jefferson Davis, Nathan Bedford Forrest, Stonewall Jackson and Jeb Stuart represented.

Far from being rabble-rousers or would-be dictators, as they are often labeled, Confederate civil and military leaders were thoughtful, well-educated men who were torn by conflicting loyalties and values. They were men who knew that they were entering the war far outnumbered, seriously outgunned and inadequately financed, yet they were compelled by love of freedom and sense of duty to defend the South. Robert E. Lee, for instance, was an American war hero who had been offered the command of the Union Army, yet reluctantly felt that his duty lay with his native state of Virginia.

My friends and I saw that the portrayals of the leaders of the South were quite negative in our school textbooks, which we noticed were published in Boston and Chicago rather than New Orleans or Atlanta. We learned from our families that the "Civil War" of our schoolbooks was actually the "War for Southern Independence" or, at the very least, the "War Between the States." The war wasn't a "civil war" because it wasn't a struggle for control of one nation's government but a simple struggle for independence for part of a nation.

To the sons of the South, our side was not the aggressor in the conflict. We knew that the South simply wanted to be left alone, that it had no desire to impose its politics or ideas on the North. But Abraham Lincoln had carefully maneuvered the South into firing the shots at Fort Sumpter. Lincoln's actions had made it clear that war was coming, and the South knew it could not win if the North held important forts on Southern soil.

We shared our ancestors' belief that the actions of our Southern forefathers were constitutional. Each state had voluntarily joined the union, and the Constitution did not prohibit any state from leaving it. True democratic principles of self-rule allow people to choose whatever government they desire. The Confederate Constitution closely resembled the Constitution of the United States, excepting perhaps its clearer protections of states' rights.

To us the War for Southern Independence was never about slavery. It was about the Southern people determining their own destiny in the same way that the American Colonies wanted self-rule rather than British hegemony. We knew that slavery had been practiced under the Stars and Stripes as well as the Stars and Bars. Even during the Great War that was supposedly to end it, slavery went on in a number of Union states. It was an issue enshrined in hypocrisy. The U.S. Constitution tacitly accepted the institution of slavery when it outlined in Article I, Section 2 the counting of slaves for census purposes. Even the Emancipation Proclamation freed the slaves only in the areas of South under Confederate rule — not in the North.

My friends and I had read the speeches of the eloquent South Carolina senator, John C. Calhoun, the addresses of the great president of the Confederacy, Jefferson Davis, and the heroic and sometimes tragic tales of battles from Bull Run to the surrender at Appomaddox. We loved the Confederacy.

Yet we had no real desire to resurrect it, for we also intensely loved America, as it had become our country, North and South. We believed that although the South had been right, its loss signaled that God meant for the nation to be united. Although we flew the Stars and Bars from our tree houses, we also got lumps in our throats from hearing the national anthem. When we recited the Pledge of Allegiance, we stood straight and tall, fixing our eyes with pride at the small American flag that hung in the corner of every classroom.

Loyal Americans in the North need to understand something that every true Southerner knows: find a bad Southerner, one who will not defend the South, and you will find an American who will not defend America.

My friends and I knew that America was number one in the world, and we were proud of that fact, proud enough to work a little harder in school, or to do a little better in sports, or even not to drop litter because we felt we were part of something much bigger than ourselves. We really wanted to earn our place in the greatest nation of the world, and we were ready to sacrifice to make that dream possible.

Today the American Dream has become synonymous with getting rich, but not so where I came from. Some of the boys from my neighborhood might have had that dream, but for most us in Gentilly Woods, comfortably middle-class as we were, our dreams were not about money. Our dreams were about affairs of the heart, not of the pocketbook. They were about becoming an astronaut or a marine biologist; or a heroic soldier, sailor or aviator. For some the dream was about designing the tallest building or writing the greatest novel or composing and singing songs that would move the hearts of millions. Athletic kids dreamed of being the best at football, baseball or track. Some dreams were about digging in the shadow of the pyramids and discovering their long-held archeological secrets or using chemistry to create a substance that would defy gravity. For some the American Dream promised poverty and hardship, for I knew a couple of boys whose dream was to give up all and be missionaries for Christ.

What about me? My dream by the age of 12 was to become a scientist. My love for the outdoors and Nature led me to want to study the capabilities of the human being. I had a loose idea of becoming an astronaut and medical researcher in the American space program. In the pursuit of that quest, I read everything I could on biology, human genetics and other scientific areas dealing with human physiology. I also read much anthropology, archeology and history.

As I read more and more, I found many of my instinctual and traditional cultural ethics under attack; I began a process that many young people experience, through the influence of television and other media: I gradually became more liberal in my viewpoints.

I was just beginning to become politically aware as the '60s burst upon us, and racial integration emerged as the biggest issue in the American political scene. The more I read and the more I watched television, the more sympathy I felt for the American Negro.

CHAPTER 4:
TRANSFORMATION

"Never run from the truth," Pinky told me. She encouraged me to admit to my folks that I had accidentally broken an old porcelain figurine they treasured. "What would Jesus say about that?" she added. I ultimately admitted my transgression to my folks and faced punishment, but I had to admit that it was better to take my medicine than to live a lie.

Our Black housekeeper, Pinky, always gave me advice such as "never run from the truth." After our return from Holland, she was the closest woman to me other than Mother and my sister, Dotti. My folks hired her to take care of the house and to watch over Dotti and me, but none of us really looked upon her as an employee. When she stayed late, we always insisted that she eat supper with us, and my father expected her to join us at the table.

Often Mother, with me tagging along, drove her home into one of the blackest parts of New Orleans, the lower Claiborne Avenue area. This was in the late '50s, when one could travel such streets safely, before the advent of the "love and brotherhood" brought by the civil-rights movement.

Pinky had the same authority over me that Mother and Father had. If I didn't obey her, my folks would punish me just as if I had disobeyed them. Pinky did housework and prepared snacks for me. We had conversations about a thousand and one subjects. She always attempted to derive every opinion from a solid Christian point of view. Scolding me for improper behavior, she would always intone, "What would Jesus say about that?" The words were really in the form of a declaration rather than a question, for the answer was always obvious: "Jesus would not approve." To Pinky there were no shades of gray to any ethical question, only clear right or wrong. Pinky influenced me to be opinionated — to think an issue over and then take a definite position rather than just sit on the fence. This is a trait that has stayed with me.

Concerning racial issues, Pinky had a traditional southern Black attitude. She insisted on using the toilet in the utility room rather than the main bathroom, and if we picked up some takeout food at a restaurant, she always used the "colored" service area. She was opposed to socializing with White folks other than in her work.

One day I asked Pinky why she had no problem with segregation. She answered simply and eloquently, "'Cause I want to be with my *own* kind." Although she was not of my "*own kind*," when she died, and I looked into her open coffin at her kind face, I saw only someone for whom I cared and who cared for me. She was someone who had made me laugh, who punished me when I went wrong, and who had encouraged me when she saw me doing something responsible or creative.

When Pinky passed away, I felt as though I had lost someone who was more family than friend. The pain of her loss was the worst I had felt since the Grand Canyon plane crash that killed my aunt and uncle and so hurt my mother. Mother and I were the only White people at Pinky's funeral.

The music and the preaching at the funeral were elemental and powerful. Pure, unrestrained emotion poured out of the pastor's mouth, almost as if the meaning of the words were secondary to the way in which he projected them. He cried with pain and sadness, he laughed deeply and warmly, he threatened us with the wrath of God, he cowered before Him, he raged in fury at the Devil, he begged for forgiveness and he passed his state of grace on to his audience as easily as a drunk would pass a bottle of whiskey. I had never experienced anything like it in the Methodist church my family attended. At my own church the emotions were restrained and subtle, while here in the Black church they were laid out raw. I was more fascinated by it all than moved. What touched my heart that day was the thought that Pinky would no longer be near when the service ended.

The tone of the service seemed out of place with my memories of Pinky. It was hard to associate her with the wild goings on in that Black church. But the way the congregation talked back to the preacher called to my mind the times Pinky would iron clothes while watching a soap opera on television, all the while interjecting dialogue as if she were in it herself. "Good goin', girl," Pinky would say, her eyes on the television, as she pressed one of Father's shirts. "He two-timin' her, yeah.... Un — huh, that's right." When I first saw *Gone with the Wind*, I knew about Mammy and Miss Scarlett — I had experienced it.

As I grew older the civil-rights movement was maturing as well, and by the time I was 11, the South was in turmoil. A social structure that had existed for hundreds of years was being completely overturned at an astonishing speed. At first I did very little thinking on the race question. I was far more concerned with my love of the outdoors, science, and my escapist world of reading (mostly of scientific books and only a little political material).

Instinctively, because of my love for the Confederacy, I initially identified with the traditionally conservative position of the South in opposition to racial integration. I saw the civil-rights movement simply as a destruction of our Southern way of life, but I hadn't thought very deeply about the issue. As civil-rights pushed to the forefront of the news in the early '60s, I began to read a great deal about the issue in newspapers and magazines, and as I did I grew more sympathetic toward the Negro cause.

Practically everything written about the subject in books, newspaper and magazine articles, as well as everything on television — led me to believe that the civil-rights movement was based on lofty principles of justice and human rights. The media proclaimed that these policies would lead America to racial harmony and material progress.

I read articles proclaiming that there is no significant genetic difference between Whites and Blacks other than skin color. Racial differences in poverty, illegitimacy, crime rates, drug addiction, educational failure, were said to be caused purely by environmental differences among the races. The media blamed Black failure and dysfunction on segregation and White racism. Ultimately, the poor circumstances of Black people were blamed squarely on White evil.

Some leading academics even maintained that there is no such thing as race; that race is an arbitrary and therefore meaningless way of classifying mankind. Other scientists went so far as to argue that the Black race is in fact not inferior, but really the progenitor of mankind — perhaps even superior to Whites. One account I read purported that the fact that Blacks have less body hair than Caucasians is a sign of evolutionary advancement and superiority.

Some stories were about the suppression of Blacks in slavery and about discrimination and brutality against Blacks since emancipation. The heart-rending accounts would provoke sympathy and outrage in any person sensitive to human suffering. At the same time I came across articles about the "great Black civilizations of Africa" and the "great Blacks in American history."

I found lessons in our nationally distributed lesson books at my Sunday school that claimed God opposed the concept of racial differences and discrimination. For the first time in the 2,000-year history of Christianity, it seemed, a new sin had been invented: racism. Many church leaders of all denominations began to speak out forcefully in opposition to racism and segregation, and they were rewarded with extravagant praise in the national media.

Even my patriotic values were enlisted in the cause of racial integration. I read articles in major magazines that maintained that racial equality is proclaimed in the Constitution of the United States. And frequently quoted were the well-known words of the Declaration of

Independence, "We hold these truths to be self-evident, that all men are created equal..."

In addition to Thomas Jefferson's words in the Declaration of Independence, the following line was used repeatedly in articles: "Nothing is more certainly written in the book of fate than that these people (the Negroes) are to be free." One summer I traveled with Father to Washington, D.C., and saw those very words inscribed in magnificent foot-tall letters on the inspiring Jefferson Memorial on the Potomac.

In the Gettysburg Address, which was quoted almost as often as the Declaration of Independence, Lincoln seemingly paid homage to the concept of racial equality: "Four score and seven years ago our fathers brought forth on this continent a new nation, conceived in liberty and dedicated to the proposition that all men are *created equal*."

For a fiercely patriotic young man who idolized men like Davy Crockett, Teddy Roosevelt, Thomas Jefferson and Abraham Lincoln, these quotations were very persuasive. My belief that America's greatest heroes had endorsed racial equality, helped influence my own attitudes.

Integration of public schools was a major issue at this time, and the media portrayed as good thing for America. Judging by what I saw on television, integration simply meant one or two little Black girls seeking to attend a formerly all White school. On the opposite hand Whites were shown unchivalrously screaming racist invectives — and attacking the quiet and well-dressed Negro children being escorted into school.

Over the years I saw on TV and read hundreds of dramatic portrayals of Blacks being hurt, oppressed, enslaved, discriminated against, falsely accused, whipped, lynched, spat upon, raped and ridiculed. Because I was idealistic and aspired to be fair and generous and chivalrous — and because I was under the influence of the media — I came to believe that racial integration would elevate the Black people to their true ability and thereby guarantee justice for them and progress for all.

There is no exaggerating the impact of television during the '50s and '60s on the issue of integration. The newness of live television coming into the home, sanctified the media newscaster and made him seem bigger than life. In awe of the technology, many people uncritically accepted what they were fed through their televisions. I was no exception.

As always, I found great enjoyment in my books and science magazines. Sometimes, under the covers with a flashlight, I would read long after Father called for lights out. I also enjoyed my chemistry set and continued to collect wild pets. When my family moved to

Jefferson Parish, far away from the swamps, I had to give up the menagerie of pets that I kept in our garage and large yard in Gentilly Woods. I set free the reptiles and amphibians and carefully adopted out the other creatures among my friends. At school I played for the junior varsity basketball team, and I began to discover the beauty and mystery of the opposite sex.

It was an exciting time for me: I was throwing off my childhood and beginning to question the accepted dogmas of the world around me. I was rebelling, challenging and questioning everything. Without knowing it, I was about to undergo a drastic change in my viewpoints.

My father often took his car to Gary's Super Service, a small Black-owned garage in a Black area just on the western periphery of the New Orleans' central business district. Like most pre-teen boys, I was fascinated with automobiles, and I was pleased when Gary offered to teach me about cars if I would do some work around the place. For months, twice a week or so, I would ride the streetcar down to his shop after school and work on cars.

I met many Black people during my after-school stays at Gary's Super Service. I often ate supper in a tiny Black restaurant three doors from the garage and talked for hours with everyday Black residents of New Orleans. It was a rewarding experience. I not only learned about automobiles; I met interesting people. And I discovered a great deal about the Black race.

What I learned about them, I liked. But it also seemed that the liberal line was not entirely correct, for it was obvious that racial differences went far beyond skin color. It would be difficult to categorize all the distinctions I noticed. In fact, I made no effort to catalogue them at the time, but their differences ranged all the way from physical characteristics to more subtle differences such as extreme aversion for work in cold weather. On cold days, when I felt invigorated, my Black co-workers seemed lethargic.

When I helped Father in his small construction firm, I had often worked side-by-side with White laborers and sometimes Blacks as well. Many of the men were needed only for some day work, so Father literally hired them off the street near the charity missions in the central city. Some of these men were good workers, some poor. But the White ones were decidedly less excitable and animated than my co-workers at Gary's Super Service.

At the garage the Blacks I encountered were very elemental, almost child-like in their dramatic emotional swings. They were quick to laugh, easy to anger, prone to cry at small disappointments or troubles, moody and temperamental — although their moods were usually felicitous rather than threatening. At risk of sounding like a narrator of *The Tales of Uncle Remus*, I vividly recall the singing, whistling, and humming that often filled the shop, and how they occasionally semi-danced as they jauntily walked from one spot to another or swayed rhythmically to their own inaudible tune right where they stood. It was no myth, they really could sing, and in Gary's shop they all did. I enjoyed their company, but I didn't sing.

A few months after Gary's shop closed, I saw the British anthropologist Ashley Montagu on a television talk show and immediately read his book, *Man's Most Dangerous Myth: The Fallacy of Race*.[4] The subject interested me enough that I read *Black Like Me*,[5] an autobiography about a White man who tinted his skin and frizzed his hair and chronicled his unjust treatment across the South, and *To Kill a Mockingbird*.[6] I sympathized with the plight of the Negro. The event that most appalled me and reinforced my egalitarian attitudes was the 1963 bombing of a Birmingham Black church where four little Black girls had been killed. For weeks the news and other media were filled with horrific descriptions of the event and the sounds and scenes of the suffering of the victims' relatives. I had become convinced that the cause of integration was a noble one and that its opponents, as evidenced by the strained faces and crude words of the protesters outside the schools and by the church bombing, represented everything ignoble, ignorant, intolerant and uncivilized.

I found it easy to be a racial egalitarian. Judging by the books, newspapers and magazines I read, all the most prominent and admired actors, singers, scientists and politicians believed in racial equality. I was proud to share the sentiments of these people of fame and accomplishment who were working to get us into the bright new age ahead. I was also aware enough to know as well that White racism may have been popular in the Deep South, but holding such views could be quite damaging to a young man who wanted to be an astronaut.

In my 13th year, I was shy and bookish and idealistic on one hand, and physically hard from my time in the outdoors on the other. I had no doubt that the civil-rights movement and integration would prevail and that when racial discrimination ended, that everything in America would work out just as wonderfully as the egalitarians predicted. The barriers were falling across the South; the Supreme Court continued to strike down Jim Crow, and Black political registration and power were growing dramatically. One thing was for sure, politics had no great interest for me.

In an eighth-grade civics class at Ganus Junior High School, the teacher gave her students an interesting assignment. We were to choose a topic dealing with current events and take a polemical position on it, then research that topic and defend it rationally in class. I chose as my topic "The Case for Racial Integration of Education." After each of us had chosen and taken a position, she told us that we had probably taken a topic we probably agreed with. So our assignment now became to research and take the opposite point of view from what we had originally chosen. The assignment set my mind in turmoil.

I went to the school library that afternoon to research "The Case *Against* Racial Integration of Education." In the card file I found listed many books on the subjects of racial equality and integration of education. I had, evidently, chosen a topic that would be easily researched. But as I examined the books, I found that one after another argued in favor of integration. Even in this small church-school library, there were at least a dozen books promoting the civil-rights movement and its heroes, but *no* books on the other side. Why? It was obvious that there was a lot of popular opposition to integration. I had seen the newsreels of its White opponents, and segregationists were being elected all over the South. Whites rioted in New Orleans to prevent integration of the schools and almost every major politician of the time opposed it in principle. Yet, amazingly, I couldn't find a book against it.

The next day I went to the Doubleday bookstore on Canal Street hoping to search out some books opposed to forced integration of public education. I found dozens of books promoting integration, and some even touting Black supremacy. But again, I found nothing opposed to integration. Even the books that supposedly offered a balanced analysis of the issue were decidedly one-sided in their presentation. Finally, to make some progress on my assignment, I resorted to gleaning the *anti*-integration arguments from *pro*-integration books.

Those arguments were uneven. The liberal civil-rights books made the arguments of segregationists seem stupid and banal. I read that Whites are opposed to integration because of sexual insecurity; that Whites want to oppress Blacks so they can keep them economically subjugated and exploited (The Marxist interpretation); that segregationists hate Blacks simply because of their color. A few of the books suggested that some segregationists thought that Blacks were less intelligent and more violent than Whites — a distinction that they argued would lead to a marked decline in American education. The liberals curtly dismissed such arguments by saying that "no scientific evidence supports the contention that Whites are smarter than Blacks," and they repeated in a litany, "The only difference is the color of skin."

I was in a quandary. I had to defend a position that had no supporting evidence and one that I morally opposed. When I opened the morning paper a few days before my school assignment was due, I saw something that gave me a glimmer of hope. The *Times-Picayune* reported a meeting held at the Municipal Auditorium by the New Orleans chapter of the White Citizens Council. It quoted Judge Leander Perez of Plaquemines Parish as saying that racial integration would ultimately destroy the quality of the New Orleans public school system.

There was little of substance in the news article, but learning about the existence of the Citizens Council heightened my hopes of finding information from the segregationist viewpoint. After school I rode the old Canal Street streetcar downtown to the Citizen's Council offices on Carondolet Street, expecting only to find a few obscure and discredited sources for the segregationist position.

A middle-aged woman, Mrs. Singleton, with bleached-out freckles and bifocals greeted me with a deep Southern accent more characteristic of neighboring Mississippi than of New Orleans. She was busy with a mailing, so I hurriedly asked if she had any books that opposed the integration of education. With a slightly exasperated manner, she pointed to bookshelves that were ten feet tall and stretched across an entire wall 15 feet across. "Take a look, " she snapped.

What I saw amazed me. They had hundreds of volumes that supported the idea that racial differences go far beyond skin color; that heredity rather than environment are the keys shapers of intelligence and personality; and that there is a historical record of racial integration and intermarriage in many nations that indicates racial mixing retards progress and leads to lowering standards.

I looked over books by prominent geneticists, psychologists, anthropologists, historians, sociologists and educators. They took the point of view that no matter how we might wish it otherwise, *race does matter*. A book by Audrey Shuey, *The Testing of Negro Intelligence*,[7] assembled 384 separate scientific studies on intelligence and race, all of them showing a marked difference between the races. Another book that caught my eye was *Race, Riots and Revolution*[8] by Teddy Roosevelt, a president whom I idolized for his conservationism and patriotism.

All of this came as a shock to me. I found an opposing viewpoint on racial integration that is literate, reasoned and intelligent — even supported by famous Americans — not simply the ranting of backwoods White supremacists. It is a viewpoint on race the popular media in America would not even acknowledge.

I didn't have much money — it was 1963 and I was 13 years old — so I asked the lady at the desk which book she would recommend. She picked up a paperback copy of *Race and Reason: A Yankee View*[9] by Carleton Putnam and put it in a bag for me with a handwritten receipt.

The voice of Pinky crept into my mind as I walked to the Canal Street streetcar, and I wondered, if I betrayed her memory by even reading such material. Was I doing her some wrong even to consider the idea that the races differ?

But then Pinky's admonishment never to run from the truth came back to me as if she had been right there speaking those words again from her own mouth. If I should not run from the truth, then I sure should not be afraid to confront a falsehood either. I imagined *Race and Reason* would be an easily refutable, shallow exposition of race prejudice. All the same, I had an uneasy feeling about it.

I had no inkling, when I walked out of the drab little office on Carondolet Street, that I was about to read a book that would change my life.

PART II

RACE AND REALITY

Chapter 5:

Race and Reason

The book riveted me. I read it on the streetcar, and then on the connecting bus all the way home, almost missing my stop. When I walked home from the bus stop, I would pause and read a couple of paragraphs and then close the book and walk while I thought about the concept. That evening, after wolfing down my supper, I bounded upstairs to my bedroom where I retrieved my book from its paper bag and read until I finished it.

The book did not convert me, but it made me think critically for the first time about the race issue, and it made me question the egalitarian arguments that I had uncritically accepted. I was not ready to give up my egalitarian beliefs, but *Race and Reason* made me realize another legitimate and scientific point of view existed.

I asked myself, *What if the things he writes are true? What if the distinctions, quality and composition of races are the primary factors in the vitality of civilizations?*

Putnam prophesied that massive racial integration of American public schools would lead to increasing Black racism, resentment and frustration, reduced educational standards, increased violence in the schools, and a resulting implosion of the great cities of America. I worried that such a fate could befall our country. I wanted to find out the truth, no matter where it might lead.

One allegation by Putnam especially interested me. He said that most of America's Founding Fathers were convinced believers in racial differences and that even President Lincoln, the Great Emancipator, stated repeatedly that he believed that there were wide differences in the races that make necessary their separation. If Putnam's allegations were correct, then I would have to acknowledge that the media had deceived me on an important matter. My generation had been taught that racial equality was enshrined in the principles of our Founding Fathers and supposedly represented even by the *Declaration of Independence:*

> **We hold these truths to be self-evident, that all men are created equal, that they are endowed by their Creator with certain unalienable rights. . .**

Most Americans can instantly identify these words. But do these words mean that Jefferson and the other patriots who put their names on that document believed that all men were truly created biologically equal; that the White and Black races had equal endowments from the Creator?

How could that be true, asked Putnam, when the same document refers to Indians as "merciless savages" who massacred innocents without regard to age or gender?

> He has excited domestic insurrections amongst us, and has endeavoured to bring on the inhabitants of our frontiers, the merciless Indian Savages, whose known rule of warfare, is an undistinguished destruction of all ages, sexes and conditions.

Anyone who used such language today from the podium of the Republican or Democratic National Convention would be universally scorned.

How could they really believe in racial equality, when many of the signers themselves, including the author, Thomas Jefferson, owned Black slaves that were considered chattel property? What of their slaves' unalienable rights? Were our Founding Fathers blatant hypocrites, or did the declaration simply say that our rights as British subjects in the thirteen Colonies were the same as those of our British brothers back in England?

After I read and re-read the rest of Jefferson's utterances on the Negro question, it seemed certain to me that he was not referring to racial equality when he penned the Declaration of Independence. Other than the "created equal" line in the *Declaration of Independence*, the most common quote by any American Founding Father used to bolster the civil-rights movement was Jefferson's classic line that reads:

> Nothing is more certainly written in the book of fate, than that these people [the Negroes] are to be free.

This declamation has been used in thousands of books, articles, plays, documentaries and movies — more than any other famous enunciation on the race issue. On the beautiful Jefferson Memorial in Washington, it is found chiseled as sacred writ on the huge interior panels of granite. The next sentence on the wall begins with the word *education*. In media articles the quotation ends with the words "are to

COMMERCE BETWEEN MASTER AND SLAVE IS DESPOTISM. NOTHING IS MORE CERTAINLY WRITTEN IN THE BOOK OF FATE THAN THESE PEOPLE ARE TO BE FREE. ESTABLISH THE LAW FOR EDUCATING THE COMMON PEOPLE. THIS IS THE BUSINESS OF THE STATE TO EFFECT AND ON A GENERAL PLAN.

The Jefferson Memorial panel

be free." Neither the articles nor the memorial's architect give the public the honesty of an ellipsis, for the quotation is clearly an intentional deception that completely alters his original meaning.

The quotation itself is only a fragment of one of Jefferson's sentences written in his autobiography:

> **Nothing is more certainly written in the book of fate than that these people [Negroes] are to be free. Nor is it less certain that the two races, equally free, cannot live in the same government. Nature, habit, opinion has drawn indelible lines of distinction between them. It is still in our power to direct the process of emancipation and deportation peaceably and in such slow degree that the evil will wear off insensibly, and their place be . . .pari passau filled up by free White laborers. If on the contrary it is left to force itself on, human Nature must shudder at the prospect held up.** [10]

When I first read the complete text of the Jefferson statement, It stunned me. Not only did Jefferson not believe in racial equality, he stated clearly that Nature had made the Black and White races indelibly different that they couldn't live in the same government, and that unless the Black race was returned to Africa, he "shuddered " for America's future. The egalitarian sources that wrote loftily of his belief in equality had brazenly deceived me.

Perhaps Jefferson was wrong in his opinion, I thought, but why have his words been twisted completely opposite to his original intent? I remembered my visit the rotunda of the Jefferson Memorial, when I had stared up in reverence at those words across from the magnificent statue of Jefferson himself. Now, I knew those words etched in granite were a lie.

The rest of those powerful words had simply gone down what the

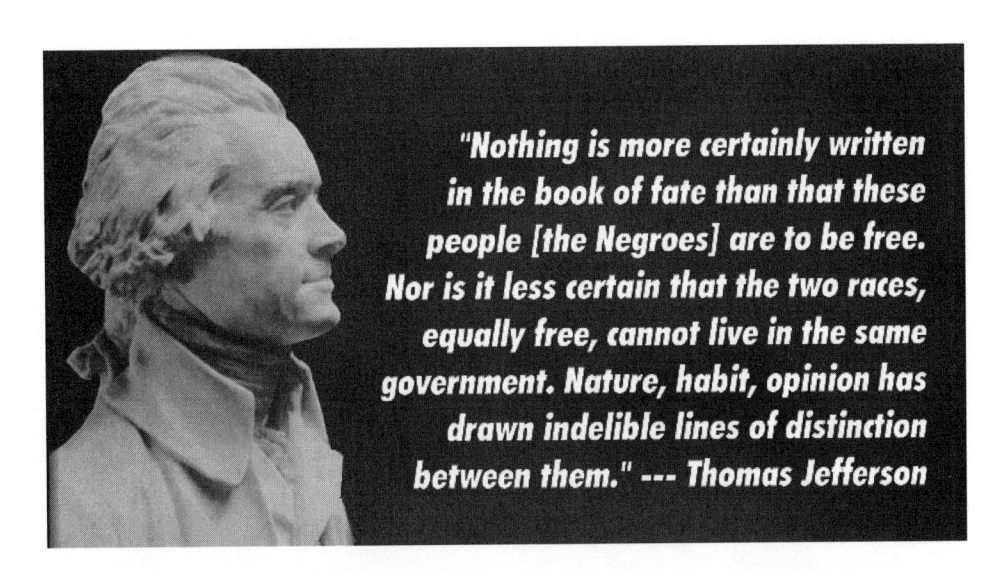

"Nothing is more certainly written in the book of fate than that these people [the Negroes] are to be free. Nor is it less certain that the two races, equally free, cannot live in the same government. Nature, habit, opinion has drawn indelible lines of distinction between them." --- Thomas Jefferson

writer George Orwell called the "memory hole" in his classic book *1984*? [11] If the establishment would blatantly suppress and distort a historical fact as important as this, I wondered if there were other important deceptions about race. Putnam exposed many more.

Martin Luther King's 1964 Civil Rights March on Washington held its rally at the Lincoln Memorial. I knew that Lincoln was opposed to the institution of slavery, as was Jefferson, but what would Lincoln's opinion be on the march for racial integration and racial equality that assembled on the steps of his imposing memorial? Here are some of Lincoln's surprising sentiments on the issue:

> **Negro equality. Fudge! How long in the Government of a God great enough to make and maintain this Universe, shall there continue knaves to vend and fools to gulp, so low a piece of demagoguism as this?** (*The Collected Works of Abraham Lincoln*, edited by Roy P. Basler, Rutgers University Press, 1953, *September 1859 (Vol. III p. 399)*) [12]

In an address at Springfield, Illinois, on June 26, 1857:

> **A separation of the races is the only perfect preventive of amalgamation, but as immediate separation is impossible the next best thing is to keep them apart where they are not already together... Such separation, if ever affected at all, must be effected by colonization... The enterprise is a difficult one, but 'where there is a will there is a way;' and what colonization needs now is a hearty will. Will springs from the two elements of moral sense and self-interest. Let us be brought to believe it is morally right, and at the same time, favorable to, or at least not against, our interest, to transfer the African to his native clime, and we shall find a way to do it, however great the task may be.** (Vol. II, pp. 408-9)[13]

In the famous Lincoln-Douglas Debates in Charleston, Illinois, Lincoln said:

> **I am not, nor ever have been in favor of bringing about in any way the social and political equality of the white and black races. I am not nor ever have been in favor of making voters or jurors of Negroes, nor qualifying them to hold office, nor to intermarry with White people; and I will say in addition to this that there is a physical difference between the white and black races which I believe will ever forbid the two races living together on terms of social and political equality.** (Fourth Debate with Stephen A. Douglas at Charleston, Illinois on September 18, 1858 (Vol. III pp. 145-461))[14]

In the shadow of the monument to the man who spoke the above words, assembled the 1964 Civil Rights march. The heavens must have laughed in irony. I searched out the text of Lincoln's Emancipation Proclamation and found to my consternation that even his speech that accompanied it called for the deportation of the Blacks from America and their repatriation to Africa:

> ...and that the effort to colonize persons of African descent with their consent of upon this continent or elsewhere, with the previously obtained consent of the governments existing there, will be continued. (From the emancipation proclamation issued from President Lincoln on Sept. 22, 1862) [15]

The following are President Lincoln's words at a repatriation ceremony in Washington, D.C.

> I have urged the colonization of the negroes, and I shall continue. My Emancipation Proclamation was linked with this plan. There is no room for two distinct races of white men in America, much less for two distinct races of whites and blacks.
>
> I can conceive of no greater calamity than the assimilation of the negro into our social and political life as our equal...
>
> Within twenty years we can peacefully colonize the negro and give him our language, literature, religion, and system of government under conditions in which he can rise to the full measure of manhood. This he can never do here. We can never attain the ideal union our fathers dreamed, with millions of an alien, inferior race among us, whose assimilation is neither possible nor desirable. (Vol. V, pp. 371-5) [16]
>
> See our present condition -- The country engaged in war! -- our white men cutting one another's throats . . . and then consider what we know to be the truth.
>
> But for your race among us there could not be war, although many men engaged on either side do not care for you one way or the other... It is better for us both therefore to be separated. . .
>
> You and we are different races. We have between us a broader difference than exists between almost any other two races. Whether it is right or wrong I need not discuss, but this physical difference is a great disadvantage to us both, as I think your race suffer very greatly, many of them by living among us, while ours suffer from your presence. In a word we suffer on each side. If this be admitted, it affords a reason at least why we should be separated. (address on Colonization to a Deputation of Negroes in Washington, DC on August 14, 1862 (Vol. V p. 371) [17]

To Lincoln the only workable long-term solution to the race problem in America is repatriation. He shared this opinion with the company of many other giants of American history, among them Thomas Jefferson, James Monroe, James Madison, Andrew Jackson, Daniel Webster, Henry Clay, and even the writer of our national anthem, Francis Scott Key. All were active members of the American Colonization Society, founded in 1817 in Washington, D.C. Even though some Americans will have a hard time believing it, African colonization by freed slaves had actually begun before Lincoln's assassination. The African nation of Liberia was formed, its name taken from the Latin word meaning freedom. Its capitol, Monrovia, was named after President James Monroe, a strong advocate of Black repatriation. Until recent times Liberia's government was ruled by the direct descendants of Black slaves from America.

Many Black leaders also supported the repatriation movement, including the much-venerated Black leader of the 1920s and 1930s, Marcus Garvey. A petition of 400,000 Blacks requesting repatriation was presented before the United States Congress in 1935; its powerful words bear repeating:

> **Given an opportunity in our ancestral Africa, the knowledge of farming and of simple farm machinery and implements, which we have acquired here would enable us to carve a frugal but decent livelihood out of the Virgin soil and favorable climate of Liberia. . .We are a liability now, and any cost of this project, no matter how great, would still, we sincerely believe, be a sound investment for the American people.** [18]

The "patriotic-American" argument for racial integration, which I had once accepted unquestionably, had collapsed, for if opposing racial integration made one un-American or unpatriotic, then unpatriotic is the man who wrote our *Declaration of Independence*, the president who ultimately freed the slaves and even the man who composed our national anthem. Our Founding Fathers were not only segregationists in the classic sense, they were *White separatists* who accurately predicted that the continued presence of Africans in America would lead to intractable social conflict. They believed the only equitable solution could be the repatriation of all Blacks from the United States, and they formed a society to accomplish that purpose. They even acquired land in Africa to become that new nation. In the end they were stymied in their quest, first by the economic power of slaveholders, who sought to preserve their fortunes, and later, at the close of the War for Southern Independence, by radical political forces who used the newly freed slaves as political fodder to maintain their control of the Congress.

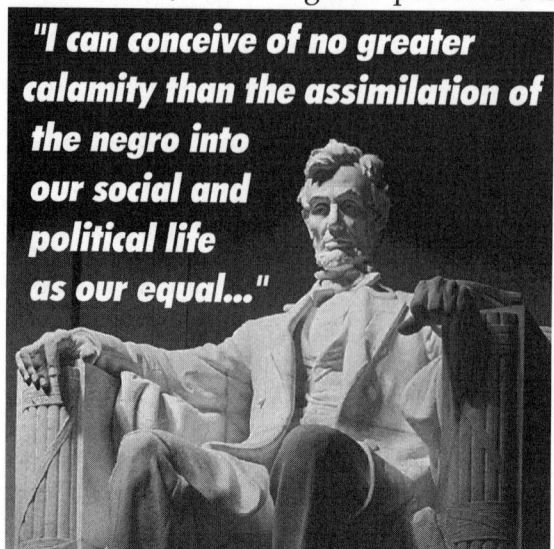

Carleton Putnam's sources on our Founding Fathers checked out right down to their punctuation marks. My mind opened to the possibility that he might be correct in more than his historiography. It alarmed me to think of the implications of race having a cardinal role in the creation and maintenance of culture and civilization. If true then replacement of the White race through immigration and race-mixing could conceivably destroy Western Civilization itself.

The egalitarians and their allies in media and government have clearly embarked upon a policy that is rapidly changing the racial composition of the United States. Even if their policy is terribly misguided, once it is fully accomplished, there is no going back. It is as if a scientist working on a cure for headaches recklessly tests his hypothetical cure on himself. If the formula turns out toxic instead of healing, he will never devise another.

The logic is clear, if Putnam is right that it is the inherent distinctions between the races that produce sharp differences in culture and values, then changing America from an overwhelmingly White nation to a multiracial, multicultural society will produce inevitable racism and conflict.

On the other hand, logic told me that if the egalitarians were right, harmony and progress will continue with the racial change.

Putnam's arguments on racial integration were just as thoughtful as his historical revelations. I summarized his argument in my civics class term paper.

> **Putnam argues that race is a distinct reality in the world. That there have been thousands of studies of racial differences which have consistently revealed profound differences in IQ, and divergent behavioral patterns between Blacks and Whites. Numerous other studies have shown many identifiable distinctions between the physical brains and craniums of Blacks and Whites, and that these differences are the root causes of poor black educational performance and anti-social behavior. It is his belief that a civilization is the product of the particular racial group that created it and that demographic replacement of the founding race, through race-mixing, immigration, and differential birthrates, will diminish and ultimately destroy the vitality of the culture and civilization.**
>
> **Putnam argues that the Supreme Court decision forcing integration of public education was a scientific and intellectual fraud perpetrated on the American public. He shows that the research of black social scientist, Dr. Kenneth Clark, was in clear contradiction to his subsequent testimony before the Supreme Court in Brown Vs. The Topeka Board of Education. The Brown decision turned on Clark's testimony that the self-esteem of Black children is seriously harmed by racial segregation.**
>
> **Dr. Clark testified that when Black children were offered a choice between playing with White dolls or Black dolls, that they overwhelmingly chose the White ones--supposedly showing the psychic damage created by a segregated society. Dr. Clark concealed the fact that while it is true that in segregated schools Black children routinely prefer White dolls, his studies also showed**

44   My Awakening

> that Black children in integrated schools were even more likely to choose White dolls.[19]
>
> In addition to harming the self-esteem of Black children, integration will actually harm the educational development of Black children. It creates a universalistic educational environment unresponsive to their specific needs and aptitudes. Putnam also argues that White children will suffer lower standards and the increased violence found in the Black community.
>
> To paraphrase Lincoln, he says Blacks and Whites "will suffer on each side."

I was not ready to accept Putnam's premise of racial inequality, but in the face of such dramatic historical evidence, it seemed outrageous to me that the popular media in America promotes the idea that our Founding Fathers believed in racial integration and assimilation. Upon realizing that they had deceived me on this issue, no longer could I take any of the egalitarian pronouncements on face value. I became determined to investigate the entire issue thoroughly, trying to set aside my egalitarian prejudice.

Egalitarians argue that there are no differences in intelligence between Blacks and Whites and at the same time that environment has the greatest influence on both mental ability and character. They furthermore maintain that skin color is the only significant difference between the races. Some of them even go so far as to allege there is actually no such thing as race at all. I knew I had a lot of reading and thinking to do if I could ever gain some balanced understanding of the race issue.

Other famous words of Thomas Jefferson inscribed on his memorial read, " I have sworn upon the altar of God eternal hostility against every form of tyranny over the mind of man." As I continued to read and find many more lies and falsehoods about race, my own hostility grew, along with my determination to discover the truth about race, wherever it might lead.

Are the differences between Whites and Blacks, as I wanted so desperately to believe, only the color of our skins? Or, do deeper, more significant mental and personality differences exist that are determined by genes rather than environment. If profound inherent differences do exist, then all the premises of racial integration become threatened.

Before I could understand whether or not there are inherent differences of intelligence and character between the races, I had to know if psychological differences are the product of heredity or environment, especially in that most important characteristic: intelligence.

Chapter 6:
A Question of Intelligence

After discovering that the establishment media had deceived me about the racial beliefs of America's founding fathers, I wondered about the premises of the race question. I was not yet ready to accept Carleton Putnam's thesis that Blacks were inherently less intelligent and less capable of sustaining civilization. It seemed unfair that God and Nature would have made one race less intelligent than another.

To understand the racial debate, I had to get down to its foundation. Were the races truly equal in intelligence and character? Before I could tackle that question, I needed to know the real sources of human behavior and performance. Was human intelligence and behavior rooted in the genes (heredity) or in conditioning (environment)? Only with that foundation could I hope to understand the racial question.

Since intelligence, more than anything else, distinguishes human beings from the animal kingdom, I decided to look into what intelligence is, how it is measured, and the real impact that it has on both the individual and society.

I began my quest by reading about the nature of intelligence, starting, as I like to do whenever I begin to investigate a subject, with a dictionary in hand.

intelligence *n.*
1. capacity for learning, reasoning, understanding, and similar forms of mental activity; aptitude in grasping truths, relationships, facts, meanings, etc.
2. manifestation of a high mental capacity: He writes with *intelligence* and wit.[20]

Intelligence is generally defined as the capacity to acquire and apply knowledge. Civilization is a product of people with a high enough intelligence to acquire and apply information, form concepts and ideas, and solve problems of language, farming, architecture, transportation, manufacturing, distribution, economics, and government. Intelligence seems even more important in the higher aspects of what we call civilization: law, religion, medicine, philosophy, literature, music, art and science.

What Is IQ?

Even though intelligence testing is now attacked by neo-Marxists as a tool of the elite, the father of the modern intelligence test was Alfred Binet, a French psychologist who in 1905 developed the test to identify and *help* children of low mental ability. Traditionally such children were barred from public education, but the French government had passed legislation ensuring that mentally deficient children would receive special educational programs. By 1911, he and his associate, Theodore Simon, had expanded the test to apply to adults. As they perfected their tests, it became obvious that they could identify children and adults who needed remedial help, but also discern those within the normal ranges of intelligence as well as those gifted in their mental abilities.

In 1912 the German psychologist Wilhelm Stern proposed dividing the mental age of a child by his chronological age to establish an overall indicator of intelligence. In 1916 American psychologist Lewis Terman introduced the IQ as the scale of scoring for his hugely successful Stanford Revision of the Binet Scales, the famous "Stanford-Binet." David Wechsler later developed the IQ tests most widely used today. He dropped the "mental age" concept and used instead the relation of an individual's IQ score to the average IQ score for his age — calling it "deviation IQ."

The critics of IQ testing were quick to point out that IQ is an abstract concept that may have no bearing on the real world. They quoted Dr. Edward Boring of Harvard, who wrote in 1923, "Intelligence as a measurable capacity must at the start be defined as the capacity to do well in an intelligence test. Intelligence is what the tests test."[21]

The statement is fundamentally true, but the same could be said of all tests. After all, a driver's license test determines only how well an individual does on the test, not necessarily how well he drives. However, no one would seriously argue that people who fail the driving test, on average, drive as well as those who have perfect scores.

Arthur R. Jensen, professor of Educational Psychology at the University of California at Berkeley, in expanding the work of pioneering English psychologist Charles Edward Spearman, substantiated the fact that all tests of mental ability have positive correlation with each other.[22] If a person scores below average in one type of mental-abilities test, he is likely to score below average in another type. Conversely, if he is above average in one, he is likely to score similarly high in another. Those who do well in reading, for instance, usually do well in math. The concept of the importance of general intelligence, or "g" intelligence as it is known academically, is accepted by a large majority of scholars and authorities in psychology.

The best way to determine whether IQ testing measures an important factor in relation to achievement is to compare large numbers of individuals' test scores with their later achievements in school and career, comparing how they match up. Researchers have done that all over the world. All of the major studies show that IQ has an important role in predicting individual achievement.

How IQ Correlates With Success in Life

Dozens of extensive studies have shown that IQ scores are at least as good as high school grades in predicting college performance. Most psychology professionals agree that learning ability is closely related to IQ. When I first looked into the matter in the early '60s, I found many scientific studies showing the importance of IQ, but the media gave the impression that the scientific community questioned its validity. In 1996 a committee of the American Psychological Association was asked to look into the IQ question. It found that IQ has a strong relation to learning ability.[23]

Numerous studies show that IQ correlates closely with grades and advancement in school; and that it even predicts an individual's success, job status and income better than does his family and socioeconomic background. Dr. Arthur Jensen — considered the preeminent authority on the practical validity of IQ — states the following in his latest book *The g Factor*:

> **Since Binet's invention, there have been countless studies of the validity of mental tests for predicting children's scholastic performance. The Psychological Abstracts contain some 11,000 citations of studies on the relation of educational achievement to "IQ." If there is any unquestioned fact in applied psychometrics, it is that IQ tests have a high degree of predictive validity for many educational criteria, such as scores on scholastic achievement tests, school and college grades, retention in grade, school dropout, number of years of schooling, probability of entering college, and after entering, probability of receiving a bachelor's degree. With equality of educational opportunity for the whole population increasing in recent decades, IQ has become even more predictive of educational outcomes than it was before the second half of this century."[24]**

Many studies show an expected correlation between a father's occupational status and his son's when he grows to middle age.[25] Most people would predict such outcomes because of the respective environments of the sons and fathers. The successful and well-to-do father is, of course, able to do more for his son than the father who is poor and unemployed. Remarkably, researchers find that a child's IQ is even a *better* predictor of child's eventual socioeconomic status than is his parent's socioeconomic status. Researcher R. B. McCall, for instance, has shown that a teenager's IQ and his eventual adult occupational status correlate at almost twice the rate as the father and son's occupational status.[26]

The Bell Curve: Intelligence and Class Structure in American Life, published in 1994 by Richard J. Herrnstein and Charles Murray, shows that a child's IQ has more bearing on his later socioeconomic status than his family's wealth.[27] It is more likely for a high-IQ poor child to reach a high socioeconomic status than for a moderate-IQ, wealthy child to reach the same status. *The Bell Curve* also shows that IQ has a strong correlation with a number of educational and societal factors, including grades in school, educational level attained, income, business success, and even social factors such as tendencies toward criminality, illegitimacy, and welfare dependence.

Another famous study examined the careers of similarly educated brothers who grew up together in Kalamazoo, Michigan. Kalamazoo has been testing all of its public school students since 1924 and offers a wealth of information. The studies showed that for brothers who had the same education and same family life, the young brothers, with an IQ difference of 15 points between them, averaged a 14 percent difference in income at middle age, with the high-IQ brother having the higher income.[28]

Job performance and productivity correlate with IQ the same way that personal success and income do. In the December 1986 *Journal of Vocational Behavior*, John E. Hunter, an industrial psychologist at Michigan State University, disclosed that high-complexity job performance correlated .58 with IQ scores. Even in low-skill jobs, intelligence correlated to overall job performance by .23. [Correlation measures how closely two properties are connected. A correlation of +1 means perfect association and 0 means they are completely independent. When the correlation is -1 that means that when one increases, the other always falls.]

Hunter argues that in all jobs intelligence predicts performance, but the factor is even more important in high-complexity occupations. From the classic studies mentioned above, to the latest research of the '90s, the results are overwhelmingly consistent, intelligence *does* matter. [29] [30] [31] [32] [33]

For all the high-minded language used by the egalitarian politicians and the U.S. Government, the commanders of the United States military readily accept the link between intelligence and later performance. Military authorities give every recruit what it calls an Armed Forces Qualification Test (AFQT). They don't call it an IQ test, but it does measure mental ability and is, in essence, an IQ test. Linda Gottfredson has pointed out that the military is prohibited by law (except under a declaration of war) from enlisting recruits below the 10th percentile level.

That law was enacted because of the extraordinary high training costs and high rates of failure among such men during the mobilization of forces in World War II."[34] A U.S. Department of Defense report states, " People with high AFQT scores are likely to achieve skill proficiency earlier in their first enlistment than those with low scores." [35]

An example of how powerfully IQ affects different areas of society can be seen in automobile accident rates. Australian psychologist Brian O'Toole showed a powerful inverse correlation between IQs and accident mortality rates. In a study of 46,166 men who previously served in the Australian armed forces, he found that those who had scores in the Army General Classification Test correlated to IQs of between 80-85, had almost *three times* the death rate due to motor vehicle accidents than those who scored in the 100-115 range. The mortality figures may be even more extreme for even lower IQ levels, but those who scored lower than an equivalent IQ of 80 were rejected from service, so there were no records for them.[36] O'Toole wrote: "[P]eople with lower intelligence may have a poorer ability to assess risks and, consequently, may take more poor risks in their driving than do more intelligent people."[37]

Death Rate per 10,000 due to Motor Vehicle Accidents for Australian Men Aged 20 to 34

IQ level	Death Rate
100-115	51.5
85-100	92.2
80-85	146.7

As I delved deeper into the IQ issue in the mid-'60s, I was amazed at the difference between the media discussion of the IQ controversy and the scientific literature on the subject. I began reading the papers of a number of psychologists who argued quite persuasively for the importance of IQ, but it seemed that these scientists and their studies received very little coverage in the popular media. Instead the media repeatedly suggested that IQ really did not mean anything. The popular media also suggested that only "racists" believe in a strong link between intelligence and heredity. There is a wealth of information on the important role of genetics in intelligence, but the media for the most part still ignores it, and repeatedly parrots the line that "there is no scientific evidence showing that intelligence is inherited." A more untrue statement has never been spoken.

Chapter 7:

Heredity or Environment?

If intelligence has a powerful impact on the success or failure of an individual, it stands to reason that the intelligence of a nation's population, as measured by IQ, affects the quality of the nation. I came to believe that the intelligence level of a nation's people is more important than its natural resources. The remaining question in my mind was whether human intelligence could be significantly raised by education and training or whether it is primarily an inherited ability. There has been a tug-of-war on the issue since man has built civilization.

Even in the earliest civilizations, a rudimentary grasp of the power of heredity to shape human character prevailed among the learned. Once man had learned to domesticate and breed specific varieties of plants and animals for unique characteristics, it was a short step to realizing that laws of heredity also applied to people.

Great thinkers throughout the ages have taken stands on the issue. In one of the oldest and most famous works of the West, the Greek classic *The Odyssey*, the author writes

> **The blood of your parents was not lost in you, but ye are of the line of men that are sceptered kings, the fosterlings of Zeus, for no churl could beget sons like you.**[38] – *The Odyssey*

French Jacobins and English empiricists such as Berkeley, Locke, and Hume[39] succinctly stated the opposing environmentalist position using the term *tabula rasa*, meaning that the mind is a "blank tablet" at birth, ready to be filled in by the world around it. The issue goes to the heart of who we are. Are our character, attitudes, talents and intelligence derived from the environment we grow up in or from the genes we inherit?

More than 100 years ago a pioneer of psychology, Sir Francis Galton, studied some families that produced generations of geniuses. Galton's research indicated that intelligence and achievement is primarily in the genes.[40]

Galton showed that high or low intelligence run in families. Since there was at that time no objective way of measuring mental ability, he based his assessments on what he defined as *eminence*, meaning illustrious achievements. Although members of the upper classes have disproportionate representation among the eminent, he found that among the upper classes themselves — although all their members are wealthy and attended the finest schools — intellectual achievement runs in certain families and their relatives the same way that mental retardation and even criminality runs in other families.

In the next few decades after Galton's work, many other scientists embraced the idea of the heredity nature of mental ability and their findings dramatically affected social policy. One of the most controversial U.S. Supreme Court cases concerned the heart of the Nature versus nurture debate. In the *Buck* v. *Bell* case, Chief Justice Oliver Wendell Holmes Jr., in deciding to approve the sterilization of mental defectives, wrote probably one of the most controversial sentences in the history of the court, "Three generations of imbeciles is enough." Holmes based his ruling on the belief that intelligence — or the lack of it — is hereditary.[41]

In contrast to the hereditarians, Marxism incorporated environmental determinism as a central part of its thesis. First perfect the environment, goes the argument, and a utopia, a worker's paradise, will arise. In 1948 the Soviet Union actually outlawed the science of genetics; all genetics not just human genetics, and reverted to Lamarckism, a pre-Darwinian theory named after French naturalist Jean Lamarck. He maintained that characteristics acquired by habit, use or disuse can be inherited. Russian scientist T. D. Lysenko, who seriously argued that you could change the strain of winter wheat to spring wheat through short-term environmental control, became the czar of Soviet biological sciences and saw to the execution of those scientists whose research contradicted his crackpot beliefs. Both Lamarck and Lysenko are today rejected by geneticists.[42][43][44]

Interestingly enough, many modern American "conservatives" have also now embraced the environmental idea by blaming the modern social ills strictly on the liberal policies of the "Great Society." It is similar to the way that liberals wholly blamed the social ills of poverty and crime on the conservative policies of previous administrations. Some conservatives have gone from a Horatio Alger, social-Darwinist philosophy (which held, expressed succinctly, that the best — meaning the strongest and smartest — would rise to the top in a free system) to the underlying principle of Communism: that all are equal, and thus everyone will rise if the environment is propitious.[45]

As a young man I had readily adopted the "environmentalist" position espoused by America's mass media. Today, as then, anyone who reads the daily newspapers or the weekly and monthly magazines and who watches television will be deluged with environmentalist polemics. Childhood and early adult environments are blamed for a violent criminal's destructive behavior, a poor person's poverty, an F student's grades, a drug addict's or alcoholic's dependency, an unemployed person's poor work habits, a welfare queen's fifth illegitimate child, a sexual deviant's weird behavior and a low-IQ child's failure to make it in school.

I had found it easy to believe the environmental argument because it offered so much hope. If only we change the child's environment, we are told, we can solve the great ills of modern society. It seemed so kind and humane to think that all people were really bright and morally good inside, only to be corrupted by an imperfect world. That sounded a lot nicer to me than to contemplate that some people were — to put it crudely — just biological slobs destined to be the inheritors of the failed societies of humanity.

By accepting the environmentalist position, I felt that I was being noble, understanding and compassionate toward the less fortunate and downtrodden. It was the same kind of thinking that leads one ultimately to think of the criminal as the victim. but, as I read more, I wrestled with the mounting evidence showing the greater impact of heredity.

A guest lecturer in one of my school classes had defended the power of environment in shaping the character and the IQ level by relating the old environmentalist argument that a child locked in a closet from birth would emerge a complete idiot. True, I had thought, but one of my classmates had had the temerity to make the crack, "But if you sent Coach [a particularly slow-witted athletics instructor] to Harvard University, he sure wouldn't come out a genius."

My classmate's statement went to the heart of the intelligence question. Are we all born equal in intelligence, excepting perhaps those children who are born with Down's Syndrome or other debilitating diseases? Can we all really be what we want to be, no matter if it's a world-class sprinter or a nuclear physicist?

Twin Studies

One way that science has emphatically answered that question is through the study of identical twins raised apart. Identical twins have, of course, an identical set of genes, whereas fraternal twins have the same genetic relationship as any two siblings, sharing only about half of their genes. If the environmental argument is correct, those identical twins separated at birth and adopted by different families should have IQ differences comparable to those in any two randomly adopted, unrelated children. Furthermore, they should certainly differ far more in intelligence and behavior than those of fraternal twins reared together.

There are many studies of twins, including a comprehensive study at the University of Minnesota by Dr. Thomas J. Bouchard Jr. that received worldwide attention. The study showed that the IQs of identical twins raised apart were much closer than random adopted children, and that they were even closer than for fraternal twins who were raised in the same home, and who attended the same schools. Not a single twin study has ever contradicted these results.[46][47]

Let me emphasize this important point — identical twins growing up in completely *different* environments — with *different* parents, *different* schools, *different* diets, *different* political and religious persuasions — have IQs closer together than those of fraternal twins raised in the *same* family. If intelligence is primarily created by environmental factors, certainly the fraternal twins raised together in the same familial, social, and educational environment should obviously have much closer IQs than twins who were raised apart.

I looked up and read more studies demonstrating the power of heredity in intelligence and found that even those focusing on identical and fraternal twins raised together yielded additional strong evidence. Because fraternal and identical twins are born only minutes apart and usually grow up in the same environment, they provide a way to measure the impact of heredity, while environmental factors are held steady.

Identical twins' IQs are much more strongly correlated than are those of fraternal twins. Correlations generally run about .85 for identical twins raised together as compared to .60 for fraternal twins. Psychologists Bouchard and McGue reviewed over 100 studies comprising 40,000 kinship pairs, almost all of that type of cognitive study reported in the scientific literature. Their correlations of IQ were:

IDENTICAL TWINS REARED TOGETHER	**+.86**
IDENTICAL TWINS REARED APART	**+.75**
FRATERNAL TWINS REARED TOGETHER	**+.60**

In all the studies comparing identical and fraternal twins — it is found that separated identical twins raised apart scored closer in IQ than fraternal twins raised together! Other sources of excellent data are found in studies of adopted children. Adopted children are closer to their genetic parents' IQs rather than with their foster parents who they grow up with.

The scientific research on intelligence has silenced all but the most belligerent egalitarians. Unfortunately the mass media in America are still promoting the unscientific and discredited environmentalist views of fringe neo-Marxist and far-left elements such as R. C. Lewontin, Steven Rose, Stephen Jay Gould, and Leon Kamin. The media almost always fail to mention these men's political affiliations, such as Kamin's former position as New England editor of the U.S. Communist Party's weekly newspaper. Similarly ignored is Lewontin's pivotal role in the pro-Marxist, Vietnam era "Science for the People," and Gould's smug recounting of learning his Marxism on his father's knee. Much of the public is still largely unaware of the overwhelming scientific evidence showing the prominent role of genetics in determining human intelligence, but the scientific community has become aware of it. Snyderman and Rothman did extensive surveys of those scientists involved in psychological research and found that by the middle of the 1980s the vast majority believed that IQ was profoundly affected by heredity.[48][49][50][51]

The Brain and Intelligence

Learning that IQ is primarily inherited made me ask the question, *What precisely is inherited?* Sophomoric as the answer seems; it is of course, the genes that construct the architecture and chemistry of the brain, along with all its overt and subtle variances. To accept the zero-heredity-impact argument of the Marxist Lamarckians, one is required to believe that, unlike any other human organ, the brain is not a product of the genes.

Scientists think that almost one-third of a human's genes are devoted to the brain, and those genes naturally vary. Intelligence is ultimately as physical as the structure that enables one to run with a football or shoot a basketball. It is rooted in the magnificent architecture and gray matter called the brain.

It is hard to imagine our minds as physically-rooted entities. After all, thoughts have no physicalness; we can't taste, touch, smell, see or hear them except in the confines of our own minds. Yet our brains are just as physical as the muscles in our arms and legs. Their construction and "wiring" is crucial to everything from our intelligence to our personality. Even our thoughts come from physical processes, both chemical and electrical, in our brains. The context of our mental abilities is dictated entirely by the structure, form, dimensions, density and chemical composition of the brain. If the structure of the brain were not important then we could teach any dog to read Dostoyevsky or any orangutan to understand organic chemistry. The more primitive structure and limited size of their animal brains prevent them from having high intelligence. Because of the structure of some people's brains, not every human can be taught to read and write, much less understand the fundamentals of organic chemistry.

There are dramatic differences between the brain of the human and that of the dog, or for that matter, the orangutan — that account for the differences in intellect between them. Even the dog and the orangutan have broad differences in their physical brains, and every zoologist would rate the orangutan as more intelligent than the dog. In fact, dog trainers report that there are sharp differences in intelligence between the different dog breeds, as well as distinctions in the breeds' temperaments and other aspects of personality.[52]

When first faced with this information about intelligence in dogs, I wondered what difference between the breeds could account for the mental differences? Only one explanation seemed feasible to me: Different genetic heritages result in physically different brains.

Just because the human brain is larger and more complex than that of the dog or even the higher primates does not make it any less subject to the same laws of genetics. Each human brain is as unique as a fingerprint. In fact, brains are vastly more complex and diverse than fingerprints. Neuroanatomist Paul Glees, in his classic textbook *The Human Brain* states that the brain is the "signature of a genetically unique person."[53] Most scientists agree that brains in higher primates and humans evolved larger over time because more voluminous and complex brains enabled problem-solving and learning skills. There is obviously a relation to the fact that a monkey has a large brain and is considered a more intelligent animal than a smaller-brained frog.

Even Charles Darwin cited numerous studies in support of his contention that "The belief that there exists in man some close relation between the size of the brain and the development of the intellectual faculties is supported by the comparison of the skulls of savage and civilized races, of ancient and modern people, and by the analogy of the whole vertebrate series."

What do the media gurus say about this? Years after I read my first article on brain size and intelligence, I read *The Mismeasure of Man*.[54] Its author is an avowed Marxist, Stephen Jay Gould. He analyzed and tried to invalidate brain-size research data from the 19th century and therefore disputed the relationship between head size and intelligence. He ignored more recent — and more scientifically precise — studies of human brains by researchers such as Todd, Vint, Simmons and Connolly.[55] There have been numerous studies since Gould's book that show a strong correlation between brain size and intelligence.

With modern MRI (magnetic resonance imaging) capabilities, extremely accurate measurements of the brains of living human beings can now be made. In a groundbreaking experiment at the University of Texas, 40 students were divided into two groups — one with IQs above 130 and another with IQs below 103. Since that time numerous similar studies have been done. A remarkably clear correlation of .35 was found between brain size and intelligence, a correlation actually higher than most traditional studies that compared head measurements and IQ.[56] It became obvious to me that intelligence was primarily hereditary simply because it was determined by the specific characteristics of the human brain.

Ego and IQ

The biggest obstacle in discussing the genetic nature of intelligence is our own egoism. Even though human beings universally blame outside forces for their failures, we consistently take credit for our successes. We don't want to think that we are limited in our horizons because of the inherent limitations of our genes, and we certainly don't want to give too much credit to our genes (something over which we have no control) for our achievements. We don't want to acknowledge that somebody else is truly smarter than we are. We can readily accept an athletic star's physical size and superiority but are reluctant to acknowledge mental superiority. Sure, many people can acknowledge an intellectual rival's educational level or experience, but most people are not as inclined to accept that a competitor has a superior mental ability. Yet hundreds of serious research studies continue to add to the evidence of genetic differences in intellectual ability. Indeed, general intelligence is one of the most highly heritable of all human traits.[57][58]

As I read the studies of IQ and understood its great impact on our lives, I realized why the IQ issue was so important among racial egalitarians. Most people — not just rural White "racists," but the leading egalitarians themselves — readily equate human worth with high intelligence. If one brings up the argument that one race is more intelligent than another, the egalitarian instantly equates that position to be saying that the Black race is "inferior." It is odd that liberals who dismiss IQ tests as meaningless somehow equate low IQ with blanket inferiority.

How less assuming it is to see intelligence as part, albeit an important part, of the whole picture. IQ is only one of the characteristics that make up the human being, for a person can possess exceptional abilities and still not have an exceptional IQ. The way a person lives his life — his responsibility, industriousness, honesty, courage, morality, and a thousand other qualities — is also vital in evaluating his worth. To say that the Black race is inferior to the White race because the average IQ is lower among Blacks is much like saying that Whites are inferior to Blacks because the average Black is faster in the 100-yard dash.

Whatever their intelligence level, Black people were genetically well suited for their historical environment in Africa. To say that their inherited capacity to adapt to that environment rather than the environment of computers and aerospace engineering makes them "inferior" human beings is a totally subjective concept. They would be inferior to what we value, perhaps, but inferior to what they naturally value, no.

At the same time I came to understand all this, I also realized that Western civilization runs on a high IQ. It is the high-octane genetically-created fuel of our culture and of our technology. I concluded that if there is a significant difference between Black and White IQs, it will have a profound impact on our society. As I read more about IQ, I found out that the real political opposition to it erupted because of the racial implications. Now that I had a firm grasp of the relationship among intelligence, heredity and environment, I began to plow deeply into the subject of racial equality with a thirst for the truth.

As for myself, it has always been easy for me to accept my own mental inferiority in relation to many brilliant human beings. I have a respectable IQ, but when I read about and consider the special genius of men like Thomas Edison, Francis Galton, Isaac Newton and William Shockley, it is hard to be egotistical. Every human being is going to be inferior or superior at some endeavor. I am philosophical about it, for it doesn't diminish my own sense of self-worth to know that there are many men and women born smarter than I am or physically stronger than I am.

Nor does it boost my self-worth to know that there are innumerable cretins on this planet. I decided at an early age to simply seek the truth, not only because it was valuable for its own sake, but also because I believed that in the unvarnished truth we can find solutions to the monumental problems facing this nation and the Earth.

All of this afforded me a useful starting point: Once I came to accept the power of genes and the validity of IQ as an important measure of mental stature, I felt that I was ready to take on the more emotionally charged question of whether or not there are significant differences in Black and White intelligence and behavior.

Thomas Jefferson's words inspired me as I delved into the most controversial subject in America. "There is not a truth existing which I fear, or would wish unknown to the whole world."

Chapter 8:

Race And Intelligence

It was easy for me to understand why the egalitarians were opposed to the studies showing that IQ is mostly hereditary, for it turns out that Blacks usually do very poorly on IQ tests. The natural inference is that if IQ is primarily inherited, and Blacks have dramatically lower IQs, then the differences between the races are likely to be genetic.

I found that there are hundreds of studies documenting the IQ differences between Blacks and Whites. Dr. Audrey Shuey, in her comprehensive work *The Testing of Negro Intelligence*, compiled more than 300 different IQ studies comparing Black and White intelligence.[59] They found that average Black IQ scores are between 15 and 20 points lower than White averages — in scientific terms, they vary between one and one and one-half standard deviations [SD] below Whites.[60]

The fact that dramatic IQ differences exist between Blacks and Whites can also be illustrated by the fact that Black activist groups have outlawed ability grouping in many schools, claiming that it "re-segregates the schools." In California it is even forbidden to use IQ tests to aid in the selection of students who would benefit from special classes for the educable mentally retarded. A courageous Black mother sued the state in an attempt to overturn the law so that her retarded child could get the remedial help she needed. In the *Larry P. v. Wilson Riles* case, the judge ruled that the tests were biased simply because more Blacks attained very low scores. Thus in the State of California it became official policy that the tests, along with ability grouping in education, are "racist" and forbidden merely because Black performance is substantially lower than that of Whites.[61] The case affords an excellent example of how efforts to artificially "equalize" the races can harm both Whites and Blacks.

I must stress that comparisons between White and Black scores are of averages of the groups. Because Blacks as a group score lower in IQ than Whites does not mean there are not some individual Blacks who score in the highest category and some Whites who score in the lowest. However, when one contrasts the overlapping bell-shaped curves of IQ performance by race and looks at the Black-White difference at different levels, it becomes obvious that the race difference becomes more pronounced at the high and low extremes of the distribution. For instance, One-half of all Blacks score in the lowest one-quarter of Whites.

On the high end of the scale, an IQ of at least 115 is considered necessary for excellent college work or for the top managerial and professional jobs in America. Only about 2.5 percent of Blacks score that high as compared to about 16 percent of Whites. About 20 times more Whites than Blacks per capita have IQs over 130, and somewhere between 50 and 100 more Whites are in the above 140 IQ range.[62] This is the IQ group that many psychologists believe is responsible for most of the greatest achievements of civilization.

Black and White IQ distribution

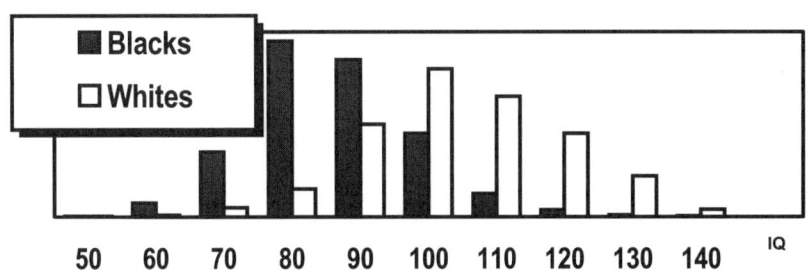

Black representation at the low-scoring end of the IQ scale has even stronger implications for society. At least 25 percent of Blacks are below 75 in IQ, and an IQ in the 70-75 range is classified as "borderline retarded" by most psychologists. Practically no one in that IQ range will graduate from high school or even learn much of elementary school basics; none will qualify for the armed forces, and few will be able to find good employment. [63] [64] [65] [66]

After learning the truth about racial differences in IQ and going public with it, for years I faced media condemnation as a "racist" for daring to say that 20 percent of Blacks had IQs below 75. In October 1994, many years after my first statements on the matter, *Newsweek* magazine did a cover story on the release of *The Bell Curve*,[67] the groundbreaking book on IQ and racial differences. *Newsweek* matter-of-factly stated that 25 percent (rather than 20 percent) of Blacks fell into that lowest category.[68] It took 24 years, but I had been eclipsed in my radical racial opinions by *Newsweek*.

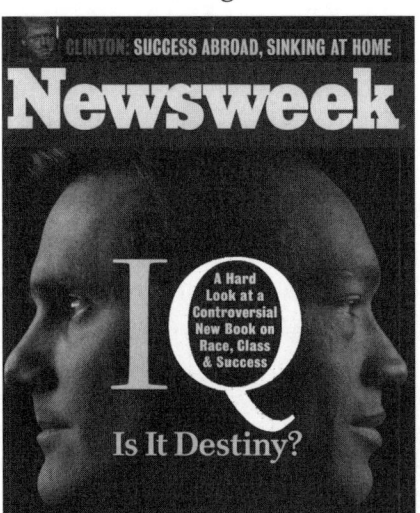

It went on to flatly assert, "If blacks are inferior to whites as a group, the dream of a truly integrated society is dead."

Even back in 1964 science had established the stark facts of White-Black IQ differences, but the media chose not to report these facts. In an analysis of 11 large studies of Black-White IQ differences, Arthur Jensen showed that there is a strong correlation between the Black-White gap on mental tests and the degree to which the tests accurately measure "g" intelligence (for general intelligence related to abstract reasoning and problem-solving ability). Blacks do relatively well on tests of rote memory (memorization of sequences of numbers or letters), but that correlates little with g.[69][70][71][72]

The popular media swept the facts under the rug, and the liberal psychologists argued that IQ doesn't really measure or mean anything and then added — as a precaution in case someone believed it did mean something — that IQ tests are culturally biased against Blacks.

Are Mental Tests Biased Against Blacks?

When I began discussing the Black-White IQ differences with my teachers and friends, I often heard the *Chitterlings* Explanation of low Black IQ scores. IQ tests were said to reflect White culture and therefore put Blacks at a disadvantage. For instance, they argue if White kids were asked questions about *chitlins* (the small intestines of pigs cooked and eaten as food), they would do as poorly as Black kids who are asked questions that use terms such as tennis.

In desperation some egalitarian psychologists have even argued that Black children would do better with testing in "Black English." Some went so far as to try to design tests that would purposely improve Black performance, but alas, when Whites took these same tests, they still scored much higher than Blacks.

Also, contradicting the cultural bias or *chitterlings* explanation for low Black IQ are studies showing that Hispanics (who on average are poorer than Blacks) and who have obvious language and cultural handicaps (many being new arrivals to our culture), score significantly higher than Blacks in the abstract sections of IQ tests. They consistently score higher in the verbal sections as well. American Indians, who in comparison with Blacks are poorer and generally more isolated from mainstream American culture and education centers, also do better than Blacks on IQ tests. Arthur Jensen in Bias in Mental Testing wrote:

> [O]n a composite of twelve SES [Socio-Economic Status] and other environmental indices, the American Indian population ranks about as far below black standards as blacks rank below that of Whites . . . but it turns out that Indians score higher than blacks on tests of intelligence.... On a nonverbal reasoning test given in the

first grade, before schooling could have had much impact, Indian children exceeded the mean score of blacks by the equivalent of 14 IQ points...opposite from what one would predict from the theory that ethnic group differences in IQ merely reflect SES differences.[73]

Blacks consistently do better on the parts of the IQ tests that have the largest cultural component and poorest on the parts that were the most culture-free. Blacks do far better on the verbal parts of IQ tests than they do on the parts with symbols measuring abstract mental abilities. If cultural bias is responsible for differences in Black and White IQ scores, then the biggest gap should be in the more culturally-loaded verbal tests. But the opposite is true.[74]

In more recent years, mechanical reaction-time tests also show strong evidence that IQ tests are not culturally biased against Blacks. Arthur Jensen and others have also found that mechanical speed of decision making correlates strongly with IQ. In these tests, subjects are set before a series of lights and respond to which one comes on. The speed of mental reaction strongly correlates with IQ test scores and is higher for White and Asian children than for Blacks. One would be hard-pressed to understand how reaction time to a flashing light could be culturally biased.[75][76]

I learned that written IQ tests actually tend to overrate Black mental abilities because a significant portion of most IQ tests are verbal, with a heavy reliance on memory and experience rather than abstract reasoning and problem-solving. If tests were more able to isolate spatial reasoning ability, the gap would grow even wider.

If an IQ test, SAT (Scholastic Aptitude Test), or Armed Forces Qualification Test (AFQT) is biased against a certain group, it would not accurately predict that group's performance. For instance, if Blacks score lower than Whites in IQ but do better in school than their IQs would suggest, this would indicate that the tests are not accurately assessing Black ability, and indicate bias against Blacks.

The reality is that IQ tests do quite well in predicting the performance of Blacks and Whites as a group. Actually, the college SAT tests have a bias somewhat against Whites in that Whites do slightly better in college than the tests indicate, and Blacks do slightly worse. It's unlikely that test designers intentionally biased tests in favor of Blacks; for if they knew how to do that, they would do more of it! Some Blacks with relatively high IQs often lack other character factors to do well at some life activities. The most prestigious scientific body in America, the National Academy of Sciences, through its research arm, the National Research Council, investigated whether there is test bias against Blacks in IQ and other intelligence-based tests such as the SAT. They stated:

> At the undergraduate college level, the equation for white students has usually been found to result either in predicted grades for blacks that tend to be about equal to the grades they actually achieve or. . . somewhat better than the grades they actually achieve. . .
>
> . . . The results do not support the notion that the traditional use of scores in a prediction equation yields predictions for blacks that systematically underestimate their actual performance. If anything, there is some indication of the converse. . . .[77]

Finding that the tests are biased against Whites, albeit modestly, illustrates once again that the truth of the matter is exactly opposite what the popular mass media regularly tells Americans. The Black-White IQ difference is not a result of the tests' cultural bias or discrimination, it is *real*.

Black IQ Is Markedly Lower, But...

As the studies of marked IQ differences between races increasingly mounted in the scientific community, racial egalitarians retreated to new ground. Many of them abandoned the *IQ is meaningless* and *tests are biased* arguments. They suggested that if Blacks had lower IQs than Whites (which had become patently undeniable), that it was simply because they grew up in "deprived" environments. The egalitarians blamed socioeconomic factors such as poverty and low parental education levels for low Black IQ scores.

However, many studies of Blacks and Whites take socioeconomic factors into account. They consistently find that even those Blacks who come from high income and well-educated families still have markedly lower IQs than Whites.[78]

SAT scores correlate very highly with IQ and the testing service has gathered information on the parental income, education, and race of its test-takers. It finds that Black students with a household income of more than $70,000 a year and who have at least one parent who is a college graduate — score *lower* on the SAT than Whites from households that make less than $20,000 annually and in which both parents are high-school dropouts.[79] [80] The most environmentally disadvantaged group of Whites who take the SAT — score higher than the most environmentally advantaged group of Blacks.

The psychological data for genetic explanations for poor Black performance in IQ are extensive and powerful. IQ studies including Blacks, Whites, and Asians have extensively correlated many socioeconomic factors, including family income, parental education level and occupation status, and school quality. Groups of low-income Whites with low parental education levels and low parental occupation statuses consistently score higher in IQ than Blacks from families of high income, high education levels and high occupation status.[81] [82]

The Harm of Ignoring Racial Differences

The argument that environmental conditions cause the difference in IQ levels between the races, admits that a *real* difference exists. If there is a *real* difference in the IQs of Black and White children — for whatever reason — it certainly suggests the ending of school integration, for it is far better for children to group them in line with their natural abilities.

A good example of the harm caused by ignoring IQ differences could be found in a classroom that has very bright and very slow-learning children side by side. The instruction is bound to be too challenging for the mentally slower child, who cannot keep up and thus becomes utterly lost and frustrated. On the other hand, the teaching will be too slow to challenge the bright child whose potential goes untapped. If such mental differences in the classroom fall along racial lines, one can imagine how tensions and ill-will can develop between the diverse groups.

Even though the races are clearly different in learning ability, the government operates on the false premise of equality. When California outlawed affirmative action in its college entrance programs, there was a dramatic decline in Black and Mexican acceptance[83] in the best academic schools. Egalitarians bewailed the results as unfair to Blacks and Mexicans. But what the lower minority numbers actually prove is that better-qualified Whites had been grievously discriminated against.

It has been more than 80 years since the first IQ studies were conducted involving both Whites and Blacks. In the 1990s Blacks score the same IQ in relation to Whites as they did in the 1920s, about 15 to 20 points lower. For 70 years, standards of living education, and employment opportunities have dramatically improved for Blacks, and they have been accompanied by massive school and social integration. Yet dramatic socioeconomic improvement has not raised Black IQ scores in relation to those of Whites.

The evidence is also clear that the IQ gap has not been narrowed by increasing educational stimulation in the Black child's early years, or by publicly-integrated schooling. [84] If there is any effect at all, it has only widened the gap. [85] The multibillion dollar Head Start preschool environmental-enrichment program, maintained primarily to help Blacks compete educationally, has resulted in no gains by Black students but a little gain by Whites. An extensive and excellent study was done by J. Currie and D. Thomas showing Head Start's abject failure.[86] Head start is the most expensive and widespread program to raise the educational performance of "disadvantaged youths.

The Scarr Study

Genetic orgins of lower Black intelligence can also be seen in a number of studies that chart proportional Black ancestry. One of the first major studies was done as early as 1916 in Virginia. Large groups of Black school children were divided in groups determined by the number of White and Black grandparents. All the Black subjects, pure or partially Black, were raised in the Black community's environment. The Blacks with four Black grandparents scored the lowest in IQ. Blacks with three Black grandparents and one White — a bit higher; Blacks with two White grandparents — higher still; and Blacks with three White grandparents scored highest in IQ among the Black children.[87] The most recent studies of the 1990s show precisely the same results.

One of the most powerful direct studies of race and environment was conducted by psychologists Sandra Scarr, Richard Weinberg and I. D. Waldman. All three are quite well known for their environmentalist opinions. The study analyzed White, Black and mixed-race adopted children in more than 100 White families in Minnesota. The study was an egalitarian's dream, because the children's adoptive parents had prestigious levels of income and education and were antiracist enough to adopt a Black child into their own family. Scarr is a strong defender of racial equality and maintained that environment played an almost exclusive role in IQ differences between the races. Scarr supports the importance of heredity in causing individual differences within a race, but she has argued that the between-race differences are mostly environmental.

The children in the study included adopted Whites, Blacks, and Mulattos as well as the biological children of the White adoptive couples. At the age of 7, the children were tested for IQ, and all of the groups, including the Blacks and Mulattos, scored above average in IQ. Scarr and Weinberg published a paper claiming to have proven the almost exclusive power of environment over race in IQ, even though they had to admit that the White children, whether adopted or not, scored well above the Black and Mulatto children and that the Mulatto children scored above the Blacks.[88]

A decade later, when the children reached the average age 17, a follow-up study was conducted that again included IQ measurements. As they matured, Black children had dropped back to an average of 89 in IQ, which is the average IQ for Blacks in the region of the United States where the study was done. The White adopted children scored an average of 106 in IQ, 17 points higher than the Black children, which is consistent with traditional studies of Black and White IQ differences. In line with genetic theory, the half-White, half-Black Mulatto adopted children scored almost exactly between the adopted Whites and Blacks.[89]

Results of Minnesota Transracial Adoption Study

Parental IQ	Biological Children	White Adopted Children	Mulatto parents adopted children	Black parents Adopted Children
IQ 115.35	109.4	105.6	98.5	89.4

Scarr and Weinberg reluctantly published their data from the follow-up survey, but they waited close to four years to do so, almost as if they were embarrassed by what they had found. Through a tortured reasoning process, they still argued that environment played a dominant role in IQ. But in their follow-up survey, unlike their first paper, they also admitted that genes had an important impact as well. Both Richard Lynn and Michael Levin effectively showed in their reanalyses of Scarr's own data, that genes clearly comprise the dominant role in intelligence levels of those adopted children.[90][91]

African IQ Studies

Genetic tests indicate that almost all American Blacks have some White genes, while only one percent of Whites have Black genes.[92][93] This probably occurred because American society classified every person with any degree of Black blood as a Negro and strictly segregated them. IQ scores in Africa (where they are presumably more purely Black) are even lower. As American Blacks are one standard deviation below Whites in IQ (about 85), pure blacks in Africa of equal schooling with Whites — average about two standard deviations below Whites (below 75).[94][95][96]

Professor Richard Lynn compiled studies in 1991 of IQ in Africa, where there is far less White genetic addition to the Black gene pool than in the United States. He found that sub-Saharan Africa Blacks have an IQ of below 75, which is almost two Standard Deviations below the White norm. By European standards, these figures mean that approximately 50 percent of Black Africans would be classified as borderline mentally retarded or below (almost twice the rate of Blacks in the United States). Since Lynn's review in 1991, three newer studies have confirmed his work. They used Raven Progressive Matrices, a noncultural-specific test that is an accurate measure of the nonverbal part of general intelligence. A Black Zimbabwean, Fred Zindi, conducted one of the studies which compared 204 Zimbabwean 12 to 14 year olds and matched them to 202 English students for sex, educational level, and class background. English students scored an average IQ of 97 while Blacks of comparable background averaged 70 in IQ.[97][98][99][100]

African IQ vs. American IQ

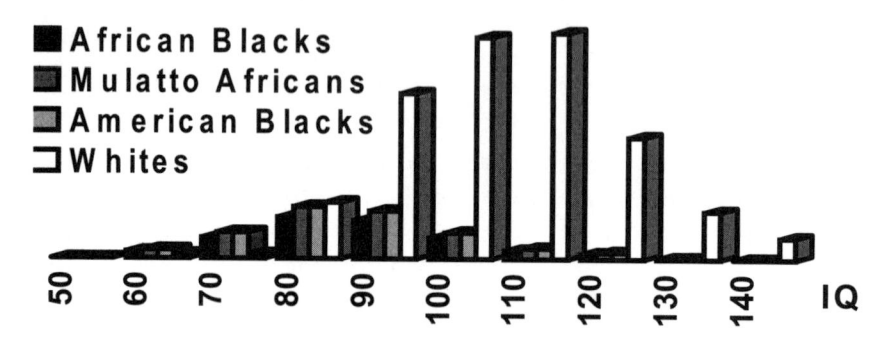

- African Blacks
- Mulatto Africans
- American Blacks
- Whites

(bar chart showing IQ distributions from 50 to 140)

Attempts to Refute The Significance of Race

A few studies have purported to prove that with the right environmental stimuli Black children would develop IQs similar to those of White and Asian children. The Milwaukee Project was the most famous of these, and inevitably it attracted plentiful media coverage in its heyday. It was reported that through intensive early childhood intervention and stimulation, underprivileged, slum-dwelling Black children had their IQs increased 30 points in comparison with the control group.[101] *The Washington Post* wrote triumphantly that the project's success "settled once and for all" the question of whether kids of poor socioeconomic backgrounds are held back by environment or by heredity.

Unfortunately for the egalitarians, their euphoric media bubble burst when the Milwaukee Project's director, Rick Haber, was convicted and imprisoned for embezzling government money. While this is not directly relevant to the results of the project, it does call into question the trustworthiness of its director. Howard L. Garber, long-time associate of Haber, in 1988 issued a report on the project that revealed the IQ gains were artificial, having been achieved by intensive practice on problems similar to those on the Stanford-Binet test, and that the kids' IQs declined steadily after leaving the program, with the gains never translating into academic success. Ultimately their abilities matched at the same level as that of the control group, which, of course, had no intervention.[102][103]

Herman Spitz, in his book *The Raising of Intelligence*, documents dozens of similar programs that failed miserably to raise the IQ of Blacks. In their initial stages, the media gave them extensive coverage and rave reviews, but little coverage of their ultimate failure. The pattern of publicity is identical to that under Lysenkoism in the Soviet Union. Over the years there were many media blitzes proclaiming the remarkable success of various early intervention programs. With embarrassing regularity the touted program was allowed to sink into quiet disrepute while the media trumpeted the miraculous results of another new approach. [104] [105] [106]

Another example of media "proof" that Black-White differences are environmental is the coverage of the Chicago Black teacher, Marva Collins. One of the most famous personalities in American education, Collins has gotten extensive media coverage, including adulatory articles in *The New York Times* and sumptuous praise on the television show *60 Minutes*. She claimed that seemingly "unteachable" inner-city children between 5 and 10-years-old had soared in standardized tests under her teaching methods and were reading and comprehending Tolstoy, Plato, and Shakespeare. In spite of such incredible claims, the media never asked Collins for hard scientific evidence to substantiate her assertions, nor has her "miracle" been successfully duplicated by any other psychologists and educators in controlled studies. These kinds of miraculous stories, ever popular in the mass media, for good reason never find their way into the scrutiny afforded by scientific journals.[107]

A Forbidden Subject

The White-Black IQ gap is forbidden knowledge in the public realm. In 1986 the American Psychological Association seriously debated whether all research on Black-White differences should be banned.[108] Much earlier, in 1962, the American Association of Physical Anthropologists voted on censuring the very book that began my search for the racial truth: *Race and Reason*.[109] Before taking the vote, the eminent president of the association, Dr. Carleton Coon, asked for a show of hands of who at the meeting had actually read the book. Only two or three hands went up. When the association approved the censure resolution, Coon resigned his post in protest. Such Luddite deliberations should raise alarm bells in the minds of all of those who seek the truth, for they are clearly reminiscent of the efforts of the Church in the Middle Ages to ban astronomical research when it challenged religious notions of the structure of the universe. What kind of truth is it that must suppress its questioner?

Scientific evidence of inherent racial differences is overwhelming and obvious. I could guess how Galileo or Copernicus felt when his tracking of the heavens convinced him that the sun did not revolve around the Earth. The evidence was so clear of the Sun is the center of the solar system that some clerics refused to look at it. One of the clerics in the controversy with Galileo, Cardinal Bellarmino, refused to look through the telescope because he said the Devil would make him see things that Galileo said were there. A narrow-necked bottle that symbolized his narrow mind became known as the Bellarmino bottle. Bellarmino's bias is perfectly analogous to egalitarian true believers that refuse to look at the mountain of evidence that challenges their creed.

In the America of 1964, as in the America of today, there was no more degrading and damaging epithet than "racist." The word was not used to mean a person who race is important in the affairs of mankind; it was and is a term associated with hatred, repression and human brutality. As Galileo's facts of the solar system were equated with the Devil, so today facts of race are associated with Hitler.

Yet for me, understanding inherent racial differences had nothing to do with hatred, and I sensed no hatred in the words of the scientists I read. They simply sought the truth. And so did a precocious 14-year-old boy reading in his room far into the night.

What is Prejudice?

When I did my report explaining the arguments against racial integration of schools, a couple of my more liberal classmates accused me of being prejudiced and bigoted. The words stung. I had no anger or hatred toward Blacks or anyone else, and I could not understand why I should be called prejudiced just for researching and reporting on a particular scientific and political viewpoint. As I shared more of what I learned with anyone who would listen, classmates, teachers, neighbors, the words prejudice—hate—bigotry kept on coming up like a mantra. When I looked up prejudice and bigotry in the dictionary, I came to realize that my slanderers were guilty of the very offenses of which they accused me.[110]

prejudge
v.t. to pass judgment on prematurely or without sufficient reflection or investigation.

prejudice
n. v. an unfavorable opinion or feeling formed beforehand or without knowledge, thought, or reason.

bigot
n. a person who is extremely intolerant of another's creed, belief, or opinion.

In one common usage of the term, *prejudice* denotes an irrational hatred or dislike toward Blacks or other racial groups. Anyone who believes in racial differences, even if the basis for his belief is scientific and reasoned, finds himself branded with this pejorative term. Most egalitarians have prejudged an idea (inherent racial differences) as I once did, before reading both sides, and they themselves are hatefully intolerant (bigoted) against those who differ with them. The press never applies the word *prejudice* to them.

I came to realize that when I so fervently believed in racial equality, it was I who showed prejudiced in the real sense of the word, for up to that time, because of the liberal press' bias, I had heard and learned only the pro-equality arguments. Until I read *Race and Reason*,[111] I had read only pro-equality books and magazine and newspaper articles. And that's not counting the hundreds of TV programs, movies, sermons and speeches that I had seen and heard that promoted egalitarian principles. I had *pre-judged* the issue before hearing both sides.

Most of those who called me bigoted and prejudiced had never read even *one* book or article questioning racial equality. They are simply not open-minded on the issue.

There is no doubt that some Whites who are opposed to Blacks are bigots, that is, they have prejudice as to their beliefs and are intolerant of the opposition. But, certainly, with the mass media presenting only one side of the racial equality argument, bigots are more likely found in the ranks of the egalitarians. Even well-known scientists and public figures have faced great difficulty, even physical suppression, for expressing their opinions about racial differences.[112][113][114][115][116] In the academic community, no egalitarian scientists have been prevented from speaking or assaulted by those who believe in racial differences, but racial free-thinkers certainly have.

It is ironic as well that the greatest support for Black and White racial equality has been found in the Whitest areas of America, and the greatest skepticism of it in the areas of the nation with the greatest Black presence. I realized that those who personally experience few Blacks but judge them as equal (and sometimes even superior) to Whites, prejudge them — while Whites who live and work among them, form their opinion after having *experienced* them. Even though most Southern Whites grow up with a constant stream of egalitarian media propaganda, they more often weigh both sides of the issue before coming to believe in racial differences. They make what could be called an *afterjudgment*.

Most racial egalitarians have good motives. They think that their position is enlightened, that it will bring goodness, and that God is on their side. But those are the same kinds of motivations that decried Galileo's astronomy as a work of the "Devil's hatred of God." In fact, the egalitarians have a special, emotionally-charged word to describe those who question racial equality: *hate*. Egalitarians love to hate the *haters*.

The ultimate word used to describe belief in racial differences is *racism*. But the word racism is loaded because it is not defined as simply belief in inherent racial differences. In most dictionaries it is also defined as "usually involving the idea that one's own race is superior and has the right to rule others," and also as "hatred and intolerance of another race or races."[117] To understand that racial differences exist does not necessarily make one want to rule over or hate other races. It is similar to the use of the term heretic in the middle ages. Astronomers who realized that the sun rather than the Earth is the center of solar system were branded heretics because the book of Genesis seems to indicate the Earth is at the center. Of course, just because an astronomer believed in heliocentricism did not make him a hater of God, any more than belief in racial differences makes one hate other races.

In later years, in a survey of academics, the authors of *The IQ Controversy: The Media and Public Policy*, Snyderman and Rothman found that 53 percent of respondents believed that both environment and genes caused the race difference. [118] [119] [120] [121]Over a period of 20 years the experts had come to the same opinion of scorned men such as Carleton Putnam, William Shockley, and Arthur Jensen back in the 1960s.

If the primary determinant of racial differences is heredity rather than environment, then genetic differences should show up in the brains of the different races. So my next focus was to explore the research on the physical differences between the races.

Chapter 9:

The Roots of Racial Difference

At the age of 10 I kept two white female rats in our garage in a large wooden box that I had built. It had a wood frame and fine-grade chicken-wire top that fit poorly. On a spring day, I discovered that one of my rats was showing signs of gestation. Even though I did not understand it, I supposed that I had mistaken a male rat for a female. I couldn't understand why the father looked so female, for I had a lot of familiarity with White rats, raising and selling them to the local pet stores and the Woolworth's store near my home.

The babies were finally born little pink sacks with four extruding legs and eager mouths but just outlines of closed eyes and ears. Each day I played with the little ones, but as they grew older they seemed decidedly different from their mother and the other rat whom I presumed must be their father. As they began to grow their new coats, the fur grew out not white but gray. More dramatically, their behavior seemed strange as well.

By the time they reached a few weeks old, equivalent to a human's teenage years, no matter how often I held them, the brood acted increasingly wild and uncontrollable. They had differences that went much further than simply the gray color of their coats. Their wildness progressed to the point that whenever I put my hand into the cage, the sawdust and wood shavings went flying as they scattered fearfully from the very same human hand that had lovingly fondled and petted them from birth. They were fast, excitable, quick to bite and physically superior to the domesticated breed. Pet white rats are very passive, slow-moving, deliberate creatures, whereas their wild rat cousins are excitable, lightning quick, aggressive and violent.

Finally I came to the realization that both white rats in the cage were actually female and that a wild rat had gnawed and squeezed into the wooden cage and mated with one of them.

A few years later, as I studied the realities of human race, I understood fully that the different breeds of rats are the genetic equivalent of human races. Breeding can occur between different races, even when there may still be dramatic genetic differences between them. The contrast between races can be in physical or psychological traits and in social or individual behavior. The behavior of those half-white, half-wild rats obviously was not a result of their environment. I had provided them with the same nurturing as for my white rats. In fact, they were suckled by their white rat mother and raised with two white rat females and constant human intervention, but their behavior was *wild*.

As a teenager looking into the race question, I looked back on the rat episode of a few years earlier. It seemed obvious that the difference in the behavior of my rats was wholly the result of genetics. The fact that the environment for the mixed-breed rats was the same as that for the completely domesticated ones suggested that there was a physical difference between the brains and hormones of the domesticated white rats and those of the breed of half-wild, gray rats. These genetic differences had powerful behavioral effects.

There were other telltale proofs of the power of heredity from my menagerie of childhood. In the course of my grade-school years, I had dozens of pets that I had captured from the swamps and forests near my home. Some breeds were amenable to domestication if reared from birth, while others were not, even though they received the same nurturing from me.

As I pondered the power of heredity and environment, another unforgettable incident of my childhood came to mind. A friend found a tiny, hungry, new born kitten in my neighborhood shortly after his pet dog had given birth to a litter of four pups. Weak and delicate, its eyes barely open, the kitten seemed likely to die. As an experiment, my friend removed one of the puppies from his mother and rubbed it thoroughly all over the tiny kitten, and then he nestled both of them among the other pups of the nursing mother. To his surprise the mother allowed the kitten to nurse. After a couple of weeks, it became healthy and robust. I loved to go over to my friend's house and see the unusual sight of a kitten nursing with and growing up among puppies.

Although the kitten had been nursed by a dog and although my friend had treated the kitten and the puppies alike, the kitten still grew up with a personality that was distinct from the rest of the litter. The kitten stalked its prey and then suddenly pounced, whereas the puppies ran headlong to their targets. In physical tussles with the pups, the kitten used its paws as its primary weapons, whereas the dogs preferred using their jaws. The kitten never attempted to mimic the sharp barks of its adopted brothers and sisters, instead preferring the feline hiss of anger or the meow of desire. After having been in the company of dogs almost its entire young life, and never having even seen another cat, she looked and behaved like a perfectly normal cat. And by the way, it never came when we called it.

Thinking back on these things, I tried to reduce what I knew to the simplest form. *Why does a dog bark and a cat meow?* I asked myself. I answered my own inquiry: *Because the dog's brain is constructed in a way that makes him bark and behave like a dog, and a cat's brain is built in a form that makes it meow and behave like a cat.*

Wanting to expand my theory, I called a friend of mine from school whose family owned a dog kennel and had bred dogs for more than 30 years. He explained to me that different breeds of dogs had distinctly different personalities. Violence, aggression, passivity, loyalty, stoicism, excitability, intelligence — all these things sharply varied in the many breeds of dogs. For example, he explained that the Chihuahua is extremely excitable and hyperactive by nature, whereas the Saint Bernard is stable and stoic. He talked about the natural violent aggression of the pit bull as compared to the naturally friendly disposition of the Golden Retriever. My friend explained why parents of small children often chose a Golden Retriever as their pet because the breed is exceptionally friendly and protective of children. Even when children torment the Golden Retriever, he told me, the breed will rarely respond violently toward them.

I also picked up an interesting little book on the history of dog breeding and found that not only did dogs have distinct personalities according to their breed, but that they were bred by man precisely for those personalities as well as for physical characteristics such as size and color. Any dog trainer would laugh if told that the only difference in breeds of dog is the color of their coats. If a dog's distinct personality characteristics are not created by solely by its training, the tendencies *must* be carried in the structure of its brain.

Armed with my newly gained knowledge, I asked my biology teacher how the classifications of breeds of dogs compared to the classifications of the races of mankind. Taken aback, she told me that she had never been asked that question by any student before, but she said *breed* and *race* are essentially two words for the same biological classification: subspecies. All dogs are members of the species Canis familiaris, of which there are at least 140 different breeds (subspecies or races). She repeated what I already knew — that the commonly accepted test for whether two groups were different species or subspecies of the same species was whether they could interbreed. The various breeds of dogs, just as the various races of humans, can interbreed in spite of obvious inherent differences.

Even though she taught biology, which included human biology, she became very uncomfortable equating differences in human races as compared with breeds of horses or dogs. It was as though I had trespassed on forbidden ground, but I saw nothing heretical about the inquiry. To understand those distinctions that separated man from the other species, and to comprehend the differences in mankind seemed important. How could we begin to understand the world around us without having an understanding of what makes us the way we are?

By then I knew that no fewer than a thousand scientific studies had demonstrated that there was a significant difference in IQ between the White and Black races, that IQ differences have a major impact on individual socioeconomic success, and that ample evidence showed that heredity rather than environment was the major source of this difference. [122] [123] [124] [125] [126] [127] [128]

Black and White Brains: The Facts

Books and articles on IQ led me to other studies revealing that significant differences existed between the brains of Blacks and Whites. In fact, the data on the racial differences in brain structure were even more cut and dried than those based on psychological testing. I found that Negro and White brains have been weighed, compared, and analyzed for decades, and the results have consistently shown Black brains to be smaller than White and Asian brains. As an illustration of the marked difference, even though Blacks are physically far larger than Asians, the latter have physically larger brains.[129]

In *The Mismeasure of Man*,[130] a popular media-touted egalitarian book, Stephen Jay Gould claimed that 19th century researchers used false methodology in comparing White and Black brains, and implied there are no differences. Gould, however, carefully left out many more recent studies that document intrinsic brain differences between Blacks and Whites. [131] [132]

In fact, ten years before the publication of Gould's book, *The Mind of Man in Africa* by John C. Caruthers showed that there had been five major studies using a modern methodological basis on Black and White brain differences, by Todd, Pearl, Vint, Simmons, and Connolly. Gould carefully avoided mentioning these more recent studies, except for two brief sentences about Pearl, whom he praised for saying that nutrition might explain the racial difference in brain sizes. Gould conveniently left out Pearl's data on Brain differences. Caruthers points out that a number of scientific studies show that Black brains are on average 2.6 percent to 7.9 percent smaller than White brains.[133]

Simultaneous with Gould's work, a 1980 study of brain weight that included data on Black and White brains showed that Black babies' brains were on average 8 percent smaller and lighter than White brains. [134] In the 1980s and '90s additional studies by Broman, et al, and Osborne have consistently shown significant differences between White and Black brain sizes. [135] [136] [137]

In the 1950s, direct studies comparing White and Black brains came to an end for a while, it being considered impolite, insensitive, and politically incorrect to contemplate such differences.[138] After a long hiatus, a number of more recent studies of brain physiology show the same evidence of differences in brain sizes between Blacks and Whites as was first reported in the last century.[139]

Perhaps the most extensive research of all was done by the National Collaborative Perinatal Project, which studied more than 14,000 mothers and children. The project was national in scope and studied mothers and their children from the time of conception through birth and early childhood. The objective of the study was to discover the main correlates of infant mortality, health, and intelligence and other aspects of child development. Subjects were tested for IQ at ages 4 and 7. Extensive body and head measurements were taken at birth and at 8 months, 1 year, 4 years, and 7 years.

Dr. Arthur Jensen analyzed the massive data from the study and found some startling things. Even within families, the higher-IQ sibling usually had the largest head size. The study also bore out numerous previous studies that had shown Blacks to have smaller heads, on average, than Whites, and corresponding lower intelligence. As a striking confirmation of the correlation between head size and intelligence, the study found that Black and White children who matched closely for IQ had, on average, little difference in head size. [140] If the size of the physical brain correlates with IQ, it makes good sense that intelligence is based on the physical structure of the Brain itself and thus has an inherited component.

Much earlier studies had shown differences in the Supra Granular Region of the brain, differences in the amount of frontal lobe area, and differences in the sulcification and fissuration of the brain between Blacks and Whites. In 1950 Connolly wrote:

> **The Negro brain is on the average relatively longer, narrower, and flatter than the brain of Whites. The frontal region,...larger in male Whites than in Negroes, while the parietal is larger in Negroes than in Whites... It can be said that the pattern of the frontal lobes in the White brains of our series is more regular, more uniform than in the Negro brain...The White series is perhaps more fissurated and there is more anastomosing of the sulci...** [141]

The importance of the brain's frontal lobes to its owner's personality was highlighted in the films *One Flew Over the Cuckoo's Nest*[142] and also in Jessica Lange's movie on Frances Farmer called *Frances*.[143] For many years some overly aggressive mental patients were given a "frontal lobotomy," an operation in which the frontal lobe area is neutralized or removed. The patient still had his memory intact, but his spirit, willpower and motivation were considerably weakened. Ward C. Halstead, biopsychologist and professor of Experimental Psychology, Department of Medicine, University of Chicago, wrote: "The frontal lobes are the portion of the brain most essential to biological intelligence. They are the organs of civilization — the basis of man's hope for the future."[144]

Most of the scientists who have studied the frontal lobes region, whether or not they make any racial comparisons, find that this portion of the brain is most responsible for fine modulation of motivation or initiative, and inhibition of primitive impulses. An increasing amount of sulcification (fissuration) of the frontal lobes suggests far more complexity of capacities; it is perhaps a measure of evolutionary development. In the lower mammals, such as the rabbit, the frontal lobes are smoother. Professor Connolly also wrote, "There is a degree of correlation between the sulcal pattern and the development status of the animal in the series of primate forms."[145]

Recent studies of the criminal brain show that criminals convicted of violent, impulsive crimes have less activity in the frontal lobes and the cerebral cortex. So not only does the frontal lobe area seem to affect initiative, it also seems to add self-control over man's passions as well.

In the middle '60s I had somewhat less evidence of inherent racial differences than is available today, but the evidence from the 1860s through the early 1960s was copious and unrefuted, it just was little mentioned in the popular press. After the Second World War, those who dared to publicly state the truth of racial differences were greeted either by media silent treatment or with slander. Yet over the years the important role of DNA and the genes in everything from schizophrenia to obesity and now even to homosexuality has been increasingly documented. A whole new academic discipline called behavioral genetics is rapidly growing. [146] [147]

There is obviously no more important organ in the human body than the brain. It is what truly distinguishes us from both our closer and more remote relatives on the evolutionary ladder. In fact, the size and form of the brain is matter-of-factly used by anthropologists as a barometer of evolutionary development. Ironically the same anthropologists who track the evolutionary development of mankind by his increased cranial capacity often insist that racial differences in brain size and morphology of modern man are not important. The evidence, however, is clear. Size, physiology, morphology and chemistry of the brain have much to do with the psychological distinctions of individuals and the broad characteristics that distinguish between the different races. Science has found significant genetic influences on intelligence, behavior and achievement in the different races. The depth of those differences we are only now beginning to grasp.

The Retreat of Racial Egalitarianism

In the racial egalitarian line of defense they have argued that:

1) **Blacks are really not less intelligent — a common popular argument) But...when critics point out that hundreds of studies show a consistent and dramatic lower IQ scores for Blacks they allege that:**

2) **Differences in IQ are the result of racially biased tests. But...when proven that they are not racially or culturally biased, they then argue that:**

3) **Lower average Black IQs are simply the result of socioeconomic factors. But...when the differences show up even when socioeconomic factors for Whites and Blacks are matched, they retreat to saying that:**

4) **Environmental stimulation of young Blacks in programs such as Head Start will bring up the Black children to the White IQ level. But...when shown that Head Start resulted in absolutely no increase in Black IQ, they postulate that:**

5) **IQ really does not mean anything anyway. But...when shown that hundreds of social scientists proved that IQ has a tremendous impact on educational and socioeconomic success — they finally retreat to an egalitarian defense that accepts the biological determination of intelligence: they allege that poor nutrition is responsible for the differences in mental development of Blacks and Whites.**

The final egalitarian defense is interesting in that it accepts that intelligence is important and is rooted in the biology and formation of the brain itself. Instead of trying to dispute the natural role of genes in the architecture and development of the brain, the egalitarians simply argue that nutrition and other biological factors of the mother and of the young child dramatically affect the brain's development. They argue that Blacks, because they are poorer than Whites, are nutritionally deprived and thus held back in the development of their brains.

European children who grew up in the starvation of central Europe, during the stress and starvation at the end and right after the Second World War, show no ill effects in lower IQ. Their IQ average compares favorably with those both the period before and after the conflict.

The scientific studies of nutrition show that there is little difference between the nutrition of Black and White children. Robert Rector showed in a survey by the U.S. Department of Agriculture that Black preschool children actually consume more protein than do average White children.[148] Children in families 75 percent below the poverty line actually consume as much of the major vitamins as children 300 percent above the poverty line.[149]

The argument that the brains of young Blacks are malnourished is almost laughable when one looks at the absolute Black domination of track and field, basketball and football. It is hard to imagine that the same nutrition that enables Blacks to develop nutritionally healthy bodies that help make them 15 times per capita more represented than Whites in these major sports, has during the same time period--*starved their brains!* [150] [151] [152]

Racial differences also are obvious in the physical realm. In the 1960s Blacks dominated the male sprinting events of the Olympics and, with integration of sports, they were rapidly increasing their numbers in professional basketball and football. At this writing Blacks now make up approximately 80 percent of the National Basketball Association, 66 percent of the National Football League, and 100 percent of the top 50 male sprinters in the world who compete in professional and Olympic 100- and 200-meter dashes. This is true although well-organized track and field is much more prevalent in White nations than Black ones and although there are far more White high-school athletes.

Some have suggested that Black overrepresentation in basketball comes from greater desire on the part of Blacks as compared to Whites. Certainly, there are just as many young Whites who desire the multimillion-dollar income and popularity of the professional basketball player, but a Black person is 29 times more likely to be in the NBA than is a White. It seems logical that the differing performance of Whites and Blacks has an anatomical and physiological basis. Scientists who have investigated the issue say precisely that.

There are numerous physical distinctions between the White and Black race. Blacks have greater proportions of muscle types that favor quick bursts of speed than Whites do. They also have less body fat, smaller body cavities, longer arms in relation to their height, and numerous other differences that contribute to their excelling in sports that favor quick bursts of speed as well as jumping ability. They are favored in sports where those traits are the most important and have a disadvantage where strength and other characteristics are favored. Whites and Asians dominate the strength sports of weightlifting and gymnastics and the higher density in Blacks' bones results in less buoyancy and a distinct disadvantage in swimming and other water sports.

For a prominent person to discuss these obvious and inherent differences between the races is as taboo as discussing the differences in the brain or the psychological traits that are so critical to the character of a society or civilization. Sports commentators such as Jimmy the Greek and baseball great and Los Angeles Dodger front office employee, Al Campanis, have been fired or publicly humiliated for saying out loud what most people know by simple observation. Harsh suppression of such obvious truths is a revealing gauge of the intolerance of the egalitarian religion. When I first thought about these things and learned the scientific basis of racial difference, I thought it much like the child's fable *The Emperor's New Clothes*. Everyone knew the emperor was wearing only his underwear, but nobody dared to say anything. It simply took the honesty of a little boy to break the bubble of denial.

If only it would be that easy, I thought. The racial picture was coming together for me. The races are profoundly different; I saw clearly that the emperor has no clothes. But seeing the emperor of racial equality in a new light was not enough for me. I wanted to know *why* the emperor came to have no clothes. I wanted to know more about the behavioral differences between the races and how they originated. I already knew enough to know that my inquiry would lead to looking into the processes of evolution itself.

CHAPTER 10:

THE EVOLUTION OF RACE

In looking into the issue of race, much of my attention had dealt with the impact of heredity on intelligence, but evidence accumulated showing the powerful role of genetics in human behavior in many areas beyond IQ.

The popular version of psychology packaged by the liberal media continued to insist that upbringing or conditioning shaped all human personality traits. It is an article of faith that criminal behavior comes from a bad environment or dysfunctional family. It seemed that every societal problem blamed poverty, poor education, or bad parenting. Some even blamed high robbery and murder rates on the availability of guns.

Few Americans know that numerous studies show that a person's disposition toward criminality can be inherited. One extensive study analyzed the data compiled from 14,427 adoptions in Denmark from 1924-1947. Over two decades of data revealed that the biological children of criminals, even when adopted by non-criminal parents, had much higher rates of criminality than that the adopted children whose genetic parents were law-abiding.

Every major adoption study of criminality in the 20th century shows similar results. Studies of identical and fraternal twins raised together show that identical twins are more than twice as much alike in their criminal behavior as are fraternal twins.[153] In a number of scientific research studies done in the 1990s, it has been shown through MRIs and electrical scans that there are differences in the functioning of the average brains of criminals as compared to the law abiding.[154] [155] The following is from the *Journal of Biological Psychiatry* in 1997 about a study of the brains of 41 murderers who pled not guilty by reason of insanity and 41 age and sex matched non-criminals. It shows that their brains revealed differences in structure between them and the non-criminal group.

> These preliminary findings provide initial indications of a network of abnormal cortical and subcortical brain processes that may pre-

dispose to violence in murderers found NGRI [not guilty by reason of insanity].[156]

Numerous studies show that extraversion, introversion, altruism, selfishness, self-esteem, dishonesty, truthfulness, and many other character traits have a strong hereditary influence. I had always believed that those kinds of personality traits were a product of environment rather than genes, but once I read the scientific journals, I found the evidence persuasive. While I learned these things as a teenager, William Hamilton and others launched a whole new scientific discipline called sociobiology. It advanced the idea that much social behavior both of individuals and groups is dramatically affected by heredity.[157] In the three decades since I first looked into the issue in the mid 1960s, what's called *behavioral genetics, sociobiology* and recently, *evolutionary psychology,* have become respected academic disciplines.

From the period of the beginning of the Second World War to the 1960s, the media associated genetic and racial understanding with the image of German Nazism. While the media dubiously attempted to shape public opinion pertaining to these matters, the scientific world learned the truth of the gene and its powerful social role. Important research findings were ignored by the mass media. However, as increasing evidence of the power of human genetics became known, the breakthroughs could no longer be kept from public knowledge.

Genes were directly linked with certain kinds of diseases such as cancers, mental conditions such as schizophrenia, and depression; and of course, intelligence and behavior. Social problems such as alcoholism and homosexuality were shown to be influenced by genes, and there was a reaffirmation, at least in scientific circles, of a genetic influence on criminality. Discoveries were made as to dramatic differences in the architecture of the male and female brain. So many possibilities opened up for the understanding and improvement of the human condition through genetics that a number of governments joined together in eventually launching perhaps the most ambitious scientific investigation of all time: the Human Genome Project, an attempt to identify all the genes affecting mankind.

Studies on identical twins, which had begun in the 1920s, suddenly began to be pursued again by psychologists and geneticists. In the 1960s and 1970s, the public was astounded to learn what many psychologists had known almost the entire century, that many identical twins separated from birth and living in entirely different environments and cultures — had remarkably similar personality traits and habits. Amazing stories filled the press of identical twins, who although growing up thousands of miles from each other, smoked the same brand of cigarettes, pursued identical occupations and had almost identical personal habits. Also, a wealth of evidence was amassed comparing personality differences between identical and fraternal twins. Below is a chart showing results of just a few of the more recent studies of behavioral genetics showing the heritibility of personality traits.

Personality Traits Shown to Have a Significant Genetic Component

The following chart shows a number of character traits are strongly influenced by heredity. If there is no hereditary correlation to a factor it would show up as around plus or minus 0. If a trait is 100 percent caused by heredity, it would show up as 1.00. Theoretically a perfect balance of heredity and environment would be represented by .5

Trait	Study	Value
Aggression	Plomin 1990[158]	.46
	Rushton, Fulker, et al. 1986[159]	.5
	Tellegen, Lykken, et al. 1988[160]	.44
Alienation	Plomin 1990	.48
	Tellegen, Lykken, et al 1988	.45
Emotional reactivity	Floderus-Myrhed 1980[161]	.56
Altruism	Rushton, Fulker, et al. 1986	.5
	Keller et al 1992[162]	.37
Cautiousness	Plomin 1990	.5
Extraversion	Plomin 1990	.3-.5
	Bouchard 1984[163]	.54
obey rules /authority	Tellegen, Lykken et al 1988	.53
Constraint	Tellegen, Lykken et al 1988	.58
Work values	Keller et al 1992	.4
Stress reaction	Tellegen, Lykken et al 1988 Rushton 1992	.53

Racial Differences in Personality

Just as all IQ studies show a marked difference in IQ between the White and Black races, psychologists report dramatic personality differences as well. In high school I had subscribed to a few racially conscious publications. They often referred to scientific studies on the race question. I had the habit of looking up the articles for myself in the journals and books that could be found in university libraries close to my home. Every month, I would go to Tulane or LSU and make Xerox copies of the articles that interested me. I have kept it the habit of reading them over the years and have found much more corroborating evidence since those early days, but there was a wealth of material available, even then.

One interesting publication I read was the *Psychological Bulletin*. I found a couple of articles from the early '60s that discussed how Blacks tend to be more impulsive and unrestrained than Whites. Dreger and Miller called some of the Black personality traits "estrangement and impulse ridden fantasies."[164]

In later years, numerous articles detailed other Black personality differences. An extreme liberal, Thomas Kochman, noted clear racial distinctions in personality between Blacks and Whites, and he expressed his preference for black characteristics. He argued that Black males perceive being ignored as the highest insult and recommends that White women should react to Black sexual aggression with sassy rejoinders just as Black women do. He even went so far as to suggest the typical non-black behavior style of White women caused violent Black male attacks.

Kochman also noted that blacks have "intense and spontaneous emotional behavior" and that the Black "rhythmic way of walking" is "a response to impulses coming from within." He criticized White debating techniques as 'low-keyed, dispassionate, impersonal and nonchallenging...cool, quiet, and without affect," while he describes Black approach to argument as "animated, confrontational,..."heated [and] loud..." and that Blacks argue not simply the idea but the "person debating the idea."[165]

After personally experiencing the Black style of argument on many occasions, I had to agree with Kochman's evaluation. However, I dispute his notion that such primitive and emotional behavior enriches our culture. After I read Kochman, I noticed the frequent news reports of Black males who argue in precisely the way he described, " heated, confrontational and loud," leading them to impulsively use their Saturday Night Specials. Our public hospitals are full of the victims of such heated and unrestrained Black styles of argument.

Many studies showed the greater levels of impulsiveness, aggression and emotionalism in Blacks as compared to Whites.[166] A study that took place in Trinidad compared Blacks and Caucasian immigrants from India. Walter Mischel conducted a study of children in Trinidad in which he gave White and Black children the choice between a candy bar immediately or a larger one a week later. Blacks almost always chose the immediate gratification while Whites usually chose to wait for the bigger reward. The inability of the blacks to delay gratification was so great in comparison with Whites, that Mischel stated that measuring it seemed "superfluous." Mischel also tried to compare the familial patterns of the blacks who almost always had female-headed households to the East Indian households, but he could not find enough East-Indian households with absent fathers to constitute a statistically meaningful study.[167]

Other books such as *The Unheavenly City Revisited* by Edward Banfield noted that inner cities' inhabitants, that include many Blacks, have less tendency to defer gratification, and an extreme orientation to the present. [168] [169] Most of the men who noted these psychological differences between the races took for granted their cultural origins, but many new studies reveal that such tendencies had hereditary implications.

One of the more interesting aspects of the study of criminal behavior I learned about was its links with testosterone.[170] Researchers have long noted that males are about ten times more often found guilty of violent crimes than are women, and high crime rates coincide with high levels of testosterone in adolescence. Criminal youths are also found to have higher average levels of testosterone than non-criminals of the same age. Interestingly enough, young Negroes are found to have significantly higher levels of testosterone than do young Whites. The Black crime rate is about 300 percent higher than that of Whites on a world-wide basis.[171]

Higher levels of testosterone could contribute to greater sexual aggression as well, contributing both to rape and assault of women as well as instability in relationships. It is also easy to see how it could damage the family. In my reading, I learned that in Africa as well as in every New World Black society, illegitimacy and promiscuity is far more common than in European societies. In the United States, for instance, the African-American illegitimacy rate is fast approaching 75 percent of all newborns.

The chronic social problem of absent Black fathers in America is found repeated on a world-wide scale. In a research paper on African marriage systems, Patricia Draper describes the parenting role of Negro fathers in Africa and the Americas:

> **The psychological, social, and spatial distance of husbands/fathers, together with their freedom from direct economic responsibility relieves them of most aspects of the parental role as Westerners understand the term.**[172]

I wanted to understand the reasons why the Black differences existed. That meant a look into the evolutionary aspects of the formations of the major races. But, before I did that, I had to answer a more pertinent question. Ashley Montagu maintained in his books and articles that Race is simply a cultural myth. In recent times this view has been parroted frequently in the media. Is race *real*, or is it a socially-contrived *invention*?

The Reality of Race

Ashley Montagu's, *Man's Most Dangerous Myth: the Fallacy of Race*[173] had impressed me before I began my look into the other side of the scientific studies on race. The "myth of race" position is essentially that skin color, hair type and other traits that influence racial classification are completely arbitrary traits of mankind and are as unimportant as are different types of fingerprint designs.

After almost thirty years of the media proclaiming the "myth of race," race-critic Jared Diamond refined the argument in the 1994 issue of the very popular *Discover* magazine. [174]Diamond chose a few traits such as lactose intolerance and fingerprint patterns that varied geographically among human populations and suggested by those traits alone, Swedes could be put in the same "racial category as the Ainu of Japan or the Xhosa of Africa. He asserted, therefore, that racial classification was nonsensical. Another media-popular disclaimer of race is Cavalli-Sforza, who in the preface of his major work, *The History and Geography of Human Genes*, gave lip-service to the arguments of Diamond and Montagu.[175] Interestingly enough, when one looks at Cavalli-Sforza's world gene-distribution maps in his book, they show the same geographic boundaries that reflect the traditional racial groupings.

I had realized back in the 1960s that the "myth of race" argument is perfectly analogous to saying that the dozens of different breeds of dogs is a myth because one can find some specific traits that exist in varying breeds. I thought about the question long and hard, and I asked myself, "Because some similar traits are found in different breeds of dogs, does that mean that there are no St. Bernards or Chihuahuas?"

If Ashley Montagu were attacked by a dog, I think it might matter to him if the dog were a Doberman Pinscher or a Toy Poodle. As the Doberman began to chow down on him, would he still insist that the differences among the breeds of the canines don't exist? Even Montagu could predict that a Doberman offers a great deal more potential danger than a toy Poodle. If Diamond wants to be technical about it, many human traits and sets of traits, can be found that exist in other mammals. In fact, humans share 98.5 percent of their genes with Chimpanzees. If one follows Diamond's rationale, there is no difference between humans and Chimpanzees because we can find sets of arbitrarily selected genetic traits we share.

A number of scientists in recent times have brought up the fact that the DNA in Blacks and Whites differs by less than a percent, and therefore such a small difference could not mean much distinction in races. Yet, with only a 1.5 percent difference in DNA between humans and chimpanzees, humans have brains that are about twice as large. Small differences in DNA can make big differences in biological structure.[176][177][178] Only a small number of genes set the structure of an organism. It is similar to the fact that only a small set of paper architectural plans make a big difference in the way wood, steel, concrete and glass construct a house.

Saying that the races are the same because similar genes make up the bulk of the physical structures of both Blacks and Whites is analogous to saying that because a shack is built of wood, steel and glass — it is the same as a skyscraper made of the same materials. The vast majority of the basic genes that make up the races are not only shared by them, but also by all mammals and even other orders of life. What makes the important distinctions are the small percentages of genes that effect the structure and composition of those life forms.

A race is a more or less distinct combination of inherited physiological, morphological and behavioral traits. J. Phillippe Rushton describes it this way:

> **A race is what zoologists term a variety or subdivision of a species. Each race (or variety) is characterized by a more or less distinct combination of inherited morphological, behavioral, physiological traits. In flowers, insects, and non-human mammals, zoologists consistently and routinely study the process of racial differentiation. Formation of a new race takes place when, over several generations, individuals in one group reproduce more frequently among themselves than they do with individuals in other groups. This process is most apparent when the individuals live in diverse geographic areas and therefore evolve unique, recognizable adaptations (such as skin color) that are advantageous in their specific environments. But differentiation also occurs under less extreme circumstances. Zoologists and evolutionists refer to such differentiated populations as races. (Within the formal taxonomic nomenclature of biology, races are termed subspecies). Zoologists have identified two or more races (subspecies) in most mammalian species.**[179]

Differences between the major races of mankind include over 50 physiological and social variables. Other than the obvious differences in skin color and hair texture, they include brain size, cranial structure, dentition, intelligence, musculature, hormonal levels, sexual norms, temperament, longevity and a wide range of personality traits. As Rushton says eloquently, "If race were an arbitrary, socially-constructed concept, devoid of all biological meaning, such consistent relationships would not exist."[180]

Science has long established different species and subspecies as a recognizable group having a common heredity. Take a look at what the Random House Webster's Dictionary has to say about the subject.

species
> *Biol.* the major subdivision of a genus or subgenus, regarded as the basic category of biological classification, composed of related individuals that **resemble one another,** are able to breed among themselves, but are not able to breed with members of another species.

race
> **1.** a group of persons **related by common descent or heredity**. a population so related.

breed
> *Genetics.* **a relatively homogenous group of animals within a species, developed and maintained by humans.**
> *lineage; stock; strain*: **She comes from a fine breed of people.**
> *offensive:* **half-breed** (emphasis mine)

Even though many scientists argue for the existence of many races of mankind, most accept the existence of at least three major divisions: Mongoloid, Caucasoid and Negroid. Obvious differences in facial features, skeletal and cranial characteristics, skin color and hair types make the three major races easily distinguishable. Blood, semen and molecular information can determine the race or even an estimate of the racial mixture in an individual. Scientific investigators can readily identify the race from just the skeletal parts of badly decomposed human remains, and the race of criminal perpetrators can readily be identified by traces of hair, semen, skin, or blood. The O.J. Simpson case gave the world a lesson in genetic racial identification.

Denying the reality of race is a good example of how egalitarians are grasping for straws. A mass of scientific evidence proves the existence of traits and features that identify the genetically differentiated breeds of mankind, just as there are genetically differentiated breeds of dogs or cats, or as I had found out years earlier in my garage — domestic and wild breeds of rat. One does not need molecular studies to know that race exists, all one must do is use his eyes and some common sense.

Imagine, for example, that a hypothetical extra-terrestrial that had no prior knowledge of humanity and no prejudices about race suddenly landed on the Earth to study its higher orders of life. He would immediately classify mankind into its different groups by the general observable differences that exist among them, just as he would the rest of the mammals and all other life forms. He would do it in the same way that we have genealogically classified the orders, species and subspecies (races or breeds) of the animal kingdom by their physical characteristics, appearance and genetic imprint. When the *Times-Picayune* ran its article, "White/Black: The Myth of Race", my campaign lawyer, James McPherson, quipped that it might as well have been called, "Light/Heavy, The Myth of Gravity."

In school, I discovered that anti-race bias had become almost like a religion with some people. They parroted back the silliest and most illogical concepts about race. For instance, someone would tell me that there are no such things as races because there are some individuals who may be racially mixed or who are not clearly of one race or another. That argument is much like saying that there is no day or night because for a few minutes every day at dusk it is hard to tell whether it is night or day.

Even a high-school teacher of mine maintained that there were no racial differences because some Whites are darker than some Blacks and that some Blacks are smarter than some Whites. Trying to negate group differences by citing individual exceptions is the poorest logic I could imagine. It is much like saying that because some grade school children are more knowledgeable than some college students, that there is no difference between the knowledge of college students and grade school students.

I have heard people say that individual variation within a race is greater than the average difference between races, so therefore race is irrelevant. One could easily take that fallacious argument to its logical conclusion and point out that since some humans unfortunately have less intelligence than some dogs, therefore there is no difference between humans and canines in intelligence. The racial egalitarians are just that silly, but like the fable of the emperor's new clothes; nobody dares to stand up and tell the truth!

Arguments erupted frequently at school, often with teachers. One teacher told me that there is no point to race because it is impossible to really know who is Black and who is White. I simply pointed out to her that the government seems to have no trouble in distinguishing between Blacks and Whites for affirmative action programs and for forced racial integration of education, and that she obviously believes that Blacks and Whites can be identified and therefore "integrated."

By far, the most popular saying among egalitarians is that Blacks and Whites differ only in color of skin. If that were true, one would be quite stupid to believe in racial differences in intelligence, and that is the direct implication. But, the idea that skin color is the only difference is patently absurd. Yet, the media consistently repeats it like a holy incantation, "We are all the same other than color of skin", How is it then, that every one of the top 16 semi-finalists in the 1996 Olympics 100 meter sprint were black, when one hundred times more Whites participate in organized track and field in the world? If the

Black difference is just a darker skin color, how could skin color make one run faster? There are genetic qualities in Black people that make them, on average, more efficient sprinters and that talent has an *association* with skin color. If there are differences that can make one group have faster runners, it stands to reason that there can be differences that make other groups have faster thinkers.

I have already argued in this volume that IQ is primarily inherited and that Blacks and Whites differ dramatically in IQ – even when Blacks and Whites come from similar socioeconomic backgrounds. I have shown that there is abundant evidence of difference in the size of the brains of Africans as opposed to Europeans or Asians. Does the fact that there are at least 40 times more Whites per capita who have a genius level of intelligence have to do with the fact that they have lighter skin color than Negroes? Lighter skin has no direct effect on the brain. Intelligence is obviously created by genetic differences other than color of skin, although there may be an association of skin color with brain size and structure as representative of racial heritage. So although lighter skin does not make one smart, it can be associated with other racial genetic features that can.

Until very recent times, American society completely segregated people with any visible degree of black blood, even those only one-eighth or one-16th Negro. Is it an odd coincidence that lighter-skinned, and Caucasian-featured Blacks have a tremendous over-representation among Negroes who have achieved prominence in academic and scientific disciplines? Or could it simply be that their lighter skin color and Caucasian facial features are somewhat indicative of their predominant White genetic component, making their intelligence closer to the White norm. As I have noted previously, in repeated intelligence testing of mulattos and full-blooded Blacks, even when environmental factors are controlled, mulattos average somewhere between Whites and Blacks.

Yes. Whites, Blacks and Yellows have obvious differences in skin color and hair texture, but also in skeletal and cranial structure, blood groups and DNA fingerprinting. The latest DNA studies in fact indicate that ancestors of Blacks and Whites split at least as long as 110,000 ago (many say 200,000) and Whites and Asians about 40,000 years ago. Subspecies, which is the scientific term for race, has always denoted a geographic genetic differentiation of a species. Europeans, Asians and Africans obviously developed on different continents under different environments. I came to the conclusion that race is certainly *real* and that racial differences are *inherent* and profound. I then wanted to better understand how racial differences originated and their possible impact on modern society. To do that I had to look into evolutionary theory.

The Evolution of Races

To understand the evolution of the races, I found it instructive to understand the genetic development of dogs. All dog breeds are members of the same species, *Canis familiaris,* just as all humans are members of the same species *Homo sapiens.* We call the different varieties of dogs breeds, and we call the different varieties of humans, races, although breed can also describe human varieties. The only difference in the two terms is that breed usually denotes genetic selection by humans, while races denote genetic selection by the forces of the geographic environment.

Selective breeding from a single species created the spectacular variety of dog breeds over a relatively short period of time, perhaps only five or six thousand years. Humans selected dogs for certain physical and personality traits, segregated them from other dogs and created the vast differences in dog breeds we see today. Before the c of the Black and White race as we know it, mankind's remote ancestors fanned out around the globe. The populations encountered vastly differing environments that selected for many characteristics, the most readily recognizable being the physical traits of skin color, hair texture and color, and eye color.

Once I understood the realities of racial difference, I realized that by learning about the evolutionary forces that created the different races, we can understand the character and conduct of the various races, our own included.

Numerous anthropological theories speculate about the origin and age of modern mankind and its varied races. The two dominant theories are called the Single Origin Hypothesis and the Multi-Regional Hypothesis. The Multi-Regionalists argue that a parallel evolution of the races has been going on since the *Homo erectus* stage of our evolution. According to this theory, Homo erectus emerged in Africa and migrated all over the Old World. In the different regions, shaped by different environmental conditions, they separately crossed the threshold of *Homo sapiens.* Homo erectus independently evolved to form the Mongoloid race in Asia, the Caucasian Race in Europe and the Negroid race in Africa. Anthropological artifacts seem to support this theory in that specimens of Homo erectus have been found in east Asia with tooth characteristics similar to those of the modern race that inhabits those regions. But, the DNA and other genetic evidence suggests a contradictory hypothesis.

Geneticists maintain that after mankind's ancestors reached an archaic *Homo sapiens* stage in Africa, they then evolved separately into two distinct genetic groups, the African and the non-African about

120,000 years ago. Later, a split between Europeans and Asians occurred around 40,000 years ago.

The latest DNA research seems to support the theory that the separate races evolved after crossing the *Homo sapiens* level, but the issue is far from decided. Whether or not the different races crossed the Homo sapiens threshold separately, the White and Black races have been divided for at least 110,000 years, even by the single origin theory. Asians and Whites, being separated for only 40,000 years have far more similarities than exist between Blacks and Whites. While scientists argue a bit about the timing, there is little doubt that the major races have been in existence for quite a long time, many tens of thousands of years, more than enough time for geography and climate to have created the profound differences that exist.

When I considered that the great differences in dogs had been created by selective breeding over only 5,000 years, it made sense to suppose that varying environments could have easily created the differences we see in mankind. [181] For example, 100,000 years is time enough for over 5,000 human generations. To cause a 15 point higher increase in the average IQ of a population, it would only have to be increased on average by a tiny fraction of one percent (.003) each generation. That is an average of less than one-one-hundredth of an IQ point per generation. Five thousand generations is at least twice the number of generations needed to make the vast differences we see in dog breeds.

The geographically separated populations of mankind facing dramatically different climatic challenges, created what we recognize as the major races of mankind.[182] [183] [184]

The Effect of Climate on the Racial Evolution

The Black race developed in the relatively warm, more tropical regions of Sub-Saharan Africa, while the European and Asian races had their origins in the colder, harsh regions of Europe and Asia. Obviously, the environment of the two regions was dramatically different. It explains the lighter skin of Whites, as a colder, wetter climate and the less available sunlight of Europe made lighter skin more advantageous for the absorption of needed Vitamin D. In the tropics, dark skin is important to protect the body from the damaging rays of the sun. Another example of climatic adaptation can be seen in the development of the protective eye fold of the Asians. The epicanthic fold is likely an evolutionary response to the extremely cold and windy weather of North East Asia.

Lighter skin color is just one of the many genetic adaptations for survival by both Europeans and northern Asians. The very harsh, cold climate also selected for certain psychological and behavioral traits that facilitated survival. A cold climate selects for mental fitness and behavior in the same way it favors lighter skin.

My interest in the effects of evolution on the races was stirred by Professor Carleton Coon, who at the time of my inquiry, was the president of the American Association of Physical Anthropologists and the premier physical anthropologist in the world. I read all of his books I could find, including *The Living Races of Man*,[185] *Story of Man*,[186] *Origin of the Races*,[187] and *The Races of Europe*.[188]

Later, I read his classics *The Hunting Peoples*[189] and in 1982 *Racial Adaptations*.[190] Coon wrote extensively in his books of the impact of the extremely cold climates on prehistoric mankind. Two other books that made a great impact on me were *Man the Hunter*[191] and *Hunters of the Northern Ice*.[192]

From my reading, I began to sketch a broad outline of life that existed in the Northern Hemisphere during prehistoric times. Much of the last two hundred thousand years the northern world has been in periods of advancing and retreating glacial ice ages. The Northern Hemisphere is currently in a lull between ice ages. Survival for prehistoric man in Europe was far more difficult, even in the lulls between the ice ages, than for man in the milder African climate. During most of the last 80,000 years, Europe endured temperatures much colder than today. Modern Europeans emerged about 35,000 years ago and met the crucible of the Würm glaciation (24,000-10,000 B.C.). Temperatures in Europe and Asia probably averaged about 18 degrees (F) colder than the present.

I traveled on a short trip with my father to Kansas City and while there experienced a snow storm on the road to Lawrence, Kansas. As I read about the trials of prehistoric Europeans, I thought about the sub-zero temperatures, and the miles upon miles of nothing but snow and ice I had seen. With that picture in my mind, I thought about how difficult it must have been for prehistoric Europeans to survive such rigors. Yet, the temperatures of the Würm glaciation would have been far colder than that of Kansas.

As the ancestors of modern man migrated further to the North, they needed a number of vital skills and behavioral qualities to survive. Unlike tropical Africa, the technology to create warm, well-made clothing and sturdy shelter became necessary for survival. The ability to make and control fire became an essential survival skill. Dealing with the deadly forces of winter demanded skills not required in the tropics. Scarcity of edible plants and small game, and even the fact that birds migrated south for the winter, posed unique problems, as early man relied a great deal on eggs and young animals for food. These were scarce in the cold months.

In Africa, numerous kinds of edible vegetation existed, as well as small rodents and insects and other varied and abundant food sources. By contrast, the ground in Europe was a frozen sea of snow and ice for many months each year and even many trees had no leaves. In the mildest of months, the inhabitants had to prepare for the harsh periods by deferring gratification and putting aside stores of food and supplies. In such cold climates, hunting large game rather than gathering edibles became the chief source of food and supplies.

PREHISTORIC EUROPEAN-ASIAN CONDITIONS	PREHISTORIC SUB-SAHARAN AFRICA
complex -sturdy shelter -- critical	minimal shelter needed for survival
winter – extremely harsh climate	no winter – comfortable climate
Warm, well-made clothing -- critical	no clothing required for survival
ability to make/control fire -- critical	fire not required for survival
Long periods of resource deprivation	resources more abundant
periods of little vegetation, few small animals or birds –hunting necessary	food gathering less problematic in tropical climes – gathering favored
foresight, planning and delayed gratification necessary for survival	little seasonal change, immediate gratification favored
in resource scarce, male-provisioned, hunting-society, monogamy favored	in female provisioned gathering society, polygamy favored.
male provisioned society, less sexual and physical aggression favored	female provisioned society favors male aggression and sexual drive
promiscuous behavior resulting in fights often leads to death of mate and children	death in fights from sexual competition not critical for survival of mates and children

Because hunting provided most resources, females and children became dependent on male provisioning, leading to a strong bond between men and their immediate family. In both Europe and Asia men had to provide for their mates and children if they were to survive.

Family Patterns of Europeans and Africans

In the more tropical climate of Africa, survival depended mostly on gathering rather than hunting. The lush vegetation and abundant small animal life provided far greater food resources than in the northern climes. The African mother could feed herself and her children with little help from the father. On a pretty fall day, there was no necessity for the inhabitants of the tropics to control an impulse to lie upon a bed of leaves with a mate and satisfy sexual desires, but in the cold north; such an indulgence could affect survival in the winter months ahead.

In the North, those who survived were more likely the ones who had the self-control to defer sexual and other forms of immediate gratification. On those pretty warm days they had to use that precious time and good weather to prepare for the extremely difficult winter days ahead. When the inevitable months of bad weather came, often they had to ration their food rather than completely satisfy their hunger.

In Europe, the prehistoric economy found dependence on several primary animals. Probably the most important were the mastodon and the various breeds of deer and reindeer. Now extinct, the mastodon was the largest animal ever to walk the Earth contemporaneous to man. A great hairy beast adapted to the cold temperatures of Europe and Northern Asia, it stood about twice the size of the great African Elephant, had huge tusks and was easily strong enough to lift weight equivalent to a small automobile. To hunt such creatures demanded technologically-effective weapons, as well as effective teamwork and planning. Much of the prehistoric economy of Europe found its base in products harvested from the Mastodon. Meat and fat, thick skins for clothing, shoes and shelter, bone and sinew for weapons and tools, oil for their lamps, organs used for thread and containers — the Mastodon provided all these products and more. Obviously, it was hunted exclusively by males. The same was true for deer and other game.

With food supplies coming mostly from hunting rather than gathering, females and children were very dependent on male provisioning. At the same time, males depended on females for much of the work involved in preparing and processing the products of the kill, as well as the gathering needs of the clan, work which could be done while caring for the children.

If the male would randomly have sexual relations with females and then abandon them and his children, they had a greatly lessened chance of survival. Dr. Edward Miller of the University of New Orleans has done much work on these concepts in his groundbreaking paper: *"Paternal Provisioning versus Mate Seeking in Human Populations."*[193] Even when surviving relatives shared some of the hunt with fatherless families, in times of scarce food resources they were likely to be the last fed. If the male had multiple mates and many children, even if he tried to take care of all of them he could have difficulty providing for them. In Africa, because women generally supported themselves and their children, male bonding and support was not nearly as important to survival. In fact, male bonding, empathy and time spent with the wife and children only lessened the male's opportunities to mate with more females. It was an environment and social system that greatly rewarded male sexual aggressiveness and infidelity. Evolutionary success for the African male found reward in his immediately gratifying his own sexual desires with as many females as possible. It favored male genes leading to strong sexual drive, aggression, and genetic advantages in fighting that comes from intense male competition for women.

Biologists call the strategy of having few children combined with high parental investment a "K" strategy, and that of having more children which is naturally accompanied by less paternal investment per child an "r" strategy. The tropical climate of Africa tended to support an *r* strategy among males and selected for males who employed it. Because of female provisioning, an effective reproductive strategy for males was to father as many children as possible since such conduct would give the most assurance that their genes would survive.

In the harsh and resource scarce environment of the cold climes, if a male were to father many children by many women, he would not likely be able to provision them. The result could well be the loss of them all. However, males having a single family and fewer children could provide greater paternal sustenance and care, enabling survival of a much higher percentage. The European environment thus encouraged a K reproductive strategy.[194][195]

Aggression as Reproductive Strategy

In any society where males attempt to mate aggressively with as many females as possible there is great potential for violence. Efforts to mate with other male's mates would encounter risk of retaliation. Any biological group in which males frequently fight for females favors genes in males that lead to combative success. Hand-to-hand fighting is very anaerobic and usually only takes a few moments to determine a winner. It favors those who have muscles favored for quick bursts of speed rather than raw strength. A fighter with longer arms than his foe has a distinct advantage, making it easier to strike his enemy while avoiding his enemy's blows. A thicker cranium allows him to withstand blows to the head which could otherwise render him insensible and vulnerable.[196] A flat nose with wider nostrils allows greater airflow needed for quick exertion, and it is harder to break than the longer nose Europeans need to warm the cold air as well as filter out viruses and bacteria.[197][198]

In prehistoric Europe, fighting could occur for many reasons, including pursuit of females and territorial conflicts, but the pattern of male provisioning of their mates and children certainly encouraged restraint. Although the European or Asian might sexually desire a female belonging to someone else, he had more reason to control his emotions and sexual urges, for if he was killed or seriously injured in a fight, his children could likely die as well. Until very recent times, most marriages were arranged by the parents, so reason would suggest that they would attempt to select males for their daughters who were more inclined to fidelity.

Many studies show that even in the modern world, woman are far more selective and reticent than men in regard to mating.[199] [200] [201] Among European and Asian women this is especially true. Just as there is a striking difference between males and females, there is also a difference between European and African women. In prehistoric Europe, choosing the right mate was critical to the female's survival. For if her mate did not provision her, she and her children would face much greater hardship and possible death.

In Africa, although there could be advantages for a woman if the male helped provide for her, it was not nearly as important to her survival. Surveys of Blacks worldwide show that Black males and females begin sexual relations earlier, have more sexual partners, more frequent sexual relations, more absent fathers, more polygamy, higher testosterone levels in males, more prominent secondary sexual characteristics, and much higher rates of sexually transmitted diseases. For instance, even in the United States, African-Americans are 50 times more likely to have syphilis, [202] and in some areas, an incredible 100 times greater likelihood of gonorrhea.[203] Blacks are 14 times more likely to have AIDS than are non-Hispanic Whites.[204] [205] "I don't think there is any question that the epidemic in this country is becoming increasingly an epidemic of color," said Surgeon General David Satcher.[206]

Physical Manifestations

In colder climates, strength and endurance became the deciding physical factors for survival rather than speed. Men had to be strong enough to build complex and heavy structures of wood or stone, or sometimes even of ice. It made more evolutionary sense for the European to have a bit more insulating body fat and a larger body cavity than Africans, as such helps protect the body from times of intense cold. Africans having a lower percentage of body fat, arms and legs proportionately larger to body size, smaller body cavities, and smaller heads — helps make them more efficient in running, jumping and fighting.

In the modern world, Black domination of boxing illustrates the physical differences created by the differing evolution of the races. Soon after Blacks were permitted to participate freely in the organized sport, they quickly asserted their superiority in it. Black athletes have muscle types that can provide quick bursts of speed, while Whites tend to dominate sports that require maximum strength and endurance. Weightlifting, for example, is overwhelmingly dominated by Europeans and Asians.

When I was looking into the evolutionary questions, one of the most heavily-promoted sporting events in history was the Mohammed Ali, Chuck Wepner fight. I remember the statistical differences to this day. Wepner stood six foot six inches in height, but interestingly, Ali, who stood three inches shorter, had a reach that was six inches longer. Wepner however, was much stronger and could lift dramatically heavier weights than Ali. It became obvious in the fight that although Wepner had a tremendously powerful blow, Ali's speed allowed him to simply strike, bob, weave and dance around his slower European-American opponent. Despite Ali's evolutionary advantage, in a courageous effort, Wepner lasted 15 rounds with Ali, and inspired the *Rocky* movie series based on his character. I was probably the only one in the neighborhood who thought about the evolutionary racial differences between Ali and Wepner as the replay of the fight came on TV.

The Roots of Higher Intelligence

In an extremely cold and inhospitable natural environment higher human intelligence is dramatically favored. Europe demanded a higher technology for survival. If a society depends almost wholly on hunting, development of advanced weapons, traps and sophisticated strategies can be critically important when there is scarce game. Effective hunting, fishing and trapping in such an environment can demand well-developed cognitive skills. The invention and rigging of ingenious traps can demand high intelligence. The skills and the tools necessary to make a fire, no easy task in a cold wet environment, can mean the difference between life and death. If a heavy shelter constructed to keep out winter collapses on its occupants because of poor design, they could well die. In equatorial Africa, if the leaves or straw huts blow away in a rainstorm, the occupants can just build another one tomorrow. If a native gets lost in the rain forests of Africa, he can live on the fauna and flora while he finds his way back, while if the European gets lost in winter he could freeze to death.

A number of writers on European prehistory believe that navigating on long winter hunts with nondescript landscapes, favored survival of Europeans and Asians with high levels of spatial reasoning. Tracking the movements of reindeer and other arctic herds from great distances demanded the intelligence to weigh past information and develop strategies to anticipate the herd movement.

Parents and prospective brides naturally tried to choose potential mates who they thought would be faithful to the wife and children. Even the female intelligence needed to detect male deception became an important genetic advantage. It was important for a female and her parents to determine if a prospective male had other families on the side. If a male had other mates and children he could well have to choose whom to provide with the dwindling stores when the shortages of winter came. On the male side, it was evolutionarily important for him to figure out if his mate was cheating and thus avoid provisioning a wife and children who were not carrying on his genes.[207]

An important aspect of intelligence is the ability to think abstractly. To conceive of winter on a warm spring or summer day is an abstract thought, as is the very concept of the future.[208] In harsh climates one must be able to conceive of tomorrow, and even more importantly, the more distant future such as next winter. In tropical zones, life is much more immediate. Without the prospect of a harsh winter, there was little need to plan for the future. If one lives only in the immediate, one is less likely to control or restrain impulsive behavior and to delay gratification.

In the long, cold hunts of the north, the hunter often had to be quiet and restrained for long periods of time, and other than occasional hunts for herds or Mastodons, he often was likely to be alone for long periods of time. Such would tend to favor restraint and introversion rather than talkativeness and extraversion. We can see this evolutionary model as represented in the strong, silent prototype of the classic European. On a popular level we find it in our attraction to the stoic heroes of our Western movies. Such is represented by men such as Gary Cooper or John Wayne, or even the classic Clint Eastwood films. That behavioral characteristic can be readily contrasted to the jive talk or the trash talk of the stereotypical Black athlete, or the sexual rap by Black males ever on the prowl in the African village or the American high school hallway.

Although a wide range of personality types are present in Europeans, on the whole, our people are quieter, more restrained, more under control. The difference between races can be seen in everything from the intricate musical melodies of Mozart as compared to the elemental beat of rap, from quiet fashion to flashy dress, from thoughtful and considerate speech, to the loud and boisterous nature that Kochman admired in his study of the Black personality.

In the cold north, as the European was more restrained and less aggressive, so the European had to develop an intense sense of community and social justice. In an African tribe of gatherers everyone can provision themselves. They can eat and indulge themselves while they gather and no one will be the wiser. They have no vital need to share or develop higher systems of social justice or common welfare. In the small hunting bands of Europe, sometimes game was so scarce that an individual hunter may not have luck bringing home any game for weeks, but one hunter's reindeer kill might fend off starvation for the whole group. Pressures for community needs and a group altruism must have been intense, creating the social conscience and ethics of Europe.

Successfully hunting the great mastodons of Europe took a tremendous group effort. Bringing one down took planning, coordination, and effective and precise communication. There was a high risk of death. Under such circumstances, the gene pool would favor genes of altruism and self-sacrifice, for each one had to take great individual risks so that the clan could survive. After the kill there had to be a well-organized effort and division of labor to process and preserve its valuable resources.

Fire became vital for survival. In inclement conditions it is much easier to keep a fire going than to light one. Some ancient bands likely lit a fire when it was warm and dry in the fall and then endeavored to keep it going all winter. To do that took teamwork, responsibility, accountability, emotional restraint and self-discipline. If just one member of the group who had responsibility for keeping the fire going fails for reasons of stupidity or irresponsibility, the whole group could die. If the exhausted hunter does not rise when it is his watch; delay his immediate need for the gratification of sleep and willfully stay awake to tend the fire, many could die.

I believe that these were some of the evolutionary forces that forged the European's intelligence, self-control, altruism and sense of social justice. From the crucible of Europe's environment came our legal systems, our government forms, our principles of self-government and freedom, as well as our social conscience.

In a hunting society where birthrates are low and death rates are high, both the female and the male must protect, provision and treasure each child. In Africa where men were driven more by sexual coupling than the love of family, and where the most honored are those with the greatest number of sexual conquests, an individual child or its mother meant little to those males who had many. When human life is too abundant it tends to lose value. On the other hand, in a struggling small band that faces the severest challenges of survival, each life becomes precious. In its rarity comes the appreciation of life's beauty. Our ancestors had that appreciation. A man who has many sexual partners is not as selective about his mate as one who must choose for a lifetime. And, in the hard climes, women and their families had to select men for their loyalty and responsibility. So evolved our race and so arose the nuclear family.

Here is a list showing a partial survey of the racial differences present today that were produced by the differences of the cold European/Asian Climate and that of more tropical Africa:

Africans	Europeans
Physical Traits:	
Darker skin	Lighter skin
Black hair and dark eyes	Some with lighter hair and eyes
Kinky hair	Thinner hair /straight and curly variety
Musculature favors speed	Musculature favors strength
Less body fat and smaller body cavity	More body fat and larger body cavity
Wide flat nose for quick intake of air	Longer nose for warming cold air
Longer arms in relation to body height	Shorter arms in relation to body height
Higher testosterone among males	Lower testosterone among males
Brain Differences	
Smaller cranium	Larger cranium
Smaller brain -autopsy data	Larger and heavier Brain --autopsy data
Smaller brain by endocranial vol.	Larger brain by endocranial data
Smaller brain by ext. head measures	Larger brain by external head measures
Fewer cortical neurons in brain	More cortical neurons in brain
Thicker cranium / lower facial angle	Thinner cranium / steeper facial angle
Less frontal lobe area / cerebral cortex	More frontal area and cerebral cortex
Brain less convoluted, sulcated	Brain more convoluted, fissurated
Larger dentition / more prognathic jaw	Smaller dentition / less prognathic jaw
Intelligence	
IQ Test scores: lower	IQ test scores: higher
Decision times: slower	Decision times: faster
Cultural achievements: few	Cultural achievements: abundant
mentally gifted: extremely rare	mentally gifted: much more common
mental retardation: more common	mental retardation: much less common
Mental health problems: more common	Mental health problems: less common
Reproductive traits	
Two-egg twinning higher	Two egg twinning one-half as frequent
Hormone levels higher	Hormone levels lower
Secondary sexual features pronounced	Secondary sexual features less
Intercourse frequencies higher	Intercourse frequencies lower
Permissive attitudes higher	Permissive attitudes lower
Sexually transmitted disease higher	Sexually transmitted disease lower

RACIAL EVOLUTION

Personality	
Aggressiveness higher	Aggressiveness lower
Impulsivity higher	Impulsivity lower
Sociability higher	Sociability lower
Dominance higher	Dominance lower
Activity level higher	Activity level lower
Cautiousness lower	Cautiousness higher
Less delay of gratification	More delay of gratification
Social Patterns	
Illegitimacy much higher	Illegitimacy much lower
Polygamy much higher	Polygamy much lower
Criminality much higher	Criminality much lower
Marriage stability lower	Marriage stability higher
Maturation Rates	
Gestation period shorter	Gestation period longer
Skeletal development earlier	Skeletal development later
Motor development earlier	Motor Development later
Dental development earlier	Dental Development later
Age of first intercourse earlier	Age of first intercourse later
Age of first pregnancy earlier	Age of first pregnancy later
Life span shorter	Life span longer

(Most of this material in this table is gleaned from the above-cited works of J. Phillippe Rushton and Edward Miller)

The races evolved quite differently. Those differences can be seen in the racial boundaries of the modern world, and the nature of the societies that thrive in them. The European race evolved into a people who have dived to the bottom of the ocean, soared through the air and into space, looked into the cell and the atom, put its footprints on the moon, and unlocked the secrets of our very Genome. The unique genotype that the cold climes of Europe fashioned has enabled European man to do all that he has done. In its understanding is the key to all that he has yet to do.

The Moral-Religious Battle

After I had a rudimentary understanding of the underlying concepts of the evolution of life, and during the time I was just becoming racially aware, I attended Clifton Ganus Junior High, a private school in New Orleans run by the Church of Christ. They taught an anti-evolutionary, creationist doctrine. Even though there were numerous competing theories of evolution, I certainly believed that all life on Earth had evolved and is still undergoing change. As a devout Christian and a science-minded geologist, my Father had the opinion that the idea of an evolutionary basis for higher life was not antagonistic to belief in God. He simply looked at Nature as the tools of God's creation. When I was very young he quoted me the first stanza of the William Henry Carruth poem *Each in His Own Tongue*.[209] I still know it by heart today:

A fire mist and a planet,
A crystal and cell,
A jellyfish and Saurian,
and caves where cavemen dwell,
Then a sense of law and beauty
And a face turned from the clod,
Some call it evolution, and others call it God.

In my Bible classes at my fundamentalist school I learned the details of the creationist belief that God instantaneously created mankind and all of Nature. At that time, most fundamentalist Christians never denied that God in his creation established the distinctions between the different races. In fact most of the main Christian denominations were segregated until the 1960s. That is one-thousand nine-hundred-and-sixty years before it was discovered that Jesus had it all wrong.

As the years passed, egalitarianism became the dogma of our times. Not only did many of the evolutionary anthropologists become egalitarians, but so did many creationists. Today, a common attitude among creationists is that God made us all the same. In reality, though, the creationist viewpoint shows God is the architect of race. For if one maintains that God made Nature and humanity as it is, then it must be conceded that he created the distinct races; gave them different features, behavioral tendencies and mental abilities. Furthermore, he segregated them from each other on different continents. From a thoughtful creationist viewpoint, to deny the reality of race and racial difference is a denial of God's own handiwork.

The reality of race is also reinforced by the Holy Bible. If the creationist uses the Old Testament as his guide to creation and as his guide to God's view of race, it is quickly apparent that the Old Testament is in fact a testament of race. It is a history of one people: the Israelites, in continuous conflict with the differing racial groups of the Middle East region. It emphasizes their own genealogy and the repeated commands not to mix their seed (an equivalent of the scientific concept of genes) with others. I have much more on this in the Race and Christianity chapter, but whether one takes the evolutionary or the creationist view, both support the reality of race.

I found it amazing to see how the mass media was able to convert both the scientific community — which espoused evolution and the fundamentally opposed creationist community — into spouting almost an identical egalitarian dogma. Their victory was complete by the time I graduated from high school.

The intellectual, secular community branded anyone who dared to publicly promote the idea of racial differences — as unscientific. Anyone in the religious community who dared to tell the truth of race was accused of being against God himself. Egalitarianism had become a de facto religion, incorporated under both the name of science and religion. Simple recognition of racial differences became a moral sin equivalent with adultery or perhaps even murder. But the racial heretics have not gone away quietly, and with each passing day more evidence emerges of the dramatic, genetically-borne, physical and psychological differences between the races. The same is true of the differences between the sexes. Today, the idea of ingrained psychological, brain-originated differences between men and women has become widely accepted among society. (See the Sex Differences chapter.) Tomorrow, the same will be true of race.

The Evolutionary Ladder

As I began to understand the evolutionary differences between the races, the question naturally arose, do the European and Asian races represent a higher level of human evolution than the African race?

Such questions are fraught with difficulty, for subjective judgments of what is advanced and what is primitive will determine many assessments of race and evolution. But, if one endeavors to be as objective as possible, a broad outline can emerge. Let us again suppose that we put ourselves into the shoes of extraterresterals here to study life on Earth from a galaxy far, far away.

Just as we would classify the phylum, orders, species and races (subspecies) of Nature, so we would include mankind in that classification structure. We would note the hard evidence of the great age of the Earth — such as the eras of geologic time it took to raise Mount Everest from the bottom of the sea and make it the highest point on the planet Earth. (we know that the rock in the highest reaches of Mt. Everest was once seabed, because of the fossils of sea life embedded deep in it) We also could look at the genetic links of all living things through DNA, chromosomes and genes. We would notice that the fossil record indicates that in the oldest geologic strata one finds the most primitive organisms and the most complex and intelligent life forms are found in the most recent geologic strata. One also could not help but notice that the closest relatives to man are the recent primates who are also relatively close in DNA. Chimpanzees, for instance, share 98.5 percent of the DNA with people.

Among the primates we would also note that the lower primates such as the lemurs are less intelligent and have smaller craniums than the higher primates such as Chimpanzees, Apes and Humans. Lemurs have longer muzzles; and that such prognathy and the cranial musculature to support it leaves smaller brains per body weight. Another difference is that lower evolutionary species have considerably faster maturation rates and reproductive rates than the higher primates. The same way we would class the higher primates on a higher evolutionary plane than lower primates, we would certainly cast the lower primates on a higher plane than most other mammals and reptiles, and reptiles than insects. Indeed, the life forms of the planet Earth represent many stages of the evolution from the simplest amino acids to one-celled plants and animals, to mankind itself. Among the races of mankind we would certainly classify the larger-brained Europeans and Asians as the most evolutionary advanced.

We could look at man's evolution somewhat like the evolution of the modern automobile. There has been improvement since the days of the human-pulled, wooden-wheel cart or horse-drawn chariot to the computer -programmed, modern automobile. Of course the evolution of man from his primitive to his modern state came from Nature, or as some might put it, God acting through Nature.

When we look at the anthropological evidence of man's development from the primitive Australopithecus to the *Homo habilis*, *Homo erectus* and *Homo sapiens* levels, it is easy to see that evolutionary development is gauged by brain size and accompanying technological achievement.[210] If the gradations in brain size from the small-brained Australopithecus to the large-brained human are important, should we now believe that differences in brain size have no corresponding importance to the different races of humanity? I think it would be safe to say that our hypothetical extraterrestrial would find that Europeans and Asians are higher than Africans on the evolutionary scale.

I also wondered how the White and Asian races compared on the evolutionary scale? There has also been evidence in recent years showing that North East Asians such as Japanese and Chinese might exceed the Europeans in some capacities. In spite of far greater cultural and language barriers than indigenous Blacks, they have shown great educational and socioeconomic success in Western nations. Many studies put their average IQ at equal to or even slightly superior to the performance of Europeans. Their high average IQ has certainly shown them capable of maintaining highly organized and efficient civilizations, and they have done so.

I do not find it demeaning to my race to acknowledge the high average IQ of the Asian race. Both races are certainly high on the ladder of evolution. There is some evidence, however, that some genetic factors cause Europeans to produce more of the highest creative achievements.

Although the Asians have a slightly higher IQ, their population IQ distribution appears to be more tightly bunched around the average. They have fewer extremely low IQ individuals and fewer with extremely high IQs. Such makes for a very competent and stable workforce. Europeans by contrast have much more widely dispersed IQs. In other words, we have far more geniuses per capita than Asians do, but it must also be noted that we also have far more imbeciles. Of course, the fact that we have far more geniuses does us no good at all if they are outvoted by greater numbers of those with extremely low intelligence. It is no advantage to us if we force a leveling equality on our schools and don't have adequate programs to develop the latent talents of the geniuses among us.

Interestingly enough, even though Europeans are outnumbered by huge Asian populations, we far excel them in seminal scientific achievements, and this is true even as we approach the end of the 20th century. The old adage that the Oriental may not have invented radio and television, but he can sure make television sets a lot faster, cheaper, and more efficiently, seems to have some basis in reality.

There are, of course, many Asians of great mental ability, and time itself will be the ultimate arbiter of evolutionary fitness. Right now the Asians seem to be far less susceptible to the egalitarian propaganda that has infected the West, and there is little threat to their genetic heritage in their own homelands — unlike that in Europe and the Americas. Both the Japanese and the Chinese also seem to have developed certain social and government policies that have a eugenic effect, as well as a educational programs designed to educate all of their populations groups to the best of their abilities.

Whatever their qualities and they are considerable, the Asians are still quite different from Europeans and their distinct genetic pattern will express itself in both their unique physical appearance and their psychological and cultural character. Europeans can look with respect to them as we hope they look on us the same way. There is no question that many Asians as individuals can fit productively into Western nations. Our nations can perhaps even assimilate limited numbers into our gene pool without a dramatic effect on our own characteristics. Such has certainly happened in historical Eastern Europe. But, if the great numbers keep coming and immigration continues in the West, we will lose our evolutionary and characteristic distinctiveness. Such would be a tragic occurrence both for our own and for all peoples of the globe. Our distinctive racial character has been responsible for the vast majority of the greatest scientific and artistic creations of Western civilization, the civilization which could accurately be described as becoming in this century, a world civilization, as many of its technological, artistic, and political tenets have come to dominate. Those contributions have brightened the lives of the intelligent and creative of all races throughout the world. There is no guarantee that any other race can continue that record of excellence. That can only be answered by time.

Aside from considerations of evolutionary fitness, it is natural for all races to prefer the company and aesthetics of their own race. I love the look and the spirit of my people, in our fair-skinned, light featured, esthetic prop we find our own concept of beauty. Whether it is the Norse-like God and Adam of the Sistine Chapel or the perennial blonde, angel-like prototype of beauty revered the world over, our race needs no justification to seek its own survival. For that matter, no race does.

The way that evolutionary fitness is ultimately decided is in evolutionary success. Right now our people seem hell bent on letting their genotype be extinguished from the planet, even in our own homelands. Here is how *The Random House Webster's Dictionary* defines three important terms:

> **genotype** *n. Genetics.*
> **1.** the genetic makeup of an organism or group of organisms with reference to a single trait, set of traits, or an entire complex of traits.
> **2.** the sum total of genes transmitted from parent to offspring. Cf. **phenotype.**
> [< G *Genotypus* (1909); see GENE, -O-, -TYPE]
>
> **genocide n**.
> the deliberate and systematic extermination of a national, racial, political, or cultural group.
> [1940–45; < Gk *géno*(s) race + -CIDE]
>
> **race suicide** the extinction of a race or people that tends to result when, through the unwillingness or forbearance of its members to have children, the birthrate falls below the death rate.

Race suicide could also be hastened when a race allows massive immigration of an alien race into its society and the loss of genetic survival through racial intermixture.

In promoting the idea of my own racial survival, I understand that all races share that same goal. If I were an African, I doubt that I would care about evolutionary gradations and where my people would rank on the charts. I'd love my own and everything that is unique about my own. An African can only be inferior in things that he is not good at, and he can always be superior in what he is born to do. If the destiny of the Black race is to live closer to the natural world, so be it. Whatever fate he seeks, it would be a destiny he would carve for himself by his own hand.

Fear of Extinction to Dreams of the Heavens

Once I had the idea that our race was vital to the evolutionary progress of mankind, a whole new perspective dawned on me. The appreciation of ecology that I gained as a very young man in the swamps and forests of south Louisiana, now helped me to fully understand how mankind is an integral part of that ecology. Understanding race is simply an understanding of what Garrett Hardin calls, "human ecology."

Not only is it not immoral to recognize the realities of race, there is no higher morality existing, than to work for the survival of your own kind. Is it not ridiculous for some of our people to work hard to preserve the unique breeds of Whales around the world while they denounce those who seek the preservation of the unique breeds of humanity? Furthermore, I realized that the high moral qualities that inspire the egalitarians were in fact created by the same race that they are so intent on dissolving into interracial soup. Do not the high morals that they tout come from the highest ideals of civilization and culture, ideals created by the European people?

Breeders of thoroughbred racehorses would be horrified to see the lines so carefully matched for speed over centuries to be randomly interbred out-of-existence with horses who could only run half as fast. Imagine if there was only one last pair of thoroughbreds on Earth. Wouldn't people do everything they could to preserve that magnificent breed of horse? Our people have been the thoroughbreds of civilization; do we really want to destroy our genetic distinctiveness, the unique heritage that has produced so much beauty on the Earth?

The opponents of racial awareness constantly parrot the idea that it is hateful and barbaric to be racially conscious, and for a White person it is said to be downright evil to desire the preservation of our own racial integrity. But, how morally supreme is the racially-mixed Black and Brown world as compared to the European World. What areas of the globe have the most brutal crime including rape, assault, robbery and murder? Which races have more concern for human rights and justice? Which races more frequently have political freedom, and among which races is despotism more prevalent? Which have better medical care for the sick and afflicted and had more concern for them? Which have more educational opportunity for their children? Which have more opportunity and fairer treatment of women? Which race leads our adventures into space? Where is the compelling evidence that the demise of the White race is really going to produce more humanitarianism, more love, brotherhood and all the catchwords of the egalitarians? Do the six thousand murders a year in racially amorphous Rio De Janeiro[211] somehow represent a moral example to the rare murders in the more racially homogenous Tokyo, Japan or Berlin, Germany?

The racial egalitarian arguments remind me of how I had learned the Communists promised freedom and equality to the Russians and other Eastern Europeans, but instead created great slave nations. I came to believe by the tender age of 15 that if I truly wanted a society capable of the love and decency that the egalitarians so value, that I had to preserve my genotype. It also became apparent that our people's right to preserve our heritage and people is perhaps the most basic right of all, the right to live.

Since I was a small boy, the media had pounded in my mind that the most terrible act of the 20th century was said to be the attempted destruction of the Jewish people during the Second World War. An attempt to wipe out a race would be an execrable crime in anyone's mind. In fact, commentators said that what made the atrocities against the Jews so terrible was not the murder of such great numbers per se, because there had been bigger slaughters in Russia and China, but the fact that there was an alleged attempt to wipe out the Jewish people. Yet, why is not the eventual destruction of our European genotype, the genocide of our race, any less terrible than that which was said to be attempted against the Jews? The ultimate result is the same.

As I recognized the genetic crisis we faced, I also became inspired with the possibilities for our people. If the genetic improvement of our race created by the ice ages, produced such great achievements, then nurturing our genetic quality offered great hope for the future.

The environmentalists, whether they be Capitalists or Communists, Democrats or Totalitarians say that the way to better the world was through better mechanisms of society. In fact, all of man's history has been about man's progress through the tools he created. The crucible of the ice ages created a genetically brilliant people that in spite of having no written language, no schools, no domesticated animals, no complex architecture, eventually created these things out of nothing. If the behavioral environmentalists were right, prehistoric man could have never built the first civilization, for his environment was far too primitive and uneducated to have ever afforded such an opportunity. Our heritage created civilization from nothing but the genetic powers carried inside of them. The achievements of the

European people can be contrasted to the centuries the African race has not even been able to copy successfully what Europeans originated. The great treasure our people possessed has always been in our genes rather than our gold or our gadgets.

The Great Paradox

While still in high school I read Elmer Pendell's classic book *Sex Versus Civilization*.[212] Pendell was a population expert who had written many books on the perils of overpopulation. He pointed out that you couldn't properly deal with the human quantity problem without addressing the human quality issue. He also made clear the strange interaction of human evolution with civilization, which I call the Great Paradox. He said that the ice ages produced the magnificent intellectual powers of what we call modern or "Cro-Magnon man," the prototype of the modern European. As the ice ages receded and the climate became less harsh, those genetically accumulated abilities flowered in the world's first great civilizations.[213] Over time, intellect combined with accumulated learning brought on the highest cultural and technological achievements. Ironically, at the same time civilization makes advancements, it fosters a dysgenic selection that in many ways is opposite to the eugenic effect of the prehistoric period.

The same sharing and social justice that helped the small hunting bands of high quality to survive, applied indiscriminately to a larger society, leads to degeneration. The least intelligent and fit reproduce faster than the best. As the most intelligent found their pleasure in their business, religious, governmental activities, as well as the arts or the various pleasures that could be purchased with affluence, they had smaller families. The poorest continued to find their greatest pleasures in the sexual acts that also increased their numbers.

The organization of civilization also meant a change in the conduct of wars. In more primitive societies, warfare could wipe away the whole gene pool and replace it with more intelligent and efficient groups. Civilization's wars tended to leave the physical and mental defectives at home, while impressing the healthiest, and fittest, who by virtue of their youth had often not yet had children. Through a succession of wars, the best and bravest traditionally led their troops and suffered the highest casualties.

As civilizations increased in power, they ranged in conquest far beyond the original boundaries of the people who built them, they sometimes brought back slaves of the conquered peoples, such as the Egyptian transport of Nubians into the heart of Egypt. Often, the genes of those non-civilized populations were slowly absorbed into the conqueror's gene pool. So for generations, sometimes even centuries, the accumulation of wealth and knowledge led to advances in civilization. But underneath, the genetic foundation of the civilization became undermined, until at last, usually more rapidly than it arose; civilization collapsed or their societies were conquered by more vigorous peoples. Its genetically weakened subjects destined to live in the ruins of past achievement.

So the Great Paradox of man is that through the barbarity of Nature over the eons, man developed his genetic capacity for civilization. Then the institutions and processes of the civilization he creates reverses the evolutionary process, weakens him genetically and eventually casts him back to barbarity. At first, learning about the chronic fate of civilization can be quite discouraging, but when one thoroughly understands the process that has repeatedly occurred, one sees the opportunity to learn from it.

I realized that the answers to the great challenges of mankind lay not in the tools or the creations of our race, but the quality of our race itself. If our people continue up the evolutionary ladder, we will become smarter, healthier and cross genetic thresholds that will someday make going to the moon seem like as simple as a child's walk across the living room. Instead of focusing on bettering the achievements of man, when we focus on bettering mankind itself, the next galaxy may someday seem as close to us as we see a neighboring city in our current era. The unleashed power of the genes will one day pass through any barrier, even the seemingly insurmountable velocity of the speed of light, for if we are advanced enough we can solve any problem. I believe that the universe is constructed so that *anything* is *possible*. Consider the great achievements that mankind has achieved with its present IQ range: It has sent probes to the stars and fixed errant genes. We cannot begin to comprehend what our people could do in the distant future with an IQ equivalent to our present one cubed.

The principle of race for me went beyond even the survival of my heritage and all the things I loved in our civilization, it became the key to the stars. I now understood that preserving my own race and its civilization was but a precondition for continuing its evolution to a higher level. As Nietzsche so eloquently advocated — that man must go "beyond man." It seemed to me that our race's struggle is similar to a man who made a long, hard climb up a high mountain. He has one more ledge to climb and the whole world and sky will be laid out before him. He grasps the utmost crag and proceeds to pull himself up, but down around his ankles are those lesser ones who keep pulling him back.

We are that climber. We have probed the bottom of the ocean and walked on the moon. We have unlocked the secrets of flight, cured the incurable, discovered even many of the secrets of life itself. We have even begun the first feeble movements toward understanding and helping to direct our own higher evolution. The future awaits, heroic and magnificent, shining as beautifully as the brightest stars on a clear night. Our fingernails are clinging to that summit, bathed in light, while the genetic forces of regression pull us down from below. Either we shall recognize race and the powers within our genes, and climb upward to a new era, or we shall tumble into the abyss never to rise again.

As a teenager, when I came to understand these things, on cloudless nights I would stare up at the milky way, no longer like a spectator to a great cosmic portrait. I was part of it all. My genes and even my atoms were part of the planet Earth and all of its life forms, and indeed, part of the cosmos. I found meaning in my life by helping, as best I could, the still primitive embryo of mankind to grow to adulthood on Earth and in the heavens. No matter how slight my contribution might be, I wanted to help form a community of my kind who shared the same vision: The continued higher evolution of mankind to the next evolutionary step toward the stars. At 16, I knew that I had to stand on the side of evolutionary advancement; not on the side of degeneration and barbarism.

CHAPTER 11:

RACE HISTORY

The racial question is the key to world history...all is race, there is no other truth — *Benjamin Disraeli.*

Science moves inexorably toward the truth of Race. Race is simply genetics as applied to the breeds of mankind and it speaks to us in blood types and genotypes, in physical traits and mental abilities, in behavior and temperament, in human achievement and human failure. It tells us more about human life than cultural characteristics do because it is the engine that makes our cultures what they are. Culture is simply a veneer reflecting the deeper genetic makeup of people. Race bequeaths diversity to the planet that affects all aspects of life. As the voices of science become more articulate on race — history and social studies speak to us just as powerfully on the subject.

Recently, a distraught friend called me and told me how Jimmy, his first-grader, had come home from school eager to tell his father that he had learned where civilization came from. The 7-year-old boy led his father to his lighted globe and immediately pointed to the heart of the African continent. He proudly announced, "That's where Black people and the first civilizations came from!" Stunned by his answer, my friend asked his child, "Jimmy, can you tell me where White people came from?" "I dunno," said the little blue-eyed boy.

The ultimate determinant of fitness for civilization is not IQ tests or psychological studies but the straightforward barometer of historical performance. Even back in the time of my initial racial awakening, there was some laughed-at babble about "great Black civilizations." Obscure Afrocentrist claims looked upon as ludicrous in the 1960s are now frequently taught in public schools.

Afrocentrism, or the idea that civilization originated in Black Africa, thrives although there is not a shred of evidence that even a single Black civilization ever developed in sub-Saharan Africa. Even ancient Egypt is being claimed as a Black civilization, despite the fact that the oldest Egyptian mummies found are distinctly Caucasian, classed as such by innumerable anthropologists and archeologists. Any modern medical investigator, such as those who identify badly decomposed human remains, would immediately deem them as White. Even the fact that prominent-nosed, fair-skinned and straight-haired Whites are the subjects of the art and hieroglyphics of the Egyptian tombs has not deterred egalitarians from desperately clinging to fantasies that ancient Egypt was an example of Black historic achievement. They have gone so far as to depict Queen Cleopatra, who was wholly of Greek lineage (the last of the Ptolemies, who ruled from 330 to 30 B.C.), as an afro-wearing Black woman. Some of the purveyors of "Black history" solemnly allege that the Greeks stole philosophy and civilization from Africa. One would be hard pressed to understand how one steals civilization. If a nation copies another's inventiveness or ideas, does that stop the originator from using it? And if a people are gifted enough to create a great civilization, art, philosophy, and mathematics, what keeps them from continuing to replenish the fountainhead of human accomplishment?

The inescapable fact is that Black Africa has neither created nor even been able to sustain a high civilization. One of the most respected historians of the 20th century, Arnold Toynbee, listed what he calls 33 historic civilizations. Most are European, some are Asian but none are Black.

Poor Black historical performance correlates with the evidence of marked differences in intelligence between Blacks and Whites. In America, school children are taught relentlessly about the great achievements of Black Americans. With a straight face, teachers recount the most important Black contributions to the modern world, and then give examples such as the traffic light and the paper bag.

The very fact that these things are listed as great Black achievements betrays their paucity. No Black is to be found in Michael Hart's *The 100: A Ranking of the Most Influential Persons in History.* [214] Perhaps even more telling is that not even one Black achievement is found in Issac Asimov's listing of 1,500 great attainments in his *Chronicle of Science and Discovery*.[215] Far from being a racist, Asimov publicly expressed a belief in racial equality and was a self-described liberal.

Can the invention of the traffic light or the paper bag remotely compare to the development of the Pythagorean Theorem, the invention of the first airplane or the first steam engine, the engineering of the Pyramids, the architecture of the Parthenon or the Roman aqueducts, the invention of the printing press, the development of the smallpox vaccine, the creation of genetic engineering, the invention of the transistor, or the mathematics and genius that took men to the moon? Such comparisons surely do not demonstrate racial equality. Instead, they suggest a disparity that goes far beyond the differences in intelligence indicated by mere IQ tests. It must be remembered that almost all of the great achievements of mankind were the products of the most intelligent four or five percent of the population. As *The Bell Curve* [216] and every other IQ study have shown, if one group has an average IQ about 15 percent lower than another, it does not mean that the lower group will have 15 percent fewer geniuses than the smarter group. The percentage of geniuses will differ by a rate of more than 44 to 1 in favor of the more intelligent group. Some researchers say it is closer to 100 to 1, depending on how high the genius IQ level is set.

The standard response of racial egalitarians to the fact that Blacks' account for only a small percentage of great achievements is that Black societies were not advanced enough or because their societies were "oppressed." Of course, such an argument is only begging the question, for what could have caused this lack of advancement or habitual "oppression" over thousands of years? If the capabilities for what we call civilization are the same among the races, why did Blacks not develop even one? In all of Black Africa beneath the Sahara, they never developed any writing and never used the wheel! There is today only one vibrant nation, the Republic of South Africa, a nation now heading rapidly to the same fate of the rest of Black Africa with the ongoing removal of White leadership and skills.

Whites dominated investment, government, education, medicine, training and communication in Africa for 200 years. But in the 40 years since the departure of Europeans, almost every Black African nation has steadily declined in its income, education, health care, sanitation, civil rights and other societal levels. The disintegration in some nations such as the Sudan and Zaire has been slowed only by the fact that once they have fallen to such low levels, there is simply little room for further decline. In their utter despair, the struggling remnants in many African nations have actually invited Europeans back, and the increased Western investment and aid should improve, even if only marginally, the current appalling conditions.

Africa's social disaster cannot be blamed on lack of resources. The continent is the greatest source of untapped resources in the world. In an age where many First World nations have exhausted their resources, Africa has had an excellent opportunity, which it has squandered. From the early 1970s to the 1990s, Black Africa's share of world trade has fallen 50 percent, its gross national product has declined about 2 percent per year, food production has declined almost 20 percent, malnutrition has increased, genocidal warfare has increased, and the continent has even less a semblance of democracy than it had just 25 years ago.[217]

Skyscrapers built and once maintained by Europeans in Nigeria now have intermittent electricity and toilets that overflow. Sanitation, hospitals, power generation and telephone services all depend on financial aid and imported Europeans must keep them running even at the most minimal levels. European colonialists who once curbed the bloody tribal warfare were no longer present to stop the Hutus and the Tutsis from murdering between 600,000 and 1,000,000 people in Zaire. European colonialists who outlawed slavery in Africa over 100 years ago are no longer present in great enough numbers to stop the enslavement of tens-of-thousands of Africans today. Slavery is technically outlawed in every country in the world, but in Africa it is still widespread. It is present to a degree in almost every African nation. Sudan, Ghana and Mauritania, in particular, are acknowledged as world leaders in the slave trade. In the Nuba Mountains of Sudan alone, 30,000 African children were sold into slavery in the mid-1990s for the price of two chickens each. [218]

Racial Egalitarians blame Europeans and White racism for the African disaster. Some have argued that the Europeans did not adequately prepare Africa for independence. Yet while the decolonization went on, some European nations adamantly maintained that more time was needed to develop the African nations before their independence. Such claims were dismissed by White liberals in the West and by African tin-pot revolutionaries as racist and patronizing. Of course, the very idea of a need for preparation for independence begs the question, for who prepared the European nations for their independence?

Of course egalitarians always have an excuse for Black historical failure. The latest apologia for the lack of African culture argues that climatic and ecological factors facilitated development of civilization in Eurasia but prevented it in Africa.[219] Jared Diamond though, does not answer the question of why successful colonization by the Arabs preserved civilized qualities for centuries (until the colonist's race was subsumed by the native Black population), and why the spark of civilization in Africa only burned when the European was there to nurture and sustain it.

Race and Nation

When the race is good, so is the place – *Ralph Waldo Emerson*

As I became more aware of the profound biological differences between the races and better understood the impact of these differences on education, crime, poverty, and other societal areas, I began to read about the historical realities of race and culture.

If racial composition can have great impact on a school, how much does it have on a nation? Can race be instructive about the development and conditions of nations? One of my friends in high school, George Cardella, came from Colombia. He spoke to me at length about the conditions of his own and other South American lands. Often his revelations of the low living standards and crude human values startled me. He was conscious of his light eyes and

European Spanish ancestry and talked frankly about the racial realities of his and other South American nations.

In geography class my teacher pointed out that South America has more potential resource development than North America. It is larger in temperate land area, richer in resources, more varied in climate and topography, and had quite a head start being intensively settled and exploited earlier than North America. The question naturally arose, "Why then are the countries south of the Rio Grande usually so much poorer, more unhealthy, less educated, and less free than those in the United States and Canada?"

South America had substantial settlements, and in some places — even universities, before the rudimentary outposts at Jamestown and Plymouth. Spain and Portugal, nations with a rich European cultural heritage, settled the region. The modern-era discovery of America by Christopher Columbus occurred the same year as the victory over the Moors, finally expelling them from all of Spain after a struggle lasting hundreds of years. The Spanish conquistadors were fit and fearless, forged by the crucible of war and a fight for freedom that spanned generations. Suddenly the national unity and purpose born of the victorious war with the Moors shifted to conquering and civilizing a new land in the New World. It wasn't long until the auburn-haired, green-eyed Isabella ruled Spanish possessions larger than the size of all of Europe.

The Spanish and Portuguese ruthlessly exploited the native population of the Americas, and those aboriginals they did not kill in war, disease often dispatched. The discovery of precious metals such as gold and silver and the vast tracts of land then in possession of the Spanish throne encouraged the Spanish to integrate with and use the native population to develop the resources. Spanish rulers were spread thin in the immense empire, a tiny minority in a sea of color. Because the physical and psychological character of the Indians adapted poorly to servitude, in some regions, to satisfy their need for laborers, they imported Black slaves from Africa.

Whether conquistador or priest, their primary task was exploitative in nature: the conquistador to cultivate the land's riches, the priest to harvest the inhabitants' souls. Living in a land with few White women but ample Indian maidens and Black slave women, mixed liaisons and marriages were common, although such unions were looked down upon by the more aristocratic classes, who often sent their sons and daughters home to Spain to find a husband or wife.

The Spanish built Mexico and their other colonies throughout the Caribbean, Central and South America in their own image. They established schools, government buildings and churches and carried the art, technology and culture of European civilization to the New World. In addition to Spain and Portugal, Great Britain, France and Holland also had colonies and possessions in the Western Hemisphere. In this vast expanse, only the 13 American Colonies and Canada had White majorities.

In North America, where there was a presence of non-Whites, whether slave or free, social intercourse among Europeans was exclusively White. In North America, Europeans came over by the hundreds of thousands, bringing their families with them, and the farming lifestyle made large families desirable, causing little shortage of women, except at the frontier. Thus America and Canada became overwhelming White nations, while the Caribbean, Central, and South Americas remained mostly non-White, except for a veneer of White leadership and control.

It seemed obvious to me that the overwhelming difference between the Canadian and American colonies, and the rest of the Americas was simply that of race. I discussed some of these facts with my geography teacher in high school, Mrs. Weir. She was a dyed-in-the-wool egalitarian who blustered that there were other factors that I failed to consider in my hypothesis. Her first counter argument was that North America was mostly Protestant and thus driven by the work ethic intrinsic to that denomination. My retort was easy: the Renaissance of Western civilization itself began in northern Italy, an exclusively Catholic society. And Quebec, a North American city, was not Protestant but had living standards far more similar to Protestant America than to Mexico or Brazil.

Next she tried to argue that it was simply the democratic traditions of North America compared to the autocratic ones of South America that have made such pronounced differences. I pointed out that history is full of examples of both tyrannies that had become democratic and democracies that had lost their freedoms. The aristocracies of Europe certainly became great and modern nations. Many of the governing constitutions of the Middle- and Southern-Hemisphere nations were modeled directly on our own U.S. Constitution, but those instruments of law did not save them from poverty, massive corruption, tyranny and assassination, continuous revolution, illiteracy, disease, and primitive lifestyles and conditions.

I asked her, "When one considers that there are dozens of nations in the Caribbean and the Americas, and there have been hundreds of revolutions and marked political changes over the centuries, are we supposed to believe that none of them ever got it right?" In response to her silence, I blurted out, "Perhaps the thing that really makes or breaks a nation is not its institutions but the race of its people. "

Race can also be seen in the differences that exist among the many different nations of the Americas. Costa Rica is readily acknowledged as the most advanced nation in Central America. It has a reputation as the least corrupt government and the highest living standard and literacy rate in the region. It also prides itself on being the Whitest nation of Central America. The most advanced nations of South America are Argentina, Uruguay and Chile — the nations with the continent's highest percentages of Europeans. The racial truth can also be seen even within nations themselves. Brazil, for instance, is much like two different nations when one considers the backward Black regions in the north and the more European-like ones in the South. When I visited Brazil in 1991, I readily noticed how the population became Blacker and poorer as one neared the traditional lands of the Black slave plantations and whiter and wealthier in the more mountainous regions. (The same is true for the old plantation "River parishes" of Louisiana as compared to the Whiter ones)

It became obvious to me that if America's demography changes into one resembling that of South America, we will become like those societies. We will lose our precious heritage and way of life. I became convinced that race is the dominant force of society, influencing every aspect of our lives. Even if a society does not overtly state it or even acknowledge it, race imprints nations — just as it does individuals — with characteristics and traits that egalitarianism cannot explain away.

The lessons of race taught by the history of the Western Hemisphere are pertinent to the history of all nations and all cultures. One can even examine prehistory and find that there have always been tribes that shared a particular gene pool and common characteristics that distinguished them. Nations arose from people who shared a common heritage. They have not always been monoracial, but they were always formed by a dominant people that made the country in their own image, their own culture, values, language and artistic tastes. Nations were not determined strictly by geography, as borders were often poorly defined and amorphous, but by the people who populated them. For instance, whether the people were Assyrians, Egyptians, Jews, Greeks, Romans, or the French, nations arose out of the races or subraces that composed them. The term *France*, for instance, came from the name of the people who rebuilt the country after the fall of the Roman Empire, the Franks. One can trace the history of nations in the racial history and character of its inhabitants.

One of the first history books my father gave me to read in grade school was H. G. Wells' classic *The Outline of History*. [220] Its theme is the rise and fall of nations. A great people arise having intelligence, strength and ambition. They create a powerful society and conquer their less fit neighbors. And then begins a process of absorbing the conquered in their nation-state. The traits that originally led them to victory and dominance are lost as they gradually absorb the defeated population. Invariably the process begins again, and another people come on the scene and conquer, only to once more be absorbed by those they had vanquished. Such a pattern was obvious to me in studying the Americas, but now, as I read more history, it became obvious to me that the race factor is present in the rise and fall of every civilization. In fact, in every fallen civilization there had been a racial change from the original founding population. The only real justification for the survival of a nation is a racial one — the survival of that specific population as a distinct genetic entity, as a source for the next generation. Otherwise, such a nation would not be worth defending in a world of many nations.

Historians such as Toynbee, Durant and Spengler have chronicled the emergence and decline of nations. Interestingly, every great civilization that has graced the Earth fell into decay and destruction. Ours is simply the last of many civilizations that have risen only to subsequently decline. The ultimate question of the historians is why civilizations have this cycle. There are many theories on why civilizations decline. Some argue economic downturns, some say political corruption, some argue military weakness and defeat, some simply say moral decay from the breakdown of religious tradition, some argue class warfare, some say wealth always breeds degeneration. There are as many theories as there are historians, but one factor is present in the rise and fall of every civilization known to man: the *race factor*. The racial group that built the original civilization lost its dominance, often even its genetic integrity.

Before I learned about race, I too had my theories, based on what I had read. Mine were based purely on the symptoms of the decline rather than on the underlying factors causing the symptoms. A book written over a hundred years ago by a French scholar, Count Arthur de Gobineau, proposed a hypothesis on the decline of civilization that had me thinking about the issue for weeks, and it ultimately led me to my world-view on the race issue. De Gobineau's *Inequality of the Races* [221] was written before Darwin's *Origin of Species* [222] and long before many of the modern principles of biology and psychology, but it put forth the startling propositions that populations were undergoing change in their biological character, and that civilization was ultimately the product of biology: the racial characteristics of its founders.

De Gobineau claimed that civilizations declined because the inherent makeup of its creators had changed. The racial quality of the people had declined. He saw it as an intra-racial and inter-racial weakening of the culture-creating race. It was inter-racial in that the cosmopolitan nature of the empire caused racial-mixing with alien peoples and declining birthrates among the founding race accompanied by overpopulation of the mixed multitudes. De Gobineau also recognized a decline intra-racially in that, he saw among the ruling race, the most intelligent and productive citizens had the fewest children, while the lower elements were extremely prolific.

De Gobineau wrote during the mid-19th century, before modern biology, which meant that his book was bound to contain errors. Yet the many principles that he got right were astounding. De Gobineau was well traveled for his time, and he had the power to dispassionately observe and interpolate what he encountered.

Once one understands race, it is easy to recognize the racial component in the history of nations and its role in contemporary societies around the world. A classic example of race history is the study of the Egyptian civilization. Purveyors of "Black history" make the ludicrous claim that Egypt was a Black civilization. They point to some Negroid features in the last of the Pharaohs as proof of this contention. It is indeed true that the last Pharaoh may have been part Black. At the end of 3,000 years, there might have been intrusion of some Black genes into the ruling family. That fact does not make the basis of Egyptian civilization Black anymore than Jesse Jackson becoming president of the United States would make the signers of our Declaration of Independence Negroes. Black genes in the Egyptian royal family signified the end of the Egyptian civilization (just as Jesse Jackson being elected president would be an epitaph for America).

There are thousands of surviving hieroglyphics depicting the builders of the Egyptian civilization as White people (some with reddish hair and light eyes). The oldest recovered mummies show the remains to be White. Egypt had a civilization in some way reminiscent of the Old South. As the aristocratic White society of the South bought Black slaves from the African slavetraders, Egyptian Whites brought Black slaves up for labor from the lower Nile. Over thousands of years licit and illicit sexual contact between the races eventually carried Black genes even into the royal family. The completion of that process coincided perfectly with the demise of the longest enduring set of dynasties the world has ever seen and the collapse of the Egyptian civilization.

Egypt today has a varied population, from the purest of Blacks to a vast mixed population and even a small White minority. The lighter elements are the educational, scientific, political, and business elite.

Few peoples have fallen as far as the once great Egyptians have. The Egyptian nation is one of the poorest on Earth, with rampant poverty and crime. There are an estimated 60,000 street beggars in

Cairo alone, and thousands of infants are purposely blinded or crippled and put on the street to beg, filling the coffers of cruel masters.

The racial story of Egypt is a clear and dramatic one because of the obvious racial impact of the admixture of the Black race. Even civilizations that underwent less dramatic racial mixing than did Egypt lost the impetus of their cultures.

Ancient Greece was probably the most culturally and artistically advanced civilization the world has ever seen. Probably 98 percent of Greek art has been lost over the last two millennia, yet we still marvel at the magnificence of their architecture, sculpture, paintings, poetry, songs, plays, philosophy, and literature. Not only were the Greeks great thinkers and artists, they were also great warriors, having conquered almost all of the known world. Alexander the Great, actually an Aryan Macedonian, at one time in his short life had even expanded the Greek empire as far as the plains of India. The Greeks accomplished all this although the total population of Athens and Sparta combined never exceeded 250,000 people.

Greek civilization is called the Golden Age, and the Greek people were described as a golden people because of the presence of so many blondes. Greek literature is full of descriptions of fair-complected, light-eyed people. Their sculptures record their physical traits, for they were a tall, magnificent people who attended to the health and beauty of their bodies just as they did to their creative minds.

The Greeks, much as the Spanish in South America, were few in numbers but conquered and administered over vast populations and land areas. Alexander decided to deal with the problem by urging his soldiers and sailors to marry the ruling-class women of the countries Greece ruled. On one occasion, 10,000 Greek soldiers married 10,000 Persian women in a mass ceremony. Although those unions were later voided, they symbolized the Greek strategy for their imperialism. Alexander thought he was binding the loyalty of the nations he subdued and simply creating more Greeks. Other Greeks came home with their foreign brides initiating a process that undermined their whole civilization. Non-Greeks from all over the Mediterranean world immigrated to Greece for the same economic and social reasons that Mexicans cross the Rio Grande. Much like the great trading cities of the world today, Greek cities became a melting pot of diverse races. Over the centuries few Greeks retained the physical characteristics described in the *Odyssey* and captured for eternity in their preserved sculptures we marvel at today. A people were lost in an alien genetic flood, and the vitality of the civilization ebbed away, only to be found in the writing, remnants and ruins of the past.

Since the fall of the Greek civilization, the peninsula has been replenished frequently by migrations from the north, and there are still genes of the original Greeks in some of its citizens today. The nation, though, is a shadow of the splendor of what once was, and still finds its highest meaning in its glorious antiquity.

In many ways the great Roman civilization resembled that of the Greeks. The founding Romans were called patricians. *Random House Webster's Electronic Dictionary* defines patrician as follows:

patrician n.
1. a person of noble or high rank; aristocrat.
2. a person of breeding, education, and refinement.
3. a member of the original hereditary aristocracy of ancient Rome, having such privileges as the exclusive right to hold certain offices.
4. (in the later Roman and Byzantine empires) **a nonhereditary honorary title** or dignity conferred by the emperor. *(emphasis mine)*

As Rome ruled the known world, the city of Rome itself became the New York City of the ancient world. Roman chroniclers talked about walking in the streets of Rome in its declining period as if it were a foreign land filled with alien appearances and languages. One can trace the decline of Roman power directly with (as the fourth definition shows) the transition of the patrician from a hereditary title to an honorary one. Another sign of the genetic basis of the original Roman civilization can be found in the common Jewish word *gentiles*, which originated from the Roman term *gens*, a term used to denote the true Roman families that built and for a time ruled the Roman empire. To the Jews of those days the *gens* or *gentiles* represented the enemy that had conquered them in Palestine. The very term *Gens* is the root of words such as *gentleman, gent, genes, genetics, genocide, genus,* and other terms of heredity.

gens (jenz), *n., pl.* **gentes**
1. a group of families in ancient Rome claiming descent from a common ancestor and united by a common name and common ancestral religious rites.
2. *Anthropol.* a group tracing common descent in the male line; clan.
3. *gens* race, people. See GENUS, GENDER

gentleman n.
1. a man of good family, breeding, or social position.

Rome never sank to the level of modern Egypt because the racial change was far less dramatic than in that north African nation, but it certainly declined. Luckily Italy enjoyed the fresh, hardy European genes of the northern barbarian invaders and conquerors who were not as culturally advanced but who had the same genetic potential as the original Romans and their patrician standard-bearers. *Barbarian* is a term that poorly describes these invaders, for they had a strong moral fiber and family life and a rich cultural heritage, as well as the intelligence and planning in war to defeat the schooled and experienced Roman armies.

When the Renaissance finally laid the cornerstones of our modern Western civilization, it found its impetus primarily not from the great city of Rome with all its history, centers of learning, and advantages, but from the northern Italian cities of Florence, Padua, and Venice. Rome still contained a lot of original Roman blood, but it was no longer the Rome of the Romans, it was now an international city, a melting pot of races from around the known world, including even some Germanic blood, Egyptians, Semites, and others. The Renaissance found its driving force where the original Roman genes still dominated. Even today, the Northern provinces are the most economically sound and robust parts of all Italy. By itself the per capita GNP of northern Italy is equal to that of the strongest economies in Europe.

One can see the racial expression of the Renaissance in Michaelangelo's masterful fresco of an Aryan depiction of God and Adam on the ceiling of the Sistine Chapel. Falsifying history has become a full-time occupation for many in the educational and cultural establishment of America. Not only has Cleopatra become Black, it appears that the great Carthaginian general Hannibal has begun to

The new version of Hannibal being taught in American schools

take on a decidedly Negro appearance. Budweiser Beer did a poster and "educational" series called "The Great Kings of Africa" in which it depicted Hannibal as resembling Black boxing promoter Don King.

Of course, Hannibal was White. Contemporary sources described him in terms that leave no doubt that he was as White as the ancient Carthaginian people he led. What's more, his death mask shows the thin nose and lips and high forehead of the Caucasian. The mask bears no Negro features.

The real Hannibal

The Black adoption of famous Europeans as their own does not end with Cleopatra or Hannibal. They have even gone so far as to ludicrously allege Ludwig van Beethoven was Black, and for that matter anyone with curly hair and swarthy is claimed by afro-centrists desperate for validation.

Liberal historians act as if civilization and advanced nations represent some cosmic accident. To them, successful nations are just lucky, and but for luck one people could be either illiterate or poor, or cultured and rich. Yet the world has abundant examples of ecologically rich nations that are culturally and economically destitute and of resource-poor nations that are culturally enlightened and economically rich. Nations can be found with long histories that are now either progressive or backward. Short national histories can herald great success or abject failure. Societies can be religiously devout or ambivalent. There are poor devout nations, rich agnostic ones and vice-versa. Constitutions and laws on the books do not really tell us how free or law-abiding a nation is, but race usually tells us a lot. There are relatively isolated nations that are wealthy and advanced, and ones in the thick of cultural and economic traffic that are poor.

Is there one sizable well-run all-Black nation where the crime rate is low, the schools good, the government free and uncorrupted? Is there one with high longevity rates and low infant mortality, or with low illiteracy and a high standard of living?

The impact of race on history and contemporary social conditions can be well illustrated by comparing two nations: Haiti, and Iceland. Iceland sits inside the Arctic Circle. It has perhaps the most inhospitable geography of any populated nation on Earth. It stands isolated and endures winter conditions that last almost three-quarters of the year. No forests grow there, and thus it has no wood or paper products. There is no oil, no natural gas and no coal. Much of the land is volcanic desert and glaciers so foreboding that the U.S. space program did training there for their lunar landings. Farming is almost impossible because of the rock-filled soil, snow-covered mountains and short growing season. Few tourists visit the little island in the north Atlantic. It's a land of clouds, little sunshine, and long winter nights. Iceland's only resource is the fish they harvest on the great cod banks in competition with many other nations. They also have natural volcanic geysers that they ingeniously use to heat their homes and businesses.

Compare this island to the island of Hispaniola and the nation of Haiti, the second oldest republic in the Western Hemisphere. It is a huge island rich beyond the dream of a poet's fancy. Warm and beautiful, with beaches, mountains and clear waters, the topography is a tourist's fantasy. It is one of the gateway islands to the Caribbean, the United States, Mexico and South America — a natural place for thriving international trade. Thick forests and rich mineral resources bless the island. The seafood in the waters around the nation is plentiful and valuable. Mild weather gives the island long and productive growing seasons and lush soil.

In the 18th century Haiti was the largest sugar producer in the world. Universities and other centers of higher learning kept the island abreast of the world's progress and advances, and it became one of the richest of France's overseas possessions — richer than any of the 13 original American colonies. Haiti came to be called the Jewel of the Caribbean.

All this ground to a halt in the late 1790s, when the egalitarianism introduced by Whites fresh from the French Revolution precipitated a Black revolt in which, ultimately, the Black revolutionaries murdered nearly every one of the 40,000 White men, women, and children on the island. In the 200 years since the revolution, under one corrupt and tyrannical regime after another, Black Haiti has become one of the most dangerous, superstitious, and backward places on Earth. The vast majority of the people are illiterate, and less than 3 percent finish primary education. It has one of the lowest per capita incomes on Earth, endemic crime and drug problems, wholesale destruction of the environment, negligible education, high infant mortality and primitive health care, and its dominant religion is voodoo.

The efforts of American missionaries and educators have proven futile. And repeated military incursions have also failed. Three times in this century U.S. Marines were sent to bring "democracy" to Haiti. The first mission began in 1915. Marines remained for 19 years, building hospitals, power stations, schools, and modern telephone exchanges, and more than 200 bridges and 1,000 miles of paved roads. Upon their leaving the island reverted back to complete ruin and despotism. In 1958 Marines returned and began the whole process over again, with the same results.

In 1994 Americans again returned to Haiti, this time with 23,000 troops as part of a United Nations peacekeeping force. At least 500 troops are expected to remain until at least the end of the century to prevent Haiti from reverting to its old ways. Even with this modern force and accompanying massive U.S. and U.N. aid, Haiti is politically corrupt, wracked by AIDS and other diseases, and chronically criminal. As Haiti approaches the end of the 20th century, the capital, Port-au-Prince reeks of human waste and rotting garbage.

At the beginning of the 20th century, a British member of the Royal Geographic Society, Hesketh Prichard, traveled to Haiti to study the effects of an entirely Black-ruled country. Upon his arrival he had strong sympathies with the natives, and he wanted to see how they fared in response to the introduction of White civilization, but without Whites ruling over them. He found that although Haiti had French laws and the workings of a civilization on paper, it was all an illusion of style without substance. The Haitian army, for instance, had 6,500 privates but the same number of generals, all with pompously adorned uniforms. They had hospitals with mud floors, train stations and tracks but no working trains, power-generating plants that generated no power, courts and laws and constitutional rights but only corruption and despotism. There were Catholic churches, but they were encumbered with primitive voodoo and animal sacrifices. Although Prichard regarded the natives as generally jovial, he found them prone to the cruelest human tortures and atrocities.

Prichard concluded that to Haitians the veneer of civilization is as important as its substance. If they could dress and speak like a European and have institutions that in form seemed like that of the European, then they viewed themselves as equal to the European.

In asking the fundamental question "Can the Haitian rule himself?" Prichard writes the following:

> The present condition of Haiti gives the best possible answer to the question, and, considering the experiment has lasted for a century, perhaps also a conclusive one. For a century the answer has been working itself out there in flesh and blood. The Negro has had his chance, a fair field, and no favor. He has had the most beautiful and fertile of the Caribees for his own; he has had the advantage of excellent French laws; he inherited a made country, with Cap Haitien [A once beautiful town on the north coast of Haiti] for its Paris.... Here was a wide land sown with prosperity, a land of wood, water, towns and plantations, and in the midst of it the Black man was

turned loose to work out his own salvation. What has he made of the chances that were given to him? . . .

At the end of a hundred years of trial how does the Black man govern himself? What progress has he made? Absolutely none.[223]

Iceland, on the other hand, even with all her disadvantages, is one of the best places to live on Earth. The nation publishes more books and journals per head of population than any other country in the world. It has some of the highest literacy rates and lowest infant mortality rates, lowest crime and drug rates, highest standards of living, best medical care, and the longest standing freely elected Parliament in the world: the Althing.

Suppose that by some incredible act, all the Icelanders were taken to Haiti and all the Haitians taken to Iceland. In five years the Icelanders in Haiti would be living in a paradise they would have built, while in Iceland...I suspect that most Haitians would be dead.

I came to the conclusion that the liberals were in a way right about the impact of environment on the individual and groups. Environment *has* shaped us, but the environment that gave us the genetic code that so deeply influences us came not in the evolutionary millisecond of the individual's short life span, but over thousands of years. That is why well-meaning efforts to improve some races of man through his environment invariably fail. And efforts to oppress other races, such as the nationalities in the former Soviet bloc, also fail in the end.

There have been many uncivilized areas of the globe that rapidly flourished to economic, social and scientific achievement after having just the slightest contact with civilization. Conversely, other areas on the borders of civilization for thousands of years never could adopt and sustain its most rudimentary characteristics. A perfect example is the traditional Sudan, an area that stretches across northern Africa just south of the Sahara. Rich in grasslands, minerals, forests, swamps

Africans regressing in the Caribbean

and even natural seaports in the east that brought trade and the learning of the civilized world, Sudan's only historical bright spots were as colonial outposts of the Egyptians, Arab Muslims and then later the modern Europeans. Contrast the Sudan of today to the descendants of Rome's colonial forays in Britain and France. Not only did those nations adopt the attributes of Roman civilization; they eventually far exceeded them.

In the Sudan, after at least six thousand years of contact, it is little better off than it was in the times of the Pharaohs, in fact it is arguably a lot worse. In the last thirty years since colonial independence, the quality of life has rapidly disintegrated as the institutions and organization set up by the west have been abandoned. The character of genes is much stronger than the institutions of mankind, for institutions come and go, while the genes are forged over millennia.

It is the genes themselves that construct the very character of the societies in which they thrive. Every nation rises or sinks according to its genes. Over time, genes override every advantage or impediment. Human genes can make nations with the poorest of resources rich, or the richest poor. They can inspire great universities or make ruins where greatness stood. They can erect tyranny over once free men or resurrect freedom from the worst of oppression. Social structures created by race can be imposed on another, but in time the genes, if preserved, will assert themselves. The power of the gene is the source of space travel or of squalor, of civilization or the jungle.

The great U.S. Senator from Mississippi, Theodore Bilbo once wrote that if a foreign nation conquered America and enslaved its people, destroyed its buildings, its crops, its schools, its farms and its economy, that as long as our White heritage remained intact — we could build it all back even better than before. But he warned that if our heritage was lost, than our nation would be forever lost as well.

It is true that when I write of the things I love and cherish that I can only be subjective, for my values are the values of my own people. Some men even dispute the virtue of civilization itself. Freedom, beauty, love, achievement, they are all subject to the eye of the beholder. An Indian American living wild and free in the American forests and grasslands had his own idea of what is good, and that concept is certainly far more sublime than the mass alcoholism found in the Indian community of today. The African's rhythmic pounding of the drum, his sexual and physical bliss, bare feet against the warm soil, and his sound sleep beneath the open stars have always answered the needs of his soul. Could anyone deny that such may certainly answer a young Black man's heart better than imprisonment in the jails of America, or the slavery of crack and heroin, or gunshot wounds suffered in the night?

Those nations left to determine their own destiny will always live more in consonance with their natural abilities and spirit. In the end genes will out. Europeans create and maintain European standards of civilization; Africans create societies much different. By our Western standards those societies do not measure up, but if Blacks are allowed to do so, they will create a society reflective of the spirit inside them, and as such can only be truly appraised by their own people. An old European proverb states, "man is happiest at home." I believe that such is true for all men and all races of men.

At the time of the French Revolution, Ernst Arndt, a German patriot seeking to resist the imposition of revolutionary-egalitarian ideology, wrote in his *Catechism for the Teutonic Armyman* that freedom was the right to live in one's own homeland in accordance with the laws and traditions of one's ancestors" (Hans Günther *Religiosity of the Indo-Europeans*).

Going through some of my old notebooks from college, I found some aphorisms that I had written on the subject of race and history. I think they are as pertinent today as they were then.

- **People make nations. They make it in their genetic image. They compose the music, write the constitutions, create business and the economy, give it its soul and its spirit.**
- **In the battle between genes and culture, genes will win out.**
- **In the struggle between the influence of heredity and environment, in the long run, heredity will always prevail except when the environment destroys the one thing that man cannot restore: his genetic oblivion.**
- **If a folk is genetically constructed to be free, no period of tyranny can ever permanently suppress them.**
- **If they are genetically amenable to live in tyranny, democracy can be imposed on them. But left to themselves, they will eventually revert to their natural state.**
- **Human ecology is as important a concept as Nature's ecology.**
- **Races have the capacity to create great social environments, but great social environments can never make great races.**
- **Intelligent peoples make great schools and universities. Higher institutions of learning can only reflect the quality of the people.**
- **The only ultimate way to improve a society is to improve the genetic capabilities of its people. The surest way to destroy a society is to have programs and policies that systematically favor higher reproduction of the genes of the least capable over the genes of the most capable.**
- **It is the sin against the quality of the flesh that causes the sin against the spirit.**
- **Widespread race-mixing is genocide.**
- **Low birthrates is race suicide.**
- **Massive immigration of alien races ultimately means genocide.**

- **Integration of the races is rapid genocide.**
- **Geographic separation creates races and supports their survival.**

History and geography spoke to me. It was not as though all these ideas were original to me, for writers and travelers from the earliest civilizations wrote and contemplated these truths, as well as many of the great thinkers of the 19th and 20th centuries. I now saw a racial picture entirely different from when I started my inquiry. America and most other White nations are following a similar course to the failed civilizations of the past and the failing racially-mixed societies of the present. When previous White empires degenerated and dissolved into the cacophony of racial mixture, there were always our racial homelands from which would come new generations to build and create civilization anew.

This time, though, the homelands of our people — all the critical fountainheads of our gene pool — are at risk. If all of Western civilization succumbs to the dark genetic flood, there is no more womb from which our people can again be born. I realized that we are in a battle not only for our own civilization this time, but also for the preservation of our expression of life on the planet.

Now it was time for me to look into the, social, economic, and political impact of race on my own nation.

Chapter 12:
Race and Society

I had become convinced.
Science spoke eloquently and persuasively:
Race is real.
It is flesh and blood; brain and hormones.
It is in every cell, in our DNA and in every particle of our being.
It creates poverty or wealth; crime or community; superstition or science; ignorance or education; tyranny or freedom.
It composes the melodies of Mozart or the obscenities of a rap song.
It creates glittering cities of promise or disease-ridden slums.
It slashes and burns the Amazon or plants a million trees.
It gives birth to Aphrodites or crack babies.
It carries mankind to the moon or casts him into hell.
It not only colors our skin, it colors the world.
It expresses itself in millions of ways overt and subtle; hateful and sublime; raw and refined.
And it rules us whether or not we want to acknowledge its power.
It is like the tide.
It will have its way.
No matter how government might try with social welfare programs, education or affirmative action, races cannot be legislated away, or made equal to each other.
No matter how the media tries to deny its power or even its existence, race asserts itself in the endemic social problems in the non-White races among us, in the technological miracles of our own people and in canyons of cultural difference between us.
Only when we understand and recognize the power of race can we solve the problems that it creates as well as reap its magnificent possibilities.

My understanding about race developed by extensive reading in psychology, biology, history and anthropology had all come together, each area supplementing the other and reinforcing the racial idea. Not only was I convinced of the underlying reality of race, I found inspiration, for I now believed that racial understanding holds the key to the progress of civilization and even the evolutionary advancement of mankind itself. I also understood that ignoring its reality could have disastrous consequences on a society. In the 1960s America earnestly embarked on a program of social and political equality for the Black race. What would be the outcome? Carleton Putnam and others applied the historical record and the evolutionary realities to America's new social policies. Because I knew that those social changes were based on the false dogma of racial equality, I came to believe that those policies were destined to fail.

Egalitarianism was little more than a modern superstition imposed by the media-political establishment. Its tenets were extremely vulnerable to rigorous challenge and debate. *But*, I wondered, *Where is the debate?*

Advocates of egalitarianism held the seats of power in academia, in politics and in the popular media. Although many in the academic community knew its scientific absurdity, few dared to speak up forthrightly. Thankfully, many continued their research, but seduced by the rhythm of the times, they avoided its racial implications as much as they could. As more psychologists rediscovered the powerful role of hereditary in intelligence and behavior, most talked about it in terms of how genetics affected the individual, while they carefully avoided the racial issue — even though their work confirmed the facts of inherent racial differences.

If one sees heredity as a primary determinant of mental ability and personality, then the dramatically lower Black IQ scores and Black social dysfunction could only be plausibly explained by genetically determined racial differences, for environmental determination could not explain all of it. The acknowledgment of heredity's powerful role in group behavior and norms struck at the foundations of the myth of racial equality, and the racial egalitarians fought it every step of the way.

Some of the few academicians who dared to discuss race in the most moderate fashion, such as Professor Arthur Jensen, were met with academic intolerance and physical intimidation. Scientific pioneers such as Nobel Prizewinner William Shockley were physically restrained from scheduled speeches at some of America's most prestigious universities. Dr. Edward O. Wilson, the premier sociobiologist at Harvard University, who tactfully avoided the race issue much as he could, found himself victimized by both character assassination and violent assault.

In spite of their struggles, the essential tenets of the sociobiologists, behavioral geneticists and hereditarians eventually triumphed in the scientific community, although few of them, even today, can afford to approach the race issue straight on. However, a great gap continues between the scientific view of race and the view posited by the popular media. The scientifically disproven views of Marxists such as Gould, Kamin and Lewontin are still presented to the public as the mainstream scientific opinion in consumer-oriented magazines such as *Discover* and The *Smithsonian*.[224] On a brighter note, however, behavioral geneticists had made great strides in educating the public in understanding the genetic basis of male and female behavior. Biologically-borne behavioral differences in men and women found popular expression in terms such as *right-brained* and *left-brained*.

In the political realm, acknowledgment of racial truth became far scarcer than in science. Every politician quickly learned never to challenge the egalitarian view. To do so would invite political banishment. America's traditional, racially structured social systems were rapidly dismantled and then restructured on the false premise of racial equality. Carleton Putnam,[225] Dr. William Shockley,[226] Dr. Arthur Jensen,[227] and many others showed how the new social experiments were failing and were destined to do severe damage to American society, but the media and government establishment only promoted and expanded the new racial policies.

Areas having large Black populations, such those in the South and in the large cities of the North and West, quickly degenerated. Social disaster struck the Black community first. As White controls and guidance were relaxed, Black crime rose to intolerable levels. Schools deteriorated. Illicit drug abuse and addiction got out of control. Illegitimacy soared and the black family disintegrated. Welfare rolls exploded. Venereal disease reached epidemic proportions.

All these social calamities were the opposite of what the egalitarians had promised would occur with the granting of political and social equality. The veneer of European-style culture and morality imposed on the Black community for centuries, crumbled in the wake of social emancipation.

Whites, of course, suffered from the changes as well. The quality of public education rapidly declined under integration. Millions of Whites were driven from public schools and ultimately from the cities they had built, fueling the rise of suburbia. Millions more fell victim to increased Black crime. Whites endured dramatically higher taxes and paid the higher costs necessary to sustain an increasingly dependent and dysfunctional Black community, and the political power structure changed as the minority-voting blocs held the balance of power.

The federal government also intensified its efforts to destroy the underpinnings of the European-American. Forced busing expanded racial integration. Discrimination against better-qualified European-Americans, euphemistically labeled "affirmative action," became institutionalized in the public and private sector. Government-funded minority housing programs systematically destroyed White communities all across America. Beginning in 1965, federal immigration policies discriminated against European immigrants while facilitating increased non-White immigration. At the same time, huge numbers of non-White, illegal immigrants were allowed to overrun America's borders. Unchecked immigration along with high minority birthrates transformed much American geography into scenes and sociology reminiscent of the Third World. European-Americans moved ever closer to minority status in our own country.

As both Black and White society suffered under these policies, no one questioned the shibboleth of racial equality, In spite of the sacrifice of their schools, neighborhoods, cities, tax money, and even many of their lives on the alter of racial equality, White people were not appreciated for their efforts, but *blamed* for the chronic Black failure. European-Americans were told that these worsening problems could be solved only by even higher expenditures for social welfare programs and education. And the egalitarians told us that the cure for what ailed America was more integration, multiculturalism and "diversity."

To the media-government establishment, whatever sacrifices Whites made were never enough. By the end of the 20th century, most family core values had dissolved among Blacks in direct correlation to their achieving greater social and political rights. As of this writing, more than 70 percent of Black children are born illegitimate, and at any given moment well over a third of all young Black males in America are in jail, on probation, or parole. Perhaps the most devastating effect of the civil-rights movement was the epidemic of crime that denied millions their most basic civil-right of all — the right not to be physically violated by intimidation, rape, robbery, and murder.

Black Crime

[Y]ou can't steal nothing from a white man, he's already stole it, he owes you everything you want, even his life.
All the stores will open up to you, if you will say the magic words.
The magic words are: Up against the wall mother f — cker this is a stick up!
Or Smash the window at night (these are the magic actions) smash the windows daytime, anytime, together, let's smash the window drag the shit from in there.
No money down. No time to pay. Just take what you want.
— from celebrated Black poet Imamu Amiri Baraka (LeRoi Jones)[228]

Perhaps the most pernicious effect of the new race-blind policies was a crime rate never before seen in Western civilization.

Up to the time I became racially aware in my mid-teens, I had never thought much about Black crime. Living in all-White neighborhoods and attending all-White schools and churches, I had no fear of crime because I had no experience of it. If I returned home late at night on the dimly lit streets in my neighborhood, the only fear I had was that of my father's punishment for being late. Crime concerns never crossed my mind. Since the enforced joys of integration and diversity, of course, every child becomes conscious of crime almost before he learns his ABCs.

Other than our housekeeper Pinky, the most contact I had with Blacks was working occasionally in Gary's Garage located on Clio Street, a Black section of New Orleans on the periphery of the business district. That was before the civil-rights movement's social changes had much impact on the mores or lifestyles of either Blacks or Whites. Of course, I knew that the Black areas of New Orleans were more dangerous. Sometimes, when I was finishing up on a job, I stayed until after dark. The first times in my life that I had a real fear of crime occurred when I walked from the shop down the trash-laden block-and-a-half to St. Charles Avenue and my streetcar stop. During the short walks, I sometimes saw a menacing stare or heard an ill-bred comment or two coming from the dark faces in the shadows. The clanging of the streetcar bell often accompanied my own sigh of relief as the steel tracks below carried me away from the dark street.

One of the reasons I stopped going down to the shop was that the *Times-Picayune* and the television news had increasing stories of crime near the area I visited. After the well-publicized robbery and murder of a deliveryman only one street down from the repair shop, my father wouldn't let me go there anymore, at least not by myself. On some Saturdays I would ride down with him when he had some repair work to be done.

Books, magazine articles, and television shows seldom discussed the "Black crime rate" and instead just referred to the rising "crime rate." When higher incidences of crime among Blacks were reported by the media, they never explicitly revealed its incredibly disproportionate levels as compared to Whites. Most White Americans even today aren't fully cognizant of them. The media offered poverty and racism as the simple explanations for Black crime. In effect, they were saying that it was White people who were ultimately responsible for it — that the repression of Blacks by the White social system caused the poverty that in turn — caused the crime. At the time, I accepted the explanation because it sounded logical, and after all, I had seen no counter evidence in the mainstream media.

Three years after first reading *Race and Reason*, by my 16th birthday, I had learned a great deal about racial differences. I had filled a decent-size mahogany bookcase in my room with the books and articles. I could have probably filled another one with the material I had read or borrowed from the public library and from the Citizen's Council shelves.

I knew of the racial difference in IQ and how lower IQs strongly correlated with higher rates of criminality. I also knew about the differences in the brains of Blacks and Whites and even the differences in hormones, such as higher levels of testosterone in Black males. I was aware of the studies showing different behavioral patterns of Blacks and Whites that could not be explained away by environment. And I had a grasp of the rudimentary evolutionary differences that had been simultaneously created over the tens-of-thousands of years of the ice ages in Europe and the tropics in Sub-Saharan Africa. Those evolutionary characteristics seemed consistent with the historical record of civilization. I liked science and history much more than politics, and that's what I concentrated on, delving into my books and articles on race every day. Now that I lived much farther from the forests and swamps of New Orleans, I spent much more time engrossed in reading.

I also developed a keener interest in the effects of racial dynamics on current events. Most of the books I found in the libraries sported the liberal interpretations, but the Citizen's Council had one of the best libraries in the South on race and related conservative issues. A number of the authors argued that the dramatic increase of crime, coinciding with the change in the Black and White social structure, warned of a dangerous future for the nation. America was declining much like the civilizations I had read about. The coming racial disaster seemed as clear to me as the increasing frequency of police sirens that interrupted the humid, once quiet summer nights of New Orleans.

At the same time that Blacks made great economic gains through the civil-rights movement, Black crime increased. By the mid-1960s Blacks, making up about 11 percent of the population, were committing almost half of the most violent crimes. The media exclaimed that poverty and justified Black resentment for "White racism" had caused the crime explosion. But none of the pundits and social interpreters could explain away the underlying inconsistencies. If poverty and its effects were the primary culprits of crime, why was it that Whites, who were close to 90 percent of the population and at least *two-thirds* of the people under the poverty level, committing only half of the crime? I pointed out to one of my teachers that it wasn't only the poor who committed crimes; sometimes middle-class people and even upper-income people violated the law. "Shouldn't nine-tenths of the population and two-thirds of the poor be committing the vast majority of the crime?" I asked.

RACE & SOCIETY 137

The next line of argument supposed to explain all Black difficulties and chastise racially impious thoughts — was the allegation of White racist injustice. But, I thought, *haven't there been millions of Whites who have been cheated or mistreated by other people and who have suffered broken families, alcoholism, child abuse, and other indignities but who don't as teenagers run out in the night and rape elderly women?* (At the time a number of elderly women, living alone, were brutally raped and abused by Black intruders). If oppression and racism causes crime, I questioned why their crime rate was far less under Jim Crow than it is today. When I brought these issues up to my teachers, they had no adequate answers.

Moreover, if one accepts that poverty causes crime, the question must also be asked, *What causes poverty?* Murray and Herrnstein, in the *Bell Curve*,[229] and many other researchers have shown that low IQ correlates strongly with poverty and criminality. Inability to delay gratification would also contribute to joblessness and poverty. Black lower IQ and less ability to delay gratification have already been thoroughly covered in this volume. Yet even if one accepts the poverty and repression argument, it could certainly not explain the incredible extent of the differences.

In 1904, when Blacks were jailed much less than they are today, the mean per capita wealth of Blacks was only 2.5 percent that of Whites. Black income is now about 20 percent that of Whites. But the crime rate has not dropped. Moreover, between 1930 and 1990, the proportion of Blacks living in poverty fell from more than 90 percent to about 30 percent.[230] During the same period, Black prisoners increased from 25 percent of the total prison population to today's more than 50 percent.[231,232] The latest analysis shows that Whites' hourly wages are on average only about a third (133 percent) higher than that of Blacks, yet Black crime rates were many times greater than just a third higher.[233]

Since my first inquiries in the 1960s, the Black crime rate has continued to increase. Some of the most recent crime figures show that Blacks, constituting about 12 percent of the population, account for 62 percent of the arrests for robbery,[234,235] 57 percent of the murders and 50 percent of all the crimes for assault and rape.[236] The per capita crime rates are much higher for Blacks than for Whites, yet most Whites and Blacks have no inkling of the vast extent of the difference.

Even though I understood the marked evolutionary differences between the White and Black races, the Black crime rate was way beyond what I had expected. I had guessed that Blacks were committing roughly 25 percent to 50 percent per capita more crime than Whites, or possibly even twice the amount of crime as Whites. A 100 percent higher crime rate by Blacks seemed exceedingly high My estimates turned out to be dramatically low. FBI uniform crime reports in the 1990s show that Blacks commit 1,200 percent, or 12 times, the per capita robbery rate of Whites and 900 percent, or 9 times, the murder rate. And despite these outrageous numbers, the government method of record keeping suppresses the true extent of the differences in the Black-White crime rate. In comparing the per capita rate of crime between Whites and Blacks, the "White" group includes Mexicans, Puerto Ricans, and other Hispanic elements who are predominantly not of European heritage. In California, where some crime tallies often separate Whites, Blacks, and Hispanics, the assault rates for Black males aged 15 to 24 are 598 per 100,000, whereas the White, non-Hispanic rate is only 27 per 100,000. That is a 2,200 percent (22 times) higher Black assault rate.[237]

The liberal media offer all sorts of explanations for the higher crime rates in the United States as compared to Europe. One of the trendiest arguments is that the easily availability of guns causes the high murder rate. They show how the homicide rate in America is 9.3 per 100,000 population as compared to 4.5 in France, 4.7 in Germany, 4.8 in Britain, 2.3 in Austria and other similar rates in the others. As such, America has a murder rate that is double that of Europe. Gun control advocates claim that Europe's strict gun laws are responsible for the lower rates.

Blacks commit 55 percent of the murders in the United States, whereas Whites commit 43 percent. At 12.1 percent of the population, the murder rate for Blacks is 44.9 per 100,000. For "Whites," which includes Puerto Ricans, Mexicans and other Hispanics of questionable white origin, the rate is 4.78 per 100,000. When one considers the disproportionate crime rate among Hispanics, and the fact that between one-fourth and one-third of our federal prisoners are not American citizens, one realizes that the crime rate for European Americans is in line with, or even less than that of the European nations. Even with the Hispanics included, the White American murder rate is slightly lower than it is in Britain — which has some of the strictest gun control laws in the world. With the Hispanics subtracted from the White murder rate, even with our millions of guns, White Americans have a lower murder rate than the European average. It is comparable to Switzerland, an all-White nation where practically every adult male citizen must by law keep a gun at home as part of the national defense forces — the homicide rate is only 3.2 per 100,000.

Within the United States, compare the tougher gun control areas such as New York to a high per capita gun-owning state such as Utah. In Utah, with more liberal gun laws and one of the Whitest populations in America, the murder rate is below one per 100,000.[238] It may be the height of political incorrectness to state it, but the facts tell us that it is not large numbers of guns that cause increased crime — it is large numbers of racial minorities.

High Black crime rates are not limited to the United States. They are confirmed on a worldwide basis. Professor J. Phillippe Rushton, professor of psychology at the University of Western Ontario ,Canada, has compiled the crime data from INTERPOL, and international police organization made up of 100 member nations. In studying the data for 23 predominantly African countries and 41 mostly Caucasian nations, the assorted crime figures composites average 243 crimes per 100,000 for Black nations and 74 for the mostly White nations. Even these dramatic figures greatly inflate the White crime rates because Black crime affects the overall crime rate in nations such as the United States, Canada, Great Britain, and France.[239]

After almost 40 years of civil rights, economic and educational opportunity, political freedom, and endless government programs, Black crime rates continue to increase to the point that *The Washington Post* reported that in our nation's capitol 50 percent of all young (18 to 35) Black males are currently felons in the criminal justice system. They are in jail, on probation or parole, currently charged with a felony or there is an arrest warrant out for them.[240]

DC has a population of 48,856 black men in this age range and 24,377 or nearly 50 percent are incarcerated, on parole or probation, awaiting trial or being sought on an arrest warrant on any given day according to the study that covered the first quarter of 1997. (Washington Post August 26, 1997)

These numbers do not include those who have completed their terms of incarceration or parole. It also does not include those who have committed crimes but who are unidentified. When one considers that the perpetrators of most crimes are never caught, it is clear that a vast majority of young Black males in Washington, D.C. are criminals. Stating such a fact might sound very harsh, but it is the plain truth. In fact, in an article by Adam Walinsky in the July 1995 issue of *Atlantic Monthly*,[241] the writer pointed out that one Washington, D.C. study estimated that upwards of 75 percent of Black males would be arrested by age 35, and 85 percent of Black males would be arrested for a felony in their lifetime. Nationally, about one-third of all young Black males are currently enmeshed in the criminal justice system, and well over 50 percent will be arrested for a felony by the time they are 35 years old.

As amazing as are the extreme differences in the crime rates between Whites and Blacks, the political and media establishment have effectively kept the facts from the public. Not only have they misrepresented the true causes of crime as guns, poverty, and racism, they have intentionally deceived the American people about its realities.

Most people have a vague idea about higher Black crime rates because they have seen the frequent Black faces of the apprehended or sought by the police in television news reporting, which relies on photos or films. Most of television programming, though, is made up of dramatic series and movies, and in those often emotionally powerful programs the percentage of Black criminals portrayed is vastly underrepresented. Television and films also portray the criminal-justice system as racist and unfair to Blacks, and hate crimes are almost always depicted as being committed by White perpetrators who prey on Black or other minority victims.

In 1983 Robert and Linda Richter published a study of prime-time television that showed that only about 10 percent of those portrayed in television dramas as criminals were Black.[242] Even more important, no viewer can help but notice that when there is a cross-race victim shown on a television series, it is almost always a Black victimized by depraved White racists. It has become a TV and movie given that when a crime has a racial motivation, the perpetrators are evil Whites.

I found out that there are many myths about Black crime. A prevalent myth is that most Black crime is committed against other Blacks, therefore, it doesn't have a much affect on the White community. That belief is shattered by recent crime data such as from 1987 showing that whereas only 3 percent of White crime is committed against Blacks, well over 50 percent of Black crime is committed against Whites. In 1987, 50.2 percent of assaults by Blacks had White victims. From the years 1979 to 1986, 2,416,696 of the 4,088,945 assaults committed annually by Blacks had White victims: a cross-racial rate of 59 percent. Proportionally this means that Blacks are at least 2,500 percent (25 times) more likely to victimize Whites than Whites are to victimize Blacks.[243] For those who say Whites should not be concerned about Black crime, those figures mean almost 2.5 million White victims of Black assault in just seven years, and that doesn't even count the estimated millions of assaults that have become so common that they often go unreported.

In murder rates, similar ratios apply. According to the FBI uniform crime reports for 1993,[244] Blacks are 2,200 percent (22 times) more likely to kill Whites than Whites are to kill Blacks. In armed robbery 7,031 Blacks were victimized by Whites, whereas 167,924 Whites had Black assailants.[245] As shocking as these figures are, I must again note that the government record-keeping makes the higher Black percentages of cross-race crime seem far less than they really are. Many crimes that are classified as "White" against Blacks are not perpetrated by Whites at all, but come from the Mexican, Puerto Rican and other Hispanic minorities, who are statistically lumped in with Whites. For instance, the shooting of a Black by Mestizo

Mexicans in a drug deal gone badly is classified as a White-on-Black crime. The rape of a Black women by a Black, Spanish-speaking Puerto Rican will be classified as a "White-on-Black" rape, or the same Puerto Rican rape of a White woman would be classified as a "White-on-White rape.

Even more tragic is the epidemic rate of Black rapes upon White women. The American Enterprise Institute analyzed rape records of the FBI for 1991 and found that while there were only 100 rapes of Black women by White men that year in America, there were 20,204 White women raped by Blacks. That's 200 White women raped by Blacks for every one Black female raped by Whites.[246][247] As nefarious as the Black and White ratio of rape is, much of the accumulated evidence shows it is far worse than the FBI's staggering numbers. A 1974 study of rapes conducted in Denver, a city of relatively low Black population, showed that Black rape of White women constituted 40 percent of all rapes and that not one case of White on Black rape could be documented.[248] Dr. William Wilbanks, a Florida International University criminologist, after sifting through large amounts of data on rape, found that in 1988 there were only ten cases of Whites raping Black women.[249]

Even if one takes the lowest possible figures for Black rape, could the reader imagine the outcry if White men in America raped ten Black women for every one White woman raped by Blacks? White rape of Black women in those numbers would cause a national scandal, congressional investigations, civil-rights marches and prayer vigils and a massive media outrage. Yet the massive numbers of Black male rapes against White women are met with silence by the media.

Another media-generated public perception is that there is not enough emphasis on White-collar crime, which is less covered because, they suggest, it is mostly White. In reality, even in so-called white-collar crimes such as embezzlement, forgery, counterfeiting and receiving stolen property, Blacks are about 300 percent (3 times) more likely to be arrested than are Whites.[250][251][252]

Perhaps the most commonly accepted racial myth about crime promoted in the media and in many universities is that America has a racist criminal-justice system. Black criminals, they say, are treated far more harshly than Whites. They point out that those who kill Whites are more likely to be executed than those who kill Blacks. Those who repeatedly quote this one fact leave out far more important statistics:

- **Even though Blacks commit far more murders than Whites, Whites have been the majority of those executed since the reinstatement of the death penalty. White murderers are about 50 percent more likely to be sentenced to death than Black murderers.**

- **Whites who kill Whites are more likely to face the death penalty than Blacks who kill Whites.**
- **Whites who murder Blacks have a greater likelihood of a death-row stay than Blacks who kill Whites.**

A typical example of the biased reporting on this subject is found in a major feature article in the *Atlanta Journal and Constitution* on April 30, 1989.[253] The article, with the provocative headline "Blacks Sent to Jail More Than Whites for the Same Crime," extended over many pages and even printed maps showing where Blacks were sent to jail in Georgia counties as much as twice as often as Whites for the same crimes. Forty-six inches into the copy the reader learns that the study ignored prior convictions. Ignoring prior convictions obviously made the study completely worthless, because criminals with prior convictions will obviously receive longer sentences than those with clean records. Blacks are far more likely to be repeat offenders, which naturally leads to longer sentencing. It is similar to the stories "proving" how Blacks face discrimination in obtaining home mortgages by showing lower approval percentages for Blacks than for Whites. Many of those stories conveniently ignore the fact that Black incomes and credit reports are generally much inferior to those of White applicants.[254]

In fact, evidence suggests that Blacks are much more inclined than Whites to acquit clearly guilty Black defendants in urban felony trials. Black jury pools convict at rates far below the national average.[255]

By a twisted logic, claims of a "racist system' are used to justify even the most brutal of Black crimes, such as O.J. Simpson's acquittal in the grisly murder of his White ex-wife and her companion. In the most publicized murder trial of the 20th century, the case turned not on the defendant's guilt or innocence but on whether one of the police detectives in the case had racist attitudes.

In many major cities, prosecutors find it increasingly difficult to convict Black criminals before Black juries. An endless parade of civil cases in the major cities find Black juries inclined to render outlandish judgments for Black plaintiffs against White defendants. When Blacks and Whites are on opposite sides of the bar in civil or criminal matters or when White and Black interests seem to conflict in cases, Whites will seldom find justice. Most successful insurance plaintiff attorneys strike potential White jurors and seek to impanel Black juries because they are known for their liberal, often outrageous, awards. A number of insurance executives have told me that the phenomenon is one of the major reasons for higher insurance rates. Blacks are far more prone to, as they say, "put it to the man."

The traditional Anglo-Saxon legal system, with its presumption of innocence, is possible only through the natural integrity of its citizens.

A legal system that is based on the natural tendency of people to be law-abiding can be much more free than one trying to maintain order in a society in which the urges toward violence and sexual aggression are more powerful than those traits favoring control and restraint. When half of the young Black men in Washington, D.C. are criminals, society has the unacceptable choice of draconian laws or barbarism in the streets, the system simply cannot work. Our justice system functioned well in the past only because most people would not commit a robbery, a rape or a murder regardless of whether there was a law against it. Now that our streets teem with those whose *only* restraint is the law, civilization becomes replaced by the law of the jungle. When the social and legal system in America became equalized for unequal people, all hell broke loose; creating a level of barbarism in our country that has never been seen in the history of European civilization except in times of war.

When I first looked over the crime figures, I began to understand just how brainwashed I had been about egalitarianism. After the 1963 bombing of a Birmingham church, when I thought of the race question, all I saw in my mind were the school photos of the four little Black girls who had been killed. It was a heinous crime to be sure, an act of political terrorism against the overthrow of Southern culture. No civilized society can tolerate such lawlessness. The misguided perpetrators of the crime did more to advance the civil-rights movement than a thousand marches. But now, I had to ask myself, was that act any more heinous than the rape and murder of thousands of White women by Black criminals satisfying their lust for sex, vengeance and blood? Since the fateful bombing in 1963, there have been thousands of White girls who have suffered at the hands of hate-filled Blacks for each one of the four Black girls in Birmingham. White victims who would have probably never experienced such a fate except for the "Civil Rights movement.

Black Panther Eldridge Cleaver wrote a book called *Soul on Ice*, which is still available in the bookstores of America. It lauds the rape and abasement of White women. Cleaver wrote:

> **And when I considered myself smooth enough, I crossed the tracks and sought out White prey. I did this consciously, deliberately, willfully, methodically — though looking back I see that I was in a frantic, wild, and completely abandoned frame of mind. Rape was an insurrectionary act. It delighted me that I was defying and trampling upon the white man's law, upon his system of values, and that I was defiling his women.** [256]

Cleaver then quotes a poem by LeRoi Jones, "come up black dada nihilismus, Rape the White girls. Rape their fathers. Cut the mother's throats." [257] Cleaver's book was praised by many literary critics for his passionate call for justice for Black people. The New York Times Book Review[258] called it "Brilliant and revealing." Eldridge Cleaver died in 1997. To his credit he renounced his wicked ways and was a convert to Christianity. However, the critics who praised it have not repented.

False Arguments of Egalitarians

How can so little be said in the national media of the Black plague of crime that has transformed so many of our streets to places of fear and so many homes to reverse jails, barred to keep out the criminal? Instead of the truth about racial differences in crime, we constantly hear things like "White people do bad things too," or "There is good and bad among all races." These two statements are true, but they are far from the whole truth. It is similar to saying that there are good people who can be found in prison and bad people found outside of prison. Should we therefore not recognize the group differences between the criminally convicted and the law-abiding?

Not recognizing group differences and acting accordingly is a prescription for disaster. In New Orleans, Black predators have murdered a number of Northern as well as European tourists who have ventured into the minority neighborhoods on the periphery of the French Quarter. Parking their cars in those areas is something that few White residents would do, because they have a local awareness of the Black crime problem. Out-of-towners that are not as aware of the racial realities of New Orleans have suffered robbery, rape and murder. For fear of being branded racist, printed tourist guides that readily offer warnings of high prices or poor cuisine, will not inform tourists of the serious threat to their lives in the Black sections. The notion that "there is good and bad in all races" and that "White people do bad things too," does not help the Whites who find torture and death at the hands of black thugs. If they would have recognized that Blacks are generally much more dangerous than Whites, many White victims could have avoided those areas and not become victims.

Patrick Sheehan,[259] writing for the Sidney, Australia, *Morning Herald* in 1995, wrote what American newspapers would not dare. He analyzed the FBI uniform crime reports for the 30 years since the civil-rights movement began and found 170 million crimes against the persons and property of White America.

> **The longest war America has ever fought is the Dirty War, and it is not over. It has lasted 30 years so far and claimed more than 25 million victims. It has cost almost as many lives as the Vietnam War. It determined the result of last year's congressional election. Yet the American news media do not want to talk about the Dirty War, which remains between the lines and unreported...**

When all the crime figures are calculated, it appears that black Americans have committed at least 170 million crimes against white Americans in the past 30 years. It is the great defining disaster of American life and American ideals since World War II. All these are facts, yet by simply writing this story, by assembling the facts in this way, I would be deemed a racist by the American news media. It prefers to maintain a paternalistic double-standard in its coverage of black America, a lower standard.

Black crime had ballooned in the middle 1960s, and I could see that it would only get worse through the last third of the 20th century as the White control over the direction of American society diminished. I thought about the social system of segregation that had Black and White water fountains and separate rest rooms and segregated schools and housing and the once strict enforcement of laws on Blacks. I wondered how the indignity of racial segregation compared to the ultimate indignities of thousands of violent rapes, robberies and murders. Millions of European-Americans have paid a high price for the so-called civil-rights revolution — far too high a price. Ironically, millions of Black crime victims have paid the price for it as well, for as the structure of White law and order broke down, they have suffered from the increased crime committed by their own brethren.

I also asked myself, *What is a civil right?* How terrible is drinking from a segregated water fountain compared to being *raped, robbed or murdered?* How bad is it for members of each race to freely go to schools of their own choice, tailored to their own needs, rather than endure the conflict, violence and educational mediocrity of the integrated one? How does the right to force one race onto another contrast to the right to live and the right to live without fear of violence?

The federal government has caused millions of White people to become crime victims in their pursuit of Black "civil rights," which were supposed to bring us peace, love and brotherhood.

The Black crime rate has always been much higher against Whites than the White crime rate against Blacks, and juveniles commit large percentages of violence. The segregated schools and neighborhoods of the past certainly did not cause Black students to be victimized by White criminals. In fact, there were no Whites in their schools at all. But integration has subjected millions of White children to predatory Black criminality, intimidation and violence.

Every American has heard a chronic recital of the mistreatment of Blacks over the years. The indignities of slavery, which ended more than 130 years ago, are repeatedly brought up, and whining Black leaders remind their own people and us of its injustices almost daily. Every American has also seen graphic photographs of African-American victims of the lynch mobs from earlier times in American history. Such chronic recital of White suppression teaches Blacks to hate White people, and the White people are made to feel an oppressive collective guilt. But how does the White lynching of Blacks in American history compare to the murderous Black crime wave of today?

Egalitarians went through mountains of historical records to put a precise number on the lynchings in the years between 1882 and 1962. The Negro Almanac proclaimed that a total of 3,442 Blacks and 1,294 Whites were lynched during that period. From 1947-1961, lynchings averaged less than one a year.[260] As terrible as lynching was, it was almost always done in response to serious criminal behavior such as rape or murder. In comparison, the Black crime wave today is levied upon the innocent, those who were never accused of any crime. Whereas lynchings almost always occurred against men, the new victims of brutality are often those least able to defend themselves: women, the young and the elderly. The days of lynching are long over, but Black crimes against White people continue to increase.

Jesse Jackson once made the powerful point that more Blacks murder and abuse each other in one year, than all the Blacks murdered and physically abused by Whites in the last 100 years. The same is true for Black crimes against Whites. More Whites are murdered and raped in just one year by Blacks than all the Blacks lynched by Whites in the last 100 years. But there is no outcry. There is no protest, no wringing of hands — only deafening silence. Nobody even protests the explicitly racist Black campaigns to end Black-on-Black crime, as if the massive brutality of Black-on-White crime didn't matter.

Whites are taught a collective guilt for slavery, even though less than 10 percent of Americans were ever slaveholders. Yet there is no collective guilt or blame ascribed to the Black race for millions of White crime victims.

Many times as a young man I would see Black victims of discrimination or physical abuse on dramatic television programs and my heart went out to them. As I grew older and learned the reality of Black crime, I began to think for myself and learned that individual injustices by fanatics can always be found to condemn any ideology. Focusing on the poignant killing of four little Black girls, the media used the tragic event as a psychological wedge for the civil-rights movement and the implementation of their social programs. If the media had been on the opposing side of the issue, they could easily have exploited the thousands of White victims of Black crime and brought many handkerchiefs to the eyes of those who would become resolved to work against the policies of integration.

Each one of those stories of the rape, or torture, or murder of innocent White victims, told with empathy and passion, could bring tears to the eyes of the hardest soul. But the telling those tragedies are counter to the media's ideological goals, so instead they affix their attention on the extremely rare White on Black crime. Hard-working Americans have lost billions of dollars of their hard-earned tax money for the social programs launched by the civil-rights movement — programs that have done nothing but spawn crime and hurt the Black family. Paying that huge tax sum has hurt the White family. Schools have been lost, fine old homes abandoned, the cities criminalized and governments corrupted.

Another scandal one almost never hears about is that of Black perpetrated homosexual rape against Whites in jails and prisons. It has become so commonplace in American jails that in some places White prisoners have filed suit trying to get the authorities to act to prevent them.[261] American comedians frequently allude to the fate met by thousands of White prisoners in the overwhelmingly Black prisons of America. Tortuous homosexual rape certainly fulfills the constitutional definition of "cruel and unusual punishment" and today, with AIDS common among Black drug addicts and criminals, it can also result in an agonizing death. Much like the disproportionate rates of rape against White women, this subject is almost never mentioned by serious news media. Charles Silberman, in his book *Criminal Violence, Criminal Justice*, writes this about the epidemic of Black on White homosexual rape:

> **A young offender, particularly a white offender, is likely to be subjected to gang rape his first night in jail. In a number of large cities, jail officials automatically place young whites in protective custody for their own safety. Sometimes the move comes too late: young offenders often raped in the van transporting them to jail...[O]ne man's defeat is another's triumph: the ultimate triumph is to destroy another man's manhood — to break his will, defile his body, and make him feel totally (and often permanently) degraded...and when the wolf [rapist] is black and the punk[victim] is white (the most frequent arrangement, by far) the wolf's demonstration of power is infinitely sweeter.** [262]

As I discovered the horrible truth about the massive homosexual rape of White prisoners by Blacks, I became incensed. The media defense of forced integration of the races as a moral imperative has resulted in the rapes of tens of thousands of White men in America's prisons. However, this terrible injustice finds no voice from the pulpits and pundits. According to their twisted sense of morality, it is better that young White men be raped by the thousands than to reveal the animalistic behavior commonly found in Black criminals.

As a young man, my heart had been manipulated by the media, but as I grew older, I began to see a more complete picture. I began to see the massive wrong being done against those of our own heritage — a great tragedy that would continue to multiply until we have the courage to face it and the power to end it. I realized that if the media tried to make me and all Whites feel angry and upset about White mistreatment of Blacks, was I not justified in being upset about the White victims of Black criminality?

As I began to gain a deeper understanding of racial differences in criminal behavior, I fully understood the injustice of integration of public education. Because Blacks are significantly less intelligent than Whites, at least ten times more likely to commit assaults than are Whites and juveniles are per capita the most violent segment of the population — White children face intolerable conditions when they are in mostly Black public schools.

The media frequently allege widespread White hatred of Negroes (for no good reason). Yet, by their chronic portrayal of White abuse and racism, they teach Blacks to hate White people. How strange it is, that when liberals put White children in schools with low-IQ, violent-prone, White-hating Black juveniles, they call it an act that fosters love and brotherhood.

Integration of Education

In 1956 President Eisenhower went on national television and announced the racial integration of the public schools in the nation's capital. Prior to racial integration, Washington, D.C. had a well-respected school system and had received many honors as one of the best in the United States. Federal officials were always anxious to have all aspects of their city serve as a showplace of our nation, and have always funded it liberally. Now they had even greater determination to make the capital and its school system the best that money could buy as they desired a showcase for the new doctrine of racial equality.

Eisenhower proclaimed that Washington's schools would prove to America that integration could work. In spite of the tremendous effort and generous expenditures to make it work by Eisenhower and subsequent presidents, D.C. schools rapidly deteriorated after desegregation. After two decades, a complete generation of Black students had passed through the school system, and it had only become progressively worse. Parents' worried concern about the pitifully low quality of education became eclipsed by even greater concerns about their children's physical safety. Police were assigned to patrol school hallways that had become as lethal as Washington's most dangerous streets.

Today, after 30 years of extravagant spending and after the flight of more than 90 percent of the White students, the D.C. school system ranks near the bottom among U.S. public schools. Although D.C. schools are second highest in spending per pupil in the entire nation, their students turn in some of the lowest test scores in America. Washington schools did become a showplace for integration — one for what's wrong with it. Forty-four percent fail to graduate from high school, and of that number 80 percent leave before the 10th grade.[263,264,265,266,267,268]

If integration and spending extra money on education were supposed to raise the Black educational performance, increase achievement and have the concomitant effects of lessening poverty, illegitimacy, venereal disease and crime, it failed. In fact, one could argue persuasively that not only had the White students been immeasurably better off in Washington's segregated schools, but Blacks had been better off as well.

By the time I had learned about race in the mid-1960s, D.C. schools were already a disaster. The transfer of power in the system from Whites to Blacks also caused many capable White teachers to flee Washington, D.C., just as the students had. By the mid-'60s the school system had to dangle large salaries — dubbed "combat pay" — before teachers in Virginia and Maryland in hopes of luring them into the D.C. schools. Integration's reality was exactly the opposite of its original promises. In spite of innumerable federal environmental enrichment programs such as Head Start, lower teacher-pupil ratios, higher teacher pay, the most modern equipment and facilities, free breakfasts and lunch in school, more public assistance and increased medical care for students — the system continues to fail miserably to this day.

In concert with the school system, the city of Washington, D.C. finds itself mired near the bottom of every statistic of societal dysfunction. The District of Columbia has the highest per capita rates in the nation for murder, robbery, rape, drug addiction, illegitimacy and AIDS. In spite of massive infusions of public money in public works and housing and a strong incentive effort to relocate minorities to surrounding communities (called "Movement to Opportunity"), some parts of the city more resemble the slum cities of Third World nations than the capital city of the leading economy in the world. In fact, it has statistics more reminiscent of a Third World nation than the United States.

In spite of the abject failure of the school-integration experiment in Washington, D.C., the federal government forced the integration of every major school system in the nation. Using the *Brown v Board of Education* case as its legal basis, it moved rapidly to forcing schools to have a specific percentage of Blacks, even if they had to be bused across town or even across county lines. Such efforts to create maximum racial mixing meant a constant shifting of the racial allocations for schools, because as fast as busing widened to include new White students, increasing numbers of Whites naturally fled the public school systems.

As the school systems in the major cities integrated, violence escalated. Today, about 300,000 high-school students in the United States are assaulted each month.[269] In Chicago, in 1991, school security guards made nearly 10,000 arrests.[270] Architects are now increasingly designing schools that resemble prisons.[271] Should we have expected less as the school population became more criminal?

When Whites could afford it, they attended private or church schools, and when they couldn't, they either endured integration the best they could or simply sold out their property (sometimes at great loses and financial hardship) and moved to White suburbs. As the cities' schools turned Blacker, the Whites increasingly evacuated them, and the cities turned darker still, which again churned the cycle of the White exodus. The White retreat, along with the burgeoning Black birthrate, created an emerging Black bloc of voters that flexed its growing political muscles and took over the city governments and school systems of many large cities. In the wake of these changes, many cities degenerated to levels of corruption that today more resemble South American banana republics rather than America's once glittering metropolises.

As forced integration afflicted America's schools, education standards plummeted. From first place in the world in many secondary school categories of educational performance, American schools at this writing are near the bottom in the industrialized world. The performance comes despite the fact that America spends more money per pupil than any country except Switzerland.[272]

Liberals tend to blame the educational decline on insufficient spending, and conservatives tend to blame it on more liberal teaching methods. But one fact is incontrovertible: School scores have fallen in concert with the demographic changes of its students and teachers. It has not dropped in school systems that have maintained their European-American racial makeup. In many European American areas test scores have actually risen. In New Hampshire's school system, which is one of the Whitest in America, excellent standards have been consistently maintained, with its students scoring the highest SAT and ACT scores in the nation. In contrast, the states with the five lowest SAT ratings have some of the highest per capita Black student enrollment. It should also be noted that New Hampshire spends less per pupil for public education than do most of the 50 states.

Here is a rundown of increasing expenditures that have accompanied integration of America's schools:

Education percent of gross national product 2.8 1970
Education percent of gross national product 6.8 1985 [273]

1970s school spending up 25 percent in real terms
1980s school spending up 40 percent.

Per pupil expenditures rose 16 and 24 percent in the 70s and 80s
From 1930 to 1980, real spending per pupil up 500 percent

Teacher pupil ratio in 1959 26
Teacher/pupil ratio in 1988 17.6 [274] [275]

In the early 1990s, symbolizing the sinking standards associated with the minoritization of our cities, the mayor of our nation's capital, Marion Barry, was caught on videotape smoking crack cocaine with a prostitute. If the actions of the mayor were not enough to show the degeneration of the city under Black dominance, it should be noted that after serving his jail time he returned to public life and was overwhelmingly re-elected by Black voters.

Even by the mid-1960s, it became obvious that so-called civil rights and integration of education were not alleviating the Black plight, and for the first time I began to consider the powerful impact of integration not just on Blacks but on White families. Integration had certainly not improved the lot of Blacks, other than providing a bit more opportunity for them to be around White people. But even that dubious goal evaporated in the face of White flight.

Although Blacks as a group had accrued more buying power than ever before and more education among its most capable elements, in the most important aspects of life Blacks suffered terribly. A generation of Blacks was growing up without fathers. Masses of Blacks are hooked on drugs, and the young have a mortality rate for murder that exceeds that of American soldiers during the Second World War. Murder is now the leading cause of death for Black males between the ages of 15 and 44, and AIDS is the leading cause of the combined death toll of Black men and women.[276]

Racial gap growing for AIDS patients

Disease now largely is a black epidemic

By SHERYL GAY STOLBERG
© 1998, The New York Times

WASHINGTON — Seventeen year. after AIDS was first recognized amon gay white men in New York and Sa Francisco, the disease in the Unite States is becoming largely an epidemi among black people, quietly devastating families and neighborhoods, yet all but ignored by leading black institutions.

African-Americans make up 13 percent of the U.S. population. But they now account for about 57 percent of all new infections

"I don't think there is any question that the epidemic in this count is becoming increasingly an epidemic of color."

[277] Blacks have about 14 times the AIDS rate that Whites have, and 50 times the syphilis rates.[278] Unemployment, especially among the young, is rampant, and most Blacks are enmeshed in the welfare system. Blacks were more violent, more prone to criminality, and angrier toward White people than ever before.

White Civil Rights?

In the 1960s the American people were told that Blacks had the right to associate with whomever they choose in the public schools. In fact, the 1954 Supreme Court decision turned on the idea that Black students would be harmed if they could not go to school with Whites. But if that were true, I thought, *doesn't it follow that White students also would be harmed if they could not attend White schools?* While it was permitted for Blacks to choose their racial associations to improve their group's well-being, Whites were told that they couldn't choose their associations. It was considered immoral to think about the well-being of Whites in the integration controversy.

Whites were told that they had to go to schools where they didn't want to go — at the force of bayonet. In forcing the races together, the government also went against the overwhelming popular sentiment. Numerous polls in the South showed that more than 95 percent of the Whites and the majority of Blacks opposed forced integration. People just felt better associating with their own heritage. Ironically, even after 40 years of forced integration, Blacks still overwhelmingly choose to associate with Blacks and Whites with Whites, both inside the integrated schools themselves as well as in the rest of society.

Forced integration of education is now so accepted that perhaps the only way I can get my point across is to drop race for a moment in the discussion.

Suppose you had a 14-year-old daughter and that there were two high schools equidistant from your home. One school we will refer to as A and the other school we will call F.

School A has children who are much like your daughter in culture, styles, dress, intelligence, law-abidingness, language, college-preparatory skills, values and morality. School F has a very different student body. Here are some of its characteristics:

- **School F's students are at least 1,000 percent more likely to commit assault, robbery, rape, and murder than the students at school A.**
- **School F students mature sexually at an earlier age.**
- **School F has students who have an average IQ of 85, and fully one-fourth who are 70 or below. Only 2 or 3 percent have an IQ adequate enough for college.**

- **School F males have higher testosterone levels, and the sexual mores of the students cause a 3,000 percent higher incidence of venereal diseases and AIDS than the students at school A.**
- **School F's predominant music is "gangsta rap."**
- **School F has more teachers who graduated from inferior colleges and have consistently lower scores on teacher qualification exams than school A's.**

Which school would you choose for your child? Would you want your teenage daughter to attend school F? Would you like her to date the boys at school F? Get her college preparation at school F? These questions are easy for any parent to answer, but the federal government answers them wrongly.

The characteristics I gave the students of School F reflect the actual statistical averages for Blacks in America. Some School F's may be a bit better, others a bit worse, but the average Black school is exactly as I described. Integration has turned many schools to F schools. The racial difference presented here is not simplistic; it is not fanciful; it exists in almost every major city and thousands of smaller ones. Is it any wonder that Whites resisted integration so vehemently and then fled when their schools were forcibly integrated? It is any wonder they fled the vibrant and cultured cities that their fathers and mothers had built. It is not hatred or prejudice that produces White flight; it is just good sense and compassion for their children.

Until I was a senior in high school, all the schools I attended were segregated. I went to an excellent grade school where the only thing we had to worry about was getting good grades, not whether the student next to you had crack or a gun in his pockets. In the span of 35 years, the New Orleans school system went from a majority White to 94 percent Black. The school system spends far more money than it did when I attended, but its educational level is far lower. It is a school system where the police are called to the schools as often as the maintenance men, where the most important part of a child's education is learning how not to get his ass whipped by the end of the day.

At this writing, the only shining star in the whole system is the magnet high school for the gifted and studious: Benjamin Franklin. Recently, the mostly Black New Orleans school board decided to scrap its tougher qualifications because the 4 percent White students in the New Orleans school system comprise 65 percent of Franklin's student body. The White percentage would be even higher except for a type of "affirmative action admission policy" for the Black public officials' children. In a couple of years the last flickering light of the New Orleans schools will also have been dimmed, as the last remaining Whites are driven out.

In another recent move, the school board voted to remove George Washington's name from a public school because, as a "slaveholder," he is an "immoral" example for the children. A leading New Orleans civil rights leader, Carl Galmon, remarked that " George Washington had as much meaning to the Black students as David Duke."[279] Not even the most radical person opposed to school integration in New Orleans in 1961 ever conceived that after only 37 years the Father of Our Country would become politically incorrect in the public schools. Care to guess what the next 30 or 40 years will bring?

European-American children face similar problems in the Mestizo-dominated schools of the Southwest. As I write these lines, a 19-year-old family friend from Brownsville, Texas, visited us and told how she faced intimidation and even physical attacks in her mostly Mexican public school. Mexican boys would frequently proposition her, sexually berate her, try to put their hands on her and call her "gringa" — a derogatory term of similar intent to "nigger." She said that sometimes she would cry and beg her mother not to send her into the school. Because of the high percentage of Mexicans, most of the teachers taught exclusively in Spanish. The lessons often degenerated into anti-"gringo" tirades. Drugs were rampant, and so many 14 and 15-year-old Mexican girls had illegitimate babies that the junior high school had established a day-care center for the students. The abuse finally forced her to drop out of high school and take the equivalency exam so that she could enroll in college.

I think about the politicians and judges who have transformed White schools into miniature versions of Black housing projects, with the gangs, the filthy language and lewd behavior, the drugs, weapons and pregnant teenagers. I would like to dispatch these hypocrites into the same hellhole schools to which they have condemned many of our White youths. Most of them would not so much as drive through such areas unless they first locked their doors and loaded their pistols — that is, unless they went during a public display of do-goodism, accompanied, of course, by news cameras and well-armed police. They do not hesitate, however, to send poor White students into such places.

Some of the students in these schools are the sons and daughters of well-to-do parents living in fortified downtown apartments. These parents have visions of urban bliss — love and brotherhood and "cultural enrichment" — for their hapless children. They babble about the school's rich diversity until their son comes home with ten stitches sewn into his scalp or their daughter has experienced a half dozen multicultural hands groping up her dress in a crowded stairwell.

Who speaks for those children? Who really cares for them? Surely not the media, not the politicians and not those who have concern only for what the establishment says they should. There are those who get emotional on cue for the politically correct cause. The only injustice they can feel is one illuminated by the lights of the TV camera. I grew more and more resentful for the way the media had manipulated my own emotions, but now, I was not only learning the facts, I was daring to use them to rethink what I had heretofore uncritically accepted.

Integrated Housing

The increasing privileges of minorities and decreasing rights of the European-American were soon expressed in the destruction of White neighborhoods and even cities. In the process, millions of European-Americans saw their property values plummet and had to abandon their homes. Others, often the elderly, unable to afford to move, have had to watch helplessly while their neighborhoods became more dangerous and dirty, their lives blighted in their final years by intimidation and alienation. They were of the wrong race for the federal government to be concerned about their human dignity. I could not understand how the government could tell a free man that he was not allowed to sell his own private property to whomever he pleased. That a neighborhood couldn't choose its neighbors or that an apartment house couldn't choose its tenants seemed against all basic rights of association. Again, the Europeans' rights were abrogated to the perceived interests and "rights" of Africans. The media did not even mention that the extremely high crime rate of Blacks made "open housing" very hazardous to one's health.

Let me construct a hypothetical example. Suppose your family lives in an all-White apartment complex in Maryland, just outside of Washington D.C. One of the factors that influenced your decision to choose the complex was that most of the tenants were European-American. A new section adjacent to your family's apartment goes up with 20 new rental apartments. Twenty Black males from Washington, D.C., apply, and then 20 White families from surrounding neighborhoods put in applications.

The undeniable fact is that more than half of all young Black males in Washington are criminals. The mathematical likelihood is that if Blacks rent the 20 apartments, at least 10 will likely be felons. You have a wife and two daughters, ages 11 and 12, and you say to yourself *I certainly don't want my family to live in an apartment complex where half the tenants have similar résumés to a prison population.* While there is no certainty that your family will become a crime victim, accepting the Black tenants over the White ones poses at least a 15 times greater chance that your family could be robbed or your daughters attacked. Are you evil and hateful because you desire that the housing complex remains all-White?

The same federal government that bans food and drugs that have only a tiny chance of causing harm to the health is determined to promote forced integration of neighborhoods and housing that results in more White victims of robbery, rape, and murder just as certainly as cigarettes will increase cancer cases. But your new Black neighbors would be far more likely to hurt you than the cigarettes the government warns you about. Forced integration is as ridiculous as if the government forced you to smoke cigarettes!

Inevitably, liberals will argue that just because someone is Black does not mean that he will engage in crimes or crank up the boombox in the middle of the night. "What about the individual Black who is not criminal or loud or rowdy?" they ask. The answer is that society can not function without recognition of groups. Drunk drivers are not allowed on the road even though the great majority of drinkers and drivers don't have accidents or break traffic laws (other than drinking too much). We ban them from the highways because they have a higher percentage of accidents. People convicted of crimes are put behind bars even though many of them will never commit another offense.

If you think about it, understanding the dynamics of probability enables us to survive. Cigarettes cause only a small percentage of smokers to get lung cancer, but many people avoid them, and for good reason. Few White people will walk across a Black housing project in Detroit. Are they racist or simply exhibiting good sense?

Liberals may retort that most criminals made choices that cause them to be treated differently, while no one chooses their race. Michael Levin, author of *Why Race Matters*, points out that the same could be said of drivers below the age of 16.[280] Many could pass the driver's test and drive as competently and as conscientiously as an 18 year old. Yet we deny the young their license because of their group norms of accidents and deaths. They don't choose to be under 16. Perhaps it is not fair to deny a careful 15 year old a driver's license, but on the opposite side, is it fair to the older groups of better drivers for them to suffer high rates of injury and death?

In terms of Black crime, being racially conscious is not a matter of racism — it can be a matter of life and death.

The federal government has now gone far beyond the first simple open housing statutes of the Civil Rights Act. Its policy is now not only to prevent White discrimination against Blacks in buying or renting homes and apartments, it now actively seeks to assist Blacks to move into White neighborhoods. Housing and Urban Development

(HUD) uses scattered-site housing to integrate Blacks into White neighborhoods and apartments with federally subsidized rent, utilities, mortgages, and many other amenities. White taxpayers endure the inequity of seeing their tax money used to pay the rent, mortgage, or other costs of Blacks to live in White neighborhoods. While the White tenants struggle to pay full value, the Blacks pay nothing or partial value for the dwelling. Not only does this often subject the White residents to higher crime brought in by the new Black occupants, often the problems associated with them drives many Whites away and ultimately depresses their property value.

In a program called *Movement to Opportunity* originated by White renegade Republican Jack Kemp, former Secretary of HUD, ghetto Blacks are given free housing in mostly White neighborhoods. Given their crime rates, they should rename the program *Predators to Prey*. As a result of such programs, Whites have continued their exodus. Many European-Americans have now spilled out into areas that are so far out from the cities, and even from suburbia, that they can be defined only as rural.

As an example of how far the federal courts have gone to destroy the racial integrity of White communities, developers have been successfully sued for simply having a White family as a model in their advertisements. The insanity can be seen in the case of an owner of a property in New York called the North Shore Towers who was sued by four Blacks who suffered no discrimination at the complex. They claimed they suffered discrimination simply because the company's advertisement did not have Blacks in it. The U.S. District Court ordered the company to pay $245,000 to the Blacks and forced them to run $200,000 worth of ads that contained at least one Black for every two Whites.[281] Even newspapers such as *The New York Times* and *The Washington Post* were found liable just for running ads whose models were not Black.[282] Should White athletes now be able to sue NBA teams for showing advertisements for some of their all-Black starting teams? Can you imagine a Black college being sued for an ad showing Black students?

The diabolical character of enforced "civil rights" can be illustrated by the federal government's recent actions against White cab drivers that are reluctant to pick up Black male customers late at night. Tens of thousands of cab drivers have suffered robbery, assault or murder in our major cities. The perpetrators are overwhelmingly Black. It is at least 1,500 percent more likely for a Black to be an armed robber than a White. Of course, those rates go up dramatically late at night when a driver is picking up young Black males. The Justice Department has threatened prosecution of cabbies and cab companies who refuse rides to potential Black customers in the major cities.

The reality is that cab drivers are trying to get as many legitimate rides as possible, because more rides mean greater income. They are not trying to discriminate against Blacks, but they are also trying to get home alive to their families. Cabbies readily will stop for a well-dressed Black man, but naturally are reluctant to stop for a ragged-looking Black youth, who more than likely could not afford an expensive cab fare anyway and may well be planning a robbery. The federal government is determined to force that cab driver to pick up that ragged Black man even if it means a high likelihood of the cabby's robbery or death. Such is the modern state of civil rights!

In spite of all the integration of schools and neighborhood, Black crime rates remain high, Black illegitimacy and venereal diseases continue to increase, Black IQ and performance continues to lag behind Whites just as it had for decades. The massive denial of White civil rights has accomplished little for Black well-being.

The Black Welfare Underclass

As illegitimacy rates among Blacks began to rise in the 1950s and 60s, the liberal egalitarians blamed the Black social problems on poverty, lack of education and the effects of segregation and racism. It did not seem at all odd to them that Black social problems increased dramatically in direct correlation with increased integration, public assistance and the end of institutional racial discrimination. As crime, drugs and illegitimacy increased, the liberals proposed their grand solution. Lyndon Johnson called the new massive welfare structure the Great Society. Welfare and whole safety net of social systems were put into place to improve the health care, diet, job training, infant care and education of the urban poor. The early '60s also introduced massive deficit-causing programs such as liberal welfare benefits, food stamps and massive public housing. The proponents noted that crime and illegitimacy had remained minimal problems in White Europe despite their liberal social welfare system. They were hopeful their programs would work among minorities here. They didn't.

The more money that poured into the minority-oriented welfare system, the worse problems became. Black social problems such as illegitimacy, sexual disease rates, criminality and drug abuse only increased. Grasping at straws, egalitarians implemented even more elaborate and expensive programs rivaling any in the world. And yet, social problems in the Black community only increased.[283] Black illegitimacy went from 15 percent in 1950 to 61 percent in 1988, to almost 70 percent in 1992, and is estimated to grow to over 75 percent by the turn of the century.[284] When I first became racially aware in the mid-1960s social researchers had already taken note that illegitimacy had begun to soar. Why? The press and government blamed it on racism, poverty, or lack of opportunity, the "legacy of slavery" — anything other than the obvious. But how could any of those issues be the cause in the wake of the greatest increase in social welfare spending and government intervention in history?

The Dissolution of the Black Family

In the middle 1960s I had read the books and research papers of a number of racially aware social scientists who predicted the Black family structure would dissolve along with lessening White cultural, social, and economic influence in the Black community. Increasingly independent Black economic, cultural, and political power gave Blacks more freedom to do what came natural to them. Divorced from White influence and culture, they reverted quickly to their genotype — increasingly typical of Black societies around the world. Males exhibited exaggerated sexual aggression and promiscuity that led to the dissolution of the Black nuclear family in America. Females reverted to the age-old African model of maternal provisioning of children.

What the race scientists could not predict in the 1960s was the rise of a historically unprecedented welfare system. Welfare and "Aid to Families with Dependent Children" as well as the housing, food stamps, medical care, and other programs that accompanied it fit perfectly into the historical model of African life. The Black female no longer needed the Black male to provision them, for the productive White masses, through welfare, provided her with housing, food, and spending money based on the number of children she had. Whatever pressure she previously had to exert upon the Black male for the support of herself and her children became superfluous. The more women Black males acquired, the better opportunity to obtain welfare money through the women, and higher numbers of illegitimate children gave them status much as it had given their forefathers prestige in Africa.

The most common liberal explanation for the dissolution of the Black family was that slavery had destroyed it. Nobel Prize-winning research from writers such as Robert Fogelman and Stanley Engerman in their award-winning book, *Time on the Cross,* showed that in the American slave system, Christianity and family values were rigorously imposed.[285] They found from plantation journals and copious slave records that, contrary to popular myths, families were almost never broken up by sales or barter, and when family members were sold to neighboring plantations, it was after the children had grown to adulthood. The lie that slavery destroyed the Black family can be easily disproven by the fact that immediately after slavery, Black illegitimacy was almost as low as for Whites. Black illegitimacy was less than 10 percent in 1890.[286] From the 1890s, Black illegitimacy grew at a slow pace until the economic and social emancipation of the civil rights movement. At that point, it exploded.

I served for over three years on the Health and Welfare Committee of the Louisiana legislature. Having complete access to the welfare records, I learned that from 1960 to 1990 welfare spending had gone up from $5 million to over $200 million, (a 40-fold increase), not counting numerous new accompanying programs. During that period of increased welfare assistance, the welfare rolls had increased dramatically along with illegitimacy, crime, infant mortality, drug abuse and many other telling social indices. I came to the realization that welfare had failed because its birthrate had outstripped the ability of the taxpayer to finance it. Children were being born into the system faster than the government could raise the taxes of the productive to pay for them all. It made sense to me that the poverty problem could only be ameliorated by reducing the welfare illegitimate birthrate. Without a reduction of the birthrate, the welfare rolls and all related societal problems would continue to grow dramatically.

The government and media refused to acknowledge the inherent racial differences that were producing a brutal crime rate, massive Black illegitimacy and welfare dependency, venereal epidemics, and Black academic failure as well as the destruction of much of the public education system. Ignoring these differences only made matters worse. And this failure came during a time of great scientific discovery as well as the dramatically increased productivity of the computer age. Fueled by an unstoppable welfare birthrate, social welfare had grown out of control. It wiped away all the potential economic gains of the American middle class. In the America of just a generation ago, a man could provide a reasonably good living for his wife and children. In the interim it had become necessary for the middle-class wife to work if the family was to have an adequate income, because a significant amount of her family's income was now lost in higher taxes and higher prices necessary to sustain the less productive, burgeoning non-White population.

Liberals often point to the small percentage of government costs made up by actual welfare payments. The argument sounds fairly convincing until one takes into account all the ancillary costs of the welfare underclass. Welfare payments themselves are only the tip of the iceberg of spending. One must consider the costs of housing, food stamps and medical care. Medical care is costly for a population with epidemic venereal disease and frequent injuries from violence and drugs as well as a high birthrate. The medical costs of minority drug problems alone amount to billions of dollars per year when one adds up the costs of drug rehabilitation, drug overdoses, and thousands of often premature, drug-addicted babies. Because at least 16 percent of Blacks fall into the mildly mentally retarded range (IQs below 70), they can qualify for large Social Security payments for each child under Social Security mental disability requirements.

One must also factor in the huge costs of public education for these illegitimate children. Each child costs a bare minimum of $5,000 per year. That's $50,000 per child in 10 years of schooling, or $50 *billion* dollars per million children. Add billions more for the costs of those children for welfare, housing, foodstamps, and medical benefits over the next decade of their lives. Costs of crime, courts and incarceration can mount to many more billions of dollars. The loss from theft alone in America mounts up in the billions of dollars, not counting the increased insurance costs for the business and individual in an increasingly criminal society. And one should not forget the incalculable loss when a productive member of society is murdered or injured in the brutal street crime plaguing America.

In these matters in 1965, I did not have the increased amount of information available today, but on the basis of the data I did have, as well as the fundamental differences that I knew existed between the races, and aided by the research and ideas of many scientific experts who looked at the Black social problems, I believed that the civil-rights movement, socially and politically would be disastrous for both Whites and Blacks.

Affirmative Action

On the floor of the United States Senate during debates on the Civil Rights Act, a number of Southern senators opposed the bill. They were also joined by the leading Republican candidate for president, Barry Goldwater of Arizona, who argued that the bill would lead to discrimination against White people. The bill, of course, specifically outlawed any racial discrimination in hiring, promotions, college admissions, contracting and public accommodations, which on its face should have prohibited discrimination against any race. After all, the bill did not outlaw racial discrimination against Blacks only but racial discrimination per se. To convince the bill's opponents that it would not result in discrimination against Whites, the following language was added to make sure nothing could be misconstrued:

> **Nothing contained in this title shall be interpreted to require any employer... to grant preferential treatment to any individual or to any group because of race, color, religion, sex or national origin. Of such individual group on account of an imbalance...**[287]

Hubert Humphrey, a leading proponent of the bill, swore that he would physically eat the paper the bill was written on if it were ever used to allow corrective hiring practices.[288] Even those pronouncements did not persuade Goldwater and others to vote for the bill, and it turned out that Goldwater and the bill's other opponents were right. Although most people think the first president who endorsed affirmative action was Lyndon Johnson, it was actually Richard Nixon[289] who in effect repealed the provision against preferential treatment by race with his own fiat allocating set asides in federal government contracting.

Later, in *Weber v. Kaiser Aluminum*, a case fought in my home state of Louisiana and ruled upon by the U.S. Supreme Court, that same provision was used to justify hiring to correct "numerical imbalance." In a tortured decision, the court ruled that because the Civil Rights Act said that preferential treatment by race would not be required, it did not forbid it. Brian Weber, an aluminum worker with more seniority and better work records, was turned down for advancement at Kaiser Aluminum in favor of less-qualified Blacks. As Jared Taylor wrote in *Paved With Good Intentions*, "Amazingly, racial quotas were blessed by the Supreme Court using the very section of the law that was included to prohibit them."[290]

The court essentially said that a bill outlawing racial discrimination allows racial discrimination if it is against Whites. On that basis it should be called the Racial Discrimination Against Whites Act, for it has been turned into a Nuremberg-type Law against the American White majority and has been used to promote or even mandate public and private discrimination against European-Americans.

Once affirmative action got under way, it became the only real way to get meaningful numbers of Blacks and other minorities into the many occupations and universities. Equal opportunity was not enough. Too few Blacks could measure up by any objective qualifications. In police and fire departments, less-qualified Negroes with lower test scores and poor work histories — sometimes even with criminal records — are hired over better-qualified Whites. Blacks are admitted to colleges, law schools, and graduate programs with qualification test scores and grades that would be laughed at if White applicants submitted them. White contractors with lower bids and better records for quality work are rejected in favor of higher-costing Black contractors who do shoddy work. The politicians, in collusion with the liberal media, won't even admit that affirmative action is discrimination, and they continue to refer to it as *equal opportunity* and *equal rights* for Blacks, even though it is blatant racial discrimination against Whites.

It is easy to prove that Affirmative Action discriminates against better-qualified Whites. The Civil Rights Act had already put the weight of the Justice Department to equally-qualified Blacks. It also established an entire body of law and a whole new cadre of lawyers "civil rights attorneys," who are offered incentives to pursue such cases with the opportunity for lucrative awards. If a company discriminated against a better-qualified Black in favor of less-qualified White person, it could face extreme financial penalties and costly judgments to the Black victim and his legal counsel. The force of the U.S. Justice Department and an incentive-driven, civil-rights legal cadre, ensures that better-qualified Blacks do not face discrimination.

The Civil Rights Act and laws can thus remedy any situation where Blacks who are truly qualified face discrimination — so Blacks who are indeed better-qualified — don't need affirmative action. It is meant to favor the clearly less-qualified Black. And that is precisely what affirmative action does. It can be illustrated in the precedent-setting Alan Bakke case in California. Bakke, a prospective medical-school student at the University of California who scored in the 90s on his qualification exams, was denied entrance in favor of minorities who scored in the 30s on the same tests.

The most recent Supreme Court action retained the Hopwood decision at the University of Texas Law School. It stopped the practice of admitting Black and Mexican students with far lower college grades and much lower scores on the Law School Admissions Test (LSAT). The opponents of affirmative action at the school showed that only 288 Blacks in the entire nation had LSATs at the median level of Whites at UTLS. To stress the point, these 288 were not the ones who applied to the school, but were the *total* number of Blacks who — out of the thousands who took LSAT exams — had scored the average of the White student at UT Law School. As incredible as it may seem, there are not enough qualified Blacks in the entire nation to fill the freshman law class of this one university.

The proponents of affirmative action continually told the American people that it was necessary because of the discrimination going on against Blacks. Yet Richard Freeman, in his book *Black Elite*, points out that

> **By the 1970s black women earned as much or more than whites [women] with similar educational attainment; black female college professors obtained a moderate premium over their white peers; young black male college graduates attained rough income parity with young white graduates, and all black male graduates had more rapid increases in income than whites...**[291]

By 1979 all Black women who were employed made 8 percent more than White women of equal qualifications.[292] When you compare Blacks by ability, such as equal IQ scores, the evidence is that the few high-IQ Blacks, when matched with Whites of identical IQ, have graduated from college at higher rates and have higher incomes than their White counterparts. Such facts show clearly that competent Blacks do not face discrimination in America. If anything, they are boosted by a racial discrimination in their favor. Affirmative action does not redress any real discrimination against Blacks. It simply stops discrimination against Black incompetence.

Not only is affirmative action grossly unfair to millions of Whites, who are denied jobs, promotions, scholarships, college and graduate admissions, it has a nefarious impact on society as a whole. Favoring the less-qualified over the better-qualified lowers the productivity of companies and governments, causing increased prices and waste. In some areas the discrimination against better-qualified Whites can even cost lives. The affirmative action deployed by many police and law-enforcement agencies opens the door for many abuses.

The New Orleans Police Department adopted an affirmative action policy in the early '70s. It still consistently favors less-qualified Black police recruits over better-qualified Whites. In addition to accepting Blacks with far lower examination scores, it frequently lets Blacks onto the force despite criminal records that would have instantly disqualified White applicants. The department also has had a policy of promoting Black officers over White officers with more

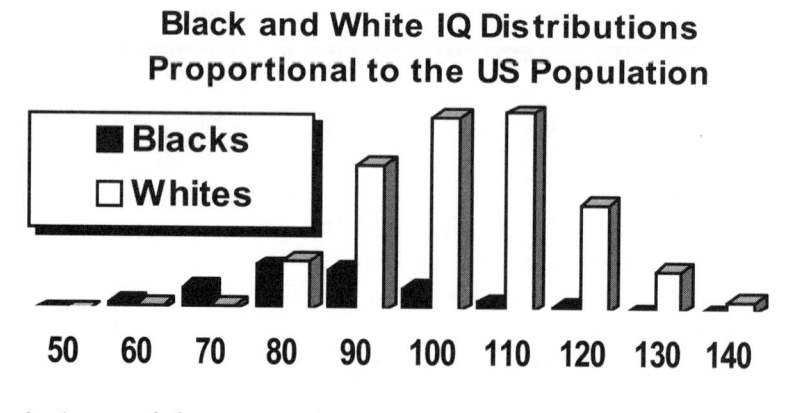

Black and White IQ Distributions Proportional to the US Population

■ Blacks
□ Whites

50 60 70 80 90 100 110 120 130 140

IQ

seniority and better performance records, a policy that the police union contested in court. What is the result of the department's affirmative action policy?

In 1995 and 1996, 50 New Orleans police officers were charged with heinous criminal offenses, which included murder, rape, drug-running, and extortion. Of the 50 officers charged, 48 were Black — and many of them were affirmative-action hires.

In one of the most horrific incidents in the history of the New Orleans Police Department, a Black woman, affirmative-action officer, Antoinette Frank,[293] committed an armed robbery of a restaurant and attempted to kill all the employees so there would be no witnesses. When her partner, White officer Ronald Williams, a husband and father of two, arrived on the scene, Frank murdered him too. Affirmative action can not only cost efficiency and deny the more deserving, it can cost lives.

The Immorality of Affirmative Action

Somehow, in the twisted morality of the New York-Hollywood media establishment and the government, it is acceptable to deny the civil rights of White people. The media forever remind us of the injustice of discrimination against mostly less-qualified Negroes, but they won't even call affirmative action what it actually is: anti-White racial discrimination.

Whites are supposed to have a collective guilt because a small percentage of White Americans practiced slavery for 89 years of the American republic (1776-1865), ending 133 years ago. Yet those advocates of collective guilt are the same ones who say that you can't blame the entire Black race for the plague of Black crime ravaging our country. No system of justice in the world would sanctify the punishment of a young person because of the sins or supposed sins of his great-great-grandfathers. But, if Blacks deem that kind of injustice as morally appropriate, it should be noted that there is far more likelihood of a Black having an ancestor who enslaved Blacks, than for a White to have a direct ancestor who enslaved Blacks.

All sorts of excuses are used to justify affirmative action. The favorite argument of the egalitarians is that not allowing for affirmative action is the same as theoretically making one runner start 10 yards behind another, but what they argue is that we actually do start the selected minority ahead of the field in a race. Is this how we should conduct the Olympics, giving the poorest athletes a 10-meter headstart in the 100-meter dash?

Do the egalitarians believe that there are no young White people who grow up in tough circumstances, in poverty or abuse or hobbled by sickness. Should these young people who have had difficult obstacles to overcome but who overcame them with their ability and their hard work now have to face discriminatory policies that favor minorities who could have actually had a less difficult life. Affirmative action distinguishes not by need but strictly by race. The wealthy, celebrity-children of Johnnie Cochran, the millionaire Black attorney who defended O.J. Simpson would enjoy preference over the poorest White person.

When I registered for Louisiana State University in 1968, the U.S. Justice Department required my university to have its new students fill out a computer card denoting their ancestry. The government wanted to make sure the numbers of minorities at the school were adequate. I noticed that I had to check off my ancestry from a series of boxes next to various racial origins. The first box was designated "African-American," followed by one next to the word "Negro," and then one next to "Black." Perhaps not to offend them, Blacks were given three choices of how to report their ancestry. Next on the list came "Mexican-American," then "Asian-American," then "Indian-American," then "Pacific Islander." After a few more obscure national origins, I finally arrived to the one I had to check as a White person. It simply read "Other."

I realized that we European-Americans, whose ancestors built our great nation, wrote our instruments of government, created our prosperity with our genius and our sweat, who had given millions of our lives so our nation could even exist — that we were now "others." We are now denied the constitutional rights that our forefathers had won. To misuse the central analogy of the of the civil-rights movement — While Blacks no longer ride in the back of the bus, White riders are now required to pay a higher fare and face a good chance of being physically attacked or robbed on that multiracial conveyance.

The Evolutionary Explanation

What I had learned about the evolutionary factors that created the White and Black races fit in perfectly with the racial differences exhibited in modern society.

Before the advent of civil rights, Blacks had lived in a society completely structured by the White man. From the time of slavery, White values, mores, religious attitudes and institutions were forced upon them. Even after emancipation, European mores were stringently enforced on the Black population, and when criminal behavior occurred, there was swift and harsh punishment. As my liberal antagonists would say, "If a Black dared to rape or harm a White person, especially a White woman, he likely would not even make it to the jail."

Every Black man knew that he would receive harsh treatment if he violated, even slightly, the social conventions of Jim Crow. Even in that repressive system, the Black crime rate was still significantly greater than that of Whites. Then, with the advent of "civil rights," the African-Americans gained legal emancipation and full political rights. With this new social emancipation, a number of interesting changes took place. The Black male came to dominate professional sports that relied on speed. The strict sexual mores imposed upon him in slavery and later under Jim Crow were relaxed by the new freedom to express his long-repressed sexual urges and aggressive tendencies. Out from under White constraints, he became free to be as sexually promiscuous as his genes suggested. Powerful White social institutions that supported legitimacy and marriage were slowly eradicated, and Blacks began to set their own moral standards.

Without the order and discipline imposed by White society, the inherent need for instant gratification overcame the White structure of delayed gratification and left Blacks vulnerable to the instant gratification of drugs and criminality. Inability to delay gratification also led to loss of employment reduced savings and other factors contributing to poverty.

Ascension of Black political power in major cities and affirmative action programs ruined schools that had been previously staffed by competent White faculty. As Black control increased, their communities diverged increasingly from European standards.

The general decline was accompanied by greater opportunity in the White establishment for those Blacks who were nearer to White abilities and behavior. Their educational and economic success, combined with desegregation, led to their exodus from the Black community, depriving it of its natural leaders. Heretofore, the more capable of Blacks had to take responsibility for the standards in their community, and they did so reasonably well. As Blacks with more intelligence and sense of responsibility were given the option to flee to White areas, they did so and the traditional bonds in the Black community were dissolved. An orgy of crime, gang tribalism, drugs, and sexual dissolution was set loose that has still not run its course.

Racially aware men such as Carleton Putnam and others, realizing the genetic difference in IQ, concluded that in education and jobs, equal rights would never be enough to achieve equal results. The vast majority of Blacks could not compete with Whites, especially in education and jobs relying on high IQs and intense self-discipline, delayed gratification and long-term study. It was not long before the egalitarian call for equal rights became one of anti-White discrimination — euphemistically called affirmative action. But even these programs were doomed to failure because of the evolutionary differences that are impervious to environmental intervention.

The deeply engraved evolutionary differences are in fact widening with time, for it is the most intelligent Black women who have the fewest children, while Black males who show the greatest ingrained sexual and physical aggression — as well as the less restraint that is accompanied by low intelligence — father the most children.

Racial Ethics of Individuals and Groups

When I discovered the broad differences between the races, I could also not deny that there are individual Blacks of good character and intelligence, and of course, individual Whites of bad character and low intelligence. My liberal friends said that for this reason there should only be consideration of individuals rather than races. The media touts this line incessantly, and many people parrot it back to me in conversation without thinking about its ramifications.

Coming from the government, the whole concept reeks of hypocrisy, for at the same time government officials spouted the argument that we are all individuals — they launched massive programs that took into account groups and races. So called civil-rights took away the rights of individuals to make their own choices of association. Even though many individual Blacks did not need the civil-rights movement to be treated fairly in hiring and promotions, it was meant to help the race *as a whole*. Affirmative action discriminated against the better-qualified European-American group, and was said to be necessary to give Blacks a hand up, even if many individual Blacks were already up and many Whites, very down.

America was almost 90 percent White at the beginning of the 1960s, and the previous immigration acts were meant to maintain the ethnic makeup. But the Immigration Act of 1965 discriminated against potential European immigrants *as a group*.

While Whites, both liberals and conservatives, were busy talking about being concerned only about individuals, every minority group in the nation had vital concerns about their *own heritage*, their *own leaders*, their *own interests*. They sought to advance their *own* people in all arenas of society, from the halls of government to the sports stadium, from the office of town mayor to the selection of the high-school homecoming queen.

While Whites talk about voting for the best person regardless of race, the Black block vote can be counted on to solidly support Black candidates even if they are convicted drug offenders such as Marion Barry. Every White candidate carefully answers specific questions about what he would do for the "Black community," or the "Hispanic community." And every White candidate is careful not to offend Black sensibilities. Any reporter who would dare ask, "How will you benefit the White community?" would be humiliated by his fellows.

Mexicans openly exhibit their own racial consciousness, expressed even in the name of their popular activist group, La Raza Unida, meaning, literally, the United Race. While learning about race, I began to notice the literally thousands of organizations devoted to race: the Black Nurses Association, the Black Police Officers Association and

African-American teachers organizations. But the courts prohibit the formation of a White Police Officers Union or the White Nurses Association.

When students both Black and White open their history textbooks in school and find references to *Black Americans* or African-Americans, it is always in a positive connotation, such as "Black Americans made substantial contributions to the culture of the United States." When the term *White race* is used, it is almost always used in the context of racial exploitation, such as "White Europeans stole the Indians' lands" and "enslaved the African." Martin Luther King, Jr. finds reference as a "great Black man," whereas Thomas Jefferson and George Washington are "great men," and never designated as "great White men."

Leaders among Blacks, Mexicans, Jews, and other minorities are forever reminding their followers of group interests, group heritage, their need to support each other and their community and their need to stick together for their own interests. Whites are told that to do the same thing is somehow evil and un-Christian.

At 16 I saw through the hypocrisies. For all the media's prattle about the "myth of race," and the promotion of everyone as an "individual," it constantly promoted pride among Blacks, Mexicans, Indians, Jews, and other groups while at the same time instilled a collective guilt in European Americans. Today the media even smiles on "Gay pride" events and parades. Would you care to guess their reaction to a "White Pride" parade.

At the same time the government pronounced its commitment to a "color blind society" it invoked race for thousands of policy decisions and programs that discriminated against European Americans and threatened our very lives, our liberty and the very existence of our future generations.

- **When Blacks defend their rights, the media depicts it as love and brotherhood. When Whites defend their civil rights, the media calls it "hatred" and "bigotry."**
- **Racial discrimination against better-qualified Whites is "affirmative action" and "equal opportunity." Against better-qualified Blacks is called "racism" and "racial discrimination."**
- **When minorities express overt pride in their heritage, its said to be good for their self-esteem. When Whites do, its proof of our ethnocentrism.**
- **When a rare White on Black attack occurs, it is media-covered "hate" crime. Millions of Black on White attacks are simply called "crimes."**
- **Discussing discrimination and century-old slavery against Blacks is "healing." Discussing the millions of White victims of Black crime is "hateful."**

- Past segregation of races in schools and neighborhoods was "morally evil." Integration, which has resulted the destruction of our major cities and in the rape, murder, robbery and assault of millions of Whites, is "morally right."
- The old film portrayal of friendly and good-hearted Black waiters and maids is "demeaning." Thousands of portrayals in today's media of unspeakably evil Whites doing all sorts of hateful things to minorities is uplifting.
- A Black revolutionary (such as Eldridge Cleaver) who boasts of raping White women is extolled as "eloquent." A White who simply points out the Black rape problem is "racist."

Double Standards

I began to see double standards and hypocrisy everywhere I turned. I didn't hate Black people. I still revered the memory of Pinky, my family's housekeeper, and I still respected the Black fellows I formerly worked with at the Gary's garage. Even after learning of the epidemic Black crime wave that had struck down so many of our people; I did not hate Blacks. I saw that their evolutionary mechanisms of behavior influenced them much as a tiger's genes made it such a fearsome predator. One doesn't have to hate the tiger to avoid his lair. Blacks do not *intentionally* do harm. They do what comes *natural* to them in an alien environment that costs them their own soul and spirit. In Abraham Lincoln's perceptive words, "In a word we suffer on each side. If this be admitted, it affords a reason at least why we should be separated."[294]

I didn't want to oppress them, hurt them, imprison them or exploit them. I simply desired to live in a society where my progeny could grow up in harmony and accomplishment, in beauty and brotherhood. I knew that those ideals were possible in a society of my European heritage, and ultimately impossible under integration and multiculturalism.

I came to the conclusion that America's founding fathers were right in the only eventual solution to the race problem is separation. It is not an easy answer, but it is the only one. The Black race can never be truly happy under our standards and control, and we could never be satisfied by theirs. No matter how much it costs, or whatever sacrifices it takes, separation is the only possible solution if America is not to transform to a land of hate and degeneration — a multicultural nightmare of conflict and irresolution.

The two most popular Black leaders of the 20th century, Marcus Garvey and Louis Farrakhan supported such a concept. The great majority of Whites, given a choice, would surely not oppose it, as they have sought to be among themselves whenever possible. Even many liberals, while endorsing racial integration with their voices have avoided it with their feet. There is nothing evil about allowing each race to pursue its own destiny among its own kind. Voluntary separation is far preferable to racial war, to racial hatred and bitterness.

I believed then and still believe that separation will come. The only question is whether it will come by negotiation or by racial war. Among the Black community there are already frequent expressions of war sentiment. One can see it in the wildly-cheered advocacy of White genocide by Farrakhan lieutenant Khalid Mohammed in a 1994 speech at Howard University,[295] to the cheering of the O.J. Simpson verdict by Blacks everywhere. Black people as well as Whites know that integration is no answer to the racial problems at hand. Even James Meredith, a man who once stood at the pinnacle of civil rights in the integration of University of Mississippi, has repeatedly decried the disastrous consequences of integration for the Black community.

It's time to right the wrongs, I thought. Blacks were taken from their homeland and brought to an alien land. The answer to that wrong is certainly not the greater wrong of racial integration and the destruction of Western Civilization. The ultimate solution is separation on this continent or elsewhere so that each people could be free to create a society attuned to its needs and spirit. Thomas Jefferson, the author of our Declaration of Independence and Bill of Rights, knew that the races "equally free, could not live on the same continent." Now it is time for each people to secure their own racial independence, their own bill of rights, the most basic being the right for each people to determine their own destiny by their own making.

It was the middle '60s, and I thought people would surely see our nation's disastrous course. I prayed there was still a lot of time to awaken our people, but then it became apparent that the 1965 Immigration Act would change America's racial composition at terrifying speed. A friend, who was a well-known author in New Orleans, sat with me at Café du' Monde in the French Quarter and made the analogy of America as the *Titanic*. He said that two things would sink our ship of state: genes and geography. I asked him what he meant, and he said the mass introduction of alien genes in America's geography.

He made an analogy of our nation as the *Titanic*; the looming iceberg was race. Our leaders pretended that the racial iceberg was just a passing cloud. When we struck the hard realities of race, we were told that the cement and steel of our constitution and our culture would keep our ship of state afloat. Even as the racial invasion began to tear into the hull under the waterline of public acknowledgment, many on the upper decks refused to believe our ship could go down. But, through the rip in the underside of our ship, the alien flood of massive immigration and unrestrained welfare birthrates poured in, drawing us down. Some parts of the vessel rapidly sank. Other sectors tilted even higher against the horizon for a while. But inevitably, the dark waters continued to mount, and the lights of civilization began to flicker and the whole ship went under.

In an animated voice, Drew Smith, author of *Legacy of the Melting Pot*, completed his analogy, the powdered sugar of his beignet dusting the air with each point he made. "Look at the rip in the hull!" he thundered at me. "It was cut by the Immigration Act of 1965. Hold onto your hat, boy, we will be up to our necks in no time."

CHAPTER 13:

THE RISING TIDE OF COLOR

By the time I was a junior in high school, I was convinced that racial differences are real and inherent and that the forced integration of our schools and society would have dire consequences. It seemed obvious that America would undergo a slow transformation to a racially mixed society with a corresponding demographic change similar to that of ancient Egypt and ancient India. Perhaps there was time, I thought — even if it took a few generations — to rally the European-American to the truth and thus prevent the looming tragedy. I hoped that the increasing scientific evidence of racial realities would eventually prevail and turn our nation in the direction of self-preservation. However, the material I read suggested we not nearly that much time.

I had read the books of Madison Grant and Lothrop Stoddard, written in the early decades of this century, which predicted "a rising tide of color" [296] and the "passing of the great race" [297] which he said would be caused by high minority immigration and birthrates. Their warnings were helpful in securing passage of the great immigration restriction bills of 1917 and 1924 and even the Walter-McCarran Immigration Bill of 1952, which passed the U.S. Congress over the veto of President Harry S. Truman. The restrictionist legislation was not meant to make America an all-White nation, it simply attempted to preserve the racial status quo in America. Shortly after the 1952 legislation passed, Eisenhower, in perhaps the high point of his presidency, acted decisively to stop a massive influx of Mexicans and returned them to south of the border.

Up until the mid-'60s, America was almost 90 percent White, a figure rigorously maintained for two-thirds of the century. So it seemed that events had at least muted some of the predictions of Grant, Stoddard and others. Most of the immigrants of the early 20th century may not have been of the founding Anglo-Saxon heritage, but they were certainly Caucasians of European origin, and by the 1960s the overwhelming majority of them had thoroughly assimilated into the Anglo-American culture. The English language reigned supreme among all European-American ethnic groups.

Then in the mid-'60s, the American government embarked on three important policies that would severely threaten the future of

European Americans. The government, under the presidency of Lyndon Johnson, inaugurated the:
1) **massive forced integration of schools and neighborhoods**
2) **taxpayer subsidizing of massive welfare-financed, illegitimate birthrates (disproportionately high among minorities)**
3) **scrapping America's immigration laws and adopting policies that favored massive non-European immigration.**

All three policies had a powerful demographic impact on America. Carleton Putnam and many others tried to warn America about the consequences of these policies. In my own way, I tried to do the same thing but as a high-school student I felt helpless.

Rather than go into all the arguments that convinced me that America's demographic change would have terrible consequences, I will relate a personal experience. After my election to the Louisiana House of Representatives in 1989, I visited my old grade-school neighborhood. Gentilly Woods, once tidy and well-kept, was now mostly Black and disheveled. Many of the homes that once had a perpetually fresh-painted look, were now blistered and peeling, and garnished by unkempt lawns of weeds and trash. I learned from the few European-American holdouts in the neighborhood that burglary, vandalism, and assault, which had once been rare, were now commonplace. As I drove slowly down my old street, groups of hard-featured Black men stood around dilapidated cars and directed hostile stares at an obviously unknown White person trespassing in *their* neighborhood.

They were right, for I was now trespassing where I no longer belonged. I looked at the burned-out shell of a home where once lived Mr. and Mrs. Aiken, and when I passed the old Markton family home, I could hardly see the place — the front yard was covered with trash and four-foot weeds.

The diehard White remnants who remained knew that things had changed over the years, but they had adapted and found a way to endure each indignity and violation. The change had been so gradual that they were no longer shocked at what went on, just resigned to it.

Even though it had been a few years since my last visit, my memories became vivid as I entered to boundaries of the neighborhood. It seemed as though I had been away only a few scant hours. Now those old memories crashed against the images of the present, causing me to feel disoriented and off balance. It was akin to visiting a healthy friend and then after only a few weeks separation, seeing him wasting away with illness. Afraid that my recollection had idealized the neighborhood of my youth, as soon as I returned to my suburban home, I ferreted out my old photographs. Those photos clearly showed a community even more attractive than I had remembered. Well-kept homes filled the album, often accented with blooming flowers and finely trimmed shrubbery; sidewalks edged closely, and homes with a freshly painted look. Polished autos dotted the clean streets. Even more dramatic were the photographs of the Tom Sawyer and Becky Thatcher-like bright faces of the children with whom I spent so many happy hours of childhood.

In my youth, these were the ruddy faces that ruled our streets and yards and parks. They were all gone now, replaced by dark, angry teenagers with scarred skin and boom boxes; often with pistols and crack in their pockets, menacing the streets where children now feared to venture. This is a picture that has been frequently repeated all over the United States of America.

The story of the remnant White residents of Gentilly Woods is much like that of the frog in the pot of water. The temperature increases so slowly that the poor creature fails to recognize the danger until the water is boiling and it is too late. Does the story not apply to the traditional American? Are White Americans too lulled by the tepid water to realize what is ahead?

Americans can glimpse their country's future by looking at the inner cities. The political corruption, failing schools, drug problems, crime, the rundown housing and even the trash in the streets — all are a preview of the coming attractions of 21st-century America. When all of America has the same racial proportions as that of the inner cities, there will be no White infrastructure, no White cornucopia of tax revenue mitigating the Third Worldism. Criminals will no longer be held in check by White police, prosecutors, juries, and judges, and the shrinking White tax base will be inadequate to the costs of the criminal justice system and the jails needed to house the lawbreakers. Those races that cannot provide for their own housing, food, medical care and schooling will no longer have them generously provided by the aging and diminishing European population. As bad as conditions are in the inner cities at the close of the 20th century, how much worse would they be without the almost sacrificial support of a productive White America? When all of America is made up of the genotypes of the inner city, America will mutate into a land somewhere between Mexico and Haiti.

The transition might be similar to the Haitian revolution. Because of the clear racial demarcation that so often accompanies the haves and the have-nots, a revolutionary proletarian fervor of the dark masses will have a clear target: people of light skin. Fires of racial hatred and envy are stoked by those who can only blame Black and Brown failure on White racism and oppression, never facing the reality of racial difference. Whether non-White ascendancy comes about through massive violence such as the genocide of the Whites in Haiti at the end of the 18th century, or by the sheer numbers in the voting booths, it will be devastating to America. Unless circumvented, the non-White racial revolution ahead will leave America a land unrecognizable and abhorrent to the remaining minority of White citizens.

As I related earlier, perhaps a true harbinger of the America of the future is the capital city of our country, Washington, D.C. In spite of almost unlimited monetary support from the whole of the American people, it is one of the most poorly educated, dirtiest, and most dangerous cities in America. The city's mayor is a crack-smoking whoremaster who was re-elected *after* his drug convictions.

An American Haiti or Mexico is not inevitable. White Americans can avoid such a fate if they once again gain control over their government, their media and their borders in the first few decades of the 21st century. Even after Whites become demographically outnumbered, because of our intelligence and organizational ability, for perhaps a generation there will still be more than enough Whites to prevail in a revolutionary physical struggle — but only if we are racially awakened and strong in will and purpose. But, the fewer our numbers, the greater the suffering and sacrifice expended in the future battle for our survival and freedom. The longer our people delay, the harder the fight that we — and even more so, our children — will face.

In the last years of the 20th century, White Americans have been incredibly indifferent to the most critical issue facing the country: its rapid transformation from an overwhelming White nation to a non-White one. In a democratic form of government, such a change has the potential to turn the society upside down, and the process is well underway in the America of the late 1990s. Not limited to America, a dramatic demographic upheaval is also occurring in Canada, England, Australia, France and many other White nations. In addition to all the racially related factors, uncontrolled immigration transforms America from a spacious and resource rich nation to a far more crowded and environmentally damaged land. No sizable nation in the history of the world has ever undergone such a sweeping population shift in so short a period.

Equally astonishing is the ignorance among the American people of this seminal change. The mass media treat this seismic shift almost as if it is inconsequential. When they mention it at all, they portray the change as one that will benefit our economy and culturally enrich us.

Some members of our heritage — those who dwell in communities and neighborhoods that are still almost all-White — think the rest of America is as unaffected as their own neighborhoods. But the change is not only in the streets of Miami, Los Angeles or Detroit. It even finds its expressions in the rising crime rates and school problems of recently all-White communities such as the remote Fargo, North Dakota, or Des Moines, Iowa. In reality, this demographic change will be catastrophic to both our genotype and the Western society that our European heritage created.

The two engines of this seminal change are massive non-White immigration and differential birthrates between Whites and non-Whites. The non-White immigration rates and welfare-spawned birthrates are not the accidental result of some natural process; they are the result of government policies that are racially discriminatory against those of European descent.

The Alien Invasion

Most experts believe that Whites will become a minority in the United States by 2050. Many projections have that landmark coming even earlier, by a decade or more, as the percentage of racial change becomes more rapid. Already the non-White population is increasing faster than predicted. Unless government policy changes — and changes radically — by the time the students of the White high-school class of 2000 reach retirement age, they and their children will find themselves outnumbered and outvoted not just in our major cities but in America as a whole.

More than 95 percent of both legal and illegal immigration into the United States is non-White. Because of the way the immigration law is structured, the highest skilled nations on Earth — those of Europe — are allowed only a tiny percentage of immigrants, while the Third World nations such as Mexico are dumping their chaff onto our American shores at the highest rate in history. Additionally, the federal government has been unwilling to enforce our immigration laws and prevent the annual immigration of more than a million illegals (overwhelmingly non-White). America also has a burgeoning welfare system that is financing a prolific non-White (predominantly Black and Hispanic) birthrate. The result is a demographic change that challenges the cultural and economic foundations that has characterized America from its founding to the present day.

Many Americans labor under the false impression that American immigration policy is selective for skills and abilities. In fact, the great bulk of legal immigration has nothing at all to do with skills. It is based on "family reunification," and the foreign reunified family members can be illiterate, insane or even HIV-positive. Because of allotment numbers, family "reunification" actually prevents many Europeans with exceptional skills and abilities from immigrating. Of course, in the area of illegal immigration, no selection standards exist at all. Many of those pouring in illegally are criminals or parasites who come here for the classic reason offered by the robber when asked why he robbed banks, "Because that's where the money is!" It reminds me of the quote of the Jewish Communist master spy Lincoln Trebisch who upon entering Germany from Soviet Russia, remarked. "I am looking for a fatherland. Where can I find one cheap?"

Even the so-called skilled immigrants hailing from Third World nations, where standards are far lower, are usually less qualified than their American counterparts. For example, better-qualified, American-born Ph.D.'s face discrimination at colleges across America that are hiring non-American, non-White university teachers to accomplish their minority hiring goals.

The mass media celebrate the racial change with constant parading of immigrant success stories. Newspapers feature stories about high-school valedictorians and successful entrepreneurs, sometimes with full-page picture spreads of the beaming smiles of the alien newcomers and their almost always-large families. But how often do the media correlate immigration with the far more common immigrant reality of crime? Every immigrant valedictorian can be contrasted to hundreds of dope dealers, robbers, murderers, and organized-crime members. Each immigrant millionaire entrepreneur can be contrasted to hundreds mired in the welfare system, their greatest productive talent being the churning out of babies nursed at the collective breast of productive Americans.

The media constantly offer up the successful immigrant as proof that the "American Dream" is alive and well, but they never offer a clear picture of the immigrant version of the "American Nightmare." Such could be the story of Colin Ferguson, a White-hating illegal immigrant obtaining residence through marriage and ultimately gunning down 25 people on New York's Long Island Railroad. Instead of being an argument to reduce immigration, President Clinton and other liberals used the Ferguson incident to call for gun control. Liberals focusing on the number of guns rather than the number and quality of immigrants is a perfect example of the incoherence of the establishment. The pervasiveness of crime in America is unrelated to the number of guns; it is related to the number of racial minorities. A comparison of American and European crime statistics clearly reveals that the eager White gun-buyers of America have practically the same crime rate as the gun-banned Whites of Europe.

A disproportionate amount of crime is committed by aliens in America. Fully one-fourth of the prisoners in federal penitentiaries are not American citizens — proportionately three times higher than it should be by their percentage of population. [298]

As staggering as these figures are, they do not include aliens who have been naturalized or the teenage or adult children of aliens born in America (who are by birth citizens). Although one might suppose that most of the aliens are incarcerated for drug importation, the fact is that upwards to four-fifths are in federal prisons for drug dealing *within* the United States.

Aliens dominate an incredibly disproportionate amount of the drug trafficking in America. In fact, from importation to distribution, combining the Nigerian heroin connection with the Russian (Jewish mafia from Russia), the South American cartels, and the Black street dealers, one of the most severe problems facing the United States is of a distinctly minority character.

America's recent experience with Nigerian émigrés offers a grim look into the current immigration policy of the federal government that could be described only as self-destructive. U.S. law-enforcement officials estimate that 75 percent of the 100,000 Nigerians in the United States are involved in serious criminal activity and account for 40 percent of all heroin smuggled into the United States. If government officials admit that three out of four Nigerian émigrés are criminals — yet they continue to let them in to prey on American citizens — it is not only the Nigerians who are criminal, it is also the federal government officials who permit it. [299] [300]

The massive immigration of the past three decades has spawned organized crime that far eclipses, in sheer numbers of criminals and criminal acts, the Mafia and other criminal syndicates during Prohibition. New ethnic criminal mafias include the Mexicans from drug importation to the street gangs, Chinese, Japanese, South Koreans, Colombians, and Russian (Jewish). Sicilian organized-crime participants are today only minor players in comparison with the new non-European mafias.

The extraordinary cost of organized crime is one more terrible cost accrued by the immigration policies of the United States. Just one aspect of organized crime, the drug problem, has a ripple effect that goes far beyond that of the criminal prosecution and incarceration of the drug dealers. How many broken lives and shattered families are its toll? How many crimes can be attributed to the addicts? How much has drug abuse and addiction affected welfare, housing, food stamps, and medical costs?

Another intrinsic cost of illegal and legal immigration is the high cost of their health care, which is routinely provided by the taxpayer. Of the 22 million Hispanics in America, at least six million are uninsured. When you add in the millions of Blacks receiving Medicaid and overflowing the public hospitals of the major cities, one begins to understand the *crisis* in "health care crisis." Those who do not pay for

180   MY AWAKENING

their medical care, whether by insurance or other means, cause health care prices to go up for those who do. Productive Americans, in paying the health care bill of those who cannot, pay spiraling taxes that increasingly burden the middle class family.

At 9.1 percent, immigrants receive welfare cash benefits at a higher percentage than do native-born Americans. In some of the heavily Black immigrant groups, the percentage goes significantly higher. For example, 27.9 percent of Dominicans are on welfare. No one knows how many more are on other noncash programs such as Food Stamps, public housing and Medicaid. In programs such as public housing, which are administered by localities, there is evidence that the immigrant numbers are even higher.

Alien immigration and welfare birthrates also increase education costs.

The Net Costs of Immigration: The Facts [301]

Public Education, K-12	$20,230,000,000
Public Higher Education	$6,260,000,000
ESL and Bilingual Education	$4,040,000,000
Food Stamps	$3,666,000,000
AFDC	$3,210,000,000
Supplemental Security Income (SSI)	$2,760,000,000
Housing Assistance	$2,980,000,000
Social Security	$25,530,000,000
Earned Income Tax Credit	$4,370,000,000
Medicaid	$14,550,000,000
Medicare A and B	$6,070,000,000
Criminal Justice	$3,080,000,000
Local Government	$20,320,000,000
Other Programs	$27,660,000,000
Displacement Costs	$15,240,000,000
TOTAL COST	**$159,960,000,000**
Less Taxes paid	$94,970,000,000
NET COSTS IN 1996	**$64,990,000,000**

California is so burdened by the bankrupting costs of large numbers of illegal immigrants in the schools that voters overwhelmingly approved Proposition 187, which limited public funding of illegal immigrants. When a segment of the school population does not pay its fair share of education costs, either the quality must go down or already high taxes must continue to rise.

When all the costs for immigration nationwide are added up, the total net cost was a staggering $64 billion in 1996. [Actually

$64,990,000,000] This figure will rise by 66 percent, to $108 billion, by 2006. For 1997 through 2006 the cumulative cost will be approximately $866 billion — and that figure is probably conservative since immigration rates are likely to rise. Government services for legal and illegal immigrants cost each taxpayer almost $1,500 in 1996. This figure will also rise dramatically, and catastrophically, in the early years of the 21st century.

Some so-called conservatives, such as the White renegade Republican politician Jack Kemp, are actually applauding the changing racial makeup of America, even though the non-White immigrants vote overwhelming for liberals. Many support opening the border even wider for the Third World masses. The liberal media are ecstatic over the change. Multiculturalism is the new catechism of our schools, offered as the new definition of what is called America.

In the American mythos, we have gone from "a nation of pioneers" to "a nation of immigrants" to a nation of "multiculturalism and multiracialism." The cost of such change is onerous for traditional Americans. We pay in crime rates so high that they challenge the term "civilized society." We pay in schools where our children are, at best, taught at a substandard level and where, or at worst, face physical intimidation and abuse. Payment is made in inordinately high taxes and a declining infrastructure to finance the machinery of welfare, food stamps, housing, medical care, and criminal justice and incarceration. White Americans pay in the racial discrimination of affirmative action. And we pay spiritually, as the media instill in us a sense of guilt and foster accusations of racism.

Future generations of our people will find it amazing that so few Whites during the last decades of the 20th century could face up to the grim reality of the racial change. Those who read these lines in the mid 21st century will think, *Why couldn't White Americans see what would happen to their society when they became outnumbered and outvoted?*

As the White taxpayer base shrinks and the number of minorities increases, non-White newcomers and newborn will demand more and more of the money spawned by White productivity. The unproductive many will vote for crushing tax rates against the productive few. The decline of society will be rapid and catastrophic. Of course, the decline will be rapid only in historic terms. For those living through it, the change will be less perceptible.

Multiculturalism is by its very definition, non-American. Either America is an American culture or it is multicultural. It cannot be both. Most White liberals I have encountered, envision America's future composition as somewhat like their own upscale neighborhoods: mostly White but with a scattering of minorities who will fit nicely into the liberals' "wine and cheese set." But continued high non-

White immigration and birthrates will not create a society in which the Third World types are present in slightly larger numbers than today. It will produce a society in which the non-Europeans will be the *vast majority*, and we, the White *minority*, will be totally under the political and cultural control of the new Third World majority.

The fact is that the notion of multiculturalism is a lie, for it demands the destruction of Western culture. When Jesse Jackson and his Black and Mexican minions demonstrated at the University of California at Berkeley, they chanted, "Hey Ho, Hey Ho, Western Culture has to go!" But even more than our culture, what is a stake here is the very survival of our life form on this planet, the very right of our people to continue the distinctions that make us as we are. In the end, we will be forced to assimilate into their culture and genotype, not them to us.

Martha Farnsworth Riche, director of the Bureau of the Census in the Clinton administration, happily offers the following comeuppance to White Americans.

Without fully realizing it, we have left the time when the nonwhite, non-Western part of our population could be expected to assimilate to the dominant majority. In the future, the white Western majority will have do some assimilation of its own. [302]

Many of those who can see what is happening cannot muster the courage to speak out openly and endure the approbation of the media. The oft-repeated refrain of American government and media is that to be opposed to unlimited immigration is "un-American," against the very principles upon which our Founding Fathers created this nation. As I researched this issue, I found that — just as on the Black-White issue — the media had embarked on a massive misinformation campaign. Of course, it is the massive non-American, alien invasion that is un-American!

Consider the following quotation from *American Heritage* magazine.

What is at stake here is nothing less than the essential nature of the United States of America. . . Only the United States takes special pride in describing the American nationality as, by definition, independent of race and blood — as something that is acquired by residence and allegiance regardless of birthplace or ancestry. [303]

In fact, America's first naturalization law, which our Founding Fathers enacted in 1790, mandated that an applicant for citizenship be a "free White person." Even the Declaration of Independence often refers to "our British brethren," "our common kindred," and our "consanguinity."

In the original Constitution of the United States, Article I, Section 2, Negroes are counted on the census as three-fifths of a human being.

John Jay, in the first essay of the Federalist Papers, refers to Americans as:

> ...one united people — a people descended from the same ancestors, speaking the same language, professing the same religion, attached to the same principles of government, very similar in their manners and customs...a band of brethren. [304]

Does one have to wonder what John Jay would have thought of gangsta rap and the Twelve Days of Kwanzaa, Mexicans crossing our borders by the millions, thousands of AIDS-infected Haitians landing on our beaches, and direction signs in Spanish along Main Street?

Another excellent example of the media distorting our Founding Fathers' real positions on race and immigration is the use of often-quoted lines by Thomas Paine proposing that America be an asylum for mankind. The lines were taken from *Common Sense*, the sensational pamphlet that so ardently argued for American independence. In it Paine made abundantly clear that the mankind to whom he referred was European.

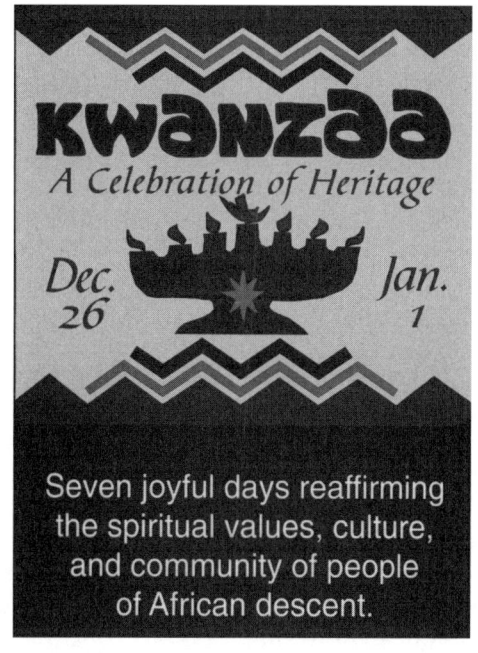

> ...we claim brotherhood with every European Christian.
>
> **All Europeans meeting in America, or any other quarter of the globe, are countrymen.**[305]

The Constitution of the United States, in its preamble, states the matter in clear language.

> **WE THE PEOPLE of the United States in order to form a more perfect union, establish justice, ensure domestic tranquillity, provide for the common defense and to promote the general welfare, and secure the blessing of liberty for *ourselves* and *our posterity*, do ordain and establish this Constitution of the United States of America...** [Emphasis added.]

As immigration author Peter Brimelow notes in his book *Alien Nation*,[306] it was the founder's posterity (ours) they wrote about, not posterity in general.

Interestingly, the same racial groups that advocate immigration in the name of "pluralism" and "multiculturalism" hunger for the day when they will be the majority. Far from willingly becoming part of the traditional Anglo-Saxon American heritage, many of the immigrants have the unabashed goal of altering America to resemble their native lands.

One of the major Mexican-American organizations over the past few decades has been the Mestizo equivalent of the NAACP: La Raza Unida. It and other organizations are titled in Spanish, and most of their publications are almost exclusively written in Spanish. Their publications often contain articles lamenting the "Anglo-American theft of the South West" and the coming political dominance of the Mestizo. Some advocate political reunification with Mexico, while others are working toward forming a new Mexican nation, to be called Aztlan in the American Southwest. No wonder Mexican-American groups refer to themselves as La Raza Unida. They don't translate the name to English, for the translation would reveal their raison d'être, for La Raza Unida means *The United Race*.

Birthrates and Race Politics

Black leaders are more open about their aspirations. Morris Jeff, director of the New Orleans Welfare Department and former president of the National Association of Black Social Workers, was asked about the social and personal damage from the high illegitimate birthrate among Black welfare recipients. Jeff, the person supposedly responsible for programs to reduce poverty and the dissolution of the Black family, asked his interviewer to look around at the predominance of Black faces in city hall and pronounced that the Blacks wouldn't control the city's politics without the high Black welfare birthrate.

Jeff said,

> **Should they have children? I don't think they should not have children. . . I think reproduction patterns are based on self-interest, although not in any conscious sense. When you look at the gains the Black community has made, it hasn't been based so much on opportunity as on the profoundness of numbers. In the political arena, you count votes. . . .**
>
> **The best self-interest of the Black community is for it to have its numbers. I could not support a position that would decrease our numbers. In some instances, this is what Darwin was talking about: The name of the game is just to be there in the future.** [307]

Jeff also states the grim reality that faces White people more honestly than does any White politician. He muses,

> **It's [referring to the high birthrate among Blacks] not just an idle concern for White people. There is a future self-interest involved in this thing. It has a profound effect on the future, and I think there**

RISING TIDE OF COLOR 185

are those in the White community who are threatened by it — not only nationally but internationally. [308]

For a generation, conscientious, well-read, environmentally concerned, high-IQ White Americans have been told that the overpopulation of America will destroy the environment and lessen the quality of life for all. Books such as overpopulation "expert" Paul Ehrlich's bestseller, *The Population Bomb*,[309] urged the renunciation of children (or at least limiting the family to one child) as an ideal of the truly altruistic. One problem with such a scenario is that the only ones intellectual enough to read such a tome — or foolish enough to sacrifice themselves — will be the practitioners of the intelligenticide. The second problem is that the hordes of legal and illegal immigrants flooding America will never read *The Population Bomb*. Even if they did, they would not refrain from their immigration nor their birthrates because of what they would consider Ehrlich's sentimental environmentalism.

Morris Jeff, national head of Black welfare workers, praises the high Black illegitimate welfare birthrate.

Race, Immigration and the Environment

Ironically, because of our immigration policy, all the environmental concern about birthrates for Americans is pointless. Americans of native stock have long had a birthrate below replacement level. Almost all of our rapid population increase comes from immigration and the high birthrates of those immigrants already here. The discriminatory policy of U.S. immigration law keeps people of very low birthrates out, such as Europeans and White South Africans, while favoring fecund Third Worlders. Additionally, most legal immigration today comes from so-called family unification provisions that simply augment the immigration from those non-White cultures that have the highest birthrates and that remain prolific in the United States.

America now spends an incredible 2.1 percent of the Gross National Product (almost $115 billion per year) on environmental protection. We are willing to lose jobs to foreign countries that have no such environmental constraints and costs. We are willing to pay more in taxes and pay higher prices for everything from manufactured products to garbage removal.

Unless immigration and the high non-White birthrate are curtailed, all that expenditure and the essence of the ecologic dream will be wasted. Nothing harms the environment more than overpopulation. Practically every scientist, biologist, researcher and writer who wants to preserve the ecology of our nation recognizes that the most critical factor of environmental quality and ecologic preservation is population size.

Resource-poor and environmentally challenged, America already has to close the gates of national parks because of the sheer number of people. The Southwest is running out of water. The wetlands of Louisiana face the ecologic Armageddon of saltwater intrusion. The great forests of America are shrinking. Every year thousands more concrete parking lots replace meadows and forests. Ecologically, America is right now on the cusp of disaster, yet out of control immigration and welfare birthrates promise 150 million more people in just the next 50 years — more than the first 300 years of European settlement on this continent. We do not want our redwood forests to become chopped down or paved over, or our wetlands drained and made barren. We curse at the morning traffic gridlock and remember a time when it was not so jammed, when there was plenty of space in American cities for a home rather than a two bedroom apartment, when one could drive cross America on two-lane roads and encounter only a couple hundred traffic lights instead of thousands. When one did not have to go to state parks to find miles of pristine beaches, uncovered by high-rises, cheap motels or the homes of the privileged elite.

Although Europeans were the first people on Earth who developed the technological ability to do wholesale damage to the environment, we were also the first to recognize it and curtail it. We are the only people productive enough to afford the high costs of environmental protection and, as demonstrated by every White population in the world, we are responsible enough to limit birthrates. The Third World has no such vision, and in their corrupt and overpopulated societies, they do not make the same choices about the future of the planet as we do.

Without question, the greatest man-made ecological disaster in the history of the world is the ongoing destruction of the Amazon rain forest. The flora of the Amazon filters the Earth's atmosphere and replenishes its oxygen much like a filter and air pump in a home aquarium. Fueled by an unbridled birthrate and widespread stupidity and corruption that permeates every level, the mixed-race multitudes of Brazil devour ever-greater expanses of the forest. Like human locusts, they leave in their wake, land scarred and exhausted, and move on to consume more of the virgin forest that has the world's richest Eden of plant and animal life.

The leaders of America and the West also must take a share of responsibility for the disaster, for their idiotic charity of aid and special trade policies have sustained both the birthrate and given the despoilers the economic incentives of this ecologic nightmare.

The unrestrained money lust of international capitalism has also been a large player. It is not surprising that the same ultra-capitalists who have historically favored the importation of slaves, and, since then, the immigration of cheap Third World labor, increasingly locate their manufacturing plants in areas of the world where labor and environmental standards are inferior to those in America and Europe.

In the Natural Order coming in the next century, we must make the rape of the Earth must become as intolerable a crime as the rape of a woman. And every policy of trade, commerce, aid or diplomacy will be greatly affected by that nation's concern for the Earth's environment and ecology.

In that Natural Order, money and the accumulation of wealth will no longer be the law, the spirit and the arbiter of human affairs.

As I write these words, I am visiting friends in Northern Italy. From my balcony, I can see the beautiful blue Lake Garda lying below the town of Torri Del Benaco. All the population around Garda is European. My days have been blessed here by seeing the harmony of the all-European schoolchildren, the trash-and-crime-free streets and highways, and the architecture of beauty and strength built to last centuries, not mere decades.

Only a few weeks before I drove through the ugly visage of miles of garish high-rises on Miami Beach, which in its pristine state must have once been one of the most beautiful beaches in the world. As I gaze out at Lake Garda, I contemplate how different it is from Miami and just soak in with my soul this emerald lake at the edge of the Alps. Quaint villages dot the green expanses of the mountains, and a few accent the shores of the freshwater lake that is truly fresh, fed only by the purity of mountain streams.

The lake is ringed in the north by magnificent mountains, their summits reaching up to the skies like white steeples. The colors are the most vivid beheld by the human eye, and in this green and blue and white house of worship, it is easy to understand how man — if he is to live — must control his greed.

Years ago the people of the lake decided that man's encroaching presence had to be curtailed. It is extremely difficult to get permission to build a house or any structures in the region. It is true that every landowner around Garda could become rich if their beautiful land would be developed like that of Miami Beach, but the people here know that if that happens the beauty is spoiled, the quality of life is crowded and lessened, the lake is polluted, ultimately replacing the perfection of Nature by the imperfection of man. Because of the ecological foresight of the people of Garda, it is possible for us now to see its true beauty. Higher motives and more vital needs than greed have prevailed here, and the lake region will be here a hundred, or a thousand years hence, as it is now. If the people do not lose their way — it will remain as it is for a thousand or even ten thousand years from now. To think that my descendents, long after my passing, will be able to come here and see it the same way that I see it now — touches a chord in my heart. The lake's beauty, resting in harmony with its people, reinforces the lessons of race, demographics, ecology and economics.

Until those who are concerned about the preservation of the Earth's ecology become concerned about the preservation of our European human ecology, the planet has no hope of environmental salvation.

What Is a Nation?

In the English Language the word *nation* is derived from *nescare*, a Latin word meaning, "to be born." Inherent in the word is a sense of generation or descent. In the common vernacular it has the following definition (from the *Random House Electronic Dictionary*):

> **nation** n.
> **1. a body of people, associated with a particular territory, that is sufficiently conscious of its unity to seek or to possess a government peculiarly its own.**
> **2. the territory or country itself.**

In the real sense then, nation means a people conscious of itself, seeking a government peculiarly its own. It is far more than simply a territory or piece of geography, a "country."

Such a definition magnificently expresses what the modern nation states came to mean, and it explains the tyranny and the ultimate disunity and strife that comes with the geopolitical state that is based not so much on a common ethnic heritage, but a political formation carved out by the force of religion, hereditary title, or simply conquest.

Each nation possesses a government peculiarly its own. Whether the nation is composed of one race or ethnic derivation or of a multitude of races. Of the Western nations, there is more harmony in those that have more ethnic unity, more strife and alienation in those that are more multicultural and multiracial. Even the small genetic differences between groups of one race can have dramatic consequences, especially in combination with religious division. One can see such in Northern Ireland and what was once Yugoslavia.

The disintegration of Yugoslavia after the fall of Communism is an example of the triumph of the national principle. Created artificially in the ashes of the First World War from the breakup of the Austro-Hungarian Empire, the only considerations used in the creation of Yugoslavia were political ones. Ethnic-cultural realities were ignored. Only the imposition of royal dictatorship in the 1920s and then Communist tyranny until the 1980s could suppress the national and spiritual longings of the various peoples. The Croats, the Serbs, the Bosnians and the other ethnic minorities all wanted a government to reflect their own heritage and character. As more democratic freedoms emerged, an inevitable conflict and division occurred as well. Democratic government brought with it a more accurate expression of the sentiments of the people as opposed to the unnatural governments imposed by power.

Governments often see one ethnic segment impose its will over another. The segment in power is usually in the majority, but it is sometimes a minority. When the majority group dominates, there is almost always less opportunity and happiness for the minority elements. When a minority ethnic group has power over a majority, political and economic suppression is inevitable; otherwise it could not for long sustain its power. The driving force of ethnic nationalism exists in all nations where there are sizable minorities, whether it be in Uganda or in the United States, in Zaire or New Zealand. The greater the respective percentages of the minorities, inevitably the greater conflict. That conflict can be lessened when the minorities have a degree of autonomy in their own regions.

Genetic differences imprinted by tens or even hundreds of thousands of years find expression in unique cultural, economic, social, and political terms. Within nations they can be manifested by social segregation, whether it be in White flight in America or distinct neighborhoods of Irish Catholics or Scottish Protestants in Northern Ireland. Differences between Scots and Irish are very minor in comparison to the gulf between Scots and Ugandans; or Irish and Ugandans, yet the differences are still enough to result in a clash of cultures and wills that results in hatred, strife, and violence. Differences between people of European origins are small enough to be overcome by intense social interaction and a unifying culture, as shown by the example of the United States. In Northern Ireland, however, the ethnic difference is exacerbated by sharp religious division, as well as by long-standing political confrontation. The combination of these three factors leads to almost irreconcilable differences.

Multiculturalism can be imposed only by tyranny; it is never a result of the free will of the people. In almost every case, governments that have embarked on multiracial immigration policies have done so in opposition to the people's wishes. Widespread popular opposition to immigration found in America also exists in every other nation enduring massive alien immigration. Canada, Britain, France, Germany and Italy have all had public-opinion polls showing strong opposition to immigration, while their governments have embarked on opposite policies.

Proposition 187, which California voters approved by a wide margin in 1994, sought to restrict taxpayer funding of government services to illegal immigrants. But the courts have prevented its implementation. What will happen to the political, social, and cultural desires of native Californians — those who made the state so attractive in the first place — when immigrants make up the majority of California's voters?

Real freedom is possible only in societies that are essentially made up of one race and oriented to the natural desires and values of that heritage.

The massive immigration in America of the last decades of the 20th century and the first few of the 21st century, combined with taxpayer-subsidized minority birthrates, will lead to conflict challenging the very foundation of America. If the people of European descent are knowledgeable dedicated, and willful, they shall prevail. If they are weak, they and all their works of beauty, all their material achievements and even their genotype itself — will be washed away in the remorseless tides of history.

At the same time that I learned of the real threat to our very existence as a people, I began to learn about the attack on our people's most basic and fundamental structure: the family. The same egalitarian forces that proclaimed racial equality, alleged that the fundamental psychological differences between the sexes were caused by environmental conditioning. They began to tear at the fabric of the family itself.

CHAPTER 14:

SEX AND SOCIETY

See Jane

See Jane. She is a fighter pilot.
See Susan. She is a firefighter.
See John. He is a nurse.
See Fred. He takes care of the house and the children while Susan fights fires.

Such is representative of the new readers found in our kindergartens. It is symbolic of the dogma of sexual equality that suggests that it is normal, in fact -- just as normal for women to be fighter pilots, combat soldiers, firefighters, carpenters, and for men to take on the role of traditional mothers. The basic premise of modern feminism is that aside from some minor biological inconveniences, men and women are psychologically identical. Differing male and female behavior and abilities are said to be solely the result of "conditioning" by their environment.[310]

In the 1960s, mainstream media and academia granted the new goddess of sexual equality a revered place beside the icon of racial equality. By the beginning of the 1990s, however, hundreds of new research studies swung the scientific pendulum toward the recognition of innate sexual, mental, and behavioral differences. Yet, the legal, social, government, and entertainment establishment ignored them and continued on their feminist way.

I was, of course, unaware of the controversy over sexual differences as I grew up in my middle-class neighborhood of Gentilly Woods. I knew girls were different in a lot more ways than just their physical appearance. At a young age, I disliked girls for their feminine ways. Ultimately, as I grew to manhood I came to thank God for their wonderful differences.

In grade school, the activities of my friends and me outside the classroom limited our intimate experience with girls. We played very rough versions of baseball, basketball, football, tag, wrestling, boxing and other hard contact sports. We would sometimes even play tackle football on the unforgiving, black asphalt street in front of my house. Nothing could excite us more than the prospect of a camping, hunting or fishing trip. We wanted war movies; the girls desired love stories.

We endeavored to take apart engines and toys to see what made them work (often failing to put them back together properly), while they wanted to dress their dolls. Our tiny toy soldiers and tanks and canon were deployed by the hundreds in great strategic battles, while the little girls we knew focused on the acute detail of the dress and the personal fantasy lives of their favorite doll. We assembled model airplanes and cars; they were interested in making things that were pretty. While they made bouquets, we made coat-hanger slingshots. While we wanted to dissect frogs and other animals and insects to satisfy our insatiable curiosity of what made them tick, they wanted to focus their love on kittens, puppies, and anything soft and cuddly, especially if it was very young and helpless.

I knew one girl who was an exception to the rule, her name was Ali Thompson and she came out and played almost as rough as we did. She'd rather climb trees than play house, and she loved my exotic pet collection of everything from toads to possums. She did, though, have a feminine side that was distinct from my friends and me, and she seemed able to move in both worlds without being perfectly at home in either one, though as she got older she became more and more feminine.

There was no place for most girls in our boyish world. To us they were alien beings. We made fun of their dainty and delicate ways, and even more fun of boys that acted like "sissies." My sister was five years older, and in the same years that I busily behaved as tough and daring as I could (and sometimes as gross as I could be), her femininity blossomed. Perfect timing! Our rooms were mirror's images of each other's in the upstairs of our cape cod, but we two siblings, unlike a mirror and its suitor, had no harmony in our opposites. Our clash of values led to terrible fights and battles. In those times, my sister convinced me that girls were to be avoided at all costs!

Because of countless examples in the classroom, I knew that girls were generally the best students, and the most articulate when the teacher had questions for the class. As I progressed in junior high school and high school, I began to get closer to girls. Some became friends, and as I matured, others became desires of the heart as I answered the call that Nature placed in me. They captivated me with their soft curves and beautiful faces, their sweet fragrances, and the elegant way they moved. When they spoke with such soft tones, sometimes their words could be almost hypnotic, and when I spoke of something that made me passionate, they listened more acutely than a boy ever could. The song of their femininity with which I was so out of tune as a young boy, slowly became a wonderful melody. By the time I was a freshman in high school, my friends and I still saw girls as very different from us, but now they had become source of attraction beautiful and mysterious.

Sexual equality was almost as pervasive in my high school classrooms and on television as racial equality was. However, it found much less popular acceptance. In the 1960's, Whites, especially those who were more educated and wealthier, seldom encountered Blacks and when they did, they were unrepresentative of the typical Negro. The lack of personal contact combined with the pervasive egalitarian propaganda contributed to beliefs in racial equality. Unlike the different races at the time, members of the opposite sex were ubiquitous. Easily observable sexual differences in behavior made selling feminism a more difficult proposition for us to swallow. It was obvious to most men and women that women differ from men more than simply the differences in sexual equipment.

The establishment by the mid-1960's insistently decreed that no vital psychological differences exist other than those induced by upbringing. [311] By the 1990's sexual egalitarians had retreated before an onslaught of scientific evidence that genetics and biology shaped the sharply different behavior of men and women.

Unlike the racial question, I didn't enter the sexual equality argument with the establishment view. By the time I developed an interest in studying the subject, I had already read many books and scientific research papers on the power of genes to influence intelligence and behavior in individuals and races. It seemed logical to think that the psychological differences between the sexes are the result of genetic imprinting, rather than simply social conditioning.

The middle of the 1980's saw a sea change in the scientific community. Many social scientists, psychologists, biologists, anatomists, physiologists, and geneticists released important new studies detailing the powerful and inherent sex differences in behavior that go far beyond those dealing simply with procreation. The evidence was so abundant that it even began to seep into popular culture. [312] People began to reference men and women as being right-brained and left-brained. [313]

Differences between the psychology of men and women were not nearly as important to me as the race question. Still, it was a fascinating subject and one that has great bearing on our lives, values, attitudes, politics, and, of course, our evolutionary development.

Brain Sex

With the development of the modern computer, electron microscope and other technological advances, genetic research and understanding increased dramatically. Later breakthroughs such as MRI (magnetic resonance imaging), ultrasound, CAT scans, and electric-impulse imaging have given scientists the opportunity to precisely measure the size, architecture, and even study the functioning brains of living people.

Although it was initially politically incorrect to study racial or sexual differences, the exploding genetic knowledge and understanding has inexorably led to greater knowledge of inherent sexual and racial differences.[314]

An example of how adjacent studies led to understanding of sexual differences is shown by the research of Psychologist Herbert Landsell in Bethesda, Maryland.[315] In studying patients who had experienced brain surgery, those who had part of the right hemisphere removed displayed strikingly different psychological effects than those who had had part of the left hemisphere removed. Landsell and many other researchers proved that the left side of the brain more influences verbal skills such as reading, writing, and speaking as well as the orderly processing of information. People who suffer injuries to the left side of the brain often have difficulty speaking and processing information in an orderly fashion. Those who have had damage to the right side of their brain lose their sense of direction, their spatial understanding and their ability to do well on abstract intelligence tests. They often get lost, sometimes even in their own homes. The right side of the brain processes visual information and spatial relationships.[316]

Landsell found that when the left hemisphere of the brain was damaged, men lost most of their language skills but those women kept most of theirs. Men were, in fact, three times more likely to lose their language skills than women who were injured in exactly the same area of the brain. When men suffered damage in the right side of their brains they lost their abilities (as demonstrated) in abstract IQ tests, while women were only slightly affected.[317]

What the research indicated was that while each side of the brain focuses on certain skills and activities, men's brains are more divided and specific in function. In women both sides of the brain engage in spatial and verbal function.

In recent years there have been many studies that have mapped distribution of electrical activity in the brain while performing certain functions. They consistently show men having electrical activity primarily in the right side of the brain while taking abstract tests, while the electrical activity in women is more balanced in both hemispheres.

One factor in this differentiation is the *corpus callosum*, the tissue that connects the two hemispheres together and handles their communication with each other. It is consistently bigger in women, in relation to brain weight, and it has more connections.[318] Research has shown that fluency and articulateness correlate with the number of connections between the hemispheres, the more connections, the more fluent.[319] Such affords a biological reason as to why in countless studies women have shown superior verbal skills to men.

Understanding the brain differences between men and women helped me to begin to understand the deep psychological differences between the sexes that are reflected in varying talents, abilities, and even different attitudes toward life.

Looking into behavioral differences between the sexes, I studied the physical differences of the brain first and then the psychological ramifications. It became obvious from the outset that the differences between the average male and female brain of the same race are far less dramatic than between the brains of the average White and Black. However, the clear sexual distinctions in the function and architecture of the brain result in clear differences in mental abilities and personality between the sexes.

It is now accepted that women exceed men on the verbal parts of IQ tests and men show more ability in the abstract parts of the tests. [320] In higher mathematics the difference is striking.[321] In the largest survey on the subject ever conducted, Dr. Julian Stanley and Dr. Camilla Benbow grouped mathematically brilliant students by sex. [322] Boys were thirteen times more likely than girls to be found in the highest category. On the other hand, girls had striking superiority in verbal skills.

Girls speak earlier than do boys,[323] and they perform better in reading, writing, grammar, spelling and punctuation. [324] They are more fluent and better communicators. Boys suffer almost exclusively from speech defects such as stuttering, and they outnumber girls almost 4 to 1 in remedial reading classes. [325] Women also are better at organizing and putting an orderly sequence to events and objects.

Dr. Camilla Benbow did not want to discover such results on sexual differences. She now believes in a biological basis for the difference. "After 15 years of looking for an environmental explanation and getting zero results, I gave up," she says.[326]

The most obvious difference between the sexes, other than their reproductive systems and body types, are the descriptions of character referred to as masculine and feminine. In the closing years of the 20th century, scientists are making discoveries that offer strong evidence that genetics and other biological factors are the primary forces that determine the differing behavior of the sexes. They show a strong biological component in homosexuality, sexual deviance and the disparate sexual behavior between men and women that causes marital disharmony. [327]

In an earlier chapter on racial evolution, I discussed the fact that the evolution of the Black race in Africa led to a different set of imperatives for Black males than for White males in Europe and Asia. In Europe, evolutionary forces favored the genes of males who protected and provided for their mates and children. The harsh climate of the ice ages also favored the nuclear family rather than the polygamy of sub Saharan Africa. Because of women's dependence on males in the cold climes, women who were less sexually promiscuous and more selective had greater chance of survival. If they more easily gave up their sexual favors to an uncommitted male, their genes and that of their children were more likely to die in the incredibly harsh conditions.

Fundamental differences between the brain architecture of men and women lead to sexual attraction, and also to societal and familial difficulties.[328] For the race to survive, men needed to have a natural sexual attraction for the females and the women for the males. So each sex has an inherent difference in brain structure that causes the male and female brain to find attraction in the characteristics of the other. Because of the division of labor between men and women, men/hunting – women/gathering and child rearing, the brains between the sexes evolved to facilitate those talents. Hunting requires more spatial skills, while mothering requires more verbal skills. Hunting requires aggression, individualism and risk taking, while mothering requires a whole set of special talents, such as altruism, risk avoidance and individual submission to the needs of the child.

If we understand these genetic drives, behaviors, and talents forged by millions of years of evolutionary development, then we can begin to understand the fundamental differences of men and women in many areas of modern life.

XY, XX — Only Part of the Sex Story

In my high-school biology class, even the most inattentive students took an interest when the teacher turned to sexual reproduction. Even the most academically-challenged of the students learned that when a mother's X chromosome matches with a Y chromosome from the father the child will be a boy and when the father's sperm fertilizes the egg with a X chromosome, it will be a boy. XX equals a girl; XY equals a boy.

Science over the last thirty years has shown that the above is not necessarily true. [329] If a genetically male XY embryo is deprived of male hormones, the newborn baby will generally look and behave like a female and even resemble a female in sexual organs. And, if a genetically female, XX embryo is exposed to large amounts of male hormones, it will generally look and behave like an almost normal male.

Near the age of six weeks the sex of the fetus is programmed.[330] If a male, the genetic blueprint of the fetus produces cells which manufacture large amounts testosterone and other androgens. These hormones in combination with DNA direct the construction of the child much as a toy manufacturer molds a doll or a toy soldier. If a female is genetically-programmed, the machinery produces a very small amount of testosterone, and the fetus develops female and a girl is born.

Whether or not the fetus develops into a male or female depends mostly on the presence, or lack of male hormones, primarily testosterone. Actually the natural brain is female in its basic form, and only the bathing of the fetus in large amounts of male hormone can change it to a male-structured organ. Male hormone at the six-week stage of the fetus is about four times the amount normally seen in childhood. It also peaks again at puberty. When the threshold changes in the brain take place, testosterone levels increase.

The amount of testosterone introduced into the fetus, as well as the timing of its addition, can dramatically affect both the physical structures of the sex organs and the brain architecture. A male fetus may have had enough male hormone to be born with male sexual organs, but not enough to pattern the brain in a male orientation. When this occurs the child becomes male in sexual organs and physical appearance but the brain is female. From the brain's point of view, it is a female trapped in male's body. On the other hand, a female fetus could develop female sex organs and then receive amounts of male hormones that could end up constructing a male-patterned brain, a male brain trapped in a female body.[331]

The process can be shown in a number of studies that have been done with laboratory white rats. In a genetic sense, they are not that far away from humans on the evolutionary continuum. They have brains and a central nervous system, similar reproductive systems and sexual organs, and testosterone. It is easy to study the hormonal effects on the developing brain in rats because they are born helpless with a minimally developed brain. The newborn rat brain is in a stage of development that corresponds to a human fetus just a bit older than six weeks: the critical time when sexual identity is established.

When scientists castrate a newborn baby male rat, he becomes essentially female. [332] He develops the characteristics of the female brain.[333] In female rats the left side of the brain is thicker, and in males the right side is thicker.[334] The hypothalamus has a distinct male and female pattern, and the different sexes have different lengths in the nerve cell connectors and the pathways to different parts of the brain.

Not only does the brain of the genetically male castrated rat develop the structure of the female brain, but his behavior mimics that of the female rats as well. He becomes markedly less aggressive than typical males, and he will groom other rats in the female pattern.

On the other hand, when scientists inject a newborn female rat with male hormones, the brain cells develop into the male architecture. The masculinized female rat will adopt male behavior patterns and attempt to mount females; she will show male-like high aggression levels.

Researchers produced an almost identical result in Rhesus monkeys, mice and a number of other animals. When they inject male hormones into pregnant mothers at the same stage of development that corresponds to the setting of the human embryo brain, genetically female monkeys form male-patterned brains[335] and later male behavior patterns of aggression and sexual behavior. Upon injecting pregnant mothers with female hormones such as estrogen, which tend to block the male hormone in the fetus, males are born with the female brain structure and show female behavior patterns.[336]

The same results can be seen in the numerous children of human mothers who have had abnormal amounts of male hormone at the time of the development of their fetus' brain. Male hormone in greater or lesser amounts than normal can come from a number of sources. The most common can simply be that the fetus' hormone production can be genetically faulty. The hormone-producing mechanism of the fetus itself can also be affected by drugs or diet. In addition, male hormones or male hormone blockers can themselves be introduced into the fetus through the mother's hormone production, or by the taking of drugs or medications. A major source of anomalous hormone levels is adrenal or ovarian tumors of the pregnant mother.

Scientists have tracked the development of children who are born to mothers who had medical conditions that produced abnormal hormone levels or who took medications that could have affected the hormone levels in their developing child at its fetal stage. The evidence from such studies is dramatic.

A condition in women called adrenogenital syndrome results in the production of a male-like hormone. Pregnant women who have this condition have had genetically female babies born with normal female organs but sometimes under-developed male organs as well.[337] Surgery can easily remedy the male anomalies, but the brain has often developed along male lines, resulting in typically male behavior. Girls born with this condition are typically more aggressive, seek the company of boys rather than girls, shun dolls in favor of toys of cars, trucks and building blocks, have little interest in feminine clothes, and exhibit slower development in reading and writing skills.

What study after study reveals is that what are traditionally described as gender roles of men and women have such a strong biological base that they often supersede a powerful environment.

John who became Joan who became John

In 1973, a sexology researcher, Dr. John Money,[338] in a well-received and much-publicized research paper, argued that gender roles are plastic and formed chiefly by conditioning.[339] His paper centered on an anonymous child whom the researcher referred to as "John." When he was only a few months old, he required an operation to repair a botched circumcism. The operating surgeon accidentally amputated John's penis. Under the doctor's advice, the parents allowed them to make the child into a girl (as is often done in similar cases, because it is easier to fashion female rather than male genitals). The doctors removed his testicles and remaining penis, and surgically constructed a vagina. John's parents raised John as girl. They changed his name to Joan, dressed and raised the child as a girl, and even later gave her female hormone treatments, never telling her the truth about the tragic accident. Even female psychiatrists were engaged to help reinforce the child's feminine identity.

Dr. Money wrote a paper about the child and ignoring a number of warning signals, reported that at an early age he (now a she) had well-adapted to the new gender role with the strong conditioning of the parents. Feminist researchers, writers and the popular media cited the case of Joan as glowing proof that gender roles were purely the result of environment rather than biology.[340]

In 1997, Dr. Milton Diamond of the University of Hawaii-Manoa in Honolulu and Dr. H. Keith Sigmundson of the Ministry of Health in Victoria, British Columbia, published an in depth follow-up on the case of John-turned-into-Joan.[341] They revealed a startling turn of events in Joan's development.

Even as a child, Joan repeatedly attempted to urinate standing up.[342] Her mother tried to show her how to put on makeup but she wanted to imitate her father shaving instead. She rejected dolls and dresses. She sought the company of boys rather than girls. At the age of 12, she was given female hormones and grew breasts. She grew intensely unhappy and considered suicide. Finally, with no knowledge of her real sexual identity, at the age of 14 she refused to continue the hormone treatments and simply refused to live as a girl any longer. At that point her tearful parents told her of the surgeon's tragic mistake. Although she was understandably bitter, her dominant emotion was relief. She said, "For the first time everything made sense, and I understood who and what I was."

Joan changed her name back to John, requested male hormone shots, had a mastectomy and ultimately, a phalloplasty to fashion a penis from skin grafts. John later married, adopted children, and is quite well-adjusted for the ordeal that he went through.

The Origins of Homosexuality

Mainstream psychology once portrayed homosexuality as a product of youthful sexual experiences, parental attitudes and behavior, even order of birth. Both the academic and popular literature was so rife with this environmental explanation; parents of homosexuals often asked the question, "What did I do wrong?" They thought that their son's or daughter's homosexuality was a result of something they did or did not do. Just as biology has explained female and male patterns of behavior, so it offers the most powerful explanation for sexual preferences as well, while acknowledging that environment can obviously play a role as well.

The pioneer in revealing role of biology with mate selection was Dr. Gunter Dörner.[343] He discovered that sex-related aspects of the brain are laid down sequentially. [344] In studies of rats, he found that the later rats are castrated the less feminine they became. On the other hand, female rats are masculinized by the introduction of male hormones at different stages of their early development. After meticulous and detailed study, he concluded that there are three levels of sexual development. He calls them 1) *sex centers* (meaning the sexual organs themselves), 2) *mating centers* (the areas of the brain which affect the choice of mating partners), and 3) *gender-role* centers (the areas of the brain that determine typical gender behaviors and skills such as spatial versus verbal skills). [345]

Each center of development can be dramatically affected during its stage of maturation. In the mating center level the sexual mating preference is established. Evidence suggests that this takes place primarily in the brain's hypothalamus. The final stage of development is the gender-role center that determines the architecture of the brain. This center affects levels of aggression; verbal and spatial skills; and individualism or group ethics.

In terms of sexual preference, Dörner found that the hypothalamus of the male homosexual physiologically behaves in precisely the same way that the normal female hypothalamus does. When injected with estrogen, the hypothalamus of females responds by producing more of it. In male heterosexuals who are injected with estrogen, there is no production of additional female hormone by the hypothalamus. However in male homosexuals injected with estrogen, there is production of more estrogen just as in the normal female. Such would seem to provide strong evidence that the area of the brain that is most concerned with sexual mating preference is physically different in many homosexuals.

There are many other studies that explain the biological role in most, but not all, homosexual behavior. One study investigated on a long-term basis 136 children whose mothers had treatment with female hormones during their pregnancy. [346] Those children had double the probability of being unmarried as those whose mothers were not so treated. Studies of girls who experienced high levels of male hormones in the womb reveal more male typical behaviors such as rejecting dolls and later in life have more likelihood of bisexual and homosexual behavior.

Even stress in the mother can reduce the amount of male hormone in the male embryo.[347] Female rats that are subjected to severe stress have male offspring that are attracted to other males. In people, corresponding periods of stress occur at times of war or devastation. In a study of male children born in Germany during the Second World War, homosexuality is found to be more common than in males born in peaceful periods before or after the war. The highest rate of male homosexuality is found in children conceived and born in the most devastating and stressful period of the war, during its last few months.

The sexual centers hypothesis also offers an explanation for some typical forms of homosexual behavior. Most homosexuals take the same promiscuous view of sex as heterosexual men; they see sex as an end in itself, not necessarily as an adjunct of a loving relationship.[348] The male brain patterning coupled with the female mating preference (preference for men) frequently results in inordinate numbers of sexual partners, with the average homosexual having many more sexual encounters with different partners than heterosexual men did. The male imprint of the gender-role is still prevalent, but the mating center, probably related to hypothalamus, is abnormal. Of course, some homosexuals are effeminate and display more normal feminine behavior patterns. In these homosexuals the gender as well as the mating center has been affected.

Arriving at an understanding of the biological factor in homosexuality affords an explanation of why it and other sexual aberrations are much more common in males than females. When one understands that the basic brain is in fact female and only the introduction of male hormones can transform it into the male form, it is obvious that much more can go wrong in the developing male brain. If little happens hormonally to the female brain, it will grow up normal. It is no wonder why males are much more likely to become homosexuals than women are to be lesbians. Males are also far more likely to be transvestites or embrace other forms of sexual deviance.

The Future of Homosexuality

Research also shows that biology is not the only factor in homosexual or other kinds of sexually deviant behavior. There are certainly some homosexuals who have had no abnormal hormonal imbalances and there are many well-adjusted male heterosexuals who have a female-biased brain wiring as a result of abnormal hormone levels in the fetal stage. But it seems pretty clear that tendencies toward homosexuality are rooted at least as much in biology as in conditioning. The homosexual brain pattern is the result of abnormal hormone levels at the time of the development of the brain structures that affect mating preference. The source of these hormone levels can come simply from the genes that affect brain architecture, or from the genes that affect delivery of the hormones that influence that architecture. In addition to the genetic factors in the fetus, the hormone levels at critical stages of the fetus can be affected by hormonal conditions in the mother's system. These conditions can be determined by the mother's genetic makeup or from pathology, diet or medical treatment.

The homosexual community has enthusiastically greeted the scientific news showing the influence of biology in homosexual behavior. [349] Their argument is that homosexuality for them is a natural condition, and that they should not be faulted for doing what seems normal to them. Some of the "religious right" see the scientific news as a threat for exactly the same reason. They do not want to accept the idea that God has made some people who are biologically oriented to homosexuality. [350] Yet, it must be bluntly acknowledged that God also allows some people to be born with the genius of a Shakespeare or the intelligence of a doorknob. Some humans are born with horrible diseases, while others keep their health to old age despite unhealthy habits.

Because some people are born with a homosexual tendency does not necessarily make it natural or normal as far as the species is concerned. It may be "normal" for them, yes, but not normal for human behavior and societal values. For some, criminal behavior is as natural an expression as musical talent is to another. But criminal behavior is certainly not desirable in a society. I am not equating homosexuality to criminality, but there are obviously many inborn traits that can be hurtful. Just because a trait is inborn does not make it necessarily healthy or "normal."

Until 1973, the American Psychiatric Association referred to it as a mental disorder, a problem to be treated as one might treat schizophrenia (In fact for many, homosexuality is a symptom that is secondary to a severe mental disorder such as schizophrenia). [351] It was only as recently as 1990 that the INS (Immigration and Naturalization Service) changed its policy that considered homosexuals undesirable visitors and immigrants. [352] Even though psychologists have had some limited success changing the sexual desires of homosexuals (primarily, these are of the "conditioned" type), they have had more success with simply helping them cope with it.

Homosexuals die decades younger than heterosexuals, from a host of maladies. They suffer mental problems ranging from depression to psychosis, and have suicide rates many times that of heterosexuals. Homosexuals and other types of sexual deviants are overrepresented in crimes such as mass-murder, child seduction and molestation. Male homosexuals have seduced and abused millions of underage boys. Their unclean sexual habits and ultra-promiscuous lifestyle have resulted in spreading the worst communicable plague in this century, the specter of AIDS, which has not only killed millions of their own, but also millions of others, including tens-of-thousands who contracted the virus from blood transfusions.

It is undeniable that irresponsible homosexual behavior fuels the havoc of AIDS. The epidemic should be viewed as a horrific scandal and a source of shame to the gay community. Instead, AIDS activists condemn heterosexuals for "not doing enough" to find a cure for AIDS.[353] The "Gay Disease" has also led to medical and other costs that have extracted billions of dollars from the economy and a disproportionate percentage of the medical research dollar. AIDS research with its politically correct and trendy status has diverted research money that is needed for diseases and conditions that afflict far more people. For example, the American government spends more on AIDS research than it does for research on cancer, a disease that millions more suffer from and die from than AIDS. And few cancer victims are ever given the chance that homosexuals have had, for AIDS "victims" contracted the disease by irresponsibly engaging in clearly high-risk sexual conduct.

All this from a virus that could have been stopped in its tracks by simple responsibility and a change in conduct among homosexuals themselves. Instead, many homosexuals continue to promote publicly their promiscuous lifestyle in often sexually immodest gay parades and confabs.

The raw truth is that homosexuality is damaging, devolutionary, unhealthy and unesthetic. It leads to disease, maladjustment, suicide and a host of other social ills. Saying that it is natural to those who practice it does nothing to alleviate its maleficence. One could easily argue that smallpox is natural, therefore it shouldn't be impeded; or even that HIV/AIDS is a life form that is also one of God's creations, and so we have no right to inhibit it. I sympathize with the unhappy predicament of homosexuals and am saddened by their loss of health, happiness and life. Although homosexuality is often portrayed as a harmless lifestyle, when its superficially humorous characterizations are put aside, homosexuality is a behavior that damages both its participants and society at large.

What could be done to alleviate both their own misery and that of society? For those who begin life biologically normal, the mores and values of our society can affect greatly the adoption of homosexual behavior. The first way to lessen the suffering associated with conditioned homosexual behavior is to change the conditioning itself. If the popular media warned of the consequences of homosexual behavior, and if flagrant homosexuals retreated a bit back into the closet by societal taboo, few biologically normal people, especially at vulnerable ages, would end up experimenting with or adopting such lifestyle. Such would help steer those on the biological-sexual margins toward the heterosexual norm. Far fewer of those without a homosexual brain bias would ever be converted to homosexuality.

The fact that homosexuality is approved today as a perfectly acceptable lifestyle by educational instruction and the media makes young people more susceptible to homosexual seduction and orientation. As noted previously, homosexual males certainly have the most sexually predatory and promiscuous of all the sexual orientations. Media approval of the degenerate homosexual lifestyle is equivalent to the media promoting the acceptability of drugs, or smoking, or drinking to children. The ugly reality is that homosexuality lessens the average life span far more than smoking, drinking, or occasional drug use. Whether or not one accepts the rights of homosexuals to conduct themselves as they see fit, certainly society should not foolishly endorse such activity.

One can understand the homosexual's pain and alienation in a society that is geared toward the heterosexual lifestyle. And one can surely sympathize with the anguish often created from the physical and mental problems that rise from his condition. But it makes no sense to lie and say that such a sexual orientation is perfectly normal. If homosexuality were in fact normal, we would not even be here, because heterosexual reproduction is how we survive. We do not shower derision on those afflicted by tuberculosis, but at the same time we certainly don't tell young people that it is acceptable to adopt a lifestyle that puts them at risk for acquiring that disease.

I am sure that there are thoughtful homosexuals who understand why such behavior can never be considered moral in a healthy society. Many who recognize their condition and their limitations can still lead productive, even meaningful lives. There are those who do not try to seduce the young into their lifestyle, and who understand why such can not be tolerated. Many do not attempt to make over the mores and morals of the society to fit their own perverted image or lifestyle. Some find a way to live with their affliction of desires in ways that do not undermine either the health of themselves or of the nation. Those who can live responsibly and tactfully, we should respect.

There is much promise that the biological causes of homosexuality can be alleviated as well. Medicine is rapidly finding ways to detect, treat, and cure illnesses and imperfections of children, even while they are still in the womb. Thousand of babies have already been cured of debilitative conditions by such techniques. It is now possible to monitor the presence of hormones in the expectant mother and in the fetus itself.

If a little girl was getting abnormally high levels of testosterone from the mother's medication or diet, such that it would likely cause the female child to be born with freakish male organs or perhaps a male-biased brain, would not any decent-minded person help the mother change her diet or medication so the child will be more normal and healthy? Or what if a male fetus was getting androgen blocking hormones which would eventually cause the boy to develop into a stunted form of manhood in which he would endure undeveloped, stunted and malformed male organs and possible sterility? Or what if the abnormal hormones resulted in a homosexual bias in the child? Would hormone treatment be justified to bring the androgens within a normal range? I can not imagine how any caring and thoughtful person could answer anything but "yes" to these questions. I am certain of what almost all prospective parents would answer.

There will be those who say that taking such steps would be tantamount to "playing God." But just try to prevent such a pontificating moralist from taking a laboratory-created medicine that he needs for his own health or well-being, and he would accuse you of bloody murder! When parents have the option to protect their children, they will. Because of that I believe that the problems of biologically derived homosexuality, organ abnormality, and sexual deviation will be tremendously lessened in the Natural Order coming in the next century.

Sometimes it appears that Nature seems far away from us in our gleaming steel and concrete cities, but she still stands inexorably in evolutionary judgment over our genotype. Bringing homosexuals out of the closet, accompanied by a full flowering of their decadent lifestyle, has resulted in the decimation of their own ranks. Decades of the AIDS virus, hepatitis epidemics and gay suicide will lessen the influence of this group in the future. Genes prone to homosexuality that have been hidden for centuries have been exposed by homosexual intemperance to a new level of vulnerability. Those genes are being extinguished in great part by the AIDS virus and other pathogens as unmercifully as wolves cull the impaired from a reindeer herd.

In addition to the pathologic enemies of homosexuality, its shameless public promotion has also engendered an intense aversion to it in the new men and women who will make the revolution coming in the next century. The epitaph of homosexuality, in part written by AIDS, will forbid it to return to a stylish acceptability. Even as I write these words, the homosexual counterculture is being decimated by its own incontinence. In the latter years of the 21st Century, homosexuality will become far less of a problem than in our decadent age.

The Inherent Sexual Differences

As is so often the case, biology wills out, even when facing the severest of environmental obstacles. Men and women differ far more than simply in preferring trousers or skirts. The difference is in the areas of the brain that affect some of the most basic skills, attitudes, behaviors, and preferences. It is true that every difference is not present in every male and every female. But, just as some men are smaller than some women and some women are larger than some men, it is still true that on average, men are physically larger than women. After decades of research and thousands of psychological studies, here are some of the *generalities* of *differences* between men and women. They are obviously not representative of every individual man or woman:

Men are better at spatial skills, higher mathematics, and map reading — Women are better at language and communication skills including reading, speech, and writing.[354]

Women are better with people, while men are better with things. In fact, men are object oriented, while women are people oriented.

Men and women have fairly close IQs, with women exceptional in verbal skills while men showing more spatial abilities.[355]

Men are better at chess. Women are better at scrabble.

Women are more empathetic, and unselfish; men are more self-centered and result-oriented. Men are oriented to the "big picture," better at overall concepts and patterns and are generally more adventuresome, curious, and risky; while women are more home oriented, people oriented and security-minded.

Women are far more law-abiding than men, and men are many times more violent and criminal than women.[356]

Men are more likely to make sacrifices of home-life for career, women are more likely to sacrifice career for home-life.

Most women find meaningful relationships necessary for sexual involvement; men are more sexually promiscuous. Men are far more sexually obsessed and more often sexual deviant[357] and have a higher frequency of homosexuals.[358]

Men tend to be more dominant, women more submissive.

Women are more group-oriented social beings, men are more individualistic. Women are more prone to be more truthful or sometimes truth bending, while men tend to tell more outright lies.

Men are more selfish, more individualistic and more often loners. Women are more altruistic, more group oriented, and more bonding.

Women are more responsive to the auditory and sensory organs, in fact they hear[359], smell[360], taste and feel[361] more acutely than men, while men are more responsive to visual stimulation and have better depth perception.[362]

Men are more single-minded and persistent[363], women more easily distracted and diverted by an external stimulus.

Men are more skillful drivers than women, but women are more responsible drivers in regard to laws such as speeding and drinking while driving. Women take fewer risks on the road.

Women and Racial Politics

Research has shown that women are far less hostile to outsiders than are males, that they are more emphatic, more giving and more altruistic. These are wonderful traits when it comes to our own societies, but are catastrophic in the multiracial quagmires of the modern Western nations. It is critical that women as well as men understand that their own best interests are indelibly bound to the survival of their own race and culture. It has always amazed me that the modern women's feminist movement has been politically allied with non-White activists. Whatever criticism is due Western man in regard to his treatment of women in Western History, and there are certainly faults to be found — in comparison to Third World societies, Europeans have been infinitely more benevolent to the welfare and well-being of women.

White-rights activist, Melissa Weaver Prince, eloquently points out that the highest attributes of the true feminine character are found in the ideals of Europe. "Women must realize that to erase the lines of distinction that have set the races apart for eons would not strengthen, but rather obliterate the rights and empowerment we have fought so hard to attain."[364]

Women are far better off in every capacity in the White nations rather than in the dark ones. In the non-White world women face horrors that Western women can barely contemplate. For instance, millions of women are brutalized and disfigured by female circumcism and infibulation. [365] In many Third World nations Women are suppressed to the status of little more than chattel property. Every aspiration of the so-called woman's liberation movement would be lost if society shifts from White to nonwhite rule.

Women should look at the epidemic levels of rape committed against them by Blacks in America, and this occurs while there is still a White majority infrastructure that somewhat holds back the criminal, sexual-impulses of Black males. Acquainted with the onrushing realities of race, only a masochistic woman could welcome the darkening of America or Europe. And frankly, only a committed woman-hater could want such a result.

The liberal media in America has cleverly appealed to the natural empathetic and altruistic instincts of women developed from the evolutionary demands of childbearing and rearing. These natural instincts have been perverted and diverted to the minorities in our midst and, indeed, all over the world. Women's kind hearts, for which all of us are thankful in our mothers, are little defense against those who are incapable of paying back kindness with kindness. Idealistic women, and many men as well, want to believe in a peaceful and harmonious world where everyone has the same talents, the same temperament, the same potential for achievement, and the same capacity for the higher love that they themselves have in their own heart. They are like lambs under the delusion that lions are vegetarians. There will always be war, whether or not it is waged on the battlefield or in the boardroom, the political campaign or the struggle for power among the groups that make up oligarchies. The world will always have contesting individuals and contesting groups, and if our genotype is to survive, we must have warriors.

The will to power and dominance is more prevalent in the male. In the less cerebral and more elemental races, that male character trait is unchallenged, raw and powerful. Right now, in America and elsewhere there is racial struggle for dominance on many different levels. If women view their world from their own gentle spirit and reference, rather than understanding that others have an entirely different reference, they will feed a lion who does not see them through the feminine eyes of empathy and love, but as the meal that the gods have laid at his table.

Women and Childbearing

One of the most tragic consequences of the feminist movement has been the genocide of many of the most gifted and talented women in the Western world. Feminism, in elevating career and denigrating homemaking, has funneled some of the most intelligent women in the West into careers that have caused the delay of childbirth and often even barrenness. White women of the highest educational, professional and income levels are the least prolific women in America. Sterilization, birth control, abortion, late marriage, non-marriage or exogamy in these talented women contributes to devolution of our genotype. By remaining childless, the very genetic treasure that makes these women so outstanding in career and work is lost forever to our people. Not only does our race suffer a genetic loss that is incalculable, but also they themselves suffer a loss in the spiritual side of life that often they do not realize until it is too late.

Women in the Workforce

A whole generation of women has been forced into the workforce. Where once almost any wife could choose to work outside the home if she so desired, now they have little choice in the matter because of economic necessity. For many women, the forced labor is not of the glamorous type portrayed in the egalitarian media. The vast majority are not employed in high-powered professions, but in jobs that often are repetitive, unexciting, and physically exhausting. When the workday is done, they return home to the traditional role of providing the primary care for children and husband. Increasingly, they face the difficult task of single parenting. Although many women through self-sacrificial effort have balanced both job and family, many more have found that it is difficult, on a long-term basis, to fill both roles to her own or her families' satisfaction. The stresses on both husband and wife often sabotage the relationship and hurt the healthy development of children.

It must be made possible for women to choose homemaking and child rearing in the early years of their married life without economic hardship. No matter the cost we must ensure this, for there is nothing more important to our society than the healthy and happy family. Nothing is more precious and beautiful than a healthy, happy and well-educated child.

Sex and Marriage

Hoggamus, Higgamus Man is polygamous
Higgamus, Hoggamus woman is monogamous[366]

The opening couplet of this was the insight of William James while experimenting with nitrous oxide. He simply stated something in a flippant way that writers and poets have known since the beginning of time. Scientific research bears out that it is universally true, and its origin comes more from the genes than from the mores instilled from society. In fact, it appears that the inherent greater promiscuity of the male and more reliable fidelity of the female is what wrote the social codes that have been called the double standard. When I was in school it was still said that if a girl slept around she was a slut, while if a boy did so he was just a healthy, red-blooded young man. In thirty years, little has changed despite the concerted effort of feminists to encourage women to be as promiscuous as men.

The old order established after the end of the Second World War attempted to construct a society in the West that was in denial of the Natural Order bequeathed by our genes. Men and women were treated as though they were potentially identical beings. When men and women are taught that they are identical in needs, desires, perspectives, actions and behaviors, there can be little tolerance when a spouse does not meet the other's standards or expectations.

"Why can't he (or she) understand why this is important to me. He (or she) must not care," might be the refrain of a disillusioned spouse.[367] This (situation) could be alleviated by the understanding and toleration that might come with knowledge of the inherent differences between the sexes. Chronic frustration often produces extreme agitation and sometimes neurosis. Men and women often try vainly to change one another into their own image. Only when we accept the differences that Nature has wrought will more harmony result.[368] That is not only true in families and relationships but in society as a whole.

The interest of girls in faces and people, and the interest of boys in things[369], carries right over to the fact that in sex and relationships girls are more interested in the relationship part of the equation and boys are more interested in the sex.[370] One writer explained it by perceptively saying that woman gives sex in exchange for love and man gives up sex for love.

In a clever survey of hundreds of college students, when attractive young survey-taking ladies bluntly offered to take their male respondents back to their apartment and have sex, over 50 percent said yes. But when attractive young male survey-takers bluntly offered the same thing for women respondents, more than 99 percent said no.[371] This Survey took place in the 1980's after decades of so-called women's liberation.

Can this difference be accounted for simply by the social codes and conditioning? Let us look at the record. Studies of male children whose fetuses in the womb had received large amounts of estrogen or other male hormone blockers, are markedly less aggressive than normal males. Males who get larger than normal amounts of male hormone are more aggressive. Studies of overly aggressive individuals reveal that they usually have a more ardent sexual drive than the less aggressive. Differences in the brain that produce variations in aggression and sexual drives have an easily understandable evolutionary origin.

The nuclear family became the prevalent feature of European and Asian societies while polygamy dominated African tribes. Genetically driven polygamous behavioral tendencies are more pronounced in the African, but such urges are still present in Europeans and Asian men as well. Extremely cold climates also select for self-control and delayed gratification. In the plentiful days of spring and summer, arduous and demanding preparations must be made for the winter ahead. Momentary pleasures and seductions must be put aside if the tribe and its members shall survive. Emotional control is clearly more evident in Europeans and Asians, contrasted to the undisciplined emotions of the African, and it can also be a major factor in the familial differences between them. Europeans, using reason and self-control have more natural ability to reign in their libidinous urges for the sake of more abstract objectives. They can delay sexual gratification and evoke behavior that serves their loved ones.

Man's genetic nature makes him far more likely to be infidelitous than are women. Yet, Western men must continue to use the cerebral areas of the brain rather than submit to the primitive limbic parts of the brain. To do so is to act in accordance with the evolutionary imperative of the healthy and happy marriage and family. In the White race it has clearly been our evolutionary path to do so, and even if the ideal is sometimes compromised, it remains the ideal for which we strive.

The radical feminist movement has promoted a female equality that consists of lowering the female of the species to the basest character traits of the male. In early days of the women's movement, it celebrated the family and acted in every way as guardians of its sanctity and well-being. Movements such as the Women's Christian Temperance Association campaigned against child and woman labor in the sweatshops of America and Europe. They also sought to restrict the societal carnage of alcohol, drugs, prostitution, and even back in the 1920s recognized the possible risks of smoking. Women's Movement pioneers such as Margaret Sanger and many others wrote and spoke of the need for eugenics to improve the quality of the race and lessen the numbers who would be born suffering from debilitating mental and physical hereditary conditions.[372]

Since the Second World War, the radical feminist movement, led by Jewish women such as Betty Friedan, Bella Abzug, and Gloria Steinem — harboring long resentment against Judaic traditions of female dehumanization, created a movement of sexual hatred and envy which they projected on Western society. Instead of raising standards to what was once considered the higher moral level of womanhood, they embraced the basest instincts of the male. They lowered the feminine standards that once made women a rock of stability and morality in a churning sea of male sexual aggression.

Instead of protecting the home, and saving women from the sweatshops and workhouses, feminism has forced women by the millions from the queenship of the home to the serfdom of menial and unrewarding labor outside of the home, all while the demands of family and children inside the home continued.

Instead of endeavoring to encourage men to be responsible in their sexual conduct, it lowered millions of women to the man's level. And how have women paid for the increased man-like promiscuity? The toll for the violation of their inner nature accounts for millions of unwanted pregnancies and the resulting devastation of abortion. They have paid in the hardship of raising children alone. They have paid in massive epidemics of venereal disease that have often resulted in barrenness. They have paid in the easier access of their married men to available women and thus even more infidelity and abandonment. They have paid in the highest divorce rate in history. As the once unassailable sanctity of womanhood and motherhood disintegrated, the rate of sexual crimes against women multiplied. In mimicking the once overwhelmingly male weaknesses of smoking and drinking, they have suffered disease and damage to their countenance and their bodies, and now they have found a pernicious equality in these addictions and in the pain inflicted upon them.

Although the gaggle of feminist crones spout their gospel of equality of men and women, by their adoption of the values and standards of men, they have become ersatz male chauvinists. Nature has decreed that women can never be as male as males, and that men can never be as female as females can be. As a whole, women will always be second-rate imitations of men doing men things, while men, of course, will be second-rate imitations of women's special qualities.

As the early women's movement leaders understood, women are absolutely superior to men doing the things that women do best. It is the feminists who decided that the traditional nature of women was inferior and the traditional characteristics and role of men are superior. When will we understand that our differences only complement each other, serve each other, enrich each other? What we find attractive in the other sex is precisely the difference between us. Instead of wailing at the differences, should we not celebrate them? Author Bryant H. McGill says, "The interlocking of the unique differences between man and woman create a higher being, and that is precisely what a good marriage is."[373]

In my childhood my favorite books were the works of Sir Walter Scott. It was before my adolescence, so I found much appealing in the courage of the knight, and paid little notice to the romantic passages. In high school, I came to love every feature of the truly feminine woman. I dug up my old worn novels and read them again. I finally realized that in the soul of the knight there could be no chivalry, no honor, no courage, no sacrifice, none of those ideals without the majesty of womanhood. It was ultimately at the root of what the knight fought for and what he would even sacrifice his life to defend. It became clear to me that women and men are ultimately simply a different part of each other. In that sacred union between men and women is the family, and in those families is the race, and in that race lies our evolutionary pathway to the stars.

America, and the entire Western world, is rushing headlong to its demise. The destruction of the race that created our civilization, along with the attack on the most elemental unit of the race : the family — can only lead to disaster. In the 1960s I could see America's fate in the into the next century as clearly as I see it now. I wondered then how this calamity could be occurring. It seemed so unnatural for a people to orchestrate their own demise. As I continued my reading, a number of sources suggested that an alien element within our society constituted the driving forces behind these changes: organized Jewry. I read a couple of articles that mentioned the fact that radical feminism was led by Jews along with the Civil Rights movement. I was appalled at the allegation which to me smacked of religious intolerance, and refused even to consider it. Then, one day at the Citizen's Council offices I encountered an elderly and very colorful lady by the name of Mattie Smith who began a whole new period of discovery in my life.

PART III

THE JEWISH QUESTION

CHAPTER 15
THE JEWISH QUESTION

In the last decade of the 20th century, to criticize the Jewish people, religion, or the nation of Israel is considered the worst of moral crimes. Jews are the most sacred of sacred cows, and anyone with a negative word about them finds himself labeled an "anti-Semite." Once a man acquires that label, true or not, nothing can redeem him from what the mass media views as the ultimate sin. So, irredeemable as I am — I have the freedom to write and speak openly about an issue that few dare to breach. I am not an anti-Semite and I reject that epithet. However, I must address what Henry Ford called the "world's foremost problem,"[374] a problem now critical to our people's survival and freedom.

It is almost impossible in our Holocaust-saturated world to even say the word "Jew" without arousing emotion. The mass media of the Western world have made that so with their unrelenting packaging and repackaging of the "Holocaust." As the respected British historian David Irving says, "It's spelled 'Holocaust' with a capital 'H' — trademark applied for."[375] The Holocaust has gone from being a sidebar of the Second World War to the point where the war has become a historical footnote to the Holocaust. During the one year before this book's publication, which is well over 50 years after the end of the war, my local (actually "local" is a misnomer, for New Yorkers own it) daily newspaper, *The Times-Picayune*, had dozens of news and feature articles exploring varying aspects of the Holocaust. In that year, the same paper had barely mentioned the Soviet Gulags where between 20 and 40 million people died, and had only one story that mentioned the Cambodian murder of three million. Not a single article appeared on the slaughter of 30 to 40 million in Red China.

Looking through old newspaper microfiche, I discovered that during the late 1990s there are at least 10 times more news articles on the Holocaust than there were in the late 1940s or 1950s. Rarely does an event become more talked and written about as time passes further from it. For instance, the subject of the Second World War took up a far greater proportion of movies, TV programs, documentaries, books

218 MY AWAKENING

and magazine articles in the late 1950s than in the late 1990s. Not so for the Holocaust: the further we seem to get away from the event, the more it bludgeons us.

It would be a Herculean task to even count all the Holocaust-oriented television news stories and specials, the documentaries and "docudramas", the books (both fiction and nonfiction), the magazine articles, movies and plays. Tales of Holocaust victims, relatives, survivors, war crimes, criminals, reparations, Holocaust-related art and literature, remembrances and memorials bombard us almost daily. A multimillion-dollar Holocaust museum stands in Washington, D.C. It is right on the most sacred soil in the American Pantheon, the Mall near the Smithsonian Institution, financed in no small part by our tax dollars. Interestingly, it was built long before there was any real effort to build a memorial to the Second World War. It is a massive, modern version of the Chamber of Horrors at *Madame Tussaud's Wax Museum*.

The Holocaust is not the only Jewish trauma of which we all must grieve, for we see many painful historical accounts and dramatic Hollywood productions about other historical persecutions of the Jews. Jews are victimized by Arab terrorists in the Mideast, by fascists in Europe, and even by Klansmen in the United States. There is a virtually inexhaustible supply of books, articles, movies and plays about individual Jews who have suffered from evil anti-Semites.

Each year, tens of thousands of stories about intelligent, compassionate, unselfish, creative, moral and courageous Jews fill two-foot TV screens and 30-foot movie screens; our newspapers, magazines, and books; our playhouses, pulpits and podiums; our radio waves and satellite transmissions. There are thousands of portrayals of persecuted Jews as innocent, noble and heroic; while their opponents are portrayed as the embodiment of evil. No group on Earth has better public relations than do the Jewish people.

Whether it is Pharaoh's army with swords unsheathed, chasing the Hebrews or the Czar with his anti-Semitic Cossacks, Hitler with his SS minions dressed in black, an unnamed Palestinian terrorist trying to kidnap Israeli schoolchildren, or the more intimate story of a sensitive Jew mistreated by an anti-Semitic businessman — we have all seen the anti-Semitic stereotype, seen the skeletal bodies, and we have all shared the Jewish pain. I know of this firsthand, for it was true for me as a young man.

At age 12, reading *Anne Frank: Diary of a Young Girl* in the school library, I recoiled from the inhumanity of anti-Semitism. By the time I had finished the book, I felt as if I had lost members of my own family. With my shirtsleeves, I covertly wiped away the moisture that had welled up in my eyes.

Only a few times did I have any discussion with my father about Jews, about whom he had only praise. He spoke about my great uncle Nathan, a Methodist minister who had converted from the Jewish faith and married my grandfather's sister, my great aunt Gussie. Father had enormous respect for Nathan and carried it over to the rest of the people he called the "Hebrews," thinking that his term carried more dignity than the word "Jews." At various times he described the "Hebrews" as hardworking, smart, thrifty, and accomplished. "Thrifty" was an accolade that made a distinct impression on me, because I knew that Father looked upon that particular trait as one of the most important. He hated waste of any kind. I learned that lesson at the dinner table a hundred times, having to eat every bite of my food before being excused. I thought thriftiness was as Scottish as the Duke family, but hearing that it was Jewish, impressed me.

Recitals of the Holocaust and Bible stories formed my primary impressions of the Jewish people. Cecil B. DeMille's movie classics, as typified by *The Ten Commandments*, led me to identify contemporary Jews with the heroic "Israelites" of the Old Testament. I formed a deep admiration for the "Chosen People."

How, then, did I go from my early fawning opinion of the Jews to being eventually described as a dangerous "anti-Semite" by the powerful Jewish advocacy organization: the ADL (the oddly-named Anti-Defamation League of B'nai B'rith)? No Jew had ever wronged me; I wasn't taught anti-Semitism by my parents or friends, nor did I blame them for the crucifixion of Jesus Christ. Although I categorically reject being labeled anti-Semitic, I certainly believe that — as any other people — Jews deserve praise for their accomplishments and, conversely, they should not be immune from criticism for their failings. The only problem is that in post-World War II, Holocaust-saturated America, any criticism of Jews as a group is viewed as the moral equivalent of condoning mass murder.

If one criticizes any part of Jewish history or conduct, of intolerant aspects of their religion, or even Israel's Zionist policies, he inevitably acquires the label "anti-Semitic," a term that could not be more damaging or prejudicial. If one speaks, however, about the routine mistreatment of Indians in American history, he is not described as "anti-American." Those who express horror about the excesses of the Spanish Inquisition are not labeled "anti-Christian" or "anti-Spanish."

The same media that prohibits even the slightest criticism of Jews has no reluctance to demean other groups. White Southerners, Germans and Evangelical Christians — these groups get more than their share of ridicule and debasement. The portrayal of the slack-jawed, green-toothed, ignorant, racist, hateful, murderous, rural White Southerner has become a stereotype in Hollywood films. One of the best-selling books of the late 1990s is the media-promoted *Hitler's Willing Executioners*,[376] a book that says the German people have something evil within them, something that makes them *all* guilty for the atrocities of the Holocaust. In stark contrast, whenever Jews are mentioned as a group, it is always with a sort of a hushed reverence. What is it about the Jewish people that evokes such unrestrained adulation and visceral hatred?

Once I became convinced that race was important and that people of European descent needed to protect their heritage and culture, I became a young member of the Citizens Council. Often, after class and on rainy summer days, I would go down to the office on Carondelet Street in New Orleans to do volunteer work.

Many fascinating publications streamed into the office from hundreds of right-wing groups all over America. One day, when I finished helping with a Council mailing, I came across some tabloid newspapers called *Common Sense*. It was a conservative, right-wing paper modeled after Thomas Paine's classic broadside; only the message was sharply different from Paine's. "JEWISH-LED NAACP PART OF COMMUNIST PLAN FOR AMERICA!" read one issue's headline. "COMMUNISM IS JEWISH!" trumpeted another. I also found some old issues. The huge headline in one of them predicted, "RED DICTATORSHIP BY 1954!" However, such a warning did not lend much credibility to the paper when looked at in 1965! I found the *National Enquirer*-type headlines ludicrous, but it was hard to resist reading something that scandalous, even if just to laugh at it.

The Sharp Words of Mattie Smith

One of the regular volunteers, Mattie Smith, an elderly lady in a flower-print dress and outlandish hat, saw me snickering at the lurid headlines and simply said, "You know, it's true."

"Red Dictatorship by 1954?" I replied with a smile.

"No," she said, "Communism *is* Jewish. They are the ones behind it."

I thought I would humor the little old lady by politely arguing a bit with her. "Ma'am. How could that be?" I asked. "Communists are atheists; they don't believe in God. Jews believe in God, so how could they be Communists?"

"Do you know who Herbert Aptheker is?" she said, answering my question with one of her own.

"No," I replied, affecting nonchalance.

She was like a tightly coiled spring waiting for release. "He has the official role of chief theoretician of the Communist Party, USA, and he's listed in the *Who's Who in World Jewry*.[377] Leon Trotsky, the Communist who took over Russia with Lenin, was in *Who's Who in*

American Jewry.³⁷⁸ His real name is Lev Bronstein. Both are atheist Communists, and both are proudly listed as great Jews in these books published by the largest Jewish organizations in the world."

Meekly, I offered, "Maybe they were listed because they were *once* Jews."

"You have so much to learn," she said with a sigh. "Under Israel's Law of Return, you can be an atheist Communist and still immigrate to Israel. There are plenty of them too. You only qualify to immigrate if you are a Jew, and a Jew is described simply as being of Jewish descent. So, you see, you can be Jewish and still be an atheist and still be a Communist — and I tell you, Communism *is* Jewish!"

"All Jews are Communists?" I retorted sarcastically.

"No, no, no," she emphatically replied, with much patience in the way she paced her words. "All Jews are not Communists, any more than all snakes are poisonous. But most leading Communists in America are Jews, as well as most of the convicted Russian spies in America, as well as the leaders of the New Left. And historically, most of the Commie revolutionaries in Russia were Jewish as well!"

What Mrs. Smith said made me very uncomfortable. Although it was not yet time to leave, I claimed that I had to catch my bus back home. I left the office hurriedly. Mrs. Smith *had* to be wrong, but I just didn't have the facts to challenge her statements. I resolved to research the issue so that I could show her why she was wrong. Something else bothered me as well, for I felt a little guilty for even talking with someone who said such things about Jews. I was staunchly anti-Communist, and to suggest that Jews were behind the horrors of Communism was, to me, such a terrible allegation that my heart told me that it just could not be true. It was the first time I had been face to face with a person I presumed was an anti-Semite. I was soon running to catch my streetcar.

During the next couple of days I avoided even thinking about the issue, and I stayed away from the Citizens Council office. Finally I picked up and read the two copies of *Common Sense* I had taken home. One copy maintained that the NAACP was a Communist front organization dedicated to the eventual overthrow of our way of life. It purported that 12 Jews and one Black had founded the NAACP, and all the founders were dedicated Marxists with decades of documented Communist affiliations. The article asserted that the only major Black founder of the NAACP, W. E. B. Dubois, was an avowed member of the Communist Party who immigrated to Communist Ghana (where he eventually was buried). Furthermore, the scandalous publication purported that the NAACP was financed by Jewish money and always had a Jewish president. It said that a Jew, Kivie Kaplan, was the current NAACP president and that he was the real leader of the organization rather than its Black "front man," Roy Wilkins. Although the public perceived Wilkins as the NAACP leader, the paper asserted that he actually had the lower rank of national secretary.

The other copy of *Common Sense* was no less startling. It had a long article asserting that international Communism was a Jewish creation and that the Russian Revolution had not really been Russian at all. Jews had supposedly financed and led Communism since its inception, and that they thoroughly dominated the Communist movement in the United States.

This *Enquirer* of the right, quoted many names, dates, and sources to support its incredible allegations. I was very skeptical of its assertions, but the information was too compelling to ignore. For I had learned early on in my racial investigations not to so easily dismiss unpopular opinions.

Despite their seemingly strong documentation, the articles just seemed too bizarre to be true. How could it be that the largest and most powerful Black organization in America was founded, financed, and run by Jews, and Marxist Jews at that — instead of Blacks? How could something so incredible be kept so quiet that most people would not know about it? If the Russian Revolution was truly a revolution led by Jews rather than Marxist Russians, how could such an enormous historical fact be ignored in our history books and in our popular media? Furthermore, I could not understand why wealthy and powerful Jews would foster race-mixing and Communism.

Father had often talked to me about the evils of Communism, and I had been thoroughly anti-Communist since reading books such as *The Conscience of a Conservative* by Barry Goldwater,[379] *None Dare Call It Treason* by John A. Stormer,[380] and *You Can Trust the Communists (To Be Communists)*[381] by Frederick Charles Schwarz. These books and others impressed upon me the penetration of Communist ideology in our society, media, and government.

The Cuban Missile Crisis had occurred just three years before, and Father's plans to build a fallout shelter were still fresh in my mind. He had even purchased food and other survival supplies for it. During that period, the idea of nuclear war went from an abstract idea to the realism of actually preparing for it. In the early '60s, most communities tested the working order of air-raid sirens by sounding them daily at noon. Sometimes, when we lost track of time in school and the noon air-raid sirens went off, we wondered for a moment if the war was actually upon us.

During the Cuban crisis, most adults rationalized that thermonuclear war would not happen because it *must* not happen — because the very thought was too monstrous to contemplate. An 11-year-old is much more prone to believe that someone might pull the switch. Years later, the world discovered that we had actually teetered much closer to nuclear war than most Americans knew at the time. The fact that Communists had put my family in real danger of nuclear incineration contributed greatly to my visceral anti-Communist stance.

One of the *Common Sense* issues mentioned a full-page newspaper article written by Winston Churchill called "Zionism versus Bolshevism: A Struggle for the Soul of the Jewish People." The article had originally appeared in the *Illustrated Sunday Herald* on February 8, 1920. Churchill had maintained that the world's Jews were being torn between an allegiance to Communism on the one hand and Zionism on the other. Churchill hoped the Jews would adopt Zionism as an alternative to what he called "diabolical" and "sinister" Bolshevism. In his well-written article, contemporary with the early years of the Russian Revolution, Churchill described Communism as a "sinister confederacy" of "International Jews" who "have gripped the Russian people by the hair of their heads and have become practically the undisputed masters of this enormous empire." [382]

The article shocked me enough that I had to check its authenticity. It turned out to be genuine. In fact, I found some Jewish references to it bewailing the fact that Churchill's article gave fodder to the anti-Semites of the world. The following is an excerpt from his amazing article.

> **In violent opposition to all this sphere of Jewish effort rise the schemes of the International Jews. The adherents of this sinister confederacy are mostly men reared up among the unhappy populations of countries where the Jews are persecuted on account of their race. Most, if not all, of them have forsaken the faith of their forefathers and divorced from their minds all spiritual hopes of the next world. This movement among the Jews is not new. From the days of Spartacus-Weishaupt to those of Karl Marx, and down to Trotsky (Russia), Bela Kun (Hungary), Rosa Luxembourg (Germany), and Emma Goldman (United States), this world-wide conspiracy for the overthrow of civilisation and for the reconstitution of society on the basis of arrested development, of envious malevolence, and impossible equality, has been steadily growing...and now at last this band of extraordinary personalities from the underworld of the great cities of Europe and America have gripped the Russian people by the hair of their heads and have become practically the undisputed masters of that enormous empire.**
>
> **There is no need to exaggerate the part played in the creation of Bolshevism and in the actual bringing about of the Russian Revolution by these international and for the most part atheistical Jews...**[383]

As an important historical figure as Churchill was, he was still only one voice. I rationalized that he could be wrong about the nature

224 MY AWAKENING

of the Russian Revolution. One of the *Common Sense* articles I read referred to a series of explosive documents (complete with file numbers) from the National Archives of the United States. I wrote to my local Congressman, F. Edward Hebert, and asked if his office could obtain copies of the files for me. A couple of weeks later, on returning home from school, I found waiting for me a large manila envelope from the Congressman.

Certified by the seal of the United States of America, the documents were from the National Archives. They concerned intelligence reports from foreign governments and extensive reports from our chief intelligence officers in Russia during the time of the Russian Civil War in the early days of the Communist revolution. The early 1920s were long before the establishment of the OSS and the CIA. The U.S. Army ran our international intelligence work at that time. One of our military intelligence officers in Russia during its revolutionary period was Captain Montgomery Schuyler. He sent back regular reports

> "There is no need to exaggerate the part played in the creation of Bolshevism and in the actual bringing about of the Russian Revolution by these international and for the most part atheistical Jews..."
> — Winston S. Churchill

ILLUSTRATED SUNDAY HERALD, FEBRUARY 8, 1920.

ZIONISM versus BOLSHEVISM.
A STRUGGLE FOR THE SOUL OF THE JEWISH PEOPLE.
By the Rt. Hon. WINSTON S. CHURCHILL.

THE JEWISH QUESTION   225

to the chief of staff of U.S. Army Intelligence, who then relayed them to the Secretary of War and the President of the United States.

Reading through the lengthy reports gave me a glimpse into a historical period of which few Americans are aware. They reported horrible massacres of thousands of Russian aristocrats and intelligentsia, murdered simply because they could provide effective leadership in opposition to the Communists. Many Americans are at least somewhat aware of Stalin's murder of over 20 million. However, many millions also died in the early days of Bolshevism under Lenin and Trotsky, for it was these men who initiated the first mass killings and the gulags.

The reports also stated, without equivocation, the Jewish nature of the revolution. In one of Schuyler's official reports, declassified in 1958, almost 50 years after he wrote and dispatched them, he states[384]

> "It is probably unwise to say this loudly in the United States, but the Bolshevik movement is and has been since its beginning, guided and controlled by Russian Jews of the greasiest type..."
>
> Robert Wilson, American Army Intelligence Officer in Russia during the revolution. (in official report)

In quoting the graphic language of this official report, my intention is not to offend; but Schuyler's report says what it says, whether we like it or not. In another report, written four months later, Captain Schuyler goes on to quote the evidence of Robert Wilton, who was then the chief Russian correspondent of the authoritative *London Times*. Wilton later went on to pen a number of best-selling books on the revolution, including the widely acclaimed *Russia's Agony* and *Last Days of the Romanovs*.[385] On June 9, 1919, Schuyler cites Wilton as follows:

> A table made up in 1918, by Robert Wilton, corespondent of the *London Times* in Russia, shows at that time there were 384 commissars including 2 Negroes, 13 Russians, 15 Chinamen, 22 Armenians and more than 300 Jews. Of the latter number 264 had come from the United States since the downfall of the Imperial Government.[386]

There was, of course, no reason to impugn the reporting of the *Times* or of Captain Schuyler. I couldn't believe my eyes as I scanned the papers dispersed across the plastic tablecloth on my dining-room table. I wondered how it could possibly be true that the "Russian Revolution" had only 13 ethnic Russians out of the 384 members of its top governing body. Churchill's description of "gripping the Russian people by the hair of their heads" came to life in the pages I received from our own National Archives.

Once I started checking out the leads I would glean from my reading, the National Archives kept spitting out the most incredible documents. Not only did our chief intelligence officer write to the president of the United States about the Jewish nature of Communism, so did our U.S. ambassador to Russia, David R. Francis. In a January 1918 cable to our government, he reported:

> **The Bolshevik leaders here, most of whom are Jews and 90 percent of whom are returned exiles, care little for Russia or any other country but are internationalists and they are trying to start a worldwide social revolution.** — David Francis, American Ambassador to Russia at the time of the Revolution [387]

The National Archives also sent me copies from its files of Communications from Scotland Yard and British Intelligence. The directorate of British Intelligence sent to America and other nations a lengthy report dated July 16, 1919, on Bolshevism abroad. It was called "A Monthly Review of the Progress of Revolutionary Movements Abroad." This lengthy report lists the Communist movements in the major nations of the world. The first sentence in the first paragraph on the first page of this British government report claims that Jews control international Communism.[388]

Years later, as a student at Louisiana State University, I took a course entirely devoted to the Russian Revolution. Neither my professor in his lectures, nor my textbook (*The Soviet Achievement*)[389] made any mention of the Jewish-Russian conflict and the Jewish domination of the Communist Party.

The Jewish role in the Communist revolution was, however, mentioned in many major Jewish publications such as the *Jewish Encyclopedia* and the *Universal Jewish Encyclopedia*. It astounded me to find them actually boasting about the pivotal role of Jews in the Russian Revolution. They even

> **"There is now definite evidence that Bolshevism is an international movement controlled by Jews."**
> — The Director of British Intelligence to the U.S. Secretary of State

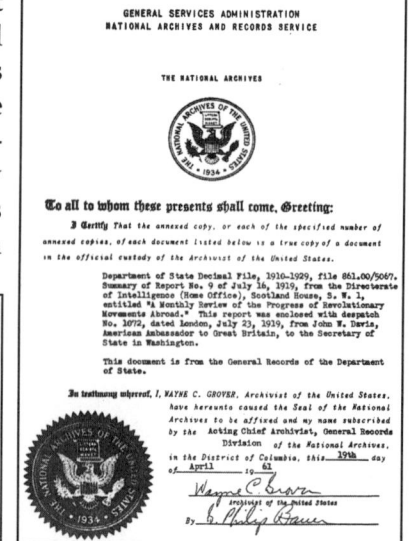

pointed out the effort of the Communist Jews to disguise the Jewish role — a successful effort — for most Gentiles in America and Europe are still unaware of it.

> **The Communist movement and ideology played an important part in Jewish life, particularly in the 1920s, 1930s and during and after World War II.... Individual Jews played an important role in the early stages of Bolshevism and the Soviet Regime.... The great attraction of Communism among Russian, and later also, Western Jewry, emerged only with the establishment of the Soviet Regime in Russia...**
>
> **Many Jews the world over therefore regarded the Soviet concept of the solution to the "Jewish question" as an intrinsically positive approach.... Communism became widespread in virtually all Jewish communities. In some countries Jews became the leading element in the legal and illegal Communist parties and in some cases were even instructed by the Communist international to change their Jewish-sounding names and pose as non-Jews, in order not to confirm right wing propaganda that presented Communism an alien, Jewish conspiracy.**[390]

Trotsky's book, *Stalin,* written in exile, attempted to show that Stalin had played only an insignificant role in the early days of the Communist takeover. Trotsky attempted to illustrate this point by reproducing a postcard widely circulated in the months following the revolution. The postcard depicted the six leaders of the revolution. Shown are Lenin (who was at least one-quarter Jewish, spoke Yiddish in his home, and was married to a Jewess), Trotsky (real Jewish name: Lev Bronstein), Zinoviev (real Jewish name: Hirsch Apfelbaum), Lunacharsky (a Gentile), Kamenov (real Jewish name: Rosenfeld), and Sverdlov (Jewish).[391] Not only does the postcard show the Jewish domination of the revolution; it also illustrates the fact the Jewish Communist leaders shown had changed their names just as reported in the *Encyclopedia Judaica.*

Although the fact of Lenin's Jewish ancestry was kept quiet for many years, Jewish writers are now taking note of it. David Shub, author of *Lenin: A Biography*, stated in a letter to the Russian émigré paper *Novyi Zhurnal*[392] that Lenin's mother was at least Jewish on her father's side and probably so on her mother's side as well.[393]

In addition, a French Jewish periodical, *Review de Fonds Social Juif*,[394] reported that a Soviet novelist, Marietta Shaguinian, was prevented by Soviet censorship from publishing evidence of Lenin's Jewish ancestry. A number of Jewish publications in recent years have disclosed Lenin's Jewish heritage, including the Jewish Chronicle.[395]

JEWISH CHRONICLE JULY 26 1991

Moscow magazine on Lenin's Jewish roots

By ZEEV BEN-SHLOMO
EAST EUROPE CORRESPONDENT

Vladimir Ilyich Lenin, the creator of the Soviet Union, often officially praised as the embodiment of the Russian national genius, had a Jewish grandfather, according to the Moscow mass circulation weekly, Ogonyok.
There have been rumours to this

The Cheka, or secret police, had a Jew, Moses Uritzky, as its first chief, and most of the other subsequent leaders were also Jews, including Sverdlov and Genrikh Yagoda (which is Russian for "Yehuda" — "the Jew") who presided over the pogroms that killed tens of millions. The Soviet propaganda minister during the war was a Jew, Ilya Ehrenburg, who notoriously distinguished himself by his Second World War exhortations of Soviet troops to rape and murder the women and children of Germany.[396] Anatol Goldberg quoted Ehrenburg in his book, *Ilya Ehrenburg* as saying, "…the Germans are not human beings…nothing gives us so much joy as German corpses."[397]

The Communist secret police, which underwent many name changes, including Cheka, OGPU, GPU, NKVD, NKGB, MGB, and KGB, was the most feared police agency in the history of the world, having imprisoned, tortured, or murdered more than 40 million Russians and Eastern Europeans. Even the more conservative Soviet historians of the 1960s were placing the number of murdered

THE JEWISH QUESTION 229

at about 35 to 40 million — figures that do not include the millions more who were dispossessed, imprisoned, exiled, tortured, and displaced. Nobel Prizewinner Aleksandr Solzhenitsyn in his opus, *The Gulag Archipelago*, using the research of a Soviet statistician who had access to secret government files, I. A. Kurganov, estimated that between 1918 and 1959, at least 66 million died at the hands of the Communist rulers of Russia. In *Gulag Archipelago II*, Solzhenitsyn affirms that Jews created and administered the organized Soviet concentration-camp system in which tens of millions died. Pictured on page 79 of the *Gulag Archipelago II* are the leading administrators of the greatest killing machine in the history of the world.[398] They are Aron Solts, Yakov Rappoport, Lazar Kogan, Matvei Berman, Genrikh Yagoda, and Naftaly Frenkel. All six are Jews.

Interestingly, though, during this period of murder and mayhem, Jews were a protected class, so much so that the Communist Party took the unprecedented step of making expressions of anti-Semitism a counter-revolutionary offense, and thus punishable by death.[399]

The Jewish Voice in January, 1942, stated: "The Jewish people will never forget that the Soviet Union was the first country -- and as yet the only country in the world -- in which anti-Semitism is a crime."[400] The *Congress Bulletin* (Publication of the American Jewish Congress) stated:[401] [402] [403]

Anti-Semitism was classed as counter-revolution and the severe punishments meted out for acts of anti-Semitism were the means by which the existing order protected its own safety.

The Russian Penal Codes of 1922 and 1927 even went so far as to make anti-Semitism punishable by death. The book *Soviet Russia and the Jews* by Gregor Aronson and published by the American Jewish

League Against Communism (1949 NY) quotes Stalin remarking on the policy in an interview in 1931 with the Jewish Telegraph Agency:

> ...Communists cannot be anything but outspoken enemies of anti-Semitism. We fight anti-Semites by the strongest methods in the Soviet Union. Active Anti-Semites are punished by death under law.[404]

The Beginning of an Ethnic War

In school, I brought these fascinating facts up with some of my teachers. They in turn were as incredulous as I had been. One suggested that the Jewish involvement in the Communist revolution might have been a result of the long-running historical persecution of Jews by the Czars and, indeed, by much of the Russian intelligentsia. For instance, Tolstoy, Dostoyevsky, and many other prominent Russian writers had criticized Jewish machinations in their books and articles. Russians didn't like it that the Jews used the Russian language for doing business among Gentiles but spoke Yiddish among themselves. Jews were also accused of having an "us versus them" mentality rather than assimilating with the Christian majority.

There had been a running feud between the Russians and the Jews for centuries, and from these conflicts arose "pogroms" to suppress the Jews. This war without borders can be illustrated by the Jewish reaction in the 1880s to the anti-Semitic Russian May Laws. The May Laws of 1882 attempted to restrict Jews from some professions and mandate resettlement of most Jews to their original area of the empire, the Pale of Settlement (a huge area, originally set up in 1772, encompassing an area about half the size of Western Europe, extending from the Crimea to the Baltic Sea, to which the Jews had been restricted).

In retaliation, Jewish international financiers did their best to destroy the Russian economy. *Encyclopaedia Britannica* describes the happenings this way:

> The Russian May Laws were the most conspicuous legislative monument achieved by modern anti-Semitism.... Their immediate result was a ruinous commercial depression which was felt all over the empire and which profoundly affected the national credit. The Russian minister was at his wits end for money. Negotiations for a large loan were entered upon with the house of Rothschild and a preliminary contract was signed, when...the finance minister was informed that unless the persecutions of the Jews were stopped the great banking house would be compelled to withdraw from the operation....[405]

In response to the economic and other pressures put upon Russia, the Czar issued an edict on September 3, 1882. In it he stated:

> For some time the government has given its attention to the Jews and to their relations to the rest of the inhabitants of the empire,

THE JEWISH QUESTION 231

with a view of ascertaining the sad condition of the Christian inhabitants brought about by the conduct of Jews in business matters....

With few exceptions, they have as a body devoted their attention, not to enriching or benefiting the country, but to defrauding by their wiles its inhabitants, and particularly its poor inhabitants. This conduct of theirs has called forth protests on the part of the people,... thought it a matter of urgency and justice to adopt stringent measures in order to put an end to the oppression practiced by the Jews on the inhabitants, and to free the country from their malpractices, which were, as is known, the cause of the agitations.[406]

So, Jews had ample reason to attempt to overturn the Czarist government of Russia, and there is direct evidence they did just that. The *Jewish Communal Register of New York City of 1917-1918*, edited and published by the Jewish community, profiles Jacob Schiff, who at that time was one of the wealthiest men in the world as head of the huge banking house of Kuhn, Loeb & Company. In the article it states how the firm of Kuhn, Loeb & Company "floated the large Japanese War Loans of 1904-1905, thus making possible the Japanese victory over Russia." It also goes on to say,

Mr. Schiff has always used his wealth and his influence in the best interests of his people. He financed the enemies of autocratic Russia and used his financial influence to keep Russia away from the money market of the United States.[407]

Jacob Schiff actually gave somewhere between $17 million and $24 million to finance the Jewish-Communist revolutionaries in Russia, a sum that would be the equivalent of many hundreds of millions of dollars by today's value. Rabbi Marvin S. Andelman, in his book *To Eliminate the Opiate*, cites two sources documenting Schiff's financial

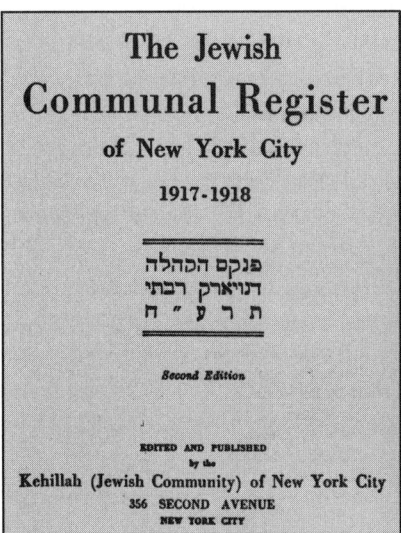

Jacob Schiff and Leon Trotsky, two key players in the Russian Revolution, both found their base of support in New York City.

support of the Communist revolution and ultimate repayment by them.

> **Jacob Schiff is credited with giving twenty million dollars to the Bolshevik revolution. A year after his death the Bolsheviks deposited over six hundred million rubles to Schiff's banking firm Kuhn & Loeb.**[408][409]

It was initially puzzling that the violently anticapitalist Communist Party would be supported by some of the most prominent capitalists in the world. But I finally realized that Russian Revolution was not ultimately about the triumph of an economic ideology, it was about the settling of an age-old struggle between two powerful peoples — the Jews and the Russians — in an ethnic war that tragically ended in the totalitarian tyranny of the Communist dictatorship. Even worse, the score was ultimately settled in the terror of the bloodwashed cellars of the Cheka and the frozen death of the Gulags.

The fact that super-capitalists such as Jacob Schiff could support a nakedly socialist regime such as Communism made me question whether there was something more to Communism than met the eye. What was it about Communism that made it so attractive to Jews, who were largely well-educated non-proletarians, when Communism was supposed to be, in Lenin's words, "a dictatorship of the proletariat"? Obviously, by-and-large, Jews were nothing like Marx's "workers of the world," for no group was more involved in capitalism or the manipulation and use of capital than the Jewish community.

I checked out the Communist personalities that Mattie Smith told me were in the Jewish Who's Who. Atheist Leon Trotsky as well as atheist Maxim Litvinov, the Soviet Minister of Foreign Affairs, are proudly listed in the directory of famous Jews compiled by the leading Jewish rabbinical groups of the world.

Winston Churchill, in his eloquent article "Zionism Versus Bolshevism: A Struggle for the Soul of the Jewish People," had argued that Communism and Zionism were distinct ideologies that were competing, as he put it, "for the soul of the Jewish people." But something didn't seem quite kosher in this supposed titanic struggle, for it appeared that many Zionists also supported Communism and, at least in the early years, many Communists were sympathetic to Zionists. Millions of Jews, even super-capitalists such as Jacob Schiff, supported the Communist revolution in Russia. The struggle seemed to be like that of two brothers who might sometimes argue amongst themselves but who always stand together against their common enemies.

In 1975, I read a book called *Trotsky and the Jews*, written by Joseph Nedava and published by the Jewish Publication Society

(Philadelphia, 1971). The book points out that before the Russian Revolution, Leon Trotsky (born Lev Bronstein) used to play chess with Baron Rothschild of the famous Rothschild banking family.

> **A Jewish journalist (M. Waldman) who knew Trotsky from the period of his stay in Vienna ("when he used to play chess with Baron Rothschild in Cafe Central and frequent Cafe Daily to read the press there").** [410]

What could the Rothschilds, the biggest banking house in Europe, possibly have in common with a leader who wanted to destroy capitalism and private property? Conversely, why would a dedicated Communist be a close friend of the most powerful "capitalist oppressor" in the world? Could it be that they saw Communism and Zionism as two very different avenues to a similar goal of power and revenge against the Czars?

A number of questions arose: 1) Could Communism simply have been a tool they adapted to defeat and rule their Russian antagonists? 2) Were there other peoples with whom the Jews believed they were in conflict? 3) Was Communism originally part of a strategic imperative that reached far beyond the confines of Soviet Russia? These were important questions. I thought that I might find their answers in the philosophical origins of Communism.

I resolved to investigate the ideological roots of Communism. I found *Das Kapital*[411] and the *Communist Manifesto*,[412] in my public library. Karl Marx's books were obtuse, especially the parts developing the Hegelian dialectic, but they made some sense if one believed mankind had a machine-like nature that Marx described. One of my teachers made the poorly thought out comment that Communism was great in theory but faulty in practice. To my way of thinking, to be a great idea it must *work* in practice, and Communism obviously doesn't. There has never been a theory that has promised more human happiness yet delivered more poverty, mental and physical oppression, and more human misery and death.

Inside Judaica
Insights on questions of Jewish interest by Dr. Frederick Lachman, Executive Editor, Encyclopaedia Judaica
Q. Was Karl Marx A Jew?
A. Born in the Rhineland town of Trier (then West Prussia), Marx was the son of Jewish parents, Heinrich and Henrietta Marx. Heinrich Marx became a successful lawyer, and when an edict prohibited Jews from being advocates he converted to Protestantism in 1817. In 1824, when Karl was six years old, his father converted his eight children, the authoritative Encyclopedia Judaica reports. Heinrich, whose original name was Hirschel ha-Levi, was the son of a rabbi and the descendant of talmudic scholars for many generations. Hirschel's brother was chief rabbi of Trier. Heinrich Marx married Henrietta Pressburg, who originated in Hungary and whose father became a rabbi in Nijmegan, Holland.

Until I looked into the foundations of Communism, I had always thought Karl Marx was a German. In fact, I had read that Marx's father was a Christian. It turns out that his father, a successful lawyer, was a Jew who had converted to Christianity after an edict prohibited

234 MY AWAKENING

Jews from practicing law. Much later, in 1977, I read an article from the *Chicago Jewish Sentinel* that revealed Marx as the grandson of a rabbi and "the descendant of Talmudic scholars for many generations."413

Not only was Karl Marx from a long line of Talmudic scholars, he also hated Russians with a passion that could be described as pathological. I looked up Karl Marx in the Jewish encyclopedias, and I found to my amazement that the man who taught him many of the principles of Communism was Moses Hess. As incredible as it might seem, contemporary Zionist leaders venerate Moses Hess as the "forerunner" of modern Zionism.

In *The Encyclopedia of Zionism in Israel*, under the entry for Moses Hess, is found the following:

> **Pioneer of modern socialism, social philosopher, and forerunner of Zionism.... Hess was thus a forerunner of political and cultural Zionism and of socialist Zionism in particular. He became deeply involved in the rising socialist movement. Karl Marx and Frederick Engels acknowledged that they had learned much from him during the formative years of the movement.... —** *The Encyclopedia of Zionism in Israel*414

After months of reading from every conceivable source, I realized that the elderly lady in the offices of the Citizens Council had been essentially right, at least about the origins of the Communist revolution. I felt as if I were sitting on the edge of a volcano. Every new piece of information seemed to both confirm and clarify the issue even more.

In *The Last Days of the Romanovs*, Robert Wilton, on assignment for *The London Times* in Russia for 17 years, summed up the "Russian Revolution" in these words:

> **The whole record of the Bolshevism in Russia is indelibly impressed with the stamp of alien invasion. The murder of the Tsar, deliberately planned by the Jew Sverdlov and carried out by the Jews Goloshekin, Syromolotov, Safarov, Voikov, and Yurvsky, is the act, not of the Russian people, but of this hostile invader.**415

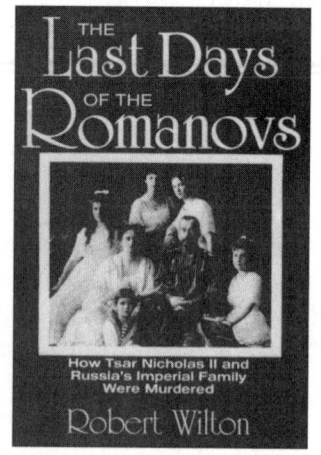

In 1990 a major New York publisher, the Free Press, a division of Simon & Schuster, published a book by Israeli historian Louis Rapoport called *Stalin's War Against the Jews*. In it the author casually admits what we Gentiles are not supposed to know:

> **Many Jews were euphoric over their high representation in the new government. Lenin's first Politburo was dominated by men of Jewish origins...**

Under Lenin, Jews became involved in all aspects of the Revolution, including its dirtiest work. Despite the Communists' vows to eradicate anti-Semitism, it spread rapidly after the revolution — partly because of the prominence of so many Jews in the Soviet administration, as well as in the traumatic, inhuman Sovietization drives that followed. Historian Salo Baron has noted that an immensely disproportionate number of Jews joined the new Soviet secret police, the Cheka.... And many of those who fell afoul of the Cheka would be shot by Jewish investigators.

The Collective leadership that emerged in Lenin's dying days was headed by the Jew Zinoviev, a loquacious, curly-haired...[416]

The once widespread knowledge of the Jewish leadership of the "Russian Revolution" has disappeared from our common knowledge — an example can be found in the *National Geographic Magazine's* May 1907 edition. An article entitled "The Revolution in Russia" describes the Jewish leadership of the terroristic Communist revolution.

THE VENGEANCE OF THE JEWS

...the revolutionary leaders nearly all belong to the Jewish race and the most effective revolutionary agency is the Jewish Bund,...The government has suffered more from that race than from all of its other subjects combined. Whenever a desperate deed is committed it is always done by a Jew and there is scarcely one loyal member of that race in the entire Empire.[417]

The facts were indisputable. An enormous fact of history has been wiped away from the intellectual consciousness of the West as thoroughly as a file can be erased from the hard disk of a desktop computer. In his classic novel *1984*,[418] George Orwell wrote about historical truth "going down the Memory Hole"; such had been the fate of the truth regarding the real perpetrators of the "Russian Revolution."

I asked myself two questions: "Why was the historical truth about the Communist revolution suppressed?" and "How, in a free world, could that suppression have been accomplished?" The first question had an obvious answer in the fact that the forces of international Jewry would not want it generally known that they were the primary authors of the most repressive and murderous evil in the history of mankind: Communism. Obviously, knowledge of that fact does not create good public relations for Jews.

The answer to the second question of "how" was more elusive. I realized that only very powerful forces could suppress important parts of the historical record and create a false impression of a "Russian Revolution" when there were only 13 ethnic Russians in the first Bolshevik government. Obviously the Jews historically did have a lot of power — as evidenced by Jacob Schiff, the Rothschilds, and others — but the power to change the perception of history — that seemed preposterous. Yet only a few months before, when Mattie Smith had told me at the Citizens Council that the Russian Revolution was Jewish, I had thought the idea was ridiculous. Now, I knew differently, and I knew I was just beginning to discover a new reality in the world.

The facts I then knew led to interesting new questions:

- **Does it make me an anti-Semite to accept the historical fact that the "Russian Revolution" was not actually Russian but a takeover of Czarist Russia by an antagonistic, non-Russian nationality?**
- **Is there a historical nationalism among the Jews that is hostile toward other peoples?**
- **Do Jewish interests and the interests of the Christian West synchronize or conflict?**
- **If those interests sometimes conflict, did the well-coordinated, worldwide Jewish effort to fiercely fight for their perceived ethnic interests in Russia have implications for Western Europe and America?**
- **How did their organized power create our "special relationship" with Israel in modern times?**
- **And, finally: Did asking these questions have anything to do with "hate"?**

When I saw programs on television about anti-Semitism, *hate* was the word almost always used to describe any negative opinion about Jews. I felt no hatred toward Jews. My investigation had been purely an intellectual exercise. I was an interloper looking into a world where I did not belong, but it was a world that intrigued me. Pondering the "hate" question, I asked a teacher at school why the word *hate* wasn't ever used by the media to describe the motivation of the mass murder of millions of Russian Christians in the Soviet Union. Certainly, it would have taken a great deal of hate to have committed such monstrous crimes. She had no answer and all I had were a lot more questions.

Once I discovered the shared roots of both Communism and Zionism, I decided to examine the history of the Jewish people, both historical Judaism and the development of modern Zionism. I felt that I had access to the best sources in the world for my investigation. I started with three excellent and exhaustive Jewish encyclopedias.

CHAPTER 16:

JEWISH SUPREMACISM

Powerful and enigmatic, intelligent and creative, idealistic on the one hand and materialistic on the other, the Jewish people have always fascinated me. Few teenagers growing up in the middle '60s, as I did, could have avoided acquiring a positive image of Israel and the Jewish people. Because of my years of Sunday school, my perception of the Jews was even more idealized than most. I was 11 years old when I saw the movie classic *Exodus*.[419] It made an enduring impression on me, so much so, that for a few months its beautiful theme song became my favorite, one that I would often hum or sing.

I remember an episode of embarrassment when my sister and her teenage friends stumbled upon me loudly singing the stirring words, "This land is mine, God gave this land to me." Heroic Israel inspired me. It was as if the Israelites of the Bible transposed themselves to modern times to live out their Old Testament adventures again. My image of Israel strongly reinforced my acceptance of the idea that Gentile intolerance had caused every historical conflict with Jews.

After I had discovered the extensive Jewish involvement with early Communism, which I had hoped was an uncharacteristic blight on Jewish history, I began to ask questions one dared not ask in polite society about this interesting people and religion. I had read about the many persecutions of the Jews throughout history, including their great suffering now called the Holocaust (in the mid-60s that term had not yet been appropriated by the Jews to apply exclusively to their sufferings during the Second World War — holocaust merely means, as it always has, destruction of anything by fire).

Mark Twain wrote, "Every nation hates each other, but they all hate the Jew." Somehow I found the impertinence to ask *why*. In a historical context, almost every major nation of Europe had expelled them, some repeatedly, after renewed waves of Jewish immigration. What was it, I wondered, about the Jewish people, *that inspired such hatred?*

Normally, when we study historical conflicts between nations or peoples, we do it dispassionately. For instance, in examining any war from long ago, we list as objectively as possible, the grievances and rationales of the opposing sides. When studying the War for Southern Independence, every American school child learns the Southern arguments for secession and the Northern arguments for forced union. In contrast, when studying the historical disputes between the Jewish people and others, only the Jewish point-of-view is acceptable.

In early 1995, Congressman Newt Gingrich, Speaker of the House, fired his newly appointed congressional librarian, Christina Jeffrey,[420] for having once suggested that history students, when studying the Holocaust should also be exposed to the German point of view. She was fired in spite of her high standing in her profession and notwithstanding her long and cozy relations with the powerful Jewish ADL (Anti-Defamation League of B'nai B'rith). The very suggestion that there could be another side to any issue affecting Jews is decried as "anti-Semitic." In both the entertainment and news media, the only permissible opinion is that Jews are always innocent victims persecuted by intolerant Christians and other "anti-Semites." *Maybe they were always innocent, and all the other peoples of the world were always unjust*, I thought. *But they weren't so innocent in the Russian Revolution.* I realized I could not evaluate the issue fairly until I had read both sides.

Looking for answers, I returned to where I had first learned my respect for the Jews: in the Holy Bible. I went back and reread the Old Testament, paying close attention to the relations between Jews and non-Jews. In contrast to the universalism of the New Testament, the Old Testament is extremely ethnocentric. It goes to great pains to identify the Israelites as a "special people," or a "Chosen People," and it painstakingly traces the genealogical descent of the Children of Israel. Many thought-provoking passages forbid the intermarriage of Jews and other tribes. In the book of Exodus, Moses responds to Israelites who had sexual relations with Moabite women by ordering their execution. In Ezra, God commanded those who married non-Israelites to cast off the wives and even the children of such unions.[421]. Some of the bloodiest writings I had ever read detailed the Jewish people's annihilation of its tribal enemies.

The massacres of Canaanites, Jacobites, Philistines, Egyptians, and dozens of other peoples are gruesomely recorded in the Bible. In today's terminology, we describe the slaughter of entire peoples as genocide. Old Testament Jews spared neither men, women, children or even the animals and pets of their enemies.[422] The following are just a few among dozens of similar passages found in the Old Testament:

> **And they utterly destroyed all that was in the city, both man and woman, young and old, and ox, and sheep, and ass, with the edge of the sword . . . (Joshua 6:21)**[423]

> Then Horam, king of Gezer, came to help Lachish; and Joshua smote him and all his people, until he had left him none remaining.
> And they took Eglon, and smote it with the edge of the sword, and all the souls that were therein. (Joshua 10:32-34)[424]
>
> And they took Hebron, and smote it with the edge of the sword, and the king thereof, and all the cities thereof, and the souls that were therein; he left none remaining. (Joshua 10:37)[425]
>
> For the indignation of the Lord is upon all nations, and His fury upon all their armies: he hath utterly destroyed them, He hath delivered them to the slaughter.
> Their slain also shall be cast out, and their stink shall come up out of their carcasses, and the mountains shall be melted in their blood. (Isaiah 34:2-3)[426]
>
> But in the cities of these peoples that the Lord your God gives you for an inheritance, you shall save alive nothing that breathes, (Deuteronomy 20:16)[427]

As a Christian, I could not explain what appeared to be celebrations of genocide. I acknowledged that God is unfathomable and unknowable. However, I could not help but have sympathy for those massacred, including thousands of innocent men, women, and children. It is easy to imagine how the few who survived those massacres felt about the "Jews." Of course, the Jews were not unique in their pursuit of ethnic cleansing; many other early peoples had visited genocide on their enemies.

With the coming of Jesus Christ and his advocacy of love and kindness as recorded in the New Testament, the Old Testament advocacy and record of genocide is little recollected by modern churches. When by chance a modern Christian stumbles across passages of the Old Testament condoning genocide, he dismisses them as the sad happenings of a remote biblical era — one now mitigated with the New Covenant of love that Christ brought.

The Israelite record on racial integrity and supremacy is quite clear:

> Neither shall thou make marriages with them; their daughter thou shalt not give unto his son, nor his daughter shalt thou take unto thy son. (Deuteronomy 7:2-3)[428]
>
> ...For thou art a holy people unto the Lord Thy God: the Lord Thy God has chosen thee to a special people unto himself, above all people that are on the face of the earth. (Deuteronomy 7:6)[429]
>
> Now therefore give not your daughters unto their sons, neither take their daughters unto your sons, nor seek their peace or their wealth for ever, that ye may be strong and eat of the good of the land, and leave it for an inheritance to your children for ever. (Ezra 9:12)[430]

Members of racial groups might argue about their comparative history, or abilities, or spirituality. But to suggest that God favors one people over all others — even to the point of advocating and committing genocide to make way for the "Chosen"? Certainly, that must be the epitome of racial supremacy.

Modern Christianity deals with the ethnocentric and genocidal parts of the Old Testament by focusing on the loving aspects of the New Testament. One example is the way that Jesus Christ moderated Old Testament law such as "An eye for an eye and a tooth for a tooth," to "turn the other cheek." The Jewish religion, however, had no comparable figure to moderate the extreme ethnocentrism of the Old Testament. Perhaps the Jewish teacher who offered the greatest moderation toward Gentiles was Maimonides, considered by most Jews as the foremost figure of European Judaism. Even Maimonides decreed that Jewish physicians should not save the life of a Christian unless not saving him would "cause the spread of hostility against the Jews." [431]

The early spread of Christianity by the Apostle Paul encouraged Christians to become more tolerant of different ethnic groups. Paul himself was a Jewish Pharisee who converted to Christianity and preached much of his life to Gentiles of diverse nationalities. The Christian faith had intolerance for other beliefs and other Gods, but not of other tribes. Evangelists of the ancient world themselves came from assorted peoples and preached across the known world. Of course, Christians could and often did harbor xenophobic tendencies, but their nationalistic or ethnocentric attitudes found their origins in their own cultures, not in the teachings of the New Testament. The book of Galatians makes the point quite well that the chosen people, "neither Jew or Greek," are now those who accept the salvation of Jesus Christ.[432] Salvation is based upon acceptance of faith, not simply on blood.

The Jewish religion had an evolution quite different from that of early Christianity. The Jewish people and their religion were entwined. Belief in God was necessary to preserve the tribe and secure God's blessings as much as preserving the tribe was important to safeguarding the religion. However, according to the Zionist State of Israel, race is far more important than religious belief. A prospective immigrant does not have to practice or believe in Judaism to immigrate to Israel, in fact he can be an outspoken atheist and Communist, he must only prove Jewish descent. Protection of the ethnic identity of the Jewish people became the main reason for Judaism's existence.

In the Middle East (and later throughout the world) the Jews mingled with many peoples, and yet they preserved their heritage and their essential customs. They are the only ethnic minority in Western nations that has not assimilated after thousands of years. In Babylon, they lived under slavery and then under domination for hundreds of years and developed a code that enabled them to survive and even prosper while living as a minority in an alien society. When they emerged from their Babylonian sojourn, they were stronger, more organized, and more ethnocentric than ever before.

The Talmud: A Jewish-Supremacist Doctrine

In rejecting Jesus Christ and the love and tolerance he preached, Judaism proceeded on its path of chauvinism. It culminated in the pages of the Talmud, an encyclopedic exposition of Jewish law and custom, compiled by hundreds of rabbis over the centuries. The *American Heritage Dictionary* describes it as "constituting the basis of religious authority for traditional Judaism." The Talmud was first transcribed in Babylonian times, and the oral tradition is many centuries older. By the sixth century AD it was put into written form, becoming the most important religious work of the Jewish people, the chief canon of their religion. In it they finally codified their most chauvinistic tendencies.

Herman Wouk, the very popular Jewish writer,[433] illustrates the influence of the Talmud as follows:

> **The Talmud is to this day the circulating heart's blood of the Jewish religion. Whatever laws, customs, or ceremonies we observe — whether we are orthodox, Conservative, Reform or merely spasmodic sentimentalists — we follow the Talmud. It is our common law.**[434]

As a 16-year-old, during one of my visits to the Citizens Council offices, I had found a book called *The Jewish Religion: Its Influence Today* by Elizabeth Dilling.[435] It interested me because the large format of the book contained complete photocopied pages from parts of the Talmud officially compiled by Jewish scholars. I remember skipping Dilling's commentary and going right to the translations. One of the first passages I read really surprised me. It said,

> **A heathen [Gentile] who pries into the Torah [and other Jewish Scriptures] is condemned to death, for it is written, it is *our* inheritance, not theirs. (Sanhedrin 59a)**[436]

If a 16-year-old boy reads something forbidden like that, he is certain to read on. The passage was completely alien to everything I had always understood about religion. Why would they not want all men to read the holy word the same way Christians want to "spread the good news?" Just what is in these scriptures that would oblige the Jews to kill a Gentile that read them? Why would public knowledge of Jewish scriptures be dangerous to Jews? I went to the library and found some old translations of parts of the Talmud. It was not long before I came across other, even more amazing passages such as:

Balaam [Jesus] is raised from the dead and being punished in boiling hot semen. Those who mock the words of the Jewish sages and sin against Israel are boiled in hot excrement. (57a Gittin) [437]

Because Christian scholars periodically obtained copies of the Talmud, Talmudic scribes hoped to deceive them by using the name Balaam to denote Jesus. In *The Jewish Encyclopedia*, under the heading "Balaam," it says, "...the pseudonym 'Balaam' given to Jesus in Sanhedrin 106b and Gittin 57a."[438] The Talmud repeatedly uses obscure words to denote Gentiles with an assortment of names such as Egyptian, heathen, Cuthean, and idolater. In the most popular English-language translation of the Talmud, called the *Soncino* edition, the practice is illustrated by the fifth footnote of the book of Sanhedrin. It reads, "Cuthean (Samaritan) was here substituted for the original goy..."[439] Christians are sometimes referred to by the code word "Min" or "Minim."[440] The footnotes of the *Soncino* edition of the Talmud as well as passages in the *Jewish Encyclopedia* blatantly mention this deception. In other passages in the Talmud I discovered a possible reason why some of the Talmud's writers had forbidden Gentiles to read it. The Talmud's words are vitriolic:

- **Only Jews are human. [Gentiles] are animals. (Baba Mezia 114a-114b.)**[441]
- **For murder, whether of a Cuthean [Gentile] by a Cuthean, or of an Israelite by a Cuthean, punishment is incurred; but of a Cuthean by an Israelite, there is no death penalty. (*Sanhedrin 57a*)**[442]
- **Even the best of the [Gentiles] should be killed. (*Babylonian* Talmud)**[443]
- **If a Jew is tempted to do evil he should go to a city where he is not known and do the evil there. (Moed Kattan 17a.)**[444]
- **Gentiles' flesh is as the flesh of asses and whose issue is like the issue of horses.**[445]
- **If a heathen [Gentile] hits a Jew, the Gentile must be killed. Hitting a Jew is hitting God. (Sanhedrin 58b.)**[446]
- **If an ox of an Israelite gores an ox of a Canaanite there is no liability; but if an ox of a Canaanite [Gentile] gores an ox of an Israelite...the payment is to be in full. (Baba Kamma 37b.)**[447]
- **If a Jew finds an object lost by a heathen [Gentile] it does not have to be returned. (Baba Mezia 24a; Affirmed also in Baba Kamma 113b.)**[448]
- **God will not spare a Jew who 'marries his daughter to an old man or takes a wife for his infant son or returns a lost article to a Cuthean [Gentile]... (Sanhedrin 76a.)**[449]
- **What a Jew obtains by theft from a Cuthean [Gentile] he may keep. (Sanhedrin 57a.)**[450]
- **[Gentiles] are outside the protection of the law and God has 'exposed their money to Israel.' (Baba Kamma 37b.)**[451]

- **Jews may use lies ('subterfuges') to circumvent a [Gentile]. (Baba Kamma 113a.)**[452]
- **All [Gentile] children are animals. (Yebamoth 98a.)**[453]
- **[Gentiles] prefer sex with cows. (Abodah Zarah 22a-22b.)**[454]
- **The vessels of [Gentiles], do they not impart a worsened flavor to the food cooked in them? (Abodah Zarah 67b.)**[455]

It astonished me to read such unmitigated hatred from the chief writings of the Jewish religion. It was obvious that these quotations were all authentic, because the copies I read were published by Jewish organizations. I could not find any rational explanation for such writings being in the Jewish sacred books; in fact, it became clear to me that most Americans don't know such writings even exist.

These quotes were hard for me to believe, as they will be for many readers. However, if anyone doubts them, an easy way to verify the Talmud's anti-Gentile is by reading the *Jewish Encyclopedia*. In its article "Gentiles," it makes very clear the Talmud's hatred toward non-Jews. Under the subtitle "Discrimination against Gentiles," on pages 617-621, it freely discusses the Talmud's attitude. Here are some excerpts:

> ...they held that only Israelites are men, ... Gentiles they classed not as men but as barbarians. (B.M. 108b)... Another reason for discrimination was the vile and vicious character of the Gentiles.... "whose flesh is like the flesh of asses and issue is like the issue of horses ..." The Gentiles were so strongly suspected of unnatural crimes that it was necessary to prohibit the stabling of a cow in their stalls (Ab. Zarah ii. 1)...."The Torah outlawed the issue of a Gentile as that of a beast...." The almighty offered the Torah to the Gentiles nations also, but since they refused to accept it, He withdrew his shining legal protection from them, and transferred their property rights to Israel. . . the presumption is that the Gentile obtained possession by seizure, . . . The property is considered public property, like the unclaimed land of the Desert. [456]

The 1907 edition of the Funk & Wagnall's *Jewish Encyclopedia* mentions a quotation of Rabbi Simon Ben Yohai (a giant of Talmudic literature) that is "often quoted by anti-Semites."

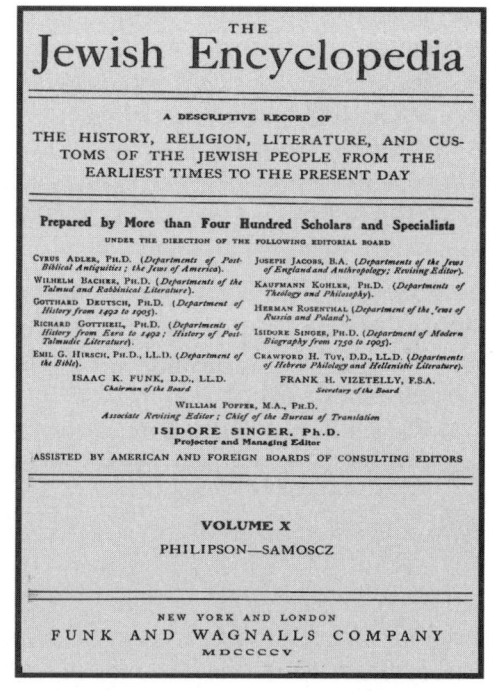

The quotation reads: "Tob shebe-goyim harog" — "The best of the Goyim is to be killed." It says that the rabbi's utterance is a result of persecution, describing this anti-Gentile statement as a result of a rabbi "whose life experiences may furnish an explanation for his animosity." Yet the passage goes on to say, "In the connection in which it stands, the import of this observation is similar to that of the two others: 'The most pious woman is addicted to sorcery'; 'The best of snakes ought to have its head crushed.' " [457]

The Talmudic quotations I reproduce here are by no means taken out of context. It is true that the Talmud is compiled from many writers and has many "commentaries" throughout. It also sometimes actually has disputes on certain issues. However, there is no mistaking the decidedly anti-Gentile tone that dominates it throughout. The exhortation that "the best of Gentiles should be killed," for instance, is found in at least three sections.

Imagine the reaction if a prominent Christian pronounced that "the best of the Jews should be killed." Would not such a statement be forcefully condemned? Imagine the media opprobrium that would be heaped on the offending words and its author — and rightfully so. Perversely, if one exposes the intolerance in the Talmud, he is the one likely to face accusations of religious prejudice and intolerance.

When I first sought to read the Talmud, I noticed a strange thing. I had a hard time finding a copy. It is not sold in bookstores, and most libraries don't have copies. Admittedly, the Talmud is a few times the size of the Bible, but certainly, in mass quantities, the Talmud could be printed for a nominal cost, much like the Bible is, on thin paper and inexpensively bound volumes. As the most holy writ of the one of the world's major religions, the interest in it must be high. Why then, must one usually go to synagogue or pay hundreds of dollars for an original Soncino edition? One must ask why it is not readily available for the public to read. The answer is probably found in the fact that the Jewish organizations that oversee such writings don't want them widely read, and when one reads the Talmudic books, one can understand their fear.

As an idealistic teenager, I was totally unprepared for this darker side of a faith that I had always respected. My impression had been that the Jewish faith had no animosity toward Jesus Christ. I was always told that they had much respect for Him as a prophet or at least as a great teacher but simply did not accept him as the Messiah. It disturbed me to have come across violently obscene descriptions of the Savior and of Christians in the Talmud. Among other things, Christ is described as a charlatan, a seducer and an evil-doer. It accuses Christ of having sexual intercourse with his donkey [458] and it describes the Virgin Mary as a whore. [459]

When I first read extensive sections of the Talmud, even with the Jewish-published translations in front of me, I did not want to believe they were authentic. I approached a Jewish acquaintance, Mark Cohen, and gave him a page of these quotations. He seemed equally upset by them. By the look on his face, I knew instantly that he was completely unfamiliar (and unsympathetic) with this Talmudic writ. He offered to ask his rabbi about their authenticity. The rabbi confirmed that the quotations were genuine but claimed that those views were not currently held by most Jews of today.

I willingly believed this, and I still do. At the same time, however, knowing that such passages existed helped me to understand why there has been so much anti-Jewish sentiment over the centuries. It also offered insight into the anti-Gentile animus that dominated Judaism. It should be noted that all rabbis study the Talmud. How would Jews react if Christian preachers studied *Mein Kampf* as part of their holy writ, but excused it by saying that the book has no effect on their current attitudes? Any open-minded reader who reads both *Mein Kampf* and the Talmud would find the Talmud far more intolerant.

When I looked up anti-Semitism in the major encyclopedias, all of them attempted to explain historical anti-Semitism purely as a Christian intolerance of non-Christian Jews. Sometimes, they even suggested that Christians persecuted Jews simply because the Gospels blame the Jews for the crucifixion of Christ. They never even suggested that one of the sources of anti-Semitism could have been the hateful and ethnocentric attitudes of the Jews themselves, as expressed and encouraged toward Gentiles in their own religious law.

Even during the life of Jesus Christ, the forces of organized Jewry opposed this kindhearted teacher who spoke of the power of love and reconciliation, rather than the militant anti-Roman measures hoped for by the Pharisees. The New Testament records faithfully the intense Jewish terror used to suppress the early Christian faith. In one of the Gospels' most chilling verses it is written:

Howbeit that no man spake openly of him [Christ] for fear of the Jews." (John 8:13)[460]

From the early centuries of Christianity, some Gentile scholars became fluent in Hebrew. They developed bitterness toward Jews based on the content of the Talmudic writings. Down through the intervening centuries, dozens of popes issued edicts and encyclicals condemning Judaism. They expressed outrage, not because the Jews crucified Christ, but because of the Talmud's vicious anti-Gentile and anti-Christian passages. Following is a potpourri of popes' views on the Jews:

246 MY AWAKENING

> **Gregory IX.** Condemned the Talmud as containing "every kind of vileness and blasphemy against Christian doctrine."
> **Benedict XIII.** His Bull on the Jews (1450) declared, "The heresies, vanities and errors of the Talmud prevent the Jews from knowing the truth."
> **Innocent IV.** Burned the Talmud in 1233 as a book of evil.
> **John XXII.** Banned the Talmud in 1322
> **Julius III.** Papal Bull Contra Hebreos retinentes Libros (1554) ordered the Talmud burnt "everywhere."
> **Paul IV.** Bull Cum Nimis Absurdum (1555) powerfully condemned Jewish usury and anti-Christian activities.
> **Pius IV.** Condemned Jewish genocidal writings.
> **Pius V.** Expelled all Jews from papal states. (1569)
> **Gregory XIII.** Said in a Papal Bull of 1581, "Moved by an intense hatred of the members of Christ, they continue to plan horrible crimes against the Christian religion with daily increasing audacity."
> **Clement VIII.** Condemned Jewish genocidal writings.

Not only did the founders of the Catholic Church take this dim view of the Jews, I was amazed to find that the great reformer and founder of Protestantism, Martin Luther, shared the same passionate opposition toward them.

As a teenager, I had a great admiration for Martin Luther, and I was keen to find out what the founder of Protestant Christianity had to say about Jews. A mail-order catalogue of books on the Jewish question at the Citizen's Council office listed a translation of a book by Martin Luther with the abrasive title *The Jews and Their Lies*.[461] The great Martin Luther was a biblical scholar who read Hebrew. He had thoroughly researched the books of the Talmud in their original language, and he had reacted to them with revulsion. Going on to read compilations of Luther's sermons and writings, I was astonished at their passionate anti-Jewish tone.

> They have been taught so much deadly hatred against the Gentiles by their parents and Rabbis since their earliest youth and continue to feed their hate during all the years of their lives, and this hatred has saturated their very blood and flesh, fills the very marrow of their bones and has become inseparable from their whole being. (Weimar 53, pgs. 482-483)
>
> Their Talmud and their Rabbis teach them that a murder shall not be regarded as a sin whenever a Jew kills a Gentile, but only if a Jew murders a brother in Israel. Neither is it a sin to break an oath sworn to a Gentile...The Jews of our days still keep to these doctrines and follow the example of their fathers, taking every opportunity to practice their deliberately false interpretation of the Lord's Word, their avariciousness, their usury, their thefts, their murders, and teaching their children to do likewise. (W. 53, 489-490-91)
>
> Maybe mild-hearted and gentle Christians will believe I am too rigorous and drastic against the poor, afflicted Jews, believing that I ridicule them and treat them with such sarcasm. By my word, I am

far too weak to be able to ridicule such a Satanic breed. (W. 32, pg. 286)

You should know that the Jews blaspheme and violate the name of our Savior day for day…they are our public enemies and incessantly blaspheme our Lord Jesus Christ, they call our Blessed Virgin Mary a harlot and her Holy Son a bastard and to us they give the epithet of Changelings and abortions. If they could kill us all they would gladly do so, in fact, many murder Christians. . . (Luther's last sermon, a few days before his death in February 1546) (Erlanger 62, pg. 189)

There were many tribes, nationalities and conflicting religious sects that migrated to the great cities of the Roman Empire. Yet, of all these groups, only the Jewish tribe elicited such relentless hostility throughout the centuries. Only the Jewish tribe never assimilated into the Roman population. Could their own Talmudic practices and their disdain for non-Jews have had something to do with the enmity they generated? It seemed logical to me that these things contributed to anti-Jewish sentiments in the West.

The Contrast of Christian and Jewish Holy Days

The contrasting holidays of Christianity and Judaism illustrate the dichotomy between the two religions. Christmas and Easter celebrate universal themes offering hope and salvation for all mankind. Christmas officially marks the birth of the Savior and celebrates the desire for "peace on Earth and goodwill toward men." Easter, a more somber occasion, represents the promise of universal salvation through the Resurrection of Christ. While Christians celebrate universal goodwill on their holy days, Jews celebrate historic military victories against their Gentile enemies.

Near the time of Christmas the Jews celebrate Hanukkah, a commemoration of their military victory in 165 BC over their hated enemy, the Greek-descended King Antiochus IV of Syria. The victory finds its remembrance by the miracle of the long-burning oil lamps in their recaptured temple. As Christians enter the Lenten Season and prepare for the celebrations of Christ's offer of salvation, the Jews celebrate Passover, a holiday that is, again, based on an ancient conflict between Jew and Gentile. Passover is an unambiguous reference to the night when the spirit of death harmlessly "passed over" Jewish homes and descended into the homes of their hated Egyptian enemies, killing every firstborn male from newborn to elderly in all of Egypt. It may be shocking to put it this way, but in reality it is a celebration of mass infanticide.

Another important Jewish holiday is the Feast of Lots, called Purim. The *Random House Dictionary of the English Language* describes it as follows:

248   MY AWAKENING

Purim A Jewish festival marked chiefly by the reading of the book of Esther and eating of hamantaschen, that is celebrated on the 14th day of Adar in commemoration of the deliverance of the Jews in Persia from destruction by Haman.[462]

The festival celebrates the Jewish massacre of thousands of Persians along with their prime minister Haman and his 10 sons. It even includes the symbolic eating of the supposed anti-Semite's ears (Haman's ears — hamantaschen) in the form of three-sided cookies. Another of the favored Purim foods is Kreplach, which is dough pockets again shaped in a triangle to denote Haman's ears, but these snacks are filled with chopped meat, symbolizing the beaten flesh of Haman. Another of their Purim celebrations involves Jews beating willow branches in the synagogues meant to represent the flogging of Haman. The following description of these practices comes from a Jewish culture organization called *Jewish Art in Context*, but is found in numerous books about Jewish culture and religious holy days. The second description is from a Jewish-cooking guide called "Bon Appetit."

> c. Special Delicacies
> 1. "Haman Taschen" (Oznei Haman = Haman's Ears).
> 2. "Kreplach": chopped meat covered with dough, also triangular in shape. The name has received a popular etymology: "Kreplach are eaten only on days on which there is both hitting and eating: Yom Kippur eve — the custom of Kaparot, Hoshanna Rabba — the beating the willow branches, Purim — the (symbolical) beating of Haman."[463]

> The reason Kreplach are eaten on Purim is interesting (if a bit of a stretch). Kreplach is also traditional for Yom Kippur ... and for Hoshannah Rabah (the seventh day of Sukkot).
> On these days it was traditional for there to be some sort of beating. On Yom Kippur in ancient times, men would be flogged before Yom Kippur and we beat the willow branches on Hoshannah Rabah. On Purim, we beat out the name of Haman. So Kreplach became traditional for Purim. (Phillip Goldwasser from "Bon Appetit")[464]

Upon learning these things, I realized that if any other group had such ceremonies, it would be called hateful and barbaric. Imagine if Klansmen observed a ritual in which they made and ate cookies shaped to represent the ears of Martin Luther King and held a holy ceremony in which they symbolically whipped him! Purim has been celebrated annually since long before the time of Christ and has certainly been important in the fomenting of hatred and suspicion of Gentiles in the hearts and minds of Jewish children. This repulsive ceremony is analogous to Christian churches teaching our children to symbolically beat the Jewish Pharisees who condemned Jesus and then eating foods symbolizing the pulverized body parts of the Jewish priests. Of course, such would be completely antithetical to the spirit of Christianity, yet such revengeful attitudes are at the very core of Judaism.

Zionism as Racism

After 2,000 years of conflict, the Jewish prayer "Next Year in Jerusalem" finally became expressed in an open political movement called Zionism. In 1862, Moses Hess, teacher to Karl Marx and the spiritual father of both Zionism and Communism, wrote *Rome and Jerusalem*. In it, he expressed the familiar Talmudic values.

> **We Jews shall always remain strangers among the Goyim [Gentiles]. . . . It is a fact the Jewish religion is above all Jewish nationalism. . . . Each and every Jew, whether or not he wishes it or not, is automatically, by virtue of his birth, bound in solidarity with his entire nation. . . . One must be a Jew first and human being second.** [465]

If Adolf Hitler had ever said the words "One must be a German first and a human being second," would not those words be often repeated as proof of his depravity? For some compelling reason, no one dares to condemn such words when they come from the man who laid the foundations of both Zionism and Communism.

I began to survey Zionist literature, from the writings of Moses Hess to the present day, and repeatedly I encountered the same supremacism expressed in the Talmud.

A prominent Zionist historian, Simon Dubnow, wrote the *Foundation of National Judaism* in 1906. In it, he expressed sentiments that would certainly be described as anti-Semitic had they come from a Gentile.

> **Assimilation is common treason against the banner and ideals of the Jewish people. . . . But one can never 'become' a member of a natural group, such as a family, a tribe, or a nation...A Jew, on the other hand, even if he happened to be born in France and still lives there, in spite of all this, he remains a member of the Jewish nation, and whether he likes it or not, whether he is aware or unaware of it, he bears the seal of the historic evolution of the Jewish nation.** [466]

In 1965, Moshe Menuhin, an Israeli who was born into an extremely prominent Hasidic family, dared to write an exposé of the Jewish hypocrisy. He wrote a fascinating book called *The Decadence of Judaism*. [467] He was a graduate of a *yeshiva* in Jerusalem and was the father of the prominent Israeli musical performer Yehudi Menuhin.

Menuhin documents the influential modern Zionist writer Jakob Klatzkin addressing the world at large in his 1921 German-language book *Krisis und Entscheidung (Crisis and Decision).* Klatzkin writes

> **We are not hyphenated Jews; we are Jews with no qualifications or reservations. We are simply aliens; we are a foreign people in your**

midst, and, we emphasize, we wish to stay that way. There is a wide gap between you and us, so wide that no bridge can be laid across. Your spirit is alien to us; your myths, legends, habits, customs, traditions and national heritage, your religious and national shrines [Christianity], your Sundays and holidays. . . they are all alien to us. The history of your triumphs and defeats, your war songs and battle hymns, your heroes and their mighty deeds, your national ambitions and aspirations, they are all alien to us. The boundaries of your lands cannot restrict our movements, and your border clashes are not of our concern. Far over and above the frontiers and boundaries of your land stand our Jewish unity. . . . Whosoever calls the foreign [Gentile] land a fatherland is a traitor to the Jewish people. . . . A loyal Jew can never be other than a Jewish patriot.... We recognize a national unity of Diaspora Jews, no matter in which country they may reside. Therefore, no boundaries can restrain us in pursuing our own Jewish Policy. [468]

Before the Second World War Nahum Goldmann, president of the World Zionist Organization, urged German Jews to immigrate to Palestine, using the following blunt words:

Judaism can have nothing in common with Germanism. If we go by the standards of race, history, and culture, and the Germans do have the right to prevent the Jews from intruding on the affairs of their volk. . . The same demand I raise for the Jewish volk as against the German. . . . The Jews are divided into two categories, those who admit they belong to a race distinguished by a history thousands of years old, and those who don't. The latter are open to the charge of dishonesty. [469]

Even Judge Louis Brandeis, the Zionist who sat on the American Supreme Court, said it succinctly: "Jews are a distinct nationality, whatever his country, his station, or his shade of belief, he is necessarily a member." [470]

Theodor Herzl, the father of modern Zionism, expresses the true causes of what he calls the Jewish Question:

The Jewish Question exists wherever Jews are to be found in large numbers. Every nation in whose midst Jews live is, either covertly or openly, anti-Semitic. . . Anti-Semitism increases day by day and hour by hour among the nations; indeed it is bound to increase because the causes of its growth continue to exist and cannot be removed. . . . Its immediate cause is our excessive production of mediocre intellects, who cannot find an outlet downwards or upwards — that is to say, no wholesome outlet in either direction. When we sink, we become a revolutionary proletariat, the subordinate officers of all revolutionary parties; at the same time, when we rise, there rises also our terrible power of the purse. [471]

The Jews' exclusivity, their resistance to assimilation, their alien traditions and customs, all these factors have contributed to a reaction from the Christian world that at times became extreme. With each persecution the Jews suffered, their own distrust and antipathy toward Gentiles became intensified in their own writings and in patterns of behavior that engendered still more persecution. A cycle of recrimination began that still continues as we approach the end of the 20th century.

A whole generation of Jews is now growing up inundated with stories of Gentile perfidy. Not only are the Germans and Eastern Europeans blamed for the Holocaust, but now there are many Jewish-authored books arguing that all the Western nations share in the guilt, as well as President Franklin D. Roosevelt, the Catholic Church, and, indeed, the entire Christian world.[472]

I discovered that to draw attention to the writings of the Talmud and to quote the very words used by modern Jewish leaders and writers, invites the charge of anti-Semitism. It seemed to me that if repeating the words of Jewish leaders is anti-Semitism, then there must be distasteful elements in the words themselves. Maybe, the historical Jewish attitude toward Gentiles should be considered when assessing the causes of anti-Semitism.

Bernard Lazare, a popular Jewish intellectual in France in the 19th century, investigated his people's role in age-old conflict with other peoples. In the widely circulated book *L'Antisemitisme*, he wrote:

> **If this hostility, this repugnance had been shown towards the Jews at one time or in one country only, it would be easy to account for the local causes of this sentiment. But this race has been the object of hatred with all the nations amidst whom it ever settled. Inasmuch as the enemies of the Jews belonged to diverse races ... it must be that the general causes of anti-Semitism have always resided in Israel itself, and not in those who antagonized it.** [473]

Some might argue that the anti-Gentile tone of the Talmud and the founding Zionists has little relevance to the Jews of today. The evidence, however, is that the core of Judaism, orthodoxy, is steadily becoming more extreme against Gentiles than in previous generations. The *Encyclopedia Judaica* [474] says as much in its articles on the subject.

Perhaps such should be expected with the advent of modern film. Cinema and television wield an enormous influence on human emotions. Serial accounts of the persecutions of Jews, all the way from the Torah to the Holocaust are now propagated in an irresistible format. In thousands of well-crafted films, from *The Ten Commandments*[475] to *Schindler's List*,[476] Jews are reminded of Gentile perfidy, while Gentiles are softened to the Jewish cause. The incessantly repeated horrific stories of the Holocaust can only serve to heighten the suspicions of the average Jew toward Gentiles while underscoring the need for Jewish solidarity.

Modern Jewish Supremacism

As I read more and more of the historical accounts of Jewish ethnocentrism, I wondered how much of this applied to the modern day. I began to devour modern Jewish books and publications. I chose their most popular and respected newspapers, books, and magazines. Because I was now beginning to see a double standard, I began to look for corroborating evidence, and what I found fascinated me. In fact, finding it was easy, and it still is. All the suspicion and condemnation of Gentiles, the anti-Christian and anti-European diatribes, the boasting of Jewish moral, spiritual, and genetic superiority, and even the ready admission that they control most of the key positions in media and government is in their literature. Any reader of publications meant for Jewish consumption will find material no less anti-Gentile than the 1500-year-old Talmudic writ I quoted. It is seldom as brazen as the old material, but the underlying themes are inevitably present and sometimes even unvarnished hatred just spills out.

Many examples of what I am talking about can be found in the largest Jewish newspaper outside of Israel, *The Jewish Press*,[477] which sets the tone of Jewish religious and cultural attitudes more than any other newspaper. One of its primary religious authorities is Rabbi Simcha Cohen, who has an instructional Dear Abby-type of column called "Halachic Questions." Not long ago, Rabbi Cohen instructed his readers that the Talmud denotes Gentiles as "animals" (as outlined by Talmudic writings from Gemara Kiddushin 68a and Metzia 114b).[478] In another section he discusses how a Jewish woman is not designated as a prostitute if she has premarital sex with a Jew, but she is a whore if she has any sexual relations with a Gentile, even if she is married.

> **Marriage to a Gentile can never be sanctified or condoned, such a liaison classifies the woman as a zona...common parlance interprets the term zona to refer to a prostitute....**
>
> **Indeed, premarital sex of a Jewish woman to a Jewish man does not automatically brand the woman a zona.... A Jewish woman becomes a prostitute or zona in the eyes of the Talmud only when she marries or otherwise has sexual relations with a non-Jew.** [479]

Another Jewish publication, the *Jewish Chronicle*, in an article called "Some Carefully and Carelessly Chosen Words," revealed that the Jewish term for Gentile woman is the offensive Yiddish word *shiksa* — meaning "whore," from the Hebrew root, *sheigetz* ("abomination"). It also pointed out that a little Gentile girl is called *shikselke*, meaning "little female abomination." [480] How would Jews react if the Gentile casually referred to Jewish women and little girls as "whores" and "little whores"?

Moreover, not only Christians but also non-Christians of all races are regarded as "supernal refuse" (garbage) by Talmud teachers such as the founder of Habad-Lubavitch, Rabbi Shneur Zalman. The Habad is a powerful movement within Hassidim. The New Republic magazine, which has a mostly Jewish staff, had some very revealing admissions in a May, 1992 edition.

> ...there are some powerful ironies in Habad's new messianic universalism, in its mission to the gentiles; and surely the most unpleasant of them concerns Habad's otherwise undisguised and even racial contempt for the goyim.
>
> As for the goyim...Zalman's attitude (was): 'Gentile souls are of a completely different and inferior order. They are totally evil, with no redeeming qualities whatsoever.'
>
> ...Consequently, references to gentiles in Rabbi Shneur Zalman's teachings are invariably invidious. Their (non-Jews) material abundance derives from supernal refuse. Indeed, they themselves derive from refuse, which is why they are more numerous than the Jews, as the pieces of chaff outnumber the kernels...All Jews were innately good, all gentiles innately evil.
>
> ...Moreover, this characterization of gentiles as being inherently evil, as being spiritually as well as biologically inferior to Jews, has not in any way been revised in later Habad writing. (The New Republic)[481]

It is true that all Jews do not have the extreme views of the Habad, who are an integral part of the Jewish Orthodox Religion. However, imagine if a movement existed within the Catholic or Methodist church claiming that Jews or Blacks are pieces of garbage who are "totally evil" and have "no redeeming qualities." Would there not be a great outcry? The Jews have demanded that the Catholic church take out of their liturgy anything the Jews deem as offensive, and the Catholics as well as other Christian denominations have done so. Yet, no one dares to insist that the Jewish faith should expunge references to Gentiles as "innately evil with inferior souls."

As I began to look at these issues from a new perspective, I saw that at the core of Judaism lies the preservation of Jewish heritage and the advancement of Jewish interests.

In examining some of the encyclopedias and biographical reference works compiled by rabbinical authorities, I found prominent Jews listed who were self-proclaimed atheists and Communists — as mentioned in the last chapter. Leon Trotsky, one of the main atheist perpetrators of the Russian Revolution, and Herbert Aptheker, the "atheist" chief-theoretician of the Communist Party USA, are proudly listed in Jewish directories such as *Who's Who in World Jewry*[482] and *Who's Who in American Jewry*.[483] These books are compiled by the leading rabbinical organizations of America.

The Jewish religion, as codified by the Talmud, is less concerned with an afterlife than with the survival and power of the Jewish people. Driven by the belief that Jews are the "Chosen People," Judaism is held together by chronic recitals of past persecutions. In a world that renounces racism, Judaism is the only creed on Earth praised for fostering genetic exclusion, elitism, ethnocentrism, and supremacism. Modern Israel is the only Western state that is openly theocratic, that unashamedly proclaims itself a nation whose purpose is to advance one religion and one unique people. Israel defines Judaism as the state religion, with little separation of church and state in its civil and religious laws. In spite of their religious state, most Jews in Israel identify themselves as "secular." But, even the non-religious Jews of Israel and America support the Orthodox-run state of Israel, and they support numerous organizations run by Orthodox Jews around the world, as a mechanism of preserving their cultural and racial heritage.

Most of us never see the reality of Jewish chauvinism and power because we have not organized the scattered facts into a coherent whole. Like a child's connect-the-dot puzzle, most of us have not yet completed the picture. The media erase as many dots as they can from our awareness, and anyone who succeeds in connecting all the dots is bludgeoned back with the ultimate moral weapon: accusations of anti-Semitism.

Given the powerful Jewish influences that have so much power in this nation's media and finance, it is amazing that any Gentiles would dare oppose them. One accused of being an anti-Semite faces an intractable enemy organized around the world — one that will do whatever it takes to discredit, intimidate, and destroy him.

After I completed a survey of readings in the Talmud and of the modern Zionist writers, I realized that the Europeans were not the only historical practitioners of racial and religious intolerance. Actually, the Jews have been quite proficient at it themselves. Once I accepted that Jewish ethnocentrism existed, again I asked the question that had arisen after my enlightenment on the "Russian Revolution": Why were we forbidden to know this?

A Jew can rightly object to slanderous criticism from Christians. Why should I, as a Christian, not be upset by slanderous criticism of my heritage by Jews? If hateful sentiments by Christians against Jews are wrong, why is the converse not just as reprehensible? Are the media right in suggesting that Christians have a monopoly on hate, while Jews have a monopoly on charity? Which religion, as judged by the evidence of its own writings, is more motivated by hatred?

Even as I write these provocative words, I harbor no hatred toward the Jewish people. There are intolerant Jews just as there are intolerant Gentiles. It is also true that there are many Jews who respect our Christian heritage. But unless the nonchauvinist Jews will work hard to bring to their own faith and community the same kind of love and reconciliation that Christ taught, the cycle of hatred between Jew and Gentile could fester. If this happens, we could see repeated the terrible excesses of the past. The government, church, and media establishment zealously work to diminish Gentile intolerance of Jews. That objective can be realized only through an equal effort to lessen Jewish chauvinism, suspicion, and anger against Gentiles. As the Israeli human-rights activist Israel Shahak wrote, "Anti-Semitism and Jewish chauvinism can only be fought simultaneously."

After reading the words of Zionism's modern founder, Theodore Herzl, I fully realized that there are, as he expressed it, "alien" power brokers in our civilization. These are people who do not share our culture, our traditions, our faith, our interests, or our values. I realized that if I desired to preserve the heritage and values of my people, I would have to defend my people from the intolerant sector within the Jewish community that seeks not conciliation but domination.

When I was 16, I never suspected that just by pointing out the powerful Jewish elements of anti-Gentilism I would be labeled anti-Semitic. I do not accept that label today, and I still believe that it is no more anti-Semitic to oppose the Jewish supremacism than it is anti-Italian to oppose the mafia.

Chapter 17:

Race, Christianity and Judaism

From the earliest times that I can remember, I was a believing Christian. My father is a devout Christian who taught me the salvation that Jesus Christ offers and about His lessons for living. Father was never dogmatic about his faith, and over the years he led my family to different churches without worrying about the denomination. At one time or another, we were members of Presbyterian, Methodist, and Church of Christ congregations. The only important consideration for Father was the quality of the minister and the congregation. When I was in grade school, my family joined the Elysian Fields Methodist Church where Father taught Sunday school. When we traveled we would almost always try to attend Sunday school and church in whatever city we happened to be in. The new perspectives we received from the different Sunday school teachers and preachers were like shots of adrenaline for our Christian faith.

At thirteen, I went to Clifton L. Ganus school, a strongly fundamentalist Church of Christ school in New Orleans. At this same time, my family and I began to attend services at the Carrollton Avenue Church of Christ, which had strong ties to the school. Although I had had an infant baptism in the Presbyterian church, my new teachers and friends convinced me that the Bible taught that a conscious decision about salvation was needed before baptism. I prayed about it and gave myself to Christ as I was lain back in the waters of the baptismal pool in our church's sanctuary. Not long after my baptism, after much pleading from me, my father found his way to the baptismal pool as well.

My experience of being a renewed Christian had a profound impact not only on my Christian beliefs, but also on my secular ones, for it seemed I saw everything in a fresh light. When a man has confidence in his own beliefs, he is unafraid to joust with contrary opinions. Being "saved" gave me a sense of security that made me more open to different ideas. When someone has doubts about the underlying validity of his beliefs, he feels threatened by challenges to them. The feeling of being "right with God and the world" gave me freedom to explore challenging ideas. It was only a few months after my baptism that I read *Race and Reason*, [484] the book that began my intellectual journey toward racial understanding.

In the early '60s, most churches in the South were still segregated, and even the Catholic church had segregated parochial schools and separate seating during Mass for Whites and Blacks. Accepting racial differences posed no moral dilemma for organized Christianity for its first two thousand years, but after only 50 years of an egalitarian-dominated media, racial attitudes began to change in the Christian establishment. Ironically, the source of this new "Christian" viewpoint came primarily from people who were, in fact, anti-Christians. At first, Christians were told that recognition of racial differences and segregation was inappropriate. When I graduated from college in the mid-1970s, increasing numbers of churches were maintaining that racism was a "sin." By the 1980s, some churches that had been totally segregated just 20 years earlier even began to consecrate mixed marriages between Whites and Blacks.

When I first questioned the idea of racial equality, it never entered my mind that understanding racial differences could be incompatible with my Christian beliefs, for almost all Christian churches in the South were then segregated. My church and its private school were entirely White.

Later, I did some real soul searching on the issue, for Christianity was not just my belief, but it was also my ultimate moral delimiter. I questioned whether my beliefs on the race issue were somehow unchristian. I began to reread the Holy Bible, paying close attention to the way it dealt with tribes, races, peoples, and nations, and I prayerfully thought about it. I read an article in a Methodist Sunday school magazine that maintained that racial segregation was unacceptable to Christians. The Scripture it used to justify its position was from Acts 17:26:

And he made from one every nation of men to live on the face of the earth...[485]

I remembered the deception used by the media concerning Thomas Jefferson's famous quote: "Nothing is more certainly written in the book of fate that these people [the Negroes] are to be free." When I thought of how they left out the next sentences affirming racial differences and supporting repatriation, I immediately opened my Bible and looked up the verse. It read:

And he made from one every nation of men to live on the face of the earth, <u>having determined their allotted periods and the boundaries of their habitations</u>. (Acts 17:26)[486]

Just as with Jefferson, important words — words that complete the meaning of the scripture — were left off. In Biblical terms *nation* is synonymous with people or race. I thought about the fact that God indeed made the many races of mankind and gave them their distinct characteristics and the "boundaries of their habitations." As I read the verse in its entirety, it did not seem to me that God favors racial integration, or racial mixing. He himself made us distinct races and He separated us by kind.

The more I reread the Holy Bible, the more obvious it became to me that God seemed very concerned about heritage. The Old Testament is about one nationality, one people: the Israelites, who are designated as a special people, a "chosen people." Life and death struggles between the Israelites and the Cannanites, Jacobites, Philistines, Amalakites, Assyrians, Egyptians, and dozens of other peoples are recorded exhaustively. Even though, as I've mentioned, I was quite surprised and dismayed by the genocide, I continued to find many more verses of the Bible (such as Joshua 6:21[487] and 10:28-10:41) [488] detailing the slaughter of entire peoples.

The Jewish stormtroopers committed their genocide under the strict guidelines established by Moses in Deuteronomy chapter 20. He told them that in the lands set aside to become Israel, they should exterminate every inhabitant, while people in surrounding nations had to be killed unless they submitted themselves as slaves to Israel.

> **When you draw near a city to fight against it, offer terms of peace to it. And if its answer to you is peace and it opens to you, then all the people who are found in it shall do forced labor for you and shall serve you. But if it makes no peace with you . . . you shall put all its males to the sword, but the women and the little ones, the cattle, and everything else in the city, all its spoil, you shall take as booty for yourselves; and you shall enjoy the spoil of your enemies . . . Thus you shall do to all of the cities which are very far from you, which are not cities of the nations here.**
>
> **But in the cities of these people that the Lord your God gives you for an inheritance you shall save alive nothing that breathes, but you shall utterly destroy them, the Hittites and the Amorites, the Canaanites and the Perizzites, the Hivites and Jebusites, . . . (Deuteronomy 20:10-18)**[489]

The wording is unmistakable. Even innocent children were to be killed simply because they were of an enemy nation.

Love Thy "Neighbor"

Since my earliest Sunday and Bible school days, I had been taught that the greatest instruction of God was to "love thy neighbor as thyself" (Leviticus 19:18)[490]. Having grown up on the Ten Commandments, the most known passages of the Old Testament, I now wondered how such Old Testament genocide could be understood in light of "thou shalt not kill," "thou shalt not steal," and "thou shalt not covet thy neighbor's house" (Exodus 20:13, 15, and 17)[491].

I decided to look up the scripture that discusses loving thy neighbor as thyself. I found it in Leviticus 19:18 in the Revised Standard Version Old Testament that had belonged to my grandmother. It read

> **You shall not take vengeance or bear a grudge against the *sons of your own people*, but shall love your neighbor as yourself... (Leviticus 19:18)**[492]

The following is the Jewish translation of the text for their bible according to Hebrew texts:

> **You shall not take vengeance or bear a grudge *against your countrymen.* Love your fellow as yourself. -TANAKH**[493]

The verse made it clear that neighbors were "the sons of *your own people*" — in other words, neighbor meant a *fellow* Israelite and not *other* peoples. The most recent Jewish translation of the verse uses "your countrymen" in place of "the sons of your own people."

The Talmud explains in Baba Kamma 113b[494] that the term neighbor specifically does not apply to a Gentile. The Jewish Encyclopedia says it clearly, "Here the Gentile is excepted, as he is not a neighbor..."[495] Years later I read an article by Dr. John Hartung in which he explained that the Ten Commandments' legal proscriptions were clearly directed at offenses against a "neighbor," which excluded non-Israelites. He pointed out that the scrolls from which the Ten Commandments were translated had no periods, commas, or first-word capitalization. Therefore, the part about "Thou shalt not kill" becomes part of a larger context. It could read:[496]

> **Thou shalt not kill, neither shalt though commit adultery, neither shalt thou steal, neither shalt thou bear false witness against thy neighbor, neither shalt thou covet your neighbor's wife and you shall not desire your neighbor's house, his field, or his manservant, or his maidservant, his ox, or his ass, or anything that is your neighbor's.**

So who are the Israelites proscribed from killing? "Thou shalt not kill thy neighbor... the children of thy people, the sons of your own people, your *fellow Israelites*." Now the mass killing and theft of other people's lands as commanded by Moses became very consistent with the laws of the Ten Commandments.

The Bible — Politically Incorrect

As much as it may surprise many of the Christians reading this, the Old Testament also supports wholeheartedly the institution of slavery. And again it is made clear that Israelites may *forever* engage in slavery of other peoples, but they are forbidden to enslave their own.

> **As for your male and female slaves whom you may have: you may buy male and female slaves from among the nations that are round about you.**
>
> **You may also buy from among the strangers who sojourn with you and their families that are with you, who have been born in your land; and they may be your property.**

You may bequeath them to your sons after you, *to inherit as a possession forever*; you may make slaves of them, but over your brethren the people of Israel you shall not rule, one over another, with harshness. (Leviticus 25:44-46)[497]

In regard to inter-racial marriage there are unmistakable passages where God commanded, "You shall not make marriages with them."

And When the Lord thy God shall deliver them before thee; thou shalt smite them, and utterly destroy them, thou shalt make no covenant with them, nor show mercy unto them;

Neither shalt thou make marriages with them; thy daughter thou shalt not give unto his son, nor his daughter shalt thou take unto thy son. . . .(Deuteronomy 7:2-6)[498]

The Bible goes on to say to Israelites who marry non-Israelites, "so will the anger of the Lord be kindled against you." (Deuteronomy 7:4)[499]

Elsewhere the Old Testament decries the mixing of the "holy seed of Israel." Jewish priests complain that "the people of Israel, and the priests and the Levites, have not separated themselves from the peoples of the lands, doing according to their abominations...(Ezra 9:1)[500] For they have taken of their daughters for themselves and for their sons; so that the holy seed have mingled themselves with the peoples of the lands." (Ezra 9:2)[501] Ezra goes on to list 107 men who renounced their foreign wives and their children by them as part of their obedience to God.

I also found that genealogies were used as proofs of untainted bloodlines. Racially impure genealogies were used to deny the priesthood to some who returned from Babylonian captivity. Every Sunday School child learns that one of the Old Testament proofs of the divinity of Jesus is his unbroken genealogy. I discovered that genocide and forbidding mixed marriages were not the only means used in biblical times to protect the bloodline of the Israelites. The Bible also clearly advocates separation or segregation.

. . . I am the Lord your God which have separated you from other people. (Leviticus 20:24)[502]

. . . Now it came to pass, when they had heard the law, that they separated from Israel all the mixed multitude. (Nehemiah 13:3)[503]

If the new egalitarian version of Christianity is right and racial separation is sinful, then by their logic God would have to be the first one condemned, for He is the one who created the racial differences of mankind. Whether one believes that God used a complex process of lengthy evolution or a simple act of immediate creation to make us, it is obvious that the different races exist and are geographically separated. If racial integrity is against the laws of God, why did he establish the races, geographically separate them, and give them distinct

RACE, CHRISTIANITY AND JUDAISM 261

characteristics and qualities? Is God supposed to have made some big mistake that man in his conceit is now to rectify through integration and racial mixing?

When I brought up the clear racial teachings of the Old Testament, my Sunday school teacher said that Jesus Christ brought a change by His coming for all mankind. I had to agree that the teachings of Jesus Christ do not concur with the harsh ethnocentrism of the Old Testament. The New Testament provides that the grace of God and the salvation of Christ are available to all people and all nations. Those who believe in Jesus Christ become the "children of God," the new "chosen people" through their salvation. Following are some often-quoted verses from the New Testament.

> **For you are all the children of God by faith in Christ Jesus.**
> **For as many of you as have been baptized into Christ have put on Christ.**
> **There is neither Jew nor Greek, there is neither bond nor free, male or female: for you are all one in Christ Jesus.**
> **And if ye be Christ's then are ye Abraham's seed, and heirs according to the promise. (Galatians 3:26-29)**[504]

Egalitarians frequently use these verses to justify their belief in racial and sexual equality. After pondering the verses carefully, I asked myself some questions. Do the verses mean that there are literally no males and females, no Jews or Greeks, and no slaves or freemen in the world? Obviously the answer is no. The New Testament repeatedly recognizes distinctions between men and women, Jews and Greeks, and servants (slaves) and freemen. In fact, although it may shock some who do not realize it, the New Testament routinely accepts the institution of slavery and says explicitly that slaveholders can be believing Christians and brethren. Examine the verses below.

- **Slaves, be obedient to those who are your earthly masters, with fear and trembling, in singleness of heart, as to Christ... (Ephesians 6:5)**[505]
- **Let all who are under the yoke of slavery regard their masters as worthy of all honor, so that the name of God and the teaching may not be defamed.**
- **Those who have believing masters must not be disrespectful on the ground that they are brethren; rather they must serve all the better since those who benefit by their service are believers and beloved. Teach and urge these duties. (1 Timothy 6:2)**[506]
- **Bid slaves to be submissive to their masters and to give satisfaction in every respect; they are not to be refractory, nor to pilfer, but to show entire and true fidelity, so that in everything they may adorn the doctrine of God our Savior. (Titus 2:9-1)**[507]

- **Servants, be submissive to your masters with all respect, not only to the kind and gentle but also to the overbearing. (1 Peter 2:18)**[508]

I do not condone slavery or any kind of oppression of people. However, Jesus Christ obviously had no opposition to it, anymore than had God when he told the Israelites that they could keep their slaves (of other tribes) forever. (Leviticus 25:44-46)[509] Jesus walked among slavery His entire life, reproaching all kinds of sin, yet He never uttered a word condemning slavery or slave owners.

An excellent example of Christ's attitude toward slavery is found in His encounter with a Roman Centurion and his slave (Luke 7:1-10). The story tells of a Roman Centurion who had a sick slave. He sent word to Jesus asking him to heal the slave, but he also sent word that the Lord need not come to him because he was sure Jesus could heal the slave from any distance. Jesus Christ did not condemn the slaveholder, nor did he instruct the Centurion to set his slave free. He simply healed the slave and praised the slaveholder effusively saying, "I tell you, not even in Israel have I found such faith." (Luke 7:9)[510] Passages such as that one suggested to me that the message Christ brought was one of personal salvation, not of liberal social activism.

"There is neither Jew nor Greek, bond or free, male or female" does not call for racial integration any more than it calls for the elimination of sexual differences or even the end of slavery. The message is very clear and very simple: salvation of Jesus Christ is open to all who believe in him, male or female, Jew or Greek, slave or free.

It became clear to me that both the Old and New Testaments acknowledge the differences in mankind. Certainly, though, the New Testament expresses a climate of love and respect that represents a change from the harsher dictates of the Old Testament. Jesus Christ and the writers of the New Testament seem to accept slavery, but slaveholders are admonished to treat their slaves kindly, and although Jesus acknowledges the different races that God Himself created and the "bounds of their habitations," He decrees that His salvation is open to all.

An illustration of how far afield some of the organized Christian churches have strayed from the words of Jesus is the push by many of them for gun control. He said in words one cannot mistake

- **. . . and he that hath no sword, let him sell his garment, and buy one. (Luke 22:36)**[511]

How would the liberal media treat someone today who said, "If you do not have a gun, sell your coat if you must, but buy one!" The liberal, Marxist-oriented, social gospel that egalitarians say is in the Holy Bible exists only in their own minds. Liberal humanism has now been grafted onto the faith of our forefathers. The wimpish and almost effeminate popular portrayal of Jesus today is a good illustration. In truth, Christ Jesus was both gentle and manly. His love came from His inner goodness and great strength. One can contrast the flower-child, hippie, media version of Jesus with the Biblical account of Christ going into the temple, turning over the tables, and driving out the moneylenders with a cat-o'-nine-tails (a scourge usually made of nine knotted lines or small cords). [512]

In recent years, liberal radicals have so perverted the meaning of Christ's message, that some church money has gone to support Communist revolutionaries. For instance, the National Council of Churches, a prestigious grouping of mainstream churches, sent money to Communists in Africa who were ultimately responsible for the murder of Christian missionaries.

Jewish Anti-Christianism

As I became more and more familiar with the role that organized Jewry played in Communism, Zionism, and liberalism, I also noticed their animosity toward Christians. Hollywood produces an abundance of movies that attack Christianity, and the publishing establishment generates prolific anti-Christian literature. For instance, in my college days I read a best-selling, highly promoted book called the *Passover Plot*, by a Jewish scholar named Joseph Schonfield.[513] He alleged that Jesus had not died on the cross, but was actually drugged by His followers to fake His death and resurrection. Jewish organizations routinely lead the fight to ban Christian prayers from schools, prohibit the mention of Christ in public facilities, and even forbid the singing of Christmas carols in our schools.

Once, when I criticized Jewish organizations for such actions on a radio talk show, a caller called me un-Christian for daring to criticize them. "After all," he retorted, "the Jews are God's chosen people." I had already done enough biblical research to know that such a statement told only half of the story. For the New Testament makes it clear that believing Christians had become the "heirs of God's promise," and that God no longer viewed the Jews as in his Covenant. [514]

Looking into the historical attitude of the Christian church toward Judaism, I found that it changed remarkably in this century. This was a period that also marked the rise of Jewish economic, political, and media power. The Christian church had a long record of conflict with the Jews. It is a record of which Jewish writers frequently complain. In the early fledgling days of Christianity, Jewish persecution of Christians, as referenced in the gospels, was still fresh in the minds of church leaders. A former Pharisee, Paul, was one of those cruel persecutors until his miraculous conversion on the road to Damascus. Eventually, Christianity became an overwhelmingly Gentile faith, and organized Jewry became its implacable enemy, claiming that Jesus was a bastard and Mary a whore, and that Christians were to be boiled in excrement. On the other side, using the New Testament, Christians blamed Jews for the crucifixion of Jesus and widespread persecution of Christians.

Many Christians think that the Jews' only religious books are those found in the Old Testament. As I described in my chapter on Judaic Supremacism, the Talmud is a collection of the chief books of Jewish commentary. The *American Heritage Dictionary* describes it as ". . . constituting the basis of religious authority for traditional Judaism."

There are three main branches of the Jewish religion: Orthodox, Conservative, and Reform. The Orthodox is the traditional source of Judaism and is considered to be at its heart. Very similar to Orthodox Judaism is the Conservative branch, but it offers some greater leeway in observance of the stringent Jewish laws. More modernistic, the Reform movement is far less bound by Pharisaic traditions than either of the other branches. The *Encyclopedia Judaica* describes the current religious picture of the nation of Israel.

> **There are very few Reform or Conservative congregations in the State of Israel. Orthodoxy is the official religious position in Israel with the majority of the rabbis belonging to the old school of talmudic jurists.** [515] ("Judaism." *Encyclopedia Judaica*, pg. 396)
>
> **The tendency within the Jewish Theological Seminary [in New York] has been emphatically . . . toward a more orthodox stance than existed within it in the previous generation.** [516] ("Conservative Judaism," Enc. *Encyclopedia Judaica*, pg. 906)

The *Universal Jewish Encyclopedia* makes it very clear that the Talmud, *not* the Torah or Old Testament, is the supreme authority for Judaism.

> **Thus the ultimate authority for Orthodoxy is the Babylonian Talmud. The Bible itself ranks second to it in reality, if not in theory.** [517] (*Universal Jewish Encyclopedia*, "Authority" pg. 637)

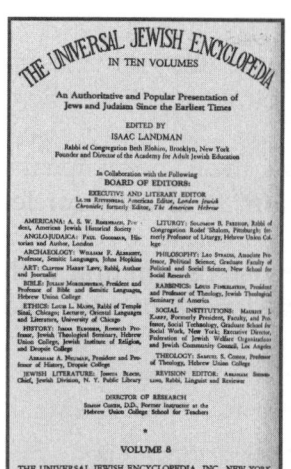

The Talmud make it clear that Judaism regards Jesus as a "charlatan," "magician," "seducer," and "deceiver." The Talmud also alleges that the biblical account of the crucifixion was a lie, maintaining that Jesus was strangled in a pit of dung, and that they hated him so much they executed him four different ways! Christ is portrayed as the bastard son of a harlot, and it even suggests that He was a Gentile. In some startling passages it boasts that the Romans had nothing to do with the death of Jesus, but that the Jews alone executed him for His idolatry. It also states that He has been conjured from the dead by a Jewish magician and then punished by being boiled in hot semen.

Below are direct quotes I confirmed from the Talmud, dealing with Jesus and Christians:

- **Balaam [Jesus] fornicated with his jackass. (Sanhedrin 105a-b)**[518]
- **Jewish priests raised Balaam [Jesus] from the dead and punished him in boiling hot semen.(57a Gittin)**[519]
- **She who was the descendant of princes and governors [The Virgin Mary] played the harlot with a carpenter (Sanhedrin 106a)**[520]
- **[Jesus] was lowered into a pit of dung up to his armpits. Then a hard cloth was placed within a soft one, wound round his neck, and the tow ends pulled in opposite directions until he was dead. (Sanhedrin 52b)**[521] Also, says they gave him four different executions in Sanhedrin 106a.[522]
- **Hast thou heard how old Balaam [Jesus] was?"...bloody and deceitful men shall not live out half their days it follows that he was thirty-three or thirty-four years old.** (Sanhedrin 106)
- **Those who read the uncanonical books [New Testament] will have no portion in the world to come.** (Sanhedrin 90a)
- **Jews must destroy the books of the [Christians].** (Shabbath 116a)

When I first encountered these Talmudic quotations in Elizabeth Dilling's book *The Jewish Religion,* such as those above and those reproduced in chapter 16, I told myself that they couldn't be accurate, that they had to be fakes or forgeries. Then I looked up the offending quotations and confirmed their presence in the *Soncino Edition* (the most popular 20th century English translation of the Talmud). The anti-Gentile quotations also received ample coverage in the *Jewish Encyclopedia,* enough so that no one could seriously doubt their authenticity. The *Jewish Encyclopedia* even details how the English translations use code words such as Amalakites, Cutheans, Egyptians, heathens, and other monikers to denote Gentiles in general, using these specific terms to hide from Gentiles how viciously the Talmud speaks of them. It also says clearly that the word "Balaam" is an alias for Jesus Christ.

As a younger man I reacted to this hidden Jewish racism first with shock and then with anger. How could the liberal Jewish pundits and media moguls condemn Southerners who simply wanted segregation, while their own Holy Writ taught hatred and violence against us, the non-Jews. When I began to talk publicly about the hatred that was in the Talmud, I was branded a hater, a bigot, and an anti-Semite by the media and by groups like the Anti-Defamation League of B'nai B'rith

(ADL). The ADL is a multimillion-dollar, worldwide organization whose whole purpose is to defame and discredit those who simply tell the truth about Jewish supremacism and hatred against Gentiles.

I became very angry, not only at the hatred that I saw in the traditional Jewish writings, but also in the Jewish leadership's hypocritical attacks on those who exposed that hatred. They attacked me for simply quoting the Talmud publicly, when I did nothing but simply read directly from their holy books. Yet, they called me the "hater."

Ultimately, the unjust and hypocritical attacks I faced only sharpened my resolve to stand up, no matter how alone, for the cause I believed in. Unexpectedly, I found that there are a number of Jews who dare to speak out about the truth about Zionism and Jewish supremacism. A much-persecuted and slandered group, they were just as appalled as I was about the intolerant and hateful strains of Judaism that had arisen in the Jewish community and the Zionist State. They included Americans such as Alfred Lilienthal, Noam Chomsky, and a courageous Jew in Israel, Dr. Israel Shahak. These scholars had dared to stand up against Jewish intolerance.

Dr. Israel Shahak risks all to bring what he calls "decent humanity" to Judaism and the Zionist State. Professor Shahak was born in Warsaw in 1933 and was liberated from the Nazi concentration camp at Bergen-Belsen; therefore, by the Jews' own definition, he is a Holocaust survivor. He immigrated to Israel, served in the Israeli army, and became a respected chemistry professor. Dr. Shahak is a lifelong human rights activist who has written on aspects of Judaism in both Hebrew and English. He has written many books, his latest in 1994 being *Jewish History, Jewish Religion*. [523] Gore Vidal wrote an excellent foreword in the current American edition. Here are some excerpts from Shahak's book exposing the attitude of the Jewish religion toward Christianity:

> **Judaism is imbued with a very deep hatred toward Christianity, combined with ignorance about it. This attitude was clearly aggravated by the Christian persecutions of Jews, but is largely independent of them. In fact, it dates from the time when Christianity was still weak and persecuted (not least by Jews), and it was shared by Jews who had never been persecuted by Christians or who were even helped by them...**
>
> **According to the Talmud, Jesus was executed by a proper rabbinical court for idolatry, inciting other Jews to idolatry, and contempt of rabbinical authority. All classical Jewish sources which mention his execution are quite happy to take responsibility for it; in the [talmudic account the Romans are not even mentioned...**
>
> **The very name Jesus was for Jews a symbol of all that is abominable, and this popular tradition still persists. The Gospels are equally detested, and they are not allowed to be quoted (let alone taught) even in modern Israeli schools.** [524]

Professor Shahak reports that the Zionists publicly and ceremonially burned hundreds of copies of the New Testament in Jerusalem on March 23, 1980. They were destroyed under the auspices of Yad Le'akhim, a Jewish religious organization subsidized by the Israeli Ministry of Religions.[525] To think that this is the same government that some Christian ministers say we should support with American tax dollars! Among other startling charges, Dr. Shahak says:

> **Jewish children are actually taught — passages such as that which commands every Jew, whenever passing near a cemetery, to utter a blessing if it is Jewish, but to curse the mothers of the dead if it is non-Jewish. . . it became customary to spit (usually three times) upon seeing a church or a crucifix. . . .** [526]

Dr. Shahak quotes the very popular, Israeli-published *Talmudic Encyclopedia*, which discusses the relationship between Jew and Goy ("Goy" meaning any non-Jew).

> **If a Jew has coitus [sexual intercourse] with a Gentile woman, whether she be a child of three or an adult, whether married or unmarried, and even if she is a minor aged only nine years and one day — because he had willful coitus with her, she must be killed, and as is the case with a beast, because through her a Jew got into trouble.**[527] **(the *Talmudic Encyclopedia*)** [528]

I knew of such hateful Talmudic laws long before I read Shahak's latest book, yet they still astonish me each time I read them. The monstrous implications still shock me. If a Jew rapes a young Christian girl, *the little girl* must be killed because she got a Jew in trouble! How does one even respond to such depravity, to such evil? Professor Shahak goes on page after page illustrating hateful Judaic laws against Christians, laws that permit Jews to cheat, to steal, to rob, to kill, to rape, to lie, even to enslave Christians.

The bulk of his book shows that Judaism in Israel, instead of moderating these anti-Gentile laws, actually becomes more openly hateful of Gentiles with each passing day. Dr. Shahak says that in order to hide their beliefs from Christians in Europe, many offending Talmudic passages and common prayers were substituted by code words (such as Cuthean for Gentile or Balaam for Jesus) by the Jewish authorities. Lists of *Talmudic Omissions* were circulated to fully clarify the code words in the viciously anti-Gentile passages. But today the passages are again being restored and published in their original form (without code words) for Israeli schoolchildren.[529]

From the earliest days of Christendom, Catholic popes issued edicts condemning the Jews for their usury, domination of the slave trade, prostitution and other vices, and their anti-Christian teachings and activities. Protestants were just as vociferously anti-Jewish. The founder of Protestantism, Martin Luther, read the books of the

268 MY AWAKENING

Talmud and called the Jews "agents of the Devil." [530] The dominant Christian viewpoint from the first century until the 1960s was that the Jewish people once had a special relationship with God, a Covenant. However, that Covenant was strictly *conditional*. In Deuteronomy 7:6-12 God states the covenant in explicit terms.

> **Know, therefore, that only the Lord your God is God, the faithful God who keeps His covenant and steadfast love to those who love Him and keep His commandments, to a thousand generations and *requites to their faith those who hate him, by destroying them — never slow with those who reject Him, but requiting them instantly.* Therefore, observe faithfully the instruction-the laws and the rules — with which I charge you today. (Deuteronomy 7:6-12)**[531]

Until very recent decades, most Christians believed that the Jews broke the covenant when they crucified and then later spurned Jesus Christ and His apostles. Jesus Christ made salvation available for Jews as well as anyone else, but there was no longer any special relationship for the people who rejected God and his Son. A New Covenant was established between God and all who accepted the salvation of Christ. The Catholic catechism and most Protestant churches persisted in this view until very recent times. Below are some of the scriptures on which this view was founded. I find the underlined passages of particular interest for this discussion.

> **For I could wish that I myself were accursed and cut off from Christ for the sake of my brethren, my kinsmen by race. . .**
> **But it is not as though the word of God had failed. For not all who are descended from Israel belong to Israel, ...**
> **This means that *it is not the children of the flesh who are the children of God, but the children of the promise* are reckoned as descendants...**
> **As indeed he says in Hosea,**
> *Those who were not my people*
> **I WILL CALL 'MY PEOPLE,'**
>
> **. . . And in the very place where it was said to them, '*You are not my people,*'**
> **they will be called '*sons of the living God.*'. . .**
> **What then? Israel failed to obtain what it sought. The elect obtained it, but the rest were hardened,**
> **(Romans 9:1–3, 6–8, 24–26 and Romans 11:7–8)**[532]

The book of Hebrews in the New Testament makes very clear that there was an end put to the old covenant and a new one formed through Christ for those who accept Him as Lord.

> **For finding fault with them, he saith, Behold, the days come, saith the Lord when I will make a new covenant with the House of Israel and the House of Judah:**

RACE, CHRISTIANITY AND JUDAISM

Not according to the covenant that I made with their fathers, in the day when I took them by the hand out of the land of Egypt; because they continued not in my covenant, and I regarded them not, saith the Lord. (Hebrews 8:6–7, 9–10) [533]

Therefore I tell you, the kingdom of God will be taken away from you and given to a nation producing the fruits of it...
And when the chief priests and Pharisees heard his parables, they perceived that he spoke of them.(Matthew 21:43-45) [534]

One can argue effectively from a New Testament perspective that the Pharisees crucified Jesus because he challenged Jewish power and practices. Judaism of today traces its lineage directly to the Pharisees. Just days before the crucifixion, Christ raised their ire by turning over the moneychangers' tables in the temple. He struggled with them all of his life and issued one of the most damning statements ever made against them, calling them the father of the lie.

Jesus said unto them, If God were your Father, ye would love me.
...Ye are of your father the devil, and the lusts of your father ye will do: he was a murderer from the beginning and abode not in truth, because there is no truth in him. When he speaketh a lie, he speaketh of his own; for he is a liar and the father of it.
...Then answered the Jews, and said unto him, Say we not well that thou are a Samaritan, and has a devil...(John 8:42-48) [535]
Behold an Israelite indeed, in whom there is no guile! (John 1:47) [536]

The gospels have repeated admonitions about the anti-Christian and misanthropic nature of the Jews. Some examples are

...for you suffered like things of your own countrymen as they did from the Jews, who killed both the Lord Jesus and the prophets, and drove us out and displease God, and oppose all men... But God's wrath has come upon them at last. (1 Thessalonians 2:14-16) [537]
This testimony is true. Therefore rebuke them sharply, that they may be sound in the faith, instead of giving heed to Jewish myths or to commands of men who reject the truth. (Titus1:13–14) [538]

These kinds of passages, the Judaized Christians seem never to quote. If anyone today would say essentially the same things said by Jesus or the apostles, he would surely be called anti-Semitic. In fact, I shudder to draw the comparison of what would happen to the person who went into a synagogue with a cat-'o-nine-tails and drove the Jews out. Yet, whoever today complains about hateful anti-Christian Jewish attitudes is quickly libeled as "un-Christian."

As the centuries passed following the crucifixion, the antagonisms between Christian and Jew grew and became even more hostile. In Rome the first great persecution of Christians occurred under Nero. The early church carefully noted that this persecution came under the ceaseless urgings of Nero's Jewish mistress, Poppaea Sabina. Even

Jewish histories record the collusion of the Jews with the Muslim Moors during their oppressive occupation of Christian Spain. In modern times Jewish Communists played a principal role in the greatest murder and oppression of Christians in history — that which took place under the Communist regimes of the Soviet Union and Eastern Europe. As I mentioned in the last chapter, Aleksandr Solzhenitsyn showed that Jews administered the gulags in Russia that murdered many millions of devout Christians. [539]

Through such evidence uncovered during my research, I came to understand fully one of the most chilling verses of the New Testament. It appears repeatedly in the Gospels:

Yet for fear of the Jews no one spoke openly of him (John 7:13)[540]

In modern America, Jews lead the effort to de-Christianize America. More importantly, Jews dominate the very un-Christian mass media. Book publishing and distribution, major newspapers, magazines, movies, and television are empires in which Jews are greatly over-represented and Christians are vastly under-represented, and those few Christians have often learned to say what they must to survive and prosper. The ancient opponents of Christ are able through their pervasive power in the media, to convince millions of Christians that they are still God's Chosen People and that God still today has an exclusive racial covenant with the Jewish people. Christians are told that to resist the Jews' anti-Christian actions would be to oppose the will of God Himself. Yet, God says explicitly in Hebrews 8:9: Not according to the Covenant that I made with their fathers, in the day when I took them by the hand out of the land of Egypt; because they continued not in my Covenant, and I regarded them not, saith the Lord.[541]

Some ministers believe that the Jewish people will eventually come to Christ, and therefore we should support Israel no matter how many terrible, anti-Christian acts it commits. That is equivalent to saying that we should give the keys to our churches to arsonists seeking to burn them down because they may someday come to Christ. The offer of God's salvation is for everyone, but that does not mean that we should not oppose the forces of evil, or that we should aid the enemies of Christ. I believe that we have a moral obligation to defend our faith against those who attack Christ and to defend fellow Christians who face persecution at the hands of Christ's enemies.

It is important to clarify that although I think we must defend our faith and heritage, we should not be hateful or spiteful ourselves. We do not need to be hateful, but we must be resolved to oppose their efforts to destroy our way of life, our Christian faith, and our freedom and our very survival as a people. In my life, I have tried to approach every individual fair-mindedly. There is no reason to treat an individual Jew with disrespect or hatred. But if he works to destroy our heritage, we have the right — indeed we must — oppose him.

Television evangelists, who obviously can be booted from the airwaves at any time the controllers choose, are very careful what they say about the "Chosen People." I remember clearly one of Jimmy Swaggart's programs long before his sexual scandals. He whimpered and cried that he had to tell us that the Pentecostals were not following the Word of God; that the Catholics were not; that the Presbyterians were not; and that the Methodists were not. Jimmy was careful not to mention the one extremely powerful religious group that openly opposes Jesus Christ. Swaggart may have lost a little by criticizing Catholics and Methodists (fellow Christians who love Christ but who differ in some interpretations of the Holy Bible), but he knew he would have risked much more (in fact, everything) by uttering the slightest criticism of Jews.

As I researched Jewish history, I became aware of the fact that the Jewish people of today share little of the heritage of the Old Testament people called Israelites. Reading the *Jewish Encyclopedia* I learned that the Jewish people classify themselves into two major divisions: the Ashkenazim and Shephardim. The Shephardim, who migrated from Palestine to the Mediterranean nations, are supposedly related to the original tribes of Israel, while the Ashkenazim first emerged from an area of Southwest Asia called the Khazar (also called Chazar) Empire and filtered into Russia and Eastern Europe.

The *Jewish Encyclopedia* contains a long article on the Khazars and admits that the Kingdom of Khazaria converted to Judaism around 740 AD. Arthur Koestler, the eminent Jewish author, in an exhaustively researched book called the *Thirteenth Tribe*[542] argues persuasively that the Khazars became the Ashkenazim branch of Jewry, which forms the great majority of the modern Jewish people. Of course, this historical inquiry is little pursued because if it could be shown that many of the Jewish people have no direct lineage to Abraham, then their "ancient homeland" justification for the state of Israel would be completely undermined.

Furthermore, many of the original Israelite tribes fell under Babylonian captivity, and Jews have been minorities in every nation of the world in which they have resided. In spite of their ethnocentrism and Talmudic prescriptions opposing intermarriage, without a doubt the Jews have intermarried with their host peoples. Even with only a slight interbreeding compounded over the last 3,000 years, the Jews probably have retained only a portion of their original genetic heritage. Yet, as they have slowly absorbed the genes of other nationalities, close inbreeding in their minority communities has certainly led to great genetic similarity among them. Exclusively

Jewish diseases such as Tay-Sachs reveal a linked genetic heritage of Jews no matter where they reside in the world.[543]

While in college I encountered the Christian Identity faith that maintains that the original Israelite tribes became the differing nationalities of the European peoples. The denomination claims that with the coming of Christ, those of the original Israelites who maintained their heritage became Christians. They believe that those who were amalgamated with the other peoples (such as the Babylonians and then later the Khazars) and followed the Talmud became what are now called Jews. I researched and prayed about the issue, but I kept my more traditional Christian attitude about Jews. Over the years, though, many Identity Christians have become my friends, and I have been impressed by their dedication to our White heritage and to the Lord Jesus Christ. I view them warmly, as fellow Christians with whom I share many sentiments and with whom I disagree on few. I am thankful that they are united with all racially conscious White people in the struggle ahead.

Whatever its ethnic origins, over the centuries Christianity adopted a European cultural overlay both in its artistic expression and its religious tones. We can see those expressions in the breathtaking paintings of the Sistine Chapel, the sculptures of the Madonna and Child, the gothic cathedrals of Europe, and even the classic Christmas carols that so deeply touch our hearts. Christianity is tightly wound within the heritage of Western man. No race is so intrinsically Christian as the European. The different Christian denominations may differ dramatically in their interpretations of the Scriptures, but all of them share their faith in Him.

In stark contrast to the European forms of Christianity, African and Black Caribbean nations veer sharply from the fundamental Christian precepts. Once White missionaries and influences are completely removed, the forms and practices of Christianity usually become almost unrecognizable in just a few short years. Idol worship, witch doctors, forms of voodoo, and other decidedly non-Christian beliefs develop and flourish, even with the church itself.

I came to understand that I was not going against the Word of God to recognize and wish to preserve the different races that he created. If anything, I was fulfilling the laws of his creation. I also firmly realized that according to the Holy Bible the coming of Jesus Christ created a New Covenant that the chosen people of God now were those who accepted him and his Father. I knew that I was right to defend my Christian heritage from the powers seeking their demise. Then, as now, I believe in freedom of speech and freedom of religion. Judaism has every right to believe whatever it wishes and be actively anti-Christian and anti-Gentile. Zionists have every right to seek their own political supremacy. But, we have the right to oppose them, to defend ourselves from their power, to preserve our heritage in the face of their attacks, and to fight for our precious freedom from their domination.

By the time I graduated from college, I had a firm orientation toward my faith and my political work. The eternal life provided by Jesus Christ has been taken care of since the day I accepted His salvation. I know little of the afterlife, but I do know about the life we experience here on Earth.

I have felt my heart beat resolutely and pump red blood through my arteries and veins. On a mountaintop, I have felt the joy of clean, cool air filling my lungs while viewing a magnificent dawn. My eyes have seen the precious beauty of a baby at the moment of birth. I have experienced the heavenly scent of sweet magnolias on a pristine south Louisiana bayou. Of the inequities that plague us, I am also aware: little boys and girls victimized by crime and brutality, the crushing of the dreams of our youth under the heel of a debauched civilization. I know, as well, of a future bright and shining that awaits our people if only we will seek it with courage.

Perhaps if I were made of sterner stuff, I would have long ago put on the minister's collar of my Christian faith, but I leave that to far more perfect men, "to the men whom God has called." My unorthodox views, the doubts that sometimes creep in, and my many flaws exclude me from that service. I will, however, use whatever abilities I have in the natural world, the living world. I will fight for my people's survival and their freedom. I cannot turn my eyes and my hands from the job that needs to be done for a saner, healthier, more noble society possible right here on Earth. Such depends totally on a higher people in body, mind, and spirit. As did our Founding Fathers, I ask God for His help and guidance in the task ahead.

Finally, I truly believe that the future of this country, civilization, and planet is inseparably bound up with the destiny of our White race. I think, as the history of Christianity has shown, that our people have been the driving force in its triumph. Ultimately, because of the genetic potential instilled by our Creator, I think that our progeny will someday travel to the stars and beyond. My life's task is to help my race toward that destiny with every bit of courage that my heart can muster. If I can help move our people just one inch toward the heavens and toward God, when I pass on, my life will have been worthwhile.

Chapter 18

Jews, Communism and Civil Rights

The eccentric woman in the Citizens Council office, who railed about the Jews and Communism, obviously had some of her facts right, even if she seemed to fit the media stereotype of the anti-Semite. The facts were inescapable: Communism and Zionism were born from the same Jewish soul, personified in Moses Hess. [544]

I slowly became aware of a dual morality permeating Jewish-Gentile relations. Jews practiced one morality for themselves and preached another for the non-Jewish world. Their own morality of racial pride taught solidarity, tradition and self-interest. But they preached diversity and liberalism for their perceived competitors. If such dualism did not exist, how could the Jewish-dominated American media:

- **Support the nation of Israel, which promotes Judaism in its schools, while opposing even the singing of Christmas carols in American public schools?**
- **Support the nation of Israel, which has strictly segregated schools, communities, and facilities for Jews and Arabs — while condemning segregated schools and housing in America and South Africa?**
- **Support the nation of Israel, with its restrictive "Jews only" immigration laws, while subverting American attempts to curtail even illegal immigration?**
- **Support the nation of Israel, which allows every Jewish citizen to carry a machine gun if desired, while advocating strict gun control for American citizens?**
- **Support the nation of Israel, which openly states its mission to preserve the Jewish people and heritage, while condemning Whites who would dare to advocate the preservation of the White race and Western culture in America?**
- **Always paint the historical relations between Jews and Gentiles with the Gentiles as evildoers and the Jews as innocent victims, while condemning White people for even defending themselves from such Jewish depiction?**

The moral hypocrisy became obvious. Powerful Jews advocate one morality for Jews; the opposite for Gentiles. If their policies of solidarity are morally good for them, why would they not be morally good for us as well? Why the double standard? If "White racists" are morally reprehensible, why are not Jewish supremacists reprehensible as well?

While Herzl and other Zionists feverishly gathered worldwide Jewish support for the establishment of the exclusively Jewish state, Jewish activists were busy trying to negate the Christian component of American culture and remove even Christmas carols from our schools. While they trumpet their belief that they are a "Chosen People" above all others, and celebrate a unique people defined by heritage from Abraham to the present — they tell White people that race consciousness is evil. While they established a Jewish nation where citizenship is based almost exclusively on the heredity of the "Jewish people," Jewish anthropologists promote the idea that the White race doesn't exist. Even though they devotedly support their own exclusively Jewish-run state of Israel, they work feverishly to undermine the White control and character of America through the "civil-rights" movement and massive non-White immigration. While they have laws in Israel prohibiting Gentiles from owning certain media, they boldly move to gain control of the great majority of the mass media in America.

Communist Ideology and Race

Mattie Smith told me that the Jews had the leading role in the efforts to destroy the very underpinnings of our race and our heritage. I had read that Jews were the leaders of the academic movement promoting the idea that races are equal in their physical and mental abilities. In looking into the foundations of racial egalitarianism, I found that adherents of international Communism pioneered the modern notions of racial equality. In America, Marxist organizations quickly gained ascendancy in the remnants of the old abolitionist movements. In South Africa, they led the fight for full "democratic" rights for the Blacks. Across the world, Communism allied itself with non-White peoples and their struggle for "liberation from White imperialism, colonialism, and oppression." I soon found out that Jews dominated the International Communist movement in modern times just as they had led Bolshevism in Russia early in the 20th century.

Jewish scribe Nathan Glazer[545] stated matter-of-factly that in the 60s and 70s the Jews comprised half of all the active Communists in the United States and four out of five of its leaders. Two Jews, Jerry Rubin and Abbie Hoffman, led the Marxist-Oriented, Yippie

Movement, and they were two of the five Jewish members of the revolutionary "Chicago Seven" group — tried for the violent disruption of the 1968 Democratic Convention. I read a book called *Behind Communism*, and I was surprised to discover that at least 4 out of 5 of all those caught and convicted of Communist espionage and treason in the United States and Canada were Jews.[546]

Probably the most infamous act of treason in American history was the theft of the atomic bomb secrets by Ethel and Julius Rosenberg.[547] They were part of the Fuchs-Gold spy ring that operated in and around the Manhattan Project and other branches of the American atomic weapons program. Seven members of the Fuchs-Gold ring pled guilty to charges associated with espionage. They were Klaus Fuchs, Harry Gold, David Greenglass, Abraham Brothman, Miriam Moskowitz, Sidney Weinbaum, and Alfred Slack. Another suspect, Morton Sobell, fled to Mexico, but Mexican authorities turned him over to the United States to face trial and subsequent conviction. A jury also convicted the Rosenbergs, and they were executed.[548] Of the ten spies most responsible for the selling of our atomic secrets to the Soviets, only one, Alfred Slack, was a Gentile.

Other major spy cases included the Amerasia Case, the Gerhart Eisler Case, the Judith Coplin Case, and the Alger Hiss Case. Jews figured prominently in these cases and made up a clear majority of the defendants. The only prominent non-Jewish spy was Alger Hiss. In the Hollywood Ten Case, The House of Representatives convicted ten of Hollywood's leading film writers of contempt of Congress. They appeared before the House Committee on Un-American Activities and refused to testify when asked if they were Communists. Jewish publications alleged the committee ruined the writers for no apparent reason. Recently a number of movies have been made defending the Hollywood Ten as unjustly and unfairly persecuted, yet six of the ten proved to be dues-paying members of the Communist Party. The other four had records of many Communist-front activities and connections. Nine of the ten were of Jewish heritage.

Julius and Ethel Rosenberg

While Jewish Marxists pursued the political part of the "civil-rights" effort, they pushed just as hard in the academic realm. Until the 1930s the biological sciences recognized the different races of mankind as surely as they did the different species and subspecies of the animal kingdom — that is, as commentator Kevin Strom says, "Until the egalitarian political wind blew into American academia, propelled by a clever, connected, and well-heeled minority with an agenda."[549]

I began to realize that the drive for race-mixing did not find its source in the Black people of America. Most Blacks were content to be separate, although they certainly wanted economic and social advancement. The most popular Black leader in the early part of the 20th century was the Black separatist Marcus Garvey, who sought repatriation for Blacks back to Africa and the foundation of a new Black nation. Against this movement of Black separatism and the effort of European Americans to preserve White America there rose a minority with an entirely different agenda.

The Racial Egalitarian Dogma

Franz Boas is the accepted father of the modern egalitarian school of anthropology. He was a Jewish immigrant from Germany with little formal training in the anthropological field, having done his doctoral thesis on the color of water. Boas introduced what he called "cultural anthropology" to the discipline. Until his arrival, anthropology fell in the realm of physical science. Boas effectively divided anthropology into the separate disciplines of cultural and physical anthropology.

Early physical anthropologists were truly race scientists because they studied man and his evolutionary development through the study of the measurable physical characteristics of the human races, past and present. Any good physical anthropologist could pick up a human skull and, based on its characteristics, quickly identify the race of the specimen. Of course, this physiological knowledge was vital in sorting out the unearthed remnants of early man and piecing together man's prehistory and evolutionary development. Cultural anthropology dealt more with the different contemporary cultures of mankind and culturally related questions of antiquity and prehistory, making it a far less precise science, and one open to wide interpretation.

Surprisingly, before he became such a prominent anthropologist, Boas expressed his acceptance of racial differences in mental characteristics. In *The Mind of Primitive Man*, he wrote:

> **Differences of Structure must be accompanied by differences of function, physiological as well as psychological; and, as we found clear evidence of differences in structure between races, so we must anticipate that the differences in mental characteristics will be found.** [550]

278 MY AWAKENING

Both of Boas' parents were radical socialists in the revolutionary movement that swept over Europe in 1870. In his biography of Boas, his student Melville Herskovits wrote that Boas' political sympathies "leaned towards a variety of socialism."[551] The United States House of Representatives cited Boas' involvement with 44 Communist-front organizations. Coinciding with the rise of Nazism in Germany and the increasing influence of racially aware anthropologists in the world scientific community, Boas began to marshal his anthropological influence in service of his political sympathies. He began to advance the quack idea that there are really no such things as individual human races. He argued that although they had variations of skin colors and features, the groups called races possessed little difference genetically and that, whatever their superficial differences, solely their environment created them. By 1938 Boas dropped the above quotation from the new edition of his book.

He gathered many Jewish disciples around him, including Gene Weltfish, Isador Chein, Melville Herskovits, Otto Klineberg, and Ashley Montagu. He also had among his followers the Negro K. B. Clark and two women, Ruth Benedict and Margaret Mead. Mead later wrote her famous book on Samoa (Coming of Age in Samoa)[552] suggesting that indiscriminate sexual relations would lessen teenage traumas and problems. (Her opus was later soundly refuted by Derek Freeman, who showed that Mead had falsified her data on Samoa.) [553] [554] [555]

Boas and his entire cadre of disciples had extensive Communist connections. He repeatedly proclaimed that he was in a "holy war against racism" and he died suddenly during a luncheon where once again and for the last time, he stressed the need to fight "racism." Boas and his comrades gained control over the anthropology departments of most universities by encouraging their egalitarian comrades to always use their positions to support their own in academic appointments. While traditional anthropologists had no ax to grind and no sacred cause to champion, Boas and his followers embarked on a holy mission to extirpate racial knowledge from the academic establishment. They succeeded.

Whenever egalitarians achieved positions of influence or power, they aided their comrades to rise in the teaching departments of the colleges and academic departments they administered. They could count on fellow Jews who held influential university positions to assist their co-religionists, as well as Gentile egalitarians, in getting professorships and research appointments and promotions. Similar collusion took place in the ranks and on the boards of anthropological associations and journals. However, the coup de grâce was the massive support given the egalitarian dogma by the media establishment, which was overwhelmingly in Jewish hands.

Racial equality was (and still is) presented to the public as scientific fact, opposed only by the "bigoted" and the "ignorant." Egalitarian writers such as Ashley Montagu and others received great praise in magazines, newspapers, and, later on television. Whether one was a Jew or a Gentile, professing a belief in racial equality became essential dogma for anyone who wanted to advance in anthropology or any other part of the academic world. Adherence to the "politically correct" line led to prestige and acclaim, money and success. Racial truth-telling led to personal attack and often economic hardship.

Ashley Montagu became the best-known spokesman for the equality hoax, superseding Boas as the most popular exponent of antiracism. His well-modulated British accent and aristocratic name added instant credibility to his racial pronouncements. I can still, after thirty years, remember his impressive appearances on the *Today* television program. His book, *Race: Man's Most Dangerous Myth*, became the bible of equality, and it profoundly impressed me before I had a chance to read the other side.[556] Montagu's real name was Israel Ehrenberg. In a brilliant exercise of psychological camouflage, Ehrenberg changed his name a number of times, finally settling on not simply an Anglo-Saxon moniker, but the name Montagu, which is one of Britain's most aristocratic and oldest medieval-titled families.[557]

By the late 1990s, Jewish writers began to brazenly write about their domination of American anthropology. In a 1997 edition of *American Anthropologist*, which is published by the American Anthropological Association, Jewish scholar Gelya Frank writes that egalitarian American anthropology was so thoroughly Jewish that it should be classed as "part of Jewish History." Frank goes on to admit that anthropology is in the service of a social agenda and that her essay focuses on Jewish anthropologists who are "concerned with turning multiculturalist theories into agendas for activism." The same breed of anthropologists who so fervently declare that "there is no such thing as race" concerning Blacks and Whites are now hypocritically affirming the unique genetic homogeneity of Jews. Moreover, increasing numbers of Jewish anthropologists have come out of the closet in celebration of their special genetic and cultural heritage.[558]

As far as Blacks and Whites are concerned, egalitarianism still dominates. Richard Lewontin, Leon Kamin and Stephen Jay Gould, are its three self-acknowledged Marxist Jews and the leading academic exponents of egalitarianism. In spite of an avalanche of fresh scientific data proving the vital role of genes in producing individual and group differences, racial egalitarianism is still the holy writ of anthropology and human psychology as characterized by the popular media. The writings of Lewontin, Kamin, Gould, Rose, and other egalitarians frequently appear in the pages of magazines such as the

Smithsonian, Natural History, Nature, Discover, Time, Newsweek, and other wide-circulation publications. Television programs often interview them as "authorities" on the subject of race — and seldom are their opponents allowed to challenge them. Most of the leading egalitarian spokesmen are self-described Marxists, a slight detail seldom mentioned in the media. Imagine if they were self-proclaimed Nazis; I suspect the reaction to them would be very different.

Despite the well-organized "part of Jewish history" control of anthropology, the scientific affirmation of race is growing so quickly that the popular egalitarians may not be able to hold back the scientific tide much longer. There has never been a greater disparity between scientific and popular understanding.

The Freudian Assault

Psychology fell to the Jewish onslaught just as anthropology had. From the days of Sigmund Freud, psychology became defined as the "Jewish science." One of his Jewish biographers put it this way:

> **History made psychoanalysis a "Jewish science." It continued to be attacked as such. It was destroyed in Germany, Italy, and Austria and exiled to the four winds, as such. It continues even now to be perceived as such by enemies and friends alike. Of course there are by now distinguished analysts who are not Jews. . . . But the vanguard of the movement over the last fifty years has remained predominantly Jewish as it was from the beginning.** [559]

Since the Great Depression, academic psychology discounted the impact of heredity and attributed almost all individual human behavioral patterns and mental ability to environmental conditioning. They claimed that environment rather than heredity is really the source of all mental and behavioral differences among the races. But, not only did the theories of Freud and his disciples attack the principles of race, they made a broadside attack on the spiritual and moral values of European civilization. Freud suggested that our Christian sexual morality was the cause of mental illness on a grand scale. He relentlessly undermined the concepts of sexual fidelity and the foundations of marriage. In 1915 he stated:

> **Sexual morality — as society, in its extreme form, the American, defines it — seems to me very contemptible. I advocate an incomparably freer sexual life.** [560]

In *Moses and Monotheism* (1939) Freud repeatedly attacks Christianity while promoting the spiritual supremacy of the Jewish people.

> **The people, happy in their conviction of possessing the truth, overcome by the consciousness of being the chosen, came to value highly all intellectual and ethical achievements.**

JEWS, COMMUNISM, AND CIVIL RIGHTS 281

The Christian religion did not keep to the lofty heights of spirituality to which the Jewish religion had soared — Sigmund Freud [561]

Just as the Communist Jews had a political war with the Czars of Russia, Freudians pursued a cultural war against Western Christian culture. Kevin MacDonald, in his classic study of Jewish ethnocentrism, *A People That Shall Dwell Apart*, points out that Freud's *Totem and Taboo*[562] reveals his role in the cultural war against Gentiles:

> **Freud's speculations clearly had an agenda. Rather than provide speculations which reaffirmed the moral and intellectual basis of the culture of his day, his speculations were an integral part of his war on gentile culture — so much so that he viewed *Totem and Taboo* as a victory over Rome and the Catholic Church.**[563]

Freud reveled in what he saw as his war against Christendom, which he compared with the Roman Empire, and suggested that he was like his idol Hannibal and was meant to sack Rome.

> **Hannibal. . . had been the favourite hero of my later school days. . . . I began to understand for the first time what it meant to belong to an alien race . . . the figure of the semitic general rose still higher in my esteem. To my youthful mind Hannibal and Rome symbolized the conflict between the tenacity of Jewry and the organisation of the Catholic Church . . .**[564]

Freud makes his Jewish supremacist viewpoint very clear in a letter to a Jewish woman who intended to conceive a child by a Gentile to heal the split in psychoanalysis. His words were:

> **I must confess...that your fantasy about the birth of the Savior to a mixed union did not appeal to me at all. The Lord, in that anti-Jewish period, had him born from the superior Jewish race. But I know these are my prejudices.** [565]

A year later the same woman gave birth to a child fathered by a Jew. Freud responded

> **I am, as you know, cured of the last shred of my predilection for the Aryan cause, and would like to take it that if the child turned out to be a boy he will develop into a stalwart Zionist. He or she must be dark in any case, no more towheads. Let us banish all these will-o'-the-wisps!**
> **I shall not present my compliments to Jung in Munich, as you know perfectly well....We are and remain Jews. The others will only exploit us and will never understand and appreciate us. (quoted in Yerushalmi 1991, 45).** [566]

Not only did Freud consciously launch an attack on our cultural values, he conveniently labeled opponents of that assault as mentally ill. In *Moses and Monotheism*, Freud portrays anti-Semitism as a mental illness that arises out of jealousy of Jewish ethical supremacy.[567]

On the deck of a ship steaming toward the United States, Freud commented to his friends that the people of America thought he was bringing them a panacea, but instead he said, "We are bringing them the plague."⁵⁶⁸

The Civil-Rights Movement

Just as Jewish academics lead the scholastic fight for egalitarianism in science and sociology, and Jewish media moguls lead the propaganda fight, the "civil-rights" movement itself found most of its leadership and financial support in the Jewish community.

Almost from the first day of its inception in 1909, the National Association for the Advancement of Colored People (NAACP) was the premier organization working for a racially mixed American society. Interestingly enough, the founding board of directors had only one prominent Black, W. E. B. Dubois (who was actually a Mulatto). Most of the board consisted of Jewish Marxist ideologues. The U.S. House of Representatives and many state investigative bodies thoroughly documented the fact that all of the NAACP's founders were activists in the Communist cause. Dubois even chose Communist Ghana as his burial site.

The NAACP's first president was Arthur Spingarn, and only Jews served as NAACP presidents from its founding until the 1970s. Noel Spingarn succeeded his brother, Arthur, and following him, Kivie Kaplan reigned over the organization. The Jewish leadership of the NAACP was little known by the public at large. When I came of age, the only name I heard associated with the NAACP was Roy Wilkins, who was its Black national secretary. Because he was so much in the press and public eye, like most Americans, I thought Wilkins was the NAACP leader. But Kaplan was the actual NAACP president during that time. Benjamin Hooks

NAACP leader Kivie Kaplan

became the first Black president finally in the 1970s. Once a Black finally made it to the presidency of the organization, no longer did the public hear much about the NAACP "national secretary." From then on the public spokesman was the NAACP president.

In the recent Black-Jewish split, liberal Jews are quick to cry foul at Black resentment against them by reciting the fact that the lion's share of the financing of the Black cause has come from Jews. They also boast that at least 90 percent of the civil-rights legal effort has come from Jewish attorneys and has long been supported by Jewish money.[569]

Practically every step of the civil-rights movement's progress came through the courts. They decreed forced racial integration of the schools, enabled illiterate Blacks to vote, and ultimately forced upon America the massive anti-White discrimination program with the Orwellian name "affirmative action." Here, too, Jews took the predominant roles.

The organization that fought many of these battles was the NAACP Legal Defense Fund, an organization separate from the NAACP itself. At this writing, Jews still lead it. Jake Greenberg has been active in the legal fund for years and was the chief attorney for Brown in the famous Supreme Court case Brown *v* Board of Education. In that nefarious decision, the Supreme Court — in one devastating stroke of the pen — initiated the transformation of the American public educational system from one of the best in the world to one of the worst in the First World.

Even in the areas where Jews were not the actual leaders, they provided much of the behind-the-scenes influence. Martin Luther King Jr. fell under the guidance of Stanley Levinson, who wrote many of King's speeches, including, some say, the "I Have a Dream" speech delivered at the March on Washington. John and Robert Kennedy warned King to disassociate himself from Levinson because of Levinson's Communist record. King, however, found Levinson invaluable and refused. The Student Non-Violent Coordinating Committee (SNCC) and the Congress of Racial Equality (CORE) also had key Jewish involvement in their formative periods, and most of the nominally White "Freedom Riders" that went South were Jews. The famous case of the three Freedom Riders killed in Philadelphia, Mississippi, involved Schwerner, Goodman, and Chaney — two Jews and one Black.

The public image of the man who called himself "Martin Luther King" (his legal name was Michael King) is a textbook illustration of the power of the media to influence America. Most people still do not know of the extent of King's involvement in Communism, in part because the media continues to ignore King's long record of Communist associations. King privately declared himself to be a Marxist,[570] and told his inner circle that his efforts were a part of the "class struggle." His personal secretary, Bayard Rustin, was a Communist. When King had to replace Rustin in 1961, he chose another Communist, Jack O'Dell. His main advisor ("handler" would probably be a more apt term), as I've mentioned, was Jewish Communist Stanley Levinson, who edited and probably wrote a good deal of King's book *Stride Toward Freedom*. Levinson prepared King's income tax returns, controlled King's fundraising activities, and was also in charge of funneling Soviet money to the Communist Party, USA.[571]

Only recently has it been revealed that King plagiarized large sections of his doctoral thesis. Boston University formed a committee to determine the extent of King's plagiarism. It determined that 45 percent of the first part and 21 percent of the second part were taken from other authors. [572] Schools regularly revoke degrees on discovery of far less cheating, but the importance of King to the civil-rights movement prevented the revocation of his divinity degree.

The media have always carefully portrayed King as a good Christian family man — the epitome of a man of God. But King had dozens of liaisons with prostitutes, White and Black, used church money to pay them and commonly beat them — all documented by the FBI and admitted by King associates.[573]

King even spent the night before his assassination copulating with and beating White prostitutes. On the FBI surveillance tapes the "Reverend King" can be heard during intercourse to say, " I'm f---ing for God!" and "I'm not a Negro tonight!" The King records are so damning that the tapes and other FBI documents were sealed for 50 years. Despite these facts, King's Jewish handlers and their allies in the media were steadfast in their laudatory portrayal of King. [574]

Jewish and Black relations have become strained in recent years as Black political sympathies have become more nationalistic in their own right. Jewish association with Black civil-rights causes originated from the days when many Communists saw the Blacks as potential revolutionaries for Communist uprising. The Communists in their creation of the Soviet State temporarily won the Jewish fraternal struggle between Zionism and Communism that Winston Churchill described in 1920. Radical American Jews envisioned the Blacks as an American proletariat, a transatlantic version of the oppressed serfs of Russia that could be utilized as allies helping to usher in a Communist revolution. Of course, even non-Communist Jews tended to support a non-racial definition of "American," since they more than anyone are aware of their status as outsiders in White society. This led almost all organized Jewish factions to support the dismantling of the laws and traditions that supported the continued existence of our race.

Zionism over Marxism

After the Second World War, two major factors began to pull the Jews away from Communism: the Russification of the Soviet State and the establishment of the state of Israel.

To fight the Germans, Stalin and the Soviet regime motivated the Russian people by calling on their deep patriotic feelings. Stalin himself, one of the most paranoid and ruthless leaders of all time, skillfully played one Jewish faction against the other until he emerged as the unquestioned authority in Russia. Leon Trotsky (Lev Bronstein), Stalin's chief rival, was forced into exile and later murdered by the Russian NKVD. Although individual Jews remained pivotal in his regime, Stalin saw all Jewish alliances as a threat to his own power. He brutally repressed any potential threat he could find, and he turned the Soviet Union to a more nationalistic course. The anthem of Soviet Communism, the egalitarian and anti-nationalist "Internationale," was replaced by a traditional Russian hymn.

Affirmative action for Jewish Communists in the early days of the revolution was replaced by a merit system in universities and the military. A lot of Stalin's maneuvers against the Jews did not become clear until long after the Second World War, and many Jews had reluctance to believe that they had lost control of the Soviet regime. Even into the late 1960s, in most countries other than Russia, Jews still constituted the majority of Marxist leadership around the world — including the United States. Many of these Jewish Communists, though, had become somewhat anti-Russian and now called themselves Trotskyites. Only a few Jewish radicals held onto the Communist vision as expressed in Russia; most others reached for a new Marxist ideology rooted in egalitarianism and, while holding onto the social tenants of Communism, began a migration to capitalist economics.

While these factors occurred in the Soviet Union, the state of Israel was created, and it seemed that the old, ethnocentric, and orthodox prophecies were finally coming about. For 2,000 years Jews had uttered the prayer "Next year in Jerusalem." Suddenly, any Jew could go to a Jerusalem once more under their direct political control. During these years, America witnessed the transformation of many New Left Jewish radicals. Norman Podhoretz and *Commentary* magazine, for example, shifted from Communist apologist to capitalist advocate — from an anti-Vietnam War dove to an unmitigated Israeli hawk. In the 1970s, a flood of these New Right Jews flooded into the "conservative movement," adapting to the tenants of economic conservatism but adding the elements of social liberalism, egalitarianism, the New World Order, and, of course, super-Zionism. Jews filtered into organizations of every conceivable political stripe, espousing different viewpoints but always keeping a keen eye for the interests of the Jews and the Israeli State.

Feminism

Simultaneous with the sacrifice of our nation upon the alter of an impossible Black "equality," came the promotion for the equally fictitious idea of sexual "equality." Women were told that they were psychologically the same as men but were just socially conditioned by their environment to be wives and mothers instead of research scientists and captains of industry. Not only did the "women's liberationists" try to convince women that nurturing and inculturating the next generation was less important than sweating on an assembly line or sweating the "bottom line" in an executive suite, they went much further by decrying the role of wife and mother altogether.

Freud also contributed to the destruction of the family in his endorsement of the supposed sexual liberation of sexual promiscuity. One of the strengths of the West has always been high-investment parenting as compared to the Third World. Freud and his Jewish purveyors of psychoanalysis conflated sex and love and justified the destruction of the family unit on issues such as unsatisfactory sexual gratification.

Women's liberation has completely restructured the American family, as most wives and mothers have been forced into the job market by the new economic standards, resulting in fewer role choices for women. Many researchers say the creation of millions of "working" mothers has had a deleterious effect on family stability and child development. As a result many women are now struggling as the sole provider for themselves and their children, and the ones in stable families often find themselves stressed and debilitated by having to do both the traditional women's roles in the home and working eight hours a day outside of it.

The most prominent of the modern feminists were Gloria Steinem, Betty Friedan, and Bella Abzug. Interestingly, all three came from one of the most sexually repressive religions on Earth: Judaism. *A Hole in the Sheet* by Evelyn Kaye, who grew up in an Orthodox home, illustrates the demeaning and often disrespectful position of women in the Jewish faith and the hatred expressed toward Gentiles outside of it. She discusses the Bar Mitzvah and the completely ascendant role of the male and writes the following:

> During the prayers which a Jewish man recites every morning are a series of blessings, which include: "Thank you, Lord, for not making me a non-Jew, for not making me a slave, for not making me a woman."
>
> In Susan Weidman Schneider's book *Jewish and Female*, Rabbi Laura Geller comments: "Menstrual taboos are responsible for real damage to Jewish women's views of themselves and their bodies. I have met many women who learned nothing about the Torah except that they could not touch the Torah because they menstruate. . . . Their sense of themselves as 'inferior' Jews has already permeated their relationship to tradition and their own bodies. [575]

Kaye also bravely comments on the anti-Gentile nature of Jewish Orthodoxy.

> The final turning point for me was anti-Goyism.
>
> The mark of a truly devout Hasidic or Orthodox Jew, as well as many other Jews, is an unquestioned hatred of non-Jews. This is the foundation of the ultra-Orthodox and Hasidic philosophy. It's as tenacious, unreasoned and impossible as anti-Semitism, racism, and sexism. And as intractable.
>
> What it says is that all non-Jews, or Goyim as the word is in Yiddish since it's the plural of "Goy," are wicked, evil and untrustworthy.
>
> There is a complete litany of all the terrible things about non-Jews which apply to every single one and which are believed implicitly by the Orthodox. These include:
> — All Goyim drink alcohol and are always drunk;
> — All Goyim are on drugs;
> — All Goyim hate Jews even when they seem to be friendly;
> — All Goyim are anti-Semites, no matter what they say or do;
> — All Goyim have a terrible family life and mistreat their wives and children;
> — All Goyim eat pork all the time;
> — Goyim are never as clever, as kind, as wise or as honest as Jews;
> — You can never trust the Goyim.
>
> There's much more. But the essence of anti-Goyism is passed to Jewish children with their mother's milk, and then nurtured, fed and watered carefully into full-blown phobias throughout their lives. [576]

The Talmud often characterizes women as unclean, whores, and as deceitful, lower beings. It even has long passages that justify adult males having sexual relations with little girls. Women are segregated in the Orthodox synagogue. Women are almost as reviled as Gentiles. Note the following talmudic references, starting with the prayer to which Kaye refers:

> Blessed be thou. . .who has not made me a goy. . . who has not made me a woman, and who has made me an Israelite. . .who has not made me a slave. Judah Ben Ilai [577]
>
> When a grown up man has intercourse with a little girl it is nothing, for when the girl is less than this [three years old], it is as if one puts the finger into the eye, tears come to the eye,... [footnote] (7) again and again but eyesight returns, so does virginity come back to the little girl under three years. (Kethuboth 11b)[578]
>
> A maiden aged three years and one day may be acquired in marriage by coition. (Sanhedrin 55b and 69a-69b)[579] and (Yebamoth 57b 58a, 60b)[580]

Yet, the Jewish high priestesses of women's liberation have made few inroads in reforming those inequities. Only the Reform part of Judaism puts women on somewhat of an equal footing. But Israel is an Orthodox-run Jewish nation, and nearly all the Reform and Conservative organizations around the world support Israel wholeheartedly. The question of ethnic heritage far overshadows any doctrinal debate. It is ironic that women from the religious culture having the most demeaning attitude toward women, should focus their efforts on promoting a sexual revolution among those of European descent. It seems to me that their time could be better spent addressing the rank inequities in their own backyard.

No Third World society on Earth venerates women, womanhood and motherhood as much as Western Christian civilization. No dark races accord women as much freedom and respect. In most Third World nations, women are treated much like chattel property. Millions are sexually mutilated with female circumcision and infibulation.[581] Physical abuse is commonplace. Women routinely provide almost all their own and their children's sustenance in Africa, where the normal behavior of the male is to sexually play — but seldom stay.

The purposely-induced antagonism between the sexes divides White Americans when it is more important than ever that we are united. The wedge driven between White men and women often divides our vote and helps minority and pro-minority candidates to win elections. Women are deceived into voting for minority candidates and liberal causes in higher percentages than men do. In spite of the wide difference between the White and Black race in the status and well-being of women, the feminist movement has aligned itself with Black "civil-rights" objectives. They've been told that the "White male patriarchy" is the enemy, causing resentments and conflicts between the sexes that could prove fatal for our people unless repaired. Many women's groups openly campaign for Jewish and Black causes, blessed by accolades of the Jewish high priestesses of feminism. But when White women form organizations exclusively for the advancement of our European heritage, they face condemnation.

White men and women who have become aware of the racial apocalypse looming ahead must make a supreme effort to reach the alienated Western woman and bring her back into unity with her own people. Her most vital interests, as well as that of Western man, lay with the preservation of her racial heritage and the Western culture in which she thrives. White nations have always afforded women the greatest degree of personal safety and physical health, the best education and economic opportunity, the most prestige, and the most stable family life.

A perfect example of the ardent minority racism dominating women's liberation groups was the halting of a demonstration against the acquittal of wife-beater turned-wife killer O. J. Simpson. A National Organization of Women spokeswoman planned a demonstration protesting the acquittal until the national office made her call off the demonstration because it would offend Blacks. Black sensibilities obviously became far more paramount to NOW than the very lives and safety of women — at least *White* women.

Women's rights are virtually nonexistent in Third World nations, where women are ruled by male tyranny and brutality. Sentiments of male chauvinism find mild verbal and cultural expression in Western nations. In the dark nations, male chauvinism is not represented by mere office chatter or humor; it is realized in a day-to-day living in which millions of women are subject to brutality, suppression, sexual mutilation, and subjugation. When women realize that their real liberation can come only in a fully Western society, the liberation of Western man will come as well. There may be debate among our people of the respective roles of men and women, but that debate can be heard only in a Western society. If our nation is remade in the image of the dark world, there will be no respect of women's rights and no possibility of debate. Even from a purely selfish, feminist point-of-view, the transformation of our society to a genetically and culturally Third World state would mean the end of any aspirations of "women's rights."

Egalitarianism and Civil-Rights as Weapons

As I uncovered more information of the Jewish domination of the anti-White, and anti-family revolution, it struck me that many powerful Jews might see White America in the same way they once viewed the Czar and the White Russians. I began to wonder whether we were destined to become a people deposed, a nation conquered not with armies and cannon but by the power of the purse and the power of the press.

If they did not view us as Theodor Herzl did — as aliens — why did so many of them attack American traditions and customs, from the structure of the family to the singing of Christmas carols in our schools? Although not all Jews participate in the crusade against our heritage, a vast majority support chauvinist Jewish organizations and back the candidates for public office who most sublimate themselves to Jewish concerns. Jewish support means far more than their voting bloc; it means full campaign coffers and the support of powerful media.

Jewish activists have been relentless in their support for pluralism of American politics and culture. The high-sounding Jewish promises of the so-called civil-rights movement — *love, peace, and brotherhood* — have been replaced with the violent obscenities of a rap song. For Blacks, once rhythmic and peaceful urban communities now echo with the sound of gunfire, a third of young Black men are in jail, probation, or parole, and millions are chained, hand, foot, and soul, to alcohol and drugs.

Whites who have fled from the cities their fathers built find themselves burdened with high taxes that disproportionately go to unproductive minorities in Welfare and in the criminal justice system flooded with minority criminals. Those unable to flee find themselves in deteriorating conditions. Their children endure the primitivism and try to adjust to the fear permeating the mostly black schools of our major cities, while their parents barricade themselves behind their locked doors and barred windows. There they often lose themselves in the make-believe world of television, where they supinely watch their history, their soul, and their spirit under an unrelenting attack as spiritually damaging as the crime on the streets is physically destructive.

What did Jews have to gain from the empowerment of minorities in America? Obviously, the Marxists saw Blacks and other minorities as staunch allies vital for the advancement of their agenda and political success. Over the past decades, the Black bloc vote has been vital to liberal politics. Perhaps more important, a Babylon-like, multiracial America suits Jewish interests. In a divided land, the most unified group exercises the greatest power. In a jumbled, kaleidoscope society, the exercise of that alien power is less apparent to the majority elements, for if a tiny minority has an agenda hostile to the majority, that minority needs to be as unobtrusive as possible. Multiracialism muddies the waters. Jews will always thrive in such a Babylon. Every blow that has broken the solidarity and furthered the dispossession of the founding and once-ruling American majority, is an opening for the new contenders to the throne.

A great deal of the degeneracy has no design at all. The alien nature described by Theodor Herzl finds its expression in thousands of jabs and body blows to the traditions and values of the Anglo-America of old. Whether it is a Nativity scene outlawed from a public square, or an all-male military academy turned coed, or morning radio programs filled with crude talk of human excretory activity, or the glamorization of drugs in films and novels, the beat goes on, drummed by people almost proud of their alien nature. The tune is the funeral march for America and the whole Western world.

They eat away at our nation's European roots, always gaining influence and power and yet always considering themselves outsiders, and that is precisely what they are: spiritual, cultural, and genetic outsiders who are now on the inside of the American power structure. Consider the following statement from a Jewish pundit who has both success and fame:

> Decades later, prowling along the river with Texas Rangers to see them catch crossing Mexicans, I stopped and sat on the ground. I said that's enough — I am one of them, the wetbacks, and not of them, the hunters. [582]

A. M. Rosenthal wrote those words, a man who has been head of the Editorial pages of *The New York Times*, America's most powerful newspaper. With all his money, power, and prestige — sitting in the dirt along the muddy banks of the Rio Grande — Rosenthal still identifies himself as an "outsider." His loyalties are not with other Americans who want to preserve our way of life. His allegiance is with the aliens who will change it.

The minority racism — the "civil rights" and the egalitarianism — that has flourished in America, had its origins in an alien ethnocentrism. Our nation, once distinctively European in nature, is fading fast. It was not brewed in the fleshpots of Babylon. But unless great change comes, it will succumb there.

Most Americans who fought against the civil-rights movement, believing correctly that it would lead to the destruction of the fabric of society, never recognized the source of its power. In the South some blamed the "Yankees," some the politicians, and some the media. Few understood that the civil-rights movement was an outgrowth of the same power that propelled the Russian Revolution, that influenced the participation of America in the First World War, that helped bring about the Second World War, and that finally created the nation of Israel.

How ironic that the civil-rights movement had its roots in racism, that it was simply a weapon wielded by the most ethnocentric people on Earth against their ancient enemies. Blacks were simply pawns in a much larger political game. Most of the non-Jewish Whites who were enlisted in the cause never realized that the struggle was not really about civil rights. These participants, like the Blacks themselves, were being manipulated in the much bigger contest of the Jewish struggle for power.

The same establishment that preaches the holy writ of racial equality and amalgamation, never lets Americans forget the right of Jews — in fact, the holy obligation of Jews — to maintain their heritage both here and in their Jewish state. It reminds us constantly, from the pulpit of television, of their unmatched godliness, their eternal innocence and victimhood. Their pundits and scriptwriters unabashedly proclaim Jewish mental, cultural, and moral supremacy. They are canonized daily by their media, while those who dare utter a contrary word are muzzled or demonized. A tabernacle of the new religion of the Holocaust stands squarely in the midst of the American Acropolis of Washington, D.C. In that shrine the American people can worship the Chosen People and feel guilt for their sins against them. There they can learn of the worst transgression of all: questioning the only true "civil right" — the Jewish right to rule us culturally, spiritually, and politically.

The alien oppression would be bad enough by itself, but our masters clearly planned the extermination of our kind. Once I understood that, I could no longer remain silent about the realities of Jewish power in the West. Their continued dominance would sweep away our folk in a rising tide of immigration, miscegenation, non-White fecundity, and White self-sterilization.

The alien-dominated media keep most White Americans completely unaware of the ongoing dispossession of our people — and another segment cheering it on. I began to see that the media was the most powerful weapon they used against us, so I focused my next inquiries on Jewish infiltration and domination of the American mass-communication media.

Chapter 19:

Who Runs the Media?

> *Such as it is, the press has become the greatest power within the Western World, more powerful than the legislature, the executive and judiciary. One would like to ask; by whom has it been elected and to whom is it responsible?*
> — Aleksandr Solzhenitsyn

In the Oscar-winning 1976 movie *Network*,[583] Howard Beale, the "mad prophet of the airwaves," becomes consumed with the idea of exposing an insidious danger facing America: the takeover of American television by Arabs through their petro-dollars.

The film was based on an Oscar-winning screenplay by Paddy Chayefsky, who depicts a dark plot by Arabs to buy and control the TV networks. Howard Beale, played by Peter Finch, is a deranged news anchorman who speaks his mind about any subject, resulting in skyrocketing ratings. Raving about the inequities and corruption in American life, Beale would cry out: "I'm mad as hell, and I'm not going to take it anymore!"

Imagine if Iraqi-American supporters of Saddam Hussein had control of the American media. Suppose they controlled the national television networks and were a majority of the owners, producers, and writers of television entertainment and news. TV is an irresistible power that reaches into every American home — the primary source by which most Americans learn about the world. Consider the dangers of that enormous power dominated by a tightly knit, Iraqi, Muslim minority that supported the Hussein regime.

If the non-television media were still free, they undoubtedly would treat Iraqi media domination as a great danger to America. Every non-Iraqi source of media would proclaim that such control threatens our freedoms. Congress would likely draft legislation to break up the Iraqi stranglehold on television. Patriots would remind Americans that if we were not free to obtain unbiased news, documentaries, and programming, democracy could not work. The power of TV controlled by one point of view would erode the foundation of all our freedoms: the freedom of speech. Pundits would be outraged that non-Americans, people with allegiance to a foreign power, had control over the American mind.

Taking the analogy further, imagine if the rest of the media were also in Iraqi hands. Suppose that the three major news magazines, *Time, Newsweek,* and *U.S. News and World Report* were run by Iraqis, that the three most influential American newspapers, *The New York Times, The Wall Street Journal,* and *The Washington Post* — as well as a majority of the remaining major newspapers and magazines — were controlled by Iraqis. Imagine that Muslim Iraqis dominated the Hollywood movie industry as well as book publishing and even book distribution. Picture the Iraqis as also holding immense wealth in business and banking, as thoroughly entrenched in entertainment and Hollywood, academia, the judiciary, and the government. On top of all this, suppose that supporters of Saddam Hussein had the most powerful lobby in Washington and were responsible for the bulk of the fundraising of both the Democratic and Republican parties. Suppose a dedicated Iraqi was head of the National Security Council at the White House. Would such a situation be dangerous for America?

If Americans awoke one morning and found Arabic names scrawled all over their TV and movie credits, on their magazine and newspaper mastheads and in the pages of their books, millions would say, "We've been taken over!" Viewers would suspect the motives of everything they see on television and read in newspapers, magazines, and books. They would be especially wary of information about issues related to Iraqis, Saddam Hussein, Islam, and the Middle East conflict. In very short order, many Americans would cry out in the fashion of Howard Beale: "I am mad as hell, and I am not going to take it anymore!"

When I came to the realization that the original Russian Revolution was not Russian, that it was financed, organized, and led mostly by Jews who were driven by a centuries-old conflict between themselves and the Russian people, I wondered how such an important fact of history had been so effectively covered up. Upon learning fully about the Communist murder of millions of Christians in Russia and Eastern Europe, I asked myself why there were so few movies, dramatic television series or documentaries, novels, books, or magazine articles about it, but endless coverage of the Holocaust.

Then I read a copy of the *Thunderbolt* newspaper, published by Dr. Edward Fields of Marietta, Georgia.[584] Dr. Fields carefully documented Jewish control of America's three major television networks, NBC, CBS, and ABC. I carefully checked Dr. Fields' sources, which included biographies published by Jews.

At the time of my first inquiry, Richard Sarnoff was the head of NBC, William Paley was the head of CBS, and Leonard Goldenson ran ABC. I was amazed to learn that all three were Jews, all were active in Zionist organizations, and all had been honored by awards of numerous Jewish, Zionist, and pro-Israeli groups. Then I discovered that the leading newspaper in America, *The New York Times*, was Jewish-owned and -edited. So was the newspaper that has more influence on the federal government than any other, *The Washington Post*. Jews also owned the largest circulation daily paper in America, *The Wall Street Journal*. They even owned my hometown newspaper, the New Orleans *Times-Picayune*.

I learned that Jews had dominated Hollywood for years. It was interesting to find out that of the "Hollywood Ten," who took the Fifth Amendment when asked before Congress whether they were Communists, 9 were Jewish. As I looked into magazine and book publishing, again I discovered a striking preponderance of Jews — most of them dedicated to Jewish interests, much like today's Steven Spielberg, director of *Schindler's List*,[585] who is an outspoken supporter of Zionist causes. In fact, the most-watched movie ever made about the Holocaust, viewed as history by millions, was entirely a Jewish production.

> **Jerry Molen — producer; Gerald R. Molen — producer; Steven Spielberg — director, producer; Kurt Luedtke — screenwriter; Steve Zaillian — screenwriter; Janusz Kaminski — cinematographer; Michael Kahn — editor; Ewa Braun- set decoration/design, production designer; Branko Lustig — producer, production designer; Allan Starski — production designer; Lew Rywin co-producer.**

Years later I read Jewish publications that boasted about Jewish domination of American media. I also read *An Empire of Their Own* [586] by Neal Gabler, a book that details the Jewish takeover of the film industry.

Ben Stein, a Jewish screenwriter (and son of Herbert Stein, an economic advisor to President Richard Nixon), wrote the book *The View from Sunset Boulevard*. In it he candidly remarks that a great majority of Hollywood's television writers and executives are Jewish and that they are adamantly opposed to Christian values and the conservatism of traditional, small-town America.[587] He wrote an article for *E!-online* in 1997 entitled: "Do Jews Run the Media" accompanied by a subtitle that read, "You bet they do — And What of it."[588]

In the '70s Dr. William L. Pierce, chairman of the National Alliance and editor of *National Vanguard* magazine, along with his staff, researched the question and documented the Jewish dominance in his essay "Who Rules America?" [589]

What I discovered was that the worst nightmare of Paddy Chayefsky and his *Network* character, Howard Beale, has been realized. A small but cohesive minority, with a 3,000-year loyalty to their own people and a fanatical dedication to their newly formed nation, dominates America's media. But it is not the Arabs who have this power; nor is it the Irish, Germans, French, English, Russians, Swedes, Danes, or Italians. It's not Muslims, Christians, Mormons, or Catholics. Ironically, it is the group made up of the Paddy Chayefskys of the world. Chayefsky — an enthusiastic supporter of Jewish causes and the state of Israel — cleverly attempts to influence viewers against Arabs by fictionally accusing them of attempting the same thing that Jews have *already* accomplished. The rest of the *Network* staff included director Sidney Lumet, producer Howard Gottfried, and editor Alan Heim. The same tribe that financed, produced, wrote and distributed the film *Network*, dominates the American media, and truly the media of the entire Western world.

Jewish media power is so extensive that one can scarcely exaggerate it. It is not simply a question of their power being disproportionate to their percentage of population — their power is breathtaking.

If you live in a major city, the daily newspaper you read will more than likely be Jewish-owned or -edited. So will the national newsmagazine you buy at the news counter. More than likely, the national cable or regular TV network you watch will be Jewish-owned, and if not, Jews will be preponderant in the executive and decision-making departments. The movie you see in the theater or watch on television will very likely have been produced, directed, or written by Jews — and often all three. The publishers of the hardbacks or paperbacks you read, even the record companies that produce the music you buy, will probably be Jewish-owned, and if not, they will very likely have Jews in key executive positions. Bookstores and libraries often select their new book purchases based on reviews by Jewish critics and publications such as *The New York Times Book Review*, another part of the Jewish-run *NY Times*.

It is certainly true that many people in media are not Jews. Nor do I allege that every Jew in media is part of some fantastic and intricate conspiracy or that every Jew is ardently Zionist. But the overwhelming domination and thrust of American media is Jewish, and no group is more ethnocentric and more organized for their perceived interests than are Jews. With these facts in mind, can any reasonable person believe that Jews present news and entertainment without a slant for their own purposes in what Gabler calls "An Empire of their Own"?

I grew up reading the New Orleans *Times-Picayune*, and from third grade on, I would read it every morning with my father. By the time breakfast ended, Father had decorated it with toast crumbs and coffee stains, and I had garnished it with oatmeal and milk. My father would take the news section first, and I would take the sports and the comics pages, and then it would be my turn to get into the headlines while he read the other parts of the paper. Up until the late '50s, the

Times-Picayune was truly a Southern newspaper. It reflected the values, standards, political viewpoints, and heritage of the South. We considered the paper our lifeblood of information about the simple goings-on around town and about the major events in the world at large. It was *our* paper — and not only because it was printed in *our* city; it represented something of *our* thinking, *our* culture, and *our* values.

When integration of schools began, the *Times-Picayune* railed against the federal intrusion into our way of life. Many articles talked about the amicable relationship between Blacks and Whites in New Orleans, about the excellent quality of life for Whites and Blacks, and about how the city included one of the largest Black entrepreneurial classes of any in America. It wrote about how, under White direction, Black educational and living standards had progressed over the last few decades. The editorial writers of the *Times-Picayune* predicted dourly that forced integration and the stirring up of Blacks by Yankees and liberal agitators would ruin one of the most beautiful and culturally rich and charming cities in the world. Integration, they maintained, would retard the progress of the Black community and threaten White standards.

After the purchase of the *Times-Picayune* by S.I. Newhouse, the paper gradually began to shift to the left. Integration was eventually depicted as "progress" and something that would increase "love" and "brotherhood." Editorials chastised those who opposed integration, referring to them as bigoted, hateful, and shortsighted. Integration, the paper claimed, would promote racial goodwill and lessen poverty and crime (which was then manageable). "What is the harm," the paper moralized, "with two little Negro girls going to a White school?"

As the city's schools and government services began to disintegrate under integration and the *Times-Picayune* became increasingly liberal, my father — who was mildly conservative — came to dislike it. I still enjoyed the paper, and as I got older, I found myself agreeing with its racial viewpoints. I didn't know that the *Picayune* was no longer a Southern newspaper, and that the owner, a Jewish refugee of Czarist Russia, resided in the New York city area.

When Newhouse died, he left a media colossus worth about $10 billion to his two sons, Samuel and Donald. Among their newspaper holdings were the *Times-Picayune*; the Syracuse, New York, morning *Post-Standard* and the afternoon *Herald-Journal*; the Mobile, Alabama, *Morning Register* and *Afternoon Press*; the Huntsville, Alabama, morning *News* and afternoon *Times*; the Birmingham, Alabama, morning *Post Herald* and afternoon *News*; the Springfield, Massachusetts, morning *Union*, afternoon *News*, and Sunday-only *Republican*.

The Newhouse empire today owns 12 television stations, 87 cable-TV systems, two dozen national magazines, 26 daily newspapers, and the *Parade* Sunday supplement that has a staggering circulation of more than 22 million.

When Newhouse bought the *Times-Picayune*, it was reported by *Time* magazine that he commented, "I just bought New Orleans." [590] In some ways, his statement is accurate. Newhouse and his employees could say anything they liked about any person or any issue with little fear of contradiction. Newhouse, secure in his monopoly, was free to push whatever social and political agenda he wished.

Even today, more than 25 years after Newhouse's purchase of the *Times-Picayune*, many in New Orleans are unaware that a Jewish New York family owns the paper. The editorial page gives a local address and says the publisher is Ashton Phelps, a descendent of the family that once owned the paper.

When I was a teenager, just learning of the Jewish control of media, I noticed that many of the *Picayune's* advertisers were Jewish-owned businesses, including Goldrings, Levitts, Mintz, Godchauxs (a French adapted Jewish name), Kirshmans, Rosenberg's, Rubinstein Bros., Gus Mayer's, Adler's, and Maison Blanche. One of the biggest advertisers in New Orleans was Sears & Robuck, and Edith Stern, a New Orleans activist in Jewish and liberal causes, was Sears' largest stockholder. I soon learned that many of the largest advertising agencies, both local and national, were under Jewish ownership and direction. These agencies could steer advertising to whatever newspaper or media outlet they desired.

Jewish advertising power not only has increased the Jewish monopolization and consolidation of American newspapers, it also greatly affects publications with Gentile management or ownership. All major publications are dependent on Jewish advertising revenue, so their features, reporting, and editorial policies must be carefully attuned to Jewish attitudes and interests. Ultimately, the free press is not free. It runs on money. The old axiom certainly holds true in the media: "He who pays the piper calls the tune."

At the beginning of this century, most major cities had two or three daily newspapers, and many had even more. There has been an alarming trend toward monopolization of daily newspapers. There are only about 50 cities in America with more than one daily newspaper, and many of those have the same parent company. The Newhouse-owned *Times-Picayune* and the afternoon *States-Item* aptly illustrate the trend; they merged into the *Times-Picayune* early and late editions.

As a result, of the 1,600 daily newspapers in America, only 25 percent are independently owned rather than part of a newspaper chain.

And only a tiny number are large enough to have even a skeleton reporting staff based outside their own communities. They are dependent on newsgathering conglomerates such as *The New York Times*, *The Washington Post*, and the Newhouse chain for their national and world news.

The Jewish domination of American media is long-standing. Even as far back as the 1920s, Jews had influence far disproportionate to their percentage of the population. And even though media operations frequently change hands and the CEOs, chairmen, administrators, and top editors change, Jewish domination is stronger than ever — and the power brokers continue to increase and consolidate their power.

Three Powerful Newspapers

The New York Times, *The Wall Street Journal*, and *The Washington Post* are positioned at the heart of American business, culture, and government. Their influence reaches out across the nation. They originate news, focus on issues of their liking, elevate public figures they approve of and denigrate those they do not. They tell us what movies to see, what books and magazines to read, what records to buy and what art to admire. They influence how we think on a thousand different subjects — and, in fact, they frequently choose what subjects we think about at all.

The New York Times is read all over America — in academia, business, politics, the arts and literary world. It sets our political, social, entertainment, literary, artistic, and fashion standards. The New York Times Company owns 33 newspapers as well as three book-publishing companies, 12 magazines, seven radio and broadcasting stations, and a cable-TV system. The New York Times News Service serves more than 506 newspapers across America.

Like so many other newspapers, it began under Gentile ownership and ended up Jewish. George Jones and Henry Raymond founded the great paper in 1851. Near the turn of the century, Jewish activist Adolph Ochs bought the paper, and now his great-grandson, Arthur Ochs Sulzberger, Jr., is CEO and publisher. Executive and managing editors are Max Frankel and Joseph Lelyveld.

Because it is so widely read by Washington's elected and appointed federal officials and bureaucrats, *The Washington Post* has a huge impact on our government. It can influence appointments, firings, legislation, and foreign and domestic affairs of all kinds. It can even be instrumental in bringing down a president, as it did Richard Nixon. The bosses of *The Washington Post* can choose to give publicity to an issue or choose to ignore it, choose to be outraged about an event or bellow in approval. The *Post* has numerous holdings in newspapers, television, and magazines — most notably, *Newsweek*.

Like *The New York Times*, *The Washington Post* started out in Gentile hands. It was founded in 1877 by Stilson Hutchins and was later run by the McLean family. Due to the McLeans' conservative policies, Jewish advertising shifted to the other Washington papers, driving the *Post* into bankruptcy. A Jewish financier, Eugene Meyer, stepped in to buy it for a trifling sum at the bankruptcy auction. As soon as it passed into Jewish hands, advertising from Jewish businesses and advertising agencies returned, and the newspaper returned to profitability.

In an effort at further consolidation of the media in our nation's capital, the Jews ran an advertising boycott of Colonel Robert McCormick's *Times-Herald*, which they detested because of its support for anti-Communist Sen. Joseph McCarthy. Unable to sell retail-advertising space, the newspaper shrunk dramatically and began losing about a million dollars a year and was finally sold to Meyer in 1954 at a bargain price. The *Washington Post* is now run by Meyer's daughter, Katherine Meyer Graham, the principal stockholder and chairman of the board. Her son Donald is president and CEO.

The third leading influential newspaper in America, especially in the business realm, is *The Wall Street Journal*, published — along with *Barron's* and 24 other daily newspapers — by Dow Jones & Company. *The Wall Street Journal* has a circulation of more than two million, making it America's largest business daily and a tremendous influence on business, banking, trade, and economic issues. The CEO of Dow Jones and chairman and publisher of *The Wall Street Journal* is Peter R. Kann, a Jew.

The Three Most-Read Newsmagazines

Time, Newsweek, and *U.S. News and World Report* are the three major weekly newsmagazines published in the United States. The largest and most respected of these is *Time*, which has a circulation of more than four million. The CEO of Time-Warner is Gerald Levin, a Jewish benefactor of many Jewish and Israeli causes.

Newsweek is the second most widely read weekly, with a circulation of more than three million. It is under the control of the *Washington Post*'s Katherine Meyer Graham, another avid supporter of numerous Jewish causes.

The third-ranking newsmagazine is *U.S. News and World Report*, whose owner, publisher, and editor in chief is Mortimer B. Zuckerman, a proud Zionist who also owns the *Atlantic Monthly* and the *New York Daily News*.

The Giants of Book Publishing

Book publishing is perhaps the part of American media least controlled by Jews. Yet they still dominate the most important parts of that industry. All one needs is a printer and some cash to publish a book, and tens of thousands of printers do business in America along with hundreds of small book publishers. Yet here too the Jewish influence is powerful, for writing a book, no matter how intelligent and provocative, offers no guarantee of it being published, and being published offers no guarantee of being professionally promoted, distributed, or even reviewed. The half dozen or so of the largest publishers and distributors handle 95 percent of the biggest-selling books in America. And in those areas of book publishing and distribution, Jewish appraisal is inevitable and Jewish approval is crucial.

According to *Publisher's Weekly*, the three largest American publishers are Random House (and its subsidiaries, including the Crown Publishing Group), Simon & Schuster, and Time Warner Trade Group (including Warner Books; Little, Brown; and Book of the Month Club). Jews control two out of three and the third (Random House, has many Jews in important positions throughout its division of the conglomerate it has joined).

Gerald Levin is CEO of Time-Warner Communications, which owns Time Warner Trade Group. The other major media, Simon and Schuster, is a subsidiary of Viacom Inc. Viacom's CEO and chairman is Sumner Redstone (born Murray Rothstein). Additionally, it should be noted that the largest publisher of children's books, with more than 50 percent of the market, is Western Publishing, whose chairman and CEO is Richard Snyder, who just replaced another Jew, Richard Bernstein.

The Major Book Publishers and Reviewers

One of the most brilliant books of this century dealing with the weakening of the American majority is *The Dispossessed Majority* by Wilmot Robertson. [591] This book is rich in research and ideas, and it is written with a command of the English language rarely seen today. But Robertson was unable to find a major publisher because he dared to write about the unmentionable subjects of race and Jewish ethnocentrism. No national or major publications would review his work, and no national distributors would handle it. Many national publications would not permit Robertson to buy advertisements for his book because it contained information unacceptable to the self-ordained Jewish censors. Despite its ban from the mainstream bookstores and not being reviewed by the major media critics, Robertson has sold well over 150,000 copies through the mail and by word of mouth.

Television

When I read the article by Edward Fields documenting the Jewish control of the three major TV networks, I was fascinated. ABC, CBS, and NBC produce the overwhelming majority of entertainment television broadcasts in America, and for most Americans they are the primary sources of news. Leonard Goldenson of ABC, William S. Paley of CBS, and David Sarnoff of NBC ran their respective networks for decades, setting the tone and breadth of the modern Jewish domination of broadcasting. Here is a condensation of Dr. William L. Pierce's "Who Runs the Media" on the current state of American broadcasting.

Who Runs the Media?

Continuing government deregulation of the telecommunications industry has resulted, not in the touted increased competition, but rather in an accelerating wave of corporate mergers and acquisitions that have produced a handful of multi-billion-dollar media conglomerates of concentrated Jewish power.

The largest media conglomerate today is Walt Disney Company, whose chairman and CEO, Michael Eisner, is a Jew. The Disney empire owns Walt Disney Television, Touchstone Television, Buena Vista Television, its own cable network with 14 million subscribers, and two video production companies.

As for feature films, the Walt Disney Picture Group, headed by Joe Roth (also a Jew), includes Touchstone Pictures, Hollywood Pictures, and Caravan Pictures. Disney also owns Miramax Films, run by the Weinstein brothers, who have produced such ultra-raunchy movies such as *The Crying Game*, *Priests* and *Kids*.

In addition to TV and movies, the corporation owns Disneyland, Disney World, Epcot Center, Tokyo Disneyland, and Euro Disney.

In August 1995 Eisner acquired Capital Cities/ABC Inc., to create a media empire with annual sales of $16.5 billion. Capital Cities/ABC owns the ABC Television Network, which in turn owns ten TV stations outright in such big markets as New York, Chicago, Philadelphia, Los Angeles, and Houston. In addition, it has 225 affiliated stations in the United States and is part owner of several European TV companies.

ABC's cable subsidiary, ESPN, is headed by president and CEO Steven Bornstein, who is a Jew. The corporation also has a controlling share of Lifetime Television and the Arts & Entertainment Network cable companies. ABC Radio Network owns 11 AM and ten FM stations, again in major cities such as New York, Washington, and Los Angeles, and has over 3,400 affiliates.

Although primarily a telecommunications company, Capital Cities/ABC earned over $1 billion in publishing in 1994. It owns seven daily newspapers, Fairchild Publications (Women's Wear Daily), and the Diversified Publishing Group.

Time Warner Inc., is the second of the international media leviathans. The chairman of the board and CEO, Gerald M. Levin, is a Jew. Time Warner's subsidiary HBO is the country's largest pay-TV cable network.

Warner Music is by far the world's largest record company, with 50 labels, the biggest of which is Warner Brothers Records, headed by Danny Goldberg. Stuart Hersh is president of Warnervision, Warner Music's video production unit. Goldberg and Hersch are both Jews.

WHO RUNS THE MEDIA   303

Warner Music was an early promoter of "gangsta rap." Through its involvement with Interscope Records, it helped popularize a new genre whose graphic lyrics explicitly urge Blacks to commit acts of violence against Whites.

In addition to cable and music, TimeWarner is heavily involved in the production of feature films (Warner Brothers Studio) and publishing. Time Warner's publishing division (editor-in-chief Norman Pearlstine, a Jew) is the largest magazine publisher in the country (*Time, Sports Illustrated, People Magazine, Fortune*).

Levin will again be the number-one media magnate when the planned deal with Turner Broadcasting System is completed. When Ted Turner, the Gentile media maverick, made a bid to buy CBS in 1985, there was a panic in media boardrooms across the nation. To block Turner's bid CBS executives invited billionaire Jewish theater, hotel, insurance, and cigarette magnate Laurence Tisch to launch a "friendly" takeover of the company, and from 1986 till 1995 Tisch was the chairman and CEO of CBS, removing any threat of non-Jewish influence there. Subsequent efforts by Turner to acquire a major network have been obstructed by Levin's Time Warner, which owns nearly 20 percent of CBS stock and has veto power over major deals. If TBS merges with Time Warner, Levin will become Turner's boss, and CNN, the only rival to the network news, will come under complete Jewish control.

Viacom Inc., headed by Sumner Redstone (born Murray Rothstein), is the third largest megamedia corporation in the country, with revenues of over $10 billion a year. Viacom, which produces and distributes TV programs for the three largest networks, owns 12 television stations and 12 radio stations. It produces feature films through Paramount Pictures, headed by Jewess Sherry Lansing.

Its publishing division includes Prentice Hall, Simon & Schuster, and Pocket Books. It distributes videos through over 4,000 Blockbuster Video stores. It is also involved in satellite broadcasting, theme parks, and video games.

Viacom's chief claim to fame, however, is as the world's largest provider of cable programming, through its Showtime, MTV, Nickelodeon, and other networks. Since 1989, MTV and Nickelodeon have acquired larger and larger shares of the juvenile television audience. Redstone, who actually owns 76 percent of the shares of Viacom ($3 billion), offers Beavis and Butthead as teen role models and is the largest single purveyor of race-mixing propaganda to White teenagers and sub-teens in America and Europe. MTV pumps its racially mixed rock and rap videos into 210 million homes in 71 countries and is the dominant cultural influence on White teenagers around the world.

Nickelodeon has by far the largest share of the four-to-11-year-old TV audience in America and also is expanding rapidly into Europe. Most of its shows do not yet display the blatant degeneracy that is MTV's trademark, but Redstone is gradually nudging the fare presented to his kiddie viewers toward the same poison purveyed by MTV.

With the top three, and by far the largest, media conglomerates in the hands of Jews, it is difficult to believe that such an overwhelming

304 My Awakening

degree of control came about without a deliberate, concerted effort on their part.

What about the other big media companies?

Number four on the list is Rupert Murdoch's News Corporation, which owns Fox Television Network and 20th Century Fox Films. Murdoch is a Gentile, but Peter Chernin, who heads Murdoch's film studio and also oversees his TV production, is a Jew.

Number five is the Japanese Sony Corporation, whose U.S. subsidiary, Sony Corporation of America, is run by Michael Schulhof, a Jew. Alan J. Levine, another Jew, heads the Sony Pictures division.

Most of the television and movie production companies that are not owned by the largest corporations are also controlled by Jews. For example, New World Entertainment, proclaimed by one media analyst as "the premiere independent TV program producer in the United States," is owned by Ronald Perelman, a Jew who also owns Revlon cosmetics.

The best known of the smaller media companies, DreamWorks SKG, is a strictly kosher affair. DreamWorks was formed in 1994 amid great media hype by recording industry mogul David Geffen, former Disney Pictures chairman Jeffrey Katzenberg and film director Steven Spielberg, all three of whom are Jews. The company produces movies, animated films, television programs, and recorded music. Considering the cash and connections that Geffen, Katzenberg, and Spielberg have, DreamWorks may soon be in the same league as the big three.

Two other large production companies, MCA and Universal Pictures, are both owned by Seagram Company, Ltd. The president and CEO of Seagram, the liquor giant, is Edgar Bronfman, Jr., who is also president of the World Jewish Congress.

It is well known that Jews have controlled the production and distribution of films since the inception of the movie industry in the early decades of this century. This is still the case today.

Films produced by just the five largest motion picture companies mentioned above - Disney, Warner Brothers, Sony, Paramount (Viacom), and Universal (Seagram) - accounted for 74 percent of the total box-office receipts for the year to date (August 1995).

As noted, ABC is part of Eisner's Disney Company, and the executive producers of ABC's news programs are all Jews: Victor S. Neufeld (20/20), Bob Reichbloom (Good Morning America), and Rick Kaplan (World News Tonight).

Westinghouse Electric Corporation recently purchased CBS. Nevertheless, the man appointed by Laurence Tisch, Eric Ober, remains president of CBS News, and Ober is a Jew.

At NBC, now owned by General Electric, NBC News president Andrew Lack is a Jew, as are executive producers Jeff Zucker (Today), Jeff Gralnick (NBC Nightly News), and Neal Shapiro (Dateline).[592]

The overwhelming Jewish control that Dr. Pierce writes about in television and movies is not a new phenomenon. It is not a short-term aberration in the entertainment and news industry. It has been prevalent for decades. Over time the names may change, but the heritage usually remains the same. If anything, the Jewish power in media continues to consolidate and grow. Jewish publications themselves often boast about their power for their own readers.

"An Empire of Their Own"

Even though it is hard to imagine now, Gentiles originated America's film industry. Thomas Edison patented many of the early cameras and projection techniques and launched the first major studio. The man who pioneered the modern movie was D. W. Griffith, a brilliant director whose techniques and films are still studied by film classes around the world. His silent classic *Birth of a Nation* [593] held the title of most-watched movie in the world until *Gone with the Wind*.[594]

Birth of a Nation is a film version of *The Clansman*, a novel by Southern writer Thomas Dixon.[595] The film depicted the fratricidal conflict of the War Between the States and the oppression of the White people during the "Reconstruction" era. It portrays the Klan as a heroic organization that freed the South from the violence and tyranny of Black and carpetbagger rule and paved the way for reuniting the American nation.

When *Birth of a Nation* appeared, Jewish organizations actually went into the courts attempting to ban the film in a number of major cities, and they applied financial pressure on theaters to keep it from playing. A special showing of the film in the White House garnered an enthusiastic review by President Woodrow Wilson and initiated an irrepressible groundswell of support. The Jewish forces in the fledgling film industry realized that it was far more effective to control the film industry from the inside than to have to fight rearguard actions to suppress films that they did not want the American people to see.

The attempted Jewish banning of *Birth of a Nation* was not the first or the last attempt at Jewish censorship in America. Many people are surprised when they learn that Jewish groups actually were able to ban a play by the greatest writer of English literature: William Shakespeare. Performing Shakespeare's *Merchant of Venice* [596] became forbidden in New York City in the early years of the 20th century at the behest of the Jewish community, which claimed that it was anti-Semitic.

In the 1990s, the Public Broadcasting System (PBS) did a running series of all Shakespeare's plays that included *Merchant of Venice*. A long editorial introduction attempted to condition the audience into interpreting the play as sympathetic to Shylock, the central Jewish character who demanded the Gentile's "pound of flesh." The lines in which Shylock defends himself in court, pleading "If you prick a Jew doth he not bleed," were emphasized to encourage the viewer to interpret the play as favorable to Jews. Interestingly, the Jews made no such interpretation of the play when they intolerantly argued for making performance of the play illegal. Recently, the *Canadian Jewish News* reported an attempt by Jews to suppress the play in a Canadian school district.[597]

As they have gone from outsiders to now thoroughly dominating the Western governmental and media establishment, many Jews have shifted from strong defenders of free speech to some of its most willful suppressers.

The Jewish students who dominated the "free-speech" movement at Berkeley in the mid-'60s sang the praises of free speech for the purpose of inviting to campus the likes of the filthy-mouthed and repugnant Allen Ginsberg and the violent, openly Communist, black revolutionary Angela Davis. Today they attempt to silence anyone who dares to speak before a student audience on the issues raised in this book.

In some cases they have reverted to similar tactics to their campaign against *Merchant of Venice*. In 1976 a national Black talk show broadcast on PBS, *Black Perspectives on the News*, invited me to Philadelphia for an appearance. After the taping, but before the show aired, the Anti-Defamation League and other Jewish organizations discovered that I mentioned the historically well-documented Jewish role in the Colonial slave trade. Jewish activists Sol Rosen, Harry Bass, and Peter Minchuck sought an injunction in the Common Pleas Court in Philadelphia, asking the judge to censor the program. The Jewish judge, Stanley Greenberg, issued an order demanding that the program not be aired until the tape was delivered to him and "approved." Luckily, the First Amendment Coalition and attorney David Marion appealed the decision to the State Supreme Court and won. However, the Jewish methods of censorship were by no means exhausted.

Jewish organizations then went nationwide in an attempt to suppress the show in each individual PBS affiliate in each city the program was to be broadcast. In a massive campaign of intimidation, Jews wrote and called local PBS stations, threatening a cutoff of donations and public support if they aired the show. If that did not work, opponents promised, picketing, harassment, and even violence against the stations. By the time they finished their dirty work, the original program aired on only a small percentage of the local PBS stations. Furthermore, the stations that did have the temerity to air the original hour show — immediately followed it with a special program attacking my positions and my character without allowing me to respond.

An example of quiet suppression, from among many I could cite, was my experience with the *Tomorrow Show* with Tom Snyder in 1974.

The *Tomorrow Show* was a late-night talkshow that went into serious topics rather than vapid celebrity banter. I did not fit the stereotypical image of the racist that host Tom Snyder had expected, and during the program he surprised me when, on camera, he referred to me as "intelligent, articulate, and charming." Snyder laughed heartily at my witticisms and repeatedly stated on air that I would soon be back on the show. His last words on the program were "David Duke will be back here."

Three days later Snyder's staff called to set up the follow-up show. They said that I would appear along with a Black civil-rights leader, a Jewish rabbi, a liberal Catholic, and a Protestant clergyman. Flight and hotel reservations were made, and I received a confirmation letter from the show. Only three days before the planned taping of the program, a staff member called and told me that she was sorry, but the program had been forced to cancel my appearance. I asked her why, and she confided in me that the Jewish executives at NBC had sternly informed the program that "David Duke will never again appear on the *Tomorrow Show*."

The program went on as scheduled, but my detractors were the only guests. They denigrated me for the entire hour with cheap insults. The rabbi, evidently well versed in Freudian psychology, attributed my racial beliefs to "sexual frustration." And so it went. The media masters had presented four high priests of egalitarianism and silenced the opposition.

The masters of the media are also adept in the dishonest remaking of classic works. Louis Mayer and David O. Selznick's film classic *Gone with the Wind* provides an excellent example of story-manipulation. I read Margaret Mitchell's novel while still in junior high school. But when I first saw the film version during high school, I noticed important differences. In the novel a Black man assaults the heroine, Scarlett O'Hara, arousing the Ku Klux Klan — which Mitchell portrays heroically — to ride for justice. In the Mayer-Selznick movie version, it is a White man who tries to rape Scarlett and a Black man who rushes to her rescue! There is no heroic ride of the KKK. In fact, the Klan disappears from the story altogether. Later I read how the producers purposefully made the change for political reasons.

Mitchell's real feelings on the KKK were explicitly written in *Gone with the Wind*:

> **But these ignominies and dangers were as nothing compared with the peril of white women... It was the large number of outrages on women and the ever-present fear for the safety of their wives and daughters that drove Southern men to cold and trembling fury and caused the Ku Klux Klan to spring up overnight. And it was against**

> this nocturnal organization that the newspapers of the North cried out most loudly, never realizing the tragic necessity that brought it into being...
>
> Here was the astonishing spectacle of half a nation attempting, at the point of bayonet, to force upon the other half the rule of Negroes, many of them scarcely one generation out of the African jungles...[598]

A film that angered me was Stanley Kramer's *Guess Who's Coming to Dinner*.[599] A beautiful young daughter of wealthy parents, portrayed by Spencer Tracy and Katherine Hepburn, wants to marry a brilliant Black doctor, played by Sidney Poitier. The film makes clear that such a marriage creates some problems but it is the morally right thing to do. Of course, Mr. Kramer produced no films promoting Jewish intermarriage with Gentiles. Many years later *Newsweek* magazine dubbed *Guess Who's Coming to Dinner* an "educational film for White Americans, who seeing their screen heroes surrender their daughter to a black male, would feel less compunction in doing the same." [600]

To catalogue the host of anti-White films produced by the Hollywood establishment would be a monumental task, but I can offer some pertinent examples. David Wolper, an ardent supporter of Israel, produced many anti-White programs, including the television miniseries *Roots*.[601] Marvin Chomsky, John Erman, David Greene, and Gilbert Moses directed the much-touted docudrama. Roots was perhaps the second most promoted and watched miniseries ever aired on television (only the *Holocaust*[602] miniseries had a larger audience due to its incredible media promotion). *Roots* found its own roots in Alex Haley's book of the same title. *Roots* is a historically misleading book and film that produced widespread Black hatred against Whites and self-hatred and guilt among many Whites.[603]

Interestingly, Jewish writer Harold Courlander sued Alex Haley for plagiarism. In writing a supposedly historically accurate book dealing with the African roots of American Negroes, Haley had stolen whole sections of Courlander's fictional novel called *The African*.[604] Haley affirmed his plagiarism in agreeing to an out-of-court settlement with Courlander for $500,000. At the height of *Roots'* popularity, most Americans never became aware that Haley based part of *Roots* on a work of *fiction*.

Freedom Road was another fantasy palmed off to a trusting public as an accurate portrayal of Southern Reconstruction.[605] The *All-Movie Guidebook*, for instance, lists it as an "historical film." When it came out in 1979, many public-school history and civic classes assigned it for homework. Muhammed Ali starred in the film as Gideon Jackson, a former slave who enters politics and forms an unlikely Southern

WHO RUNS THE MEDIA   309

coalition of freed Blacks and poor Whites. He is then elected to the U.S. Senate from South Carolina and finally leads his poor White and Black followers in a struggle against their wealthy White oppressors until slain in a shootout with the Ku Klux Klan.

History records that there has never been a Black senator from South Carolina. Only two Black senators served during Reconstruction, both from Mississippi, and both died of natural causes. *Freedom Road* takes on added perspective when one learns that the producer of this historical fantasy was Zev Braun, and the director was J'an K'adir. "Chosenite" Howard Fast wrote the original fictional novel. Fast also happened to be a longtime member of the American Communist Party, and his autobiography is titled *Being Red*.[606] Teachers, probably unaware of Fast's ardent Communism, ordered millions of public-school children to watch and do reports on this alleged "docudrama." Is it any wonder that so many White Americans have such a distorted view of their history and of the race issue? Could one expect less, knowing that they are getting a Communist interpretation of American history?

Not surprisingly, the most slavishly promoted miniseries of all time was also the most important film of all to the Jews: *The Holocaust*. The film was a thoroughly Jewish production. It was directed by *Roots'* director Marvin Chomsky. Gerald Green wrote the screenplay. Morton Gould composed the music. The producers were Robert Berger and Herbert Brodkin. *TV Guide* remarked that during filming in Europe, the writer's father died. Rather than return home for his funeral, Green felt he was honoring his rabidly pro-Zionist father by staying in Europe to work on *The Holocaust*. For a dozen hours, the film, a work of extreme ethnic hatred, portrayed Germans and other Eastern Europeans as either bloodthirsty or spineless, and of course, it portrayed every Jew as a paragon of virtue, love, and kindness. Never had a television production received more advance coverage or more praise than *The*

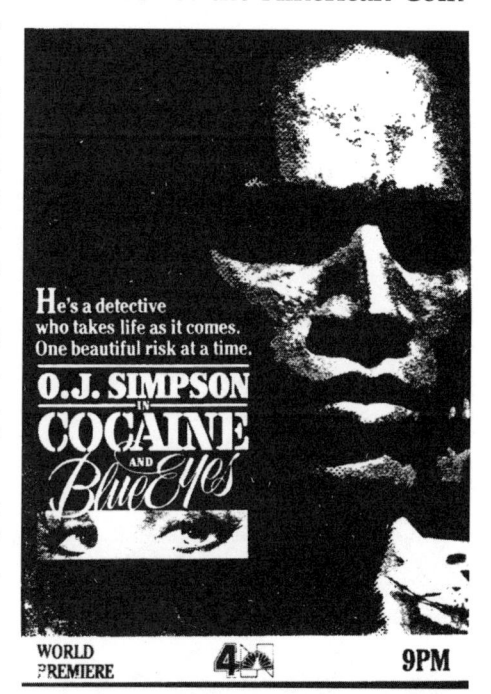

An ad for a TV movie featuring OJ Simpson as a Black cop fighting White crime — the TV world as compared to the *real* world.

Holocaust. Jewish-run publications and pundits acted as though it was the most important piece of drama in the history of cinema.

While I was still in college, I attended a so-called Black-exploitation film called *Farewell Uncle Tom*.[607] I read about the film before its showing in New Orleans, where it played in a mostly Black movie house downtown. Expecting a difficult situation, I drove down from Baton Rouge with two of my bravest and most dedicated LSU friends. In 90 minutes, at a matinee filled with Blacks, my friends and I received an emotional and graphic education on the heinous impact of the Hollywood anti-White movies.

Set in the antebellum South, the film portrayed slave life as an orgy of White mutilation, starvation, murder, and rape of Black men and women. A Black revolt occurs, and the screen erupts with revenge-minded Blacks hacking to death White men, women, and children. With each bloody outrage, the audience howled with approval. "Right on!" some screamed. "Rape the Bitch!... Kill 'em!" The Black crowd laughed and cheered during the goriest scenes of mutilation, rape, and murder.

To make sure the film's point was clear to its patrons, the film's ending flashed to the present day, showing afro-wearing Black men in leather jackets and sunglasses, sneaking into the bedroom of a White couple. The camera depicts the couple's horror as the attackers hack them to death with a hatchet. In slow motion, the hatchet falls repeatedly, splattering blood and brains across the room. Even after 20 years, I vividly recall the film and the raw hatred it engendered in the Black audience.

At the sight of the murders, the audience worked itself into frenzy. As soon as the credits appeared, my friends and I, sitting in the rear of the theater, grabbed our coats and left quickly. We were somber as we drove back to LSU because we knew that *Farewell Uncle Tom* was intended to incite Blacks to murder and rape Whites across America.

In researching the film, I discovered that Cannon Releasing Corporation had released it and that Cannon's president was Dennis Friedland. His associates included Marvin Friedlander, Thomas Israel, James Rubin, and Arthur Lipper. I found out later from a film review that most of the Jews involved with the White-hating film actually had their names removed from the films credits.

The time I spent in that dark theater touched my emotions so powerfully that I swore to myself and to God that I would make whatever sacrifices I must to someday stop the brutal attacks against our flesh and blood as symbolized in that hateful film. I also resolved to stand up against filmmakers who create a climate of anti-White hatred.

During my hundreds of interviews over the years, whenever I mentioned Jewish media domination, my interrogators first would deny the Jewish preponderance of power. Then, when that defense sank beneath a sea of facts, they acted shocked that anyone could even suggest that Jews might use their media power for their own advantage.

The domination of America's news and entertainment media is so obvious that some Jewish media have begun to acknowledge it, but they suggest the Jewish domination makes no real impact on content. The cover of the August 1996 issue of *Moment* magazine was blazoned with the headline, "Jews Run Hollywood, So What?" The article, written by well-known Jewish film critic Michael Medved, includes the following comments: "It makes no sense at all to try to deny the reality of Jewish power and prominence

312   My Awakening

in popular culture. Any list of the most influential production executives at each of the major movie studios will produce a heavy majority of recognizably Jewish names." Medved reports about how Walt Disney studios hires only "highly paid Jewish moguls" such as Jeffery Katzenberg, Michael Ovitz, and Joe Roth as producers. He goes on to state that:

> **The famous Disney organization, which was founded by Walt Disney, a Gentile Midwesterner who was alleged to be anti-Semitic because he spoke out against the pernicious Marxist-Jewish influence in Hollywood, now features Jewish personnel in nearly all its most powerful positions.** [608]

Interestingly, in spite of the attempts to besmirch the name of Walt Disney as an anti-Semite, his films were the most morally spiritually uplifting and educational in the industry. All this while Michael Eisner's new Disney and its subsidiaries continue to make anti-Christian and sexually degenerate films such as *The Priest* [609] and *The Crying Game.* [610]

Not only do the Jewish producers create a plethora of pro-Israel and pro-Jewish propaganda along with their anti-Christian, anti Gentile hate films and documentaries, they are careful to monitor films made by both Jews and Gentiles. For example, Jewish censors of the fact-based film, *Seven Years in Tibet*, felt that the main character, an ex-Nazi explorer from Austria, was not repentant enough about his past. They had the filmmaker invent a repentance scene and insert it into the "true story." [611]

Michael Medved writes in his article that "Jewish writers and directors employ unquestionably flattering depictions of Jews for audiences that react with sympathy and affection." It goes without saying that they depict those who oppose Jewish supremacism as thoroughly evil.

A 1998 made-for-television film documentary aired on the Arts & Entertainment cable network boasted of the preeminent Jewish role in media and the shaping of our society to their purposes. It was made by Elliot Halpern & Simcha Jacobvici Productions, and written and directed by Simcha Jacobvici. The documentary tells how Jews overcame the Gentile filmmakers such as Thomas Edison and D.W. Griffith, and gradually replaced their traditional American themes. Movies such as Griffith's *Birth of a Nation* which honored our White heritage, became replaced with paeans to the immigrant and multiracialism. They interview Jewish author Neil Gabler, who frankly tells how they replaced the "real" America.

> **They created their own America, an America which is not the real America…But ultimately this shadow America becomes so popular and so widely disseminated that its images and its values come to**

devour the real America. And so the grand irony of all of Hollywood — is that Americans come to define themselves by the shadow of America that was created by the Eastern European Jewish immigrants who weren't permitted in the precincts of the real America.

The narrator goes on to say that the Hollywood Jews became almost godlike in their power and set up a system to raise their prestige in the eyes of Americans.

> Where there were new Gods there must be new idols. So, the studio heads began a movie guild with the lofty title of The Academy of Motion Picture Arts and Sciences. It was Mayer's brilliant idea to create the Oscars where the movie moguls' guild honor themselves by giving each other awards. In this way, they went from being a group of immigrant Jews to award-winning American producers.

Jewish power is such that they can make craven even the greatest of Hollywood icons. During an appearance on the Larry King television show, actor Marlon Brando said that "Hollywood is run by Jews. It is owned by Jews." Brando contended that Jews are always depicted as humorous, kind, loving, and generous while they slander every other racial group, "but are ever so careful to ensure that there is never any negative image of the Kike."[612]

Jewish groups came down hard on Brando, stating in their press releases that they would see to it that he "would never work again." No one in the Jewish press seemed to notice that the threat simply validated Brando's observation of their unchallenged media power. Brando was so intimidated that he had to arrange an audience with Wiesenthal himself. Brando cried and got on his knees and kissed Wiesenthal's hands, begging for forgiveness for his truth-telling. Wiesenthal absolved him for his sin, and Brando has said nothing but positive things about Jews ever since.

There can be no renewal for our people until that kind of intimidating power is broken. No regeneration of our society can occur until our people again have true freedom of speech and press.

Once I discovered the Jewish power over the American media, I resolved never to surrender my freedom of speech in deference to it, no matter what it would cost me. I became determined to oppose the media masters who seek to destroy our way of life and our very life form. I am confident that in time my kinsmen will likewise rise up in defiance rather than kneeling in dishonor — like Marlon Brando — to our would be masters.

Chapter 20:

The Jewish Influence in Politics

> The U.S. has no longer a government of Goyim [Gentiles], but an administration in which the Jews are full partners in the decision making at all levels. Perhaps the aspects of the Jewish religious law connected with the term 'government of goyim' should be re-examined, since it is an outdated term in the U.S. (From the major Israeli newspaper *Maariv*) [613]

In recounting my learning about the Jewish power in the government of the United States, I will skip ahead about five years to an event I saw on television on April 15, 1973. Senator William Fulbright appeared on the CBS *Face the Nation*[614] program when, in discussing American policy in the Mideast, he stated, "Israel controls the United States Senate."

Since the middle 1960s I knew enough about the pro-Zionist policy of the U.S. government to realize that what he said was true, but I was shocked that he would say such a thing openly. I wondered what impact such a charge would make on the public. After all, he made one of the most sensational charges ever spoken by a U.S. Senator, an allegation with incredible implications — that a foreign power controlled the highest legislative body in America.

In a matter of just a few days, Fulbright's accusation of Zionist control disappeared from the press almost as if it had never happened. However, Senator Fulbright, a popular personage in his home state, who had been re-elected easily during highest patriotic passions of the Vietnam War, suddenly found himself in political hot water.

In his next election, he paid dearly for his truth telling. Huge amounts of Jewish money poured into Arkansas to defeat him, and Jews with any position of influence in business, government, or media — both inside and outside of Arkansas — rallied to help Israel-Firster, Dale Bumpers. One of the remarkable aspects of the affair was that most Jews had liked Fulbright early on because he took a position on the Vietnam War that they endorsed. Jews overwhelmingly opposed the war, from the radical Communists in the street such as Jerry Rubin and Abbie Hoffman to the influential Jews of *the New York Times* and *The Washington Post*.

Senator Fulbright dared to say that just as it was not in our true interest to be in Vietnam, neither was it in our true interest to be embroiled in the Mideast conflict. Ironically, many Jews had called Fulbright a hero for casting the lone Senate vote in the early 1950s against continuing the funding of Wisconsin Senator Joe McCarthy's, Permanent Investigations Subcommittee.[615] They owed him a great debt, but all of Fulbright's past support for the liberal policies of Jews meant nothing to them when he refused to pledge unquestioning subservience to Israel. By criticizing the U.S. government's policy in the Mideast, he lost his Senate seat.

As I learned about the Jewish domination of the news and entertainment media in the late 1960s, I also came across copious evidence of their enormous political power. I found it to be two-headed. Obviously, through their domination of the media, they have tremendous influence on elections and on public issues. Not only can they influence the public's perceptions by weighting propaganda for or against a candidate or an issue, they can essentially determine whether certain issues will even be discussed at all. The second way they influence politics is more direct. They have become became, by far, the most powerful players in American campaign financing — their support is crucial to every major candidate. Those who cater to them with the most servility receive support, and they withheld it from those whom they deem less servile. They could deliver great rewards for those who played along and politically annihilate those who would not.

In the 1970s, I read a *Wall Street Journal* article entitled "American Jews and Jimmy Carter" by James M. Perry. He writes, "Jews are generous with their money. The White House's Mr. Siegel previously a longtime employee of the Democratic National Committee, estimates that as much as 80% of the big gifts that sustain the party, year in and year out, come from Jews."[616] Another article in the Wall Street Journal about campaign financing frankly stated that most of the money of the Democratic Party came from Jewish contributors, and half of the Republican war chest came from Jews as well. Campaign contributions to politicians are like oxygen; they are necessary for political life. Is there anyone who thinks that such money does not buy influence? Because Jewish money and organized Jewish support is so essential, Jewish advisors and assistants also become absolutely vital.

Not long after Sen. Fulbright's statement claiming Jewish control of the Senate, the highest-ranking military officer in the United States — General George Brown, Chairman of the Joint Chiefs of Staff — spoke unguardedly at Duke University about the Jewish control of the American government, media, and economy:

> **We have the Israelis coming to us for equipment. We can say we can't possibly get the Congress to support a program like this. And they say don't worry about the Congress. We will take care of the**

Congress. This is somebody from another country, but they can do it. They own, you know, the banks in this country, the newspapers. Just look at where the Jewish money is.[617] — (General George S. Brown, Chairman of the Joint Chiefs of Staff)

As I discussed in my chapter on Jewish group strategy, they ethnocentrically support each other until they come to dominate most organizations they are brought into. Such is also true of the American government. From the "advisory" roles of Bernard Baruch and Louis Brandeis to President Woodrow Wilson, to the complete domination of Bill Clinton's National Security Council, Jewish power has grown steadily as the century has grown old.

My awakening to Jewish power came in the mid-'60s, during the administrations of Johnson and Nixon. During the Johnson era, I was particularly aware of Wilbur Cohen who as head of the Health, Education, and Welfare Department, was pushing racial integration and the baby-factory welfare system that I saw as an inevitable disaster for America. I also knew that Zionist partisan Walt Rostow was one of Johnson's chief foreign advisors, and the ambassador to the United Nations, Arthur Goldberg.

Despite Richard Nixon's supposedly crypto anti-Semitic views as exposed by the Watergate tapes, he feared their power and readily placated it. He surrounded himself with high-level Jewish advisors and cabinet members. He made Henry Kissinger, Secretary of State, appointed James Schlesinger as Secretary of Defense — both crucial positions of course, in regard to Israel. In the economic realm he appointed Arthur Burns, chairman of the Federal Reserve Board, Herbert Stein as his chief economic advisor, Laurence Silberman, as deputy Attorney General, and Leonard Garment, as legal council and head of the White House civil-rights department.

The Zionists covered all their bases, as they usually do, by also having key positions in the inner circles of the other party. Hubert Humphrey's closest advisor, E. F. Berman, and his 11 largest contributors were Jews.[618] George McGovern's top advisor was Frank Mankiewicz.

After Nixon's resignation, Gerald Ford kept Henry Kissinger and brought in an old Stalinist sympathizer, Edward Levi, as Attorney General, and he named Alan Greenspan as his chief economic advisor. Jimmy Carter continued the disproportionate Jewish representation by appointing Harold Brown as Secretary of Defense and adding a troop of the "Chosen" to the National Security Council and important economic positions. Reagan and Bush added to the Jewish onslaught with the appointment of a host of other Jews to positions throughout the bureaucracy always reserving many key roles for Jews in foreign and economic policy. From the early days of the 20th century, Jewish power has steadily progressed until as it winds to a close, it can only be called breathtaking. As Jewish power became more entrenched, the Jewish-dominated media found less need to deny its clout, in fact they may find it somewhat to their advantage to boast of it in the elite circles so as to make sure no Goyim will dare challenge it.

The major Israeli newspaper *Maariv* ran a story called "The Jews Who Run Clinton's Court" on September 2, 1994, in which it boasts of the Jewish domination of Clinton's advisors and cabinet. It quotes a prominent Washington rabbi to the effect that the government of the United States is no longer a government of Gentiles.

> **The U.S. has no longer a government of Goyim [Gentiles], but an administration in which the Jews are full partners in the decision making at all levels. Perhaps the aspects of the Jewish religious law connected with the term 'government of goyim' should be re-examined, since it is an outdated term in the U.S.**[619]

The article boasts of their complete domination of the administration, and describes many top officials around the president as "warm Jews" on whom Israel can always count.

> **In the National Security Council, 7 out of 11 top staffers are Jews. Clinton had especially placed them in the most sensitive junctions in the U.S. security and foreign administrations: Sandy Berger is the deputy chairman of the council; Martin Indyk, the intended ambassador to Israel, is a senior director in charge of the Middle East and South Asia; Dan Schifter, the senior director and adviser to the president, is in charge of Western Europe; Don Steinberg, the senior director and adviser to the president, is in charge of Africa; Richard Feinberg, the senior director and adviser to the president, in charge of Latin America; Stanley Ross, the senior director and adviser to the president, is in charge of Asia.**
>
> **The situation is not much different in the president's office which is full of warm Jews: the new Attorney General, Abner Mikve: the president's schedule and programs manager, Ricky Seidman; deputy chief of staff, Phil Leida; economic adviser, Robert Rubin; media director, David Heiser; staff director, Alice Rubin; Ely Segall, in charge of volunteers; Ira Mezina, in charge of the health program. Two Cabinet members, Labor Secretary Robert Reich and Micky Cantor in charge of international trade agreements, are Jewish. They are joined by a long list of senior Jewish officials in the State Department, headed by the head of the Middle East Peace Team, Dennis Ross, and followed by many deputy secretaries and even more senior secretaries' chiefs of staff.** [620]

Bar-Yosef begins the article by pointing out those "warm Jews" (dedicated Zionists) who every day go over the most secret intelligence information presented to the President of the United States. One wonders why Israeli spy Jonathan Pollard is locked up in federal prison when extreme partisans for Israel, such as Sandy Berger, have daily access to America's most secret intelligence.

318 MY AWAKENING

Even by my college days, it was obvious to many people that the Jewish lobby had a tremendous impact on Capitol Hill and in the White House. A real dichotomy existed between what the politicians would do and say. Even though Nixon ran on a conservative platform, which emphasized issues such as victory in Vietnam and opposition to forced busing, his administration began the first affirmative-action programs. Although he gave lip service to ending busing for racial integration, he appointed the officers in the Attorney General's office who continued to push for it in courts across America. His Jewish Secretary of State, Henry Kissinger, helped frame the Paris Peace Accords that led to the inevitable victory of the Viet Cong and a peace with "dishonor," making meaningless the sacrifices of hundreds of thousands of American fighting men. Interestingly, many of the same dovish voices decrying the napalming of Viet Cong soldiers were Israeli hawks cheering the use of the same weapon on women and children in the Palestinian refugee camps.

The Israeli newspaper also makes it clear that effective Jewish control includes both Democrats and Republicans:

> **Incidentally, although the Jewish power in the current Democratic Administration is so huge, there are also many warm Jews heading for the top positions in the Republican Party.**[621]

The first use of Jewish power in Washington obviously regards Zionist interests, such as our pro-Israel policy. In that area, Israel has all her bases covered. They have the President's top security advisors such as Sandy Berger and Leon Perth, they have the Secretary of Defense William Cohen, and Secretary of State Madeleine Albright. When the United States mediates Mideast peace talks between the Palestinians and the Israeli Prime Minister, Dennis Ross is the chief arbitrator — a nice, as they say, "warm" Jew. Is it any wonder that the Palestinians feel that they do not get a fair shake when the so-called mediators of the conflict are just as much dedicated Zionists as the official representatives of Israel. The hypocrisy goes on and on.

Salon Magazine, in a February 17, 1997, article by their Washington correspondent, Jonathan Broder (a writer for the *Jerusalem Report*), began this way:

> **WASHINGTON--following the recent revelations about Madeleine Albright's Jewish roots, the new U.S. Secretary of State faces a new conundrum: All her top candidates for a slew of senior positions in the State Department are Jewish--and male.**
>
> **A number of foreign policy experts have been quick to note the exquisiteness of the irony. "It suggests that we've come a long way in this country from the days when the foreign service was reserved for a very WASPy elite," says former National Security Council Middle**

East advisor Richard Haass, who now directs foreign policy studies at the Brookings Institution.[622]

When Albright traveled to the Balkans, she attacked the immorality of Croatia for not allowing refugees to return. But, of course, she makes no similar moral demands for Israel to allow in the million Palestinian refugees it has banned for decades.[623]

As any group seeking power would understand, economic prowess is the next important component of control after directly-administered political power. Jewish power in the economic processes of our country is extreme.

Many of these positions, of course, change from time to time, but as of this writing in the last term of President Clinton, Jews hold all the most powerful economic positions. The most powerful position of all is the Chairman of the Federal Reserve Board, and it is interesting to note that this critical economic appointee, Alan Greenspan, has remained in office through both Republican and Democrat administrations.

- **Chairman of the Federal Reserve Board** — Alan Greenspan and Vice-Chairman Alan Blinder
- **Treasury Secretary** — Robert Rubin and Under Secretary David Lipton
- **The National Economic Council** — Laura Tyson, and her new replacement Gene Sperling
- **The Chairman of Council of Economic Advisors** — Janet Yellen, later Joseph Stiglitz
- **Trade Representative** — Charlene Barshefsky

Jews hold all these positions and many others, including the Secretary of Labor, Robert Reich, a position with tremendous impact on business. Even the Secretary of Agriculture, Dan Glickman, is a Jewish appointee who has never had any farming experience. You can bet the individual who sets agricultural policy has a tremendous impact on commodity markets and commodity foreign trade. Robert Kessler holds the position of chief of the Food and Drug Administration, another position that has tremendous economic implications for thousands of businesses and industries.

Are Americans so naïve as to believe that this cohesive, ethnocentric people of immense wealth do not share information and network with their brethren for their own benefit? In the section on Jewish economic strategy in my chapter on the origins of anti-Semitism, I point out how in the economic sphere, early knowledge of government policy or even access to government's knowledge — is worth countless billions of dollars. As I discovered these things, I asked myself, "Do these Jewish economic czars have an opportunity to advance their common interests?" Does not reason suggest that they have pressed their own economic interests in the same way they have advanced their interest in America's pro-Israel policy?

320 MY AWAKENING

Survey of Jews in Key U.S. Government Positions

Secretary of State	Madeleine Albright
Secretary of the Treasury	Robert Rubin
Secretary of Defense	William Cohen
CIA chief	George Tenet
Head of National Security Council	Samuel Berger
Secretary of Agriculture	Dan Glickman
Chairman of the Federal Reserve Board	Alan Greenspan
Health Care Chief	Sandy Kristoff
Head of Voice of America	Evelyn Lieberman
Under Secretary of State for Europe	Stuart Eisenstat
U.S. Trade Representative	Charlene Barshefsky
Chief Aide to the First Lady	Susan Thomases
Heads National Economic Council	Gene Sperling
Heads National Health Care Policy	Ira Magaziner
Deputy Secretary of State	Peter Tarnoff
Ass. Sec. of State for Congressional Affairs	Wendy Sherman
On Board of Economic Council	Alice Rivlin
On Board of Economic Council	Janet Yellen
Presidential Advisor	Rahm Emanuel
Council to the President	Doug Sosnik
Deputy National Security Council	Jim Steinberg
NSC Senior Director for Speechwriting	Anthony Blinken
Drug Policy Coordinator	Robert Weiner
Special Liaison to the Jewish Community	Jay Footlik
Presidential Personal Chief	Robert Nash
Presidential Attorney	Jane Sherburne
Asian Expert on Security Council	Mark Penn
Communications Aide	Robert Boorstine
Communications Aide	Keith Boykin
Special Assistant to the President	Jeff Eller
National Health Care Advisor	Tom Epstein
National Security Council Member	Judith Feder
Asst. Sec. of Veterans Affairs	Richard Feinberg
Deputy Head of Food and Drug Admin.	Herschel Gober
White House council	Steve Kessler
Asst. Secretary of Education	Ron Klein
Director of Press Conferences	Margaret Hamburg
Director of St. Dept. Policy	Karen Alder
Member National Security Council	Samuel Lewis
Member of the National Security Council	Stanley Ross
Director of the Peace Corps	Dan Shifter
Deputy Chief of Staff	Eli Segal
Dep. Director of Man. and Budget	Jack Lew
Under Secretary of State	James P. Rubin
Under Secretary of the Treasury	David Lipton
Special Council to the President	Lanny P. Breuer
Special Representative to NATO	Richard Holbrooke
Chief of Social Security	Kenneth Apfel
Deputy White House Council	Joel Klein
Special Advisor to the First Lady	Sidney Blumenthal
Chief of Food and Drug Administration	David Kessler
Acting Solicitor General	Seth Waxman
Presidential Pollster	Mark Penn
Special Middle East Representative	Dennis Ross
General Counsel for the FBI	Howard Shapiro
White House Special Counsel	Lanny Davis
Secretary of Management and Budget	Sally Katzen
Heads FBI Equal Opportunity Office	Kathleen Koch
Deputy Chief of Staff	John Podesta
Vice Chairman of Federal Reserve Board	Alan Blinder
Heads Council of Economic Advisors	Jane Yellen

JEWISH POLITICAL INFLUENCE 321

Their perceived interests, of course, go far beyond Israel and economic policy. The top advisors to the President of the United States influence every area of American life from welfare to taxes, immigration to criminal justice. Consider their influence on the appointment of federal judges alone. In my own federal court district, the Eastern District of Louisiana, which has only a very small Jewish population, Jews constitute a third of the sitting federal judges. On the Supreme Court of the United States there are currently two Jews and seven Gentiles. They often have had specific agendas in the areas of civil rights, immigration, feminism, homosexuality, religious beliefs, the arts, gun control, and many other areas of American life. Invariably, Jews have insinuated themselves into positions of great power and influence which impact government policy on those and many other issues.

It is not only President Clinton's top advisors and councilors who are Jewish, vice-president Al Gore's Chief of Staff is the Jew, Ron Klain — they are even prepared in the event of the president's death or impeachment. Perhaps one of the most telling indications of the special status of Jews in the U.S. government is the startling fact that Clinton has appointed an official position of "Special Representative to the Jewish Community."

Jay Footlik's position is a unique one as there is no "special representative" for any other ethnic, racial, or religious group. There is no representative exclusively for the Irish, Germans, or Italians or, for that matter, even Christians. But there is one for the Chosen, and it is easy to see why when one considers their incredible power. It is a power clearly understood by every President of the United States. A partial list of the key governmental positions occupied by Jews is printed in this chapter. This list by no means shows their complete power. It is anybody's guess how many bureaucrats are like Madeleine Albright — Jews who supposedly don't know they are Jewish until after they are appointed to office. I Dr. Edward R. Fields of the *Truth at Last and I* publicly talked about her Jewish pedigree over two years before she supposedly knew of it.

One of the many low points of the Clinton administration was the pandering of the White House Lincoln Bedroom for big campaign contributors. The newspaper *Jewish Week* proudly reports that:

> "There was a definite Semitic aspect to the list." Said Johns Hopkins University political scientist Benjamin Ginsberg. In fact, half or more of the White House visitors listed were Jewish, ... from the new DNC [Democratic National Committee] chair and former president of the pro-Israel lobby, Steve Grossman, to superstar singer Barbara Streisand.

That result was hardly surprising, given the special character of Democratic party fund raising, Ginsberg said.[624]

Not only do Jews exercise great power inside the government bureaucracy and diplomatic corps, they also have disproportionate power in the lobbying organizations that most influence government. The three most powerful foreign-policy lobbying organizations on Capitol Hill are pro-Zionist organizations, plus the heads or key administrators of many other special interest groups are Jews. They also have great influence in many foundations and organizations that in turn affect politicians and government. They include such groups as the American Civil Liberties Union, the American Medical Association, the American Bar Association, and many more. Of course, they wield immense power in the press, such as Katherine (Meyer) Graham's *Washington Post* and the Sulzberger's *New York Times*, as well as having immense influence in television. This constitutes the most powerful lobby in the world: that wielded by the media.

> ### List of donors who slept at the White House reveals many with Semitic-sounding names.
>
> Last week, The New York Times published a list of donors to the Democratic National Committee who also enjoyed overnight accommodations at the Clinton White House. Republicans have charged that the administration was literally renting out the Lincoln Bedroom as a fundraising gimmick for high rollers.
>
> Jewish observers quickly noticed one striking fact.
>
> "There was a definite Semitic aspect to the list," said Johns Hopkins University political scientist Benjamin Ginsberg.
>
> In fact, half or more of the White House visitors listed were Jew-
>
> *The Lincoln bedroom, located on one of the private residence floors of the White House.*

Their power in government and media has grown so great that they seem to think they are unassailable. Upon the reelection of Bill Clinton to the presidency, *Jewish Week*, on January 24th, 1997, reported that they gathered in Washington, D.C., at the Jewish Community Center, for a "Jewish Leadership Celebration." The article makes the case that in years past:

> Jewish leaders would not be so bold in celebrating Jewish political involvement...The worry was that acknowledging Jewish successes would only reinforce anti-Semites. . . Jews feel secure enough in their accumulated clout...Politically we've come out of the closet...comfortable enough with our own achievements to celebrate them openly
>
> ...the Jewish community has reached a kind of critical mass in politics that guarantees that many of the gains of the Clinton years will remain, no matter who occupies the White House.[625]

No matter who occupies the White House, they boast, their immense power will remain. The implication being that no one could even attempt to become President without subservience to their power. I certainly can't refute these Jewish pundits.

Perhaps the most telling barometer of how the American government has become a Zionist Occupational Government, referred to as "ZOG" by those in the know, is their representation in the diplomatic corps. If, after all, the government is in reality a "Jewish Occupational Government," it certainly makes sense that its key representatives overseas would reflect that fact. Here is a partial list and it does not include the multitude of Jewish bureaucrats and under-ambassadors serving lower-level positions as of 1997:

Ambassadors for Whom?

North America

Mexico	Jeffrey Davidow
Canada	Gordon Griffin
Cuba	Diplomat Michael G. Kozak

Europe

France	Felix Rohatyn
Belgium	John C. Kornblum
Germany	Alan J. Blinkin
Denmark	Edward R. Elson
Norway	David B. Hermelin
Sweden	Thomas L. Siebert
Switzerland	Madeleine Kunin
Poland	Daniel Fried
Hungary	Donald M. Blinken
Romania	Alfred H. Moses
Belarus	Kenneth S. Yalowitz

Others

Turkey	Marc Grossman
Egypt	Daniel C. Kurtzner
Israel	Martin Indyk
India	Frank Wisner
New Zealand	Josiah H. Beeman
Morocco	Marc Ginsberg
South Africa	James A. Joseph
Singapore	Timothy A. Chorba
Brazil	Melvyn Levitsky

America's emissaries to its three closest neighbors, Canada, Mexico, and Cuba, are Jewish. They are: Ambassador Gordon Griffin for Canada, Jeffrey Davidow for Mexico, and our "U.S. Interest Diplomat" for Cuba is Michael Kozak. In the Middle East, America has a Jewish Ambassador to Israel and Egypt.

Jewish diplomatic hegemony is equally impressive in Europe. Its two largest nations, France and Germany, have Jewish ambassadors: Felix Rohatyn in Paris and John C. Kornblum in Berlin. It hardly ends there, as Jews also serve as ambassadors to Belgium, Denmark, Norway, Sweden, Poland, Hungary, Romania, Belarus and Switzerland. Switzerland is at the center of a tremendous tug of war between itself and Edgar Bronfman's World Jewish Congress over supposed Holocaust bank accounts. America's Jewish Ambassador, Madeleine Kunin, as reported by *The New York Times* of October 4, 1997, "...doggedly pursues the Swiss on the issue of Gold for Holocaust survivors."[626]

Just as they have come to dominate the advisors and appointees of the President of the United States, they are accomplished at team politics in the lower echelons of power as well. They hold a vastly disproportionate share of positions of influence in groups from social clubs to labor unions. Their domination of many labor unions is an ironic display of their power, for no group in the United States is less disposed to physical labor. Such leadership may explain why Union administrators have often sold out their overwhelmingly European-American membership by supporting programs such as affirmative action and taking only half-hearted actions in opposition to free trade and immigration. Once in positions of great power, they are not reluctant to use their positions to advance an agenda that conflicts with the interests of the overall membership. In my campaigns for the U.S. Senate and for Governor of Louisiana, Jewish officials in diverse groups from Insurance companies to tourism — would use their influence in the organizations to promote their own political agenda against me.

Jewish political tactics similar to those used on the local and national level are employed in the international arena. Jews in critical positions in the U.S. government can use their influence to blackmail other nations of the world to support Israel. Foreign aid, trade status, and other U.S. policies are used like a carrot and a stick to coerce other nations to support Israel's position in the United Nations. They are also used to support actions against the enemies of Israel such as Saddam Hussein or Muammar Kaddafi. They also have demonstrated the power to buy off, with a huge expenditure of American taxpayer's money as foreign aid, Israel's enemies such as Egypt and Jordan. America, with her great might, has become a surrogate strong-armed enforcer for Israel and the Jewish people worldwide. The tail wags the dog.

In Switzerland's battle with Edgar Bronfman's Jewish World Congress, Zionists in the United States used our government to blackmail the Swiss into going along with Bronfman's extortion of $1.2 billion dollars, by threatening to have the United States government shut down Swiss banking in the United States.[627] Even city governments were used in the blackmail effort, and of course, New York City as a center of banking can severely punish the Swiss for failing to accede to Jewish demands. To quote the *Times-Picayune* of August 13, 1998, "A number of cities and states in the United States had threatened to impose sanctions on UBS. AG and the Credit Suisse group if they did not agree to an acceptable settlement."

When I began my chapter on the Jewish domination of American media, I asked, "What if Iraqis who supported Saddam Hussein, controlled the American media?" Americans would correctly see that situation as dangerous to our freedoms and our national interests. Suppose for a moment that the same Iraqis that were loyal to Saddam had the most powerful lobby in Washington, were the top national security advisors to the president, and practically controlled the economic policies of the United States. No true American patriot aware of that alien domination would tolerate it.

Is this situation any less tolerable that these men and women are not Iraqis, but fanatical Zionists reared in the catechism of anti-Gentile, Jewish Supremacy?

Few in America seem to ask these important questions. The silence is understandable, however, when one discerns the tribe who decides what questions are to be posed and what facts are to be given to the American people. It is also understandable, considering the real-life examples of the political consequences of telling the truth about Jewish supremacism and power. Men such as Senator William Fulbright, Senator Charles Percy, Representative Paul Findley and I have paid a high price for frankness. Congressman Findley wrote an excellent book detailing the incredible intimidation and suppression exercised against those who stood up against the Israel Lobby: *They Dare to Speak Out*.[628]

Perhaps the Jews have every right to try to influence the American government and its policy. But we, the great majority of the American people, have the right to demand that our government be "ours" and not "theirs." Such is the most basic of all political freedom. A government manipulated against the best interests of its people on behalf of a tiny minority, is called tyranny. When some of my friends in the Movement coined the term *Zionist Occupation Government*, or *ZOG*, I thought the term a bit extreme, but after much reading and thought, I realized that it is a pretty apt description of the sad state of affairs in Washington, D.C.

The quotation from the Israeli *Maariv* newspaper should put a shiver up the spine of every loyal American. I will quote it for the second time, and I will do so again and again in my political life, until the American people understand its importance:

> **The U.S. has no longer a government of Goyim [Gentiles], but an administration in which the Jews are full partners in the decision making at all levels. Perhaps the aspects of the Jewish religious law connected with the term 'government of goyim' should be re-examined, since it is an outdated term in the U.S.**[629]

So America no longer has a "government of Goyim," and the only ones who make a point of saying it publicly are Zionists boasting for the edification of their fellow Jews in Israel. It is my belief that there are still millions of Americans, who, if they have the opportunity to read these lines will become as angry much like the character of Howard Beale in the movie *Network*.[630] They will become "mad as hell" and they will do what it takes so that the next generation of Americans will not have to "take it anymore."

The human instinct to protect one's family, race, and nation is called patriotism. It beseeches us to oppose any alien group seeking the control our nation's government, whether it be Zionists, Iraqis, Germans, or even, theoretically, the fanciful notion of invaders from outer space. Such impulses are not anti-Semitism but simply good patriotism. We have every right to stand up for *ourselves* just as Jews stand up for *their* own. In America and the Western world, only Jews are allowed to exhibit true patriotism — for those of us whose patriotism dares to go beyond enjoying the fireworks on the fourth of July, we are attacked relentlessly. Jews who seek to exert control over *other* nations are never condemned, but we Gentiles who simply desire to control *our own* nations, are branded as anti-Semitic and hateful. Such hypocrisy can thrive only when the media covers it up and treason prospers.

Chapter 21:

The Roots of Anti-Semitism

[Anti-Semitism] is an understandable reaction to Jewish defects – Theodor Herzl, the founder of modern Zionism (From his diaries, as quoted by Arthur Kornberg [631])

When I became aware of the existence of Jewish supremacism and its powerful influence in the United States government and the American media, I spoke openly about it. In a high school civics-class, I made a remark that Jewish bureaucrats who authored American Mideast policy had a potential conflict of interest. In an effort to quickly dismiss me, my teacher quickly pointed out that the President of the United States was a Gentile. I recounted to her what I thought was an impressive list of important government positions that were held by Zionist Jews who would likely put Israel's interests over that of strategic American interests.

My teacher, frustrated in trying to rebut my points, dropped an intellectual atomic bomb. "That's the kind of sentiment that led to the deaths of six million Jews," she said. "You don't want to give us the impression that you're an anti-Semite, do you?" The usually restless and boisterous class became still, and I fell silent. I feared being accused of anti-Semitism. What was anti-Semitism? Had I become an anti-Semite for simply opposing elements of Jewish Supremacism?

That very afternoon I went to the school library and found some books on anti-Semitism. Jews wrote all of them, and from what I could discern, most of the writers were Zionists. I looked up anti-Semitism in the four encyclopedias on the library shelves, and found that *all* of the articles on anti-Semitism had Jewish authors.

As illustrated by the popular *Microsoft Encarta Encyclopedia* by Funk and Wagnall's, such is still true today. The *Encarta* article on anti-Semitism has a Jewish author, Nahum Norbert Glatzer, a revered scholars in the Jewish community and author of the very supremacist and ethnocentric *Jewish History*. *Encarta* also has a recommended reading list on anti-Semitism. I reproduce it here.

Bein, Alex. *The Jewish Question: Biography of a World Problem*. Fairleigh Dickinson, 1990. History of anti-Semitism worldwide.

Belth, Nathan C. *A Promise to Keep: A Narrative of the American Encounter with Anti-Semitism*. Various publishers. Historical account of anti-Semitism in America and Anti-Defamation League efforts to combat it; for general readers.

Furet, François, ed. *Unanswered Questions: Nazi Germany and the Genocide of the Jews.* Schocken, 1989. Balanced collection of essays covering a variety of issues on the Nazis and Jews of Europe. *("balanced"? It is anything but balanced)*

Gerber, David A., ed. *Anti-Semitism in American History.* Illinois, 1986. Collection of essays focusing on hostility towards Jews in America.

Katz, Jacob. *From Prejudice to Destruction: Anti-Semitism, 1700-1933.* Harvard, 1980, 1982. Recommended historical survey of anti-Semitism in France, Austria, Germany, and Hungary.

Lewis, Bernard. *Semites and Anti-Semites: An Inquiry Into Conflict and Prejudice.* Norton, 1987. Analysis of anti-Semitism in the Islamic World.

Poliakov, Leon. *The History of Anti-Semitism.* 3v. Vanguard, 1964-75. V.1, Christ to Court Jews; V.2, Mohammed to Marranos; V.3, Voltaire to Wagner; V.4, Suicidal Europe, 1870-1933; translated from the French.

Reinharz, Jehuda, ed. *Living With Anti-Semitism: Modern Jewish Responses.* Brandeis Books/University Press of New England, 1987. Essays on varied reactions over 200 years, arranged geographically.[632]

The theme common to the article and all Jewish-authored books recommended by the encyclopedia is rather simple: Throughout history, Jews have been innocent victims of evil Gentiles. In hundreds of civil, national, and religious reactions against the Jews outlined by these books, there is never a hint that Jews could have done anything of a disreputable nature that could have spawned such horrendous reactions. Christians, Muslims, Zoroastrians, Pagans and other antagonists are all said to be motivated by religious or ethnic intolerance and hatred of Jews. The books also argue that innocent Jews are universally made into scapegoats for social and economic problems. Just so the reader understands that *Encarta* is not an exception, I also reproduce here the suggested reading list at the end of *Grolier's Encyclopedia*'s article on anti-Semitism.[633] Erich Rosenthal wrote its article and presumably picked out the reading list.

Bibliography:

Almog, Shmuel, *Anti-Semitism through the Ages* (1988)

Arendt, Hannah, *The Origins of Totalitarianism* (1951; repr. 1983)

Curtis, Michael, ed., *Anti-Semitism. (*1986)

Katz, Jacob, *From Prejudice to Destruction* (1980) *in the Contemporary World* (1985);

Dinnerstein, Leonard, *Anti-Semitism in America* (1994; repr. 1995)

Gager, J. G., *The Origins of Anti-Semitism* (1983)

Gerber, D. A., ed., *Anti-Semitism in American History*

Poliakov, Leon. The History of Anti-Semitism, 4 vols.

Aren't these suggested reading lists equivalent to recommending articles on the Arab-Israeli conflict written only by Palestinians or articles on anti-Communism written only by Communists?

It is suggested by some of the authors that inherent Jewish superiority in ability and morals causes Gentiles to be jealous and spiteful. Many books on anti-Semitism even argue that anti-Semitism is a manifestation of mental illness and that it is an inherent defect among Gentiles. In discussing the universal, oft-repeated anti-Jewish attitudes of the past 2,000 years, Glatzer, Rosenthal, and the other writers fail to recognize a few things. They never make the slightest suggestion that the Jewish people may have been at least in part responsible for the almost universal negative reactions to them. One would also never suspect that Jews themselves held any intolerant attitudes toward Christians and other Gentiles. Without exception, in every conflict between Jews and Gentiles, the Gentiles and Christians are depicted as evil, while the Jews are depicted as paragons of goodness.[634][635][636][637]

Glatzner, Rosenthal, and the other Jewish partisans have a one-sided point-of-view. None of their books mention that the negative Christian reaction to Judaism arose out of the Jewish anti-Gentile rhetoric of the Talmud and the persecution of early Christians by Jews such as Paul (Saul) until his conversion. Viciously anti-Gentile, Jewish teachings long predated the anti-Jewish Christian writers. None of these Jewish authors mention this important fact.

The more I read, the more I realized that the articles and books castigating Europeans as anti-Semites are racist in the most pejorative sense. To portray a race of people as inherently psychotic and murderous is just about the worst thing someone can say about a race. And yet, the mainstream Jewish media characterizes European Christians precisely that way.

So this is how I am supposed to get to the truth about anti-Semitism, I thought. *Jewish chauvinists must explain it to me*. If that is good logic, then we might as well learn about the Second World War only from the perspective of Nazis or the history of the Palestinian people only from followers of Menachem Begin. How could anyone discover the truth about the causes of the Gentile-Jewish conflict from reading only the Jewish side of it, or from only those Gentiles who endorse the Jewish view? Gentile writers cannot help but learn early on that there are great advantages to adopting the Jewish point of view in getting their books accepted by the major publishers or reviewed in the thoroughly Jewish *New York Times Book Review*. The same is true if they want to be interviewed on programs such as the Jewish-produced *Today Show*. And, of course, they must promote philo-Semitism for their works to become "recommended reading" by the encyclopedias.

Why, in all the mainstream media, are people not allowed to hear the reasonable view that anti-Semitism has frequently been a reaction to Jewish supremacism and misanthropy? Certainly, there have been intolerant outbreaks of anti-Semitism in which innocent Jews have suffered or died. That being said, we must also acknowledge that Jews have had more than their share of anti-Gentile intolerance.

However, we never hear about the Jewish excesses. To end the recurring cycles of anti-Semitism, we must try to learn its real causes.

Is anti-Semitism an irrational response that finds its genesis in the mental pathology of its adherents, or does it find its origin as an understandable reaction to Jewish behaviors? It is reasonable to think that Jewish supremacy and anti-Semitism nourished each other over the generations, ultimately producing the modern horrors of the Second World War, the Holocaust and Zionist imperialism. The conflict may well reach a dehumanizing crescendo in the 21st century unless we learn the true roots of the conflict between Jew and Gentile.

To understand what has motivated Gentile opposition to Jews as a group, it is important to be aware of Jewish patterns of behavior that Glatzner and other authorities on anti-Semitism fail to acknowledge. So-called anti-Semites have alleged over the centuries that, as a group, Jews have disproportionately engaged in unethical and exploitative practices such as usury, the slave trade, prostitution, fraudulent business schemes and various other criminal enterprises. Many have alleged that Jews use unethical business practices and collusion to gain control over commerce. Anti-Semites have charged that many historic examples exist of Jews collaborating with the foreign enemies of their host nations. Charges of Jewish disloyalty are common since the time of their sojourn in Egypt, and have continued right up to the present controversy of Jewish spies convicted of Israeli espionage.

It was time for me to dig into the roots of anti-Semitism.

Religious Intolerance or Economic Jealousy?

When I delved into the great body of popular Jewish authors on anti-Semitism, two themes emerged. The first and most popular theory is that anti-Semitism stems from the fact that Gentiles blame Jews for the crucifixion of Jesus. To quote the *Encarta Encyclopedia*, "Jews from the fourth century and perhaps even before were viewed as the killers of Jesus Christ." The second theme of Jewish and philo-Jewish writers is that anti-Semitism arose from Gentile jealousy of Jewish economic and social success. Jewish writer Arthur Hertzberg shows how blaming anti-Semitism on Christian intolerance has a strategic advantage:

> **To blame Christianity and only Christianity for most anti-Semitism has certain advantages for Jews. Their sufferings through the centuries can be conceived as noble martyrdom; the attacks on Jews are not to be connected with their own distinctive beliefs, culture, and patterns of behavior, and in some cases their faults, but only with their faith. –Arthur Hertzberg** [638]

Any thorough study of the Jewish problem makes obvious the fact that blaming the crucifixion of Christ on the Jews had only a minor role in ancient and modern anti-Semitism. For instance, biblical passages asserting that Jews crucified Jesus Christ did not prevent Christians from trying to convert Jews and bring them into the Christian community. Obviously, the Christian Church did not see Jews as irredeemable because of the actions of their pharisaic ancestors. Early multiethnic Christians opposed Jews not on the basis of race or ethnicity, but primarily because of Jewish beliefs and practices. In regard to religion, Jews as a group were opposed primarily because of the intractable anti-Christian and anti-Gentile character of the Talmud and concomitant anti-Christian acts — illustrated by the mass persecution and murder of Christians by the emperor Nero's Jewish mistress, Poppaea Sabina.[639] [640]

In stark contrast to the ethnically more tolerant Christians, Jews based their opposition to Gentiles on race. While Christians repeatedly tried to convert Jews, Jews made no real attempt to convert Christians. Instead, they erected barriers to conversion, and the small number of Gentiles who did convert were designated, according to Jewish law, as bastards. Jewish priests were forbidden to marry Jews who were converts or the even descendants of converts, a policy still in effect today.[641] In all of Jewish history in Western civilization there is not one Gentile convert who became a significant Jewish leader.

Christianity evolved from a precarious, fledgling faith into the state religion of Rome, and later Europe itself became synonymous with Christendom. Once secure in its own power, Christianity became more tolerant of other faiths — even if disapproving of them. Hostility toward Jews found its base in economic, social, ethnic, and political issues, and there is a much evidence that these factors dominated anti-Jewish attitudes even during times of little religious turmoil. For instance , anti-Semitism was not historically limited to Christians but found virulent expression before the Christian era and in many non-Christian lands. Religious antagonism often seemed to be a rationalization of economic and social hostility.

I sought out the works of the giants of European literature, philosophy and

From the *Times-Picayune*, July 9, 1998

Study affirms genetic link in Jewish priestly class

By MALCOLM RITTER
AP science writer

NEW YORK — Scientists have found fresh genetic evidence that Jews who consider themselves part of the priestly class known as Cohanim really are part of an unbroken line extending back thousands of years.

The Cohanim are said to be descended from Moses' brother, Aaron. Originally they had primary responsibility for offering sacrifices and serving as arbiters and mentors.

Today, in Orthodox and some other Jewish congregations, Cohanim are still accorded special duties and privileges. They are given the honor of reading first from the Torah during a service and presiding over a traditional ceremony for some first-born boys.

Cohanim aren't allowed to marry widows, divorcees or converts. Because of the Jewish belief that the Temple in Jerusalem will be rebuilt and that Cohanim will serve again as priests there, they try to remain spiritually pure. So they stay away from dead bodies, not attending funerals except for those of immediate family, for example.

Many Cohanim have surnames such as Cohen, Kahn, Kane or similar variations. But not all men with such surnames are Cohanim.

Last year, scientists who studied the Y chromosome in modern-day Cohanim reported evidence that the designation has been passed from father to son. The Y chromosome is inherited that way, making it useful for such studies.

More evidence appears in a new study, reported by Israeli and British scientists in today's issue of the journal Nature. They looked for variations in the Y chromosome from 306 Jewish men, including 106 self-identified Cohanim, from Israel, Canada and England.

Most Cohanim had the same version of the Y chromosome or close variants that differ because of random mutations. That shows there has been "reasonable adherence to the policy of father-son inheritance," said researcher David Goldstein of Oxford University.

By studying how long it would take for the variants to develop, researchers concluded the inheritance of Cohanim status has gone on longer than 700 years and maybe as long as 3,000 years, as tradition maintains.

The sample also contained 81 self-identified Levites, a designation that began with the Levi tribe after the Exodus and also is supposed to pass from father to son.

The study could not confirm that. The Levites showed too much variety in their Y chromosome variants. That could mean that non-Levite Jews took up the designation in the past, or that the original Levites had a lot of variety in their Y chromosomes, Goldstein said.

Rabbi Raphael Butler, executive vice president of the Orthodox Union, an umbrella organization of Orthodox congregations, said he doubted the study would affect the designations of Cohen or Levite today. But it's "enlightening" that the results agree with the Jewish tradition, he said.

science on the Jewish issue. Sometimes I would spend hours in the library looking up "Jews" and "Judaism" in the indexes of the books of some of the greatest Western writers. I found that many had things to say that would be considered anti-Semitic today. It would be impossible to list them all, but a few of them include Milton, most of the popes, Shakespeare, Kant, Goethe, Tolstoy, Dostoyevsky, Voltaire, Shaw, Emerson, Melville, Dickens and even my favorite American author, Mark Twain made some interesting comments. Most of Twain's remarks on the Jews in an 1899 *Harper's* magazine article are extremely flattering to the Jewish people. But some parts of his essay are impermissible today.

> **In the cotton States, after the war, the simple and ignorant negroes made the crops for the white planter on shares. The Jew came down in force, set up shop on the plantation, supplied all the negro's wants on credit, and at the end of the season was proprietor of the negro's share of the present crop and of part of his share of the next one. Before long, the whites detested the Jew, and it is doubtful if the negro loved him...**
>
> **The Jew is being legislated out of Russia. The reason is not concealed....He was always ready to lend money on a crop, and sell vodka and other necessaries of life on credit while the crop was growing. When settlement day came he owned the crop; and next year or year after he owned the farm, like Joseph...**
>
> **In the dull and ignorant England of John's time everybody got into debt to the Jew. He gathered all lucrative enterprises into his hands; he was the king of commerce; he was ready to be helpful in all profitable ways...**
>
> **Religious prejudices may account for one part of it, [anti-Semitic Prejudice] but not for the other nine.** [642]

Jewish authors gave me more insight into Jews than did Gentile ones. To my amazement, Jewish histories, which are intended mainly for Jewish eyes, frankly record cases of Jewish economic exploitation from ancient times to the present. I found the Jewish historians far more enlightening on the issue than the Gentile writers. They had no prejudice against Jews; if anything, they had a strong bias for their own people that was clearly supremacist. Many of them practically gloated about their financial victories over the Goyim.

USURY

> **Jews are a *nation* of usurers . . . outwitting the people amongst whom they find shelter. . . . They make the slogan 'let the buyer beware' their highest principle in dealing with us — Imanuel Kant**[643]

The philosopher Immanual Kant was not the first Westerner who made the charge that the Jews are a nation of usurers, and that their economic practices were often exploitative. Since the Israelite sojourn in Egypt, non-Jewish politicians, theologians, and chroniclers have spoken of Jewish avarice and exploitative practices. Even Shakespeare immortalized the Jewish usurer in the *Merchant of Venice* through his character Shylock, who, in absence of the money due him, demands the Christian's "pound of flesh." There are numerous examples of medieval governments receiving huge percentages of their revenues from the taxation received on the profits of Jewish usury. In the Diaspora (the Jewish people living outside of Palestine) there is a pattern of Jews being employed by Gentile kings and governments as tax farmers and revenue collectors, and of their being utilized as the administrators of foreign occupational governments.

By their very nature, farming and ranching require periodic infusions of capital. Diseases, insect infestation, and natural disasters can place the cultivator of land or animals at the mercy of those who have ready money to lend. This is especially true among those who draw little more than their essential sustenance from such pursuits, which was true for most people from ancient times right up to the modern era. Historically such needs for capital were often provided by cooperatives and intervention by the civil authorities, but more often such needs went unanswered, resulting in times of severe suffering and want. In all business, capital is crucial to smoothing out the jagged cycles of prosperity and recession. Into this legitimate need stepped the Jewish community, far more skilled and knowledgeable in the manipulation of money than their customers.

There was little financial regulation of lending practices until fairly recent times, offering many opportunities for the unscrupulous. It should be made clear that the term *usury* means not simply a fair and moderate interest rate but an *excessive* one. Usury would be what one would call loansharking today — with exorbitant interest and compound interest rates.

usury *n.*
1. the lending or practice of lending money at an exorbitant interest.
2. an exorbitant amount or rate of interest, esp. in excess of the legal rate.
3. *Obs.* interest paid for the use of money.

loansharking *n.*
the practice of lending money at excessive rates of interest
Random House Webster's Unabridged Electronic Dictionary 1996

Jews themselves understood the exploitive nature of their usurious practice on the Gentiles. Maimonides, who is considered the greatest European Jewish teacher, wrote the following in his important *Book of Civil Laws:*

334 MY AWAKENING

> It is permissible to borrow from a heathen or from an alien resident and to lend to him at interest. For it is written *Thou shalt not lend upon interest to thy brother* (Deut. 23:20).[644] — to thy brother it is forbidden, but to the rest of the world it is permissible. Indeed, it is an affirmative commandment to lend money at interest to a heathen. For it is written *Unto the heathen thou shalt lend upon interest* (Deut. 23:21).[645] (*The Code of Maimonides, Book 13, The Book of Civil Laws*, ch. V:1, 93)[646]

> *Nesek* ("biting," usury) and *marbit* ("increase," interest) are one and the same thing. . . . Why is it called nesek? because he who takes it bites his fellow, causes pain to him, and eats his flesh. (*The Code of Maimonides, Book 13, The Book of Civil Laws*, ch. IV:1, 88-89)

The usury practiced by the Jews of the medieval world are outrageous by modern standards.

- In *A History of the Jews in England*, Cecil Roth finds Jews charging interest rates between 22 and 43 percent.[647] In northern France the interest rate was limited to 43 percent in 1206 as the authorities tried to reduce the prevailing rate of 65 percent plus compounding.[648]

- In *The Jews of Poland: A Social and Economic History of the Jewish Community in Poland from 1100 to 1800*, writer Bernard Weinryb shows similar outlandish rates in Poland in the 14th and 15th centuries.[649]

- In the 1942 book *The Jews in Spain: Their Political and Cultural Life During the Middle Ages*, the Jewish author A. A. Neuman writes that in Castile the authorities allowed Jews to charge an interest rate of 33 1/3 percent. When farmers desperately needed to purchase seed during the great famine in Cuenca in 1326, the Jews refused to lend money unless they were allowed 40 percent.[650]

The most important political document from medieval England and perhaps in the history of Western civilization, the *Magna Carta* (revealing their common presence) declares that widows and orphans have first claim on estates over Jewish moneylenders.[651]

In *The Social Life of the Jews of Northern France in the XII-XIV Centuries as Reflected in the Rabbinical Literature of the Period*, Louis Rabinowitz notes how the Jewish usurers themselves saw their occupation as far more profitable than farming or artisanry.[652] Many Jewish historians have documented the tremendous wealth accumulated by the Jews through usury. Rabinowitz points out, for example, that the taxes on Jewish usury alone amounted to more than the rest of the ordinary royal revenues in France in 1221. King Louis IX, who vigorously denounced the Talmud, had more concern over the Jewish economic predatory behavior. In 1254 he barred Jews from moneylending and said they should live by trade and manual labor. As an illustration of the far-reaching impact of Jewish usury, Achille Luchaire shows that in medieval Europe even many churches and monasteries were closed because of debts owed to the Jewish moneylenders.[653]

Jacob R. Marcus, one of the world's leading Jewish historians, in his *Encyclopaedia Britannica* article "Jews," states, "the floating wealth of the country was soaked up by the Jews, who were periodically made to disgorge into the exchequer." [654]

Gentile opposition to Jewish predatory economic activity, far from always being pathologic and hateful, was more often rational and compassionate. Today loan-sharking is viewed as a pernicious activity that deserves criminal prosecution. It has been also shown that in communities that limited such activity, anti-Semitism was also mitigated. Davidson quotes two patricians in 16th century Venice as saying that moneylending is the way that the Jews "consume and devour the people of this, our city." [655] The Venetian authorities eventually codified precise regulations of Jewish economic activity, including a maximum interest rate of 5 percent on loans.[656] Brian Pullen quotes a rabbi of the times who, after elucidating the causes of anti-Semitism elsewhere, noted:

> **Usury makes them unpopular with all the orders of the city; engaging in crafts with the lesser people; the possession of property with nobles and great men. These are the reasons why the Jews do not dwell in many places. But these circumstances do not arise in Venice, where the rate of interest is only 5 percent, and the banks are established for the benefit of the poor and not for the profit of the bankers.** [657]

Arthur Kornberg, in *Theodor Herzl: From Assimilation to Zionism*, quotes extensively from the founder of modern Zionism, Theodore Herzl — including fascinating parts of his diary. Herzl writes that anti-Semitism arising from Jewish financial domination was completely understandable and insisted that "one could not expect a majority to 'let themselves be subjugated' by formerly scorned outsiders whom they had just released from the ghetto."[658] In another section he quotes Herzl as saying that Jews had been educated to be "leeches" who possessed "frightful financial power" and were a "money-worshipping people incapable of understanding that a man can act out of other motives than money." [659]Herzl commented, " I find the anti-Semites fully within their rights."[660]

Modern Jewish writers on anti-Semitism never acknowledge the possibility that Gentiles have a basic right to defend themselves from "frightful" Jewish financial power and that anti-Semites could be "fully within their rights." If a Gentile described Jewish financial predators as "leeches," — even when such is acknowledged by one of the leading lights of Zionism — he would certainly be called an anti-Semite.

Is it any wonder that a thoughtful Christian such as Saint Thomas Aquinas, who was considered a great exponent of love and charity, would also speak out against the Jewish practice of usury?

> **The Jews should not be allowed to keep what they have obtained from others by usury; it were best that they were compelled to work so that they could earn their living instead of doing nothing but becoming avaricious." — THOMAS AQUINAS, Saint. 13th century scholastic philosopher.**[661]

As I read more Jewish histories, I learned that usury was just one of many predatory financial practices in the commercial sector that spurred opposition in the Christian community.

Jewish Commercial Activities

Usury was the greatest source of Jewish power and certainly the well-spring of the Jewish banking families that dominated Europe for hundreds of years, but Jews also found profit in many other activities, both credible and contemptible.

While Jewish religious teaching forbade usury to fellow Jews as a pernicious practice, it encouraged Jews to engage in usury against the Gentiles. The same principle extended to every economic competition between Jew and Gentile. Financial acumen combined with powerful group cohesion and economic strategy provided powerful weapons in the battle for commercial dominance in Europe and later in America. The fact that Jews practiced a dual set of ethics — an altruistic one for themselves and a predatory one for Gentiles — contributed to their economic domination even in the more ordinary business endeavors.

Many of the most egregious practices were condemned by a (Jewish) Frankfort synod of 1603 in order to prevent *hillul hashem* (disgrace of the Jewish religion). "Those who deceive Gentiles profane the name of the Lord among the Gentiles."[662]

That statement has been much quoted by those who dismiss anti-Gentile financial measures as representative of a bygone era. However, a subsequent rabbinic *responsa* clarified the issue as a result of a dispute between two Jews who contested the spoils of the deception of a Gentile. It held that exploitation and deceit against Gentiles is permissible as long *hillul hashem* does not occur; that is, if the act does not damage the Jews as a group. Jacob Katz says, "Ethical norms applied only to one's own kind."[663] Just as it was morally wrong to practice usury on fellow Jews and morally commendable to be usurious with Gentiles, it is decreed morally ethical for Jews to engage in profitable unethical acts toward Gentiles as long as they can do so without harming the Jewish community.

The following passage from the vital *Code of Maimonides* clearly shows the dual economic morality in business dealings. It should not be forgotten that Jews consider Maimonides their greatest philosopher during the enlightenment.

A heathen cannot prefer charges of overreaching because it is said "*one his brother*" (Lev. 25:14).[664] However, if a heathen has defrauded an Israelite he must return the overcharge according to our laws (in order that the rights of) a heathen should not exceed (those of) an Israelite. (*The Code of Maimonides, Book 12, The Book of Acquisition*)[665]

Jewish teaching commanded Jews to aid their brothers and not to compete with one another in attempts to exploit Gentiles. Jacob Katz traces a large body of Jewish literature forbidding competition between Jews. They were barred from interfering with monopolies controlled by other Jews and from underbidding fellow Jews. They were always to cooperate with other Jews in the face of Gentile competition so as "not to lose the money of Israel."[666]

It is difficult to overstate how much Jewish economic solidarity and, when they deem them necessary, economic boycott or hostility can impact commercial enterprise. In my chapter on media control, I discussed the well-coordinated Jewish takeover of the Gentile-owned *Times-Herald* in Washington, D.C., which was accomplished by quietly mustering Jewish advertisers and agencies to leave the *Herald* and drive it into insolvency and then returning their revenue after the newspaper was safely in Jewish hands. Such is indicative of the many ways that group strategy can have tremendous economic impact on almost any business enterprise.

Take, for example, the impact that government has on almost any major corporation in America. Key bureaucrats can influence government contracts, environmental compliance, civil rights, tax liability, and regulations on items such as food and drugs. If a Jewish government administrator has hostility toward a particular corporation — or a vested interest in it — obviously he can have a tremendous impact on its financial health. If a Jew has an important corporate purchasing authority, he can choose to buy a product from either a Gentile firm or one owned by fellow Jews. His decision will have a profound effect, for good or ill, on the two entities. The Gentile in this instance has been conditioned to think that everyone must be judged on his or her merits and that it would be immoral to be biased for his own race. Furthermore, he learns that his primary mission is the good of the company or government agency he serves. The Jew, on the other hand, has been conditioned from early life to think in terms of the good of his group and of Gentile perfidy from Pharaoh to Hitler. Is it any wonder that the Jewish manager is likely to choose the Jewish firm to fill the contract or the Jewish applicant to fill the important executive vacancy? Such actions might seem altruistic, but they are also self-serving, for just as he knows he will assist a fellow Jew when he can, he knows that somewhere along the line he will be assisted in the same way.

Historically there are many examples of this "team effort" utilized for economic and political advantage. Roth discusses the appointment of a Marrano Jew, Diego Arias Davilia, as state treasurer in 15th century Spain.[667] The terms "Marrano" and "New Christian" are used to denote Jews who falsely converted to Christianity, while practicing Judaism covertly.[668] Roth points out that through Davilia's influence many other "New Christians" rose to high positions. He also shows that the Marranos also controlled all New World imports and exports as well as their distribution in Spain. If Roth is right and the Jews, as a closed syndicate, controlled all the trade during that period, would not that cause hostility from Gentile merchants?

All over Europe the Jews used their common languages and organizations to gain a competitive advantage over Christians and Muslims in the Mediterranean region. In his book *The Jews of the Ottoman Empire and the Turkish Republic,* Stanford Shaw shows how Jews had a system of bills of exchange honored only by other Jewish traders and bankers, giving them a competitive edge.[669]

A case study in Opatow, Poland, during the 17th and 18th centuries by Gershon Hundert called *The Jews in a Polish Private Town: The Case of Opatow in the Eighteenth Century*[670] illustrates how the Jews came to dominate commercial life. There were constant complaints that the Jews refused to join the craft guilds; that they controlled the trade and prices of raw materials; that they imported finished goods into the town, undercutting the local Christian artisans; that they did not buy from Christians; that there were complaints . . . that Jews had pushed Christians entirely out of commerce, with the result that Christian merchants were forced to move elsewhere.[671] Hundert writes that "Jewish domination of the town's commerce . . . was almost complete."[672] He also notes that Jews came to dominate all phases of the alcoholic beverage business, including its manufacturing, distribution and retail.

Some Jewish writers even implied that Jewish union leaders in America were more inclined to be conciliatory to management if their union membership was mostly Gentile rather than Jewish.[673] If that is true, then one could presume that Jewish firms would be likely to get more favorable labor agreements than Gentile firms. One can easily see the powerful advantage such firms would have over their Gentile competitors. There are many ways that group cohesiveness and loyalty can corrupt and ultimately pervert supposedly free markets.

Banks and Stock Exchanges

The first family of banking over the last two centuries has been the Rothschilds. From them came the most powerful banking houses of Europe. The founder of the House of Rothschild, Mayer Amschel Rothschild, was born in 1743 in Frankfurt am Main, Germany. Amschel studied first to be a rabbi and then decided to go into moneylending and finance instead. He ultimately became the financial agent of the British government during the Napoleonic Wars and launched the greatest banking houses in Europe, with his sons going to the continent's major capitals and establishing banks there.

I read a very flattering book on the Rothschilds that related the story of Mayer Amschel's most famous financial coup. During the great battle between Napoleon and Wellington at Waterloo, the London stock market suffered as traders worried about the possibility of Napoleon's victory. Amschel saw the important battle as an unparalleled business opportunity. Knowing that if Napoleon won, the stock market would crash, and that if France lost, the market would soar, Amschel set up a system whereby he would learn the outcome of the war before anyone else got the news. Using carrier pigeons over land and a series of boats with signal lanterns at intervals of a mile or so across the English Channel, he learned before anyone else that Napoleon had lost at Waterloo. He then had his confederates put out the false information that Napoleon had won. This lie led to a devastating crash of the London stock exchange. Valuable stocks sold for pennies on the dollar. Amschel and his Jewish associates, knowing that Britain had actually won, bought up the stocks for a pittance. Overnight, as the London market learned of the British victory, these stocks became worth a huge fortune.

The book presented the Rothschild's fraud as clever and admirable. One must pause to think about the fortunes lost — fortunes that had been acquired by years of toil and genius — of businesses literally stolen from their creators, of lives broken. Did the author think that this huge fortune simply materialized out of the air? Did the author care that money comes not only from those who create and lead companies, but also from the hard work of thousands of laborers? Such a theft affects salaries, working conditions, employment and many other factors. Many hundreds of thousands ultimately had to pay the high cost of Rothschild's swindle.

Mayer Amschel used the enormous wealth he acquired through his Waterloo scheme (among others) to establish his five sons, Amschel, Salomon, Nathan, Karl, and James, in their own banking houses across Europe. As discussed in my chapter on the Russian Revolution, the Rothschilds have readily used their massive wealth to influence nations on behalf of Jewish interests, as when they ripened Russia for revolution by canceling loans in protest over the Czar's May Laws.[674] Rothschild's ill-gotten wealth also effectively bought his family the first Jewish seat in the British Parliament and even membership in the British aristocracy. By combining the power of their own family's huge banks and other Jewish-owned banks, they could literally bring a nation's economy to its knees. By dominating international banking, they could set their own financial terms to cash-hungry nations and amass even greater riches.

Because of the competitive advantages of Rothschild's international contacts, Jews dominated private banking throughout Europe. For instance, there was almost a complete absence of Gentile banking firms in Prussia in the late 19th century. In 1923 Berlin there were 150 Jewish banks and only 11 non-Jewish banks.[675] [676]

In the stock market, schemes similar to Rothschild's Waterloo ploy have been used for generations, finally resulting in the center of world trading, Wall Street, becoming dominated by Jewish stock and investment-banker operations.

In the book *Our Crowd* and a relatively recent one, the *New Crowd: The Changing Jewish Guard on Wall Street,* Jewish writers Judith Ehrlich and Barry Rehfeld fawningly relate the overwhelming Jewish takeover of the nexus of the American economy.[677] [678] Ivan Boesky and Michael Milken, who stole close to two billion dollars between them, are essentially praised for their brilliance and market savvy.

When I was in high school, my father had some modest stock investments. His broker was a politically conservative Jew, R. Newmann of the firm of Kohlmeyer & Company. I got a job working for Newmann, "plotting curves" — the term for charting stocks and commodities. At the time of my employment, I was racially aware but had little understanding on the Jewish issue. I liked Newmann, and he always seemed to have a pertinent statement handy in opposition to the latest outrages of the Black movement. Newmann had made a fortune in the market, and while I worked for him I discovered the real secret of making money in the market and the reason Jews have come to dominate the brokerage industry.

Newmann was constantly on the phone with his fellow Jews in New York, Chicago, and Washington, D.C. Each member of his circle knew other Jews as well as a few Gentiles in business, government, and media and at the critical junctures of the market. In his conversations Newmann often spoke using words that I could not understand: they were *Yiddish*. Occasionally, after the telephone conversation, he would quickly write out an order for a major stock or commodity purchase and have me run it to the clerk for submission. I remember frequent transactions that netted him tens of thousands of dollars. I asked him what his secret was, and he told me that he had no secret. "Information," he said, "that's how you make real money in the market. You have to get the information before the crowd gets it. Once it is in the newspapers it's too late."

He felt safe bragging to a quiet high-school student, and I listened and learned a lot.

"Let's take the government," he said. "Imagine you knew someone in the Federal Reserve who had inside information that Arthur Burns planned to raise interest rates. After all, someone has to know these things before the world knows. How could you do in the bond market or, for that matter, a dozen other markets that are extremely interest rate sensitive? Or how about if you knew someone in the Department of Defense, and he knew if Lockheed or McDonnell-Douglas would get the new fighter-plane contract. Face it, someone must know ahead of time. Think you could make money? Or how about if he knew where the next military base would be opened. Think you could do pretty well in real estate? Or say you knew someone at the Justice Department who lets you know that they will drop their antitrust litigation against IBM. When that news comes out, what happens to the stock? Would you buy IBM stock? And it's not just government information that can make you a king's ransom. For instance, if you had a friend at IBM and knew before anyone else that IBM was going to give a contract for a hundred thousand computer cases to a small company, what do you think might happen to that penny stock? There's a million ways," he would tell me, "how information means money."

I asked Newmann if insider trading was illegal, and he told me, "They might as well make breathing illegal." He said it was technically illegal but that it was almost impossible to prove — and that it was not really even looked into except in the most blatant cases — usually involving huge amounts of money.

Years later, such manipulation of enormous sums of money led to the biggest stock-market scandal in history. In 1986 Dennis Levine, Ivan Boesky, Martin Siegel, and Michael Milken were charged with insider trading of stocks and bonds worth billions of dollars. Boesky admitted his guilt and was fined $100 million, and millions more were eventually paid by Milken, who after all the fines and litigation and some jail time, still came out a very rich man. In 1987 Milken made $550 million for his activities the year before — more than all but the top 41 of the Fortune 500 companies earned that year. Levine, Boesky, Siegel, and Milken were guilty of the greatest financial fraud perpetrated since the Rothschild's theft of the English stock exchange. It should also be noted that with his Jewish lawyers, and facing

Jewish judges, they served light sentences in minimum security federal jails for their enormous crimes.

It is instructive to note how the Jewish power structure reacted to the Boesky affair. Some top Jewish leaders, including Laurence Tisch (who later became top man at CBS), Felix Rohatyn (now U.S. ambassador to France), and David Gordis, executive vice-president of the American Jewish Committee, came together to do damage control. The *Palm Beach Jewish World* quoted Rabbi Gordis as saying that because of the arrests, Jews would be seen as "exploiters of the economy and profiteers."[679]

If my friend Mr. Newmann was right and information equated to "money" in a modern market economy, how would that bode for the most cohesive and organized group in the world? Many Jewish young people are as knowledgeable in finance from an early age as many Gentile kids are familiar with the star players of the Super Bowl or World Series? Ivan Boesky is exceptional only in the magnitude of his theft. Insider information of one sort or another is incredible power in the hands of people who know how to make use of it. Around the corner, or around the world, it is the greatest weapon in an economic war. The spoils of that war are not only the luxuries that money can buy, but also the enormous political and media power it purchases.

Criminal Behavior

I grew up on movies. I never failed to go to the Saturday matinee, and over the years movies have been my main form of entertainment. My idea of an evening out is still dinner and a movie. Of the hundreds of films I have seen over the years, I have many recollections of gangster films. Because of those films and many newspaper and magazine articles and novels, I long associated organized crime with Italians — specifically, with Sicilian-Americans. It is a common association. Gangsters are synonymous in almost everyone's mind with Italian features and Italian accents.

In high school I came across an article about Murder, Inc., a huge criminal syndicate based in New York City that was one of the most evil and powerful crime organizations in the history of the United States. It specialized in murder-for-hire and ran every kind of criminal racket, generating hundreds of deaths and the theft of tens of millions of dollars. Thomas Dewey (later a presidential candidate) helped break up the organization. The cast of characters of Murder, Inc. amazed me, for they were almost all Jews. Its original members became the leaders of organized crime through the 1980s and included crime boss Meyer Lansky.

ROOTS OF ANTI-SEMITISM 343

I then read that the biggest boss of organized crime since the time of Al Capone was Jewish. I thought he would be a Sicilian as depicted

Colorful Members of Murder, Inc.

Al GLASS	Carl SHAPIRO	"Nig" ROSEN
Max 'The Jerk" GOLOB	Irving "Chippy" WEINER	"Fat Sidney" BLATZ
"Abbadabba" BERMAN	"Waxey" WECHSLER	Allie "Tick Tock"
Bo WEINBERG	"Tootsie" FEINSTEIN	TANNENBAUM
Emanuel "Mendy" WEISS	Hyman KASNER	Max SHAMAN
Sholem BERNSTEIN	Mickey COHEN	"Happy" MELTZER
Jacob "Hooky" ROTHMAN	"Pittsburg Phil" STRAUSS	Al SLIVERMAN
Charlie WORKMAN	'Jack" GOLDSTEIN"	Harry "Big Greenie" GREENBAUM
Mert WERTHEIMER	Abe" WAGNER	Jacob SHAPIRO
'Pretty" AMBERG	"Bugsy" GOLDSTEIN	Sam GASBERG
"Dopey Benny" FEIN	"Bugsy" SIEGEL	Arnold ROTHSTEIN
Frankie TEITELBAUM	Benny "The Boss" TANNENBAUM	Joey SILVERS
"Lulu" ROSENKRANZ	Meyer LANSKY	"Fatty" KOPERMAN
Charlie SOLOMON	"Gangy" COHEN	Izzzy FARBSTEIN
Lou COHEN	"Puggy" FEINSTEIN	Lou GLASSER
Abe SLABOW	"Dandy Phil" KASTEL	Willie SHAPIRO
Yasha KATZENBERG	"Longy" ZWILLMAN	Max BLECKER
Max RUBIN	Isidore "Curley" HOLZ	Harry MILMAN
Charlie YANOWSKI	Paul BERGEN	"Muddy" KASOFF
Moses "Moey Dimples" WOLINSIKY	"Wolfie" COLDIS	Hyman YURAN

in the movies. The book *Lansky* by Hank Messick documented a view of organized crime far different than I saw at my Saturday matinees.

The top law enforcement sources and investigative reporters agreed that Lansky was the master gangster in America. He had been the most powerful person in the American crime syndicates for four decades, yet most Americans — who certainly know the names Al Capone and John Dillinger — have never heard of Meyer Lansky. The most notorious gangster was not Italian; he was in fact Jewish

Jews objected to the cover on the left pointing out that Jews control organized crime in the United States.

and an ardent supporter of Zionism. *Newsweek* reported the following:

> Each year, Lansky and his underworld associates pour vast sums into the Israeli bonds and Israeli philanthropies. As the daily *Ha'aretz* saw it, the government seemed afraid of losing the millions of dollars in illicit money first "laundered" in mob-controlled institutions and then funneled into Israeli business and industry.[680]

Investigative reporter Jack Anderson talked about the issue in *The Washington Post*:

> This underworld boodle — much of it raised from nefarious enterprises in the U.S. — is "laundered" before it arrives in Israel.[681]

In *Lansky*, Messick reveals the relationship between Israeli and American Jewish gangsters

> Certainly Jewish gangsters have long and openly supported Jewish causes and the state of Israel. On the night Lansky's ex-partner, Bugsy Siegel, was executed, the Flamingo was taken over by Moe Sedway. When asked how he so conveniently happened to be in Las Vegas, he explained that he was there to arrange a United Jewish Appeal fund drive.[682]

As an illustration of how Jewish gangsters are treated in the Hollywood media, one only has to look at the treatment accorded the notorious gangster Bugsy Siegel in the film *Bugsy*.[683] The film downplayed his Jewishness and portrayed one of America's most bloodthirsty and merciless murderers as a handsome and playful romantic, a man of vision, portrayed by the thoroughly Anglo-Saxon-looking Warren Beatty. Siegel was portrayed as a kind-hearted man who had a somewhat rough side. Even though I was familiar with the horrible deeds of the real Bugsy Siegel, while watching the movie I found myself liking him. It did not surprise me to learn that the film had been written by James Toback and directed by Barry Levinson.

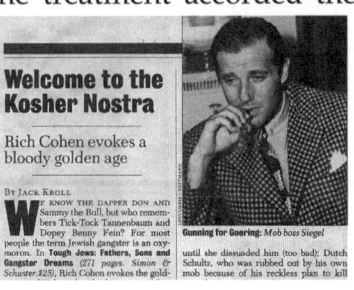

Bugsy Siegel

Messick sums it up well when he writes:

> The real leaders of crime have remained hidden while the nation's law enforcement agencies have chased minor punks. . . . Research reveals that non-Mafia leaders of crime have been hiding behind the vendetta-ridden society for decades. . . . I have been smeared as anti-Semitic from coast to coast by gangsters who used religion as a cloak.[684]

"Russian Revolution" and/or "Russian Mafia"

In the final years of the 20th century, the most dangerous criminal organization in the United States and all over the world is the

"Russian Mafia." Much like the truth about the so-called Russian Revolution, the "Russian Mafia" is neither Russian nor Mafia. In a word, it is: Jewish.

Just as the media downplayed the huge role of Jewish organized crime in America throughout the 20th century (from Murder, Inc. to Meyer Lansky's Syndicate), so they have hidden from the American people the truth about the modern crime syndicate called the Organizatsiya — the most powerful criminal organization in the world.

The members of the Organizatsiya come from parts of the former Soviet empire, but they don't identify themselves as Russian, and certainly not as mafia. They are exceedingly proud Jews who support Jewish causes with the same exuberance shown by Meyer Lansky and his cohorts.

In the mid-'70s I read *Hustling on Gorky Street*, a book written by Yuri Brokhin, a former Jewish pimp for one of the crime organizations in Russia.[685] Konstantin Simis, a prominent Jewish lawyer for organized crime, wrote another important book on the subject called *USSR: The Corrupt Society*.[686] Both books make clear the Jewish control of organized crime in the Soviet Union. Brokhin brags that Jews are the only ones intelligent enough to run large-scale organized crime. Slavs, he says, are capable of only street crime. Of course, neither book mentions the advantages of Jewish criminals having allies in the heavily Jewish Soviet bureaucracy. When the Communist regime fell, the already powerful and Jewish crime groups grew dramatically, so much so, that it could be said that no nation has ever suffered more in the grip of organized crime than Russia does today.

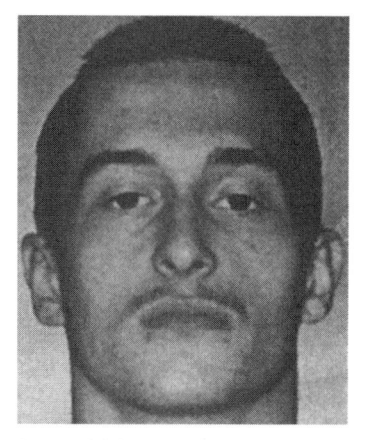

Mikail Markhasev, convicted slayer of Bill Cosby's son, labeled as Ukranian by the media, is actually Jewish.

Even the Russian President, Boris Yeltsin, is clearly under the thumb of organized crime, as evidenced by his appointment of Jewish organized crime figure Boris Berezovsky to Russia's National Security Council. Yeltsin had to rescind Berezovsky's appointment after some of Russia's non-Jewish newspapers made an issue of his crime connections. Berezovsky is thought to be the richest person in Russia, followed closely by his fellow tribesman, Vladimir Gusinsky, who has become the most powerful media boss.

Since the fall of the Soviet Union, the Jewish mob spread rapidly all over the world, and many authorities in law enforcement now considered its American branch as the most powerful and dangerous crime organization in America. After the murder of comedian Bill Cosby's son in Los Angeles, the press identified the alleged murderer as Mikail Markhasev, a Ukranian immigrant, when in fact he was a Jewish member of the so-called "Russian Mafia." Invariably, Jewish film and television producers portray the gangsters as blond, blue-eyed Russians, with not even a scant suggestion of their real Jewish identity. Casting these Jewish criminals as Russian is a double lie. It is inaccurate as to their Jewish origin, and it libels the Russian people. Again, the contradictions of Jewish power come to the fore. The masters of the media will not tolerate even a truthful exposé of Jewish perfidy, yet they perpetuate false and pernicious images of others.

Occasionally, though, the truth breaks out, even if it isn't in the movies. *The Village Voice*, on May 26, 1998, ran a story called "The Most Dangerous Mobster in the World" by Robert Friedman.[687] He writes:

> **According to the FBI and Israeli Intelligence, Semion Mogilevich rules over an arms trafficking, money-laundering, drug-running and art-smuggling red mafia, the most dangerous mobster in the world...**
> **The leader of the Red Mafia is a 52 year old Ukranian born Jew. He is a shadowy figure known as the brainy Don — he holds an economics degree — and he has never been exposed by the media.**

Robert Freedman, himself Jewish, writes that the Organizatsiya has even brought in ex-commandos from Israel as gunmen, and they are so ruthless that some policemen will not work the cases because they won't hesitate to go after a cop's family. Freedman goes on to write:

> **Jewish organizations have lobbied the Justice Department to downplay the Russian Mob, fearing that adverse publicity will jeopardize the mass exodus of Russian Jews to Israel.**[688]

As well it might. But what about the exodus of "Russian Mafia" Jews to America? Obviously there is no concern about that, for the interests of the Israeli state to augment its Jewish population — and the sacred interests of Jewish public relations — are far more important than the rights of the people of the United States to defend themselves from this horrific Jewish organized-crime syndicate.

The Jewish 2 percent of the population has the dubious distinction of producing the lion share of organized crime in America in the 20th century, from Murder, Inc. to Lansky's Syndicate to the "Russian Mafia" of Semion Mogilevich. This hidden fact suggests the possibility of similar behavior in former times.

In looking into the history of Jewish criminal behavior, I found many major historical figures and chroniclers who feared Jewish criminal organizations. (If this volume could afford the space, the below sampling could expand a hundred-fold):

Roman statesman Marcus Cicero: Flaccus, a friend who was a customs official found himself persecuted for stopping the illegal flow of gold from Rome to Jerusalem. Cicero in defending Flaccus condemns such early smuggling and money-laundering and the efforts to intimidate an honest public official from doing his duty. He says, Softly, Softly! I want none but the judges to hear me. The Jews have already got me into a fine mess, as they have many other gentlemen. (Oratio Pro Flacco)

First century Roman philosopher Lucius Seneca referred to the Jews as that "most criminal nation."

Napoleon: The Jews are the master robbers of the modern age; they are the carrion birds of humanity. . . . We ought to ban the Jews from commerce because they abuse it. . . . "

Daniel Defoe: The works *Roxana, Robinson Crusoe,* and *The Military Memoirs of Capt. George Carleton* have frequent allusions to greedy and unprincipled criminal Jews whose stock in trade is "fenced stolen articles."

William Prynne, a Puritan writer opposing Cromwell's efforts to allow the Jews back into England, describes Jewish offenses as "usuries and deceits, clippings and falsifying monies." (from *A short Demurrer to the Jewes long discontinued Remitter into England*).

Charles Dickens had the classic characterization of the criminal Jew (Fagin) in *Oliver Twist*. The character would enlist Gentile children to pickpocketry and an assortment of similar criminal enterprises.

Tacitus Among themselves they are inflexibly honest and ever ready to show compassion, though they regard the rest of mankind with all the hatred of enemies. . . (*The History* 5.4,659)

There is much evidence of a Jewish-dominated criminal underworld that has existed for hundreds of years. One of the most amazing things I discovered was a book published at the time of Protestant reformer Martin Luther. Europe was so plagued by organized crime that the authorities felt compelled to publish a lexicon of criminal terms. Luther supported its publication as a means of fighting crime and wrote an introduction to the lexicon in which he noted that the vocabulary of criminals was full of Hebrew words.

In the preface Luther wrote:

> **I consider it useful that this book be widely read, so that it may be seen and understood how the Devil rules this world, so that men may be wise against him. It is true that this Rothwelsche Sprache (underworld slang) comes from the Jews, for it contains many Hebrew words, as those who know Hebrew will observe.**[689]

The Slave Trade

44 As for your male and female slaves whom you may have: you may buy male and female slaves from among the nations that are round about you...

> **46 You may bequeath them to your sons after you, <u>to inherit as a possession forever</u>; you may make slaves of them, but over your brethren the people of Israel you shall not rule, one over another, with harshness. (Leviticus 25:44)**[690]

Although the institution of slavery existed throughout most of human history, trade in human flesh has never been looked upon as a noble occupation. Compassionate men and women have long decried cruel mistreatment of slaves, especially of women and children, by slave-traders and holders. Many agreed with Christ's admonitions to slaveholders to treat their slaves kindly. In contrast to the benevolent image assigned to them by the media, Jews historically dominated an international institution that touched the darkest aspects of human exploitation: the slave trade.

My introduction to the important Jewish role in slave-trading came from an article about Jews written by a leading Jewish historian and apologist, Jacob Marcus, in the *Encyclopaedia Britannica*. Marcus casually remarked about the Jewish control of commerce in the Middle Ages — particularly in the slave trade.

> **In the dark ages the commerce of western Europe was largely in his [the Jew's] hand, in particular the slave trade....**[691]

The Jewish mastery of the slave trade did not go unnoticed to Christian writers of the middle ages. I read poignant accounts of European children who suffered sexual and other abuses from Jewish slavetraders who acquired them. In Roman times they often followed the path of the conquering Roman army and enslaved enemy soldiers and civilians. Chroniclers of the ancient and medieval periods wrote of their preference for fair women and children, and of their frequent sale in the Levant. The Jewish slavers were more than happy to satisfy the Middle Eastern taste for White flesh. Horrified by reports of abuse of Christian women and children by Jews, a number of Christian principalities issued edicts detailing these abuses and forbidding Jews to own or trade in Christian slave women and children. Jews, in writing their own histories, have matter-of-factly acknowledged the Jewish role in slave trading, looking at it as simply a lucrative Jewish commercial venture. *In A History of the Jew: From Babylonian Exile to the End of World War II*, published by the Jewish Publications society of America, the author writes very emphatically:

> **Jews were among the most important slave dealers [in European society].**[692]

ROOTS OF ANTI-SEMITISM 349

What really surprised me was that Jews played a prominent role in American slavery. In the early '70s I came across a book called *Who Brought the Slaves to America* by Walter White.[693] I could understand the role of Jews in the slave trade of the Mediterranean region, but it seemed unlikely to me that the very small Jewish population in the early American Colonies could dominate such a large enterprise. I also retained, at that time, Hollywood's image of White men, perhaps even Southerners, sailing to Africa and rounding up Black natives for the slave trade. In movies, articles and books, slavers were Anglo-Saxons with names like Smith or Jones. Usually they were hard drinking, uncouth Southern types. Later I learned that slavery was ubiquitous in Africa among native Blacks themselves, and that they were seldom rounded up by Whites. Usually, Black African slave-holders were the ones who sold them to the slavetraders.

Who Brought the Slaves to America steered me to the library collections that housed the records of the slave ships, contemporary accounts, and a number of Jewish historians who documented the role Jews have played in slavery. The Jewish writers I read were prideful in their accounts of the great Jewish slave-traders. A good case in point is Marc Raphael's *Jews and Judaism in the United States a Documentary History*.

> **Jewish merchants played a major role in the slave trade. In fact, in all the American colonies, whether French (Martinique), British, or Dutch, Jewish merchants frequently dominated.**
>
> **This was no less true on the North American mainland, where during the eighteenth century Jews participated in the 'triangular trade' that brought slaves from Africa to the West Indies and there exchanged them for molasses, which in turn was taken to New England and converted into rum for sale in Africa. Isaac Da Costa of Charleston in the 1750's, David Franks of Philadelphia in the 1760's, and Aaron Lopez of Newport in the late 1760's and early 1770's dominated Jewish slave-trading on the American continent.**[694]

In North America, the slave trade had its most powerful center in Newport, Rhode Island. Newport formed a pivotal part of the triangular slave trade of rum and molasses from New England to Africa for slaves and back to the West Indies and the Colonies with the human cargo. I discovered that it was no coincidence that Newport, center of the slave trade, had the oldest synagogue in America and the largest thriving Jewish community in the American Colonies.

Aaron Lopez, a Portuguese Jew of Marrano descent and a resident of Newport, was one of the most powerful slave-traders in the Americas. He owned dozens of ships and imported thousands of Blacks into the Western Hemisphere. In an account of just two voyages of one of Lopez's ships, the *Cleopatra*, at least 250 Blacks

350 My Awakening

perished.[695] Such horrendous loss of life in such a dirty business did not prevent Jewish chronicler Jacob Marcus from praising Lopez: "What can be said about this most attractive figure.?"[696] Although Lopez acquired riches in the Colonies, he violated the anti-British non-importation trade agreements during the revolutionary period, supporting Britain's interests rather than the Colonies.'[697]

Jews dominated the slave trade not only in the American Colonies but all over the New World. In a major Jewish history of the early Americas called, *New World Jewry, 1492-1776,* one can find the following passage:

> **They came with ships carrying African blacks to be sold as slaves. The traffic in slaves was a royal monopoly, and the Jews were often appointed as agents for the Crown in their sale....[They] were the largest ship chandlers in the entire Caribbean region, where the shipping business was mainly a Jewish enterprise....The ships were not only owned by Jews, but were manned by Jewish crews and sailed under the command of Jewish captains.**[698]

Many Jewish writers chronicled the Jewish role in slavery, often boasting of their shrewdness in the business.

> **The West India Company, which monopolized imports of slaves from Africa, sold slaves at public auctions against cash payment. It happened that cash was mostly in the hands of Jews. The buyers who appeared at the auctions were almost always Jews, and because of this lack of competitors they could buy slaves at low prices. On the other hand, there also was no competition in the selling of the slaves to the plantation owners and other buyers, and most of them purchased on credit payable at the next harvest in sugar. Profits up to 300 percent of the purchase value were often realized with high interest rates....If it happened that the date of such an auction fell on a Jewish holiday the auction had to be postponed. This occurred on Friday, October 21, 1644.** [699]

Although certainly indefensible by today's moral standards, slavery in the United States was many times preferable to the incredibly cruel and murderous conditions of African slavery. The greatest inhumanity of Black slavery is associated with the passage to America. Some say that 10 to 15 percent of Black slaves died in the cramped and filthy conditions on the ships. Since the Jews have dominated the slave trade from ancient times, I realized that it is not only Blacks who have suffered from those inhuman conditions, but also untold numbers of White people of the Mediterranean region. It should also be pointed out that not only were Jews the principal slave-traders, they had a markedly higher per capita holding of slaves than non-Jews.

> **All through the eighteenth century, into the early nineteenth, Jews in the North were to own black servants; in the South, the few plantations owned by Jews were tilled with slave labor. In 1820, over 75 percent of all Jewish families in Charleston, Richmond, and Savan-**

nah owned slaves, employed as domestic servants; almost 40 percent of all Jewish householders in the United States owned one slave or more. There were no protests against slavery as such by Jews in the South, where they were always outnumbered at least 100 to 1....Very few Jews anywhere in the United States protested against chattel slavery on moral grounds.[700]

Considering that less than 10 percent of colonists owned slaves, Marcus reveals that individual Jewish Households (40 percent owned slaves) were far more likely to own slaves than were Gentiles. With their comparative greater numbers in the Mediterranean world, Jews constituted disproportionate slaveholders in the ancient and medieval world just as they were in the Colonies. The importation of slaves to America is a relatively recent historical phenomenon that lasted about 200 years. From before the time of Christ, to the African trade of the 1700s, most of the slaves owned and bartered by Jews were White.

Steven Spielberg's movie about the slave trade made no mention of the predominant Jewish role in the Newport, RI slave trade.

When I learned of the Jewish role in the slave trade, it seemed to me that it could have certainly added to the resentment against the Jews felt by their host populations. Being known as the greatest perpetrators of the slave trade is not the best of public relations for Jews. It is no wonder that the Jewish-dominated media have avoided the issue. Only Jewish scholars, who faithfully record Jewish history, primarily for Jewish readers, are allowed to travel on to such forbidden historical ground.

After my first efforts on national television in the early 1970s to expose the Jewish role in slave trading (on PBS's — *Black Perspectives on the News*), the Nation of Islam also did extensive research on the issue. Their historical research department came up with a tremendous amount of documented material on the subject that they published in the book called, *The Secret Relationship between Blacks and Jews*.[701]

Today, simply by repeating the words of prominent Jewish historians on the Jewish role in slavery, one becomes guilty of anti-Semitism. It was only when the public began to learn some of the little-known facts previously reserved for Jewish scholars, that the ADL found it necessary to counter such "anti-Semitic" propaganda. The ADL and other Jewish organizations have responded by trotting out a number of prestigious Jewish scholars who have publicly announced that the Jewish role in the colonial slave trade was "minimal."

In Spielberg's blockbuster movie on the slave trade, *Amistad*,[702] there was hardly a Jew to be found in the film. Although the Jews dominated the Newport, Rhode Island slave trade, all the slavers in the film seemed conspicuously Christian. A number of articles that discussed *Amistad* and the slave trade, including *Time* and *Newsweek*, went out of their way to deny a major Jewish role in slave trading. Unfortunately, most of *their* readers were not told what prominent Jewish historians themselves wrote on the matter before it became an embarrassing issue.

Few will read the words of the editor of the magazine of the American Jewish Historical Society; "Jewish merchants played a major role in the slave trade. In fact, in all the American colonies, whether French (Martinique), British, or Dutch, Jewish merchants frequently dominated. This is no less true on the North American mainland…"[703]

White Slavery

Prostitution, or White slavery as it is aptly called, is another institution as old as civilization. Even in ancient times, the fair-skinned beauty of European females and little boys brought a premium from the purveyors of perhaps the most brutal kind of slavery of all: the sexual defilement of one's body. The subjection of countless innocents to the filth and pain of sexual degradation is a crime of enormous magnitude.

Just as they dominated the organized slave trade, Jews dominated prostitution. It originally came about as a natural adjunct to slavery, as it took no special commercial acumen to realize that a female or young boy slave could be rented out for sexual purposes. And fair European maidens could fetch great prices from the sultans of the darker nations.

From the days of the concubines of King David to the modern "madams" Xaviera Hollander and Heidi Fleiss, Jews have dominated the sex business. The Talmud is obsessed with sexual "connections" of what it calls "natural and unnatural" kinds, of sexual relations of adults with little boys and girls, with bond maidens, and with harlots. In the modern age, Freud and his colleagues in academia brought this perverted view of our natures into the classrooms and living rooms of America. Freud, with the help of the Jewish-influenced media, told Western society — with a straight face — that sexual and excretory organs are the most important factors in life and that every male secretly desires to have sexual relations with his mother.

In looking into the history of prostitution, I read about a maleficent deception Jews would use in Central Europe during the last century. During times of famine or economic hardship, well-dressed, fast-talking Jews would go into peasant communities and tell the parents of attractive Christian teenagers that their children could have a better life in America, which had a shortage of household labor. The Jews told the parents that after a short time their children could pay off the cost of their passage and begin a new life in the land of freedom and plenty. In spite of the pain of being separated from their children, some of the parents would consent to such an arrangement, wanting the best for their daughters. Instead of finding a bright, new life, tens-of-thousands ended up suffering in the brothels of the New World.

In his book *Prostitution and Prejudice*, Jewish historian Edward Bristow writes about the world prostitution network and clearly shows the prominent Jewish role.[704] [705] It is not hard to conceive of the reaction of many Eastern Europeans to the Jewish enslavement and degradation of tens of thousands of Christian girls. Bristow reveals that the center of the Jewish trade in Gentile women from Poland and surrounding regions was a small town called Oswiecim, which the Germans called Auschwitz. That simple revelation can bring much understanding of the recurrent Jewish and Gentile conflict.

Jewish domination of White slavery continues. In fact, it is on a larger scale now than ever before in history. The New Orleans *Times-Picayune* on January 11, 1998, ran an article titled "Slave-traders Lure Slavic Women." It (written by Michael Specter and distributed by the Jewish-run New York Times News Service) documents a Jewish-run White slave operation of huge proportions. The piece begins with a poignant story about how a beautiful blonde Ukrainian girl hoping to escape the poverty and despair of her village life answered an ad in a small newspaper in her hometown promising work and opportunity abroad. She wound up a slave in Israel.

> **She was 21, self-assured and glad to be out of Ukraine. Israel offered a new world, and for a week or two everything seemed possible. Then, one morning, she was driven to a brothel, where her boss burned her passport before her eyes.**
>
> **"I own you," she recalled his saying. "You are my property, and you will work until you earn your way out. Don't try to leave. You have no papers and you don't speak Hebrew. You will be arrested and deported. Then we will get you and bring you back."**[706]

In Israel the government does little to end the brutal slave system other than deport a small percentage of the girls they find with no immigration papers. Almost 1,500 Ukrainian women have been deported from Israel in the past three years. The deck is completely stacked against the Gentile woman and in favor of the slavemasters, for if they file a complaint against the slavemaster, they must remain in prison until a trial is held. Specter quotes the prison director at Neve Tirtsa as saying she did not know of a single girl who chose to testify against her Jewish slavemasters. The White slaver is thus protected by the Israeli system, while the victims are punished.

Specter identifies both the prostitutes and their masters. He quotes an Israeli White slave master, Jacob Golan:

> **The women who work there, like nearly all prostitutes in Israel, are Russian, their boss is not.**
>
> **"Israelis love Russian girls," said Jacob Golan.... "They are blonde and good looking and different from us," he said, chuckling.**[707]

Of course, Israel is not the only destination of the Eastern European women. The Jewish gangs in Russia have strong connections with Jewish organized-crime syndicates all over the world. According to the Ukraine's interior ministry, an estimated 400,000 women under the age of 30 were lured from the Ukraine in the past decade — and that is just one of the former Soviet states. Specter quotes the International Organization for Migration as estimating 500,000 Eastern-Block women are trafficked into Western Europe and around the world annually.[708] It is a tragedy of huge proportions that gets very little press.

Moment magazine, the "Magazine of Jewish Culture and Opinion," had an article on page 44 of the April, 1988 edition, called "Hookers in the Holy Land."[709] In it they discuss the thriving prostitution with blonde Russian girls as a "national institution." It goes on to talk about the customers who even include rabbis riding bicycles to the whore houses.

> **A good percentage of the customers — or Johns, in the lingo — are ultra-Orthodox Jews, pious men whose lives are guided by halachah (religious law), which tells them when they can or cannot have sex with their wives. So, on Thursday afternoons, (boys night out in Israel) busloads of Orthodox Jews travel from Jerusalem, Haifa, and points beyond to Tel Aviv for a few precious moments of passion in a massage parlor, behind a sand dune, or in an alleyway. Other customers are accountants, lawyers, policemen, and politicians. "The entire spectrum of Israeli society is keeping the hookers in business." Claims Detective Shachar, a cynical veteran on the Tel Aviv vice detail...Tel Baruch is so very absurd and so very Israel.**[710]

It blatantly goes on to describe the girls, who are mostly East European Gentile women along with some Palestinians, are virtual slaves who are put on a slave auction block.

Roots of Anti-Semitism 355

> Once the girls arrive in Israel, the crime bosses take over. The girls are usually taken to an "auction house," where the owners of the various massage parlors can bid on the talent — each one offers a price, and the highest bidder gets the girl....The girls are virtual slaves.[711]

The article goes on to note that many of the prostitutes in Israel, especially those of Arab descent, encounter physical abuse from Jews who abuse them as an expression their "racial-nationalist fervor."

> ...find that their Jewish customers only come to them after a Palestinian terrorist act to get their own brand of sexual revenge laced with racial-nationalistic fervor. "...and they do it with hate and anger."[712]

In discussing the forged documents used to smuggle the girls into Israel, Specter notes that they have often been obtained from "elderly Jewish women in the Ukraine." Even so, Specter casually refers to the Jewish perpetrators of this international White slavery ring as "Russian crime gangs" or "Russian mafia." It would be bad for Jewish public relations if the *Times-Picayune* had titled the article "Jewish Slave-traders Lure Gentile Women."

Jewish writers on anti-Semitism never mention the Jewish domination of the slave trade or of prostitution over the centuries. They never point out that such Jewish activities could understandably lead to unfavorable attitudes toward Jews.

Imagine the world-wide media reaction if Gentiles were enslaving hundreds of thousands of Jewish girls, putting them on auction blocks, and subjecting them to indescribable brutalities? Consider the outrage that would bellow from the Jewish media. Yet, with millions of Christian girls becoming the victims of Jewish criminals, there is no moral outcry — no international cause trumpeted by celebrities and politicians.

After my discussion of these issues on the national PBS program *Black Perspectives on the News*, attacks on me as an "anti-Semite" became even more shrill. As a young man, when I read about slavery in the South, my heart was touched by the tales of cruelty and suffering, so much so that I felt guilty. But as I learned the truth about the slave trade, I noticed that the same Jewish writers and producers and publishers who had instilled guilt in me never once suggested that Jews had any "collective guilt" for a 2,000-year record of plying their trade in human flesh.

Apparently, in the new morality of the Jewish press, learning about White exploitation of Blacks is "history," and learning about Jewish exploitation of both Whites and Blacks is called "hate."

Disloyalty

Historically, the most common term other than *moneylender* associated with Jews has been *tax collector*. There are many examples, all the way through the 20th century, of Jews being the main instruments of tax collection that ruling bodies used to raise revenue. The Jewish historian Josephus, in his *Antiquities of the Jews*[713], tells the story of a Jewish tax collector named Joseph in the court of the Ptolemies who was so ruthless and effective in collections that he bid twice the amount of anyone else for the right to collect taxes. In those times kings often took bids from tax collectors, and the one who promised the highest set amount would obtain the commission, and he would keep for himself all he collected over the amount he promised the king.

Joseph's success came in no small part from the fact that he would kill and confiscate the property of those who refused to pay what he demanded. Josephus described his success as "stripping Syria to the bone." Yet he showed no restraint in his praise: "Joseph was a good man, and of great magnanimity; and brought the Jews out of a state of poverty and meanness, to one that was more splendid."[714]

Rulers of multicultural empires often used Jews as administrators because the ruling powers knew that they would have no loyalty to the non-Jewish people of the lands where they resided. Jews made excellent tax collectors. They had good financial acumen, and they had the required trait of all good tax collectors: little sympathy for the taxpayer.

In the Muslim world, the practice of using Jews as occupying administrators can be seen in the Arab conquest and rule of Spain in the eighth to 11th centuries, in the Fatimid rule over Tunisia in the 10th century, the Merinid occupation of Morocco in the 13th through 15th centuries, during Mongol rule in Iraq, and in the 16th century Ottoman period. The practice has continued even into the 20th century — in Morocco, where the French used them in this role over the Muslims, in the post-World War II satellite states of the Soviet Union in Eastern Europe, and even in the control exercised by King Faysal in Iraq.

One of the most repeated charges that anti-Semites have made is that, in retaining loyalty to their own perceived group interest, Jews have historically betrayed their host nations in times of war, occupation, and hardship. Byzantine history affords an example of a relentless conflict between the Jews and their host people during wartime.

Constantinople: A Story of Repeated Betrayal

- **Jewish writers Gedalia Alon[715] and Michael Avi-Yonah[716] show that Byzantine authorities prophetically feared that their Jews would aid Persian invaders. They also were correct in fearing that they would assist Muslim armies as well.**
- **Jews were killed in great numbers after the uncovering of a Jewish plot to deliver a city to the Persians.[717]**

- **Jews sided with the Persian invaders of the early 7th century and in collusion with the Samaritans massacred 100,000 Christians.**[718]
- **When the Christian Byzantines retook the city, Jews were forcibly converted to Christianity.**
- **The Jews supported the Arabs when they conquered the area in 636-40.**[719] [720]
- **In the 12th century, the Byzantine Jews supported the invading armies of Seljuk Turks.**[721]
- **In the 14th-century they supported the invasions of the Ottoman Turks — the final conquest of Constantinople occurring through a Jewish quarter with the active assistance of the Jews.**[722]
- **In gratitude for their support, the Sultan imposed Jewish economic domination over his Christian subjects and Jews immigrated into the area from throughout the Diaspora.**[723]

A great deal of evidence exists that Jews supported the Saracen conquest of Spain[724] and served as the harsh administrators of the repressive Muslim occupation government.[725] [726] [727]

After the Second World War, Jews became the prominent administrators and secret police of the brutal regimes installed by the Soviets in Eastern Europe. In his 1981 book *Uprising*, David Irving shows that Jews so dominated in the secret police that tortured and murdered hundreds of thousands in Soviet-controlled Hungary, that "anti-Semitism" was one of the motivations of the anti-Communist uprising.[728] Considering the Jewish involvement in the murderous specter of Communism, it should be no puzzle that Eastern Europeans are the most "anti-Semitic."

In Russia itself, Jewish Communists were the forces that dispossessed the Russians of their own government, that made up the leadership of the murderous KGB, and who murdered the Russian royal family, including the children. America experienced one of the most treacherous acts of treason in the annals of history when Julius and Ethel Rosenberg and their Jewish co-conspirators stole America's atomic bomb secrets and gave them to the Soviets. During the Vietnam War, the Jewish-dominated New Left led pro-Viet Cong demonstrations while American boys died from Viet Cong bullets and bombs. The two most famous of the Vietnam era seditionists were Abbie Hoffman and Jerry Rubin. Jewish spies for Israel such as Jonathan Pollard have stolen some of America's most closely guarded secrets.

Perhaps the classic example of their role as administrators and exploiters of an oppressive government is found in their own chronicles of the Story of their sojourn in ancient Egypt.

The Story of Joseph

Every Sunday school child is familiar with the biblical story of Joseph, his "coat of many colors," and his betrayal by his brothers, enslavement, and subsequent rise to great power in Egypt. When I was in college a friend recommended that I read the account of Joseph and the Israelite sojourn in Egypt in the light of my new understanding of historical Jewish behavior. I took out my Bible and turned to the last pages of Genesis and the first of Exodus, and after reading and reflecting on what I had read, I think I finally understood why God was so often put out with the "Chosen People."

Genesis introduces Joseph at age 17, tattling to his father Jacob about his brothers' wrongdoing. Jacob is so taken by Joseph that he gives him a coat of many colors that evokes jealousy in two of his brothers. The brothers are also disgusted by Joseph's self-aggrandizement in relating his dreams of his future superiority. In one dream, Joseph tells how he is in a field binding sheaves and how his sheaf stood up, whereas his brothers' sheaves were gathered all around it, bowed low.[729] Soon afterward, he relates a dream in which the sun, the stars, and the moon bow down before him. Even Jacob rebukes Joseph for that display of insufferable chutzpah. His brothers hate him so much that they decide to kill him and subsequently throw him down an abandoned well. However, when they see an Ishmealite caravan bound for Egypt, they decide to sell their brother into slavery instead.[730] Joseph is taken to Egypt and eventually sold to Potiphar, captain of the Pharaoh's guard.

Joseph's glib tongue and financial acumen lead to his rise as overseer of an entire household. Potiphar trusts him with every detail. One day, while Potiphar is away, his wife cries out that Joseph is trying to rape her, and when the other servants come running, they find Joseph's clothes, left behind as he fled. Joseph claimed it was he who was victim of an attempted rape, but an enraged Potiphar throws him into prison anyway.[731]

Again using his cleverness and acumen, Joseph rises to become the top trustee of the prison and virtually runs the jail and has all the prisoners under his control. In the prison were several of the Pharaoh's servants. From them Joseph undoubtedly learns all the gossip and goings-on at the royal house. Two of Pharaoh's servants, a butler and a baker, have dreams that Joseph cleverly interprets. The butler is eventually reinstated, and after the Pharaoh has a disturbing dream, the butler tells Pharaoh about Joseph's abilities. Brought before the Pharaoh, Joseph interprets the famous dream of the seven fat beeves and the seven thin ones. Intelligently understanding the cyclical nature of prosperity and famine, he tells the Pharaoh that there will be seven good years and seven bad ones. Joseph then suggests that Pharaoh appoint a man "discreet and wise, and set him over the land of Egypt (Genesis 42:33).[732] Pharaoh then makes Joseph the most powerful man in Egypt other than himself and has him gather up the crops of Egypt.

For the next few years Joseph collects vast amounts of grain from Egyptian farmers and ensconces himself as the "Lord of Egypt" and "ruler of Egypt," acting in the name of the Pharaoh. When drought and famine finally hit, Joseph hatches a scheme to increase his and the Pharaoh's wealth and power. As the starving Egyptians appeal to the Pharaoh to get back some of the grain they have deposited over the years, the Pharaoh tells them to go talk to Joseph. He tells them that they must pay for the grain and "gathers up all the money that was found in the land of Egypt" (Genesis 47:14)[733]. A severe depression occurs when the currency fails. Following are a few of the powerful verses:

15: And the money failed in land of Egypt, and in the land of Canaan and all the Egyptians came to Joseph and said, Give us bread, for why should we die in thy presence? For the money faileth.

16: And Joseph said, give your cattle, and I will give you food for your cattle, if money fail.

17: And they brought their cattle unto Joseph: and Joseph gave them bread in exchange for horses, and for the flocks, and for the cattle of the herds, and for asses, and he fed them with bread for all their cattle for that year.

18: When that year was ended, they came unto him the second year, and said unto him. We will not hide it from my Lord, how our money is spent: my lord also hath our herds of cattle: there is not ought left in the sight of my lord but our bodies and our lands.

19: Wherefore shall we die before thine eyes, both we and our land? Buy us and our land for bread, and we and our land will be slaves unto Pharaoh...

21: and as for the people, he made slaves of them from one end of Egypt to the other...

So Joseph first takes away all the money of the free Egyptians, then all their domesticated animals, then their homes and lands, and finally he puts them back on the Pharaoh's new land as slaves with 20 percent of their crop going to the Pharaoh. The Pharaoh is ecstatic with this arrangement, for his treasury is overflowing, and Joseph has taken away all the lands of the people and put them back on it working essentially as sharecroppers. At the same time the Egyptians are going through this misery, Joseph sends for and brings all the Israelites to Egypt. Genesis makes it quite clear that Joseph gives the Israelites bags of gold and food and "live off the fat of the land."

> **45:18 And take your father and your households, and come unto me; and I will give you the good of the land of Egypt, and ye shall eat the fat of the land.**
>
> **47:6 The land of Egypt is before thee; in the best of the land make they father and brethren to dwell: in the land of Goshen let them dwell;**
>
> **47:13 and there was no bread in all the land; for the famine was very sore, so that the land of Egypt and all the land of Canaan fainted by reason of the famine.**
>
> **47:27 And Israel dwelt in the land of Egypt, in the country of Goshen; and they had possessions therein, and grew, and multiplied exceedingly.**

One can imagine what the Egyptians thought about Joseph taking all their lands and possessions and reducing them to slavery while the foreign Israelites are given gold, free food, and the best land in all of Egypt. The Egyptians had built a grand civilization with magnificent artistic and cultural achievement, and advances in mathematics, engineering, architecture, astronomy and agriculture. They had built the most enduring architectural creations in the world: the pyramids. How they must have chafed under the absolute power of this foreign tribe. According to Genesis and Exodus the arrangement persisted for a long time, suggesting that the Israelites were the privileged administrators of Egypt during that period. The Pharaoh could count on them having no loyalty to the native aristocrats or merchant class of Egypt, and they might have served the Pharaoh's purpose by directing the wrath of the people toward the Jews rather than toward the Pharaoh himself. At any rate, eventually the numbers and political and economic power of the Jews grew so excessive that even the royal family felt threatened — a pattern that has often been repeated in Jewish history. Note the following passages from Exodus.

> **1:7 And the children of Israel were fruitful, and increased abundantly, and multiplied, and waxed exceedingly mighty, and the land was filled with them.**
>
> **1:8 Now there arose up a new king over Egypt who knew not Joseph.**
>
> **1:9 And he said to his people. behold, the people of the children of Israel are more and mightier than we:**
>
> **1:10 Come on, let us deal wisely with them; lest they multiply, and it come to pass, that, when there falleth out any war, they join also unto our enemies and fight against us, and so get them up out of the land.**[734]

The Egyptian Pharaoh was not the last who sought to expel Jews from his land. Following is a partial list of the expulsion of Jews from European kingdoms:

Expulsions of Jews from European States		
Mainz, 1012	Upper Bavaria, 1442	Naples, 1533
France, 1182	Netherlands, 1444	Italy, 1540
Upper Bavaria, 1276	Brandenburg, 1446	Naples, 1541
England, 1290	Mainz 1462	Prague, 1541
France, 1306	Mainz, 1483	Genoa, 1550
France, 1322	Warsaw, 1483	Bavaria, 1551
Saxony, 1349	Spain, 1492	Prague, 1557
Hungary, 1360	Italy, 1492	Papal States, 1569
Belgium, 1370	Lithuania, 1495	Hungary 1582
Slovakia, 1380	Portugal, 1496	Hamburg, 1649
France, 1394	Naples, 1496	Vienna, 1669
Austria, 1420	Navarre, 1498	Slovakia, 1744
Lyons, 1420	Nuremberg, 1498	Moravia, 1744
Cologne, 1424	Brandenburg, 1510	Bohemia, 1744
Mainz, 1438	Prussia, 1510	Moscow, 1891
Augsburg, 1439	Genoa, 1515	

Zionist leader Chaim Weizmann wrote the following about frequent hostile reaction to Jewish presence:

> Whenever the quantity of Jews in any country reaches the saturation point, that country reacts against them. . . . [This] reaction . . . cannot be looked upon as anti-Semitism in the ordinary or vulgar sense of the word; it is a universal social and economic concomitant of Jewish immigration and we cannot shake it off. [735]

According to the popular Jewish version of history, in every case Gentiles were at fault in the conflict. After tolerantly allowing Jewish immigrants into their nation, Gentiles are accused of unreasoning hatred against Jews, who are depicted as blameless sources of economic and social benefit.

When I read of the hostility toward Jews in dozens of different locations and historical circumstances, it seemed analogous to a man who is charged and convicted of dozens of rapes in several states over the course of many years. The man claims that he is always innocent, and that the dozens of rape convictions are merely the results of an unreasoning "hate" that the victims had for him. One perceptive writer, Joseph Sobran, said it well when he suggested that the term "anti-Semite" no longer means someone who dislikes Jews — it now means someone whom the Jews dislike.

The Jewish View of Anti-Semitism

As I continued my reading, I discovered what Jewish scholars believe is the historical origin of the Jew-Gentile conflict. If one delves back into the pages of Genesis preceding the story of Joseph, one comes upon the striking story of Isaac and Rebecca and their two sons, Esau and Jacob. The Jewish faith says that the two sons represent the two separate nations of Jew and Gentile.

From Genesis chapters 25:

> 23 And the Lord said to her. Two nations are in your womb, and two manner of people shall be separated from thy bowels; and the one people shall be stronger than the other people, and the elder shall serve the younger...
>
> 25 And the first came out red all over like a hairy garment, and they called his name Esau, and after that came his brother Jacob and he took hold on Esau's heel...
>
> 27 And the boys grew; and Esau was a cunning hunter, a man of the field; and Jacob was a plain man, dwelling in tents...
>
> 28 And Isaac loved Esau, because he did eat of his venison, but Rebecca loved Jacob.
>
> 29 ... And Esau came from the field, and he was faint [sick]. And Esau said to Jacob, feed me I pray for I am faint. Feed me with the same red pottage: Afterward he was called Edom. (after the red pottage)
>
> 31 And Jacob said I will feed you for the price of your birthright
>
> 32 And Esau said, I am at the point of death, what good then will my birthright do for me?
>
> 33 And Jacob said, Swear to me your birthright and I will feed you. Esau swore to him and sold his birthright. And Jacob fed him bread and pottage, and when Esau ate and drank, and got better, he went away...[736]

Esau's good and faithful conduct causes him to remain Isaac's favorite. Ailing and of poor of eyesight, Isaac calls Esau and asks him to hunt down and bring him some venison, saying that after he did he would offer him the blessings of God. Rebecca, upon hearing this, schemes with Jacob to pretend that he was Esau and bring Isaac ram meat prepared to taste like venison. Jacob disguises himself to feel and even smell like Esau. Jacob then lies to his father and presents himself as the firstborn Esau. Ultimately, from this deceit, he receives his father's blessing.

> 19 Jacob said to his father, "I am Esau your first-born. I have done as you told me; now sit up and eat of my game, that you may bless me..."
>
> 21 Then Isaac said to Jacob, "Come near, that I may feel you, my son, to know whether you are really my son Esau or not."

22 So Jacob went near to Isaac his father, who felt him and said, "The voice is Jacob's voice, but the hands are the hands of Esau..."

24 He said, "Are you really my son Esau?" He answered, "I am..."

29 Let peoples serve you, and nations bow down to you. Be lord over your brothers, and may your mother's sons bow down to you. Cursed be every one who curses you, and blessed be every one who blesses you![737]

Returning from the hunt with the venison, Esau discovered that his brother had deceived his father, and cheated him out of his blessing.

33 . . .I have eaten before you came, and have blessed him, yes, and he will be blessed.

34 And when Esau heard the words of his father, he cried with a great and exceeding bitter cry, and said to his father, bless me also, oh my beloved father.

35 And he said. My brother came in deceit and took away my blessing. . .he has robbed me two times, for he took away my birthright and now he has taken away my blessing. Father, have you not reserved a blessing for me.

37 (Isaac) Behold, I have made him your lord and all his brethren have I given to him for servants. .

38 . . . And Esau lifted up his voice to him and wept. . .

39 And by your sword shall you live and serve thy brother, and it shall come to pass when you have dominion, you will break Jacob's yoke from your neck.

Jacob and Esau found reconciliation 22 years later, but according to Jewish commentary, Esau's descendants became the Gentile Edomites, while Jacob's became the Jews. Jewish scholars later referred to the Romans as Edomites, and the term *Esau* became synonymous with Europeans and all Gentiles. The story of Jacob and Esau is an allegory of the Jew and Gentile with which the Jewish religion still identifies. Allusions to Esau are found in Raphael Patai's popular book *The Jewish Mind* and hundreds of other Jewish works.[738] Sholem Aleichem, the famous Yiddish-language author, wrote in his autobiography about a crude Russian ferryman,

> Esau! Only a Goy could do work like that, not a Jew. The Bible says of Esau, 'and thou shalt serve thy brother.' It is good that I am a descendant of Jacob, and not of Esau.[739]

Popular Jewish intellectual Sidney Hook recounts how he questioned his Jewish teacher about the injustice of Jacob's actions against Esau. He quotes his rabbi as saying, "What kind of question is that? Esau was an animal."[740]

Jacob, who became renamed "Israel," is considered the father of the Jewish people. Esau is seen as the archetype of the Gentile. Because Jews suggest that Jews are always blameless of the anti-Semitism inherent in Gentiles, Esau's hatred of Jacob is considered the origin of anti-Semitism as well.

A sermon by Rabbi Leon Spitz, quoted in the *American Hebrew*, illustrates the depth of hatred of many Jews for Esau and his descendants:

> **Let Esau whine and wail and protest to the civilized world, and let Jacob fight the good fight. The anti-Semite. . .understands but one language, and he must be dealt with on his own level. The Purim Jews stood up for their lives. American Jews, too, must come to grips with our contemporary anti-Semites. We must fill our jails with anti-Semitic gangsters. We must fill our insane asylums with anti-Semitic lunatics, We must combat every alien Jew hater. We must harass and prosecute our Jew-baiters to the extreme limits of the laws. We must humble and shame our anti-Semitic hoodlums to such an extent that none will wish or dare to become their fellow travelers.** [741]

When I understood that Jacob and Esau are an apt Jewish allegory for the eternal conflict between Jew and Gentile from a Jewish perspective, I realized that Gentiles might learn from it too. Is not the fact that Esau worked hard in the fields while Jacob stayed in tents, symbolic of the history of Jew and Gentile? It corresponds perfectly with the Europeans' inherent love of Nature, the outdoors and land — with the Jews' love of urban life.

Even reading the account written from the bias of Jacob's descendants, would not any fair-minded person find Esau's tears and rage justified? Is Jacob blameless and innocent or was Esau the one cheated? Shylock asking for a "pound of flesh" in Shakespeare's *Merchant of Venice* represents no less avarice and cold-heartedness than does Jacob withholding food from his sick brother so he could steal his birthright. In addition, consider Jacob's disguising of himself to defraud both his father and brother. Is that what the Jewish scholars see as justice? Is Esau's anger "hate" and "anti-Semitism"? Is it anti-Semitic to note that by it's own account, Israel found its earliest roots in fraud, treachery and deceit — and that it boasts about it?

Perhaps Isaac was prophetic when he said that Esau would be a servant to his brother until he obtained dominion (complete control over the land in which he lived) and thus broke "Jacob's yoke" from around his neck. Even though the philo-Semitic version of history is one long tale of Jewish woe at the hands of Gentiles, Jacob's descendants are certainly not the only ones who have suffered.

Esau's children have lost untold billions to the descendants of Jacob in usury, fraud and organized crime. Millions of Gentiles have suffered torturous slavery, degradation and death at the hands of the Jewish masters of the slave trade and prostitution. Esau's tears have fallen for the murder of millions of Christians at the hands of Jewish Bolsheviks in Eastern and Central Europe. They have been shed for millions of combatants and civilians who died in the fratricidal World Wars, encouraged in no small part by Jewish power. Is not Esau's justifiable rage found in the Palestinian people who lost their land, their freedom and, for so many, even the lives of their children?

If the story of Jacob and Esau is what the Jewish rabbinate say it is — the story of the genesis of the Jew and Gentile — it is a story of Jewish deceit against those whom they consider Gentiles. Such deceit must end. If it continues, it is only a matter of time until Esau's rage rekindles once more, just as it has a thousand times since the "sons of Jacob" first entered our lands.

Thoughtful and intelligent Jews must recognize that just as certainly as Jews have grievances against Gentiles, Gentiles have real grievances against Jews. Those Jews must take sincere action to mitigate Jewish supremacism and destructive anti-Gentilism. They have the power of the media and wield great influence in government — certainly enough to break the cycle of Jewish supremacism and anti-Semitism. We do not ask Jews to sacrifice their identity and heritage. In fact, we understand their natural urge for the survival of their cultural and genetic heritage, but we demand that they recognize that same fundamental right for the peoples among whom they dwell.

For instance, how hypocritical it is of them to secure the banning of Christmas carols from our public schools, while at the same time urging support of an exclusively Jewish religion and culture in Israel — financed by the tax dollars of American Christians! They campaign to open America's borders to the riffraff of the Third World while working to send American tax money to a nation that denies immigration to those not of Jewish blood, denying return even to those who were born there and whose families lived there for generations!

If farsighted Jews would refrain from such hypocrisies and abide by our standards of morality while living among us, if they would stop the manipulation and exploitation, then we could avoid the tragic anti-Semitic reaction that has erupted repeatedly in so many nations.

From the lessons of Jewish history that I have learned from the works of the Jews themselves, it seems unlikely that their leadership will see the wisdom in my proposal. History teaches harsh and often bloody lessons, but few heed them.

I also know that we of European descent cannot rest in the vain hope and trust of the magnanimity of our traditional enemies. No, we have the right to be masters in our own house. We have the natural right to have our Western nations reflect our own soul, our own spirit, our own esthetics, our own art, our own values, our own desires, our own interests, our own destiny.

As always in history, one can never negotiate successfully from weakness, only from strength. It is our task to become strong. Knowing the truth will make us strong. We must understand that we are in an evolutionary, life-or-death struggle — and we must understand that if we fail in this effort, all the beauty and greatness purchased by the blood and sacrifices of our ancestors will be lost, and along with them all hopes for the future for our people.

As the Bible says so elegantly, only when Esau has dominion will Jacob's yoke be broken. I seek no yoke upon the Jewish people. I only seek our own dominion in our *own* lands, free of Jewish political, intellectual and cultural domination and deformation.

Jews may be able, theoretically, to trace their lineage to Jacob, but obviously, the White Peoples of the Earth were not born of Esau. Our progenitors had already built the Egyptian, Mesopotamian, Babylonian, Mycenaean, Sumerian, Hittite and many other civilizations when Rebecca had her twin sons. Our ancestors designed the great pyramids and the complex astronomical observatory at Stonehenge long before the Jews established the kingdoms of Solomon and David.

I am an Aryan (a racially conscious White person dedicated to the survival and freedom of his people). I and my kinsmen seek no war against the Jews. We ask only to live and let live, but it must be made clear: We do intend to live! Only when Jewish supremacism abates will anti-Semitism disappear.

Aryans will not accept neither the deceit nor the supremacy proclaimed by Jacob. We will not wear the yoke of subservience. Our dominion shall be won. We have earned the blessings of God and Nature by our genius, our hard work, our creativity and our faith. We will not shrink from the fight for our freedom, and we reject the label of anti-Semitism from those who are themselves the embodiment of ethnocentrism, intolerance, and anti-Gentilism.

I am not an anti-Semite. I am simply an Aryan who strives for the life and freedom of our people. While having respect for those Jews who act honorably, I must oppose Jewish supremacism in our nations. It is as simple as this: Because I love my people, I have no choice but to oppose those who harm us or threaten our survival.

CHAPTER 22:

ISRAEL: JEWISH SUPREMACY IN ACTION

Jesus Christ couldn't please them when he was here on Earth, so how could anyone expect that I would have any luck. — President Harry S. Truman under pressure to recognize the newly announced Zionist state in Israel.[742]

For all its disappointments, Israel is who we are, uncamouflaged and unadorned. — Hillel Halkin [743]

American Jews must have the courage to declare openly that they have a double loyalty — to the country in which they live, and to the state of Israel. The Jew must not let himself be talked into merely being a good patriot of a country in which he lives.[744]
In the Zionist movement's new campaign to 'conquer the communities of Free Diaspora, the government of Israel will give every moral and political support...to the limits of its capacity.[745]

As I delved deeper into the Jewish question and Zionism, attempting to get a clear understanding of this enigmatic people, I realized that exploring the foundations and policies of the modern nation of Israel would answer some of my questions. For the first time in over 2000 years, Jews had their own sovereign state, a nation created entirely in their own image.

By the time I began my inquiry, it was obvious to me that the press and the entertainment industry were very pro-Israel. They had induced in me an early prejudice in favor of Israel. I now noticed that the reporters covering the stories for the TV networks and for the major newspapers are usually Jewish. Suspecting that much of my pro-Israel sentiment had come from biased sources, I sought to learn the undisputed basics of the Mideast conflict, and I first turned to my encyclopedias.

I found in my encyclopedias, information similar to what one will find today in the "Israel" article in the very popular *Encarta Encyclopedia*.

Of the more than 800,000 Arabs who lived in Israeli-held territory before 1948, only about 170,000 remained. The rest became refugees in the surrounding Arab countries.[746]

In 1948, the year the Israeli nation was set up, more than three-fourths of the entire Palestinian population living in the Israeli-held territory had become refugees. According to *Encarta*, 630,000 people were no longer able to dwell in their homes and to work on the land where their families had lived for thousands of years. Since then, Israel expanded its borders in the wars of 1956, 1967, 1973, and in the Lebanon invasion in 1982 — creating hundreds of thousands of additional Palestinian refugees.

Would people voluntarily leave their homes, their businesses, their farms? I asked myself. *Would they freely choose to live as penniless, stateless people in squalid refugee camps?* Obviously, the Zionists had driven them from their homes and property; and furthermore, the expulsion had obviously been intentional, for the Palestinians were forbidden to return to their homes after the fighting ended.

While in high school I wrote to a Palestinian information organization in Washington, D.C., and asked for some books giving their side of the Israeli-Arab conflict. From them and from libraries I obtained many well-documented sources — including some amazing Zionist ones — that gave a very different answer to the Mideast question. I learned that the fledgling Israeli government had passed regulations forbidding the expelled Palestinians from returning to their homes and property. They also enacted a special law that deemed this Arab property "abandoned" and subject to confiscation without compensation. The Nazis of Hitler's Reich could not have disposed of the problem with any more cold-blooded efficiency.

I checked the figures compiled by the British Census in 1922. At that time, Jews accounted for only about 10 percent of the population. In the last such census, taken the year before the establishment of Israel, Jews had made up only about half of the population within the area that subsequently became Israel. The Palestinians then owned 93.5 percent of the land. The facts were inescapable and damning: Zionist immigrants had forced their way into Palestine against the wishes of the inhabitants and then, through the weight of arms and terror, had driven the residents from their homes, robbing them of their land and possessions.

The facts could not be plainer. The Zionists, with help from their cohorts all over the world, had stolen a whole nation: the nation called Israel. No equivocation, no mountain of pro-Israeli propaganda, no playing of "Exodus" on the radio, and no replay of millions of feet of Hollywood films showing Arabs as brutal terrorists and Jews as innocent victims — none of this could change the obvious and inescapable facts.

The pro-Israeli propaganda I read suggested that Palestine was essentially an empty country. Tell that to the more than one million people who have been driven out of it since 1948. Zionist leaders understood from the beginning that Israel was going to be acquired by colonization and conquest. The dedicated Zionist leader Vladimir Jabotinsky makes this clear in his 1923 book *The Iron Wall: We and the Arabs*.[747]

> Zionist colonization must either be terminated or carried out against the wishes of the native population . . . an iron wall... to resist the pressure to the native population. . . . A voluntary reconciliation with the Arabs is out of the question...for without an armed force ...colonization is impossible. . .Zionism is a colonization adventure . . . It is important . . . to speak Hebrew, but... more important to be able to shoot... [748]

Israel: Founded on Terrorism

The first obstacle to Zionist objectives was that Britain envisioned a Palestine as portrayed by the Balfour Declaration, a society that would protect the civil and religious rights of all who lived there.

To dislodge the British, whom the League of Nations had mandated to govern Palestine, the Zionists developed to a fine art the use of terrorism as a modern weapon of political revolution. Menachem Begin, Abraham Stern, Yitshak Shamir, David Ben-Gurion, and many others began a campaign of bombings and assassination. They hanged and garroted British soldiers with piano wire and left their mutilated bodies to be found by the British authorities. Israeli terrorists blew up the King David Hotel in Jerusalem, killing more than 100 people. Their operatives invented the letter-bomb technique. Jewish hitmen even assassinated the UN mediator in Palestine, Count Folke Bernadotte, because he dared to express concern for the rights of the Palestinians. In his final report to the UN before his death, Bernadotte scathingly referred to

> Zionist pillage on a grand scale and the destruction of villages without apparent military need. [749](U.N. archives)
>
> It would offend basic principles to prevent these innocent victims of the conflict from returning to their homes, while Jewish immigrants flood into Palestine . . . threatening to permanently replace the dispossessed Arab refugees who have been here for centuries. [750]

The Zionist campaign worked. Eventually tiring of the terrorist campaign waged against them and despairing of a world press that covered up these crimes, the British finally threw up their hands and announced their withdrawal from the region. With the British gone, the Zionists could have their way with the native peoples who had dared to live on the land they coveted. No force was left to restrain them. Aided by both the military and financial support of both the capitalist U.S.A. and the Communist U.S.S.R., as well as by the huge sums of money that poured in from Zionist coffers from all over the world, the Jewish blitzkrieg rolled over their enemies as decisively as the Biblical account of the Red Sea rolling over the Egyptians.

With military victory certain, two significant problems still confronted the Zionists. The first was that there were hundreds of thousands of Palestinians who obviously would not sit back and let the new Jewish State take away their rights and their lands. Secondly, Palestinians owned more than 93 percent of the land of the new nation — a serious roadblock to the new "Greater Israel."

Quoting literally from the Book of Joshua, Jewish religious leaders warned that Israel must drive the Palestinians out of their borders:

> **Else if ye do in any wise go back, and cleave unto the remnant of these nations, even these that remain among you, and make marriages with them, and go in unto them, and they to you; know for a certainty that the Lord your God will no more drive these nations from out of your sight; but they shall be a snare and a trap unto you, and a scourge in your sides, and pricks in your eyes, until ye perish from off this good land — (Joshua 23:12-13)**[751]

Zionists fanatics ultimately solved their "Palestinian problem" with mass expulsions, murder, and well-planned terror. Palestinians who were born there and whose ancestors had lived there for countless generations were rounded up by the Israeli stormtroopers and driven over the border. Told they could never return to their homes, those expelled had little more than the tattered clothes on their backs. Many who refused to leave their homes were massacred by the Israeli military, and the Zionists publicized the massacres, intentionally causing widespread panic and flight among the Palestinians.

Committing atrocities against the Palestinians became an integral part of the Israeli strategy. When Jewish terrorists raped and massacred the residents of Arab villages, those in the surrounding villages naturally gathered up their children and fled for their lives. Once the Zionists set up their state and secured their initial borders — minus approximately 630,000 pesky Palestinian men, women, and children — the beneficent government of Israel forbade them ever to return to their homes, businesses, fields and flocks. By the time the Israeli "War for Freedom" ended, only about 170,000 Palestinians were left within Israel's borders.

The Jews, of course, had prominent and powerful spokesmen and supporters all over the world, especially in media, telling of the courage and righteousness of "little Israel." By the 1960s there were millions of adults and children around the world who, like me, were enthralled by the heroic story of Israel — a story romantically retold by the Academy Award-winning movie *Exodus*.[752] At that time I, just as most Americans of today, had scant knowledge of the gross injustice committed against the Palestinians.

The most well known atrocity of the first Israeli war was the massacre of Deir Yassin. On April 9, 1948, after cessation of fighting in that small village, the Zionist terrorist Irgun Gang, led by Menachem Begin, murdered 254 people, most of them women, children, and the elderly. For two days these Zionist terrorists had murdered men, women, and children, raped women, crushed the stomachs of pregnant women, and stolen their possessions. A Red Cross doctor, Jacques de Reynier, chief representative of the International Committee of the Red Cross in Jerusalem gave a chilling account of the massacre in his official report.[753]

De Reynier arrived at the village on the second day and saw "the mopping up," as one of the terrorists put it to him. It had been done with machine guns, then grenades, and was finished off with knives. They decapitated some of the victims and maimed 52 children in the sight of their mothers. The terrorists cut open 25 pregnant women's wombs and butchered the babies in front of them.

After his retirement in 1972, Israeli Haganah officer, Colonel Meir Pa'el, stated the following about Deir Yassin in *Yediot Ahronot*, a major Jewish publication:

> **The Irgun and LEHI men came out of hiding and began to 'clean' the houses. They shot whoever they saw, women and children included, the commanders did not try to stop the massacre...they were taken to the quarry between Deir Yassin and Giv'at Shaul, and murdered in cold blood...**[754]

The commander of the Haganah unit that controlled Deir Yassin after the massacre, Zvi Ankori, made this statement in the Israeli newspaper *Davar*:

> **I went into six to seven houses. I saw cut off genitalia and women's crushed stomachs. According to the shooting signs on the bodies, it was direct murder.**[755]

Albert Einstein, along with other concerned Jews, wrote a letter to the New York Times in 1948 decrying Begin as having: "openly preached the doctrine of the Fascist State." He went on to describe Deir Yassin in these words:

> **On April 9, terrorist bands attacked this peaceful village, which was not a military objective in the fighting, killed most of its inhabitants — 240 men, women, and children, and kept a few of them alive to parade as captives through the streets of Jerusalem...the terrorists, far from being ashamed of their act, were proud of this massacre...**

Menachem Begin boasts of the importance of the massacre of Deir Yassin in his book *The Revolt: The Story of the Irgun*. He wrote that there would not have been a State of Israel without the "victory" of Deir Yassin. "The Haganah carried out victorious attacks on other fronts... In a state of terror, the Arabs fled, crying, 'Deir Yassin'." [756].

Israel's first Prime Minister, David Ben-Gurion — no slouch at Jewish supremacy himself — was quoted as describing Begin with these words:

> **Begin undeniably belongs to the Hitlerian type. He is a racist, ready to destroy all the Arabs in his dream of unification of Israel, prepared to resort to any means to realize this sacred goal.**[757]

The instigator of the mass murder, Menachem Begin, later became the Prime Minister of Israel and even received the Nobel Peace Prize. Such an award is symbolic of the incredible worldwide Jewish media power, for Begin had been guilty of crimes not dissimilar to those of Nazis whom Jews are still hunting and prosecuting today. Yet instead of facing trial and punishment for crimes against humanity, Begin received what many would consider the world's highest honor.

The massacre at Deir Yassin was not the only one Israeli forces committed. In its May 6, 1992 edition, the Hebrew daily *Ha'ir* published an article by Guy Erlich called "Not Only Deir Yassin" that outlined a pattern of terror and murder. Erlich quotes the Israeli historian Aryeh Yitzhaki as saying the following:

> **'The time has come' he says, 'for a generation has passed, and it is now possible to face the ocean of lies in which we were brought up. In almost every conquered village in the War of Independence, acts were committed, which are defined as war crimes, such as indiscriminate killings, massacres and rapes. I believe that such things end by surfacing. The only question is how to face such evidence.'** [758]

Erlich and Yitzhaki point out that Israeli authorities are still covering up the murders. Nor did the massacres cease after the establishment of the Jewish State; they continued in times of both peace and war. Following are the names of some of them: Sharafat Massacre, Kibya Massacre, Kafr Qasem Massacre, Al-Sammou' Massacre, the Sabra And Shatila Massacre, Oyon Qara Massacre, Al-Aqsa Mosque Massacre, the Ibrahimi Mosque Massacre, the Jabalia Massacre.

There were further killings and expulsions of the Arabs as theJewish State expanded. In subsequent wars and military incursions, Israel drove more hundreds of thousands of Palestinians into relocation camps. Plagued by hunger and disease they bore remarkable resemblance to wartime concentration camps. Lebanon also fell victim to Israeli aggression in the 1980s and '90s, when it was bombed and invaded. Estimates of civilian casualties in Lebanon exceeded 40,000.

ISRAEL: JEWISH SUPREMACISM 373

The Zionist State also surreptitiously helped create and support rival factions in the Lebanese civil war.

The extraordinary diaires of Moshe Sharett, who had once shared the prime ministership of Israel with David Ben-Gurion, reveal Israel's machinations in the Lebanese Civil War. Sharett had been forced out the cabinet because he would not go along with what he felt were Ben-Gurion's clandestine and immoral actions. After Sharett's death, his son published the diaries despite a long battle of intimidation and legal maneuvers by the Zionists. Jewish author Livia Rokach quotes Sharett's diaries in her book *Israel's Sacred Terrorism*. The diaries tell how Israel purposefully created the Lebanese "Civil War" to further Israel's imperialist ambitions.[759]

In May, 1955 passages, Sharett's dairy describes Israel's plans to destabilize Lebanon's government, a plan that eventually produced the 1978 Lebanese War. Sharett quotes Moshe Dayan, Ben-Gurion's defense minister, at a secret cabinet meeting on May 16th planning to foment Lebanese civil war as an excuse for Israel to go in and annex land with water rights to the Litani River.[760][761]

In the first invasion of Lebanon in 1982, 30,000 civilians died and one half of a million people were driven from their homes. In the course of the fighting, Israeli forces devastated the city of Beirut, which before the war was described as the garden city of the Mideast. During the Israeli invasion, The *U.S.S. New Jersey*, sitting offshore, fired shells into some of the Lebanese towns. The U.S. involvement in Israel's 1982 war destroyed what little credibility America had left in the Mideast and cost our taxpayers billions; it also cost the lives of 300 U.S. Marines. More than 1,000 women, children, and elderly people were butchered in the Sabra and Shatila refugee centers under the watchful eyes of the Israeli invaders. Israel's General Ariel Sharon, who was directly responsible for this mayhem (it should be said that thousands of honorable Israelis marched in the streets in protest against it), was relieved of his command, although he was later rewarded with a cabinet post.

A more recent massacre was at Qana, a small town in southern Lebanon. Here are some excerpts of a British journalist's eyewitness account of the action so that the reader can fully understand that behind the cold statistics are real people, people who have faced a horror no less real than those who were murdered in the Oklahoma City bombing.

> **Qana, southern Lebanon - It was a massacre. Not since Sabra and Chatila had I seen the innocent slaughtered like this. The Lebanese refugee women and children and men lay in heaps, their hands or arms or legs missing, beheaded or disemboweled. There were well over a hundred of them. A baby lay without a head. The Israeli shells**

had scythed through them as they lay in the United Nations shelter, believing that they were safe under the world's protection. Like the Muslims of Srebrenica, the Muslims of Qana were wrong.

In front of a burning building of the UN's Fijian battalion headquarters, a girl held a corpse in her arms, the body of a gray-haired man whose eyes were staring at her, and she rocked the corpse back and forth in her arms, keening and weeping and crying the same words over and over: "My father, my father." A Fijian UN soldier stood amid a sea of bodies and, without saying a word, held aloft the body of a headless child.

...When I walked towards them, I slipped on a human hand...

Israel's slaughter of civilians in this terrible 10-day offensive - 206 by last night - has been so cavalier, so ferocious, that not a Lebanese will forgive this massacre. There had been the ambulance attacked on Saturday, the sisters killed in Yohmor the day before, the 2-year-old girl decapitated by an Israeli missile four days ago. And earlier yesterday, the Israelis had slaughtered a family of 12 - the youngest was a four-day-old baby - when Israeli helicopter pilots fired missiles into their home.

Shortly afterwards, three Israeli jets dropped bombs only 250 meters from a UN convoy on which I was traveling, blasting a house 30 feet into the air in front of my eyes. Traveling back to Beirut to file my report on the Qana massacre to the Independent last night, I found two Israeli gunboats firing at the civilian cars on the river bridge north of Sidon...

A French UN trooper muttered oaths to himself as he opened a bag in which he was dropping feet, fingers, pieces of people's arms...

We had suddenly become not UN troops and journalists but Westerners, Israel's allies, an object of hatred and venom. One bearded man with fierce eyes stared at us, his face dark with fury. "You are Americans", he screamed at us. "Americans are dogs. You did this. Americans are dogs."

President Bill Clinton has allied himself with Israel in its war against "terrorism" and the Lebanese, in their grief, had not forgotten this. Israel's official expression of sorrow was rubbing salt in their wounds. "I would like to be made into a bomb and blow myself up amid the Israelis", one old man said...[762]

Unlike the bloody scenes of the aftermath of Palestinian suicide bombers in Israel, Americans and Europeans never saw the butchery that Fisk describes. The media very seldom draw our attention to sufferings inflicted *by* Jews, it is suffering inflicted *on* Jews that they focus on. Those who wear the six-pointed star and who bomb United Nations shelters, ambulances, civilian refugee camps and civilian automobiles are never described as terrorists. They are simply referred to as "commandos" or simply "military forces." In contrast, Palestinian fighters outside the borders of Israel are, of course, routinely described as terrorists.

The remarks of the unknown old man at Qana that he "would like to be made into a bomb and blow myself up amid the Israelis," proved tragically prophetic, for just a year and a half later a number of Palestinians, desperate to exact revenge, sacrificed their lives to do just that in a Jerusalem marketplace. No one can defend any acts that kill or maim the innocent, but it is important to understand the horror that has induced hundreds of Palestinians to sacrifice their own lives to strike their feeble blows at those who have murdered their loved ones and stolen their homeland. In their grief and rage they also commit acts of violence against the innocent. The Zionist leaders also know full well that such Jewish losses, stroked by their media airing the blood-splashed video around the world, only increases Jewish solidarity and augment non-Jewish sympathy for the eternally suffering Jewish people.

When Saddam Hussein tried to take back Kuwait, which just a few decades before had been part of Iraq, the Western world went to war — encouraged to do so most notably by Israel. Were Iraq's actions any more imperialistic than Israel's against the Palestinians or the Lebanese?

Other than the scale of the conflict, what is the difference between Israel's perpetual war of conquest compared to Nazi Germany seeking Lebensraum in the 1940s? Germany treated no nation worse than Israel did Palestine, with its terrorizing and driving out three-fourths of its Palestinian residents. No populations of any European nation, other than those in some of the Soviet-occupied sectors of Germany, had been so massively displaced. It is Interesting to note that Jews also directed the terror against the Germans as well, but in that war they wore the uniform of Soviet commissars rather than that of the terrorist Stern Gang or Haganah.

Within the borders of Israel and her occupied territories, under the heel of a harsh military occupation, Israel continues to expropriate land from the Palestinians, settlement by settlement. Naturally the Palestinians resist such confiscation. The greatest uprising in recent years was the Intifada. The statistics of Palestinian casualties are ominous. Here are the figures compiled by the major French magazine *Le Monde*:

> **1,116 Palestinians have been killed since the beginning of the Intifada (the stone-throwing revolt) on 9 December 1987, shot by soldiers, policemen or settlers. The figures break down as follows : 626 deaths in 1988 and 1989, 134 in 1990, 93 in 1991, 108 in 1992 and 155 from 1 January to 11 September 1993. Among the victims were 233 children under 17 years old according to a study carried out by Betselem, the Israeli association for human rights.**
>
> **Military sources give a figure of nearly 20,000 for the number of Palestinians wounded by bullets and the U.N. Relief and Works agency for Palestine Refugees (UNRWA) gives a figure of 90,000.**

...This humanitarian organization also indicates that at least 20,000 detainees are tortured every year during interrogation in the military detention centers.[763]

No country in peacetime — not even the Soviets or the Red Chinese in the heyday of their gulags — has held as many prisoners per capita as the nation of Israel. It is one of the few nations that will not officially renounce the use of torture. It has long been high on the list of the offenders compiled by Amnesty International. The *London Times Magazine* did an extensive exposé on Israeli torture in both the 1970s and the '80s. The inescapable fact is that Israel was born and built by invasion, murder, and theft. Such injustice requires the use of force and terror to maintain its power.

Meanwhile, Americans and Europeans grow up on mother's milk and the sacred intonation that Israel is the "only democracy in the Middle East." But does our Jewish-dominated media ever ask what kind of democracy simply expels three-fourths of the residents who might vote the wrong way? The terrorizing, dispossessing, imprisoning, killing and expelling have taken away from the Palestinians a lot more than just their votes, for the exiles have lost their country.

The Historical Roots of Israel

Israel was born of the Holocaust, but it was sired thousands of years before. For at least 2,000 years Jews prayed, "Next year in Jerusalem." And until the middle of the 20th century, such prayer was only a religious metaphor. Then, dramatically, in 1948, the possibility of "next year in Jerusalem" became a possibility for every Jew in the world. The political machinations of the Zionist State are testimony to the cohesive and pervasive Jewish power in the West. In its operation, Israel lives as testimony to the very supremacist nature of both Judaism and its partly secular son, Zionism.

Jewish messianic tradition goes back as far as their recorded history. Even when the Jews were one of the smallest tribes of the Middle East, they fashioned a faith that designated themselves a special people, a chosen people, a people who were promised to rule the world. These messianic intentions are not paranoid delusions of anti-Semites, they are written plainly in their own Hebraic scriptures, and since that time they have been dutifully appended all the way to the present. Compare the following Biblical quotation to the messianic words of Israel's first Prime Minister, David Ben-Gurion.

> **. . .and kings shall come from you and shall rule wherever the foot of the sons of man has trodden. I shall give to your seed all the earth which is under heaven, and they shall rule over all the nations according to their desire; and afterwards they shall draw the whole earth to themselves and shall inherit it for ever' (Jub. 32:18-19)**

In *Look* magazine in 1962, Ben-Gurion stated his prediction for the next 25 years, a prediction of amazing prescience:

> **The image of the world in 1987 as traced in my imagination: The Cold War will be a thing of the past. Internal pressure of the constantly growing intelligentsia in Russia . . . may lead to a gradual democratization of the Soviet Union. On the other hand . . . transform the United States into a welfare state with a planned economy. . .With the exception of the USSR as a federated Eurasian state, all other continents will become united in a world alliance, at whose disposal will be an international police force. All armies will be abolished, and there will be no more wars. In Jerusalem, the United Nations (a truly United Nations) will build a Shrine of the Prophets to serve the federated union of all continents; this will be the seat of the Supreme Court of Mankind.** [764]

Many people are amazed to discover that most Jews in Israel are "non-religious," just as was their first great leader David Ben-Gurion. However, these mostly atheistic Jews tolerate a religious state. Apparently, Jews who have no belief in God support Judaism as a state-sponsored institution that preserves both Jewish culture and the Jewish genotype. Other than a few intolerant fanatics, the Jewish Orthodox institutions allow a wide range of religious belief, from atheism to forms of the occult called Kabbalism. Only the Talmud, could have a passage where a rabbi claims to have argued with God and defeated him. To Jewish orthodoxy, biblical and theological interpretations may vary greatly as long as Jewish tradition and Jewish heritage is scrupulously preserved.

Is God a Zionist?

Israel supports its claim on Palestinian land by saying that God gave it to the Jews. A corollary secular argument is that the remote ancestors of the Jewish people lived 2,000 years ago on parts of what is now Israel. They argue with a straight face that this gives them the right to take that land away from whoever has lived on the land during the intervening years.

That argument is much like saying that because the Romans had ruled the Mediterranean 2000 years ago that Italians now have the right to conquer the entire Mediterranean Basin and drive out three-fourths of its population. Furthermore, the Jewish people cannot claim they were first people dwelling in the "Promised Land." The Bible clearly records Jewish invasions and genocide in the region. The Palestinian people are descended from the same peoples who lived in the area before the Jewish conquests. If the claim that whoever lived on the land first has the rightful claim, then the Palestinians should have the primary claim to the land because many of their ancestors lived on it long before ancient Israel even existed.

The allegation that Jewish rule over Palestine today is God-ordained poses a more difficult question, especially for contemporary Christians. It is difficult because the Jewish powerbrokers have been able to completely change 2,000 years of Christian interpretation of the Bible. Servile Judeo-Christian preachers have made alliances with the Zionists because of their media power. They quote liberally from Old Testament verses that proclaim a covenant between God and the Israelites that bequeaths to the Jews the land referred to as Israel.

The Christian Church of our fathers, though, from its earliest history up to recent times, has always refuted that claim. Christian scholars, from the writers of the New Testament itself to the midpoint of the 20th century, pointed out that the Bible makes it very clear that all promises made by God are conditional upon faithfulness. God says clearly in the Old Testament that if the Israelites reject him, he will requite them. The New Testament emphatically makes the point that the Jewish nation, by rejecting God and his Son, has dissolved the Old Covenant. New Testament scriptures quote God as making a *New* Covenant with a *new* promise of salvation of Christ for *all*. As I have previously quoted, the scriptures cannot possibly be any more explicit than in Hebrews 8:10, in which God says the Jews are no longer in the covenant he made in the Old Testament.

> **8:10 Not according to the covenant that I made with their fathers, in the day when I took them by the hand out of the land of Egypt; because they continued not in my covenant, and I regarded them not, saith the Lord.**

Is it any wonder that Jews reject the New Testament and that Israel forbids even quoting from it in their schools? Government-funded groups have even organized public burnings of copies of the New Testament, and laws provide for criminal prosecution and five-year imprisonment for Christians who seek to convert Jews. It seems quite odd, in light of these facts, that many denominations of the Christian Church are now busily adopting the view that Jews are still today the "chosen people."

It is understandable that supremacist Jews who reject Christ and the New Testament would say that God sanctions their terror against the Palestinian people, but it is scandalous that Christians could possibly support them in their bloody adventure. Many of those who suffered from the Zionist onslaught were Christian Palestinians. Israel's crimes have significantly hurt the Christian component among the Palestine people. The fact that a some Christian leaders lend moral and financial support to a nation that hates and oppresses Christians is testimony to the penetration and subversion of Zionist power and influence — even into the highest councils of various Christian denominations. In doing so they have undermined the Christian faith in the entire Mideast. And, indeed, in the entire World.

The Israeli claim that God gave them the land of Israel is ludicrous when one considers that at least three-quarters of Israelis don't believe in God in the first place. (Israeli government statistics say 85 percent do not believe in God.) How can a God that they don't believe in, promise them land. Far from being a religious promise, Israel's creation came not from divine intervention, but from Zionist intrigue that began during the First World War.

The Balfour Declaration

The First World War laid the political foundation of the Zionist State. Britain was having a tough time of it. For years, the war had droned on with a horrendous cost of life. Despite oceans of spilled blood, the front lines had moved only a few kilometers back and forth on the Western front.

Jewish loyalties were somewhat divided during the war. Some Jews favored the allies for business or other reasons. Others favored the Germans for the main reason that German success against Russia would weaken their long-time enemy, imperial Russia and the Czar. Just a decade earlier, financiers Jacob Schiff and Bernard Baruch led a campaign to finance the Japanese in the Russo-Japanese war, resulting in a defeat for Russia. Now Jewish powerbrokers around the world hoped for an even worse Russian defeat in the Great War as their opportunity to overthrow the Czar and establish a Jewish-Bolshevik government.

The Germans, desperately fighting a war on two fronts, knew that a revolution in Russia might remove Russia from the war. Toward that end Kaiser Wilhelm approved one of the most treacherous deeds in the annals of Western civilization. In his zeal to defeat Russia, his ministers assisted Lenin, Trotsky, and hundreds of other Bolshevik revolutionaries, mostly Jewish, to cross Germany in a sealed train toward Russia. Allowing the Bolshevik terrorists and assassins access to Russia unleashed the greatest period of human oppression, torture, and murder that the world has ever experienced.

Britain and her allies fought to a stalemate against Germany, but as Russia weakened, the allies knew that her defeat would allow the entire German army on the Eastern Front to almost double their army in the West, dramatically tipping the military balance toward the Central Powers. Britain understood that it was critical that they bring the United States into the war on the Allies' side to counter the Russian collapse.

Onto this stage of crisis, stepped the British Lord Arthur Balfour. He met with the Rothschilds, and made an agreement that in return for pledging Britain's support in the creation of a Jewish homeland in Palestine, the Jews would use their great international power and influence to draw the United States into the war. Lord Balfour drew up a document — the Balfour Declaration — that called for the Jewish homeland. Even our popular encyclopedias admit the reason for the Balfour Declaration:

> **It has been commonly accepted that the Balfour Declaration was a unilateral undertaking by the British government. The immediate purpose was to win for the Allied cause in World War I the support of Jews and others in the warring nations and in neutral countries such as the United States.[765] (Encarta Encyclopedia)**

Read what David Lloyd George, Britain's wartime prime minister, wrote about the Balfour Declaration. Note his pointing out that the Jews of Russia had been the "chief agents in the betrayal of the Russian war effort" as well as "the disintegration of Russian society — later recognized as the Revolution."

> **Another most cogent reason for the adoption by the Allies of the policy of the Declaration lay in the state of Russia herself. Russian Jews had been secretly active on behalf of the Central Powers from the first... by 1917 they had done much in preparing for that general disintegration of Russian society, later recognized as the Revolution. It was believed that if Great Britain declared for the fulfillment of Zionist aspirations in Palestine under her own pledge, one effect would be to bring Russian Jewry to the cause of the entente.**
>
> **It was believed, also, that such a declaration would have a potent influence upon world Jewry outside Russia, and secure for the entente the aid of Jewish financial interests. In America, their aid in this respect would have a special value when the Allies had almost exhausted the gold and marketable securities available for American purchase. Such were the chief considerations which, in 1917, impelled the British Government towards making a contract with Jewry.[766]**

Samuel Landman, in his book *Great Britain, The Jews and Palestine*, confirms the Jewish role in bringing America into the war. Landman, a leading Zionist and secretary of the Zionist Organization from 1917 to 1922, confirms from the Jewish perspective exactly what Lloyd George says:

> **... the only way (which proved so to be) to induce the American President to come into the War was to secure the cooperation of Zionist Jews by promising them Palestine, and thus enlist and mobilize the hitherto unsuspectedly powerful forces of Zionist Jews in America and elsewhere in favor of the Allies on a quid pro quo contract basis...[767]**

Some of President Woodrow Wilson's top advisers during the period were the Jewish Supreme Court justice Louis Brandeis, Rabbi Stephen Wise, and the powerful banker and international financier of New York City, Bernard Baruch. Although Wilson had campaigned for president on the slogan "He kept us out of the war," once the Balfour Declaration was proposed, Jewish influence quickly pushed him to an interventionist path. When Balfour came to the United States in May 1917 in hopes of pulling America into the war, he ignored the U.S. State Department (which created much resentment) and met with Brandeis, who had no authority to speak on foreign relations.[768]

The Jewish protagonists for war were also aided in their jingoism by a number of American magnates who saw American participation in the European conflict as writing a blank check for the military-industrial complex. The press that was Jewish-owned or Jewish-influenced agitated unashamedly for war, running lurid tales of German atrocities, and promoting stories that Germany planned to invade the United States through Mexico — even though, in four years of war, it had been unable to even take Paris.

In short order, the Germans — although racially and morally no different from the British and Americans — were labeled "Huns" and "baby-killers." The Allies, despite Britain's and France's non-democratic foreign empires, were said to be fighting for "democracy." Even though Germany had electoral institutions similar to those of the Allies, it was called tyrannical.

The two prominent slogans of the greatest and bloodiest war in all of history up to that time were, "The War to Make the World Safe for Democracy" and, incredibly, "The War to End All War!" If those were truly the Allied objectives of the First World War, it is easy to see the fruits of their victory. As the 20th century rumbles to a close, democracy around the world still seems to be in precious short supply, and war since 1918 has done a thriving business.

Most historians now agree that the First World War was not the result of aggression or dictatorship or any sinister force other than entangling alliances structured to preserve the balance of power. Essentially, it was prompted by nothing but national fears and bravado. For most of that internecine conflict, America sensibly stayed out of the war's insanity, but finally, Jewish power, whose concern, as always, was only its own interests — tipped the scales for war. After all, what were the lives of a few hundred thousand young Americans compared to the interests of the Chosen?

The media kept Americans blind to the Jewish influence in our participation in the First World War, just as they had cloaked the pivotal Jewish involvement in the Russian Revolution. To this day, few

Americans are aware of the Jewish influence in America's joining the First World War.

The Balfour Declaration was innocuous-sounding enough, and it took pains to state,

> **...that nothing shall be done which may prejudice the civil and religious rights of existing non-Jewish communities in Palestine, or the rights and political status enjoyed by Jews in any other country.** [769]

The Zionists, though, did not want a homeland containing a significant non-Jewish community. From the outset, they were determined *not* to set up a multicultural, pluralistic democracy that they were so busy planning for America and the rest of the European world. They wanted a chauvinistic, ethno-religious, purely Jewish state, but they could not reveal this until they had attained power. Among themselves, though, they made clear their intentions to create an ethnic state — one amazingly similar to the nation they most hated: Nazi Germany.

Zionism/Nazism: Born in Each Other's Image

In the Nuremberg War Crimes Trials, Julius Streicher, the notorious publisher of the crudely anti-Semitic *Der Stürmer*, gave the following testimony when asked if he had helped develop Germany's racial laws:

> **The accused (Streicher) : Yes,...I had been writing that all mixing of German and Jewish blood had to be prevented in the future. I wrote articles to that effect, and I have always repeated that we had to take the Jewish race, or the Jewish people, as a model. I have always repeated in my articles that the Jews were to be regarded as a model by other races, for they have given themselves a racial law, the law of Moses, which says: "If you go unto foreign lands, you must not take foreign wives." And this, Gentlemen, is of great importance in judging the Nuremberg laws. It was these Jewish laws that were taken as a model. When, centuries later, the Jewish legislator Ezra saw that, despite this, many Jews had married non-Jewish wives, these bonds were broken. This was the origin of Jewry which, thanks to its racial laws, survived for centuries, whereas all the other races and civilizations were destroyed.** [770]

The racial awakening in Europe of the 19th and 20th centuries grew in great part because of the presence of the Jewish people. There were no Blacks or Orientals in Europe, but there was no shortage of Jews. Scientific and social observers noted that their character and appearance differed from those of the indigenous races of Europe.

One of the first major figures to recognize the dynamic power of race and write extensively about it was the British prime minister Benjamin Disraeli, who himself was of Jewish heritage. He stated:

"The racial question is the key to world history...all is race, there is no other truth." Scholars who recognized the role of race in history knew that the power and perseverance of the Jewish race rests in its ethnocentrism and prohibitions against intermarriage, enabling it to survive after 2,000 years of living among Gentiles. As Stretcher's testimony proves, the formulators of European racial ideology had learned a lot from studying Jewish institutions and history. Although Zionists and Nazis saw each other as mortal enemies, many of the leaders of both movements saw similarities of ideas, and some collaborated in pursuit of mutual aims.

The National Socialists wanted their own nation free of Jewish influence, and the Zionists sought nonassimilation with Gentiles and a nation of their own. (Even today in modern America and Europe most major Jewish organizations oppose intermarriage.) At first glance, it seems unbelievable that Zionism and Nazism sometimes had worked together, but the historical record reveals fascinating evidence.

Most Jews in Europe and the rest of the world virulently opposed Hitler and National Socialist Germany. In fact, as Hitler gained power, the World Jewish Congress, claiming to speak for Jews worldwide, declared economic war on Germany and announced their intention to do everything in their power to destroy Germany and National Socialism.[771]

Within the Jewish community, however, there were many Zionists who saw the anti-Semitic policies of Germany as an aid to the creation of the Jewish state. They saw those policies as encouraging emigration to Palestine and increasing Jewish anger and solidarity. And, interestingly enough, they viewed the racial thinking of Hitler as analogous to what they desired for their own people. For these Jews, collusion between the Zionists and the Nazis served the interests of both.

Britain had difficulty dealing with the increased Jewish immigration into Palestine in the 1930s, as it caused marked unrest in the Arab sectors of the mandate. To lessen tensions, the British attempted to limit Jewish immigration into Palestine. Into this opportunity stepped Hitler and Nazi Germany. Even though Hitler had misgivings about Israel becoming a center for international Jewish power in the same way the Soviet Union had become one for international Communism, and although he had concerns about damaging German relations with the Arab world, he saw the emigration of the Jews from Germany and all Europe as paramount. In his mind, a Jewish state in Palestine might be a practical destination for Europe's Jews.

From the earliest days of Hitler's rise to power, the leading Zionist organization in Germany sought out common ground with him. Within months of Hitler's achieving the chancellorship, the Zionist

384 MY AWAKENING

Federation of Germany presented him with a statement suggesting that Zionism could solve the "Jewish Question."

> **In the foundation of the new State, which has proclaimed the race principle, we wish to adapt our community to these new structures...**
>
> **Our recognition of the Jewish nationality allows us to establish clear and sincere relations with the German people and its national and racial realities. Precisely because we do not want to underestimate these fundamental principles, because we too are against mixed marriages and for the maintaining of the purity of the Jewish group...**
>
> **...Zionism believes that the rebirth of the national life of a people, which is now occurring in Germany through the emphasis on its Christian and national character, must also come about in the Jewish national group. For the Jewish people, too, national origin, religion, common destiny and a sense of its uniqueness must be of decisive importance in the shaping of its existence...**
>
> **...We are not blind to the fact that a Jewish question exists and will continue to exist. From the abnormal situation of the Jews severe disadvantages result for them, but also scarcely tolerable conditions for other peoples.** [772] [773] [774] [775]

Joachim Prinz, a German Zionist who emigrated to the United States and who later became head of the American Jewish Congress, wrote in his 1934 book *Wir Juden* [*We Jews*] [776] that the National Socialist revolution in Germany meant "Jewry for the Jews." Prinz in later years also scathingly wrote about Adolf Hitler's view of the importance of race, but hypocritically showed no reluctance to defend the concept of the "Jewish race."

> **We want assimilation to be replaced by a new law: *the declaration of belonging to the Jewish nation and the Jewish race*. A state built upon the principle of the purity of nation and race can only be honoured and respected by a Jew who declares his belonging to his own kind...No subterfuge can save us now. In place of assimilation we desire a new concept: recognition of the Jewish nation and Jewish race.** [777]

In the key book of modern Zionism, the *Jewish State*, Theodore Herzl maintained that the Jews were much more than a religious community; they were a *people*. Herzl even used the well-known German racialist word *Volk* to describe them. Volk was also one of Hitler's favorite words. With it he described his ideal state, the "Volkishe Staat." Herzl wrote, long before Hitler's rise, that anti-Semitism is a natural reaction of Gentiles to Jews. He advocated a separate state as the only real answer to the conflict. [778] [779] [780] [781]

> **The Jewish question exists wherever Jews live in noticeable numbers, Where it does not exist, it is brought in by arriving Jews. ... I believe I understand anti-Semitism, which is a very complex phenomenon...I consider this development as a Jew, without hate or**

ISRAEL: JEWISH SUPREMACISM 385

fear. . . . It is a national question. To solve it we must, above all, make it an international political issue. . . . a final solution of the Jewish question.

The leading German Zionist paper, *Judische Rundschau*, in 1935 even went so far as to express approval of the "Nuremberg Laws" designating Jews as an alien nationality and forbidding intermarriage and sexual relations between Germans and Jews.

> The new laws give the Jewish minority in Germany its own cultural life, its own national life. In the future it will be able to shape its own schools, its own theatre, and its own sports associations. In short, it can create its own future in all aspects of national life . . .[782]

Georg Kareski, the former head of the largest Jewish community in Western Europe (that of Berlin) and leader of the Zionist State Organization and Jewish Cultural league, made the following comment to the Berlin daily *Der Angriff* at the end of 1935:

> For many years I have regarded a complete separation of the cultural affairs of the two peoples [Jews and Germans] as a precondition for living together without conflict. . . . I have long supported such a separation, provided it is founded on respect for the alien nationality. The Nuremberg Laws . . . seem to me, apart from their legal provisions, to conform entirely with this desire for a separate life based on mutual respect. . . . This interruption of the process of dissolution in many Jewish communities, which had been promoted through mixed marriages, is therefore, from a Jewish point of view, entirely welcome. [783][784][785][786][787]

Other leading Zionists around the world spoke similarly. Rabbi Stephen S. Wise, president of the American Jewish Congress and the World Jewish Congress, speaking before a rally in New York in 1938, said:

> I am not an American citizen of the Jewish faith, I am a Jew. I am an American. I have been an American for sixty-three sixty fourths of my life, but I have been a Jew for 4000 years. Hitler was right in one thing. He calls the Jewish people a race and we are a race.[788]

Not only was there cooperation in words, there was a collaboration between the Zionists and the Nazis up to and even during the Second World War. The Nazi government set up a series of 40 agricultural centers throughout Germany to train young Jews for kibbutz life in Palestine. It supported immigration of Jews into Palestine until prevented by the war. The official SS newspaper, *Das Schwarze Korps*, supported Zionism in front-page editorials.[789]

The SS collaborated with the Haganah, the Zionist underground military in Palestine, with help in Jewish immigration and even provided smuggled guns for the Zionist forces. Despite misgivings, Hitler continued to support Zionist objectives in Palestine.[790][791][792][793]

Hitler told his army adjutant in 1939 and again in 1941 that he had asked the British in 1937 about transferring all of Germany's Jews to Palestine or Egypt. The British rejected the proposal, he said, because it would cause further disorder.[794]

As the British government became more restrictive on Jewish immigration into Palestine in the late '30s, the SS made a pact with the secret Zionist agency Mossad le-Aliya Bet to smuggle Jews into Palestine. As a result of this collaboration, Jewish migration, both legal and illegal, from Germany (including Austria) to Palestine increased dramatically in 1938 and 1939. 10,000 Jews were scheduled for emigration in October 1939, but the beginning of the war prevented it. During 1940 and 1941, and as late as March 1942, Germany still assisted with indirect Jewish immigration to Palestine and had at least one officially authorized Zionist "kibbutz" training camp in Germany for potential emigrants.[795]

In the economic sphere, the Ha'avara agreement between Nazi Germany and the Palestine Center of the World Zionist Organization was vital to the Zionist cause. It began in 1933 and lasted throughout the 1930s and allowed the transfer of Jewish wealth to Palestine. Through this pact, Hitler's Third Reich did more than any other government during the 1930s to support Jewish development in Palestine.[796,797,798,799,800,801]

Probably the most telling document of the willingness of some Zionist factions to enter an alliance with Hitler was the offer made in 1941 by the Fighters for the Freedom of Israel, popularly called the "Lehi," or the Stern Gang. One of its top officials was Yitzhak Shamir, who became its leader and chief terrorist after Stern's death and who later became Israel's prime minister in the 1980s. The Stern gang considered the British to be Zionism's biggest enemy because Great Britain tried to protect the civil rights of the native Palestinians and attempted to slow the insurgent Jewish immigration.

In one of the most amazing facts of modern history, the Lehi actually made a formal proposal to the Germans of a military alliance between the Jewish revolutionary organization and the Nazis. In effect, they formally proposed to join the war on Germany's side. Here are portions of the text of their communiqué with the Nazis.

> **In their speeches and statements, the leading statesmen of National Socialist Germany have often emphasized that a New Order in Europe requires as a prerequisite a radical solution of the Jewish question by evacuation. ("Jew-free Europe")**
>
> **The evacuation of the Jewish masses from Europe is a precondition for solving the Jewish question. However, the only way this can be totally achieved is through settlement of these masses in the homeland of the Jewish people, Palestine, and by the establishment of a Jewish state in its historical boundaries.**

> The goal of the political activity and the years of struggle by the Israel Freedom Movement, the National Military Organization in Palestine (Irgun Zvai Leumi), is to solve the Jewish problem in this way and thus completely liberate the Jewish people forever.
>
> The NMO, which is very familiar with the good will of the German Reich government and its officials towards Zionist activities within Germany and the Zionist emigration program, takes that view that:
>
> 1. Common interests can exist between a European New Order based on the German concept and the true national aspirations of the Jewish people as embodied by the NMO.
>
> 2. Cooperation is possible between the New Germany and a renewed, folkish-national Jewry.
>
> 3. The establishment of the historical Jewish state on a national and totalitarian basis, and bound by treaty with the German Reich, would be in the interest of maintaining and strengthening the future German position of power in the Near East.
>
> On the basis of these considerations, and upon the condition that the German Reich government recognize the national aspirations of the Israel Freedom Movement mentioned above, the NMO in Palestine offers to actively take part in the war on the side of Germany.
>
> This offer by the NMO could include military, political and informational activity within Palestine and, after certain organizational measures, outside as well...
>
> The indirect participation of the Israel Freedom Movement in the New Order of Europe, already in the preparatory stage, combined with a positive-radical solution of the European Jewish problem on the basis of the national aspirations of the Jewish people mentioned above, would greatly strengthen the moral foundation of the New Order in the eyes of all humanity.
>
> The cooperation of the Israel Freedom Movement would also be consistent with a recent speech by the German Reich Chancellor, in which Hitler stressed that he would utilize any combination and coalition in order to isolate and defeat England. [802] [803] [804]

No records exist of the German response to the amazing proposal, but by the time it was offered, Germany had already committed itself to a pro-Arab posture in an attempt to undermine Britain's position in the Middle East.

When I first saw this document, I noticed the ideological similarities between Zionism and National Socialism, right down to the use of that favorite Nazi word "folkish" (Volk) to describe the foundations of the state they wanted to create.

It fascinated me to read about Zionist collusion with Nazi Germany. Zionist-Nazi collaboration has long been a dirty little secret — one that speaks volumes about the ideological foundations of Israel and the lengths to which Zionist extremists would go to secure its creation.

Zionist fanaticism had little regard for human lives, including that of Jews, when it came to the establishment of Israel. Israel's first prime minister, David Ben-Gurion, made the following statement when German Jewry was threatened by Hitler.

> **If I knew that it would be possible to save all the children in Germany by bringing them over to England, and only half of them by transporting them to Eretz Yisrael, then I would opt for the second alternative. For we must weigh not only the life of these children, but also the history of the People of Israel.** [805]

If Israel's first prime minister's regard for Jewish life was such that he would rather see half the Jewish children of Germany die than be transported to England instead of Israel, how much value could one expect him to place on the life of a Palestinian child? How would we react to a Nazi who would say that he would rather see half the Jewish children die rather than simply go to another country?

Another classic example of a low regard for human life, even Jewish life, can be seen in a 1940 terrorist act by Ben-Gurion and the founders of the Zionist state. The Haganah, led by Ben-Gurion, blew up a ship of Jewish refugees from Hitler. The British had been taking them to Mauritius rather than allowing them to disembark in Haifa, Israel. To arouse indignation against the British, the Zionists blew up the ship on Christmas day, 1940, causing the death of 252 Jews as well as the ship's English crewmen. If Nazis had blown up a ship of refugees in the waters of Israel, the Mossad would have hunted the perpetrators to the ends of the Earth if need be, so that they could be brought before the Israeli "war crimes" courts. There would be well-publicized, annual remembrances of the terrible act of terrorism. Instead, Israel chose the murderer as its first prime minister.[806]

Zionism and Nazism are torn from the same cloth, their banners stained with blood. Zionists, though, are a lot better at public relations.

Israel: A Racist State

On November 10th 1975, a plenary session of the United Nations declared that Zionism is a form of racism. Howls of protest went up across America and throughout the world from the (once again) poor, persecuted Jews. They were furious that such a charge could have been made against the "only true democracy in the Mideast." But what exactly is Zionism if it is not racism? Even David Ben-Gurion, in discussing the "Hitlerism" of Menachem Begin, wrote, "He can be accused of racism, but then one will have to put on trial the entire Zionist movement, which is founded on the principle of a purely Jewish entity in Palestine." [807]

The International Convention on the Elimination of All Forms of Racial Discrimination, adopted by the United Nations General Assembly in 1965, has now been ratified by most member states. Article 1 of this Convention defines the term *racial discrimination* as

> **. . .any distinction, exclusion, restriction or preference based on race, color, descent, or national or ethnic origin which has the purpose or effect of nullifying or impairing the recognition, enjoyment or exercise, on an equal footing, of human rights and fundamental freedoms in the political, economic, social, cultural or any other field of public life.** [808]

Israel was and is a nation set up exclusively for Jews. By the Israeli "Law of Return," a Jew is defined not by his religious beliefs, but by his Jewish ancestry, proven by the heritage of his parents. Although it is possible for Gentiles to convert to Judaism, the obstacles are so great that the "converted" make up only a tiny percentage of the Jewish population. As I write these lines, Jewish Orthodoxy, the state-sanctioned religion of Israel, is in a major controversy with American Reform and Conservative factions because the Orthodox in Israel will not even recognize conversions from these two branches of Judaism.

A Palestinian who was born in the boundaries of what is now Israel, and whose family lived there for thousands of years before being forced out by the Israeli army, cannot return to his homeland and become a citizen of Israel. In contrast, an atheist Jew born in New York City and who speaks no Hebrew, can immigrate to Israel and be given instant citizenship. In addition, the Israeli government offers him help in housing, living expenses, education, and numerous other benefits to immigrate.

In 1948, nearly 94 percent of the land of Israel was owned by Palestinians. Since then, Palestinian-owned land has been systematically confiscated by the Israeli government. Most of the Palestinian land went into what Israel calls the "National Jewish Fund," and was declared by law to be "Land of Israel." It has become "Jewish" land, and by law it can never be sold to a non-Jew, rented to a non-Jew, or worked by a non-Jew. Much of the land has been given at no cost to Jewish settlers. The Zionist army forced the Palestinians from more than 350 cities and villages in Israel and the Occupied Territories and then bulldozed the homes. Even ancient Palestinian cemeteries are often plowed under.

Two other laws concern the Keren Kayemet ("National Jewish Fund" Law passed on 23 November 1953) and the Keren Hayesod ("Reconstruction Fund" Law passed on 10 January 1956). The president of the Israeli Human Rights League, Doctor Israel Shahak, a professor at the Hebrew University of Jerusalem, in his book, *The Racism of the State of Israel*,[809] tells us that there are in Israel whole towns (Carmel, Nazareth, Illith, Hatzor, Arad, Mitzphen-Ramen, and others) where non-Jews are forbidden by law to live.

The Palestinians who remained in Israel, although ostensibly citizens, suffer intense discrimination. They are given citizenship-identification cards that have no Israeli nationality designation; nationality is listed only as Arab or Jewish, lending itself to the many discriminatory policies in the Jewish state. In Israel there are whole cities and settlements in which it is illegal for Palestinians to live. There are segregated housing areas and complexes, schools, and recreational facilities where Palestinians are not allowed. This segregation is not de facto; it is official government policy. Palestinians are not permitted to serve in the military, and even though Palestinians are between 15 and 20 percent of the Israeli population, there has never even been one Palestinian in the Israeli cabinet.

Israeli law does not recognize the legality of marriage between Jews and Palestinians, as marriages and other aspects of civil laws are decided by religious courts, which do not recognize such marriages. Whenever I see Jews in the American media glorifying and encouraging intermarriage between Blacks and Whites, I think about their hypocrisy in supporting a nation in that will not, by law, recognize a marriage between a Jew and an non-Jew.

Haim Cohen, a former judge of the Supreme Court of Israel, noted

> **...the bitter irony of fate which has led the same biological and racist laws propagated by the Nazis and which inspired the infamous Nuremberg laws, to serve as a basis for the definition of Judaism within the State of Israel.** [810]

The Treachery against the Liberty

The Jewish people and their history fascinated me. I did not remain quiet as I educated myself about the Jewish question. I discussed what I read with my family, friends, and teachers. Pointing out Jewish hypocrisy caused me to be accused of hatred, intolerance, racism, religious bigotry, and of course anti-Semitism.

It became clear to me that despite the media image of Jews as the most holy and Godlike people on Earth, the Jewish infrastructure has maintained an extreme form of ethnic supremacism. Their supremacism was coupled with intense hatred toward others, nursed from the time of their sojourn in Egypt to the post-Holocaust modern age. Such chauvinism has repeatedly erupted in intolerance and repression. Anyone who dares to expose this record of Jewish hypocrisy, racism, and hatred is defamed by the "Anti-Defamation League" as a hater.

When I would bring up Jewish racism or quote from Jewish scriptures or current Jewish leaders, my teachers were at first taken aback, but would later assure me that such sentiments were part of a remote past or a tiny minority in the *present*. They told me that Jews of the modern era really did not follow the ethnocentric way of their forefathers. But studying Israel helped me to realize that Jewish supremacism is very much in their present. One of the things that really brought it home to me was an Israeli act of war against America — a treacherous act that elicited only obsequiousness and treason from America's media and government.

On July 8, 1967, an American Navy intelligence ship, the *U.S.S. Liberty*, patrolling off the waters of Israel and the Gaza Strip, came under the fire of jet fighter aircraft and torpedo boats. I recall that I heard the news from my transistor radio while I was on my summer job, scraping the old paint off of a house in New Orleans' Lakeview section. The attack occurred during the Israeli-Arab war of 1967, a war in which America supported Israel. The first news accounts did not identify the attacking parties, and I assumed that the Egyptians, in a supremely brutal and stupid attack, had struck a U.S. vessel in retaliation for our massive support of the Israeli military. A few elected officials had already begun to call for immediate military retaliation on Egypt.

USS Liberty with gaping hole from Israeli Torpedo Attack

In spite of my growing knowledge of the pernicious nature of Zionism, my deeply embedded patriotism came pouring out. I became angry at Egypt for daring to attack an American vessel. Later on, the reports began to filter in that it was the Israelis who had attacked the American ship, resulting in 171 Americans wounded and 31 dead. The official excuse was that the Israelis had mistaken the *Liberty* for an Egyptian ship. Over the next few weeks, a great deal of evidence emerged revealing that the attack had been deliberate. But by then the story of the *U.S.S. Liberty* and the 171 American casualties had dropped from the headlines.

The crew had been ordered not to divulge any information about the attack. When the silence was finally broken years later by Lieutenant James Ennes, an officer aboard the *Liberty*, that the overwhelming evidence pointed to a cold-blooded attack by the Israelis on an American ship.

The *U.S.S. Liberty*, a lightly armed intelligence ship whose mission was to intercept foreign radio communications, had been sailing in international waters off the Egyptian town of El Arish, which Israeli forces had just captured. Israel knew that the *Liberty* was monitoring its transmissions and was fearful it would learn of preparations for an invasion of Syria the next day.

On the clear and breezy morning of June 8, Israeli fighter jets circled the *Liberty* numerous times, coming in so low and close that the ship's crewmen waved at the pilots and could actually see their faces. The *Liberty* was clearly marked with its large U.S. Navy identifying letters, and it had a large American flag flying stiffly in the breeze.

With no warning, at 2:00 p.m., unmarked Israeli jets attacked the *Liberty* with rockets, cannon fire, and napalm bombs. Their first target was the radio room, which they destroyed along with the *Liberty*'s antennas. The fighters made repeated passes, attacking the ship until they ran out of bombs and ammo and broke off the attack. At that point the men of the *Liberty* replaced the first American flag, which had been shot away, with an oversized 7- by 13-foot flag.

The Israelis obviously knew the ship was American as they intercepted and tried to electronically jam the *Liberty*'s radio signals for help. Incredibly, the ship's radio men had managed to rig a new antenna and get through a distress call identifying the attackers and requesting help from the Mediterranean Sixth Fleet. The carriers *Saratoga* and *America* sent messages that help was on the way and dispatched fighters to defend the *Liberty*.

The beleaguered and bloodied crew of the *Liberty* waited in vain for the promised fighter support as Israeli torpedo boats then attacked, trying to sink the *Liberty* and finish off the crew who were now fighting the napalm fires on the decks and tending to the wounded. The Israelis raked the *Liberty* with 20 and 40 mm cannon fire and struck the ship with a torpedo at the waterline, killing 22 more sailors below decks. The torpedo boats came in close enough to machine-gun the crew tending to the wounded on deck.

Despite 821 holes bigger than a man's fist, napalm bombs exploding on the decks and in the superstructure, and a gaping hole and serious torpedo damage at the water line, miraculously, the *Liberty* remained afloat (no thanks to the U.S. fighter support, which never came; they had been called back by orders of President Lyndon Johnson before they could intercept the attackers).

Israel obviously intended to sink the *Liberty* and kill everyone on board. In violation of international law, Israeli torpedo boats even machine-gunned the *Liberty*'s deployed life rafts. They sought to knock out the *Liberty*'s communication room and jam her radio signals to prevent her from identifying her attackers, then to send the American ship and her crew to the bottom so no one could refute the natural supposition that the treacherous deed had been committed by the Egyptians. The Zionists knew that by knocking out the *Liberty* they would have more of a free hand in Syria, and the indignation over the sinking of an American ship by the Egyptians would garner unconditional support for Israel's most radical war aims. Only the courage and resourcefulness of the men of the *U.S.S. Liberty* prevented that further miscarriage of justice.

In his recall of the U.S. Navy jets sent to protect the Liberty, Johnson committed of the most treasonous acts of betrayal in American history. He cared more about preventing a public breach between the U.S. and Israel than saving the lives of American fighting men. The survivors of the *Liberty* have stated clearly that had the jets not been recalled, the torpedo boat attack could have been stopped, saving many American lives.

Captain William McGonagle, the *Liberty*'s commanding officer, although seriously wounded, showed exceptional heroism that eventually won him the Congressional Medal of Honor. Usually the president awards the nation's highest honor in a White House ceremony along with a citation recording the details of the heroic deed. President Johnson called the Israelis to see if they had any objection to the awarding of the medal and then decided not to take part in the ceremony or even allow it at the White House. The Secretary of the Navy ended up awarding the medal at the Washington Naval Yard, and the citation did not even identify Israel as the attacker. *The Washington Post* had no story about Captain McGonagle receiving the award. The U.S. Navy conducted a perfunctory court of inquiry (lasting only four days), and failed to call even one Israeli to testify. In contrast, the attack on the *U.S.S. Stark* merited a nine-month-long investigation.

Lieutenant James Ennes, one of the *Liberty*'s officers, wrote a detailed book about the incident called *Assault on the Liberty*, published in 1979.[811] It exposes the tremendous evidence showing how the attack was a calculated and deliberate attempt to sink a ship the Israelis knew was American and kill any survivors so there would be no American witnesses. The U.S. ambassador to Lebanon at the time has also come forward and stated that when he was on duty in the Middle East, he heard U.S.-intercepted Israeli communications with the attacking Israeli fighters acknowledging the ship was American. Many prominent leaders of the U.S. Navy courageously have gone on record to demand a real inquiry on the *Liberty*, and the head of Navy Operations said that the evidence clearly pointed to a planned attack. Secretary of State Dean Rusk, Admiral Thomas Moorer and the surviving crew of the *U.S.S. Liberty* all say that the attack was clearly deliberate.

Perhaps one could understand such a treacherous act from the enemies of this country, but not from a supposed ally. The fact that Israel had attacked the forces of the nation that has supported it more than any other — in money, diplomacy, good will, and even military arms (including weapons that were turned against our men) — has to be one of the most egregious acts of military betrayal in the history of nations.

I asked myself how Israel could be so reckless as to attack an American vessel. The obvious answer was that they knew their operation against the *Liberty* held very little risk, for if the attack succeeded and the ship and all its crew were destroyed, Israel would get everything it wanted in the war. If they failed in their mission to sink the *Liberty* and blame it on the Egyptians, the Israelis knew they could pass it off as a mistake. They also knew that their massive influence in government and the press would help them cover up. After sweeping the terror and dispossession of a million and one half Palestinians under the rug for half a century — the Liberty was child's play.

Not only has our noble ally, Israel, attacked American forces, it has had highly placed spies in our government for decades. One example is the Pollard Affair, in which a highly placed Jew in American intelligence passed over huge amounts of top secret material to the Israeli government. When Pollard was duly tried, convicted, and imprisoned, the Israeli government established a fund to help secure his release and reward him for his service. Since the Pollard affair the Zionists have not needed low-level spies, for they now have highly committed Zionists dominating the highest intelligence levels of the United States — in the president's National Security Council.

When I learned the full truth of the *Liberty* treachery years after the actual attack — I remembered how incensed I felt at 17 when I heard on my transistor radio how the Egyptians had apparently attacked an American ship. Those moments of anger had long passed when I read Ennes's book. However, as I read Lieutenant Ennes's poignant accounts of the dead and dying men aboard the *Liberty*, my anger rose again only to give way to profound sadness for my country. As a young and proud American, I could not understand how our president could treasonously stop the defense of American men under fire, or how our government would cover up the treachery of the intentional Israeli murder of American young men — and even reward the murderers with even more billions of our taxes in foreign aid.

At that moment, I realized that Israel is not just a Palestinian problem. It is an American problem. Israel is a problem not just because of the $50 billion it has drained from our treasury; or because of the hundreds of billions of dollars in higher oil prices spawned by our Israeli-first policies; or the damage it has done to our good name around the world; or even just because of its treacherous attack on the

Liberty. Our Israeli policy is a symptom of a pervasive Jewish power in our government and the press that threatens the very foundations of America itself.

While Zionists in Israel were dispossessing the Palestinians, Zionists in America were busy consolidating their power in all the Western nations also, promoting policies that would weaken the identity and the will for self-preservation of the founding Gentile elements. They had even set about to make us a minority in our nation, just as they had made the Palestinians a minority in Israel. I knew the day would not be far off when we, like the Palestinians, would become an oppressed minority in our own land. The fact that the ship attacked by Israel was named the *Liberty* has a bitter appropriateness, for I knew that if the Zionists succeeded in their ultimate objectives they would destroy our people's life and liberty.

The structure and form of modern Israel proves that Jewish supremacism is not an ideology of the past, but a ominous reality of the present, overtly expressed in every sinew of the Israeli state. The fact that the Jewish power structure in America and around the world intensely supports it offers convincing evidence that little had changed in the struggle between Jew and Gentile over the last 2,500 years. Moreover, the fact that Jews have been able to get the Western world to support Zionism in all its glorious hypocrisy is testament to their power of over all forms of media and over our nation's governments. The European race cannot survive unless that power is broken.

Chapter 23:
A Holocaust Inquiry

After I became aware of the ethnocentrism that permeated Judaism and Zionism, and of the pervasive Jewish presence in the media, I read some books and articles that hinted that the stories of German atrocities during the Second World War were exaggerated and misconstrued. Some suggested that the persistent saturation of the media with what is now called the Holocaust, decades after the war, was motivated by the strategic interests of Israel. At first, I rejected the idea that some of the allegations against the Germans could be false, for I had seen the gruesome photos and films that seemed to make German atrocities self-evident. The following is an account of how I came to question some aspects of this somber episode of European history.

I wrote an essay for an English class at Louisiana State University on the liberalization of American sexual morality. I recounted how I had never seen a picture of a frontally viewed, completely nude woman until I was a freshman in high school. That reminiscence may sound strange to young people of today, but even *Playboy* magazine omitted the most private sexual area until the mid-'60s. After I wrote the essay, a right-wing friend who read it told me that I was mistaken about not seeing full nudity in my childhood.

"You have seen fully nude women," he said, "graphic pictures of nude men and women, often emaciated, in horrible scenes of death. You saw many photographs and films of the Jewish victims of Nazi atrocities."

On reflection, I had to admit that he was right. Television and print media of the late '50s and early '60s were much more prudish than they are today, but during the years of my childhood, the media often showed horrific photographs and newsreels depicting graphic scenes of mutilated and emaciated nude Jewish victims of the Second World War. They burdened the pages of magazines such as *Look* and *Life*; they never failed to appear in television documentaries on the war, and even daily newspapers reprinted them — including my hometown newspaper, the Jewish-owned *Times-Picayune*.

In a time of innocence when my friends and I had never seen a photograph of a completely disrobed woman, the media showed us cadavers, often of nude women or the small frames of children, piled up like so much cordwood being bulldozed by Allied troops into mass graves. Those photographs were powerful, for even today those images remain vivid, etched deeply by the emotion in them.

THE HOLOCAUST: AN INQUIRY 397

My friend suggested that there was a political reason why the media repeatedly showed me the Jewish victims of the Second World War. "Was it accidental?" he asked rhetorically. "If it was just for the sensationalism of nudity and death, why are Jewish victims practically the only ones shown?"

When the movie *The Faces of Death* [812] opened in theaters across America in 1974, millions lined up to see actual film footage of real people in the throes of death. Seeing a human being in the maladroit pose of death is perhaps the most riveting sight a human being can witness. Parents shield their children from such scenes, and television news programs seldom show the most gruesome pictures of a homicide. Despite the media's frequent use of sensationalism to boost ratings, even after the crash of a passenger airliner they usually show only general footage at the scene rather than severed heads and torsos.

In the 1990s many voice concern that television programs and movies are too violent and gory for young children, yet the horrific scenes of the Holocaust have become mandatory viewing for some school children by state law. Jewish groups have lobbied to pass laws to require "Holocaust Studies" in public schools, and many thousands of local school systems, at Jewish urging, have simply mandated it. The bloody violence of the rankest of fictional movies or television programs could not possibly be more graphic than the gory scenes of the Holocaust. Would those same schools show films of the bloody victims of airline crashes to their young charges? Would they show the massacres of Palestinian women and children butchered at the Sabra and Shatila camps in Israeli-occupied Lebanon or the victims butchered by the Communists in Cambodia, to 9-year-olds? *For what reason*, I asked myself, *must they show little children these horrible scenes of Jewish victims of half a century ago?*

Proponents of "Holocaust Studies" for school children say that the trauma is necessary to teach them about the dangers of racism and anti-Semitism. Yet they show no victims with their brains blown out to teach children about the horrors of committing armed robbery, no scenes of the millions of corpses starved or butchered by the Soviets to teach children the dangers of Communism. No colleges have a "Gulag Studies Department," and no public high schools require studies about the Gulags to graduate.

One of the arguments used by those who promote Holocaust Studies for our young children is that the Holocaust shows the evils of racism. It reveals, they say, that mass murder is the ultimate consequence of racial consciousness. They fail to point out that far more human beings have been slaughtered in the name of equality than in the name of racism. From the days of the bloody excesses of the French Revolution, to the millions butchered by the Soviets in their gulags, the murderous Red Guards in China, and the killing fields of Cambodia, no doctrine has killed more people than Communism — and at its very heart lies fanatical devotion to egalitarianism.

The awful scenes of Jewish suffering and death touched my heart as a young man, and they still do. They spawned revulsion at the inhumanity that produced such horrors. Indeed, it arouses anger in all of us against those responsible for the carnage. Nevertheless, as I became more aware of the early Jewish domination of the international Communist movement, I wondered why the media's focus was almost entirely on Jewish suffering, with little attention afforded the other victims of mass murder.

The only victims of whom I was really conscious were Jews. They were the victims I read about, the victims I saw in television dramas, the victims I saw in the graphic photographs and newsreels.

No greater human crime exists than the slaughter of the innocent. British historian David Irving labels it "innocenticide." Yet I eventually learned of an innocenticide far more extensive than even the terrible crimes of the Nazis. This knowledge did not come from television documentaries or docudramas or from well-publicized trials of war criminals or searches for them, but from the quiet pages of books and documents little discussed by the popular media.

Communists in Russia, Eastern Europe, and China killed at least ten times more innocent people than alleged by the Nazis. As a young teenager, those victims of Communism were outside my awareness. I heard occasional comments about atrocities by the Communists, but I saw no newsreels or photographs of the victims of Communism. I cannot recall even one. I saw no documentaries, nor did I read any diaries of young girls (or anyone else, for that matter) who had suffered at the hands of the Communists. Thus, I had no emotional involvement with the Christian victims of Communists, but I had strong emotional ties to the Jewish victims of the Second World War.

Spurred on by my anti-Communism, I read about the greatest human slaughter in world history: the murder of tens of millions of Christians in Communist Russia. I read with fascination about the horrible murder of Czar Nicholas and his family by Jewish Bolsheviks and the mass murders begun by Lenin and climaxing in the unparalleled slaughter committed by Stalin. Lenin's classic statement about mass murder by the Soviet state illustrated the cold-blooded nature of these killings. He said, "You can't make an omelet without breaking some eggs." By the early 1960s, published information from the Kremlin itself acknowledged that the early leaders of Communism had organized the liquidation, by the Communist Party's own estimates, of 25-to-40 million people. During this period, the establishment remained focused on the suffering of Jews, with little sympathy or attention left over for the other victims of totalitarianism. I found it amazing that the media lavished so much attention on atrocities against Jews while showing indifference to the mass murder of millions of Christians by Jewish commissars in the Soviet State.

The muted response to Soviet atrocities seemed unexplainable considering the fact that at the time, America was in a "cold war" with the Communists. What psychological weapon could have been better used against the Communists in that worldwide ideological cold war than exposing the historical truth of their massacre of tens of millions of human beings?

The Western press kept mostly silent on the Soviet mass murders even while millions still suffered in Communist Concentration Camps. They killed millions more in Red China during the "Cultural Revolution," in many nations of Africa, in the jails of Cuba, in the killing fields of Cambodia, and in the "re-education camps" of Vietnam. Yet, through all these liquidations of millions, all we seemed to see was the endless parade of stories about Jewish suffering of decades before.

At the same moment Jewish pundits were screaming "Never again!" about atrocities committed by a solitary regime dead and gone for decades, millions of innocent people faced torture and death in dozens of Communist tyrannies around the world. While the murders continued, we heard only a few whispers about them, but the shouting about 1945 goes on to this day. During the late '60s and early '70s I attended meetings of anti-Communist Cubans and many Eastern European nationalities who had suffered grievously at the hands of the Communists. Latvians, Estonians, Lithuanians, Ukrainians, White Russians, Romanians, Hungarians, Czechs, Poles, Croatians, Serbs, and many other refugees told a story of oppression, torture, and murder that received only a fraction of the media coverage of the Holocaust — yet it concerned the suffering of even greater numbers of people.

While the media trumpeted the search, capture, and trial of German war criminals, modern-day Communist war criminals continued incarcerating, torturing, and murdering millions in concentration camps across the world. The Jewish-dominated media made no effort to prevent the destruction of the lives that still might have been saved, nor did they make a righteous call for the prosecution of Communist war criminals past or present.

After I learned of the great massacres organized by the Jewish Bolsheviks in the Soviet Union, I wondered why I reserved such special rancor for the Nazi perpetrators of war crimes. *Why, I wondered, did I reserve special enmity for one mass murderer over another?* Whether it is a commissar murdering the Czar and his children, an SS commander in war-torn Eastern Europe liquidating Jews, a Chinese Maoist Red Guard murdering thousands in the so-called Cultural Revolution, a Jewish member of the Stern Gang massacring Palestinians at Deir Yassin, or an Arab terrorist blowing up a commercial market in Tel Aviv, are not all equally depraved? Yet undeniably, it was for the Jewish victims that I had the most empathy, and for their anti-Semitic persecutors, I had the most disgust and anger. I asked myself, *what brought that on?*

At that point I began to understand how I had been manipulated. Because of Jewish influence in the news and entertainment media, it was *their* story I saw on television and in the movies; it was *their* heartbreak I shared in books, *their* mangled bodies I saw in pictures and filmstrips, *their* horror I heard from teachers and preachers. How powerful is the impact on a 9- or 10-year-old of the first nudity he sees in media, a nudity accompanied by authentic scenes of death worse than he could have imagined?

I began to ask other politically incorrect questions about the Holocaust. Even if everything the media say about the Holocaust is true, why does it occupy our attention a thousand-fold more than the massacre of many more people by the Soviets? Now that Communism has fallen, why is there no clamor for Nuremberg-type trials for the Communist mass murderers?

Other questions began to plague me. If putting an innocent Jewish civilian in a gas chamber was the epitome of evil, was the aerial firebombing of millions of German and Japanese civilians morally wrong too? Is there an ethical distinction between murdering the innocent by poison gas and murdering the innocent by burning them alive? Does it make it morally acceptable that America firebombed civilian women and children because we were at war with the Germans and Japanese? By that standard, would Second World War German atrocities against Jews be somehow acceptable if they considered themselves to be at war with the Jews?

I read a book by David Irving called The *Destruction of Dresden.* [813] It exposed the murderous firebombing of Dresden in the waning days of the Second World War. Most Americans have heard much about the bombing of Nagasaki and Hiroshima, but few are aware that more people perished in Dresden than in either of the cities obliterated by atomic bombs. Dresden was an Allied "experiment." They wanted to discover if they could create a "firestorm" by dumping tons of incendiary bombs on the city center. Dresden was a city of priceless artistic and cultural treasure that had been untouched up to that point during the war. The bombing set the entire inner city ablaze, creating hurricane-like winds that fed the flames. Asphalt bubbled and flowed in the street like lava.

The Holocaust: An Inquiry 401

When the aerial attack was over, around 100,000 people had perished. To avoid the spread of disease, the authorities burned the ghastly remains of tens of thousands of people in grotesque funeral pyres. Dresden had no military significance and when it was bombed, the war was practically won. If anything, the bombing only stiffened German resistance and cost more Allied lives. I sincerely asked myself, *was the bombing of Dresden a war crime?* Was it a crime against humanity? Were the children who suffered the cruelest death of all, being burned alive, any less wronged than, say, Anne Frank, who was unjustly placed in a concentration camp, where she ultimately succumbed to disease?

Today the British government admits that their Air Ministry, from February 1942, embarked on a policy of targeting German civilians for bombing. More than 600,000 men, women and children perished,.

The United Nations now defines deliberate bombing of civilians as a crime against humanity. The double standard that seemed to exist in all things dealing with the Second World War nagged at my sense of fair play. An example of the media's morality of convenience is the treatment of the Oklahoma City bombing as compared to the tremendous civilian bombing in the Second World War. I still remember the refrain in the hours of the aftermath of the Oklahoma City carnage, and the incredulity that echoed in the trial of Timothy McVeigh. In essence, it went, "What kind of monster would bomb and burn to death innocent children?"

Was the burning alive of tens of thousands of innocent German babies any less horrible and morally wrong than the murder of two dozen children by Timothy McVeigh? We give one bomber of children medals, and the other we give the death penalty. As for me, I view the intentional mass murder of women and children by anyone, any cause, or any government — as unjustifiable.

Even after the war's end, for many months the Allies allotted an official calorie ration for each German civilian that was less than could sustain life. Hundreds of thousands of civilians died in those months of hunger, exposure, and disease. The Soviets forced millions from their homes in German lands in the east. In violation of the Geneva Convention and long-standing rules of war, millions of German soldiers were held long after the war's end and thousands died from starvation, exposure and illness in the Allied-administered camps. Those deaths occurred after the fury of war had ceased and while massive stores of food and medicine were close by, stockpiled in Allied warehouses.[814]

I found a perfect example of the "us and them" double standard of morality in a book I learned about in college called *Germany Must Perish!* [815] by an American Jew, Theodore N. Kaufman. Published in

1941 before America's involvement in the war and before the allegation of any German extermination program against Jews, the preface states:

> This dynamic volume outlines a comprehensive plan for the extinction of the German nation and the total eradication from the earth of all her people. Also contained herein is a map illustrating the possible territorial dissection of Germany and the apportionment of her lands.

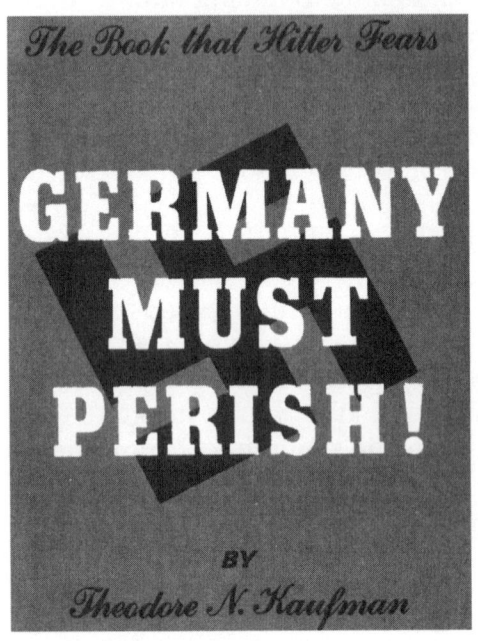

Both *Time* magazine and *The New York Times* reviewed the book rather than simply dismissing it, and neither publication seemed too outraged at its open call for genocide. How would today's moralists react if the Nazis had published a book called *Jews Must Perish*, and major magazines and newspapers in prewar Germany had publicized a book calling for "the total eradication from the Earth of all the Jewish people"? Would not they offer it as proof of the moral depravity of Germany?

As a teenager, although I was fiercely patriotic and pro-American, I began to see that in war no side had a monopoly on virtue. And in total war, in which one side annihilates the political and cultural establishment of the other, only the victors write the history. The adage applies here that "In War, truth is the first casualty." So what of the truth of the Holocaust?

I knew that America's mass media had deceived me about the origins and driving force behind Soviet and international Communism, and about the extent of Communist mass murder. It certainly seemed possible that the Jewish-dominated mass media would be just as deceptive on an issue immensely important to them.

By the time I looked into the nuts and bolts of the Holocaust I had already learned that the media-generated image of the always innocent Jewish religion and people was false. Yet I still found it difficult to look at the Holocaust objectively, for not so many years before my eyes had misted with tears when I read *Anne Frank- the Diary of a Young Girl*. [816] I was — and still am — deeply moved by the scenes of human carnage from the Second World War.

THE HOLOCAUST: AN INQUIRY

On the surface, it seemed the evidence of the Holocaust was overwhelming. Mountains of books, magazine and newspaper articles, movies, sermons and speeches, and documentaries proclaimed it with nary a word of contradiction. In addition, as a fiercely proud young American, with a proud military history in my family, I was prone to believe all the war propaganda about my country's enemies. My father, a full colonel who still participated in the active Army Reserves, viewed his participation in the Second World War as the most meaningful period of his life. He would not hear of any mitigation of German guilt.

The Holocaust was part of Father's belief system and it became part of mine. However, I discovered that a number of distinguished Americans had made statements dissenting somewhat from the establishment version of World War II history. They included such men as Senator Robert Taft, Charles Lindbergh, General George Patton, and former Supreme Court chief justice Harlan Fiske Stone.

I read the interesting views of Paul Rassinier, a holocaust survivor who spoke out against what he called the lies of the Holocaust. A French political opponent of the Nazis, Rassinier suffered greatly during the war. In a number of concentration camps during the war, he never saw any evidence of human gas chambers or any program to exterminate the Jews. After his liberation, he read sensationalized accounts that he knew were false. Although he had little respect for his German captors, he felt it was his ethical duty to tell the truth about the camps and refute the exaggerated and false claims being made in the world's press.

In addition to the poignant accounts of his own experiences and observations, he began to research the entire issue after the war. Rassinier contended that the death toll in the camps was far lower than alleged and that the deaths were primarily caused by the poor conditions of the camps — the unintended effect of the loss and devastation of a nation crushed in a catastrophic war. He also called the allegations of gas chambers "classic examples of war propaganda that had no basis in fact." Rassinier had nothing to gain personally in postwar France by taking such an unpopular position. In fact, he had a lot to lose, and after suffering all the hardships and privations of the German concentration camps, he then suffered intense persecution for his courageous writings.

Holocaust survivor and revisionist Paul Rassinier.

Three Famous Victims the Holocaust

Years later, read a pamphlet outlining the inconsistencies and improbable content of *Anne Frank: the Diary of a Young Girl*. [817] Dr. Robert Faurisson, a liberal professor who specializes in the authentication of literature at the University of Lyon, France, made a strong case that the book's form and content made it unlikely that a girl in her early teens had written it, at least in its published form. It also amazed me that this girl, the most famous victim of the Holocaust— who spent most of the war at Auschwitz — did not die in the gas chambers. Near the end of the war, the Germans evacuated her, along with many others, to Bergen-Belsen. In the last months of the war, she succumbed to typhus. Anne Frank's sister, Margot, and her mother were not gassed either. They both died from typhus as well. Her father, Otto, fell ill while at Auschwitz and was nursed back to health in the camp hospital. Near the end of the war the Germans evacuated him to Mauthausen and he was liberated there. Otto Frank himself attested to these facts.

These facts seemed at variance with the stories I had read about Auschwitz. Books and movies portrayed the camp as an assembly line of murder. A place where whole trainloads of Jews were taken straight from the arrival platforms to the gas chambers. The Nazis supposedly inspected the new arrivals and sent the able-bodied to work; the young children and the sick to the gas chambers. If these stories are true, why then were the young Anne and her sister, who arrived in Auschwitz at the supposed height of the killing, not gassed?

The other famous survivor of Auschwitz is the high priest of the Holocaust, Elie Wiesel, the man who won the Nobel Prize for his writings about it. Wiesel, like Anne Frank's father, also had a sojourn in the camp hospital during the end of the war. In his autobiographical work *Night*, Wiesel relates that in January 1945, at the Birkenau section of Auschwitz, he had surgery on an infected foot in the camp hospital. His doctor suggested two weeks of rest, but the Russians were soon to liberate the camp. Hospital patients and all others who were considered unfit to travel, where given the option by the German authorities to remain in the camp to be liberated by the Russians or be evacuated with the Germans. After discussing it, Wiesel and his father decided to evacuate with their supposed "killers." [818 819]

I should also note that the third most famous survivor of the Holocaust is Simon Wiesenthal, who has become famous for fighting those who dare to have doubts about some aspects of the Holocaust. Much like Anne Frank's father and Elie Wiesel, Wiesenthal also had a sojourn in the Nazi camp hospitals. Wiesenthal wrote that while incarcerated by the Nazis he tried to commit suicide by cutting his wrists.[820] The Nazis — who he alleges were trying to kill all the Jews of Europe — did not let him die, instead they sent him to the hospital where they carefully nursed him back to health.

If the Germans were the fiendish brutes that Wiesel suggests in his books, and they were truly dedicated to the extermination of all Jews, why would he and his father have chosen to leave with the Germans rather than waiting for the Soviets? When I read of this admission by Wiesel, I was incredulous. Why would they send Anne Frank's father to the hospital, and why on Earth would they endeavor to save the life of a Jew who tried to commit suicide? Upon learning these things, I realized they were completely inconsistent with the Holocaust story as normally presented.

I wondered if the Holocaust story had changed over the years. So the first thing I did was pull out my much-thumbed volumes of the 1956 *Encyclopaedia Britannica*.[821] It had only one reference to Nazi atrocities against the Jews. The extensive Second World War article made no mention of Nazi pogroms against the Jews. The edition also had no articles devoted to the "Holocaust." In an article titled "Jews," there was a short section on the Jews in Europe during the war. This article, written by Jacob Marcus, perhaps the preeminent Jewish historian in the world at that time, cited many Jewish writers and authorities as sources, including *Encyclopedia Judaica, Judishe Lexicon, the Jewish Encyclopedia,* and the *Universal Jewish Encyclopedia*. A pro-Jewish perspective dominated the article, and Marcus described Jewish conditions under the Nazis with these words:

> **In order to effect a solution of the Jewish problem in line with their theories, the Nazis carried out a series of expulsions and deportations of Jews, mostly of original east European stock, from nearly all European states.**
>
> **Men frequently separated from their wives, and others from children, were sent by the thousands to Poland and western Russia. There they were put into concentration camps, or huge reservations, or sent into the swamps, or out on the roads, into labour gangs. Large numbers perished under the inhuman conditions under which they labored. While every other large Jewish center was being embroiled in war, American Jewry was gradually assuming a position of leadership in world Jewry.** [822] [found in the 1947, 52, and 56 editions]

Imagine my surprise to find this description of what is now called the Holocaust in the 1956 edition of the encyclopedia, published within 11 years of the war's end and after the most important of the Nuremberg War Crimes Trials. I had expected to read a detailed article about the "greatest human carnage in history." The article certainly painted a grim picture of human suffering, but, importantly, it did not mention the famous six million figure or gas chambers or even the word *Holocaust*. Instead, *Encyclopaedia Britannica* simply stated that the Nazis put Jews into concentration camps and made them work in labor gangs where many perished from the terrible conditions. I thought, *what a far cry from today's image of the Holocaust.*

It seemed curious to me that the most famous and respected encyclopedia in the world would report the Jewish suffering in that way. It sparked my first real glimmer of doubt about the whole question and began to open my mind to new questions. I went to the public library in 1970 and again looked up the heading, "Jews," in a 1967 edition of the *Encyclopaedia Britannica*. [823] In stark contrast to its 1950s editions, it stated unequivocally that the Germans attempted to exterminate all of European Jewry and had employed a method that was "more efficient and economical than shooting or hanging: poison gas." What did the *Britannica* know in 1967 it did not know in 1956?

Why the change from the earlier editions? I asked myself. Had new evidence been uncovered decades after the war? If the efficient Nazi war machine controlled Europe's Jews and aimed to kill them, how could so many have survived? In fact, millions of Jews have applied for and received compensation from the German government. How did all those survive? I also noted that in Wiesel's famous autobiography, published in 1956, the same year as the *Britannica* article, even though he mentions crematories at Auschwitz, he never mentions gas chambers even once. In fact, he writes that Jews were killed in mass by being thrown alive into burning pits, a horrific allegation to be sure, but far different from modern claims.

Wiesel also quotes accounts of Jews being murdered at Babi Yar, where for "month after month the ground never stopped trembling" and "from time to time, geysers of blood spurted from it."[824] I thought, *Is this from the man who will tell me the truth of the Holocaust?*

Other impertinent questions occurred to me. Did the Nazis, while in the midst of the war effort, really construct huge and complex gas chambers; transport millions of Jews to camps, and exterminate their victims in this manner? If their intention was to kill them, why wouldn't bullets, costing a few cents apiece, have killed them more efficiently and saved them the huge requirements of their transportation housing, food, and medical care? I asked myself, *If the Nazis really intended to kill all the Jews, why would they even need to build concentration camps.*

I was uneasy asking myself these questions. I wondered if I was somehow defending mass murder by questioning whether the atrocity tales had been exaggerated. I had seen survivors on television telling the stories of Jewish victims' skin turned into lampshades and their bodies made into soap. A wall of sympathy sometimes came up, causing me to drop my inquiry for a while.

I finally decided to continue my reading and think about the issue. The search for the truth is never wrong. The only sin is to lack the courage to follow where truth leads. I began my inquiry into the Holocaust by looking into the Nuremberg Trials, the international proceedings that supposedly proved the nature and extent of the Holocaust.

The Nuremberg Trials

My father was a traditional Republican who admired Senator Robert Taft of Ohio. Taft agreed with many American military men that the Nuremberg Trials set a dangerous precedent that could endanger American military personnel captured in future conflicts. If the victorious armies of the Second World War could prosecute their defeated enemy for war crimes, he thought the same could happen someday to captured American soldiers. I saw the award-winning movie *Judgment at Nuremberg* and read a book that depicted the trials as dispensing justice to war criminals who deserved the gallows or the firing squad.

Interestingly, the first alternative view I read about the International Military Tribunal at Nuremberg, came from a man whom I viewed as an enemy of the South: President John F. Kennedy. In the pages of his Pulitzer Prize-winning book *Profiles in Courage*,[825] Kennedy wrote of the political heroism of Senator Taft, whose personal code of honor required him to denounce the Nuremberg Trials at the risk of jeopardizing his lifelong quest for the presidency. Despite vociferous opposition and an unprecedented smear campaign against him by the Jewish-influenced media, Taft questioned the fairness of the Nuremberg Trials.

He contended that they were not the shining example of Western jurisprudence that the mass media had led me to believe. Taft conducted a Senate investigation in which many American witnesses disclosed that there had been widespread torture of German defendants. Such conduct appalled Senator Taft and he had the temerity to suggest that one could not trust such confessions. He went on to question the very foundations of the trials and the image of justice they were supposed to represent.

In *Profiles in Courage* Kennedy quotes Taft speaking at Kenyon College in Ohio. On page 238 Kennedy writes,

> The trial of the vanquished by the victors," he [Taft] told an attentive if somewhat astonished audience, "cannot be impartial no matter how it is hedged about with the forms of justice." [826]

Kennedy goes on to quote at length from Taft's speech.

> About this whole judgment there is the spirit of vengeance, and vengeance is seldom justice. The hanging of the eleven men convicted will be a blot on the American record we shall long regret.
>
> In these trials we have accepted the Russian idea of the purpose of trials — government policy and not justice — with little relation to Anglo-Saxon heritage. By clothing policy in the forms of legal procedure, we may discredit the whole idea of justice in Europe for years to come.[827]

Kennedy comments,

> Nuremberg, the Ohio Senator insisted, was a blot on American Constitutional history, and a serious departure from our Anglo-Saxon heritage of fair and equal treatment, a heritage which had rightly made this country respected throughout the world. "We can't even teach our own people the sound principles of liberty and justice," he concluded. "We cannot teach them government in Germany by suppressing liberty and justice..." [828]

Taft's argument was that the victor's justice is no justice at all. Although the media gave the trials an appearance of fairness in a courtroom setting, it was superficial. Real justice cannot be found when the accusers had control over judges, prosecution, and defense? Our Western concept of law rests on the idea of impartial justice. Is that possible when the judges are the political enemies of the accused? Is it possible when men face persecution for acts of war that the Allies themselves had committed? When the trials allow massive amounts of testimony without cross-examination of witness? When so-called evidence consists of confessions exacted through torture? When witnesses for the defense could face arrest for showing up at court? When men are tried for violations of laws that did not even exist at the time of their alleged commission?

Judge Edward Van Roden was a member of the Simpson Army Commission that investigated the methods used at the Dachau Concentration Camp. In the January 9, 1949, *Washington Daily News* and in the January 23, 1949, London *Sunday Pictorial* he told of some examples of the use of torture.

> ...The investigators," he said, "would put a black hood over the accused's head and then punch him in the face with brass knuckles, kick him and beat him with rubber hoses. . . . All but two of the Germans, in the 139 cases we investigated, had been kicked in the testicles beyond repair. [829] [830]

Much of the "Holocaust proof" offered today by historians is the "confessions" extracted at the war crimes trials. I thought, *Can we trust the "confessions" of those whose testicles were damaged during interrogation?* I was also shocked when I learned that Russian KGB officials, who themselves had committed extensive crimes against humanity, sat as judges.

THE HOLOCAUST: AN INQUIRY   409

One of my friends at the Citizens Council told me that an American judge who was president of one of the tribunals exposed the injustices of the Nuremberg Trials. I found out that Iowa Supreme Court justice Charles F. Wenersturm had resigned his appointment in disgust at the proceedings. He charged that the prosecution prevented the defense from obtaining evidence and preparing their cases, that the trials were not trying to create a new legal principle but were motivated solely by hatred of Germans. Additionally, he said that 90 percent of the Nuremberg Court consisted of persons who, on political and racial grounds, were biased against the defense. He contended that Jews, many of whom were refugees from Germany and newly made "naturalized" American citizens, dominated the staff of the Nuremberg Courts and were more interested in revenge than justice.

> **The entire atmosphere is unwholesome. . . . Lawyers, clerks, interpreters and researchers were employed who became Americans only in recent years, whose backgrounds were embedded in Europe's hatreds and prejudices.** [831]

I also found out that my military idol, General George S. Patton, had opposed the war crimes trials. For example, in a letter to his wife he wrote

> **I am frankly opposed to this war criminal stuff. It is not cricket and is Semitic. I am also opposed to sending POW's to work as slaves in foreign lands, where many will be starved to death.** [832]

The armies of our allies, the Soviet Union, raped almost all the German women in their occupied areas — from young children to the elderly. They murdered millions and forced millions from their homes in the winter of 1945. East Prussia, a German land for centuries, had its entire German population expelled or murdered by the Soviets. In the 1990's, Jewish researcher, John Sack, documented the Jewish mass murder of tens-of-thousands of Germans in the months following the war.[833]

It wasn't just the Soviets and the Jews who committed war crimes. The Western allies had their share of them as well. One of them was Operation Keel Haul, which deported hundreds of thousands of Russian and Eastern European anti-Communists to torture, slave labor and mass murder in the Soviet Union. When they learned of the forced repatriation planned by the Allies, scores of them committed suicide. Another was the Morgenthau Plan, which the Allies implemented for a while after the war. The plan called for each German civilian to receive a ration of food that was less than that alleged to have been allotted to inmates in Germany's concentration camps.

It sickened me to read of German mothers who were forced into prostitution to feed their children. After the war was over, hundreds of thousands of German civilians and soldiers died in the first year of the harsh Allied occupation. [834] When I began to understand that war created these kinds of injustices on both sides, it broke down my concept that Germans were uniquely guilty of wrongdoing during the Second World War.

Discovering that the Allies also committed atrocities reminded me of vicious anti-Southern propaganda emitted when Yankee forces liberated Andersonville Prison Camp in the War Between the States. Many Northern prisoners there had died of disease and malnutrition. This came about because the Southern forces had literally nothing to feed their prisoners. Many Southerners themselves suffered terribly from the scorched-Earth policy of William Tecumseh Sherman, the destruction of railroads, and the naval blockade of the South. Under such circumstances, it isn't surprising that the prison camps were Hell-holes, and no malevolent plan or conspiracy is required to account for it. While still in college I learned that although the North suffered no food shortages, the conditions in Yankee-run prison camps were little better than those in Southern camps. When I read of Lincoln's direct order to forbid Yankee prisons from giving their captured Southerners the food parcels and blankets sent from concerned relatives, I learned the bitter truth that the victors always portray themselves as just and the conquered as unjust.

When I considered the patent injustice of the Nuremberg Trials, it became easier for me to view the Holocaust objectively, for its foundation lay in the allegations set out by the International Military Tribunal at Nuremberg.

One example of Nuremberg's shabby evidence is the purported confession of Rudolf Hoess, the former Nazi commandant at Auschwitz Concentration Camp. For years, Holocaust historians cited the Hoess' "confession" as proof that the Nazis purposefully exterminated the Jews. In fact, it formed the foundation of the Auschwitz allegation of mass gassings. Chief Holocaust historian, Raul Hilberg, heavily relied upon it, but when its full-unedited content became widely known in the 1960s, many Holocaust experts became embarrassed by it, and by the 1990s some admitted its obvious unreliability. Historian Christopher Browning admitted in a *Vanity Fair* article that:

> **Hoess was always a very weak and confused witness. The revisionists use him all the time for this reason, in order to try to discredit the memory of Auschwitz as a whole.** [835]

The first problem lay in the numbers. In his alleged confession, Hoess said there were more than 2.5 million Jews gassed at Auschwitz. Nearly all so-called authorities on the Holocaust, including the current curator of the museum and center at the Auschwitz camp,

Dr. Francizek Piper, now say that the figure was 1.2 million. Why should Hoess have lied?

Hoess also confessed to things that were impossible. For example, he alleged that after hundreds of victims were gassed with potassium cyanide, workers immediately entered the nonvented rooms and removed the bodies without wearing gas masks. He described how they smoked and ate snacks as they performed their task. By comparison, in modern times, the State of California vents its gas chamber for hours after an execution. Even then, workers cannot enter the room without gas masks and body suits to avoid the toxic substance that can kill just by entering the pores. Anyone in the camps who immediately entered a large room saturated with deadly potassium cyanide that had killed hundreds of people would have quickly found himself among the victims. In his confession, Hoess also alluded to a concentration camp that did not even exist — Wolzek.

Hoess wrote his memoirs while awaiting trial and execution in a KGB-run Communist prison in Poland, with all that implies.

Rupert Butler, in his anti-Nazi and anti-Hoess book *Legions of Death*, vividly describes Hoess' capture. Here is Butler's account of Hoess' torture and arrest:

> At 5 p.m. on 11 March 1946, Frau Hoess opened her door to six intelligence specialists in British uniform, most of them tall and menacing and all of them practiced in the more sophisticated techniques of sustained and merciless investigation...
>
> We discovered later that he had lost the cyanide pill most of them carried. Not that he would have had much chance to use it because we had rammed a torch [flashlight] into his mouth...
>
> Clarke yelled: "What is your name?" With each answer of "Fritz Lang," Clarke's hand crashed into the face of the prisoner. The fourth time that happened, Hoess broke and admitted who he was...
>
> The admission suddenly unleashed the loathing of the Jewish Sergeants in the arresting party...
>
> The prisoner was torn from the top bunk, the pajama ripped from his body. He was then dragged naked to one of the slaughter tables, where it seemed to Clarke the blows and screams were endless. Finally a medical officer urged the Captain: "Call them off, unless you want to take back a corpse..."
>
> [Hoess] was dragged back to Clarke's car, where the sergeant poured a substantial slug of whiskey down his throat. Then Hoess tried to sleep. Clarke thrust his service stick under the man's eyelids and ordered in German: "Keep your pig eyes open, you swine..."
>
> The party arrived back at Heide around three in the morning. The snow was swirling still, but the blanket was torn from Hoess and he was made to walk completely nude through the prison yard to his cell. It took three days to get a coherent statement from him. [836]

412 MY AWAKENING

Another powerful example of the inaccuracy of the Nuremberg Trials was that the Allies had represented as fact that 300,000 people had perished by gassing at the Dachau Concentration Camp near Munich. Today no authorities on the Holocaust claim that the Germans gassed even one person at Dachau, and the official death toll has been reduced to approximately 30,000 from all causes. Approximately half the death toll occurred from disease epidemics that had ravaged the camp, and many of the deaths occurred even after the Allies took control of it.

Even after the liberation of the Dachau camp, thousands of inmates died of typhus as the Allies struggled to get the epidemic under control. Allied photographs at the time show speed limit signs in Dachau that read, in English, SPEED LIMIT 5 MPH. DUST SPREADS TYPHUS.

War-torn Europe suffered widespread and catastrophic typhus epidemics. German authorities fought lice infestation with disinfestation chambers for clothing and personal articles, just as American jails fight lice by disinfecting prisoners with a delousing spray. Zyklon B was used only on clothes and other articles and it had to be used within in a custom-built, well-ventilated airtight chamber so as not to endanger anyone.

Because I read the Holocaust literature extensively, both the old and the new material, I began to see cracks in its foundation that threatened the whole edifice. Most of us have read or heard accounts of American soldiers who have related that they knew what the Nazis had done because "they saw it with their own eyes."

What did American soldiers actually see? They saw terrible scenes of human suffering and death. They saw piles of corpses emaciated from hunger and disease, just as Yankee troops saw the same at Andersonville during the War Between the States. Nevertheless, did any Americans see gas chambers? According to accepted authorities on the subject, including the famous Nazi hunter Simon Wiesenthal, Americans saw no such sights in Germany — nor could they have — because the only gas chambers used on Jews were in Eastern Europe.

One classic picture shown around the world depicts a helmeted American soldier at Dachau standing next to a heavy metal door painted with a skull and crossbones and the German warning CAREFUL, LIFE THREATENING. The photo caption read "Gas Chamber at infamous Nazi death camp at Dachau." No one from Moscow to San Francisco could be blamed for thinking they had seen a picture of

The Holocaust: An Inquiry 413

a gas chamber in which Nazis had murdered human beings. When I first saw the photograph, I thought the same thing. Years later I found that it was indeed a gas chamber — one used for the fumigation of clothing to kill lice, the vermin that spread typhus and other diseases that killed concentration camp inmates. In fact, many hundreds of Allied soldiers died from those vermin-spread diseases during and after the war. The soldier in the famous photograph stood next to a disinfestation chamber intended to save inmate's lives, not take them.

Napoleon said, "In war, the mental is to the physical as three to one." Near the end of the war, Allied governments had to paint the German enemy in the worst possible light. Rumors abounded; exaggerations exploited. It was not a big leap for war propaganda to represent disinfestation chambers for lice as gas chambers for humans.

American camp liberators, who had read and heard a thousand times over about Germans gassing Jews, came to believe that they had seen the results of gassing with their own eyes. It is a psychological phenomenon familiar to judge and journalist alike. After having seen the psychological shock of the horrible scenes of death at the camps, no one could be blamed for believing the "official explanation" as touted by the media. Many

Famous Dachau gas chamber door photo shown to the world turned out to be disinfection chamber for lice.

years after the war, long after it became known that no American soldiers had seen a single gassed victim, the media still support the myth. Newspapers and magazines frequently quote soldiers who "know" that the Germans gassed the Jews because they "were there" and they "saw it with their own eyes." Yet, no editor corrects the error.

In the late '60s and early '70s I noticed the beginnings of a significant revision of the Holocaust story. "Death camps" where hundreds of thousands had supposedly been gassed suddenly became "concentration camps" where there had been no purposeful effort to exterminate the prisoners. Camps such as Dachau, which were formerly

414 My Awakening

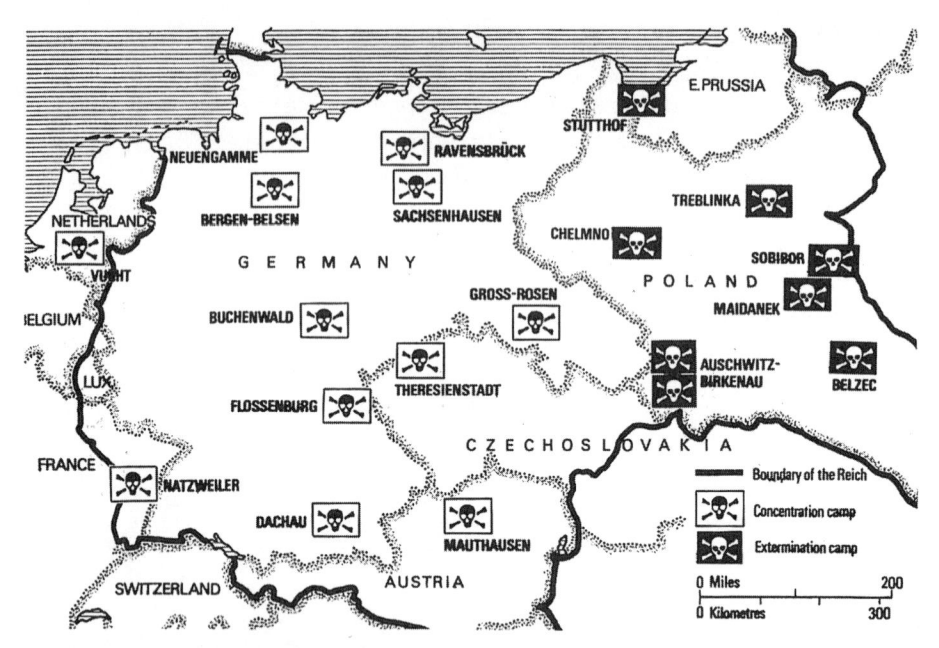

The much-published map of concentration camps (white) and "death camps" (black). Note that all the "death camps" were all Soviet-captured..

alleged to have gassed Jews, suddenly dropped any mention of gassing and their death figures were revised downward. Plaques on the camp gates showing old inflated numbers of victims were quietly replaced. Even the professional "Holocaust historians" began to classify Dachau as a "concentration camp" rather than a "death camp."

Under greater scrutiny, the previous claims of human gassing in camps on German soil became exposed as a war propaganda falsehood. Much of the popular press still supports this inaccuracy, even though the official chroniclers of the Holocaust had shifted the gas chamber allegations entirely to the "Communist-liberated" camps of the east. The so-called experts who now say that all death camps were in the East, had just a few years earlier claimed the same in the west.

The Jewish Soap Story

The outlandish story that the Nazis made soap from the bodies of Jews is perhaps one of the most startling examples of the fraudulent nature of the evidence and conduct of the Nuremberg Trials — as well as falsehoods contained in the Holocaust story. During the Nuremberg Trials, L.N. Smirnov, chief counselor of justice for the U.S.S.R., declared:

> The same base, rationalized SS technical minds which created gas chambers and murder vans, began devising such methods of...the

production of soap from human bodies and the tanning of human skin for industrial purposes...[837] (Nuremberg exhibit U.S.S.R.-197)

Allied prosecutors produced affidavits that alleged that Dr. Rudolf Spanner, head of the Danzig Institute, had called for the production of soap from the bodies of concentration camp inmates. Dr. Spanner's supposed formula for human soap was presented (Nuremberg document U.S.S.R.-196), and actual soap presumed to be made from humans was submitted to the IMT (exhibit U.S.S.R.-393).

Sir Hartley Shawcross, chief British prosecutor, in his summation to the court stated, "On occasion, even the bodies of their [the Germans'] victims were used to make good the wartime shortage of soap." As part of the Nuremberg verdict, the judges stated, "attempts were made to utilize the fat from the bodies of the victims in the commercial manufacture of soap."[838] This sensational allegation made headlines all over the world and is still often repeated today.

After the Nuremberg Trials, the Jewish soap story grew with each recounting. Survivors recounted washing their bodies with Jewish soap.

Nazi hunter Simon Wiesenthal wrote about the human soap during the Nuremberg Trials. In 1946, in the Austrian Jewish Community paper *Der Neue Weg*, he wrote:

> **During the last weeks of March the Romanian press reported an unusual piece of news: In the small Romanian city of Folticeni twenty boxes of soap were buried in the Jewish cemetery with full ceremony and complete funeral rites. This soap had been found recently in a former German army depot. On the boxes were the initials RIF, "Pure Jewish Fat." These boxes were destined for the Waffen-SS. The wrapping paper revealed with completely cynical objectivity that this soap was manufactured from Jewish bodies. Surprisingly, the thorough Germans forgot to describe whether the soap was produced from children, girls, men or elderly persons.** [839]

The allegation that the Nazis made soap out of Jews during the last years of the war was presented simply as a grim fact of the inhumanity of the Germans against the Jews. It was repeated in books such as the greatly media-touted, William Shirer's *Rise and Fall of the Third Reich* and in thousands of articles, documentaries, and even in textbooks.[840] In Israel, there have even been Jewish funerals for bars of soap alleged to be the remains of Jews. The soap bars, wrapped in funeral shrouds, were interred according to solemn Jewish ritual.

Every article, statement, affidavit and drama about the Germans making soap from the bodies of Jews has been shown false. After the war, the Allies initiated indictment proceedings against Dr. Rudolf Spanner. After a lengthy investigation, the prosecutor's office found no evidence that the Danzig Institute had ever made soap of human bodies, and they dropped charges against him.

416   My Awakening

It turns out that the initials "RIF" that appeared on the soap in question did not stand for "pure Jewish fat" but for the official name of the government agency that distributed soap and other cleansers. "Reichsstelle fur Industrielle Fettversorgung" means simply "Reich center for Industrial Fat provisioning." In fact, "Pure Jewish Fat" would be "RJF" (**R**ein **J**udisches **F**ett), not "RIF," but in the hysterical anti-German atmosphere at the end of the war, the authorities on the Holocaust story would not let simple facts get in the way. When "Holocaust revisionists" confronted the atrocity-mongers with the truth, they had to admit the soap lie or lose credibility.

Jewish historian Walter Laqueur, in his 1980 book *The Terrible Secret*, acknowledged that the human soap story was a fantasy.[841] Gitta Sereny, another famed Jewish historian, noted in her book *Into That Darkness*[842] that "the universally accepted story that the corpses were used to make soap and fertilizer is finally refuted by the generally very reliable Ludwigsburg Central Authority for Investigation into Nazi Crimes." Deborah Lipstadt, professor of modern Jewish history and Holocaust Studies at Emory University, wrote in 1981 that "the Nazis never used the bodies of Jews, or for that matter anyone else, for the production of soap."[843]

Finally, in April 1990, the man acclaimed as the world's foremost Holocaust historian, Professor Yehuda Bauer of Israel's Hebrew University, as well as Shmuel Krakowski, archives director of Israel's famous Yad Vashem Holocaust Center, stated that the human soap stories were not true. Bauer said that camp inmates "were prepared to believe any horror stories about their persecutors." In his interesting statement, Bauer blamed the whole human soap story on the Nazis. Krakowski commented that "Historians have concluded that soap was not made from human fat. When so many people deny the Holocaust ever happened, why give them something to use against the truth?"[844]

Historian Mark Weber writing in the Journal for Historical Review sums up his article on "Jewish Soap" stating, "That so many intelligent and otherwise thoughtful people could ever have seriously believed that the Germans distributed bars of soap brazenly labeled with letters that indicating that they were manufactured from Jewish corpses shows how readily even the most absurd Holocaust fables can be — and are — accepted as fact."[845] Just as the "Jewish Soap" story turned out to be a gigantic falsehood, there is a wealth of information that also contradicts many of the other popular beliefs. Many researchers, drawn to the contradictions and implausible scenarios of the Holocaust story, independently came up with new findings. The body of inquiry that challenges the Holocaust story — "Holocaust

THE HOLOCAUST: AN INQUIRY 417

revisionism" — continues to uncover new evidence even as I write these lines.

The Holocaust experts have countered the revisionists with invective and suppression. Just a few years ago, those who dared to question the Jewish soap story were called Nazis and haters. Even today anyone who dares to question any part of the Holocaust package: its nature, numbers, or policies — is condemned as a "Holocaust Denier" (a term that will probably be trademarked and written with a capital "D," just as Holocaust has come to be spelled with a capital "H").

To call anyone who questions the Holocaust dogma a "Holocaust Denier" is to suggest that he is a witless (or evil), anti-Semitic lunatic. How could anyone deny what, after all, everyone has seen with their own eyes — the photos and newsreels of gassings and shootings, the mounds of Jewish bodies.

In reality, I discovered that no responsible revisionist denies that large numbers of innocent people, including many Jews, died at the hands of the Germans and their allies during the Second World War. No one denies that the Germans rounded up the Jews from all over occupied Europe and put them into deplorable concentration camps. Revisionists do not deny that Nazis committed atrocities against Jews; they do, however, contend that the numbers of those killed have been grossly inflated. More importantly, they maintain that there was no central program, plan, policy, or order by the German government to exterminate all of the Jewish people. Revisionists claim that the Nazis created the camps to confine Jews because they considered them a security risk, much like the American government rounded up and incarcerated Japanese for security reasons.

Revisionists argue that scientific and documentary evidence supports their position and that the proponents of Holocaust orthodoxy must ruthlessly suppress debate if the Holocaust story is to survive. Finally, they argue that there are powerful political and economic motives for the creation and perpetuation of the Holocaust story.

Suppression of Holocaust Heretics

In the 1990s, hundreds of individuals all over the Western world, including many scholars and researchers, have been harassed, intimidated, physically attacked, fired, fined and even jailed simply for offering evidence that challenges parts of Holocaust orthodoxy. Professors, judges and teachers have been fired from their jobs. Some have been fined tens of thousands of dollars merely for expressing politically incorrect opinions. Professor Robert Faurisson at France's University of Lyon-II, for example, has been fined thousands of francs for his opinions and had his face crushed and doused with acid in a brutal attack. Often the victims are well educated, respected men who were never accused of anti-Semitism until they researched and wrote about the Holocaust.

A prime example of the persecution of the Holocaust questioners is the story of historian David Irving. His books are found in almost every library in the world. Irving has written more than thirty volumes on the Second World War published by a half dozen of the most prominent publishers in the Western World, including: The Viking Press; Harper & Row; Little, Brown; Simon & Schuster; and Avon Books.

The most respected historians in the world, including A.J.P. Taylor, Trevor Roper, Gordon Craig, and Stephen Ambrose have praised his works. He has researched in the German State Archives for more than thirty years, as well as in the U.S. National Archives, the British Public Records Office, the government archives of Australia, France, Italy and Canada; and even the former Soviet Secret State Archives. He was the first historian to challenge the validity of the widely heralded (and later debunked) *Hitler Diaries*.[846] In the course of his wide-ranging research, Irving has uncovered many documents that challenge parts of the Holocaust orthodoxy.

While he was in Germany, Irving quoted the videotaped admission of the head curator of the Auschwitz State Museum, Dr. Francizek Piper. Piper had admitted that the facility shown to the world (and more than 40 million visitors) for 40 years — as a genuine Nazi-built gas chamber — is not authentic. Polish Communists had actually built it after the war. For simply quoting Piper's admission, the government charged Irving with "Defaming the memory of the dead."

Although he had clear evidence proving the truth of his statement, Irving was forbidden to present it at his trial or even to call Dr. Piper as a witness. For making his statements of historical fact, the German government fined him 30,000 marks. In "the German State's interest" they banned him from using the German State Archives where he had labored for more than thirty years, and to which he had donated priceless collections of original documents.

The German government has now banned him from the country. Canada, France, Austria, Italy, South Africa, Australia and many other nations have subsequently banned him at the behest of the Jews. His publishers have been harassed and intimidated into canceling contracts. He has been physically attacked and has had lectures broken up by pipe-wielding thugs.

In Canada, at the request of the Simon Wiesenthal Center, the authorities seized, shackled, and deported him from the country in handcuffs. *The Toronto Globe & Mail* asked why he had been handcuffed and then answered its own question, "Did someone think he might use his typewriter?"

With the American tradition of First Amendment rights, few realize that in the so-called "Free World" it is possible for a historian to be jailed simply for voicing an opinion about a historical event of 50 years ago. Speaking inside his home near the U.S. embassy in London, Irving did an interview with a French television station, again repeating the fact that the main gas chambers shown to tourists at Auschwitz are fakes. For making this statement in his own living room in London, he was prosecuted in the Paris courts. In France, it is illegal to challenge any of the crimes against humanity as alleged in the Nuremberg Trials Charter of 1945 — even if one does so in his own home and in another country.

There are those who say that we should not debate aspects of the Holocaust anymore than we should debate those who say the world is flat. Yet, would any knowledgeable person be afraid to debate an advocate of the flat Earth theory? Would he urge the passage of laws to prevent the advocate of that theory from speaking, writing or publishing? Would he try to have his livelihood destroyed, have him fined thousands of dollars, and if that did not work, cast him into prison?

I believe in freedom of speech because I am not afraid. I believe that my ideas are well reasoned and that I can back up my opinions with logic and evidence. In an atmosphere of free and open discussion, I fear not, for there is not a truth that I dread. What do the opponents of David Irving, or of all revisionists, fear?

Our libraries and schools are extremely well stocked with Holocaust literature. Newspapers and magazines surge with an endless stream of related stories. Theater and television screens light up with drama, commentary, interviews, and images of the Holocaust. It would seem that with this much overkill, there should be little to fear from the David Irvings of the world — unless of course, they think that his evidence is convincing, his reasoning sound and his presentation eloquent. Thus, to protect their popular version of the Holocaust, they seek to hound this man to the ends of the Earth.

What "historical fact" is so weak that it must be protected by terror, by jail, and deportation? What do the opponents of David Irving and the other revisionists fear? Are the revisionist arguments so convincing that their opponents must use naked political oppression to silence them?

Auschwitz: The Centerpiece of the Holocaust

The Holocaust story centers on the Auschwitz concentration camp in Poland. For years, it was presented to the world as a death camp where the Nazis gassed three to four million Jews as well as millions more non-Jews. Whatever doubts visitors might have about the enormity of the Holocaust, and the veracity of the gas chamber stories — are wiped away by the camp tours. About a half-a-million tourists each year see what guides purport to be the actual gas chambers where millions of Jews were murdered. From 1945 to 1989, a plaque at the front gate proclaimed in many different languages that 4.1 million victims had died there. During a visit to the camp in June 1979, Pope John Paul II stood before this monument and blessed the four million victims' souls. It turned out that three million of the souls were imaginary.

Shortly after the pope's visit, with no fanfare or publicity, the camp historians removed the plaque and replaced it with one reflecting the new official figure: 1.2 million. For many years, the officially declared six million Jewish victims of the Holocaust included the four million supposedly killed at Auschwitz. Interestingly, when the Auschwitz figure was reduced by about three million, there was no rush to correct the encyclopedias or the endless stories quoting the six million figure.

When the "experts" made the Auschwitz reduction, they did something for which revisionists have been jailed: They revised the Jewish casualty rate downward. However, they had no real choice. They had to radically lower their figures or lose credibility. It was one thing to make fantastically ludicrous claims when Auschwitz was a little-visited Communist Party-controlled site of the '50s and '60s, but with greater access came more questions. By revising the figures, the camp curators were in effect admitting that the Communists and the subsequent camp museum officials had fabricated numbers and that they were just too big to be believed.

Jewish revisionist David Cole traveled to Auschwitz in September, 1992. Wearing a Yarmulke, he interviewed the curator, Dr. Francizek Piper, who admitted that while the "official tour guides" tell the visitors the gas chamber is exactly as it was when the camp was liberated, it is actually a "reconstruction." That revelation is just one of the gaping leaks in the bow of battleship *Auschwitz*, the mothership of the Holocaust fleet. Cole was subsequently beaten up and his life threatened repeatedly.[847]

In response to repeated revelations catching Holocaust promoters with their pants down, new books rewrote the story and admitted what people such as David Irving had been condemned for saying. Interestingly, in the most authoritative and exhaustive book on Auschwitz yet published, *Auschwitz: 1270 to Present* by Robert Jan Van Pelt and Deborah Dwork, it is admitted by the two Jewish Holocaust upholders that the gas chamber at the main Auschwitz camp and that the one shown to tourists was a fake built by the Polish Communists long after the war. [848] The authors, however, go on to allege that there were gas chambers in another Auschwitz camp.

The overthrow of Communism in Russia brought to light many documents that were hitherto inaccessible to Western researchers. Startling pieces of evidence have recently turned up in the Moscow State Archives. When the Soviets had "liberated" the camp, the Germans had hurriedly abandoned it, leaving behind tons of documents. Among the items recovered by the Communist troops was the Auschwitz *Death Register* — chronologically bound volumes of death certificates of those who had died in the camp. For 45 years, these crucial documents had languished in the secret files of the KGB, Russian president Mikhail Gorbachev authorized release of the ones researchers had located, 46 bound volumes. The volumes show that doctors and other medical personnel meticulously recorded each death at Auschwitz. The records included descriptions of the cause of death, which ranged from execution (generally shooting or hanging) to disease, heart attack and similar causes. Most of the deaths were from disease. The incomplete *Death Register* volumes contain records that add up to approximately 74,000 deaths, of which approximately 30,000 were Jews. The rest were Poles, Russians, and other nationalities.

The *Death Register* raised immediate questions. If the authorities recorded executions by shooting or hanging, then why not those by gassing? More importantly, why had the books been kept hidden for so many years? Had the Soviets suppressed the books because they knew that they did not correlate with their official KGB versions of Auschwitz?

Powerful evidence from Allied sources also conflicts with the fantastic alleged murder rate at Auschwitz. In the mid-1970s, the U.S. government released war-time aerial photographs of the Auschwitz camp. Jewish historian Raul Hilberg, in his article for *Encarta Encyclopedia*, writes, "In 1944 the camp was photographed by Allied reconnaissance aircraft in search of industrial targets; its factories, but not its gas chambers, were bombed."

The United States Air Force took the photographs over a lengthy period, and they are so remarkable in their clarity that vehicles and even people can be distinguished in them. Many of the photographs had been taken during the supposed height of the alleged killing. The surveillance flights took many at mid-morning on typical workdays. Not one of the photos taken over a number of days shows huge pits or piles of human bodies; nor are there any fires suggesting their burning or smoke billowing from the chimneys of the crematoria.

Thousands of tons of coke would have been needed to fuel the crematoria if the murder and cremation of millions of people had been in progress. Yet the photos show no mountains of coke, and there are no long lines of railway cars filled with the fuel. No lines of people are assembled outside the doors of the alleged Auschwitz gas chamber, and no holes appear on the very roof where allegedly Zyklon B was supposedly tipped in on top of the victims.

Another startling piece of evidence surfaced with the release of the British "Enigma Secret." Using computers, the British broke the supposedly indecipherable ultra-secret code that the Germans had relied on to send communiqués between the battlefront and the high command. Cracking the code helped turn the tide of war, for the British and Allied forces knew the German's military plans and orders — sometimes even before the German field commanders themselves.

Sir Frank H. Hinsley, master of St. John's College and professor of International Relations at Cambridge University, published a special appendix to Volume II of his magisterial *British Intelligence in the Second World War: Its Influence on Strategy and Operations*.[849] In the section titled "German Police Cyphers," Hinsley reveals that during 1942 and 1943 British intelligence intercepted daily coded communications for Dachau, Buchenwald, Auschwitz, and seven other camps. Every day each camp reported the number of people brought in, the number transferred to other camps, and the numbers who were born and those who died. It also reported executions by shooting or hanging.

"The returns of Auschwitz," states Hinsley, "the largest of the camps with 200,000 prisoners, mentioned illness as the main cause of death but included references to shootings and hangings. There were no references in the decrypts to gassing." The numbers of dead in the decoded messages correlate with the records of the death books and the amount of coke consumed. More importantly, if gassing had been taking place, why would they have not been reported, just as shootings and hangings were? Since the Germans dutifully reported executions or killings to their superiors, and their reports were made in top secret transmissions, why would they hide the method of execution used?

Interestingly enough, the British Intelligence also intercepted the communications of German commando forces called "einstatzgruppen" that were locked in an horrific partisan war in the east against the Communists. In those decrypts are graphic descriptions of mass murders of Jewish partisans and groups of civilians. Why would those secret messages include grim accounts of the murder of civilians, but not the decrypts from Auschwitz?

Scientific Evidence

In a criminal trial, scientific evidence is usually the most powerful because it can be validated in an objective, scientific manner. There is no scientific evidence indicating mass gassing at Auschwitz or any other German camp. The United States Army had toxicology experts do autopsies on hundreds of dead in the Nazi concentration camps. Human remains can show signs of cyanide poisoning for years. No scientific evidence existed that even *one* of the victims was gassed to death. Nor do records of autopsies by Russian doctors in the Eastern European camps show any evidence of gassing. Although autopsies had been performed, the results were not presented at Nuremberg. Why? Such would not have served the prosecution because none of the deaths could be blamed on poison gas? In every murder trial doesn't the prosecution show the cause of death. In the most publicized murder trial of all time (the IMT) proof of the cause of death is conspicuously absent. If the Nazis had really gassed people by the millions, would not the prosecution have produced at least one autopsy proving the cause of death to be poisoning by the cyanide produced by Zyklon B?

Holocaust gurus purport that one "proof" of the gassing of human beings is the great quantity of Zyklon B used at Auschwitz during the war. Attempting to rebut revisionist questioning of gas chambers, Jean Claude Pressac, a French chemist, in his book *Auschwitz: Techniques and Operation of the Gas Chambers*, supplies data showing the large consumption of Zyklon B at Auschwitz.[850] A logical explanation is that the Germans used the chemical in an effort to control the epidemics that ravaged the camps.

Additionally, the data published by Pressac himself shows that the per capita amount of Zyklon B used in the Auschwitz concentration camp was similar to Zyklon B consumption in German camps such as Oranienburg, where the experts admit that no human gassing took place. If Auschwitz was the great center of extermination, and if Zyklon B was the poison used, how could it be that records of the chemical's purchase and usage show no greater consumption at Auschwitz than at the concentration camps where Zyklon B was used strictly for lice infestation and where there were no alleged gassings? Pressac also inadvertently revealed that coke consumption was no greater per capita in Auschwitz than the camps in Germany where extermination is not alleged.

In February 1988, the Canadian government charged Holocaust questioner Ernst Zundel with violating an archaic law against "spreading false news." Defense attorneys in this criminal case commissioned an American engineering consultant on prison gas chambers,

Fred Leuchter, to make a scientific examination of the alleged homicidal gas chambers at Auschwitz. Leuchter, an apolitical person, is perhaps the premier authority in the United States on the construction and use of execution equipment, and he was actually in charge of the design and construction of execution facilities used in a number of American prisons.

In his investigation, Leuchter surveyed the construction of the alleged gas chambers and researched the chemical properties of the Zyklon B fumigant. He found that Zyklon B is a compound that, when exposed to air, releases deadly potassium cyanide gas. It clings to surfaces and has a tendency to react chemically with materials containing iron (ferric compounds), creating a ferricyanide. If Zyklon B is used in iron chambers or in red brick structures, it reacts with ferrous (iron) material to produce a distinctive blue color. The printing ink industry has used these chemical reactions for many decades to produce a distinctive color called Prussian Blue. *Random House Webster's Electronic Dictionary*, 1992 edition, defines it as follows:

> **Prussian Blue n. 1. a moderate to deep greenish blue. 2. a dark blue, crystalline, water-insoluble ferrocyanide pigment, used in painting, fabric printing, and laundry bluing.**

Not only did Leuchter find that the supposed homicidal gas chambers at Auschwitz were structurally unsuitable for gassing, he also took samples from the walls and had them chemically analyzed. Independent laboratories in the United States found no evidence of the ferricyanide compounds. Yet, when Leuchter examined the rooms used as disinfestation chambers for clothes and luggage, he readily observed the distinctive blue coloring associated with ferricyanide. After further chemical analysis of the samples, he proved that the disinfection walls had heavy concentrations of the ferricyanide caused by exposure to cyanide.

Leuchter also pointed out that the disinfestation chambers used for delousing clothes were well made, airtight, and designed for safety. On the other hand, the supposed human gas chambers were shoddily constructed. He asked why gas chambers for killing lice would be properly engineered, whereas chambers allegedly for killing millions of people would be improperly engineered and constructed — and dangerous for its operators.

The Fight against Revisionism

When Leuchter published his report, Holocaust authorities reacted predictably — with defamation, suppression, intimidation and even imprisonment. Leuchter became the victim of an intense international campaign to discredit him and ruin him financially. Jewish groups wrote defamatory letters to all of his state penitentiary clients urging them to cancel his contracts. They were able to get authorities to prosecute him in his home state of Massachusetts, in spite of his obvious expertise and his patents, under an arcane statute of practicing engineering without a license.

The German government jailed Leuchter for six weeks simply for reporting his technical findings in a lecture in November 1991 at Weisshiem. For simply translating and commenting on Leuchter's speech, Mr. Günter Deckert, a former high-school teacher with a clean record, was sentenced to a year's probation. In their verdict, the judges, Dr. Orlet and Dr. Muller pointed out that Deckert was a city councilor who graduated with distinction in law from Heidelberg University and was of high moral character. Because they did not sentence Deckert harshly enough according to the international press, the judges themselves faced intimidation and efforts were made to overturn their sentence.

Frau Saline Leutheusser-Schnarrenberger, the German minister of justice, called the verdict a slap in the face for every victim of the Holocaust and had the two judges suspended and placed on "sick leave." Mannheim prosecutor Hans Klein appealed the verdict with the result that Deckert received a two-year jail sentence. Klein also promised to go over the wording of the verdict in search of anything that might be grounds for prosecuting the two judges. It is obviously not a free system if a Judge can face termination, or even be criminally charged for stating why he is lenient within the bounds of his authority.

It seems that little has changed in Germany during this century. In America it is hard to imagine someone going to jail simply for translating a scientific lecture, or having judges suspended or threatened with arrest for rendering a verdict or sentence deemed politically incorrect. Nevertheless, such are the methods of protecting the Holocaust story. Germany is not the only violator of free speech in this matter. Some time later, the frail and spectacled Fred Leuchter was also incarcerated and forcibly deported from Great Britain.

A year after the Leuchter controversy, the Auschwitz Museum itself secretly duplicated Leuchter's tests and arrived at the same scientific results. They do not, however, discuss these scientific facts in their guidebooks. Their feeble explanation for the lack of ferricyanide in the human gas chambers is that somehow it dissipated over time — a chemical impossibility. They offer no explanation why the ferricyanide did not dissipate in the disinfestation chambers. Another Holocaust expert argued that it takes less cyanide to kill humans than it does to kill lice, therefore there would be less in the human gas chambers than in the disinfestation chambers. Yet, they allege huge amounts of Zyklon B were used to kill hundreds of thousands of people in a veritable "factory of death."

The Holocaust revisionists, with almost no help from the press, have caused such a stir by the Leuchter Report and releasing the details of modern Auschwitz's own chemical study, that the Auschwitz staff authorized a new investigation that purports to refute Leuchter and their own earlier study. However, they will not allow any independent studies by scientists and engineers, although it would be relatively easy and quick to obtain samples and do analysis of the alleged gas chambers' walls. Repeatedly in the study of the Holocaust, those with a personal stake in maintaining their version of events are opposed to academic or scientific inquiry. They endeavor to prevent a physical inspection of records or scientific studies of sites, and they make even the public reporting of scientific or historical investigations punishable by imprisonment.

Even a well-respected Jewish historian who believes in the existence of the gas chambers offers a somewhat revisionist viewpoint. In his 1988 book *Why Did the Heavens Not Darken?: The "Final Solution" in History*, Princeton University professor Arno J. Mayer pointed out that there are many questions about the Holocaust. Mayer, who himself lost close family in the Holocaust, writes:

> **Many questions remain open. . . . All in all, how many bodies were cremated in Auschwitz? How many died there all told? What was the national, religious, and ethnic breakdown in this commonwealth of victims? How many of them were condemned to die a "natural" death and how many were deliberately slaughtered. . . ? We have simply no answers to these questions at this time. (pg. 366)**
>
> **From 1942 to 1945, certainly at Auschwitz, but probably overall, more Jews were killed by so-called "natural" causes than by "unnatural" ones. (pg. 365)**
>
> **Sources for the study of the gas chambers are at once rare and unreliable.** [851]

I must repeat that Mayer strongly believes that gas chambers did exist at Auschwitz, but he points out that "Most of what is known is based on the depositions of Nazi officials and executioners at postwar trials and on the memory of survivors and bystanders. This testimony must be screened carefully, since it can be influenced by subjective factors of great complexity" [852] Mayer's statements would be grounds for prosecution in France and Germany.

Witnesses to the Holocaust

As Mayer points out, much of the Holocaust story is based on eyewitness accounts. Revisionists argue that so-called eyewitness testimony is not always reliable. They give as an example, the John

THE HOLOCAUST: AN INQUIRY   427

Demjanjuk case. Demjanjuk, a naturalized American autoworker from Eastern Europe, was accused of being Ivan the Terrible, a nefarious concentration camp guard at Treblinka concentration camp who allegedly murdered hundreds of people.

Demjanjuk maintained his innocence, but hundreds of Jewish eyewitnesses testified that he was Ivan. The witnesses screamed, cried, and postured, telling the most incredible stories of cruelty and sadism. They swore under oath that they clearly remembered that Demjanjuk was Ivan. Ultimately, Demjanjuk was deported to Israel, an Israeli court tried and convicted him, primarily on "eye-witnesses" testimony. But new evidence came forward that proved that the Soviet KGB had framed Demjanjuk. Documents that supposedly showed him to be a guard proved to be Soviet forgeries. When faced with a worldwide scandal, even the Israeli Supreme Court had to agree that the eyewitness accounts were not credible and that Demjanjuk was innocent.

Those Incredible Numbers

In examining the Holocaust, I found that sources varied wildly in their estimations of the number killed, ranging from 4 to 24 million. Reproduced below is the entry under *Holocaust* in the *Compton's Multimedia Encyclopedia, 1991.*

> **As Nazi Germany gained control of one country after another in World War II, there was much killing of civilians and maltreatment of soldiers that can be classified as war crimes. These crimes, however, pale in comparison to the massive, deliberate, *and well-planned extermination of more than 15 million persons* in what is termed the Holocaust. This genocide of staggering proportions was carried out with scrupulous efficiency by a well-coordinated German bureaucracy in which nothing was left to chance.** [853]

Elsewhere in the same Compton's Encyclopedia (under the topic *Concentration Camp*) is the following statement:

> **The most horrible extension of the concentration camp system was the establishment of extermination centers after 1940. They were set up primarily to kill Jews. This slaughter is known as the Holocaust. It is believed that from *18 to 26 million people were killed in them*, including 6 million Jews and 400,000 Gypsies.** [854]

Holocaust chroniclers assessing German crimes obviously see no need for accuracy or even consistency. But regardless of which set of numbers is used, the figures are so fantastic that they strain credulity. If 18 to 26 million people were murdered and cremated in the "extermination centers" of Poland (most of them at Auschwitz), the daily count would have had to be in the tens of thousands. As cited previously, the expert cited by the Holocaust scholars themselves, Prassac, now estimates the death toll at Auschwitz of all victims to have been between 600,000 and 800,000. How do these figures, which themselves could be greatly exaggerated, square with the wild numbers for Auschwitz bandied around in the popular encyclopedias? When a nation is accused of such terrible crimes, shouldn't there be at least a demand for accuracy and consistency? If not, then any people could be accused of any transgression without fear of reproach.

About the time I noticed the discrepancies in Holocaust numbers, I saw a television interview of a Zionist who attacked Holocaust revisionism by saying that "Whether it was ten million or one million, 100,000 or 1000, it does not make the crime any less abhorrent!" The truth is that if hundreds of thousands rather than up to 26 million were killed, and if most of those deaths were caused by the expected brutalities of war rather than a calculated plan of extermination, then the prevalent version of the Holocaust story is grossly inaccurate.

Other Holocaust Questions

The main component of the Holocaust story is that the Nazis had a plan or program for exterminating the Jews. But even though the Allies captured Germany's government and military headquarters and most of the concentration camps with their records intact, there has never been a single order or instruction found that calls for the gassing of Jews or that indicates a plan to exterminate all of European Jewry. No blueprint has been found for the construction of a human gas chamber, or instructions or orders written for gassing human beings.

On this subject, as on others, the Holocaust story has undergone revision. No longer do the experts claim the Nazis gave direct orders to exterminate the Jews. Raul Hilberg in the 1961, first edition of his major work on the Holocaust, *The Destruction of the European Jews*, wrote that in 1941 Hitler had issued two orders for the extermination of the Jews. In Hilberg's revised three-volume edition of the book, published in 1985, all reference to such orders had been removed. [855] In a review of Hilberg's revised edition, historian Christopher Browning, himself an "exterminationist historian," wrote:

> **In the new edition, all references in the text to a Hitler decision or Hitler order for the "Final Solution" have been systematically excised. Buried at the bottom of a single footnote stands the solitary reference: "Chronology and circumstances point to a Hitler decision before the summer ended." In the new edition, decisions were not made and orders were not given.** [856]

A Holocaust under the Nose of the Red Cross?

Jewish leaders have recently directed anger toward the International Red Cross for not revealing and doing anything to stop the Holocaust. They point out that international teams of Red Cross inspectors visited and inspected all the major German concentration camps, including Auschwitz, right up to the end to the war. On one hand, the Holocausters expect us to believe that the Germans were murdering tens of thousands of people a day in a super-secret plan that they dared not mention even in their top-secret orders. On the other hand, they expect us to believe that the Nazis would let the International Red Cross inspect those same camps at the same time they were supposedly killing many thousands each day. Here are excerpts from a telling *U.S.A. Today* article:

> **Many Jewish leaders and Holocaust experts long have contended that the Red Cross failed spectacularly during World War II — mostly by not raising an alarm about Nazi atrocities — and compounded the failure later by refusing to acknowledge it...**
>
> **In fact, in a Nov. 22, 1944, letter to U.S. State Department officials about the visit, the Red Cross said: "(We) had not been able to discover any trace of installations for exterminating civilian prisoners...**
>
> **In this case, the documents show, the Red Cross failed at every possible turn. Not only had Red Cross officials neglected to grasp the situation, but they then passed along bad information to the Allies.**
>
> **A TENDENCY TO DISBELIEVE HORROR STORIES**
>
> **Several Red Cross documents suggest that the organization was reluctant, at least initially, to put much faith in tales and rumors of Nazi brutality. Like the general public, Red Cross officials didn't comprehend the true extent of the Nazis' crimes...**
>
> **"There is no doubt that the Red Cross let itself be used by the Nazis," says Radu Ioanid, director of the Holocaust Survivors Registry at the U.S. Holocaust Memorial Museum. ``There is no doubt they were fooled."**[857]

Obviously, if the grievously high death toll was from lack of medicine, shortages of insecticide (for killing disease-spreading lice), and food — because of the destruction and disruption of the war — the Nazis would have had no fear of International Red Cross inspectors and volunteers in the camps any more than the British would have feared them helping in the ruins of East London after an air raid. Do the promoters of the Holocaust story believe the members of the International Red Cross were part of an anti-Semitic, Nazi-Holocaust conspiracy? Or did their members, in spite of visiting the camps during the war and delivering to prisoners 973,000 packages and parcels (as their own records show), simply see no evidence at all of mass gassings or burnings or "extermination facilities" or for that matter, any effort on the part of the Nazis to purposefully exterminate the Jewish people?

While helping hundreds of thousands of refugees, Red Cross volunteers undoubtedly heard stories of Nazi brutality and rumors of mass gassings and they noted those rumors and kept an eye out for any evidence of them, but they saw nothing to indicate that the rumors were true. At the end of the war, in camps such as Buchenwald, they saw great numbers of bodies, but their own reports laid the horror on disease epidemics, epidemics that even the British occupiers and the Red Cross itself had tremendous trouble controlling. For instance, the British estimated that more people perished *after* they assumed control of Bergen-Belsen than *before* the camp's liberation.

Jewish forces condemn revisionists who raise common-sense questions about the Holocaust, such as "How could there have been a Holocaust right under the noses of the International Red Cross?" It's no wonder they want such questions quashed and the questioners imprisoned. Their version of the Holocaust story cannot afford such inquiries.

Why No Debate?

The official keepers of the Holocaust wage an international campaign to silence the disturbing questions. Most people never even hear the revisionist position because Jewish forces dominate the media and block mainstream access to material that questions Holocaust orthodoxy.

Among the most potent of such forces is the worldwide "Anti-Defamation League of the B'nai B'rith," which has a $37 million annual budget in the United States devoted to defaming those who criticize Israel or question parts of the Holocaust tale. The ADL instructs its spokesmen never to debate any aspect of the Holocaust. If their version of the Holocaust is so overwhelmingly documented, why do they fear free and open discussion?

An honest debate between the high priests of the Holocaust and Holocaust questioners would reveal that the latter are not crackpots or hatemongers but people with legitimate questions and arguments based on sound evidence. Such a debate would reveal that revisionists do not deny that Jews, like the Japanese in World War II America, were unjustly incarcerated in concentration camps. Revisionists acknowledge that the conditions in the European camps were horrendous near war's end, and they maintain that many thousands of Jews died in the camps, mostly from malnutrition and disease. Finally, revisionists also freely admit that some massacres of innocent civilians took place and that such horrors should be condemned.

Revisionists maintain that while there were certainly Germans who committed what is today defined as "war crimes," the Allies

THE HOLOCAUST: AN INQUIRY

themselves, which include the Soviets, were guilty of them to at least an equal degree. Revisionists point to the Allied intentional firebombing of civilian populations as well as to the Soviets' mass rape, expulsion, and murder of millions of Germans and other peoples of Eastern Europe. They also point out that many of the deaths in the concentration camps in the last years of the war were caused by Allied bombing of rail lines vital for transportation of food and medicines. They point out that specific targeting and destruction of pharmaceutical factories that produced medicines and medical supplies increased the death rate among German civilians, soldiers and also among those in the camps.

To challenge the popular perception of the Holocaust, obviously, does not condone mass murder. Those who refute the popular conception of the Holocaust make clear that they view atrocities against innocent Jews or any other people as crimes against the moral values of Western civilization. Revisionists simply contend that the Jews were not the only victims of the world's most horrific war. Many revisionists also argue that the motive for a horrific Holocaust story is the furtherance of the economic and political objectives of Israel and the Jewish organizations.

When I began to learn of the many disturbing facts that influenced my perception of the Holocaust, I asked myself how the Holocaust story began and why it so ubiquitous more than 50 years after the end of the Second World War. Usually, there is a great deal of bitterness and hatred at the end of any war, but as time passes, the hysteria lessens and cooler heads prevail. Yet there seems to be as much frenzy about German war crimes today as immediately after the war. Just months after the war's end, a U. S. Senate leader, Robert Taft, condemned the International Military Tribunals as a "blot on the American record we will long regret."[858] The Chief Justice of Supreme Court of the United States, Harlan Fiske Stone, said of Justice Jackson, who left the court to lead the tribunal:

> **Jackson is away conducting his high grade lynching party in Nuremberg. I don't mind what he does to the Nazis, but I hate to see the pretense that he is running a court and proceeding according to the common law. This is a little too sanctimonious a fraud to meet my old-fashioned ideas.** [859]

Fifty years later, one would be hard-pressed to find even one American congressman who would dare condemn the war crimes trials, for even if he secretly harbored that opinion. He would know that uttering it would bring upon his head such wrath that his political career would be over.

What is it, then — the motive that keeps Holocausters striving to keep the story so ingrained in our minds and hearts?

Motives for the Holocaust Story

Pressure was placed on the Allied powers to establish a permanent haven in Palestine for Jewish survivors. The establishment of Israel three years after Germany's defeat was thus an aftereffect of the Holocaust. [860] –Encarta Encyclopedia article on Holocaust by Raul Hilberg, leading Jewish Holocaust historian

During every war, there is war propaganda. In modern war, it is developed to a high art. It is a weapon that has no necessary relation to truth, for it is simply an instrument of power used on the psychology of a nation's own forces — just as the physical weapons of war are brought to bear on the enemy. During the First World War, the British War Office issued dispatches saying that the German soldiers would enjoy themselves by hoisting up the babies of Belgium on their bayonets, and, furthermore, that they boiled the babies' bodies to derive the phosphates used in munitions. After the war, the British War Office confirmed that these stories were blatant falsehoods.

During the Second World War — in the age of radio, movies, and mass-circulation newspapers and magazines — propaganda was far more refined and powerful. Jews, who exercised considerable power in the American and British media, started circulating stories about German atrocities even back in the 1930s, and the stories escalated as the war wore on. Just as Germans were accused of boiling babies in the First World War, Germans were accused of making soap from the bodies of their murdered victims in the Second. However, this time it took almost half of a century for the truth to vanquish the lie about the soap story, and yet blatant falsehood is still often repeated.

As a student, in the basement of the Louisiana State University library, I surveyed a great many magazines published between 1945 and 1950, and I found compelling reasons why the war propaganda did not stop after the end of the war. Scarcely after the guns in Europe had been silenced, a new war began that was vital to the worldwide Jewish community. A massive Jewish invasion and ensuing war began in Palestine for the creation of the Zionist State of Israel. Its success depended to a great degree on the Holocaust story. In his *Encarta Encyclopedia* article, Raul Hilberg accurately depicts the establishment of Israel as an "aftereffect of the Holocaust." Actually the establishment of Israel was not so much an aftereffect of the Holocaust as it was an aftereffect of the Holocaust *story*. The realities of the Holocaust were not important — but the perception that there *was* a Holocaust was crucial.

Today there are important historical questions concerning the sinking of the *Maine* preceding the Spanish-American War; the Gulf of Tonkin Incident preceding heavy American involvement in Vietnam; and whether the *Lusitania*, which the Germans sank in the First World

The Holocaust: An Inquiry 433

War, was illegally carrying munitions. Their importance at the time was not the truth of the events as much as the public perception of them. The same is true of the Holocaust. The Zionist dream of Israel needed a "Holocaust" — the most monstrous Holocaust imaginable — to further their national aims.

Israel could not have been born, but for the story of the story of the "six million." The creation of the Jewish state depended on the massive invasion of Jews from all over the world into Palestine and a successful war of terror against both the British who administered the region under a League of Nations mandate and against the region's native inhabitants. The displaced Jewish populations of Europe were a tremendous source of immigration to Palestine. Without that emigration, it is doubtful that the relatively small prewar Jewish population there could have wrested control from the British and the native Palestinians.

The Zionist military takeover of Palestine required vast economic, military, and political support from around the world. It entailed the terrorization of the Palestinian majority, driving them from their homes and lands and denying them their civil and political rights. Only the perpetuation of the Holocaust story could make these crimes tolerable in world opinion. Sympathy for the Jews, deeply stirred by recollections of the Holocaust, made whatever grievous offenses committed against Palestinians, no matter how unjust, seem trivial.

The Holocaust story has generated tens of billions of dollars of aid from the United States and even greater amounts from Germany in reparations. Perhaps most importantly, the Holocaust was the fuel that fired the flame of Jewish Zionism all over the world. Recital of the Holocaust united Jews worldwide and elicited the huge monetary and political support necessary for the establishment and maintenance of Israel. After 50 years of almost unbroken conflict with the Palestinians and her Arab neighbors, Israel still completely depends upon American and German support. Israel remains America's biggest annual recipient of foreign aid, just as it has been since her foundation. Constant harping on the Holocaust keeps the money flowing from both Jews and non-Jews and forms a subtle excuse for every injustice committed against the Arabs.

Nahum Goldmann, president of the World Jewish Congress, wrote a popular book called *The Jewish Paradox*, published by Grosset & Dunlap in 1978. Goldmann writes dramatically of the impact of German reparations for Israel.

> **The Germans will have paid out a total of 80 billion…Without the German reparations that started coming through during the first ten years as a state, Israel would not have half of its present infrastructure: All the trains in Israel are German, the ships are German, and the same goes for electrical installations and a great deal of Israel's**

434 MY AWAKENING

> industry... and that is setting aside the individual pensions paid to survivors. Israel today receives hundreds of millions of dollars in German currency each year.... In some years the sums of money received by Israel from Germany has been as much as double or treble the contribution made by collections from international Jewry. [861]

In this amazing book, Goldmann admits that even during the war the Zionists were planning war crimes trials and reparations from Germany.

> During the war the WJC (World Jewish Congress) had created an Institute of Jewish Affairs in New York (its headquarters are now in London). The directors were two great Lithuanian Jewish Jurists, Jacob and Nehemiah Robinson. Thanks to them, the Institute worked out two completely revolutionary ideas: the Nuremberg tribunal and German reparations.
>
> The Institute's... idea was that Nazi Germany ought to pay after its defeat, ...The German reparations would first have to be paid to people who had lost their belongings through the Nazis. Further, if, as we hoped, the Jewish state was created, the Germans would pay compensation to enable the survivors to settle there. The first time this idea was expressed was during the war, in the course of a conference in Baltimore. [862]

The Nuremberg Trials were presented to the public as an effort by the Allies to levy justice on war criminals. In *The Jewish Paradox*, Goldmann admits that the Nuremberg Trials and the idea of German reparations were originated not by the Allies but by Zionists before any evidence of a Holocaust, and that the compensation would be vital to the foundation of Israel.

Since the Second World War, the Holocaust story has engendered tens of billions of dollars from the United States and even greater amounts from Germany in reparations. The staggering sum, easily exceeding $150 billion, would certainly provide a powerful motive to Israel and World Zionism to perpetuate the sensationalized Holocaust story.

Another possible motive for keeping the propaganda alive became apparent to me as I read the stacks of 1940s magazines in the LSU library. Repeatedly I found stories predicting the eminent rebirth of Nazism. Stories abounded about secret hordes of gold to fund the neo-Nazi movement in Germany and elsewhere, possibly even in South and Central America.

Associating the Holocaust with Nazism was certainly the most effective way to rebuke the National Socialist philosophy. Of course, the Holocaust not only rebukes the Nazis, it insulates the Jews from criticism. It is also a psychological weapon in the hands of the Jewish-led egalitarian movement, for the mass media never seemed to miss an opportunity to link racial thinking and science to the Nazi horrors.

THE HOLOCAUST: AN INQUIRY 435

In advancing the Holocaust story, the Jewish-dominated media had a willing partner in the Allied governments. At the end of the war, with Europe in ruins, tens of millions dead, and half of Europe under the Communist tyranny, many could be forgiven for asking if involvement in the original Polish-German war had been worth it. The Holocaust story provided powerful emotional justification.

I enjoyed reading Raymond Chandler murder mysteries when I was in college. When studying the Holocaust, I remembered that in making a criminal case, the prosecution shows the defendant has motive to commit the offense and the opportunity to do so. Powerful Jewish interests certainly had the motive to create and promote the Holocaust story in its most extreme version, and with their domination of the media they certainly had the opportunity.

There are literally thousands of books in print focusing on aspects of the Holocaust and thousands more articles, speeches, sermons, documentaries, novels, and movies tell us of its terror. An overwhelming number of the authors of material on the Holocaust are themselves Jewish. Is it likely that Jews, who passionately and emotionally believe in the unspeakable horrors of the Holocaust, can write objectively about it? Could Elie Wiesel write an unbiased account of Nazi Germany or the Holocaust any more than Adolf Hitler, were he alive, could write an unbiased one of Wiesel and the Second World War?

Elie Wiesel writes:

> **Every Jew, somewhere in his being, should set apart a zone of hate — healthy, virile hate — for what the German personifies and for what persists in the German. To do otherwise would be a betrayal of the dead.**[863]

Imagine if a Russian survivor of the murderous Gulags under Jewish Bolshevism made a statement saying that,

> **Every Russian, somewhere in his being, should set apart a zone of hate — healthy virile hate — for what the Jew personifies and what persists in the Jew. To do otherwise would be a betrayal of the dead.**

I don't believe he would have won a Nobel prize.

The real power of the Holocaust story has been in the human emotion it evokes. It is the tearful remembrances of elderly Jewish survivors, the coquettish words of Anne Frank, and the photographs and newsreels of emaciated and mangled bodies that are ingrained in the consciousness of us all. It is the pictorial record that is the real "proof" of the Holocaust, for we have all seen its victims in their terrible poses of death. However, we could see similar pictures from many wars. We could see the millions of victims of Communism under Trotsky's Red Army or Stalin's purges. We could see the women and children who died by the thousands in the British-run concentration camps of the Boer War. We could see the remains of the tens of thousands of men, women, and children who were burned alive at Dresden or Hamburg. We could see the dead of the killing fields of Cambodia or the blood-drenched jungles of Rwanda. But we do not see these victims in photographs and films day after day, year after year. These other victims of war have no multimillion-dollar memorial among the monuments of Washington, D.C., no political lobby, no Hollywood promoters. To remember them doesn't suit the agenda of those who decide such things.

During the coming century, as communications flow with greater ease and rapidity, more people will challenge the premises and allegations of the Holocaust story. The errors and falsehoods will fall before vigorous cross-examination and intellectual challenge. And each day, as the story becomes a little less factually tenable and a bit more tattered and weakened, the truth will grow stronger. When it is finally free to be heard, the truth will prevail. When that day arrives, truth will not need terror or suppression to protect it.

I cannot say with certainty that the Holocaust did not occur just as the leading "exterminationists" allege. They may be right and the revisionists wrong, but certainly there is now enough contrary and reasonable evidence to open inquiry and debate on some parts of the Holocaust story.

We cannot know the truth until opinion and inquiry into the Holocaust is free. There may be many of the most respected historians who harbor doubts about aspects of the Holocaust story. But they know what would happen to them if they spoke openly about it. They don't want the David Irving treatment.

After reading and questioning aspects of the Holocaust story, I came to realize that those who challenged parts of it were no more lunatics than those who disputed the establishment's version of the Kennedy lone assassin theory. The difference is that there is little political, economic, social, or religious repercussion to refuting the Warren Commission findings. To simply ask pertinent questions about some aspects of the Holocaust story will bring upon oneself the unbridled wrath of those who dominate the media and who support Israel. I have already paid dearly for my apostasy, and this book will probably exact even a greater cost. In America, if one dares to privately publish and hire halls to discuss the issue, it could result in the loss of one's livelihood, and even physical endangerment. In Canada and Europe it has meant revocation of university degrees and loss of employment, judgeships, pensions, businesses, and, in addition to all that, imprisonment and physical attacks.

As I write these words, news has just come to me that the French nationalist leader Jean-Marie Le Pen has been convicted by a French court and fined thousands of dollars for simply saying in a conversation with a journalist that the gas chambers were a "footnote" of the Second World War.[864] Sir Winston Churchill, in his monumental six-volume *The Second World War*,[865] has not a mention of gas chambers. In fact, Churchill did not even give them a footnote. The same can be said for Eisenhower's *Crusade in Europe*.[866] Perhaps the Zionists can arrange for a posthumous trial for these two "Holocaust Deniers."

After Le Pen's comment, the European director of the Wiesenthal Center demanded the waiver of Le Pen's European Parliament's immunity to make him liable for prosecution and to make him ineligible to run for elective office.[867]

A society that does not allow free discussion, inquiry, and debate is not free. A government or media establishment that suppresses certain ideas fears those ideas, not because they are weak, but because they are powerful; not because those ideas are refutable, but because they are convincing. If we are to know the true story of the Holocaust, there must be freedom of inquiry, freedom to question, and freedom to doubt. If a historical viewpoint cannot withstand challenge, it is not true. Those who seek to suppress a potential challenger betray their own weakness. A "truth" that is afraid to be questioned fears itself false.

If there is one thing I have learned in my political life, it is to question. We must have free speech and press, free inquiry and discussion. Before we can know what is true or untrue, fact or fiction, we must hear both sides. This holds for every issue before us, including the historical event that produces such incredible passion: the Holocaust, spelled with a capital "H."

The Holocaust increasingly assumes the dimensions of a religion. It is a sort of death and redemption theme that takes on the image of an innocent people being slaughtered but rising in an aura of unassailable holiness. It finds its shrines in the refurbished concentration camps, its pilgrimages to them, its saints and sinners, and its temples, such as the Holocaust Museum in Washington, D.C. Anyone who questions even the slightest detail of it is a heretic who deserves scorn and derision at the least, but more suitably loss of livelihood and imprisonment. The writings of the blasphemers must be burned; if not that, then simply silently banned from our publishers and distributors. If the heretical works somehow, to some small degree, find their way to the public, they must be uncovered and extirpated from our bookstores and libraries.

The Holocaust legend lives on, fueling intense ethnic solidarity among Jews and suspicion and hatred toward Gentiles. Among Gentiles, the chronic replay of the Holocaust story destroys our most elementary defenses against Jewish supremacism.

Ironically, the biggest Holocaust born of ethnocentrism was the mass murder of tens of millions of Christians by the Jewish-led Bolsheviks in the Soviet Union and Eastern Europe. It seems so ironic to me that this chapter on the Holocaust deals so little with that horrible crime. As is prevalent in our age, things are defined as the Jews define them. The Holocaust remains the exclusive preserve of the Jewish victims of the Second World War. The Jewish Holocaust is sacredly held apart from all other loss of life. There are Jews and then there is all the rest of humanity — the small "g" gentiles of the world.

The Mother of All Holocausts

It would be far more appropriate to describe the entire Second World War as a Holocaust, than simply the sufferings of the Jews in it. The bombing and burning of Europe's most beautiful cities and artworks, the death of tens of millions of the bravest and fittest young men, and the ruthless uprooting, starvation, rape and murder of tens of millions of innocent civilians from all nations and ethnic groups of Europe — that was the greatest Holocaust the world has ever known. The civilized world will feel the cultural and genetic effects of the Second World War for many generations to come.

The British Prime Minister, Neville Chamberlain, said it succinctly when he said that the German-Polish border dispute wasn't worth the blood of one English grenadier. All of those born during and since the conflict grew up with the catechism of parents and press about what is called the "good war." If the death of 50 million human beings is a good war, then what exactly is a bad one? Naturally, the same forces that have publicized the Holocaust have told us of the necessity of the war, and the Nuremberg Tribunals decreed the ultimate war guilt of the Germans. Seeking to end the 20-year Polish subjugation of eastern German territory, Germany invaded Poland. At that point, it was a border war, with minimal loss of life and little bombing of cities or civilians. The war widened as France and England declared war on Germany, and soon it was a World War, ultimately the greatest human carnage in history.

In every nation there were those who wanted war. There were Germans looking to the east for Lebensraum; Poles, who would rather have war than give back their German territory. Among the French, there were those insanely jealous of their German rivals; and among the British, those who were fearful of the economic, political, and military power of a united Europe. All those forces created the Holocaust of the Second World War.

And, by all means, we must not forget one other group that bears a heavy responsibility for this Holocaust: the worldwide forces of organized Jewry. In 1933, the World Jewish Congress proclaimed war on Germany.[868] For six years, in every nation of the West, they exacerbated every national grievance and paranoia. They ran inflammatory articles about Germany in the Jewish Press. They used their great financial power. They used their powerful political and media influence to agitate for war and feed the fires of hate, a fire still stoked by the media 55 years after the fact.

We Americans, along with British, Germans, French, Poles, Russians, Italians, and others slaughtered millions of European women and children, killed and maimed our young men, and burned our most sacred works of beauty in the European cradle of our kind. When I was very young, I developed a feeling of guilt for slavery and Jim Crow. I shed that guilt as I came to realize that our race has given far more to the people of the Earth than it has taken. As I came to understand the realities of the Second World War, feelings of guilt came upon me again, but this time, not for what my race has done to others, but for what we have done to ourselves. Ultimately, we have no one to blame for that carnage more than ourselves.

The Second World War was perhaps the most destructive and devastating occurrence in the long history of European mankind. Communism raped half of Europe and was propelled across the planet, killing and enslaving millions more before it expired. With their victory, Jewish supremacists consolidated their power, with the result that the 20th century closes with Zionist hegemony in the highest echelons of media and political power. The White world has dissolved its empires and now finds its own shores invaded by the Third World to the point that even the homelands of our people are now threatened with demographic and genetic catastrophe. An ancient hatred is now being settled by the people who "never forget and never forgive."

And today, although our Jewish antagonists appear on the threshold of complete victory as they busily lay the foundations for their New World Order, it is still not their power that condemns us. It is our own weakness. Our Achilles' heel has always been our naiveté. If we learn the truth of the Holocaust, such naiveté will end, and we may yet avert the plans for the eradication of European mankind.

We men and women of the West must not sacrifice our birthright upon the altar of the Holocaust.

Chapter 24:

The Jewish Led Alien Invasion

Give me your tired, your huddled masses,
Yearning to breathe free.
The wretched refuse of your teeming shore.
— Emma Lazarus

The influx of Europeans into North America led the Indian populations to displacement and eventually to consignment on reservations. Similarly, relentless Jewish immigration into Palestine was against the interests of the Palestinian people, but it was necessary for the Jewish takeover of the region. It laid the foundation for the Zionist State.

Any tribe, race or nation desiring to preserve its culture, group interests and sovereignty must preserve its predominant status in the geographic region in which it dwells. Most nations have had a fundamental understanding of that fact from the time of the earliest civilizations, and every modern nation has sought strict control of its borders and immigration.

Most Americans view the Indian historical record of resistance to European colonization as morally justifiable, but in the skewed ethics of today, some find European-American attempts to preserve our unique genes and culture from non-European immigration — morally reprehensible. Nevertheless, despite pervasive propaganda promoting multiculturalism and the media-touted joys of diversity, opinion surveys in America show overwhelming opposition to unrestricted immigration. Similar public sentiment holds true in every European nation.

It was not until the 1965 Immigration Act that the U.S. Congress ignored the majority's wishes and began a policy that discriminated against potential European immigrants, and encouraged massive non-European immigration. From that time forward, the federal government also showed less willingness to enforce our immigration laws and police our borders. These policies resulted in a flood of non-White immigrants, legal and illegal. Immigration and higher non-White birthrates have transformed the American population from almost 90 percent European in the early '60s to a projected less than 70 percent at the turn of the millennium. The U.S. Census Bureau has predicted that by the middle of the 21st century, well within the lifetime of many reading these words, European Americans will be a minority in the United States. We are already a minority in most of America's major cities and will soon be one in California and Texas.

Policies similar to those enacted in the U.S. have introduced large numbers of non-Europeans into Canada; Negroes into Britain; North Africans and Asians into France; Turks in Germany; and a potpourri of alien races into Scandinavia, Spain, and Italy.

As I grew racially aware, it was certainly obvious to me that the new immigration policies of the United States and Europe would greatly damage our societies. Only a short time after the change in immigration policy, crime problems escalated in all the affected nations. The quality of education suffered and social welfare problems increased. As this planned racial transformation accelerates, these ills will reach catastrophic proportions.

What groups had anything to gain from this demographic Armageddon? The individual foreigners who could benefit from the economic opportunities afforded by the Western societies had little political or economic clout inside the Western nations. As I looked into the American fight over immigration laws during the last 100 years, the driving force behind opening America's borders became evident: It was organized Jewry, personified by the poet Emma Lazarus whose lines I quoted to begin the chapter.

By the time I was a junior in high school, I had become convinced that massive non-European immigration poised the greatest short- and long-term threat to the America that I loved. I saw that the Immigration Act of 1965, unless repealed, would eventually ring the death knell for my country. Much of the material I read pointed to a long history of organized Jewish efforts to change America's immigration laws. I contacted Drew Smith, an elderly New Orleans attorney who had written the book *The Legacy of the Melting Pot,* and who had already taught me a lot about the immigration issue.[869]

Smith and I met one rainy day after school at the Citizens Council offices. He explained the history of American immigration law. After quoting the Lazarus lines from the base of the Statue of Liberty, he asked me, "Whose interest could have been served to have America flooded with 'wretched refuse'?" He quickly answered his own question. "It was in the perceived interest of a cohesive people who use racial solidarity like a weapon, a weapon they want only for themselves. The efforts to change the American immigration law and ultimately displace the European majority has been led almost exclusively by Jews."

Smith explained that Emma Lazarus — like many other immigration activists — was a Jewish partisan who supported the creation of an exclusively Jewish Zionist state in Palestine, but who supported "diversity" for America. He pointed out to me how Jews such as Lazarus have even changed the modern meaning of the Statue of Liberty. The beautiful jade-colored colossus had no original connection with immigration and predated the Ellis Island immigration center. It was a gift from France to commemorate the American Revolution, not to honor the arrival of "wretched refuse" on America's shores.

Emma Lazarus had been best known for her fulminations against Russia's pogroms following the assassination of Czar Alexander II in 1881. The irony is rich: A woman dedicated to the foundation of an elite Jewish State in Palestine was anxious to make America into a refuge for the castoffs of the world. Drew Smith had many books on the immigration issue, including some by Jews where he had underlined important passages. I borrowed them and passionately delved into them.

Jewish organizations such as the American Jewish Congress led (and still lead) the effort to open American immigration and stop restrictionist legislation. In 1921, 1924, and 1952, Congress passed legislation that simply attempted to maintain the racial status quo in America. Interestingly enough, even though Anglo Americans were in a vast majority of the American population as well as in Congress, they did not attempt to increase their own percentage of the American population, but simply sought to fairly maintain each group's percentages. In the early legislative battles, Jews were the leading advocates of open immigration and vehemently opposed legislation that would maintain the status quo of America as an ethnically European, Christian nation. In the House of Representatives, Adolph Sabath, Samuel Dickstein, and Emanuel Celler led the fight for unrestricted immigration, while in the Senate, Herbert Lehman and in later years Jacob Javits coordinated the effort.

In the early struggles, Representative Leavitt clearly outlined the Jewish involvement in remarks before Congress.

> **The instinct for national and race preservation is not one to be condemned. . . . No one should be better able to understand the desire of Americans to keep America American than the gentleman from Illinois [Mr. Sabath], who is leading the attack on this measure, or the gentlemen from New York, Mr. Dickstein, Mr. Jacobstein, Mr. Celler, and Mr. Perlman.**
>
> **They are of the one great historic people who have maintained the identity of their race throughout the centuries because they believe sincerely that they are a chosen people, with certain ideals to maintain, and knowing that the loss of racial identity means a change of ideals. That fact should make it easy for them and the majority of the most active opponents of this measure in the spoken debate to recognize and sympathize with our viewpoint, which is not so extreme as that of their own race, but only demands that the admixture of other peoples shall be only of such kind and proportions and in such quantities as will not alter racial characteristics more rapidly than there can be assimilation as to**

ideas of government as well as of blood. (*Congressional Record*, April 12, 1924.) [870]

Sociologist Edward A. Ross, in his influential 1914 book *The Old World and the New: The Significance of Past and Present Immigration to the American People*, quotes the famous pro-immigration leader Israel Zangwill as suggesting that America is an ideal place to achieve Jewish interests. Ross then bluntly writes about the Jewish influence.

Jews therefore have a powerful interest in immigration policy: Hence the endeavor of the Jews to control the immigration policy of the United States. Although theirs is but a seventh of our net immigration, they led the fight on the Immigration Commission's bill. . . . The systematic campaign in newspapers and magazines to break down all arguments for restriction and to calm nativist fears is waged by and for one race. Hebrew money is behind the National Liberal Immigration League and its numerous publications. [871]

In 1924 Congressman Knud Wefald pointed out the Communist ties of many of the Jewish immigrants and stated that many Jews "have no sympathy with our old-time American ideals."

The leadership of our intellectual life in many of its phases has come into the hands of these clever newcomers who have no sympathy with our old-time American ideals . . . who detect our weaknesses and pander to them and get wealthy through the disservices they render us.

Our whole system of amusements has been taken over by men who came here on the crest of the south and east European immigration. They produce our horrible film stories [and] they write many of the books we read, and edit our magazines and newspapers. (*Congressional Record*, April 12, 1924. [872]

The last important congressional legislation passed to protect the status quo of America was the Walter-McCarran act of 1952. Congressional opposition was led by the Jewish troika of Celler, Javits, and Lehman. Every major Jewish organization (as well as the Communist Party USA) also lined up to oppose it, including the American Jewish Congress, American Jewish Committee, the ADL, National Council of Jewish Women, and dozens of others. During congressional debate, Francis Walter noted that the only civic organization that opposed the entire bill was the American Jewish Congress. Representative Celler noted that Walter "should not have overemphasized as he did the people of one particular faith who are opposing the bills." (*Congressional Record*, April 23, 1952.) [873]

When Jewish Judge Simon Rifkind testified against the bill in joint hearings, he emphasized that in supporting breaking down U.S. immigration law, he represented "the entire body of religious and lay opinion within the Jewish group, religiously speaking, from the extreme right and extreme left."[874]

It thrilled me to read the courageous remarks of Mississippi Congressman John Rankin during the debate. Today such truthful comments by any elected official would bring a torrent of abuse that few could withstand.

> **They whine about discrimination. Do you know who is being discriminated against? The white Christian people of America, the ones who created this nation. . . . I am talking about the white Christian people of the North as well as the South. . . .**
>
> **Communism is racial. A racial minority seized control in Russia and in all her satellite countries, such as Poland, Czechoslovakia, and many other countries I could name.**
>
> **They have been run out of practically every country in Europe in the years gone by, and if they keep stirring race trouble in this country and trying to force their Communistic program on the Christian people of America, there is no telling what will happen to them here. (*Congressional Record*, April 23, 1952.)** [875]

Finally, in 1965, the goal first advanced by Jewish organizations in the 1880s came to fruition when Congress passed the Immigration Act. It has resulted in immigration becoming 90 percent non-European. America went from an immigration program meant to be proportionately representative to all groups in the United States to one that discriminated against Europeans. As with earlier legislation, Jewish representatives and senators as well as powerful Jewish lobbying organizations led the assault. It succeeded because during the 41 years since 1924, Jewish power had increased dramatically in almost all spheres of American life.

In 1951 Senator Jacob Javits authored an article called "Lets Open Our Gates."[876] that called for massive unrestricted immigration. Javits and Representative Celler figured prominently in the passage of the bill in 1965. Nine years before passage of the 1965 Immigration Act, the American Jewish Congress initially proposed the essential elements of the bill and praised President Eisenhower for his "unequivocal opposition to the national quota system." In a 1956 editorial they praised him for "courageously taking a stand in advance of even many advocates of liberal immigration policy and embraced a position which had at first been urged by the American Jewish Congress and other Jewish agencies."[877]

Jewish Motivation Behind Immigration

It would have been stupid and counterproductive for the Jewish organizations that pushed for open borders to admit that they were motivated by interests that conflicted with those of non-Jewish Europeans. They had to promote open immigration as patriotic. From the early days of the century, they make public pronouncements that multiculturalism and diversity would be beneficial to the United States.

After the passage of the open immigration statutes of 1965, Jewish authors such as Naomi W. Cohen felt much safer in revealing some of the real Jewish reasons for promoting such policies. She wrote that, beginning with the persecutions in Russia in the 1880s through the Nazi occupation of Europe and into the Cold War conditions in Eastern Europe, open immigration in Western nations served Jewish interests because "survival often dictated that Jews seek refuge in other lands."[878] Cohen also wrote that a U.S. internationalist foreign policy serves Jewish interests because "an internationally minded America was likely to be more sensitive to the problems of foreign Jewries"[879] Perhaps even more important, Cohen intimated that Jews saw open immigration policies as breaking down the homogeneity and unity of America, creating a pluralistic society in which Jews could thrive.

In his monumental book *A History of Jews in America*, Howard Sachar notes that pluralism supports "legitimizing the preservation of a minority culture in the midst of a majority's host society."[880] So, in effect, by breaking down the integrity and cohesion of America, Jews could increase their integrity and cohesion. Sachar goes on to explicitly show how pluralism intensifies Jewish solidarity:

> **But Kallen's influence extended really to all educated Jews: Legitimizing the preservation of a minority culture in the midst of a majority's host society, pluralism functioned as intellectual anchorage for an educated Jewish second generation, sustained its cohesiveness and its most tenacious communal endeavors through the rigors of the Depression and revived anti-Semitism, through the shock of Nazism and the Holocaust, until the emergence of Zionism in the post-World War II years swept through American Jewry with a climactic redemptionist fervor of its own.** [881]

Social psychologist Kevin MacDonald pointed out in *A People That Shall Dwell Alone* that major anti-Semitic movements are usually found in ethnically homogeneous nations and that "ethnic and religious pluralism serves external Jewish interests because Jews become just one of many ethnic groups. . .and it becomes difficult or impossible to develop unified, cohesive groups of Gentiles united in their opposition of Judaism." [882] [883]

In his 1985 book *A Certain People: American Jews and Their Lives Today*, Charles Silberman writes that

> **American Jews are committed to cultural tolerance because of their belief, one firmly rooted in history, that Jews are safe only in a society acceptant of a wide range of attitudes and behaviors, as well as a diversity of religious and ethnic groups. It is this belief, for example, not approval of homosexuality, that leads an overwhelming majority of American Jews to endorse "gay rights" and to take a liberal stance on most other so-called "social issues."** [884]

John Higham, in his book *Send These to Me: Immigrants in Urban America*, states in clear terms that Jewish-sponsored changes in

446 My Awakening

immigration law were a defeat of the political and cultural representation of "the common people of the South and West."[885]

During the decades leading up to opening the borders in 1965, Jewish groups had piously stated that there should be no discrimination against any group in immigration and that such policy would be good for America. Richard Arens, staff director of the Senate subcommittee that produced the Walter-McCarran Act, points out that Jewish forces who themselves endorsed open immigration more than any other group, opposed ethnic immigration they deemed clearly dangerous to their own interests.

> **One of the curious things about those who most loudly claim that the 1952 act is "discriminatory" and that it does not make allowance for a sufficient number of alleged refugees, is that they oppose admission of any of the approximately one million Arab refugees in camps where they are living in pitiful circumstances after having been driven out of Israel.** [886]

Apparently organized Jewry not only wants to exclude Arab refugees from returning to their homes in Israel, they oppose them coming to the United States as well. Could it be that they see the displaced Palestinians as potential political opponents? They promoted only forms of multiculturalism that would destroy Gentile cohesion while not threatening their own group power.

Jewish-dominated political and media influences have long promoted the demographic invasion and dissolution of America. While the Jewish media demonize as "racists" those who oppose non-White immigration in America, in Canada and all the European nations, nary a word of criticism is evoked for Israel's immigration policy that excludes non-Jews. In Israel a million Arabs fled their homes in the wake of the Israeli blitzkrieg takeover of Palestine. Palestinians cannot return to the homeland of their forefathers. Many are forced to live in refugee camps that are little more than concentration camps of want and squalor.

A. M. Rosenthal has for decades been an editor on the staff of the most influential newspaper in America, the long-time Jewish-owned *New York Times*. An hawkish supporter of Israel, his only complaints about the Zionist state occur when it is not Zionist enough for his taste. In a 1992 *The New York Times* editorial, Rosenthal pronounced the following concerning Germany's immigration policy:

> **They would do better to set a quota on immigrants and nurture a more pluralist society by adopting a formula for citizenship based on residence than blood ties.**
>
> **Equally distressing is Bonn's failure to revise an outdated naturalization law rooted in ethnicity. Under the existing system, a Turkish guest worker who has lived in Germany for 30 years and speaks German fluently is denied the citizenship automatically granted a Russian-speaking immigrant who can prove German ancestry.**[887]

Rosenthal goes on to compare current German immigration policies to that of the Nazis. Yet, is Israeli immigration law really any different?

Not only Germany, but every White nation is a target of Rosenthal's immigration advocacy. Only Israel's immigration policy — the most draconian of all — is immune from criticism. In America, Rosenthal identifies himself as the offspring of an illegal immigrant (his father) and even touts the immigration of Haitians (who are often drug using and HIV-positive).

> **Almost always now, when I read about Haitians who risk the seas to get to this country but wind up behind barbed wire, I think of an illegal immigrant I happen to know myself, and of his daughters and his son [himself]....**
>
> **Even reluctantly recognizing some economic limitations, this country should have the moral elegance to accept neighbors who flee countries where their life is terror and hunger, and are run by murderous gangs....**
>
> **If that were a qualification for entry into our Golden land, the Haitians should be welcomed with song, embrace and memories.**[888]

As a chronic reader of *The New York Times*, I have yet to read a Rosenthal editorial calling for the entry into Israel of the million or more Palestinians who live in the hunger of the refugee camps. Nor, unless I have overlooked it, has Rosenthal called upon Jews to welcome Palestinians into Israel with "song and embrace." Rosenthal is not stupid, but he is hypocritical and diabolical. He knows that making full citizens of all the Palestinians currently in Israel and all those in refugee camps outside of its borders would rapidly sweep away the Zionist political state in the same way that non-White immigration erodes the America of our forefathers. When it comes to America, Rosenthal proudly identifies himself with the aliens.

Rosenthal knows what he and many other Jews are: aliens as much as the wetbacks with whom he identifies. He lives here, partaking of all the advantages of American citizenship, but he will not — and cannot — become a real American.

As the Jews become more brazen in their exercise of power, some now boast of their role in dispossessing the European-Gentile American. Earl Raab, executive director emeritus of the Perlmutter Institute of Jewish Advocacy, an associate of the ADL (Anti-Defamation League of B'nai B'rith) and writer for the San Francisco *Jewish Bulletin*, wrote:

> **It was only after World War II that immigration law was drastically changed to eliminate such discrimination. In one of the first pieces of evidence of its political coming-of-age, the Jewish community has a leadership role in effecting those changes.**[889]

Raab goes on to celebrate the coming minority status of Whites in America. Once that has happened, he looks forward to "constitutional constraints" (restriction of freedom of speech?):

> **The Census Bureau has just reported that about half of the American population will soon be non-white or non-European. And they will all be American citizens. We have tipped beyond the point where a Nazi-Aryan party will be able to prevail in this country.**
>
> **We have been nourishing the American climate of opposition to ethnic bigotry for about half a century. That climate has not yet been perfected, but the heterogeneous nature of our population tends to make it irreversible and makes our constitutional constraints against bigotry more practical than ever.** [890]

As Raab says, Zionist Jewish activists who have supported an exclusively Jewish-run national state have been nourishing massive nontraditional immigration into America , and they look forward to the time when the voting demographics of the United States reflect that transformation.

I wonder if Zionist Israel Zangwill — who coined the term "melting pot" — envisioned his Jewish state as a melting pot of Jew and Arab, of Islam and Judaism? Given the ethnocentrism of Zionism, such a question goes beyond absurdity. One American cartoonist wrote that the problem with a melting pot is that "The bottom always gets burned, and the scum rises to the top." It is true that America has seen a melting of the different nationalities of Europe into the traditional American framework, but in spite of the pervasive race-mixing propaganda of the Jewish media, there has been no great melting of the White and Black, and only marginal melting of the fringes of the Mestizo and Anglo. But what these Zionists have not yet been able to accomplish through their advocacy of racial-mixing, they are achieving through massive immigration and differential birthrates.

Jews have also promoted, through "zero-population" advocates such as Paul Ehrlich, smaller families among the natural leaders of the American majority. Their promotion of the women's liberation movement and abortion on demand has lowered the birthrate of America's most intelligent and educated classes. Their blunt desire is the dissolution of the White race in the West by any means necessary. Continued massive non-European immigration satisfies these aims.

Massive non-White immigration has been an effective weapon of organized Jewry in its cultural and ethnic war against the European American. We cannot win this war until our people realize that we are embroiled in an ethnic war — and our side is suffering great losses. To lose this war would mean the destruction of our American culture, heritage, and freedoms. It would mean nothing less than the destruction of the very genes that make it all possible. We are quietly witnessing the genocide of our people. The time is late. We must speak out now and defend ourselves and the futures of our children or be forever silenced.

Chapter 25:

Jewish Evolutionary Strategy and Claims of Jewish Superiority

In the early 1970s, a period of rampant egalitarianism, I read the *Geography of Intellect*[891] by Jewish partisans Nathaniel Weyl and Stephan Possony, and also a popular book called *The Jewish Mystique* [892] by Ernest Van Den Haag. They claimed outright that Jews were genetically, culturally, and morally superior. They said brazenly what the mainstream Jewish histories had implied. In 1969 popular British scientist-turned-novelist C. P. Snow gave a speech to Hebrew Union College in which he claimed that because of "inbreeding" Jews were "superior to all other living peoples." [893]

In explaining Jewish success, some Jewish authors suggested that the structure of Judaism had a positive genetic effect on intelligence. Assertions of Jewish genetic superiority had a warm reception by the same media that caustically condemned as immoral and evil what they called "the theory of Caucasian genetic superiority."

Weyl argued persuasively that Jewish traditions had a eugenic effect, citing the fact that the most successful Jewish scholars and thus the most intelligent in the Jewish community, the rabbis, were supported by their fellow Jews in having the largest families. He compared the high rabbinic birthrate to the celibacy of the Catholic clergy, which he felt had a dysgenic effect among Gentiles.

I could certainly see how such reproductive patterns would be beneficial to Jewish intelligence, and I was certainly willing to acknowledge that Jews are intelligent. What struck me then was Weyl's thesis that Jewish social patterns and practices could affect their intelligence. I had long believed that both intelligence and behavioral tendencies have an important genetic component, but for the first time I began to think seriously about the underlying differences between Jews and Gentiles. Were they cultural-religious or genetic in origin? To get to the bottom of it, I looked at applications of evolutionary biology to the development of the Jewish people.

Charles Darwin's *The Origin of Species*[894] dealt with the effects of natural selection on the individual level, but even more importantly, on the selection process involving species and subspecies (races). He studied the origin of groups of genetically related individuals and studied their fitness to survive in their respective environments. The subtitle of his masterpiece reads, *Or the Preservation of Favoured Races in the Struggle for Life.*

Few understood the mechanism of group selection in regard to human evolution. Perhaps the best early stab at it was Sir Arthur Keith's dynamic 1948 book *A New Theory of Human Evolution*.[895] Keith explained that just as individuals were subject to evolutionary pressures, so were competing groups. Beginning in the early '60s, researcher W. D. Hamilton and others began the modern inquiries into the genetic basis of social behavior, now referred to as sociobiology.[896]

The principles of sociobiology, first propounded by G. C. Williams in the 1960s, became scientifically embedded in the principals of behavioral genetics and in the landmark work of Dr. Edward Wilson in his seminal *Sociobiology: A New Synthesis*.[897] I read Wilson's book just a few months after it came out and found it magnificent. Although Wilson deftly sidestepped the application of his theories to the human races, he offered powerful evidence that behavior in the most elementary creatures such as ants and ranging to the complexities of mankind itself had a biological basis driven by the urge to preserve the genotype. Genetic kinship turned out to be a powerful factor in evolution and behavior. In such a context, group loyalty and altruism become understandable from an evolutionary perspective in that the individual may sacrifice his life and his individual reproduction to ensure the survival of those who are genetically similar to him.

Richard Alexander, J. Phillippe Rushton, D. S. Wilson, Kevin MacDonald, Edward Wilson, Edward Miller, and many others over the next two decades pushed the envelope further, showing that human groups differing in their genetic makeup experience similar social pressures to those experienced by competing animal species or subspecies. The new scientific discipline called behavioral genetics continues to break new ground, showing the intimate relation of heredity to human behavior on both the individual and the group level.

The insights of sociobiology and behavioral genetics greatly increased our understanding the development of racial differences. It is easy to understand the evolutionary impact of the harsh northern climate on more than 5,000 generations of Europeans and the effects of the milder climate of Africa on the Black race. It makes sense that the social taboos, customs and social organization of human beings since the beginnings of civilization can also have a dramatic impact on reproductive patterns and genetic makeup.

Since the relatively recent domestication of the dog, mankind has produced, through selective breeding, hundreds of breeds that differ as much as the St. Bernard, the hairless Chihuahua, the German Shepherd, and the Pug. All come from one original species, and all are capable of interbreeding. Here is how *Grolier's Encyclopedia* characterizes the varieties of dog and how selective breeding has affected both appearance and temperament:

> **Dogs vary more in outward appearance than in anatomical structure. An adult dog may weigh 2 to 99 kg (4 to 220 lb.), depending on the breed, and range in height from 12.5 to 90 cm (5 to 35 in.) at the shoulder. Other differences in conformation include length of leg; length of muzzle; size and attitude of ears; length, shape, and carriage of tail; and length, density, color, and character of hair. Over time, the various breeds were also selectively bred to produce temperaments suited to the tasks they performed.**[898]

The same way that people could selectively breed genetically different breeds of dogs, certain social structures and policies can affect human evolution. Social structures, especially those that influenced marriage patterns, could have a dramatic impact on survival and reproduction rates. They could certainly affect human temperament and behavior in the same way that dog breeders have created breeds as stoic as the St. Bernard or as hyperactive as the Pekinese. We all know people who are naturally as aggressive as a Pit Bull, or as friendly as a Labrador Retriever.

Is the Jewish behavioral pattern a product of cultural institutions such as Judaism and its secular offspring, Zionism, or is there something in their genotype that inclined them to the consistent behaviors that they have exhibited across greatly differing cultures over three millennia? I wondered how the structure and nature of Judaism across the centuries affected the genetic characteristics of the Jewish people.

Just as two species of animals occupying a particular geographic area naturally develop a group evolutionary strategy to compete for resources, so human groups can do the same — even in the civilized societies. They can develop certain behavioral traits that give them competitive advantage and greater reproductive success. In human societies, when genetically distinct groups interact, they can assimilate and lose their genetic distinction, or they can develop ethnocentric ideologies and behavior that favor the distinct characteristics of their own gene pool. An ethnocentric group could even develop a religion that rationalizes its evolutionary response to other groups.

I wondered if the Jews had become genetically distanced from the other peoples of Europe and, if so, how deep the divide was. Had their supremacist and ethnocentric tendencies become ingrained in their genetic code, or were they simply a result of the cultural attitude of their religion and the separate societies they created? Did genetic impulses create the ideology of Judaism that reinforced and intensified the Jewish genotype? Years later, in the 1990s, the same Jewish-dominated anthropology that rejected the importance of

European racial consciousness and sense of identity has reasserted Jewishness and the "Jewish identity." In "Jews, Multiculturalism, and Boasian Anthropology," in *The American Anthropologist*, Jewish writer Gelya Frank celebrates American Boasian antiracist anthropology as "Jewish history." [899] She points out that the central Jewish role was intentionally whitewashed for fear that Gentiles would realize that Jews had a radical agenda.

> **There has always been a lively, if sometimes hushed, in-house discourse about American anthropology's Jewish origins and their meaning. The preponderance of Jewish intellectuals in the early years of Boasian Anthropology and the Jewish identities of anthropologists in subsequent generations have been downplayed in standard histories of the discipline...**
>
> **This essay brings together strands of these various discourses on Jews in anthropology for a new generation of American anthropologists, especially ones concerned with turning multiculturalist theories into agendas for activism....**
>
> **There has also been a whitewashing of Jewish ethnicity, reflecting fears of anti-Semitic reactions that could discredit the discipline of anthropology and individual anthropologists, either because Jews were considered dangerous due to their presumed racial differences or because they were associated with radical causes. –Gelya Frank**

Now, with the political and cultural victory of racial pluralism over European solidarity, Frank discloses that Jewish anthropologists are reasserting their Jewish ethnicity and group identity.

> **Any number of scholars are reasserting Jewishness in the academy, simultaneously attempting to discover and define what Jewish identity can mean in that most universalist of institutions. Some relevant examples from the long and growing list of sources, in addition to several already cited, include: Behar 1996; Boyarian 1992, 1996; Eilberg-Schwartz 1990, 1992, 1994; H. Goldberg 1987, 1995; Kleebatt 1996; Nochilin and Garb 1995; Prell 1989, 1990, 1996; Robin-Dorsky and Fisher Fishkin 1996; and Schneider 1995.**
>
> **The reappearance of Jewish difference(s) raises the stakes for Jewish anthropologists engaged in multiculturalist discourses.**[900]

The article floored me. The same Jewish-driven anthropology establishment that tells Europeans there is really no such thing as race and that racial identity is silly at best and a moral evil at worst, quietly promotes Jewish "differences" and " genetic identity." Frank's article goes on with unrestrained praise of the Jewish pride in the writing of Barbara Meyerhoff in *Number Our Days*.[901]

When I first looked into the issue of Jewish genetic relatedness, I did not have the benefit of Frank's article. At that time, I thought that the best way to investigate the issue was to see how similar the geographically separated Jewish populations are to each other and to the Gentile populations among whom they live. Do Jews differ from the other Europeans the same way that, say, an Englishman differs from a Frenchman or a German from a Russian? Or are they altogether different from all European subraces?

Substantial work had been done on the issue, much of it from Jewish researchers who were busily studying their own people's genetic makeup. Over the years, they enlightened me on this subject in much the same way that I had gained an interesting perspective on Jewish history from Jewish chroniclers.

The first thing I found was information on the set of genetically borne diseases that occur almost exclusively in the Jewish community, such as Tay-Sachs disease. Their presence certainly indicated a genetic variance specific to the Jewish population and illustrated a genetic difference from the Gentiles. Soon I found scientific papers dealing precisely with the issues I sought. [902] [903]

Genetic researchers Sachs and Bat-Miriam discovered amazing similarity between the Jewish populations of nine countries of North Africa, the Middle East, and Central Europe. Conversely, they found sharp differences between Jews and non-Jews from those same countries. [904]

In studying blood group data, Mourant, Kopec, and Domaniewska-Sobczak wrote in a book called *The Genetics of the Jews* that

> it may be said that, in general, blood group data…support the relative homogeneity of the main historical Jewish communities.[905]

Now, *get this*, their mainstream Jewish anthropologists and geneticists, the same group who chronically preach to us that there are no great differences between Blacks and Whites, boldly assert that the Jewish people are genetically homogenous! Their assessment is that although there are some differences between the Ashkenazim and the Sephardim (the two main ethnic divisions among Jews), essentially Jews are a single people who have little genetic resemblance to the European populations among whom they dwell. [906]

- In blood group data, two major studies, one in 1977 by Bonné-Tamir, Ashbel, and Kenett and one by Karlin, Kenett, and Bonné-Tamir in 1979, found when using fourteen polymorphic loci, no significant difference in Jewish populations from Iraq, Libya, Germany, or Poland. They estimated that the genetic distance between Gentiles and Jews living in the same area is three to five times greater than for Jews living in the different nations studied. In the 1977 study, the researchers state "not much admixture has taken place between Ashkenazi Jews and their Gentile neighbors during the last 700 years or so." [907] [908]

- Mille and Kobyliansky discovered in studies of dermatoglyphic data that Ashkenazim (Eastern European Jews) are much more similar to Shephardim (Middle-Eastern and European Jews) than they are to the non-Jewish Eastern Europeans. [909]

JEWISH EVOLUTIONARY STRATEGY 455

- **Kobyliansky and Livshits in using cluster analysis on 25 morphological characteristics, estimated that Jews in Russia were six times more distant from Russians than Russians were from Germans. They also found the Jews to be completely separate from the twenty-four other ethnic groups studied in Russia, Germany, and Poland.** [910]

- **Another study compared modern Jews and those of 3,000-year-old Jewish skeletons discovered in the Middle East. Sofaer, Smith, and Kaye studied dental morphology from Morocco, Kurdish Iraq, and Eastern European countries. They found more likeness between the widely scattered Jewish populations than for the Gentile groups living near them. The ancient Jewish skeletal group turned out to be far more similar to the three Jewish populations than for every non-Jewish group studied except for one, an Arab Druse group from the 11th century.** [911]

One researcher summed up the overall genetic differences by saying that there was probably at least three times more genetic difference between an average Jew in France and his Gentile Frenchman neighbor than between an average French Jew and a Jew living in Russia or the Middle East.

The Jewish studies amazed me. I would not have guessed that Jews were that genetically different from all Europeans. I knew a few Jews who were indistinguishable from the potpourri of other European-Americans. From their appearance, it seemed impossible that they were three times more different from us than from their fellows in remote regions of the world. The research proved that a wide genetic difference existed, but I wondered why their appearance did not seem all that radically different.

Fritz Lenz suggested back in the 1930s that Jewish resemblance to the European populations did not mean that their genes were similar.[912] He suggested that their similar external resemblance could have emerged from the natural selection of genes within the Jewish gene pool. These genes could simply be a small cluster of genes that lay dormant in the Jewish pool or that were introduced by limited genetic mixture with Gentiles, and which then were selectively favored by the social environment. Genes that caused a greater corporeal resemblance to that of the Gentile host could have favorable results in acceptance, wealth, and social advancement and thus on reproductive success. It is a similar process by which some distinct species of butterflies, not closely related, come to resemble one another without narrowing their genetic distance. Only a small set of genes influencing appearance within the Jewish population could thus be favored, causing a greater similarity of appearance to the Gentile population while not narrowing their overall genetic alienation from their host population. Over many generations the external resemblance to Gentiles could increase while the parts of the brain that affect behavioral tendencies and abilities could be unaffected.

According to evolutionary genetics, it is possible that Jews have come to more resemble their hosts in their external appearance while at the same time becoming even more distant in their mental and behavioral characteristics. Whatever the questions of physical appearance, there seemed little doubt that Jews are indeed very different from Europeans and that they had maintained that genetic difference for a very long time.

I also ran across a number of popular sources arguing that high Jewish-Gentile intermarriage would end that genetic distinctiveness from European Gentiles. As in so many other matters dealing with the Jews, there is a wealth of information on the issue indicating that the underlying reality is very different from popular perceptions.

Will Intermarriage End Jewish Ethnocentrism?

It is often said that the high rates of intermarriage between Jews and Gentiles, especially in the United States, will diminish ethnocentrism and cause assimilation of the Jewish population into the Gentile gene pool. The highly publicized and popularly promoted book *The Myth of the Jewish Race* by Ralph and Jennifer Patai makes that contention. They suggested that Jewish intermarriage has steadily increased since the Enlightenment. [913]

It is true that many Jewish groups and leaders have raised a great commotion about the dangers of intermarriage. Major Jewish publications often have articles and even ads decrying intermarriage and imploring Jews to marry only other Jews. Steve M. Cohen writes the following in *The Jewish Family: Myths and Reality*:

> **Vigorous effort by organized Jewry to try to halt or reverse recent demographic changes . . . to get large numbers of Jews to change their family-related decisions — that is, to marry young, marry each other, stay married, and have many children.** [914]

Pinches Stolper cites the Union of Orthodox Jewish Congregations of America promoting only strong pure Jewish marriages. In describing the threat of a beautiful Gentile girl living just a few houses away, he asserts:

> **Intermarriage is a tragedy the Jewish people cannot tolerate. The person who marries out of the faith has turned his or her back on the Jewish people. Our tradition regards such a person as spiritually dead, and the family sits *shiva* [observes a period of mourning] for him or her.**
>
> **Such marriages rarely work, even when accompanied by a so-called conversion to Judaism, and certainly can never work when the Jewish partner is seriously concerned with his or her Jewishness.**

For the families involved, the result is heartbreak and tragedy, and for the children, a life of frustration, conflict, and strain. [915]

David Landau shows that Jewish fundamentalism is rapidly increasing in the Diaspora. He quotes one of the opponents of a mild change in Reform law allowing tracing of genealogy through the father rather than the mother as "one of the most evil crimes, almost akin to Hitler. It destroyed the integrity of the Jewish People." [916]

Rising fundamentalism has also meant a rise in birthrates among the most committed Jews. In an essay in the book *The Jewish Family: Myths And Reality*, Cohen notes that through high birthrates and by "using insulating mechanisms, the Hasidim have achieved a high degree of success in offsetting the assimilative tendencies of the larger society." [917]

Therefore, it can be seen that organized Jewry has made a concerted effort to encourage endogamy among Jews. Orthodox groups are certainly the most extremely opposed to intermarriage, but even the newspapers and magazines published by Reform groups strongly discourage it. The Jewish researcher Ellman comments in the journal *Jewish Social Studies* that the only ethnic or religious community in the United States that continues to attempt to limit and discourage conversions and intermarriage is the organized Jewish community. But Ellman — along with a number of other authors who are strongly opposed to intermarriage — also believe that the seemingly high rates of intermarriage are no real threat to the Jewish heritage. He suggests that it strengthens the traditional Jewish culture and genotype by eliminating those Jews who have assimilationist tendencies. [918]

Ellman points out that intermarriage has little effect on the core of Judaism. He points out that intermarriage is far more frequent for second and subsequent marriages in which the couples are unlikely to have children. He also cites the much higher rates of divorce in intermarriage. More than 90 percent of intermarriages results in nonconversion and thus the intermarried do not become part of the Jewish community. Only a small percentage of children of intermarriage are raised as Jews, and more than 90 percent of them do not marry Jews. Ellman also reports that Jews of higher socioeconomic status are more likely to marry other Jews, thus the community will continue to be dominated by a pure Jewish elite core while lower-class Jews, who do not represent the desired traits of ethnic solidarity, are much more likely to marry outside and leave the community.

Barry Kosmin and other Jewish researchers, in *Highlights of the CJF 1990 National Jewish Population Survey*, found that 91 percent of intermarriages were made up of nonconversionary couples, that only 28 percent of the children of such couples were raised as Jews, and that even this small minority's descendants would not be likely to marry Jews. [919]

Not only are intermarried Jews far more prone to leave the Jewish circle, evidence suggests that they often encounter hostility in Jewish society. Jewish authors such as Michael Meyer [920] and C. Waxman [921] cite "tacit rejection" of the mixed couples. All these factors indicate that mixed marriages have little effect on the Jewish gene pool other than affecting the overall number of Jews.

Higher rates of intermarriage will probably have the long-term effect of strengthening traditional Jewish genetic characteristics. Jewish elements prone to assimilation are being removed while at the same time there is a resurgence in Jewish orthodoxy and high birthrate among the most committed of the Jewish elements such as the Hasidim. Additionally, religious Jews in Israel are almost all Orthodox, and there is almost no intermarriage in the world nexus of Jewry — the nation of Israel.

Perhaps the best way to describe the Jewish community is how the distinguished Jewish writer Daniel Elazar does in *Community and Polity: Organizational Dynamics in American Jewry*. [922] He proposes a model of concentric circles. The inner circle is a hard core of about 5 to 8 percent who lead what he calls "fully Jewish lives." Next are 10 to 12 percent of Jews whom he calls "participants." They are often employed in "Jewish civil service," working tirelessly for Jewish causes. Third, he identifies 25 to 30 percent of Jews whom he calls "contributors and consumers." These make regular contributions to Jewish causes and make use of the Jewish community for things such as weddings, bar mitzvahs, and funerals. Elazar calls his last group the "peripherals and repudiators." They make no contributions to Jewish causes, but sometimes the inner circles pull them in to participation or they are peeled off, leaving the Jewish core at the center and the whole of Jewry more committed than ever. [923]

Because of copious publicity of high rates of Jewish intermarriage, some Gentiles may come to believe that Jews are becoming less ethnocentric. But in reality the opposite is true. Those Jews left at the core are less disposed to assimilation. At the same time, the out-marrying Jews who are amenable to Gentile values also serve an important role in causing Gentiles to believe the Jewish group is more similar to them than it actually is.

More importantly, some Jewish researchers see a degree of intermarriage as having a functional value in Gentile environments. Mark Zborowski and Elizabeth Herzog say that it serves as a bridge to the Gentile community, but one that does not threaten the Jewish core.

The peripheral area which serves as a bridge to the surrounding cultures fills several functions. It is an avenue to invasion, a buffer

and a source of renewed vigor. Each impact that chips at the outer edge may serve simultaneously to strengthen the core. [924]

Lieberman and Weinfeld, in their article "Demographic Trends and Jewish Survival," view relatively high levels of intermarriage as a successful strategy in securing greater support from the Gentile community for their political and social goals such as political support for Israel.

> The successful exercise of influence is best achieved in a community with a large subset of members interacting with politicians and opinion leaders. Through intermarried Jews themselves, and certainly through their social networks involving Jewish family and friends who may be closer to the core of the community, Jewish concerns, interests, and sensibilities can be articulated before a wider, more influential audience. In a recent interview, Presidential aide Robert Lipshutz traced the origin of Jimmy Carter's concern for Israel to his close friendship with a first cousin, an Orthodox Jew (Carter's aunt married a Jewish man, and their two children were raised as Jews). Intermarrying Jews, while perhaps diluting the community in one sense, perform compensating strategic functions in another. [925]

Obviously, if intermarried Jews serve as a "bridge to the Gentile community," those who are outside of the Jewish community but are conscious of Jewish blood will often have warm feelings toward that heritage and be well disposed to Jewish interests. They will also express less solidarity with European issues and interests.

Far from solving the Jewish-Gentile conflict, intermarriage only tends to reinforce the core Jewish genotype and nurture more extreme political and cultural solidarity. By sending their allies into our culture and body politic, they are better able to secure Jewish interests. Among Gentiles intermarriage has the opposite effect. Because they are absorbed almost wholly into our society, our own solidarity is weakened while giving the appearance that the Jewish community is less impenetrable and ethnocentric. There is no real threat to the Jewish genotype; if anything it becomes more "Jewish" each generation.

Once I learned that Jews had a different genetic heritage than Europeans and that this difference was intensifying, I wanted to understand what that could mean in terms of Jewish behavior and evolutionary strategy.

A Historical Summary

This book has so far shown that Jewish history, from the earliest periods recorded in the Bible up to the present tribal jingoism of Israel, has been a long story of supremacism and ethnocentrism. Jews learned to thrive as a distinct minority in overwhelmingly non-Jewish nations, and they learned to preserve both their cultural and genetic heritage in the face of often intense pressures toward assimilation from the host societies. To avoid the process of assimilation that swallowed every other people living as a minority in ancient nations, they nurtured an ideology of intense inward group loyalty and love, and outward ethnocentrism and hatred.

Through their sojourn as a powerful minority in Egypt early in their history, they created a strategy of survival and racial purity. Later, in a region composed of many distinct peoples, they refined their ethnocentric policy and created a mythology that this policy was decreed by God. It is a strategy that finds its purest expression in Judaism, a this-worldly religion that promises dominion and power for the Jewish people rather than personal reward of an afterlife to deserving individuals.

To resist assimilation by the much larger societies in which they lived, Jews developed a theology that fostered the belief that they were a superior people "chosen by God" and made "separate from other peoples" with a divine-ordained right to rule the world, accompanied by a sacred obligation to keep both their culture and genotype pure. Non-Jews were characterized as unclean inferiors and even as murderous foes who were determined to destroy them either by extermination (as commemorated annually in Passover and Purim) or by assimilation (as commemorated in Hanukkah).

To survive as a minority in other nations — often as newcomers with little or no land and a religiously born disdain for physical labor, they needed to develop skills in other areas. They became proficient at usury, finance and administration, as well as legal and criminal forms of commercial enterprise. They discovered that with an altruistic team effort they could come to dominate important areas of Gentile social structure. It also became apparent that it was in their interest to maintain an ethnocentric team strategy and at the same time to weaken Gentile solidarity. They also developed complex strategies to hide their hostility from their Gentile hosts.

By the end of their Babylonian captivity, a period of hundreds of years during which they flourished as a powerful minority in an alien nation, their Judaic strategy had developed to a fine art that they codified in the Tanakh (Old Testament) and ultimately the Talmud.

Jews developed distinct cultural, dietary, and ritual traditions to keep them separate from Gentiles. Distinct from the other two major world religions, Judaism sought no converts and, although ostensibly permitting conversion, erected barriers making conversion difficult. The Jewish community did not fully accept converts or even their descendants. (Many rabbis in Jewish scripture say it takes ten generations or more in the Jewish community to be fully accepted, and Jewish law refers to offspring of the converted as "bastards.") The vast majority of Jews who out-married did so with nonconverted Gentiles, and thus were expelled from the Jewish community.

In other words he was deprived of civil and political rights to which every Israelite had claim, even those such as bastards who were of seriously blemished descent. [926]

As a cohesive minority in Gentile nations, Jews needed to hide their true ethnocentric beliefs. One aid to that process was their maintenance of the Hebrew language among their scholars and their limiting of translations of their texts into Gentile languages. (As mentioned elsewhere, in modern times they even developed code words to disguise the more hateful anti-Gentile quotations in their Talmud and rituals, even to the extent of publishing companion guides to the Talmud showing Jewish students the real anti-Gentile meaning of the disguised terms.)[927] Jews also learned to make themselves as politically cryptic as possible, often content to direct policies from behind the scenes so as not to awaken Gentile ire. In these endeavors they often failed to restrain their rapaciousness, leading to intemperate anti-Semitic reactions.

The Judaic community had historically emphasized education and highly praised Jewish scholarship of the Talmud, rewarding such scholarship with prestige and economic security. Such policies had a profound impact on their genotype. Just as favoring the best scholars favored those with high verbal IQs, so a number of other aspects of their social structure favored other traditional Jewish characteristics.

J. Philippe Rushton, in his groundbreaking 1995 book *Race, Evolution, and Behavior*,[928] has shown in studies of data dealing with twin research, that even tendencies toward group altruism and ethnocentrism have strong genetic components. Jewish law has for hundreds of generations expelled Jews who have assimilated with Gentiles, thus removing them from their gene pool. Such policies would certainly strengthen any Jewish predisposition to ethnocentrism by removing those who had a more conciliatory attitude or even attraction to Gentile aesthetics or values.

As the Jews became more proficient at usury, monopolistic business practices, tax farming, criminal enterprises and acting as oppressive intermediaries or the administrators of occupational governments, Gentile reactionary anti-Semitism reinforced the siege mentality of Jews. Their antipathy toward their Gentile hosts encouraged Jewish communities to support foreign military incursions and occupation of the nations in which they lived. Such actions in turn spawned greater animosity toward Jews, deepening the vicious cycle that continues to the present day.

Jews reacted to the threat of assimilation by becoming more ethnocentric. In sharp contrast, living in their mostly homogeneous communities in the heart of Europe, our ancestors never developed the siege mentality of the Jews. As trade, slavery and foreign immigration increased into Europe, at first they were ill prepared for the differences in populations and beliefs burgeoning within their borders. Gentile societies of the ancient world often permitted varied religious expression, including the allowance of the Jewish community and faith, whereas the Jewish people demanded strict adherence to their faith within the confines of their society.

The Jewish community has continued through the centuries as an authoritarian society that has continually and consciously promoted Jewish cohesion. Even through the Middle Ages, many Jewish communities exercised the death penalty for those Jews deemed to have betrayed Jewish interests. The execution of Jesus is a perfect example of the eradication of one who they felt was a threat to their homogeneity. Other historic tools used to maintain their ideological and genetic purity were excommunication and expulsion. While Europeans coming from a more homogenous society could afford a more individualistic ethic, Jews maintained an intense collectivism. In modern times, they have increased their lines of communication and solidarity while supporting individualism and atomization of Gentile allegiances.

To thrive as a small minority in an alien society also requires a talent for deceit. In Christian Spain of the Middle Ages, Jews responded to demands for Christian conversion by becoming Marranos, supposed converts to Christianity who secretly practiced Judaism. They developed elaborate schemes of deception that lasted for centuries. Many secret Jews successfully deceived Gentiles as to their Christian impiety. At any rate, the most convincing Marranos thrived and prospered, while those less skilled in such duplicity often suffered or perished in the Inquisition and other persecutions.

Jews developed patterns of dual morality: one morality for themselves and their kin and another for their Gentile hosts. Conversely, Gentiles in the homogeneous societies of Europe tended to develop what they conceived of as a universal morality that often led to assimilation when alien populations immigrated to their lands or when they conquered other nations. Ancient Greece exemplified that tradition by carrying a doctrine of universalism to their conquered lands. The same values of within-race altruism that Jews revered for themselves existed among European populations. However, because no other competing races were usually present, there was no need to develop intricate competitive or deceptive group strategies. In the day-to-day commerce and social interaction of Europe, truthfulness was held as an ideal and as a way of life. In times of war with foreign entities, a dual morality for one's own nation and the enemy nation would flourish, but the normal course of affairs was interchange primarily among one's own kind rather than among alien people. Thus our people never learned well the art of dual morality except in the exigencies of war. The migration and presence of alien Jewish elements, has however, contributed greatly to the modern development of European racial consciousness.

The Present State of Jewry

Churchill put it succinctly in 1920 when he described the Jewish takeover of Russia as having "gripped the Russian people by the hair of their heads and become the masters of this enormous empire."[929] By the last decade of the 20th century, they now grip America in the same way.

They thoroughly dominate the news and entertainment media in almost every civilized nation; they control the international markets and stock exchanges; and no government can resist doing their bidding on any issue of importance. They can coalesce against any state that resists their power, whether it economic extortion of a billion dollars from Switzerland or the violent carpet bombing of Iraq. The cohesion of the Jewish people is indeed the context of the New World Order, and with it they propose to extend their totalitarian denial of free speech from Europe and Canada to the nation that was once the most free in the world: the United States.

Those who state the facts of Jewish power are called believers in "The Jewish Conspiracy," as if to conjure the ridiculous image of Jews in caftans and yarmulkes peering behind their earlocks at a candle-lit globe as they plot world domination. But it is not the fanciful Learned Elders of Zion we have to fear. It is those who wield the Jewish power brazenly.

There is no conspiracy. There is not even much secrecy about it. Jewish power is ubiquitous. Every politician is so aware of it that he knows he cannot dare mention it! Jewish organizations, Jewish media, and Jewish political agents ruthlessly seek their perceived interests without remorse and without introspection. Just as single-mindedly as they once orchestrated the Russian Revolution, they now coordinate their power over the goyim. No Jewish leader has to direct his minions to seek political control of Gentile nations; they do it as naturally as the blue jay appropriates another bird's nest. No one has to tell Jews to destroy Gentile pride, heritage, honor, loyalty, tradition, while at the same time building up their own. It is in their programming. There does not have to be a master plan to destroy the Gentile sexual mores and family structure, for Freud and his intellectual descendants and media purveyors just do what comes natural to them. No Learned Elder of Zion has to tell the Jewish bureaucrats to open America's and Europe's borders to the riffraff of the Third World; they know almost instinctively that in a nation of diversity, they can dominate. They also know that if they can destroy our genetic integrity and racial solidarity of the European, there will be no one with the capacity to challenge their rule.

No, it is not a conspiracy. It is simply two nations — Jew and Gentile — in a state of ethnic war. Of course, most Jews and Gentiles do not even realize that we are at war. But while we Gentiles are unknowingly taught cultural and political sedition, Jews are taught allegiance to their kind and hatred and mistrust of us. Only a small portion of Jews are on the cultural and political battlefront but, through Jewish institutions and organizations, the homefront supports its troops. Of course, there have been Jews who have adopted the thinking meant for the Gentiles. Some have even become seditious, such as Benjamin Freedman and Alfred Lilienthal, two men of Jewish descent who know that Zionist leadership will lead them to disaster. The peace movement in Israel harbors many such Jews. In those Jews we may find Jews who, while still desiring preservation of their own genotype, seek to evolve it toward a policy of peaceful separation and coexistence rather than Jewish absolutism. They know that Jewish supremacism will eventually destroy them.

Although we understand the Jewish supremacist character of both Judaism and Zionism, we must also acknowledge that there are individual Jews who embrace neither doctrine and who are not engaged in any kind of culture-destroying or degenerative activity. A good example is Israel Shahak, a Jewish survivor of Nazi concentration camps and a professor in Israel who has suffered greatly for daring to speak out about Zionism and Talmudic Judaism. He tells the world about the Jewish misanthropy not only on behalf of justice for Gentiles and to save his people from the consequences of their actions.

Jews such as Israel Shahak offer hope of a mutually beneficial resolution of the Jewish-Gentile conflict. But Shahak and those like him remain a despised, tiny minority among their brethren. Fair resolution of the conflict can surely never come from Jewish hegemony. Only after we depose Jewish power in our own nations can we negotiate with them successfully. At this point in the conflict, although an ethnic peace conference would be the best solution for all parties, history tells us that it is unlikely. Tyrannies defer only to greater power.

If they truly represented what is noble in man, maybe it would be in the order of Nature to have our people replaced by the Jewish prototype. However, history reveals that as a group Jews have far more often been the harbingers of darkness than of light. This can be seen in the doctrines of the three most influential Jews of the 20th century: Freud, Marx and Boas. These three Jews came to debase mankind, not to ennoble it.

They have enormous power — power born of both talent and unscrupulousness. They are strengthened by what weakens us. Our power can reassert itself only from dedication to truth and justice, from expressions of courage and nobility. When we violate our own morality, we grow weak and exploitable, as we are now.

Somewhere in our genotype lay the dormant genes of survival, and those genes are now expressing themselves in a new awakening. I see this awakening wherever our people are. It is especially strong in our young. They have a vision of the Aryan society they want to build. It is a vision that persecution and hatred cannot destroy. Somewhere, at this moment, a fair baby sleeps peacefully in his cradle, unaware of the great battle now raging for his right to grow up and live in his own land and by the values of his own people.

Are Jews Superior?

What about intelligence, how do Jews compare to Europeans as a whole and to select European groups?

There has been a fair amount of study on the issue, primarily by Jewish researchers. They show a higher general IQ for Jews. But the difference comes almost exclusively from the verbal parts of IQ tests. Most studies show that Jews have a markedly higher verbal IQ, but Europeans often score higher on the more abstract and spatial components of IQ. Brown found Jewish children higher in verbal IQ and Scandinavian children higher in spatial-visio IQ. Levinson found the same thing among Jewish and Gentile children in a 1960 study, and Backman shows significantly higher verbal IQs and significantly lower IQs for Jews on visio-spatial reasoning. [930] [931] [932] [933] [934] [935] [936]

That Jews seem to be superior in the verbal mental skills seems perfectly consistent with their evolutionary strategy. Verbal skills are obviously important for communication, commerce, teamwork, administration, and mediation, all of which were vitally important in the societies in which they prospered.

Werner Mosse, a celebrated historian of European Jewish history, has even suggested, citing studies from Germany early in the century, that Gentile manufacturers tend to be artisans whereas Jewish manufacturers tend to be from trading or banking families. He argues that the character of Jewish involvement in manufacturing in Germany of the 19th century was:

> less in outright innovation or invention than in a special aptitude for economic "mediation" in the forms of the export of German goods, of "secondary innovation," technology transfer through the introduction into Germany of processes and methods observed abroad, and new techniques for the stimulation of demand. [937]

Richard suggests that visio-spatial abilities and verbal abilities are negatively correlated and that more of the cerebral cortex is devoted to one set of abilities. Another researcher, Richard Swartzbaugh, in his book *The Mediator*,[938] suggests that Jews are natural mediators in a multiethnic, multireligious, multinational environment, that the natural clashes between the antagonistic groups produces a tremendous demand for mediation. Such mediation finds expression in law, negotiation, arbitration, stock exchange, and government administration — all of which are responsive to Jewish verbal skills and intelligence.[939,940,941]

Jews have received a disproportionately large percentage of awards for scientific and cultural enterprise. From Academy Awards to Pulitzer Prizes to Nobel Laureates, the Jewish presence is ubiquitous. Disproportionate Jewish success among scientific and cultural awards is a reflection on both their abilities and their team strategy. Both the Academy Awards and the Pulitzer Prizes have a large contingent of Jewish voters who have from an early age been taught to favor their own. As mentioned in my chapter on ZOG, Jews are especially prone to join the governing bodies of any social organization in which they participate, and thus would tend to increase their ability to recognize and reward their own in their respective professions. Additionally, the Jewish-dominated news and entertainment media consistently elevate their own for praise and recognition.

Barbara Streisand may not have been the best pop singer in the country, but she certainly was in the eyes to the Jewish press. *Schindler's List* may not have been the best movie, but it was important to Jewish social and political objectives. The appalling choice of Jewish terrorist Menachem Begin for the Nobel Peace Prize depended on the groundwork laid by the Jewish press around the world. Even in the scientific sphere, in an era of tremendous scientific advancement and great numbers of the deserving researchers, publicity and public perception of a scientist's work is now probably just as critical for the earning of a scientific award as the work itself. In this arena, Jewish scientists have by far the most self-promotion and loudest cheering sections. Even today, with geneticists and psychologists rapidly proving the crucial role of heredity and race in intelligence and behavior, the Jewish media continue to tout the behavioral environmentalist viewpoint. The media give fringe egalitarians such as Lewontin, Kamin, and Gould preference over the quieter but more cogent scientists.

The three most influential Jewish intellects in politics, psychology, and race in the 19th and 20th centuries have been Karl Marx, Sigmund Freud and Franz Boas. All three were intelligent men, yet each had a catastrophic effect on European society. Karl Marx laid down the foundations for the most destructive and murderous ideology of all time. Sigmund Freud undermined the foundations of the family and European values. Franz Boas was the father of the egalitarian movement that now seeks nothing less than the destruction of our genotype.

The Ultimate Gauge

Even the so-called moderate wing of Judaism preaches a Jewish supremacy of morality and intellect. In an article in *Reform Judaism* titled "Relax. It's Okay to be the Chosen People," Arthur Hertzberg (the editor) and Aron Hirt-Manheimer discuss their victimization as youngsters at the hands of Christians. They go on to assert the specialness of the Jews, even those liberal Jews who don't want to admit it. In the article they quote the words from the founder of the Israeli state, David Ben-Gurion.

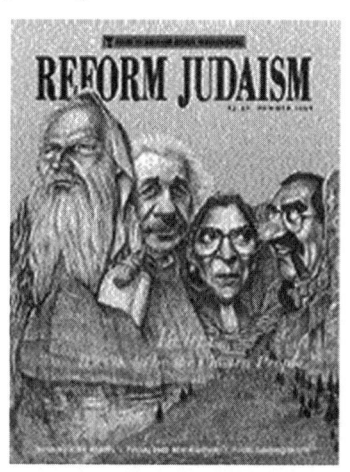

> **My concept of the messianic ideal and vision is not a metaphysical one but a sociocultural-moral one... I believe in our moral and intellectual superiority, in our capacity to serve as a model for the redemption of the human race. This belief of mine is based on my knowledge of the Jewish people, and not some mystical faith; the glory of the divine presence is within us, in our hearts, and not outside us.**[942] (emphasis mine)

It would be interesting to see the reaction if the President of the United States made a statement that he believed in the moral and intellectual superiority of the White race. Not only does the Ben-Gurion quotation show a supremacist attitude, it also shows that for many Jews their sense of supremacy is not born of believing they are "chosen by God" but simply egotism.

Before self-proclaimed assertions of Jewish superiority can be taken seriously, it is important to remember that the ultimate gauge of worthiness is historical performance. The European record is magnificent. Caucasians laid the foundations of astronomy, physics, mathematics, engineering, biology, geology, and medicine. It was we who designed the pyramids, the Parthenon and the Roman Coliseum. It was our Greek ancestors who wrote the first novel, developed drama as an art form, and gave the world the philosophy of Socrates and Plato. It was our race that unlocked the secrets of the Copernican universe. It was our folk who built the Roman Republic and who wrote the Magna Carta, the Declaration of Independence and the Constitution of the United States. Our people created the great art of ancient Greece and propelled the beauty of the Renaissance. Michaelangelo had our blood in his fingers as he reached out to God on the ceiling of the Sistine Chapel and in Leonardo's hands our blood pulsed as he formed in cold stone the warm beauty of *The Madonna and Child*.

From our genes came the compositions of Bach and Mozart and Beethoven and Wagner. Our people invented the automobile, the airplane, the steam engine, the internal combustion engine, the jet engine, the electric light, telephones, radios, and cameras — and even the tools now used as weapons against us: the motion picture camera and television. Men of our heritage invented the transistor and even the sources of the computer age, the semi-conductor and integrated circuit. Our people developed the math and physics and the chemical propulsion through which we have left our footprints on the moon.

I could go on and on recounting the great achievements of our European heritage. In the greatness of the Greece of Pericles, or the Rome of Caesar, or the England of Shakespeare there was almost no Jewish influence. Western civilization would still have scaled the heights without their presence. But could we have plumbed the depths of Marxism, Freudianism and Boasian egalitarianism without them?

The difference between Jews and Gentiles finds expression in the kind of films made by Walt Disney and the type made by the current Jewish head of Disney Studios, Michael Eisner. While both Disney and Eisner made technically proficient films, Disney made films accenting the beauty and nobility in man and the wonders of Nature. Eisner steered Disney away from the Nature-film business and toward degenerate films such as *The Crying Game* and *The Priest*, two films wallowing in sexual deviance and depravity, films that Walt Disney would not have even watched — much less produced.

While the Classical Greeks and the Europeans of the Renaissance were producing great art and sculpture showing the ideal beauty of the human form, Jews rejected art as graven image. Now they sponsor and promote degenerate art that prizes the misshapen and the weird over the well formed, noble, and heroic. While the European's Faustian spirit has penetrated the deepest oceans and the highest mountains and even ventured into space, the Jews have seldom been pioneers. While we revere the soil, the Earth, the very natural world by which most Europeans gained their daily bread until very recent times, the Jews have collected around the golden calf of a soulless and parasitic urban life.

While Freud held up the genital and excretory organs as the keys to the meaning of life, the Gentile Karl Jung dismissed Freud and developed the concept of the racial soul. While Jews still enshrine the dictum of an eye for an eye, the Europeans embrace, perhaps dangerously, the doctrine of "turn the other cheek."

Whether such characteristics are superior or inferior depends on subjective definition. In terms of intelligence, Jews are superior to the European people in verbal skills. They are a fast-talking, clever people well versed in the arts of manipulation and mediation. But they are certainly not superior in the qualities of character that have created the greatness and sublimity of our people. The Jewish genotype has certainly been resilient and adaptive, and they may yet inherit our Earth as their dominion. The contest, though, is far from over. There is a wealth of wonderful genetic material in our people that shall yet prove itself worthy of survival. When our people awaken and apply our genius, our idealism, and our courage to the struggle for our survival, victory shall be possible.

Jews have adapted to the vagaries of multiculturalism while preserving their own genotype. But while they have *adapted*, we have *created*. We have created both technology *and* art. We have found great beauty in both the body *and* the soul. We have embraced both God *and* Nature; science *and* religion. We have learned how to balance both government *and* freedom.

The ultimate clash of these diametrically opposed genotypes and cultures fast approaches with the new millennium. Jewish will-to-power pushes them on to domination as it has for the last 2,000 years. Their evolutionary strategy has been perfected to the point that we Europeans now suffer under Jewish hegemony on a global scale. We cannot help but fully recognize their present superiority in political and social power, but we also know that their power represents the devolution of our civilization. Its persistence can only lead to our eventual extinction, and that fact gives our task the importance of life or death and makes it urgent.

We Aryans are those of European descent who are racially conscious and who have committed our lives to our people's survival and evolutionary advancement. We shall do our duty. We shall not surrender our freedom and our very existence to Jewish or any other power. We shall preserve our heritage and our hard-won rights and freedoms. We shall guide our people up the evolutionary stairway to the stars.

Part IV

The Fight for the Truth

CHAPTER 26

MY BEGINNING ACTIVISM

In 1966, my father was hired as an engineer for the U.S. Agency for International Development in Vietnam. As I prepared to enter my junior year in high school, he felt it would be better for me to attend military school while he was overseas. Although I wanted to follow in his footsteps, eventually serve in the military and become an officer, I did not want to leave New Orleans. He enrolled me in Riverside Military Academy, as he thought that my mother's illness would prevent her from providing me adequate supervision.

I adjusted unevenly to my new life at Riverside. At home I knew freedom. I could go out into the swamps and forests whenever I wanted, or read late into the night. I could go to the library, swim in the lake or spend some time volunteering at the Citizens Council. With my Father often working and my mother mostly bedridden, I could do pretty much what I wished.

All that came to an abrupt end. My loss of freedom at military school hit me hard. It seemed to me that the school tried to control as much of its students' time as it could in order to keep us out of trouble. In the regular military one could get a pass or furlough for a few days, but in military school it seemed every hour was pre-arranged from the reveille at 6:30 a.m. to lights out at 10:30 p.m. We had inspections before breakfast, after breakfast, before supper, and again after supper. There were study periods, athletics and drills. Time seemed to grind away in boring rituals of meaningless activity.

I always used my Saturday pass, and while most of my buddies usually headed for town, I usually headed off for the beauty of Lake Lanier and its surrounding mountains. The Louisiana bayou country had made me intimate with the great variety of life found in Nature, for no part of America has more life per square mile than the lush swampland. But the mountains of North Georgia gave me a different view of Nature. They rekindled my early memories of the Alps and the trips our family took to America's national parks.

The mountains were so different than the humid marshes back home. In the forests and swamps I could seldom see farther than just a few hundred feet. Even on clear nights the ambient lights of New

Climbing the hills of north Georgia, I could see for miles in the crisp air of autumn. In the evening, the stars seemed close enough to touch, almost as close as the leaves of the live oak trees back home. It seemed as though I could climb into the stairway of the Milky Way as I had the branches of those oaks. That fall, the wilds of north Georgia also gave me a show of the most vivid autumn colors I had ever seen, and painted them in heroic scale in the sweep and grandeur of the mountains. As the wetlands made me focus on the varied forms of life and the love that springs from it, the mountains and stars inspired me with a sense of the awesome power of Nature and the call of the infinite.

After the wild horse in me had been broken, I adapted quite well to the discipline at Riverside. I realized that there was a relation between discipline and honor, for discipline is ultimately exercised in the power of one's word. I learned lessons that have stayed with me all my life. I learned to do what I had to do rather than what I wanted to do, and I learned that complaining or whining about unpleasant tasks did no one any good, especially myself.

At Riverside I continued my inquiry into race. I ordered book after book from Noontide Press, and my favorite publication was *Western Destiny.* Willis Carto's introduction to Francis Parker Yockey's monumental book, *Imperium,* inspired me.[943] Actually I liked Carto's introduction better than the book itself, for it was a beautifully written, succinct summary of our struggle for Western mankind. I was lucky to have two really fine teachers who were open-minded on the race issue and who willingly read the books on the subject that I brought to them. One was Lt. Bell, my history teacher, and the other a brilliant, elderly English teacher with the old New York family name of Van Houten, a name he was very proud of. He was

Getting ready for an Atlantic dive with Lt. Bell.

one of the few teachers who carried no military rank at the school. While Bell stimulated my love of history, Van Houten focused our class on the great classics of literature, including the classics of ancient

Greece. I stayed long after class on many occasions to discuss a great range of topics, so much so, that despite our age differences and station, they became my friends — and treated me as an intellectual equal. I would often spend a Sunday afternoon, or a weeknight study period at their offices discussing with them everything that came to mind in the arts and sciences. One of the unique aspects of Riverside is that, after Christmas break until Easter, the school would relocate to its campus at Hollywood, Florida. After class, Lt. Bell and I would go frequently to the beach — don our scuba or snorkeling gear — and swim out to the reefs 200 yards offshore. The appreciation for Nature that I had acquired as a very young man in Louisiana bayou country helped me appreciate the wonders of the ocean. Soon, I had all sorts of shells and aquatic specimens scattered about my dorm room. The racial truths I had learned fit in perfectly with my love of the Natural World. I became aware of the difference between being observing or enjoying the wonders of Nature, and being conscious that my genotype was truly a part of Nature, an integral part. It became apparent that such elemental understanding affords a basis for getting our race healthy again.

When I returned home the next summer, I found the swamps and cypress forests just as beautiful as I remembered. On my first day back I found some heart of palm, caught some fish and crabs and roasted them all in a shady place. Nothing had tasted so sweet in months. After I had my fill, I stretched out on the grass in the shade of a cypress tree, feeling the beads of perspiration sting my eyes. I thought about the cool breezes that swirled in the hills and mountains around Gainesville, and how much that coolness had exhilarated me. I also thought about the purplish peaks and the rays of sun that broke through clouds like spotlights raking the mountainsides. Only in mountains can one really get a sense of the magnificent architectural sweep and power of the Earth. I still loved the life I found in the swampland, but I came to the realization that I loved the esthetic and power of the mountains even more, and in the mountains I have since found my greatest inspiration.

The summer of my return, I used the experience I had gained building houses with my father to land a summer job working with some local house painters. I also found a sizable paper route opening in the uptown section of New Orleans. It was about a 15-minute drive from my house, which I drove in my rickety old Ford Falcon. After a few months on the paper route, I sold the car for a profit. So, with my newspaper profits and some of my savings, for about $1,200 I bought a 1963 white convertible Ford Galaxy that needed a lot of work. That was an excellent deal in those days. After a month's time I had it in perfect condition, complete with a new convertible top I had installed myself.

Every morning I would drive to my route about 4 a.m. and throw my 200 newspapers, stopping at the end of each block and walking around it with my bulging paper bag slung from my shoulder. I worked for the same newspaper I despised for its incessant egalitarianism and hypocritical, pro-Zionist position: the Newhouse-owned *Times-Picayune*. But strangely, I did not think about its ownership or ideology in connection with my job. There was only one daily in New Orleans, and I had thrown papers during a number of periods since fifth grade. For me, throwing the paper was a way of life, disconnected from its ownership or politics.

Winter that year was extremely cold; remembrance of it comes to me every time a rubber band breaks in my fingers. When the editions ran thick and heavy, the red rubber bands would often pop in the cold temperatures as I stretched them around the thick papers. When they struck my cold fingers, they felt like a bee had stung them. In New Orleans, the humidity makes the summers feel hotter and winter nights and early mornings seem colder. In the winter I shivered, and in summer I sweated, but it was a great job for a high school student.

I was 17. In six months, by the laws of Louisiana, I would be deemed a man. For the first time in my life I attended an integrated school, John F. Kennedy. It was a newly constructed school of mostly middle-to-upper-income White students in New Orleans near the Ponchartrain lakefront. Kennedy also had about a 10 percent Black makeup. Although the numbers of Black students were small compared to most New Orleans schools, there were still some problems.

I had a chance for the first time to observe a number of teenage Blacks in a close environment, and it seemed every behavioral trait that I read about in psychological studies came alive right in front of my eyes. I noticed many differences between the White and Black students. Black girls and boys, on average, were a lot louder than the Whites. They wore their emotions as flamboyantly as they did the styles of their clothing, and they seemed to oscillate between broad toothy smiles or closed-mouthed frowns. When they became upset or angry, their nostrils would flare like a bull ready to charge.

Even though their anger was a terrible sight to behold, their temperament seemed more jovial than morose, and the hallways often reverberated with Black girls or boys singing or chanting some jingles that always ended with the slapping of hands and spastic body movements. Academically, most of them performed poorly, but I do remember one Black girl in my civics class that I thought was an excellent student. In sports, they excelled in numbers disproportionate to their percentage of the student body, and the coaches energetically recruited them for the athletic teams.

A friend, who had a large paper route he was giving up, offered it to me. I ambitiously added 225 new newspaper deliveries to my own 200. My first day with it fell on a rainy Sunday morning. I found it difficult to both read my address sheet and make out the house numbers on that cold, dark, wet morning. To compound my troubles, I had gone out the night before to a drive-in theater with a girlfriend from school and didn't get home until after midnight. I arose at 2 a.m. so I could handle the new route. At about 7 a.m., completely exhausted, I started the drive home. I had nodded off driving once or twice on previous occasions, but an internal alarm always woke me up, and the adrenaline rush kept me alert the rest of the way home.

On *that* Sunday morning when I dozed off, I nearly never woke up again. Coming off the New Orleans Ponchartrain Expressway onto Lakeshore Boulevard, the road curved a little to the left while I kept going straight at 45 miles per hour. I struck an eight-foot diameter oak tree that didn't give an inch when my Galaxy hit it head-on. My head and body broke through the steering wheel, and my head shattered the windshield. I ended up slumped over the steering column, pieces of steering wheel lying in my lap. I remember nothing about the accident, other than that the blood, soaking my shirt, had turned cold, and hands pulling my body out of the wreckage and loading me into an ambulance for the trip to Oschner Hospital.

After a few hours, my face had begun to swell to the point that I could barely peer out of my eyes, and the doctors had suspicion of internal bleeding. After the extreme discomfort of my introduction to a urinary catheter, the doctors were surprised that there were no signs of blood. I did, however, have a crushed nose and chin, an eight-stitch cut on the right side of my upper lip, as well as a concussion. I stayed in the hospital for the rest of the day, and then they sent me home. With my father in Vietnam and my mother in poor health, I tended to myself for the most part. However, my girlfriend Evelyn came over to nurse me a little during the next two weeks while I remained out of school. When she first came into my room and saw my head swollen like a huge turnip, with my forehead and cheeks so swollen that they almost obscured the sight of my eyeballs, she burst into tears. Of course, her reaction helped neither of us feel any better. The policeman who had pulled me from the car came by to visit. He told me that he had seen a lot of car wrecks and was really surprised that I had survived. He said that he had expected to find me decapitated when he arrived on the scene and saw the smashed windshield. I can still remember, feeling as bad as I did, talking to him about the race problem. It was a subject I always managed to bring up.

While at home I continued to read, despite some blurred vision, but finally I put down my books and just closed my eyes. I thought deeply about my beliefs. I realized that the racial concepts I read about and understood were not just some sort of intellectual game without any practical meaning for the real world. Racial dynamics constituted the essence of both mankind's history and his future. Our race faced the greatest genetic danger of its long history. Because of our nonsustaining birthrates, our people all over the world were committing race suicide. Even the homelands of our race were being inundated by massive immigration and proliferating non-European genes. Intermarriage was also increasing because of its media fashionableness. I knew our people were liable to be a minority in America, and even in our European homelands, in a couple of generations. We were in a struggle for our heritage, culture, freedom, and very existence.

I saw America being rapidly transformed from an extension of European values and culture to one being reclaimed by the Third World. There were no government projections then of non-White American majorities, but all the racial writers I had read saw the coming minority status of Whites in America. It would not be until the 1990s that the Census Bureau would confirm a projection of White minority status for 2048.[944] In the Immigration Act of 1965, all the liberal Senators swore that the act would have no effect on the ethnic population percentages of the United States, but again, writers such as Drew Smith[945] and others said what the Census Bureau finally admitted 30 years later.

On a more visceral level, I saw the destructive changes taking place in our schools, on our streets, in our government and in the media. An alien wave was sweeping away the values of our forefathers. New Orleans streets were exploding with crime, the new schools built by ever-higher taxes were bright and new on the outside, but mostly full of dull faculty and even duller students on the inside. Welfare financed minority birthrates and non-White immigration flooded and overwhelmed our social infrastructure, from educational costs to housing, from maintenance to medical care. The resulting economic drain caused a steady decline in living standards for the American middle class family, forcing both spouses to work with devastating impact on both marriages and children. Thousands of White men, women and children were falling victim to Black crime that swept the major American cities like a medieval plague.

The mass media levied a concentrated attack on the mores of Western Civilization, beginning to glorify everything from wholesale promiscuity, to homosexuality, to alcohol and drug abuse. It was obvious to me that the propaganda would only increase with time. The quality of elected officials declined with the introduction of vast hordes of minority voters who seldom read anything more intellectual than the TV listings, if even that.

I saw the handwriting on the American wall. But what was I to do? I was just one 17-year-old high school student. What I did know was that I had to do *something*. I could not selfishly pursue my own dreams to be a doctor or an astronaut. My race was in the greatest crisis in its long history. I also knew that I could not just continue to sit on the sidelines devouring my books and spreading the racial truth to anyone who came within earshot. I knew that no cause could ever triumph without organization. Ultimately, I looked to history to guide me in the present fight, for I was enthralled by the historical success of the Ku Klux Klan of the Reconstruction South.

I wanted to join an organization that stood up for the things I believed, and the Citizens Council seemed too passive, for it would not address the issue of Jewish supremacism, even though they were certainly aware of it. I felt the subject had to be addressed.

The only group that seemed to stand up forthrightly on race was the Klan. The historical "Klan" I had read about was very different from the Klan image I saw on television and in the movies. The mass media presented the Klan as nothing but a collection of ignorant, green-teethed, violent Southerners who would just as easily lynch a Black man as look at one. I rejected that image because I knew then that the Klan's fundamental recognition of racial differences, although categorized by the media as false, actually was scientifically correct. By almost any measure, races are unequal in mental ability, and this difference is clearly a product of their genetic makeup, rather than poverty or racial suppression. As for the Jews, Klansmen understood that, as a group, they were the real supremacists, and they were the driving force of one-world egalitarianism and multiculturalism, while they maintained a hypocritical doctrine of ethnic superiority for themselves and their beloved Israel.

True, some Klansmen little understood the genetic or psychological evidence on the race issue. Few were well educated on the historical aspects of the Jewish ethnic war against Western man-

Gen. Nathan Bedford Forrest.

kind and our religious and cultural institutions, but the ones I came in contact with were overwhelmingly good people — mostly hardworking, church-going, family men. A high proportion had farms or small businesses, and in their self-discipline and responsibility for themselves and their families, they also took responsibility for the society in which they lived. In the heavily Black-populated Deep South, they made close observations of the Black race that conflicted with the egalitarian dogma of the media, and they trusted their senses and their own experiences rather than the media-concocted image. They thought for themselves.

The Historical Record

Even before I met my first Klansman, I had already read both the Northern and Southern views of the "Radical Reconstruction" of the South. Though there were hardly any books in print in the 60s supporting the Southern viewpoint, I found many in the libraries, written in earlier decades, that showed the corruption and destructive qualities of the so-called Reconstruction Period. From about the turn of the century until after the Second World War — most histories of the period depicted Reconstruction as a regressive, corrupt period that ended only after the success of groups such as the Ku Klux Klan.

The popularity of that view is illustrated by the two most-watched movies of the 20th century, *Birth of a Nation* and *Gone with the Wind*. They both depicted Black Reconstruction as a violent and corrupt period. In contrast to the modern historical portrayal of the Klan, *Birth of a Nation* presented an unapologetic, heroic image of the Klan, and *Gone with the Wind* presented an image of heroic Southern resistance against the evils of Reconstruction.

The negative view of the Carpetbagger

At the close of the War for Southern Independence, the South was treated like a conquered province. Any Southerner who served in any civil government or in the ranks of the Confederate Army (constituting most White males of the South) was disfranchised. No women's suffrage existed at that time, so the great majority of Southerners were denied the vote. Blacks, who were nearly all illiterate and who had little experience with running either businesses or government, were suddenly given the right to vote. Opportunities for corruption were rife under those circumstances. Carpetbaggers swarmed into the

> In Downtown New Orleans in 1874 a great battle (called the Battle of Liberty Place) was fought against the illegally installed Reconstruction Government of Louisiana.

South to exploit the easily corruptible Black vote for their own gain. The Southern brand of such scoundrels — the scalawags — also exploited both the newly franchised Negroes and the prostrate White Southerners. Rapacious taxes destroyed productive Southern families and transferred vast amounts of property to corrupt officials. Black crime ravaged both towns and countryside; while newly constituted Black juries routinely freed those guilty of atrocities against Whites. Illiterate and venal elected officials who flaunted their corruption had flooded the Southern legislatures. The Black and Radical-controlled Louisiana legislature, for example, appropriated $10,000 dollars, a huge sum for those times, for cigars and whiskey.

Into this maelstrom rode the Ku Klux Klan, a secret organization dedicated to restoration of Western civilization in the prostrate South. Well-educated men in Pulaski, Tennessee formed it first as a social club. From their knowledge of Greek, they called their group the Ku Klux Klan, after the word *kýklos*, meaning circle or assembly. They adopted the traditional garb of the Christian ascetics (which is still maintained in Spain) who wore the peaked hoods to symbolize doing good works in anonymity. When the superstitious Blacks mistook the robed Klansmen for the ghosts of Confederate soldiers, the costumes became a powerful psychological weapon.

An oft-repeated story is told of an incident in which a Black was accused of burning some barns near the Klan headquarters in Pulaski. He was visited one moonlit night by the eerily clad, white-robed horses and men. Under the speaker's robe was a rubberized tube leading to a treated pouch. He demanded his frightened host bring him a pail of water. The Klansman would then appear to drink the entire bucket of water, saying that this was "his first drink since the battle of Shiloh." It is said that the Negro was never again suspected of any further mischief.

The legendary Confederate general, Nathan Bedford Forrest, who pioneered modern guerrilla warfare tactics, and who had the distinction of never having lost a battle while in an army that lost a war, became the first Grand Wizard of the organization. When Radical Republicans moved to outlaw the group by federal law, in a brilliant tactical maneuver, General Forrest formally disbanded the South-wide Klan, knowing that it would simply continue on the local level wherever needed. More than 500,000 Southerners joined in the Reconstruction-era Klan, making it a veritable secret army against Radical Reconstruction. Mere possession of a Klan robe could be punished by death. Yet the Klan, state-by-state, quietly overthrew the Black Reconstruction governments. Within 20 years of the Klan's founding practically the entire Southland had become free from Black and Radical Republican control. Because of the terribly bitter feelings generated by the radicals in the Republican Party during the period, the South remained a solid Democratic South for 100 years — until Republicans such as Barry Goldwater and others announced their opposition to forced integration and the Civil Rights Act.

In the period following Reconstruction, the American people, along with the federal government, eventually came to understand that the Klan was right, and the 1896 *Plessy* v. *Ferguson* Supreme Court decision upheld racial segregation in the South and elsewhere.[946] *Birth of a Nation*, which portrayed the successful KKK as reuniting North and South as one nation of White brotherhood, was so well received that it spawned what is commonly called the Second Era Klan. It became one of the most powerful American social organizations in 20th century America. At its height it garnered millions of members, with many becoming U.S. senators, congressmen and state governors in both the North and the South. Upon a special showing of *Birth of a Nation* in the White House, President

Woodrow Wilson effusively praised the Klan for saving civilization in the South and thus preserving it for all of America. From *History of the American People:*[947]

> Adventurers swarmed out of the North as much an enemy of one race as of the other. To coerce, beguile and use the Negroes...In the villages the Negroes were the office holders — men who knew nothing of its use of authority except its insolence.
>
> The policy of the Congressional leaders wrought a veritable overthrow of civilization in the South...in their determination to put the White South under the heel of the Black South...
>
> The White men were roused by the mere instinct of self-preservation... until at last there had sprung into existence a great Ku Klux Klan — a veritable empire of the South to protect the Southern country.[948]

President Woodrow Wilson

To illustrate the universally expressed high esteem for the Ku Klux Klan, the *Encyclopaedia Britannica*, in a turn-of-the-century edition, characterized the Reconstruction KKK as a chivalrous organization. The article begins by stating, "Ku Klux Klan is the name of an American secret association of Southern whites united for self-protection and to oppose the Reconstruction measures of the United States Congress." It ascribes the reasons for the Klan's rise as:

> ...the absence of stable government in the South for several years after the Civil war... the corrupt and tyrannical rule of the alien, renegade, and negro...the disfranchisement of Whites... the disarming of whites...outrages of white women by negro men...[949]

The reborn Knights of the Ku Klux Klan of the 1920s, much like the Klan of Reconstruction, had a membership that included the most educated and prominent elements of society, but this time, of both the North and the South. Thousands of politicians joined, as well as many clergy and businessmen. In its heyday, its successful recruitment strategy was to enlist the leaders of the community in business, education, politics, and the church. Compared to the Reconstruction Klan, which had no anti-Catholic bias and had some entirely Catholic units in south Louisiana and a few other areas, the Klan of the 20s capitalized on the fear among the Protestant clergy of the growing Roman Catholicism fueled by the new immigration waves. Protestant ministers were frequently the most avid Klan backers and supporters. In the Third Era of the Klan (during the civil rights revolution of the 1950s and 1960s), Protestants still dominated the Klan in the largely non-Catholic South, but most Klan groups discarded prohibitions against Catholics and saw the need for White Christian unity in response to Jewish supremacism and anti-Christianism. In heavily Catholic south Louisiana, membership in my Klan was mostly Catholic, reflecting the general population. In recent years, some national Klan organizations have even had Catholic leaders.

Immigration concerns fueled Klan growth in the 1920s, and when the restrictionist acts of the 1920s caused immigration to dwindle, the Klan's appeal lessened. Also, growing Jewish media power launched a propaganda war against the Klan, consistently portraying Klansman as evil characters, and portraying any individual Klan member who broke the law as typical of all Klansmen.

Some independent Klan organizations had continued unbroken and little changed from Reconstruction, passed down from father to son. Others fell under the umbrella of the 1920s Klan and adopted its unique titles and rituals, along with its political and religious beliefs, many of which differed from the original Ku Klux Klan. Most Klans of the '20s and '30s evolved into more of a social club than a revolutionary organization. Although the violence necessary in the Reconstruction was no longer condoned by Klan policy, some Klansmen did respond aggressively to particularly heinous crimes, especially when the victims were women or children.

Lynchings and beatings were not limited to Black lawbreakers, however. The criminal-justice system during that period seldom dealt with wife-abuse, but the Klan had a code of chivalry that held sacred the sanctity of womanhood and motherhood. They viewed the physical violation of women as the most terrible of crimes. A drunken bout of wife-beating by a White man could be punished by a small group of concerned citizens, sometimes Klansmen, who gave the abuser a taste of what he had given his wife.

Klansmen of that period would be shocked that in our "tolerant" society there are such frequent attacks against women, and that non-Whites now rape more than 20,000 White women each year. They could not have imagined the growing physical abuse of women in Western nations — increasingly like that of the Third World.

The Third Klan era arose in the late 1950's when the civil rights movement overturned a social system that had lasted for centuries. Thousands of independent Klan groups sprang up across the South and in all parts of the United States. The Klan name and symbols had been in the public domain for many years, so no group could claim exclusive use of them. As a result, many different Klan groups sprang up with widely varying philosophies and tactics. There were the U.S. Klans, the United Klans, the White Knights of the Ku Klux Klan, the Knights of the White Camellia, and many simply called Knights of the Ku Klux Klan. Most Klan groups were law-abiding, but some believed that violence was the only way to stop integration.

Their violent actions were minor compared to the endemic violence that social equality of the races would unleash, and they could not understand that bloodshed only created sympathy for the enemies they despised. The media solemnly publicized those cases, never missing the opportunity to portray the opponents of "civil rights" not only as opposing the principles of liberty, but also as immoral men of brutality and violence. In the name of civil-rights for Blacks, a social system was overturned that resulted in the loss of civil rights for millions of Whites who became victims of Black violence and crime.

One afternoon at the Citizens Council, I met the Klan leader who came to have a great impact on my life: James Lindsay. He was a fascinating man who led a double life. Lindsay was one of the most successful stockbrokers in New Orleans, having a fine home in the exclusive uptown section of New Orleans, but quietly — he led a dedicated Klan group under the pseudonym Ed White. His organization had members in the states of Texas, Tennessee, Louisiana, Mississippi and Alabama. He put me in touch with a couple of students at Kennedy High School whose fathers were active in a Klan Den. Lindsay told me that illegality and violence would not be tolerated in our group, and he repeatedly pointed out that much of the violence in some of the other Klans around the country had been instigated by government *agent provocateurs*. The federal government, he contended, encouraged violence as a means to destroy the Klan, and at the same time to discredit and make our cause appear immoral in the eyes of the public. Years later when the U.S. Congress had hearings on the federal government program called Cointelpro[950] (counterintelligence program) it discovered that the federal government had done exactly what Lindsay claimed — that its agents had promoted violence and illegality among both right-wing and left-wing groups as a means of destroying their viability.[951]

I was invited to a small meeting, and Lindsay gave a brief, but moving speech describing his love of our heritage and country. He passionately spoke of the dire fate that awaited us if the Anglo-Saxon became overwhelmed by the masses of the Third World. Lindsay was not only savvy at business and very well read, but he had distinguished himself as a boxing champion while in the U.S. Navy. He was well spoken, sincere, and had the heart of a boxer who never gives up, even when far behind in the final rounds. He was a man of the world, and with my father halfway around the world, Lindsay became much like a second father to me. I also admired how Lindsay did his Klan work in spite of the risk it posed to his social standing and business. It was interesting how deftly he moved between both worlds. From the minute we met and he saw the depth of my knowledge and commitment, he treated me as an equal despite our age difference. I was his apprentice in many ways, for he taught me about the intricacies and psychology of people, and he helped to sharpen my racial education and rough knowledge to a smooth edge.

Finally, the important day came. In a room lit only by flickering white candles on a wooden cross, with White-robed men standing at attention — I approached the altar where lay a sword and a Bible open to the book of Romans. There I took a sacred oath to my Christian faith, to America, to the Constitution of the United States, to the White race, and to my Klan brothers. I swore to always protect the sanctity of womanhood, the innocent, the elderly, and the ultimate treasure of our people: the children.

Just to be sure that every Klansman in his organization knew clearly our position on violence, Lindsay also required each Klansman to swear that he would not conspire to commit any illegal acts of violence, a section that remained in the oath of my Klan during my entire tenure. From the time when I first joined to the time I resigned from the organization years later, no member of my Klan organization had ever committed an act of illegal violence against a racial minority. Even the ADL in their attacks against me in later years, grudgingly admitted that my Klan was nonviolent. Of course, to them, our strict legality simply made us more dangerous than other Klans because we were more able to influence the public and the political process.

Chapter 27:
The LSU "White Tiger"

After the thrill of my Klan initiation, our Klan den activities seemed rather mundane. The Klan seemed more of a social club than anything else. Occasionally we printed flyers and distributed them. Usually we used the piggyback method of distribution, that consisted of getting stacks of free newspaper giveaways, and affixing our Klan leaflets with a rubber band and then throwing them on the lawns of selected neighborhoods. We also had some cross-lighting ceremonies, usually in St. Bernard or St. Tammany Parish. Cross-lightings were generally referred to as "cross-burnings" by the media, implying that they were anti-Christian sacrileges.

Calling cross-lightings anti-Christian was a hypocritical and deceitful tactic used by the anti-Christian, Jewish-dominated media. Actually, cross-lightings represent an illumination of the cross. For centuries before the advent of electric lights, Christians had been stirred by the beauty of candles arranged in the shape of the cross. The Scottish clans, who also had a strong Christian orientation, used it as a symbol in opposition to tyranny. For us it was a sacred ceremony and not meant as an intimidation tactic of any kind. But the media portrayed it as a sign of terror. Some Whites, usually kids, unfortunately picked up on that symbolism presented by the media, and they would light crosses to show opposition to integration of schools or neighborhoods.

I began to drift away from the Klan in the later part of my senior year in high school. Although I admired Lindsay and loved the valiant heritage of the Klan, it just seemed that the Klan was simply too mired in the past and was not ready to adopt new strategies for victory. Even before I joined the Klan, I had read some of the literature of George Lincoln Rockwell, the leader of the American Nazi Party. Rockwell was an interesting and compelling personality. He was a U.S. Navy fighter pilot who achieved the rank of Commander fighting against the Germans during the Second World War. After the war, he became active in the conservative movement, at one time working with William Buckley. Rockwell, while still a conservative, became awakened to a thorough understanding of the race issue, including Jewish supremacism, but felt frustrated that so many conservative leaders refused to say publicly the things that they said privately. He decided on a bold strategy of raising the swastika banner, even with all its negatives, in order to use its sensationalism to bring attention to the critical issue of Jewish supremacism. He explained it as political Jujitsu, or the art of using the overwhelming power of an opponent against himself.

Commander Rockwell cultivated the image of a humorous buffoon and as an incredibly radical person in short media sound bites, but when he appeared on talk shows and before college audiences, he presented a reasonable and appealing image. In college speeches he shocked his audience with Churchill's *Illustrated Sunday Herald* article on the Jewish leadership of Communism, as well as pertinent documents from the National Archives, describing the Jewish takeover of Russia. He exposed Jewish supremacy and hypocrisy, and the efforts by Jewish groups to suppress the truth.

He impressed me with his intelligence and bravery, and I began to correspond with him in the months before an assassin's bullet struck him down. I told him that I was traditionally Southern and intensely proud of both our Southern and American heritage. I let him know that I understood the race and Jewish issues, but that I was also fiercely patriotic and believed in the Constitution and protections of free speech and press. Rockwell replied that his group endorsed a strictly pro-Constitution position and was not totalitarian like the Germans.

His effective uses of radical tactics to make people confront the racial truth impressed me. He wrote that, "The White race had to be shocked out of its lethargy and racial suicide." After his death, I felt torn between the traditional Klan approach and Rockwell's more unconventional methods to break through on the issues. Rockwell's legacy drove me to my later action when I was 19 years old, during my freshman year in college. William Kunstler, the Communist Jewish lawyer, came to speak at Tulane University in the spring of 1970. Kunstler had been the main lawyer for the "Chicago 7" defendants, who were charged with rioting at the 1967 Democratic National Convention. He had also been involved with hundreds of Black legal actions, trying to force destruction of White schools and neighborhoods. One of the things that really disturbed me about Kunstler was that the media seldom mentioned his Communist activism and beliefs. Instead they presented him as an "activist," or "civil rights lawyer," never as the Communist revolutionary that he was. I wanted to do something to call attention to his Communist pedigree.

I heard about his scheduled appearance at Tulane University, only a day before the event. My good friends Ray Leahart and Louis McWilliams asked me if I wanted to do anything, and I thought about it quickly and proposed that we picket him. We three made up one large sign reading KUNSTLER IS A COMMUNIST JEW. To add to the drama and prevent the press from ignoring it, I decided to try the Rockwell tactic and use a swastika armband to demonstrate against the Communist traitor. We went to the location of his speech at McAllister auditorium on the Tulane campus, and found ourselves greeted by three dozen members of the Black Panther Party, all of them wearing berets and black leather jackets. To picket, I would have to walk right through their gauntlet. Only one unarmed Tulane campus security guard was on hand as Ray and Louis unwrapped the sign from the shopping bag. I hoisted the provocative sign and started to walk toward the Blacks. I knew that I was doing a foolish and dangerous thing, but at the same time I felt exhilarated, for it felt good to stand up and express publicly my opposition to a man whom I felt was a traitor. Kunstler was a man who had stabbed the American fighting man in the back in Vietnam by his support of the Viet Cong.

As I stepped out on the sidewalk, it seemed everyone stood frozen for a moment. The White students were looking on in disbelief, and the Black Panthers couldn't believe that a lone White teenager would dare stand up to them. Within moments, TV and newspaper cameramen descended on me, and the security guard powered up his radio with desperate pleas for back up officers. Each time I walked passed the Black gauntlet, their obscenities and threats grew louder. Four more security guards arrived, and a police car with lights flashing roared up on the sidewalk in front of the auditorium. A campus security guard stopped me, asked if I was a student, and then said I had no right to be on campus. I responded that I had a right to be there because this was a public event at a University that receives some public funds. Within 20 minutes, a half-dozen more police cars showed up, and about 10 police officers were present while I walked just a few feet from the black-beret revolutionaries. Ray and Louis also took the sign for a round or two and then we left, our point made.

My father was furious when he found out what I had done. He made me promise that I would not join the Nazi Party, and I never did. Of course, that single rash act of picketing Kunstler came back to haunt me many years hence, for it gave my enemies another chance to attack me by association, rather than confront the ideas and the issues themselves. At the same time, I felt relieved that I had acted publicly, I had crossed my Rubicon and I felt there was no going back from my chosen path.

At Louisiana State University

My father had worked his way through both high school and college. Ultimately, he had a distinguished military career; also successful civilian careers as a petroleum engineer, homebuilder, and oilman. He later worked for the State Department, USAID, program in Southeast Asia, and then embarked on a final career position with the U.S. Department of Energy, working into his mid-70s. Father had noticed in his reading that self-made men seldom seemed to have sons as successful. He thought that this occurred because their sons seldom endured the challenges that had brought out the best in their fathers. Even though he certainly had the financial ability to pay my college expenses, he thought it would be better for me to develop the resourcefulness and work habits required by doing it myself. I learned his lessons well, for he taught me that my life's future success or failure was ultimately my own responsibility.

In school, I met a lot of students who blamed their parents for all the problems in their lives. I was thankful to mine for teaching me that I was the ultimate source of how my life would turn out. I believe that a man does not have to simply be affected by outside forces, that he can create the story of his life by simply the power of his own will. A book that really influenced me at the time was *The Master Key to Riches* by Napoleon Hill.[952] The book really wasn't about money, it was about the real riches of life that come from accomplishment.

I decided to design my life just as someone would write a play or a novel. It hasn't always turned out as I have planned it, but I found it empowering to consciously direct my life rather than just floating through it, buffeted by the winds and the tides. A man doesn't have to be carried helplessly like a raft on the river of life, but can actually *be* the river, a directed and powerful river of purpose. For me, my own sense of accomplishment could only find meaning in advancing the cause of our people.

From the time my father and mother taught me to read, they had emphasized higher education. My grandfather, Ernest M. Duke, frequently gave me a little spending money when he came to visit, but Father encouraged him to make his gifts for my college savings account. From early grade school I worked with my father on his home building. In addition, I mowed yards, threw papers, and sold the reptiles I captured in the swamps to the snake farm in Slidell. In high school, I worked some afternoons for Randy Newmann at Kohlmeyer and Company, a stock brokerage firm in New Orleans.

After my wreck in my senior year in high school, I no longer had a car and a paper route. I found a tiny, old and rusted Fiat. I bought it for $200 dollars and brush-painted it military green. The engine was so small it had a maximum speed of about 70 miles per hour. Beginning the summer of 1968, I still needed to earn a lot of money for tuition, books, and the price of room and board on campus. I decided to go into business for myself and donned my old, paint-spattered overalls and painter's cap and drove around my neighborhood looking for homes with blistering or peeling paint. I'd knock on the door, introduce myself as a college student working his way through school, tell of my experience painting houses with my father, and offer to paint the home for about half of what a typical commercial firm would cost. I did a competent job and after I had done a few houses, word-of-mouth recommendations kept me busy all summer.

It was the hardest summer in my life. I would rise about 5:30 a.m. to be on the job by 6 and then work until about 8 every evening. Stormy days were my only days off and I welcomed them. Most of my work was outside, and words seem inadequate to describe the stifling, humid heat of New Orleans during that time. The work that I most hated involved preparing the wooden surfaces. Often I would be high on a ladder, straining and reaching over my head in the heat for hours — paint dust and chips covering and sticking to my sweat-soaked face and body. Working the underside of eaves was especially difficult. I was six feet tall and still growing, but the all-day intensive work in the New Orleans outdoor summer steam bath left me weighing only about 155 pounds. In the evening, I would return home and take a long hot shower and then read for about three hours until I fell asleep, usually dozing off in the middle of a page somewhere. I had little social life; I was simply not up to it. But I knew I had to work hard in order to pay for a large portion of the entire college year in only three months of work.

Painting houses in 1968, helped out by a visiting activist friend, Bill Kirstein.

When I finally left for school in late August 1968, I loaded down my little Fiat and started the 80-mile drive to the LSU campus in Baton Rouge. About three-quarters of the way, I smelled burning rubber and looked in my rear-view mirror to see black smoke and flames coming from the rear engine compartment through the cardboard and cloth-covered deck behind the back seat. I pulled over, quickly dumped my gear out of the car, and frantically threw dirt and mud on the engine. But I couldn't stop the flames. By the time I snuffed out the fire, my car looked like it had been bombed. A tow truck stopped by and the driver wanted to know if I needed his services, and I told him that if he wanted the car he could have it for towing it away. I signed the back of my title and watched him tow away my planned transportation for my freshman year. While driving to LSU, an acquaintance saw me, pulled over and gave me a ride to my dorm room at the north stadium.

I settled into my room later that evening, still smelling of smoke and oil, and quickly made friends with my four new roommates in my five-man room. Not a night from the first one onward seemed to pass without an argument or discussion on the race issue. North stadium was a wild place in those days, with booze flowing freely, occasional firecrackers going off, and big-pot, Cajun Bourre card games going on every evening somewhere in the dorm. Loud rock and roll music seemed to permanently play, and occasional fisticuffs added to the excitement. One could become burned-out in that dorm, but never bored. Everybody seemed to have an opinion about everything, and no-holds-barred heated discussions took place on everything from religion to politics, from sex to ethics, from space travel to sports.

A hierarchy developed among the students, not based on who their parents were or how much money they had, but on how they presented themselves, how fit they were, and how well they kept their word. I became known as the dormitory "Klansman," and most of those in my dorm agreed with my basic sentiments, but they were not as committed or vocal about it. At least three-quarters of the male students loved the confederate flag. I soon discovered that a few hated me because of my racial beliefs, but as they got to know me and came to realize that I wasn't a hatemonger or baby-killer, a number of them became my friends in what was then, an all-White dorm.

We could discuss anything in those days, and we did so. I think people in that era were far more committed to real freedom of speech and thought than in today's era of political correctness. No subject was off-limits, in fact if a student got his feelings hurt; he was simply viewed as a wuss. Instead of crying to the authorities about politically incorrect insults, you learned how to defend yourself point-by-point, with repartee — or by your fists if necessary. Today, on some campuses uttering politically incorrect sentiments can get a student expelled. Once in a great while, participants could become so agitated or angry that a fistfight broke out, but it seemed when it was all over, there was a mutual respect for those who acted like men.

A College Radical

By the time I had finished high school, I knew what I wanted to do with the rest of my life — I wanted to become a leader in the cause of our racial survival. I also had some high personal goals. I had attended military school one year and looked forward to the ROTC program at Louisiana State University, which had a reputation as one of the best in the country. At that time ROTC was compulsory at LSU for all freshman male students, but I would have joined it anyway, for I wanted to follow in my father's footsteps and become an officer in the United States Army. Although I had serious doubts about our involvement in a war halfway around the world, I saw Communism as an archenemy that threatened us all. I also knew that its influence had to be curtailed, and since my days as a child in my Gentilly Woods neighborhood, I had wanted to be tested. I looked forward to the challenges of Vietnam, to fighting for my country in the battles I had dreamed about when I was a young Boy. I also joined the Special Forces-oriented, extracurricular part of the ROTC program at LSU called the Bengal Raiders, with its rigorous training and special sessions at regular Army facilities.

On the academic side, I majored in *race*. I worked toward a BA in history, but if the curriculum I tailored for myself had been included in the university catalogue, it could have been called *The Dynamics of Race*. During my college career, I took courses in American and European history, one dealing with the Russian Revolution (taught by an open Marxist) and two courses centering on the American Revolution. I took biology, geography, and anthropology for a base in the biological aspects of the racial question. I took sociology to better understand the liberal arguments, and I took philosophy, logic, advertising, and speech to understand the underlying philosophic issues and how to express them. I took English and journalism to learn how to better express my beliefs, and I took three German classes as a gateway language for European studies.

I often challenged my teachers in class. Many of them taught the egalitarian viewpoint. I had read enough and thought enough about the topics to dare to debate them in class. Most classes at LSU were very open and discussion-oriented, and I soon developed a reputation for asking impertinent questions and sometimes sharply disputing the teachers' assertions. Instead of just lying low and parroting back what the teachers expected, I wrote dissenting opinions even on some of my essay tests in history, sociology and other humanities courses. I always carefully backed up my assertions.

Most of the professors who disagreed with me still graded me fairly, but I had a few who hated my challenges and graded me down for daring to express a contradictory point-of-view. Even though I had concern about some teachers knocking down my grades, I found it impossible to remain quiet in class when I heard things that I thought were simply untrue and destructive of our racial well-being. I did not want my fellow students to be misled, and I believed I had an obligation to speak out. An instance comes to mind, in a Philosophy 101 course, a good portion of it centered on Sigmund Freud. I liked to call him Sigmund *Fraud*. On one occasion the professor asked why Freud believed that potty training was so instrumental in the formation of the personality. "Maybe because he had chronic constipation," I quipped, to a good laugh from the class. It incensed me that hundreds of students in the class were being seriously told that anal fixation is a key factor to the personality.

At the same time, I developed good relationships with many of my teachers, including some liberals who were open-minded. My German teacher, Professor James Hintze, was very liberal, and I spent many hours after class in his office in spirited discussion and often-friendly debate. He was open to many of my perceptions as I was to his, and although we sharply disagreed on race, we found common ground in our desire to preserve the environment and reform the corruption inherent in the current political system.

During my freshman year at LSU, the Young Americans for Freedom sponsored a speech by Black spokeswoman, Julia Brown, on the dangers of the American Communist movement. Brown was an eloquent and moving speaker who had remarkable insight into the infiltration of Communism in the American government and the mass media. In the question-and-answer session that followed her speech, I pointed out that most of the Communist personalities she mentioned were Jews, and I asked her if she had any thoughts about the fact that Jews were the driving force behind Communism from its inception to the current day. She smiled and said that she knew exactly what I was talking about but that she "couldn't get into that."

Babs Minhinnette a few months before her death. She was a tireless patriot.

Immediately after the meeting, I met Babs and Virgil Minhinnette. They had rushed up to me and said that it was great that I had pointed out the connection between Communism and Jews. Babs, her son Tommy and her husband practically adopted me as part of the family, and I have spent countless hours with them over the years. Babs became a leader in her own right in the cause for our racial survival, and she headed up my campaign for Governor in Baton Rouge. I am thankful for her and her family's sacrifice for the cause over the years. She died of cancer in July of 1998, and her spirit shall stay with me as long as I live, and truly with all those she touched and inspired.

I had very little open political activity my first year. I just kept up my reading and applied myself to my favorite subjects. LSU had an area between the LSU Union and the theater called Free Speech Alley. It came alive every Wednesday at noon. There was a strong antiwar movement at LSU, similar to most major universities in the late 1960s,

One of the first organizational tables we set up at LSU. Ray Leahart hands out leaflets.

and left-wing activists had dominated Free Speech Alley for years. Although I spoke out in class and had participated in some anti-Communist street demonstrations, I had never really given a speech or participated in a formal debate outside the classroom. My nature was always more quiet and personal. It was one thing having a discussion with a few guys in a dorm room, quite another to contemplate giving a speech.

Up to my college years, I found my greatest joy in the solitude and silence of the many days I spent in the South Louisiana wilds. I also found that there is quite a difference between reading and speaking. Perhaps the most valuable thing that college did for me was enhance my communication skills. Many well-read, self-educated people have problems when they begin to communicate in an intellectual environment. Sometimes, intelligent people are not the best natural communicators; there is a distinct difference between spatial and verbal skills. It is not rare to encounter people who can understand the proofs of the Pythagorean theorem, but who have difficulty speaking fluently. They sometimes mispronounce words that they are familiar with and understand only from reading. A great thought spoken in bad grammar and with mispronunciation is more likely to be dismissed in the academic community than a ridiculous thought expressed with eloquence.

I also learned the power of humor. I have seen many profoundly illogical concepts effectively promoted by people who were humorous and endearing. The truth also needs those weapons, especially if one is expressing an unfashionable truth. Another lesson I learned from frequent debating is that people are far more convincing when they simply state their beliefs with sincerity. Sincerity and enthusiasm are always more persuasive than cleverness.

I discovered in college that racial egalitarians, although scientifically wrong, are often more eloquent than White activists. This is partly because of the powerful social pressures against anyone who speaks out on the race issue. Openness about the truth of race can cost someone his social standing and sometimes even his job advancement and livelihood. The best educated and most accomplished have the most to lose from political incorrectness, and too many remain silent. Many of those who dare to publicly tell the truth about race are from society's lower rungs — people that have little to lose by their outspokenness. They often lack the style to present their arguments well in an intellectual environment.

In my second year of college I resolved to no longer let the antiwar and egalitarian activists dominate the LSU political climate. I started a group called the White Youth Alliance and published a tabloid newspaper called *The Racialist* (a subtle distinction from the pejorative term *racist*) — *racialist* meaning *racial-idealist*. I saw the WYA as a more modern version of the Ku Klux Klan. We used the traditional Klan symbol, the kýklos, or crosswheel, which historically has symbolized the sun or enlightenment. On campus, our group would eventually grow to about 300 members, and we were able to start chapters at about a dozen other schools, and by the time I left college, it grew to a national membership of about 2,000.

I resolved to go to Free Speech Alley and speak; determined to tell the truth about racial differences and expose Jewish supremacism. Free Speech Alley usually had just a few dozen spectators, except when major student controversies arose. One quiet Wednesday at noon, I stood up on the soapbox and began to tell the whole truth as I knew it. I spoke frankly about racial differences and about the Jewish involvement in Communism, as well as their domination of our government and media. There were only about 15 students present when I started, but after I had spoken for about 10 minutes, about 300 people had gathered; in 20 more minutes there were about a thousand. They stood high on the cement planters, while others leaned over the second and third balconies of the Union for a better view.

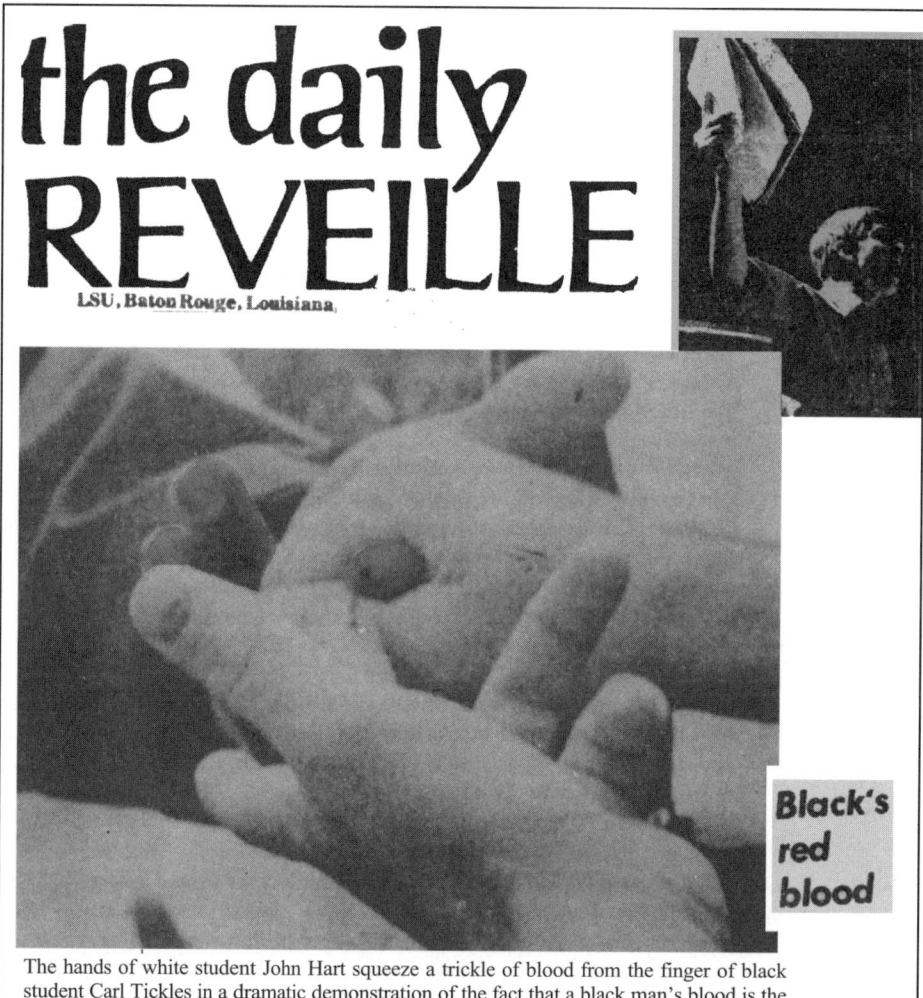

the daily REVEILLE
LSU, Baton Rouge, Louisiana

Black's red blood

The hands of white student John Hart squeeze a trickle of blood from the finger of black student Carl Tickles in a dramatic demonstration of the fact that a black man's blood is the same as a white man's. The demonstration took place at yesterday's Free Speech Alley.

The longer I spoke, the more easily the words seemed to come together and the more confident I became. In the uncontrolled atmosphere of the Alley, heckling and interruptions punctuated the speeches. Sometimes even projectiles whistled over my head. To win the debate you not only had to have good arguments; you had to respond to humor with greater humor, and to satire with counter-satire.

My opponents just *knew* I was wrong in challenging racial equality, but they had difficulty arguing the facts and concepts I presented. The fact that they could not effectively refute my points caused them such frustration that they went over the edge. At one point, attempting to refute my assertions that there were significant genetic differences between Blacks and Whites, they became so incensed and irrational that they began cutting themselves and holding up their bleeding fingers: Black and White (a photo of their cut fingers appeared on the front page of the campus newspaper the next day), all to prove, I suppose, that each race bleeds just as red.

I countered by telling the crowd that I could go over to the biology laboratory across the street and get any of the lab rats, and they would bleed red too! I also told them that they didn't have to cut the rats to prove that the rats were as intelligent as they were, for the rats were undoubtedly far superior — as rats would never stupidly cut themselves! Although I preached a supposedly discredited and unpopular doctrine, even most of the liberals reluctantly agreed that I won the debates. Of course, they explained it by suggesting that I was simply a more effective speaker than any of my liberal opponents. They certainly could not give any credit to the logic of my racial heresies. In truth, I had no greater skills than my opponents did. Many of them had stronger speaking voices and more ingratiating styles than I. My secret was having the racial truth on my side, and although the truth certainly does not always win every argument, it is a great advantage. With each passing week, more people began to stand up with me and support my position, until finally, *The Reveille* questioned the entire relevance of Free Speech Alley — saying that it had become simply a forum for racism and suggesting that it should be done away with. No longer a forum for liberalism and Marxist ideology, free speech became expendable.

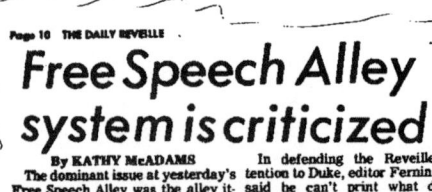

At the end of the 1960s, LSU, like many other colleges, had a strong contingent of Communist radicals, and even some members of the Students for a Democratic Society (SDS). It also had some very radical Black students who at one alley session, frustrated at their loss of a debate with me, picked up a stack of my newspapers, *The Racialist*, and burned them. The incident helped to wake up a lot of White students at LSU to the realities of race. As my popularity grew among many White students, radical Blacks and Jews hated me all the more. Death threats were slipped regularly under the door of my dorm room. One note threatened to pour gasoline under my dorm room door as I slept and light it. Bomb threats emptied my dorm on a couple of occasions.

During the spring semester of my sophomore year, Dean French called me into his office, concerned for my safety and also for the university's reputation. Students with no family in Baton Rouge were required to live on campus until their senior year, but the dean decided to make an exception in my case. He told me that I could live off campus if I wished.

I took a studio apartment on Chimes near Nicholson Drive and did maintenance work for the apartment complex for a reduction of my rent. The apartment manager, whom I knew only as Mr. Fryday, introduced me to Raymond Chandler crime novels and the wonderful writings of Casanova, which I found to be a tremendous study in human psychology. Mr. Fryday became one of my biggest boosters all through college.

In my junior year the Student Government Association invited radical opponents of the Vietnam War, including Dick Gregory and Dr. Benjamin Spock, to speak on campus. My group, the White Youth Alliance, organized protests against each of the featured speakers, and I attended the speeches and challenged them with questions. Before the speeches, I read up on the leftist spokesman, and I was surprised to learn of the many Marxist affiliations of Dr. Spock, the Jewish doctor who wrote the bible of childcare. I also read some critiques of his libertarian, anti-discipline style of child rearing, a style that fit in perfectly with the dissolution of the youth of the 1960s.

Benjamin Spock delivered an anti-Vietnam War diatribe before a packed Union Theater. He alleged that our soldiers were "war criminals" in Vietnam, and he also sounded traditional Marxist economic themes, supportive of equalized incomes for all Americans. He argued that his life was committed to seeing to it that babies he helped raise did not grow up to die in wars or to suffer in poverty, and he also told us that raising taxes and equalizing incomes could permanently end poverty. We could keep babies from dying, he claimed, by refusing to give any assistance to the anti-Communist war effort in Vietnam.

I made it to the microphone first for his question-and-answer session. My lengthy question went like this:

"Dr. Spock, you say that you are against the war in Vietnam not for political reasons, but because you did not want to see the babies you helped raise grow up to be killed in the brutality of war. As you know, the Vietnam War is winding down; our troops are beginning to come home. There is little you can do about that conflict now, but there is a new conflict brewing in the Mideast between Israel and her neighbors. There is potential danger for all the world's people by the confrontation of the superpowers in the Mideast. Frankly, I have doubts that your motives are really as you say — simply against the carnage of war. If it is war and the weapons of war you really oppose, would you make a public statement here and now that you oppose any more American involvement in the Israeli-Arab conflict, that you oppose any more weapons to Israel, just as you oppose arm shipments to South Vietnam? Or, Dr. Spock, is it only war waged against Communists that you oppose?"

Spock stuttered and was shaken. He mumbled something about the Mideast being an age-old conflict. There were factors, he said, that made the region "different" from Vietnam. I knew that the paramount difference to him was that Vietnam is Vietnamese and that Israel is Jewish.

I got back in line, and right before the question-and-answer period ended, I asked my second question of the night.

"Dr. Spock, you have told us tonight of the terrible suffering and hardship of America's poor, especially the Negro poor, and that we need to tremendously increase taxes and eventually have an equalized income for all Americans. Isn't it true, good doctor, that you own an entire island in the Bahamas, that you own a private jet and have a net worth of tens of millions of dollars? If you are so concerned about the poor and believe that the government should forcibly confiscate money and property from hard-working Americans, my question is, why don't you go ahead and teach us by example and sell your island and give it to what you call the deserving poor. I challenge you here publicly to do voluntarily what you want to force from the rest of us. Will you sell your island and your jet and give the money to the poor?"

The audience became ominously silent during a long pause, and Spock seemed flustered by the question. He feebly mumbled that he financially helped causes that he believed in, but the moderator rushed to his rescue. He announced that the program was over, and that Spock had to go to the reception. I looked at the dismayed faces of his Marxist followers and knew that I had struck a blow at his hypocrisy. Later that week, in a column in *The Reveille*, one of its liberal writers wrote that he thought I had asked the best questions of the evening. Although the liberals didn't agree with me, I earned a lot of respect from them, and they knew that I was a sincere person with a legitimate point of view.

Challenging the icons of the left and spreading the truth of race is exciting and deeply satisfying for me. It is like competing in the Olympics of ideas. Winning these jousts helped wake up my people and I must confess they were intensely pleasurable on a personal level.

There were aspects of my notoriousness, however, that were not so pleasant. I dated a number of intelligent and attractive women during the period, and more than once I had lost a friend. One teacher publicly ridiculed a girlfriend in class for dating me. Some teachers lowered my grades whenever they had the chance. The threats against my life seemed to grow more serious. Coming from a class one night, four men jumped me and struck a number of hard blows before they ran away into the darkness.

Sometimes the media treated me fairly. More often it did not. In one memorable Free Speech Alley session in which I was hammering at the Jewish hypocrisy of being doves toward the Vietnam War and hawks for Israel — a feminist, Jewish anti-war Marxist with hair shorter than mine — began screaming obscenities at me at the top of her lungs. "You f----- bastard, you son of a bitch, you...," she bellowed. Usually I try to turn such events away with satire or ridicule. I played on her obvious Jewishness by saying, "You are not giving us a good image of a Jewish-American princess." At this comment, she began bellowing obscenities even louder. At that I told her, "You had better stop using obscenities or we'll get the idea you really are Jewish."

She then jumped up on the bench and attempted to kick me in the groin. As it was, she kicked me really hard in the shins and on my knees, but I knew that if I punched her out, — that tomorrow's headlines would read "Klansman Attacks Jewish Girl." So I held her at arms-length until the campus security officer who was standing by could get over to drag her off. Of course, she wasn't arrested, but instead of lauding my restraint, the campus newspaper tried to make me look like I wimpishly had to be saved from the diminutive girl. I can imagine what the response would have been if I had struck the Jewess. It became obvious that once you get on the wrong side of the media, you are doomed to being painted wrong by the press, no matter what you do.

At the end of my second year at LSU, I was happy with my progress on all fronts. I had the respect of many liberals, some of whom I even called friends. Conservatives liked my outspokenness. While some professors docked my grades, others, even a few

Chloê Hardin at "No Vietnam in Mideast table"

of my ideological opponents, spoke well of my classwork and sincerity. Even a couple of the Black leaders on campus came to respect my racial honesty, which they thought was lacking in many Whites. They viewed the White race as exploitive and evil, but because they had an honest concern about their own heritage and interests, they could understand my concerns as well. They knew that I was unlike the liberals. I was not trying to subsume the Black race and culture into the White. I realized that I could best preserve the integrity of my own race by fostering the integrity of both.

Finding a Kindred Spirit

In my sophomore year the White Youth Alliance had a literature table with materials opposing America's pro-Zionist, Middle East policy. My friend Ray Leahart watched the table for me while I was in class. A cute coed had come by and expressed interest and he lent her a book. She promised him that she'd call me and return the book after reading it. A couple of days later, I heard from her and we met for dinner to discuss the book. Chloé was strawberry blonde, beautiful and charming — pure Southern girl, she could have sparked any man's interest, but even more important to me, she had a natural affinity to my beliefs. She had been a member of the conservative group Young Americans for Freedom on campus. When she read my literature on the race issue, she quickly understood its vital importance to the conservative values she cherished. She told me that she readily

Chloê Eleanor Hardin in 1970

understood that if the White race was not preserved, that neither could conservative principles be saved.

I ended up spending the entire rest of the evening with her. We drove around and talked. About 10 p.m. we parked by the largest campus lake; walked out to a moonlight peninsula and lay back in the cool grass — gazing up at the stars. By midnight, I was telling her my dreams for the future and about the things that I so fervently believed. I could see that my words expressed her own feelings, and that they burned just as bright in her own heart. From that night we were inseparable. In the next year, she came back very distraught from summer break at home in Florida, for her folks were upset that their daughter had become involved with a "radical" such as me. It seemed as though we would lose each other, but after many tears, we decided to continue to see each other. The next summer I traveled down to West Palm Beach and, although her parents, Jim and Eleanor Hardin, still had a lot of concern about her, they accepted me and realized I was not the monster the media made me out to be.

Military Madness

In ROTC I got along well with the Black cadets and indeed with both the corps and the teaching staff. After the first year, I had distinguished myself on the drill field and in class. Through the recommendations of both drill and classroom instructors, I won the Outstanding Cadet Award, and achieved the highest rank possible in a class of about 3,000 basic cadets at LSU. I must mention that fact so that you can understand the greatest disappointment of my college career. From the time I first saw my father in his uniform, I had wanted to serve my country and become a military officer. I looked forward to serving honorably in the Vietnam War and really fighting the Communists I had campaigned so hard against here at home. I relished every hardship of the Bengal Raiders Special Forces ROTC training organization. My hopes, though, were about to be crushed.

Colonel Joseph Dale, commandant of cadets at LSU, called me in for a meeting. He made the ultimate determination of who would be accepted in the advanced program and thus obtain their officer's commission. Colonel Dale offered me a chair and told me that a number of Jewish people in the community had called him and that they were dismayed that a member of the ROTC cadet corps had expressed what they called "anti-Semitic and racist viewpoints." Colonel Dale said he couldn't give the corps a bad name and therefore, despite my perfect ROTC record, he could not accept me in the advanced program. He acknowledged that I had not taken my political beliefs into the ROTC classroom or drill field. His words shocked and hurt me, and I knew that nothing I could say would dissuade him. I reacted by telling him that he was acting unfairly and in an un-American fashion. "By your standards," I told him, " the first Commander-in-Chief of the American armed forces, George Washington, would have been barred from service."

Having to tell my father was the worst part of my rejection. He so looked forward to my being commissioned an officer. By this time he had been transferred from Vietnam to Laos and in a phone call by a radio hookup requiring the saying of "over" and a delay after each statement, I told him of my disappointment. He responded by telling me that everything always works out for the best in life, if you just believe it to be so. Then he told me that he knew of some ways that I could help the war effort even though I wouldn't be in the military. He told me that he would try to help me come to Laos and participate in an important program there in support of the war. I hung up the telephone. It stormed outside. Although it was only about three o'clock in the afternoon, I drew the blinds, turned the air conditioner on high, took off my clothes and got under the covers, where I remained until dawn the next day.

The next day, I wrote Congressman F. Edward Herbert, whom my father and I both knew well, and asked him about my military prospects. He told me there was nothing he could do about my commission and suggested that if I tried to qualify for any kind of service I would end up getting an "unsuitable for service" classification, which might brand me for life. He offered me a student deferment and told me that he always had a lot of respect for me. "There are a great many traitors in our government," he told me frankly, and he told me bitterly that he thought traitors in Washington were determined that Vietnam would be the first war that America would lose outright. "Your father and I will find a way for you to support the war effort," he promised. I will always remember his last words to me. "But, David," he said, "you must realize that the most important fight for America ultimately won't be in Vietnam, but will be right in our own country; in our own neighborhoods. Frankly, I am in the Washington cesspool of government, and from that vantage point I can see what's in store for the nation — plain as day."

I redoubled my efforts against the Vietnam War Moratorium Committee at LSU and was determined that until I went to Southeast Asia, I would do my best to oppose those at home who were stabbing our soldiers in the back.

The war in Vietnam was entering a critical phase as the 1970s began, and I wanted to do whatever I could to help the fight against Communism. It seemed obvious that even after the sacrifice of tens-of-thousands of American lives, Kissinger and Nixon planned to abandon Southeast Asia to the Communists.

My father was with the USAID program in Laos where he helped the anti-Communist government with public-works programs. He contacted the U.S. State Department run school in Vientiane for Laotian military officers. It had to be ostensibly run as a civilian operation because Laos, although anti-Communist, was officially neutral in the war. The anti-Communist Royal Laotian forces controlled only about 20 percent of the nation, while the Pathet Lao (Communist forces) controlled the remainder. But the anti-Communist forces controlled the major cities of Vientiane, which was the administrative capital, and Luang Prubang, the royal capital. The Royal Laotian anti-Communists, who controlled the major capitals, were at war with the Pathet Lao Communists who controlled most of the countryside. The U.S. government surreptitiously supported the anti-Communists. The school needed instructors in Vientiane at the American Language School, where Laotian army and air force officers were instructed in basic and military-oriented English. It was a basic program that enabled them to be further instructed by actual American military advisors in the field or at American bases in Southeast Asia or in America. With my job arranged, my father arranged for my passage — as his dependent — to Laos.

Chapter 28:
Around the World

My plane tickets to Laos had arrived! The prospect of living with my father excited me. It would be my first time living with him since before I went to military school — and he to Vietnam — in 1966. I was also enthusiastic about being finally able to make a modest contribution to the anti-Communist war effort. I looked forward to seeing firsthand the nations and races I had read about in my quest for racial understanding. I felt like a botanist making a first trip to the Amazon. I arranged my itinerary to take me to nations I had long desired to visit and I left weeks earlier than my assignment began so I had a chance for a lengthy visit to the nations I had chosen. After a two-day stopover in Hawaii, I headed to Japan, Hong Kong, Saigon, Bangkok, and finally Vientiane.

The first great impression of my trip was flying into Tokyo. As the plane came within 50 miles of Tokyo Harbor, cruising at 35,000 feet, the dawn sky was crystal clear. On the horizon I could see ships and tankers strung in endless lines. They were steaming in filled with raw resources and leaving bursting with finished business products and consumer goods. Once the plane had landed, I noticed that the airport was spotlessly clean — and so were the people. I rode on the subways and found them filled with well-dressed and well-groomed men and women. Not a single derelict was in sight. Many of the people had a good knowledge of English, and I spoke to as many as I could, trying to get a feel for their culture and their lifestyle. The people had no fear of crime, and I could see the natural harmony of the nation everywhere. There are few dissidents and angry elements in Japan because the nation is truly a reflection of its people's spirit. Seldom did I see so much as a gum wrapper on the pavement and once when I saw a tiny wrapper blow away from a man in a wind gust, three people passing by jumped at once, almost knocking into each other, to pluck it from the gutter.

On relating the gum wrapper incident to a Japanese student I had met named Toshi, he told me that all the Japanese feel a kinship with each other. The sense of a common heritage and a common destiny makes the Japanese nation somewhat like a huge family. Certainly the greater Japanese family has its squabbles, but when threatened by outside forces or common problems they band together to solve them. "You want to know why Japanese don't litter?" Said Toshi; "It's because throwing litter in the street is like throwing trash in a relative's home!" I asked him about Japanese students' study and work habits. He told me that every Japanese person is taught from the time he is very young of the noble history of the Japanese people, and each child learns that he is a vital part of that tradition, and that he and others like him are now its guardians and keepers. They teach him that if he personally fails, that his family and tradition fails as well. Not only is he responsible for himself, but he must take a personal responsibility for his own nation, and ultimately, even for the meaning of their ancestors' sacrifices. Worship of one's ancestors is common throughout Japan. The rich racial and cultural tradition, and artistic continuity, unites the people in a sense of brotherhood unparalleled in the world.

Japan's history also refutes one of the main explanations used to explain Africa's lack of development. Afrocentrists say that sub-Saharan Africa failed to develop into modern civilized states because of its isolation from the rest of the world. Yet, many Black African states were near the great ancient civilizations, and the Arab world colonized Africa for millennia. In stark contrast to Africa, Japan completely cut itself off from the rest of the world in the modern era (from 1603 to 1867), the Tokugawa Shogun period. By 1900, only about 30 years after reestablishing contact in 1867, Japan emerged as a world power. In 40 more years it became a manufacturing giant. Then, after the almost complete destruction of its industry and a terrible loss of life in the Second World War, its economy became second in the world only to that of the United States. And it must be remembered that Japan accomplished these gains despite being a small, crowded, and resource exhausted nation.

Could Japan's secret be partly that it is all-Japanese? The largest minority group in the entire nation is Korean, and they constitute only about 2 percent of the population. They differ from the Japanese in a similar, slight degree as say the Irish do from the English.

I walked around Tokyo one day during my visit and did not see a Caucasian or a Negro — that is, until I went to the top of the Japanese Tower. On the observation deck, I saw my first White man of the day, and when he turned around, I saw that his female companion was Black. I wondered if the couple was a symbol of American racial diversity, and indicative of the degeneration of our social health in comparison with that of the Japanese.

My next stop was Hong Kong. Going from the airport into Kowloon and seeing the uncountable numbers of people in the streets, I gained a true sense of the incredible population of Asia. I talked to some tourist guides who told me that many of the Chinese in Hong Kong live in apartments by the shift. They sleep and cook there for a

508 MY AWAKENING

third of the 24-hour period and then leave the apartment for the other two shifts of tenants, who do the same thing.

I took the tram to the top of the beautiful Hong Kong Island at dusk and saw one of the most magnificent views of my life: the dark hills of China up against the bright lights of Kowloon and the well-lighted ships dotting the magnificent harbor below. It was a romantic scene, but I was a long way from Chloê and felt even lonelier soaking in its beauty by myself. I then noticed a White man on the observation walk. He turned out to be the same one I had seen in Tokyo! And, yes, the same Black female accompanied him. *Is there a point to this coincidence?* I thought.

From there I flew to South Vietnam and the beautiful city of Saigon. I looked up a couple of my father's friends and they helped me understand the lay of the land. No one I talked to thought Nixon's Vietnamization program would work. George McGovern, Nixon's opponent in the upcoming elections, promised to get the US out of Vietnam, while Nixon promised to win the war. But after winning re-election, Nixon let Kissinger give South Vietnam away to the Communists. He had promised Americans peace with honor, but his tenure had only meant more American lives lost in a war that the government never had the guts to do what it took to win.

Next I went on to Bangkok, the Venice of the Orient. The city impressed me greatly, and I had an opportunity to go to the beautiful

On a boat on the Mekong River in 1971

coast at Padua. Boiled seafood halfway around the world from my home in New Orleans looked, smelled, and tasted exactly like what I was used to back home — and I had some other dishes with very similar French-style cooking. I noticed that Bangkok, for all its historic places and special beauty, seemed to have a more primitive character about it than Vietnam. Finally, I boarded a train for Vientiane, which was just across the Mekong River from northern Thailand.

Laos

As the train rumbled north from Bangkok, cultivated landscape increasingly gave way to thickening jungle. Sturdy brick and wood houses diminished to bamboo huts with thatched roofs. The further north we traveled, the children wore less clothing — while the adults wore more jewelry. They wore their savings accounts around their necks in an almost pure form of 24-carat, reddish-tinted gold. Finally, about dusk, we came to the station, which was near the Mekong River. I grabbed my bags and found out that I had to hail a water taxi across the river to Vientiane, Laos. The boats seemed almost as narrow as a Louisiana pirogue, but they had big gasoline-powered automobile engines ingeniously mounted on a swivel in the boat with a 12-foot propeller-ended driveshaft trailing in the water behind it. They turned the boat by turning the engine on its swivel, and when they gunned the engine, these boats put on an incredible burst of speed that could practically knock you off the boat if you were not braced for it.

The pilot had a large transistor radio blaring the ending of some sort of Asian song broadcast from one of the nearest Thai radio stations. About halfway across the river, at the very same moment when I considered the fact that I was almost exactly halfway around the world from my beloved Louisiana, the radio came alive again. *"When I was a little bitty baby, / My momma would rock me in the cradle, / In them old cotton fields back home/ It was down in Louisiana / Just about a mile from Texarkana, / In them old cotton fields back home."* Then before we arrived at the other side of the river, the next song was Creedence Clearwater Revival's *Born on the Bayou*.[953] It seemed I wasn't so far from home after all.

Vientiane had some paved streets but a lot of dirt ones, and it had a thriving American community that was part of the American Aid effort. Unlike Vietnam, Laos was officially neutral and had embassies from all over the world, including Communist China and Russia as well as the U.S.A. Quietly, American personnel under the cover of USAID and other programs were aiding the war between the Royal Laotian Government and the Communist Pathet Lao. I got across the river an hour later than scheduled, but I could see Father patiently waiting for me, standing besides his 1968 Chevrolet Caprice station wagon. It was wonderful to see him. It had been eight months since his last visit to the States. He had a two-bedroom white stucco bungalow in a modest neighborhood near the embassy district. At the door was his housekeeper-cook, a freckled and thin Laotian named Mething who spoke broken English, but had a wide smile and only had a few missing teeth.

My third day there, I awoke to find a young cobra in the living room. It had squeezed in under our door. With a carved, 3-foot decorative fork plucked from the living room wall, I got to practice the skills I had honed long ago in Louisiana. I captured him and set him free down the road in some thick underbrush.

While Father worked at the Civil Engineering section closer to town, I took the car to the English-language school on the northern outskirts of town. My students in advanced military English were all army and air force officers, the cream of the Laotian upper classes and

My Laotian Army and Air Force officer students

generally very intelligent. All of them were intensely anti-Communist. We taught with a repetition and illustration method that is used in teaching English to people of any language around the globe. Some of my students would go on to further training in the United States, usually at Fort Hood or Fort Knox. Others would use their increased language skills in their advanced military training by American military advisors.

Laos is the crossroads of Southeast Asia, and many different racial groups exist there. Among my students I had very light-skinned and fairly tall Chinese — to darker and smaller Thai types. I had many that were simply called Lao, who looked like a cross of the two. I had a couple of students who looked like the primitive Montagnards, as well as some Vietnamese. The different Asian races had quickly discernible features and personality characteristics, and they differed in intelligence ranges as well.

The Chinese in my classes typically caught on the fastest, followed by the Vietnamese, the Lao, the Thai, and generally last came the Montagnards. The pattern held up fairly consistently, as the lighter-skinned Laotian usually excelled over his more Thai-like, Laotian counterpart. Some of the Thai were very dark, with wide, flat noses and large lips, with a strongly Negroid appearance even though their hair was straight. I wondered if they were at least partially descended from the same ancient race that fathered the Australian aborigines. On the opposite hand, some of my higher-ranking Chinese students had skin as light as any White man's, along with sharp features and thin lips. It was only their epicanthic fold that gave them away, and in many of them, their eyes had only a slight fold somewhat like Mexicans or Indians who happen to have a lot of White blood.

I wanted to know if there had been many White incursions in the Chinese gene pool in the provinces where these lighter Chinese came from. My anthropology textbook at LSU showed a line of prehistoric Caucasian migration all the way across China, and there is now evidence that early Aryans introduced the wheel and the chariot as well as domesticated horses to ancient Asia.[954] Recent findings of extremely ancient Caucasian mummies show the advanced cultural attributes of Europid settlers of the region.[955]

Like most Third World cities of any size, the auto traffic in Vientiane could become harrowing. One afternoon, while I was driving down the narrow streets near the embassies, a bicyclist darted out from between two parked cars directly into my path. I threw on my brakes and swerved to the right to avoid her, but my car clipped the fender of a stopped automobile. I was surprised to see a tall, blond Russian get out of the car. He could speak rather good German and a little English, and although I couldn't speak Russian, I knew a bit of German from my college courses, and through the two languages we communicated pretty well. After he and I discussed the minor accident, he introduced himself as Peter, and we went next door into a French coffee shop and began to talk about our respective nations and the politics of each. I mentioned that I was opposed to Nixon's initiative to the Red Chinese. Peter grinned and said, in words I well remember to this day, " Ja." He said, "We White men must stick together!"

I was dumbfounded. I thought, *I'd love to hear an American diplomat say that!* After a while we both felt comfortable and discussed many serious things and even shared some jokes. I decided to ask Peter about the Jewish influence in the Soviet Union. At first he did not understand what I was talking about, but then he smiled and took his

512 My Awakening

forefinger and drew an imaginary semicircle out from the bridge of his nose, an instantly understandable international description. He told me that Jews still had a lot of influence in Russia, but that it had greatly declined since the days of the revolution. He also told me that they dominated organized crime, which he said was a serious problem in his nation. He told me that their crime network had even extended to a handful of Jews in Laos, who imported drugs into Mother Russia. He also told me that Zionism had gained much ground in the Soviet Union, and now that Jews had slipped from the pinnacle of power they once held, many were trying to undermine the state, thinking that in chaotic times they could work their way back into power.

As I stood listening to this Russian in the streets of this Third World capital far away from our respective nations, I began to see more clearly than ever that political forms have very little importance compared to the racial currents underneath them. If what Peter said was true, and the Jews had turned against their baneful creation of Communism, then their organized opposition around the world, plus their still considerable power inside the Soviet State, could well result in its fall. That was an unheard of thought in 1971, for then it seemed Soviet Russia was as solid as steel. As an American, for years I had been taught about the Russian "enemy," and even after I learned about the true nature of the Russian Revolution (that it wasn't really Russian), I still had negative feelings toward Russians. Perhaps I still held the rape of Eastern Europe and Germany against them. My meeting with Peter, however, made me understand more clearly that it was not the Russian people who were our fundamental enemies. They had been used and exploited the same way that American policy had been perverted in the Mideast.

In addition to my teaching, I was anxious to do something more to directly help the anti-Communist war effort in Laos. I traveled to some of the outlying areas of Laos with my father, flying with Air America pilots to the most remote regions of the country. Air America was a quasi-US Government airline that supported the anti-Communist effort in South East Asia. It was a rag-tag group of aviators. Some were veterans and some were novices who flew both aircraft and helicopters in support of anti-Communist civilian and

View of Mekong River at flood stage from the helicopter open cargo bay from which I would drop supplies.

military forces. Once, we flew to the far northwest village Ban Houi Sai, only about 10 kilometers from the Chinese border.

I made friends with some of the Air America pilots and hitched rides with them as they made their rice and munitions drops to the anti-Communist villages and military forces of Laos some of them deep in enemy territory. These pilots included some of the best in the world, many having flown during both the Korean and the Second World War. A couple of times our plane encountered some fire. Once, during a low altitude rice run, I was readying for a drop near the open back cargo doors when we suddenly encountered some flak. I felt as though someone had just punched me in the side. I thought I had been hit seriously until I saw a small glistening fragment of shrapnel protruding from my thick-webbed canteen belt. I dug the shrapnel out with my pocketknife and examined it. It was no bigger than a split lima bean, but left a bruise the size of a half-dollar. Father had been worried about my safety on the missions, so I didn't tell him

Getting ready to go on an Air America rice-run to supply anti-Communist troops and civilians in the remote regions of Laos.

about that experience until after I stopped doing them near the end of my stay in Laos.

The stark beauty of the country enthralled me. Flying up to Luang Prabang, the Royal Capital, one could see granite spires reaching hundreds of feet out of the jungles — covered by the greenest of exotic vegetation that seemed to scratch against the clouds. Hiking back into the jungle, I found more varied wildlife than I ever saw in my Louisiana swamps. A lot of the terrain was practically inaccessible for hundreds of square miles. It was sparsely populated, often by tribes that seemed barely out of the Stone Age. It was no wonder the Pathet Lao guerrillas controlled most of the countryside; no government could ever control those who chose to dwell in such an environment. I also realized why the Communists were able to provide for their forces in South Vietnam despite the heavy bombing of the Ho Chi Minh Trail. If the terrain was as thick and as mountainous as what I saw in Laos, it would have been almost impossible to detect the Communist enemy, and then, only a direct hit of a thousand-pounder could do any real damage.

Living with my father in Laos I felt closer to him than I had since I was a young man working beside him on the homes we built. He was in his late 50s and he looked much younger, and acted the same way. He always had a way of putting everything in the best light, and he loved to point out that temporary disappointments could work out for the best in the long run. He set it up in his own mind that any disappointments *would* work out for the best, that there is a good purpose for everything if one just leads his life with sincerity.

In late August, I said goodbye to father and Laos and left for further adventures in India, Israel and Europe.

At a grass airstrip in a remote region of Laos.

Chapter 29:

My Indian Odyssey: A Ghost From India Haunts Me Still

Armed with a camera and a frayed notepad, I trotted out of the YMCA at about 5:30 in the morning. After a humid, sweaty night, the cool air enlivened me as I walked briskly toward the center of New Delhi. Thousands of chirping birds serenaded me as I strolled along the main boulevards. A fat, bushy-tailed squirrel crossed my path a few inches from my shoes, exhibiting no fear. Such an abundance of small birds and animals was in stark contrast to what I had seen in Laos and Thailand. Indo-Chinese cities have a scarcity of small game because people eat almost any non-poisonous, four-legged creatures available. In India, however, small game has the rigorous protection of religious taboo — a power far greater than hunger.

Small animals were not the only beings in great abundance. So were people. Along one long sidewalk, I saw hundreds of wooden shelves about the size of a refrigerator lying on their sides. Each served as home for at least one person. Even less fortunate souls lay on the grass or in the brown dirt with a tattered blanket serving as their only shelter. Some had only rags to protect themselves from the elements. About a block from the YMCA, an old man grunted as he squatted and defecated in the gutter. A little further on, a bony couple engaged in mechanical sexual intercourse while two children sat beside them, taking little notice of their parents as they played in the dust. Millions in India live out their lives on the public streets awash in the dried mud. There they are born, and there they bathe, eat, sleep, excrete and copulate. As attested by the teeming population, the one thing they seem to do best is breed.

As I penetrated deeper into the center of New Delhi, I saw many modern structures. Most of the structures housed branches of European firms doing business in India. Many Indian government buildings had been constructed in the Colonial style of the twenties and thirties under the auspices of English imperial rule. The contrast between abject human debasement only a few steps away from such esthetic architectural achievements was disconcerting; but my eyes

516 My Awakening

slowly got used to the stark disparity as I headed for one of the main commercial squares.

At about 8:30 a.m. I reached a main square where I planned to inquire about bus service to Agra, site of the Taj Mahal, one of the Wonders of the World. The streets buzzed with activity. A large white bull pulled a cylindrical lawnmower over the grass on the boulevard's center ground. Dressed in white of a shade that matched the animal's hide, a turbaned Indian guided it patiently. At the cabstand I learned that I could ride to Agra and back in a taxi cab (a round trip of about two hundred miles) for only $12. I met a young English student from Cambridge traveling during his summer vacation, and we decided to share a cab after getting some breakfast at the main coffeehouse on the square.

Six Indians behind the counter worked at a furious pace, serving hundreds of patrons. Each worker had a separate job. Only one of them washed dishes, and cleanliness was not one of his finer points, for he looked as though he moonlighted as a gravedigger. Crusty black dirt trimmed the tips of his long fingernails; the lighter spots on his face and neck, on closer inspection, turned out to be streaks where sweat had washed off some layers of muck. After hundreds of swabbings from the same filthy water, his dishrag resembled what I imagined were mummy wrappings. The man wiped the filthy plates and utensils according to their immediate necessity right before the eyes of the customer.

Upon deeper consideration, I discovered that I no longer had any hunger. But Rodney Johnson, my new English friend, wolfed down the coffee and fried eggs without the slightest suggestion of discom-

A photo I took at the time -- a sacred cow pulling a lawn mower

fort. He seemed oblivious to the unsanitary conditions. I told him that I had never imagined British Colonial grit was the foreign matter found in their food.

We hired a rundown taxi of a make I could not identify. Some sort of strange religious symbols hung from the rearview mirror, and the clear plastic seats immediately stuck to our bare legs as the three-hour trip to Agra began. The dozen books I had read on India had not prepared me for the panorama of horrors unfolding as we sped from the business district of New Delhi. By the roadsides I saw hundreds of rickety, bug-eyed children, and even a couple of emaciated corpses lying on the street, treated by passersby like so much refuse to be hauled away. The bargaining and squabbling of the marketplace were strange and annoying to my ears, and I could not get accustomed to the stenches. Sometimes the odors came from the fires made from briquettes of bovine and human dung. Amid the ruins and rubble lay intermittent piles of ancient garbage through which the starving picked in search of even the tiniest of rotting morsels.

Once in a while an old temple or structure would heave into view out of this sea of desolation and offer a brief glimpse into a high culture that had once flourished here. Visiting India for the first time, I decided not to be depressed by the ugliness and the decay, and gradually, in the midst of the ruins and putrefaction, I resurrected in my imagination the once beautiful, magnificent empire of India. I could feel the vitality and creativity that had ruled this land thousands of years ago. In my mind's eye, see the farmers and tradesmen, the artisans and musicians, the road builders and architects, the noblemen and the warriors.

As the cab began to wind out of the stifling city and escaped into the countryside, I wrestled with what I knew about the once great Indian civilization. Green rice fields sped by the window of my cab as I weighed what I had learned from books on ancient Indian history and from conversations I had with some New Delhi college professors I had met during the previous few days. The historical facts mingled in my mind with the impressions harvested by my own eyes.

Aryans, or Indo-Europeans (Caucasians) created the great Indian, or Hindu civilization. Aryans swept over the Himalayas to the Indian sub-continent and conquered the aboriginal people. The original term *India* was coined by the Aryan invaders from their Sanskrit word *Sindu*, for the river now called the Indus. Sanskrit is perhaps the oldest of the Indo-European languages, having a common origin to all the modern languages of Europe. The word *Aryan* has an etymological origin in the word *Arya* from Sanskrit, meaning noble. The word also has been associated with gold, the noble metal and denoted the golden skinned invaders (as compared to the brown skinned aboriginals) from the West.

Composed in about 1500 B.C., the Hindu religious texts of the *Rig Veta* tell the story of the long struggles between the Aryans and the aboriginal people of the Indian subcontinent. Sixteen Aryan states were partitioned by the sixth century A.D., and Brahmanism became the chief religion of India. The conquering race initiated a caste system to preserve their status and their racial identity. The Hindu word for caste is *Varna*, which directly translated into English, means *color*. Today the word is usually associated with occupation or trade; but that is because occupations evolved on the basis of skin color and ethnicity. The most pale skinned were called the Brahmin. These were the warrior-priest class, the top of the social ladder. The Untouchables (or Pariahs) were the racially mixed in the bottom caste.

Over the past few centuries the clear racial differences have faded, but one can still notice the lighter hues and taller statures of the higher castes. Many scholars consider Sanskrit the oldest and purest of the Indo-European languages. In modern India, the greatest insult one could pay a fellow Indian is to call him "black."

In spite of all the organized government and media efforts to root out racial feeling, there is still ample evidence that race does matter in modern India. Rodney Johnson showed me the personal ad columns that catered to the English-speaking Indians. The skin color of the advertiser is always described very precisely. I found that many of the ads emphasized the degree of lightness of the prospective husband or wife.

The average Christian conservative of the Western world would be aghast at the exuberant interest displayed by the ancient Indians in sex and in the ways they publicly displayed sexual experience through art. Hindu history, though, seems to indicate that it was not preoccupation with sex that brought down the high culture as much as it was the racial impact of that obsession. In spite of strict religious and civil taboos, the ancient Aryans crossed the color line. Slavery, or a similar system, had made servant women easily obtainable and proved a dangerous temptation for some of the basest of the slaveholders. Only a small percentage of each generation had sexual liaisons with the lower castes, but over dozens of generations a gradual change in the racial composition occurred. Such changes are almost imperceptible in a single generation. But they are dramatic after a millennium.

One of the problems of the Indian civilization is that the most creative, most intelligent, and most successful people have many avenues of fulfillment, while the lower classes consider sex a form of recreation. Sex is the one highly enjoyable pastime the poor can always afford. Every civilization has a lower average birthrate among its most talented elements, while its less intelligent and unproductive tend to proliferate. Ancient India was no exception.

Even traveling 45 miles per hour with all the taxi's windows down, it was still so hot and dusty that my British friend and I felt as though we could not get enough air. However, India was not the dry, desert-like expanse that I had pictured. Certainly India has its arid areas, but great portions of the country are humid and wet. During my stay I saw beautiful seaports, green fertile valleys, thick forests and jungles, mountains that glittered with the reflection of their vast mineral wealth. The countryside we traveled through was far from dry. Rice field followed rice field, and there were many watering holes — usually filled with cows cooling their sacred hides.

At midmorning we decided to stop for a little refreshment, and the cab driver pulled off the highway by a little shanty cafe. By this time my hunger had overcome my lack of enthusiasm for Indian dishwashing. Rodney, undaunted as ever, ordered some fried eggs. I optimistically thought that eggs fried in a hot skillet — albeit it dirty — would not do much harm, so I put my order in. Since the coffee was boiling hot, I consented to have some of it as well.

After letting them cool a bit, I ravenously consumed a yellow spoonful of eggs. A feeling like liquid fire spread from my tongue to the roof of my mouth and clear back to my larynx. It spread from my throat into my esophagus and stomach. My eyes watered. My nose ran. I tried to swallow, but I could not. I looked at the swarthy, beady-eyed driver, then at the proprietor of the shanty, and for a fleeting moment I imagined a criminal conspiracy between them. I pictured the authorities finding my poisoned, pain-contorted body in a rice paddy a few days later, stripped of identification, passport, camera, and cash.

Then, through a blurry film, I saw Rodney wolfing down his eggs like they were milk chocolate. Maybe what I had taken for British bravado was only his true affection for this land and its traits.

I believed that I had stumbled onto the reason why almost all the food in India is intolerably hot, for as famished as I was, that one bite was more than enough for me that morning. Suddenly I had no more hunger. But it was no longer fear of dirty utensils that killed my desire to eat, for I figured that few germs could have survived the heat of the little red infernos the Indians call peppers. Growing up in south Louisiana, I had often eaten spicy and hot food, but those Indian peppers are indistinguishable from glowing embers of lava. Only the English could have colonized this place, I thought, for only they, like Rodney, had the stomach for it.

Near the shanty where we ate were hordes of small children. A number of them had deformities such as full or partial blindness and amputated limbs. The cab driver told me that many parents purposely mutilate their own children to increase their intake from begging.

As we drove on, I found the poverty of New Delhi duplicated in the countryside. We passed many settlements teeming with rag-swathed, skeleton people. Children were starving everywhere. Cruel, open sores spotted their bodies, and the unrelenting flies swarmed the children to feast on their festering wounds.

The probable first impulse of any Westerner who learns of India's plight is to send money and food. But by sending such assistance, he actually only compounds the agony. The reason that so many Indians are starving is their chronically high birth rate combined with their low ability rate. The resulting overpopulation outstrips the ability of the people to feed themselves. Unless the givers tie aid to absolute guarantees of population control, the increased food simply feeds another reproducing generation that in turn only multiplies the problem. Despite this self-evident fact, Western nations have poured seemingly unending food and medical supplies into India. The purpose of the relief at its start early in this century was to help the thousands who were starving. Paradoxically, because of our generosity we can now report that tens of millions starve in India. The sunken faces of the malnourished, sick, and mutilated children around the nation are the results of misplaced humanitarianism that has only increased human suffering and death.

At our next stop on this trip to the Taj Mahal, was a small roadside bazaar. The cab driver apparently had an arrangement with some of the ceramic and leather shops to bring in tourists. In addition to the shops, also present were fakirs, snake charmers, and animal trainers. One turban-crowned Indian had what he called a "dancing bear." A worn, leather leash was tightened around the bear's neck, causing him to choke and gag. It was stifling hot, and this poor creature's heavy coat contributed to his severe skin infections that scarred his body and had removed large patches of fur.

This bear was so emaciated that he had an eerie appearance, for as he would stand and perform his tortured dance, he resembled a man. When the trainer whipped the bear with his stiff cane pole, the animal placed its paws over its head to protect itself from the blows. Streaks of red blood colored his digits.

I moved through the crowd with my fists clenched. It would have been so easy to wrench that pole from that puny little torturer and give him a dose of the pain he was inflicting on the pitiful bear. One more strike at that bear and I will have at him, I thought. Then I felt a tug on my arm and heard the calm, evenly modulated voice of the

Englishman whispering that he felt exactly the same way I did, but then looked directly into my eyes and said, "What are you going to do, David — go to war against the whole Indian nation?"

I stumbled back to the cab, wondering how many times in a man's life he must turn his head when justice demands he act. Regardless of how much pity I have for the people of India, it is true that every people ultimately have responsibility for its own condition, for its general health and well-being. After gazing on the poor, mistreated animal that had no control over its destiny, a profound sadness came over me.

On both sides of the highway to Agra were cattle — thousands of them. The driver explained that they were sacred. As he told us about their religious sanctification and protection, I thought about the great cattle industry the nation could have. Later, in the shops of Agra, I saw rats and birds scampering around the food in the bins and not receiving a second glance from the proprietors or their skinny customers. In some areas of India, not only the cattle but even the rats are sacred.

Agra and New Delhi are far cleaner cities (by Indian standards) than the other large cities, such as Calcutta and Bombay. In northern India the people are taller, lighter skinned, and more sturdily built than are those of the hot coastal areas. Occasionally I encountered a native Indian who could easily pass for a southern European — or perhaps a Louisiana Creole.[956]

Anticipation welled up in me and tingled like a cool breeze across my sweaty body as we neared the Taj Mahal. My father had described the structure to me a number of times, and for years I had been eager to see it. As we passed through the shaded arches of the outlying buildings, the whitish-blue sky became bright with glare. Then the great temple itself came into view, gleaming, white and magnificent in the sun. I had stepped out of the filth, rot, and decay of modern India into an earlier era of beauty, order, and high art.

Rodney and I sat on the edge of the reflecting pool to cool off and rest. We rested quietly, our eyes drawn to the water. We looked at the reflection of the great structure, overwhelmed by its beauty, and then at the building itself. Although Rodney and I were both usually quite glib, we sat motionless and mute. When Rodney finally spoke, the words came out in whispers of reverence for the splendor of the Taj Mahal. And then reality slowly began to crowd in on me. I knew that most of the modern-day Indian visitors I saw around me were poor reflections of the men and women who had walked these grounds centuries before. The temple — actually a memorial built by a man for his dead wife — had been constructed as a Muslim temple long after the great flowering of the Aryan civilization but contains many of the architectural and artistic qualities of the earlier era. I thought, as I approached the temple, how it might be taken as a metaphor, a funerary monument to the memory of a people who had given the world such great beauty. As I viewed the structure in the sharp sunlight of afternoon, it occurred to me that the rounded dome, with its features like sun-bleached bone, resembled a great skull. The temple might represent the spiritual cranium of the Aryan people, I thought — one that had once held talented and disciplined minds but which now served only as a magnificent gravestone of a deceased culture and genetic treasure now degraded beyond redemption.

On the long road back to New Delhi, Rodney slept, while I rested my head on the window frame and peered into the dusty countryside, taking in the sights and sounds as nonchalantly as if I had traveled the road a thousand times before. Half asleep, I dropped Rodney off after we had exchanged addresses, but somehow in my travels it became lost, and I never saw or heard from him again after that day. When I got back to the YMCA, I took off my shoes, curled up on my musty cot, and fell asleep with my camera still around my neck.

The next day, I decided to explore some of the other temples that dotted the countryside. I hired a cab, and it wasn't very long before I spotted a suitable target. I began walking across a dry grassy area toward the huge structure in the distance. A few hundred feet from the paved highway, I literally stumbled across another road. It was extremely old, and only a part of road was visible through the overgrowth and sediment. It was a magnificent road of stone carved into perfect blocks and laid over a base of gravel. The surface of the road was as level as a billiard table and would still have been usable if the weeds that had grown up in the cleavages of the stone had been cut.

As I walked over the ancient road and through the patches of dry weeds toward the temple, I reviewed all that I had read about India and all that I had seen firsthand. I recalled the fact that the highest classes were the lightest-skinned, that nothing was more insulting to an Indian than calling him "black," that "Varna" (*caste*) is the Indian word for color. The original language of the ancient Aryan invaders, Sanskrit, is an ancient Indo-European language with direct links to every other European language. Ancient Sanskrit literature even has descriptions of Aryan leaders as having light eyes and hair. As I neared the temple, I thought about the splendor that once was and about the dreadful squalor I had witnessed since my arrival in the India of today.

I noticed that the temple's dome had partially caved-in. Only two walls remained standing. Still closer, I saw thousands of pockmarks eroding the structure. Each of them had once housed a precious stone, but these had long ago been pried loose and picked clean. I wondered if all the monuments of Europe and America would eventually endure the same fate as this one.

Around the corner of the temple, on the partially shaded side, I saw something that will forever remain in my memory. In the shade sat a little, brown, half-caste Indian girl. She was thoroughly emaciated and resembled some sort of hideous doll except that she moved slightly, and her animated bones and skin had a terrifying effect. She was so malnourished that her face had not developed properly, but her eyes were very large, and in their own way they were hauntingly beautiful. On one cheek was an open sore the size of a quarter. More sores covered her arms, chest, and legs. Dozens of flies covered each sore, jockeying with each other to feast on her flesh. Occasionally the little girl would brush her frail hand over one of the sores, causing the flies to retreat. Inevitably, though, once her hand had passed, the flies returned like iron filings to a magnet. The child held her hand out to me, begging for a few rupees. I dug my hand deep into my pocket, pulled out all the Indian coins I had, and carefully tipped them into her dark, skeletal hand. I turned and stumbled back out into the hot Indian sun, my eyes blinded by tears.

On the way back to my room I wondered if, in a few hundred years, some half-black descendant of mine would be sitting among the ruins of our civilization, brushing away the flies, waiting to die. Every day our nation grows a little darker from the torrential immigration of non-Whites, high non-White birthrates, and increasing racial miscegenation — and with each passing day, we see the quality of our lives decline. Crime is ever on the increase, drug activity proliferates, educational quality declines, and the American standard of living suffers. There are those who ridicule the healthy racial values of our forefathers and replace them with the pseudo-science of egalitarianism. Treason to our heritage thrives, and corruption feeds in the highest places.

All that keeps our society afloat are the small number of scientists and technicians (predominately Caucasian) who continue to create technological wizardry that cushions the impact of the economic slide caused by lower individual productivity and the dependency of the growing Welfare underclass. Somehow, the increasingly hard-pressed, White middle class keeps the wheels turning (and taxes flowing into the social structure) — but with decreasing efficiency.

To the plaudits of the media, the Pariahs — the Untouchables — are slowly replacing the Brahmin of America and the entire Western world. The hideous skeletal girl in that prophetic setting of that Indian temple was my glimpse of the future of the Western world. If that bleak future is to be avoided, it will require each person who understands the racial truth to act with resolve and a sense of urgency.

The nation of India, like most of the Third World, has already passed the point of no return. She cannot feed or otherwise adequately take care of herself, not even with repeated injections of Western capital, aid, and technology. The huge populace of modern-day India cannot sustain the level of culture and economic well-being that its high-caste forebears created.

It is not, however, too late for America and the West. No matter how dark our destiny may appear, there is enough genetic treasure among our people to fashion a road to the stars. Those who know the racial truth often excuse their inaction by expressing pessimism. Suggesting that "the battle is already lost" is often simply an excuse for cowardice. Our race's struggle for survival and evolutionary advancement became the meaning of my life when I looked into that little Indian girl's forlorn face, for I then knew exactly what I must do. Prospects of victory or defeat became irrelevant to my responsibility and my honor. I resolved to live my life in the original meaning of the term Aryan, a noble life of dedication to my people. My life from that moment onward has been in the service of my people and the Promethean task ahead. I became determined that my life would be about awakening the Aryan inside of every European.

When I grow weary in this battle and I find my character smeared or my personal life attacked, that girl's gaunt face is there to haunt me, to drive me onward. When my personal safety — or that of my loved ones — is threatened, that girl's pleading countenance is there to remind me, in the most graphic terms what failure would mean for our progeny. I learned that it was my responsibility to do all that I could for the survival of my heritage. In the crisis our race now faces, all of us who know the truth must carry that same personal responsibility, and with it the understanding that any individual danger or suffering must be endured when the fate of our whole people is at stake. Such was the altruism that brought our forebears through the crucible of the ice ages of prehistoric Europe, and now we must draw from that genetically imprinted trait as we stand on the brink of being inundated by the masses of the Third World.

Before my journey to India, the racial ideals that I believed in were abstract concepts and principles. In the moment I saw that emaciated child in the ruins, all my ideas were dramatically transformed into the reality of flesh and blood. I finally realized that my cause is different than that of an athletic contest, business competition, winning of an election, or even struggling for an important new scientific discovery. It is not about being right or wrong about ideas, but about the very essence of life itself — the natural laws that provide its beauty, character, and meaning. Seeing the child in the temple changed an intellectual commitment into a holy obligation.

A passage from the Bhagavad Gita[957] comes to mind:

**Likewise having regard for duty to your caste
You should not tremble;
For in a warrior, there exists no better thing than
A fight required of duty** (Chapter 2, Verse 30)

I realized that day, in the scorching Indian sun outside that ruined temple that I had to adopt the spirit of an Aryan warrior who understood the current struggle of our race transcends the centuries. Selfish pursuits seemed trivial, and my life became interwoven with the Cause, a Cause that I knew I could not abandon.

Through years of heartbreak and hardship, physical weariness and character assassination — but also in the exhilarating moments of success and acclaim — my heart has remained true. The flame that ignited in me on that hot August day in India in 1971 is still white hot and imperishable.

It was at that point that I realized who I am. I am an Aryan — a word that has evolved through the centuries to denote those of our race who are racially aware and racially committed. Before I saw that half-breed little girl in the ruins, I was a racially conscious White person. Afterward I was a White person who had become completely committed to the preservation and evolutionary advancement of his people. Not only was I awakened to the truths of race, I was awakened to the sacred purpose of all those who came before us, and those who will follow us in the unbroken spiral toward the heavens. I had become an Aryan.

Chapter 30:
A Taste of Israel

I have never dwelled on the negative. As far back as I can remember, life to me has been about possibilities for achievement, rather than opportunities for failure. I wanted to learn, to accomplish, to be respected. Perhaps my positive attitude, even from an early age, was a defense mechanism for the hurt of my mother's difficulty; or maybe it is simply in my genes as inherently as my light green eyes. I have never wasted much time on trying to psychoanalyze myself. Why I am the way I am — is less important than whether my ideas are sound and my conduct honorable. Many times I have not lived up to my own standards. And when I fail, I am tougher on myself than my critics could ever be.

At 21 I possessed a dangerous combination of naiveté and positive attitude. Although I could competently discuss many aspects of science, religion, philosophy, and politics, it seemed I was often oblivious to real dangers. To me, life was as elemental as a historical novel or a good movie. Life did not seem to demand a lot of distracting details, just a strong enough commitment. I sincerely believed that somehow right and justice would ultimately triumph in the world, as if there is an intrinsic power in justice — independent of the physical world. My father told me repeatedly that everything works out for the best, proffering examples from his own life and career. Probably the biggest fault of idealists and the chronically positive is that they are seldom inclined to look at what can go wrong. Instead, they focus on what they want to go right. That attitude is fine for a golf swing but is poor for a chess game or a war. My full-speed-ahead mentality almost cost me my liberty, and perhaps even came close to costing my life in 1971.

While I was in Laos, I carefully planned my trip home. I was hungry to see Burma, India, Pakistan, Israel, Istanbul, Greece, Rome, Munich, and London. In Europe I had planned meetings with right-wing leaders in Greece, Rome, Germany, and England. I had one suitcase crammed with books and literature on the racial and Jewish issues for my contacts in Europe. I also had dozens of copies of newspapers and leaflets that I had written on race and Jewish Supremacism. And to complete my potpourri of "racist" items, I had dozens of brass swastikas I had purchased in India.

India's most common symbol is the swastika. It can be found on autos, ships, government buildings, bicycles, and almost anything else imaginable. One can buy this ancient symbol of the Indo-European race in shops and from curio stands all over the country. For a few pennies apiece, I picked up a handful of beautifully carved and engraved brass swastikas, thinking that they would make appropriate gifts for the European racialists with whom I had appointments.

On the long flight from Pakistan to Israel, it began to dawn on me that I was deeply into a very stupid mistake. I was headed to the nation of Israel, flying to the most security-conscious airport in the world at Tel Aviv, and my bags were full of swastikas and "anti-Semitic" literature!

For years I had been aware of the suppression, torture, and terror going on in Israel against Palestinians and their sympathizers. American tourists that made the mistake of simply having Palestinian friends or associates back home have been arrested as spies for simply taking tourist photos while in Israel. I knew the history of how the Israelis treated their enemies, and how they were cited by the *Daily Telegraph* as frequently using torture on their political prisoners. I knew too that the Anti-Defamation League kept extensive files on anti-Zionist activists in the United States and that they shared the information with the Mossad (Israel intelligence). Since my racial awakening, I also knew that anti-Semitism was a serious crime in Israel. I practically kicked myself for the perilous spot I had put myself in.

I realized the gravity of the situation only during the in-flight meal on the trip from Pakistan. I spent the rest of the night in nervous agony. I could not finish my food, and I could not sleep. I found it impossible to read my travel book. My life flashed before me like an old Edison moving picture — interspersed with contemporary, full-color news accounts of my impending tragic fate in Israel. The longer I went without sleep, the more intricately my imagination painted a picture of my demise.

Articles I had read from the British press, particularly the *Daily Telegraph*, about the Mossad's torture of thousands of Palestinian detainees came flooding back to me. Daydreaming, I could see beady-eyed agents attach the electrodes to my fingers and toes. I could feel the warmth of an overhead aluminum-hooded light as it cast dark shadows on their faces, making their eyes darker and more sinister. I saw visions of my lifeless body being dumped on the side of a dusty, desert road, and I pictured my father reading a Mossad-authored telegram that stated, regretfully, that his son had been a victim of Arab terrorists and that arrangements would be made to send the body home.

A lady cloth importer, who was traveling to Israel from Pakistan, told me that since the recent Lod Airport bombing by the Japanese Red Army terrorist gang, all incoming passengers and their luggage were thoroughly searched.

After hearing that bit of bad news, I wrote a short but melodramatic letter to Chloê and one to my mother and father telling them of my love for them and the White cause. I cursed my stupidity and explained what might happen to me. I wrote that I would call them as soon as I landed in Israel, so if they did not hear from me by phone before receiving the letter, I was probably in Israeli custody or dead. I wrote a fake name and the return address of a friend on the envelope and gave the letters intended for my parents and Chloê to an American passenger who was from a small town in Georgia. He was connecting to a flight to New York City and then home. Thinking these words might be my last; I conjured all the poeticism I could muster.

I can see the last orange streaks of the sun give way to the darkness of the desert kingdoms below, and I know that when this plane descends, my own sun may burn out as well. If you read this after hearing from me by phone, you'll smile at my anxious moments shared with you by these words, but if you read these words without hearing my voice beforehand, then you will be anxious about me, for you will be fearful for me because of my own stupidity.

. . .Contact the U.S. State Department immediately if the Israeli government is holding me. They need to know that you know they have me — so I won't meet with any untimely accidents blamed on 'Palestinian terrorists.'

. . . I know that my racial activism has caused you a lot of worry and frustration over the past few years, but I do believe that if you were confronted with the information I have acquired, you would have acted similarly. Maybe there is a fine line between the foolish and the heroic. I am sure that I am more on the foolish side of the line. Yet I am just as convinced that the ideas to which I am dedicated are honorable, correct, and important. The facts and ideas vital to the survival of our heritage must be the most important information in the world, because they determine the fate of millions and truly the sum of human evolution.

If you don't hear from me again, send my love to all, and tell them that if they want to remember me, they can do that best by fighting for the survival of our heritage . . .

The last line I desire to write in this letter is the expression of my deep and abiding love for you both.

Finally, at dawn, I forced myself to eat breakfast, thinking it could be my last decent meal — maybe my last meal ever. It struck me as funny that an airline meal might be my last, and I laughed out loud, earning strange looks from the passengers around me.

We disembarked and walked down the stairs into the terminal, escorted by Uzi-toting police in brown khaki uniforms. They were sharp and well disciplined as they made sure no passengers wandered off the tarmac and away from passport control.

As I stood waiting for my bags to emerge from the rubber-curtained baggage doors, I overheard a couple of the passengers comment that security was tight because of the massacre that had taken place in the same terminal only a year or so before.

I waited awhile to claim my bags, wondering if I could slip through customs with my smaller clothes bag and maybe get away before they discovered my seditious suitcase. But I saw that the security forces were matching up the passengers with their baggage before allowing entry to customs and immigration. There was no way around it. I was stuck like a pig on a spit.

Then my eternally positive nature kicked in, and I hoped against hope that the inspectors would not notice the titles of my books or the nature of the brass trinkets. But as I moved through the double-doors into a large room, I saw something that chilled me. A shiver passed through my chest as I saw suitcases lined up, opened-wide, on long wooden tables. Israeli Customs was going through the luggage item by item, examining everything, including the luggage itself, and then hastily repacking the bags. Sometimes, when the agents could not force all the items back into tightly packed suitcases, they simply put the excess items in plastic bags that they handed to the bewildered arrivals. A number of passengers had already lined up at a curtained area, where, one at a time, they would disappear behind it so as to completely disrobe.

I closed my eyes and said a silent prayer. Finally, I resolved that if my life were to end now, I would face it in a fashion worthy of my forefathers. A strange calm came over me. I was ready to face whatever God had in store. Instead of racing, my heartbeat seemed to be slower and stronger as I pulled my head back in an erect fashion and looked directly into the eyes of the Israeli agent. I slowly placed my passport on the desk. The agent opened it, glanced quickly at my photo, and without a word motioned me through the checkpoint. I picked up my bags and rushed so quickly out into the main terminal that my breathing came hard. It was then that my heart beat quickly, and my fingers trembled. Barely able to suppress shouts of relief, with about eighty pounds of bags I practically danced my way across the floor, looking for a door out to blue sky and freedom.

I asked myself what had happened. It dawned on me that because I had worked for the U.S. State Department in Laos in the American Language School, I had a red government employee passport rather than the standard green. I had been treated as a diplomat. I had not realized until then that my passport would exempt me from customs. I thanked God for saving me from my own stupidity in the land of Israel.

I had arrived in Tel Aviv on the Jewish New Year, and parts of the airport were closed. I must have looked like an easy mark for a short, moon-faced cab driver who solicited a ride in his taxi. My student finances permitted only a bus ride, so I inquired where the bus stop was. The cabby protested that there was no bus service because of the

Jewish holiday. When I said I still did not want to hire his cab, he pressured me. "I told you there is no bus service into the downtown district. Don't you trust me. . . ? You think I lie to you? Come," he insisted. "I will take you into town, only 20 American dollars."

Instead of simply telling the cabby that he was right, that I didn't trust him, I made a lame excuse about calling a friend to pick me up. A couple of exit doors and a hundred feet more down the corridor was a door marked TRANSPORTATION in Hebrew and English. At the curb sat a practically new Mercedes-Benz bus with a sign in the front window reading TEL AVIV. It cost me $2 to get to my destination.

From the time of that first bus ride into Tel Aviv until the time I left Israel, I noticed little heavy industry in the country. I saw numerous little Jewish shops, but in most of them the great percentage of goods had labels indicating foreign origin, except for numerous Palestinian handicrafts.

I had read extensively about the kibbutz system of collectivized farming. American media are full of stories about how the system has made the desert bloom, but the stories seemed to have little to do with reality. Israel does have a large citrus industry, but the media image of the kibbutzim is far from the truth. I usually avoid tourist bus tours, but this time I took one to a few of the kibbutzim. In the main building of one, the first thing I noticed was a large poster-size picture of Karl Marx. Another room had a portrait of Leon Trotsky.

The tour included the kitchen area, where I dallied. I opened the food locker and was amazed to find it loaded with American food products, including a shelf full of Campbell's Chicken Noodle Soup. We toured some of the Jewish living quarters, which were as lavish as any fancy American apartment. On a Wednesday at 10 o'clock in the morning, the community center was filled with adults. In the fields, we were introduced to a Jewish foreman who was supervising about two dozen workers. They were all Palestinians.

I rose before dawn one morning and went immediately to the beach in Tel Aviv. I was surprised to see many Jews, of every physical type, on the beach, exercising and running along the edge of the surf. Physical health and fitness is part of the ethic Israel teaches its citizens. That morning I had a long conversation on the beach with a Jewish woman doctor who was visiting from Atlanta. She had had a very liberal upbringing and opposed the Israeli policies against the Palestinians. She spoke at length about the rigidly segregated nature of the country. Jews have exclusively Jewish state-financed schools, neighborhoods, and settlements. She reiterated what I already knew, but it interested me to hear it from a Jew. The government does not recognize marriage between Jews and Gentiles. Immigration is permitted for Jews living anywhere in the world (Jews by birth — not necessarily religion, as many Jewish citizens are atheists), while hundreds of thousands of Palestinians who were born there are not allowed to return. Citizenship and its rights are seldom accorded to Palestinians, and they can be jailed and held indefinitely without charge.

The government is theocratic. It instills a strong religious-ethnic-national patriotism in every aspect of Israeli life. There is a much stressed "ties to the soil" land movement. Militarism and social order are represented by universal military service. An interesting mix of capitalism and socialism, combined with an intense nationalism, guides the country. Concentration camps and jails house many of the Palestinians, and there is a myriad of laws that sustain Jewish supremacy in all walks of life, including the media, which has strict laws that maintain Jewish ownership. Israel has many such Nuremberg-type laws, but the American media, which are dominated by Zionists, would be horrified at the comparison.

Before visiting Israel, I believed that Nazism had perished in 1945. But during my 1971 visit, I saw that it was alive and well in the streets of Tel Aviv, in the schoolrooms of Haifa, in the kibbutzim of the highlands, in the militarism, and in immigration policies.

As days passed I began to reassess and refine my comparison of Israel with Nazi Germany. It almost seems the whole mythos of the nation is a huge stage play, built with money from America, Germany, and, truly, from all over the globe. Israel is not an organic state but an artificial one, with little productivity and a great portion of its national budget coming from outside. Other nations provide its economic prosperity and its military defense. There is no nation like it in the world.

Even Israel's forms of racism seem to be a corruption of the racial idealist philosophers of Europe, for their racism is essentially of an exploitative nature: exactly what the American media accuse Whites of practicing, and it is truly a supremacist rather than a separationist doctrine. While most Whites want to separate themselves from non-Whites, Zionist racism is based on exploiting other races close at hand. While racially aware White people are motivated by love of their heritage, Zionists are psychologically dominated by the wrongs, real and mythical, that have been committed against them. Hatred of their perceived persecutors consumes far more of their attention than love expressed for their own kind and creations. No people on Earth have created such an all-consuming cult of their persecution.

I attempted to talk to a number of the Palestinian merchants in Jerusalem about their situation in Israel, but they were suspicious of my motivations and often were reluctant to say too much. It is hard for them to trust anyone with Northern European features because some Jews also have that kind of appearance. Their fear of the Mossad and other police and army-intelligence groups was ubiquitous, so only a few talked with me about the terrifying aspects of the Zionist regime. During my stay I met some Palestinians who had been jailed, tortured, and abused. Some of them had lost all their possessions; others lost their homes and property simply because their son or daughter was accused of being an anti-Zionist.

A young Palestinian college student named Rahid who had been studying in America but was home visiting his parents, talked with me at length about the Arab-Israel conflict while we drank coffee strong and thick as mud. He told me how most of his extended family had been forced out of their homes and lands in 1948. Many of his cousins, aunts, uncles, nieces, and nephews could not even visit the land where their forefathers had lived for 4,000 years — since even before the first ancient Israelites of the Bible arrived. From our table in the outdoor coffeehouse we could see the streets being patrolled by soldiers armed with Uzis and — even worse, in Rahid's view — average Israeli citizens carrying submachine guns, while almost all Palestinians were forbidden to have even a pistol. He told me, "We don't call it Israel. It is 'occupied Palestine.'"

During my stay, I also started conversations with Jews and I frankly discussed some of the issues with them, being careful to not argue, only inquire. I tagged along with a typical tourist group near the Dome of the Rock and was surprised to hear the Israeli guide tell a number of Palestinian jokes, equating them with imbeciles and animals.

Twenty-four hours before I was scheduled to leave the country, I

At the Dome of The Rock in Jerusalem

returned to my hotel after another journey to Jerusalem, only to have the clerk (with whom I was friendly during my stay) tell me that immigration authorities had come earlier in the day and asked questions about me. The clerk told me that she had admitted them to my room, where they stayed for about 30 minutes. My room looked undisturbed, but when I opened my largest suitcase, I noticed that the top book was not, as I remembered it, Oswald Spengler's *Decline of the West, Vol 1*. I knew the top book had been Spengler's because I had been reading it and had placed it on top at the last second in New Delhi. I was relieved to be leaving Israel the next day, but I began to wonder why, since they obviously found these seditious books, they had not arrested me. Could they have received the records of the Mossad and the Anti-Defamation League in the United States about my "anti-Semitic" background?

I slept uneasily that night, and the next morning I had the feeling that things were just not right. I surveyed the streets behind me as I made my way to the beach. *They might be following me*, I thought. The saying "If they're really out to get you, you're not paranoid" came to mind and made me smile. I decided to enjoy my walk and not to worry. Within a few hours I nervously settled into my seat on the flight to Istanbul on El Al, Israel's national airline, and breathed a long sigh of relief as the jet lifted off and began to climb over the Mediterranean. I had a chicken salad sandwich and then napped halfway across the Aegean. I arrived at my hotel room in Istanbul at about 11 that night and found the hotel restaurant closed. I got a bottle of sealed sparkling water from the bar and went upstairs and crashed on the lumpy old bed. I planned to see the historic Bosporus the next morning, and fought for sleep as I excitedly considered my itinerary.

I woke at 5:30 a.m. with a dull headache and quickly showered and shaved. I refused to let the headache deter me from visiting the historic edge of Europe. A few aspirins for my head, some fresh bread with bottled water, and I was off for the Bosporus Peninsula. I rode about 40 minutes on the bus, feeling increasingly ill. I practically forced the driver to pull over and let me off at an Esso gas station — where I rushed for the rest room and retched. Pale and drawn, my head feeling as though it would burst, I ignored my student budget and caught the first taxi back to the hotel. I managed to call up the American Embassy and asked if there were any American hospitals in Istanbul. They told me that Athens had the best facilities.

At this point I knew that I was seriously ill — life-threateningly ill. I thought about going to a hospital in Istanbul, but had heard they were wretched. Even though I was doubtful that I could make it to Athens, I decided to try. I gathered up my belongings, hailed a cab, and told the driver to take me to the airport as fast as he could. Afraid that if the ticket writers knew I was sick they would not let me board, I washed my face and combed my hair, went to the airline counter, and asked them to change my tickets to the next flight to Athens. By late afternoon when the plane landed in Athens, fever had me on the edge of delirium. I forced myself to act as though I was not ill when presenting my passport. To this day I am surprised I made it through customs. Stumbling through the airport exit doors into the warm Athens sunshine, I collapsed into the back seat of a cab and told the driver to take me to the U.S. Naval Hospital.

I woke up a few days later. For a few moments nothing made any sense. *What I was doing there — was I alive or dead?* Then a pretty, American nurse came in to take my pulse. The doctor told me that I had come into the facility semi-conscious with a fever of 105, my body reeling from toxins. He said that I had been the victim of a rare and often deadly form of food poisoning, and he went on to describe it as "sophisticated." "You are lucky," he said, "that you came to Athens." The U.S. Naval Hospital had the latest equipment to analyze the toxins and produce antidotes. The doctor said that in my condition, my chances of survival would have been one-in-a-thousand had I remained in Istanbul.

As I recovered, I thought about the fact that the Anti-Defamation League had files on my anti-Zionist activities in the United States and how they are directly linked with the Mossad. My embarkation records may have been matched with my American records a few days after my arrival, eventually leading to the agents visiting my hotel room. On confirming my identity, they might easily have poisoned my food on the aircraft, expecting that I would die days later in some hovel in Istanbul. There would be one less enemy of the Zionist cause, and no possible blame or repercussions for mother Israel.

No proof exists that agents of Zionism attempted to murder me. It is certainly possible that I had merely eaten a tainted chicken salad sandwich on the plane, as airline food can be pretty poor, but I have just never had it that bad. But from consideration of the events that occurred, suspicions are natural. I had survived my naiveté. I resolved to be a lot more careful in future. Lying in my hospital bed, pensive thoughts turned to what lay outside my window: the land of ancient Greece. I decided that upon recovery I would make the most of my time left in Greece, and savor its beauty as thankfully as my first breath upon waking from the fever.

Chapter 31:
Greece: A Celebration of Life

Free at last in the in the magnificent land of Greece! On the morning of my release from the Athens hospital, I set off to see the Parthenon. Weak and dehydrated, I somehow managed to walk up the Acropolis, a hill that takes its name from the ancient Greek fortifications. At the top, a bright September sun warmed me as I rested against the beautiful columns of the Parthenon, and eventually stretched out on the straight-cut, square White stones between them. The looming pillars above framed a brilliant sky. Such a luminescent blue should be named a whole new color, as the simple word *blue* seemed a poor description of its stark beauty. The ancient Greece that I had dreamed about as a young boy reading Homer's *Odyssey* and *Iliad* kept filling my imagination. Impressions of the Greek authors, such as Herodotus, Aristotle, Euripides and of course Socrates through the works of Plato, now flooded back. It seemed I was present 2,500 years ago, and that at any moment Socrates would stroll up the stairs, students at hand.

Even before reading the *Odyssey*, the Greek myths and fables entranced me as a small child. Later I read the history of Sparta and Athenia; the melding of history and myth in the story of Helen of Troy; the stories of perhaps the greatest conqueror of all time, Alexander; and the courage of Leonidas and his Spartan warriors at Thermopylae. They all came alive in these magnificent temple ruins. To think that many of the Greek heroes had sat here where I now rested. Could it be true that the first time they saw this sight, their hearts were filled with the same awe and reverence that these columns evoked in mine? Maybe they had lain between these Doric pillars and stared up at the Aegean sky with the same appreciation felt in my heart in that exquisite moment.

Having had a close brush with death, a keener appreciation grew in me for life and the love of life the Hellenes promoted. I felt reborn in the land of our Western cultural genesis. The Greek unbridled reverence for life that I had read about found meaning in my own thankfulness to be alive. While in the hospital the previous few days, I read only Greek histories and literature. My nurse kindly went to the base PX and bought about ten paperback editions of different English translations of Greek writings. They touched such a chord that although I was sick and alone in Athens; no melancholy came over me. The words I read nursed me back to health as much as the medicine I swallowed.

Every American young person should travel the world. They must let their knowledge become animated in the feel, taste, smell, sight, and sound of the geography and history that they learn about. Even seeing a film of a place is not the same as being there, for film is just cellulose or electrically charged videotape. Actually being there makes the place and its history become real. Once a man is physically present, he becomes part of a greater reality rather than just an observer. Facts of history grow alive in the young mind. It makes the racially conscious realize that they are not mere observers or even cheerleaders for their heritage — they are participants, the last link in a chain spanning the centuries and the generations. It makes a man realize the value of his inheritance, as well as his dutiful obligation to pass it on.

Growing up in an era in which our civilization regressed and our race retreated can cause melancholy because of the seemingly insurmountable difficulty of our task. But, learning of the terribly hard times in the history of the Greeks, and their subsequently heroic periods, encouraged me. Knowledge of the heroism and achievement of our forefathers sparks those genetic traits in us. Being physically present in historic places makes the words in musty old books come alive in flesh and blood. To feel beneath my own feet the hard stone upon which Socrates once stood — made his words and wisdom more immediate and pertinent.

Around 3,000 B.C. our Aryan ancestors, speaking various forms of the Indo-European language, invaded what is now the Greek peninsula. The Aryan tribes included the Achaeans, who overran the Peloponnesus; the Ionians, who migrated to Attica; the Aeolians, who settled Thessaly; and the Cyclades, who assimilated with the Helladic people. The Dorians left their mountain homelands and became the dominant Indo-European tribe in Greece, but all the tribes eventually became known as Hellenes, or Greeks. Greek mythology explains the genealogy of Greece as the descendants of Hellen; hence, the word *Hellenes* denotes the Greek people.

Somewhere around the 12th century B.C., about the time of the period depicted in the *Iliad* and the *Odyssey,* and coinciding with the Iron Age, Greek civilization began to make its powerful imprint on the ancient world. As the Aryan tribes invaded and established their kingdoms, the tribal chiefs became the kings of the conquered lands and ultimately were replaced by aristocratic oligarchies, which in turn gave way to alliances among rich commoners and some disgruntled aristocrats. It seems that all of Greece fell under such cycles over the centuries. Dictators replaced periods of liberal democracy; later overthrown by aristocrats; later replaced by a meritocratic middle class. Dictators then succeeded them in turn. It should be noted that even in the most democratic periods, democracy was never democratic in the modern sense. Greek democracy was always limited to a narrow and privileged class called "citizens," and voting was never an inherent right, but a privilege earned either by hereditary line or based on ability and accomplishment. Slavery was an accepted fact of life in Greece, but those who were free were perhaps freer than any people who ever lived. In any event, throughout all the political upheavals and frequent warfare of ancient Greece, the cultural and artistic level soared to heights, most nobly expressed in the Periclean Age, that has never been equaled.

We now know that the earliest ancestors of the Greeks had the first bronze metallurgy in the Balkans thousands of years before anywhere else on Earth. We know too that the Golden Age of Greece was indeed an age of golden people, being that Greek literature and art clearly depict a fair-complected, predominately light-eyed people.

The Greeks were trade-conscious and imperialist, and as Greek civilization rose, it began to conquer and negotiate an empire that stretched throughout the known world. Alexander the Great, technically a Macedonian, arose as a despot in the last imperial stage of their fading greatness in the third century before Christ. He used a unique system to incorporate new lands and peoples into his empire. He would often require his soldiers to marry into the ruling classes of the kingdoms he conquered, thinking that by inculcating them into Greek families and culture he was making more Greeks. Upon the defeat of Persia, he presided over the marriage of thousands of his soldiers with the daughters of Persia's ruling class. Even though, after Alexander's death, most of those mixed "Susa" marriages were dissolved by the more thoughtful Greeks back home, other racial threats increased. Commerce, immigration and increasing intermarriage between Greeks and foreigners slowly transformed Greece into a melting pot of the Mediterranean world, and the vitality of the Greek civilization faded over time.

The mixing in Greece was not as dramatic as had occurred in Aryan India, but substantial change did occur. Many of the people of Greece today retain traces of noble ancestors and are indeed worthy of their heritage, but the Golden Age was lost as the light of the genes of the Hellenes became dimmed with the absorption of the alien.

Although primitive in comparison with the scientific accomplishments of the modern world, the ancient Greeks reached the pinnacle of civilization in the arts, philosophy, and government. The intellectual and artistic level of the intelligentsia surely exceeded that of any society before or since. Today we have only scant traces of the poetry and literature, painting, sculpture, theater, and architecture of a society from which we still learn so much — 3,000 years after its greatest flowering. It amazes me to think that the plethora of magnificent art, architecture, philosophy, and literature emerged from city-states that probably never had a combined population that exceeded 250,000.

As I grew healthier, I began to travel about the magnificent country and was impressed with the beauty, the hospitality, and loveliness of the land and people. I felt as if I were viewing an earlier time through the filter of the modern world.

Near the time of my departure, I traveled to the plains of Marathon and then to Thermopylae — once a narrow pass but now a wide flood plain. I reverently walked across the blood-drenched fields of that great battle 2,500 years ago. The story of King Leonidas offered a magnificent example of a man of our race who will defend his heritage regardless of the personal cost.

The words I had read years before from the world's first true historian, Herodotus, came to life before my eyes. The Persian kingdom, a rich empire dominated by Indo-Europeans but with a largely non-Aryan population of Asia Minor from which to draw an army, had its sights set on the beauty of ancient Greece. King Darius' army began its invasion soon after Ionia and some other Greek coastal states revolted against Persian rule. Ultimately, his forces found defeat on the Greek plain of Marathon, but his son Xerxes I soon assembled an even larger force: the largest army and navy in the history of the ancient world. In 481 B.C. Xerxes and his army crossed the Hellespont Strait on a bridge of boats and headed south toward Athens.

The Asian invasion could not have occurred at a worse time. The Greeks were largely unprepared and bickering among themselves. At the moment of the invasion, the Spartans were engrossed in the most important of their religious festivals. Leonidas, a Spartan King, saw the danger clearly and marched with a small force of about 7,000 to the most naturally defensible position on the Greek mainland: Thermopylae, a pass only about 50 meters wide. The Spartans were the most skilled soldiers in the world and had a code of honor unbreakable even in death. Leonidas decided that Greece could survive only if he and his warriors held the pass long enough to allow the rest of the city-states to organize their defense. Two days went by and Leonidas' band held the pass despite being outnumbered hundreds-to-one. With each day he bought time for his people, and he knew too that his example would rally his countrymen. Near the end of the siege, Leonidas discovered that a Thessalian traitor named Ephialtes had shown the Persians a hidden path over the mountains, enabling the encirclement and doom of Leonidas and his men.

Knowing that his position would eventually be overrun, Leonidas ordered most of his fellow Spartans to leave the battlefield and prepare for the battles he knew would lay ahead. Looking over the ancient battlefield, I recalled Leonidas' response to a soldier who said that the air would be so filled with Persian arrows that they would "blot out the sky." He responded that they would then just have to "fight in the shade!" With only 300 of his finest Spartan soldiery and about 1,100 others, mainly Thebans and Thespians, who refused to leave his side, Leonidas, in an act of heroism that has inspired our race countless times over the centuries, chose to die so that his people might live. The Greek epitaph over the dead at Thermopylae is simple and powerful: "Stranger, tell the Spartans that we lie here in obedience to our duty."

Greece reeled under the Persian advance, but after the sacking of Athens, Greek forces rallied. Under the command of Themistocles, the Greeks destroyed the Persian navy at Salamis, and mostly Spartan forces later defeated Xerxes' army at Plataea. The heroism and sacrifice of Leonidas lived in every Greek's heart and drove them on to victory in much the same way that shouting "Remember the Alamo!" inspired the men who defeated Santa Anna at San Jacinto. A Persian victory could well have meant the end of the West and the traditions we now cherish. Such is the power of one man's will to change the course of history.

Overlooking the battlefield, I wondered where the Leonidases, the Colonel Travises and the Crocketts of our day were. There are millions of men and women of our heritage who know that non-White immigration and birthrates will mean our own racial genocide unless we alter our current course. If the media masters and the corrupt men who control our Western governments have their way, our unique genotype will be lost forever. A devastating flood of non-White genes will drown our civilization and threaten even our very existence as a people. Yet with such a racial catastrophe looming, too few are willing to make a sacrifice of even modest amounts of their time or money for something that should be far dearer to them. Countless millions of our progenitors in history have risked their lives, and when one considers the many who knowingly gave their lives so that we could be here today, how can we not make at least a meager sacrifice so that our descendants will be here tomorrow? Every day we tarry will mean greater loss of our people's precious blood in the future.

Looking upon the fields of Thermopylae brought home to me the fact that I should not complain about any price I had to pay, for those battlefields were consecrated by the bodies and blood of men who gave so much more than what is asked of us. Their sacrifice enables us to be what we are: Men of the West. I also understood that if we should fail in the struggle, even their gift of long ago would be in vain, forever muted by our own cowardice. For if we are no longer here to venerate these men, no one will.

It is not the Ephialtes of the present who really disturb me. There will always be traitors who will sell out their heritage and birthrights. But I am most disheartened by those of our kind who know the truth but refuse to act. They do not join the ranks of the enemy, but neither do they devote themselves wholeheartedly to our vital cause.

Leonidas did not expect all of Greece, or even all of his men, to die with him. Once he knew the battle was lost, he sent many of them away so they could fight more effectively at another time and place. Not every White man and woman can be expected to make the sacrifices or take the risks that their leaders must, but every racially conscious White person must take *some kind of action* for our cause. Every true Aryan makes the cause of our heritage and freedom every bit as important as the rest of his or her basic human needs. The cause must become an integral part of the life of every racially aware White man and woman. Only when one becomes committed to the survival and advancement of our heritage and *acts upon it*, does he or she deserve the title *Aryan*.

Many stories of sacrifice similar to Leonidas' have been written. At Tours by Charles Martel, at Turbingen with the Teutonic knights against the Huns, at Blood River in South Africa, at the Alamo, at Stalingrad, and at a thousand more battlefields, European men willingly laid down their lives for the lives of their people. Certainly the men of the present can afford the risk of their reputations.

One other thing that profoundly moves me every time I delve into ancient Greek history is the futility and fratricidal character of the Greek conflicts. When they were racially strong and united, the Greeks dominated the known world. Only the Greeks could destroy the Greeks — and, truly, they extinguished themselves by their own hands. They did it both by internecine warfare such as the Peloponnesian Wars and by a cosmopolitanism and internationalism that eventually took a genetic toll from which they could not recover.

Modern scientific knowledge will eventually create moral codes that will preserve and advance our genotype, but I suspect halting the fratricidal conflicts that have decimated our people will be far a more difficult task — one that will require considerable contemplation. Our European heritage has survived despite the War Between the States and the First and Second World Wars, but it cannot survive any more Peloponnesian conflicts. It is absolutely our duty to put aside any regional and cultural animosities that exist between Europeans anywhere in the world. While still cognizant and protective of individual White cultures and traditions, we must unite to confront our common enemy, the internationalists who would destroy all of our national traditions and even our very genotype itself.

I do not know of any more courteous and friendly people than the modern Greeks. I have seen the light of our race in their eyes. As the Greeks as well as the other Europeans eugenically face the future, the genes that created the ancient Greek civilization will again come to the fore and illuminate the Greece of the next age. They will certainly share its light with the reborn artistic firmament that shall bathe the Western world.

My last memorable visit while in Greece was to an old unnamed marble temple on a hill overlooking the Aegean. Looking out from the broken white columns toward the horizon, where the aqua-blue of the water mistily joined the perfect blue of the sky, I felt the spirit of the people that built these monuments. I shared in their blood — their genes were in me. For a day, in the shadows of the ancient columns, with a cool breeze coming up from the sea, I read passages from Herodotus, Thucydides, and Sophocles. I realized that although the Greeks would risk and suffer death for their honor and their duty; yet, at the same time no people on Earth loved life more. They had perfect union of body and spirit.

In the ancient world of toil and tyranny, where death was simply a relief from the pain of living, many ancient cultures concentrated their thoughts on the afterlife. The Greeks, on the other hand, created a world of art and architecture, heroism and beauty, and thus celebrated life. The miseries of the ancient world made previous societies elevate the unworldly and the unseen, but the Greeks reveled in the beauty of mankind or, more correctly stated, in that spark of the divine that they could find in man. As Egypt was a society mesmerized by the world of the dead, their greatest expressions being the cold, deep tombs of the pharaohs, the Greeks worshipped the noble urges of life. Their temples were open and executed in the scale of the living, not in the encumbered rooms of the dead. Living men and women came together beneath the elegant and monumental architecture to commune with God, to venerate life, and to inspire them to nobility in spirit.

Aristotle expressed the Greek love of life and beauty in a way that every Aryan can understand intuitively.

> **We take pleasure in a statue's beauty, should not the living fill us with delight? And all the more if in the spirit of the love of knowledge we search for causes and bring to light evidences of meaning. Then Nature's purpose and her deep-seated laws be revealed in all things, all tending in her varied work to one form or another of the beautiful. (D. A. Thompson,** *The Legacy of Greece*)[958]

In contrast to the secrets held by only the Egyptian priesthood and the magical arts that ruled the Mediterranean, the Greeks believed in open inquiry, with no holy man to mediate between man and God. To them there were no revealed truths but only the natural truth toward which all men had a duty to aspire. An evening of the learned in the age of Pericles found men engaging in spirited conversation and debate about the Nature of life itself. The poet John Keats summed up the Greek ethic in his great lines from "Ode on a Grecian Urn": "'Beauty is truth, truth beauty,' — that is all / Ye know on Earth, and all ye need to know."

Edith Hamilton, an authority on ancient Greece wrote that by having no "vital lies," meaning no "revealed truths," the Greeks could afford an open-mindedness unlike that of any other ancient civilization and much less superstitious than our own. They had no holy writ in constitution or in sacred texts. They found their ultimate guidebook inscribed in the Nature around them, a vision of Nature that included them. They could afford to put every idea at risk, for they had no fear from an inquiry into truth. I thought about the vital lie of racial and sexual equality in our modern civilization and about how anyone who challenged it was excommunicated from accepted society as surely as any heliocentric astronomist faced condemnation in the Middle Ages. And I thought how Socrates would have laughed at the idea that any story such as racial equality or the Holocaust should be immune from examination.

Euripides said it so clearly: "A slave is he who cannot speak his thought." To me, Periclean Greece represented the true ideals crafted by Thomas Jefferson in the Bill of Rights. In the early days of our American Republic, not only were the Bill of Rights revered, they were practiced in principle in the minds and hearts of men. Such can be shown by the often-radical writings of Thomas Paine, whose pronouncements were freely read in his times but whose sentiments no politician could today express without utter ruin. Political and religious free thought and speech are the most vital of men's rights. Without free thought and speech no other rights can be safe, nor can we ever truly strive for truth.

The one great commandment of the Greeks was to "know thyself." If we men of the West are to find our way again to the greatness of spirit that represented Greece, we must learn who we are and make our sacred identity the banner we wave in the winds of the cultural war.

And how did the Greek see himself? A knowledgeable man was one "versed in Nature," and the Hellenes saw mankind as a vital part of Nature. They sought no relief from Nature's ravages, but to delve into her very bosom and swim in the eternal sea of life and wisdom. They were the first scientists and the first to understand the interrelatedness of all living things. The Greek also saw himself apart from other men. Plato wrote, "The Egyptians and Phoenicians love money, while we love knowledge."[959] But in a later age they egotistically thought they could make the whole world Greek simply by teaching their truths and sharing their vision of beauty. They failed in that quest, but their truths were picked up from the dust of history by men whose genes made are moved by the same spirit. The spirit of the ancient Greeks is our spirit, or the best of it, and only Western man can truly feel what the Greeks felt.

The Greek intellectuals argued for harmony between the intellect and the spirit. Their art and architecture reflects it. In her wonderful book *The Greek Way*,[960] Edith Hamilton relates the story of a famous Greek artist who painted a picture of a boy holding a bunch of grapes so lifelike that birds flew down trying to peck at them. The populace hailed him as a master artist. "If I were," he answered, "the boy would have kept the birds away." As Hamilton says so eloquently, "Grapes were to be painted to look like grapes and boys to look like boys, and the reason was that nothing could be imagined so beautiful and significant as the real." How that attitude conflicts with the alien and Jewish-inspired modernistic art that pervades the West today, where a chimpanzee's scratchings can sometimes fetch a king's ransom. A cult of ugliness has pervaded the spirit of the West that wrenches us from our own culture. To all true men of the West, the contemporary alien way of the arts is as base and ugly as the Greek way is noble and beautiful.

Reading of the Greeks' unrestrained joy of life made me think of the doomsayers and humorless people in our own movement who never allow themselves to see the good and the beautiful. They become so wrapped up in the horrors accompanying the demise of the

West that they lose sight of their own inner nature which, like the Greeks, can dance in the face of annihilation. Embracing the dance of life affords us the effrontery to prevail against great odds. Living in these challenging times is no terrible burden — it is a great privilege and adventure. It is our great chance to realize a vision of the beautiful world we can create. It is not hatred of our enemies that really gives us power, it is the sweep and grandeur of our vision that drives us forward. And it is that appreciation of beauty that keeps us going and living fully — despite the darkness of the modern world.

We strive, even in our own imperfect lives, toward the development of the divine in man that can lead to, as Nietzsche said, an evolutionary step beyond man. Long ago, Aristotle talked about developing those qualities.

There is a life which is higher than the measure of humanity; men will live it not by virtue of their humanity, but by virtue of something in them that is divine. We ought not to listen to those who exhort a man to keep to man's thoughts, but to live according to the highest thing that is in him, for small though it be in power and worth it is far above the rest. (Eth.,X,7,7.)

The illness that struck me as I left Israel could easily have killed me. *Life is so fragile and so short*, I thought. *Why not do what I'm meant to do?*

The demands of my cause and the hardships I knew were inevitable no longer loomed as a burden but as simply the small price I would pay for living a life of rapturous struggle rather than of resignation. I began to see the striving as a thing of joy and beauty rather than of hardship. I rejoiced in Euripides' notation that "A man without fear cannot be a slave." My close call in Israel, coupled with the wisdom of the Greeks, had set my spirit free.

I stayed on in southern Greece for a few days, slowly regaining my strength. Although in much discomfort, I never complained. Instead, I was thankful that I was able to have such feelings. Every bit of pain was now a signal that my physical body was alive and growing stronger. I had a reason to live, and the sacred cause in my heart only grows more vibrant the longer I live.

I had a reason to rejoice, for I felt I was now in the close company of those men of antiquity who had fought, in their own way, for the same things I now fought for — the survival and advancement of our people, our culture, and our freedom.

On the plane heading for Rome, above the engine's drone, the words of Aeschylus played in my head:

**For Freedom, sons of Greece,
Freedom for country, children, wives,
Freedom for worship, for our father's graves.**
Aeschylus, pers 402

Chapter 32:
TO EUROPE AND HOME

On Flying from Greece to Rome I felt that I was going from the philosophical home of the West to the imperial side of it. Ancient Rome was arguably the world's greatest historical empire. A practical people of great organization and accomplishment, the Romans gave us the foundations of our legal precepts and even offered models of government we use to this day. Italy was also the birthplace of the Renaissance, where the fading values and beauty of the Greek and Roman civilizations were rekindled in more modern times.

I slept in an old and inexpensive monastery boarding house in Rome and enjoyed the simple food, table wine and the ambiance of a small, wood-raftered room at least 1,200 years old. Perhaps the most moving part of my sojourn was a reverential visit to the Sistine Chapel. I stared upward at the beautiful vision of an Aryan Adam reaching to the European-visaged God the Father.

Much of the Renaissance had Old Testament themes, but the images and stories emphasized were those that meshed more perfectly with the European psyche. Most of the churches had both paintings and sculptures of armored, sword-wielding knights and kings. Michaelangelo's St. Peter's basilica in Rome is far from the Sermon on the Mount and the unwashed proletariat; it is a palace of a higher order of mankind. Its steeples reached to the skies in its times as heroically as *Apollo 7* did in ours. Although the early church fought the heresies of heliocentrism, Faustian battles were inevitable, for the people of the Renaissance loved beauty and art, they treasured knowledge, and they revered courage in battle. They were also on a collision course with those who viewed Christianity as the victory of the underclass. Christianity as expressed in the Italian Renaissance was a religion focused on a people striving toward their Father in Heaven through their courage, their faithfulness, their art and their monumental works. Their continuing of the evolution of mankind to a higher cultural level, as they would say, "toward perfection," was their way to communion with God.

I thought about whether the plain wood and stone Protestant reformation was a step back from those aspirations expressed by the Renaissance in such physical power and beauty. I realized that the Reformation's representation in movements such as the Calvinists and as represented by the Puritans in America, were simply a different form of that same Promethean striving, but in the form of an unfettered individual's, Siegfried-like test for his own spiritual perfection. They celebrated a will-to-power over the physical self and the world around them. One part of the Christian faith found its expression in the striving of its art and music and architecture and all the power of its creations; the other in the disciplined individual, a philosophical vision as stark and hardy as the ice-bound prehistoric landscape from which our ancestors emerged.

Walking the streets that were those of ancient Rome filled me with awe of its greatness, a glory that still seemed to be. Its still-living spirit touched my soul. The Gens (The Roman founding fathers) who built it still have their genes alive in millions of us. If we but allow it, we can feel their presence, and hear their words and deeds echoing in the chambers of our own hearts and minds — resonating in deepest part our soul.

Circling the Coliseum, brushing my way through the hundreds of cats that now inhabit it, I thought about the sacrifices made by the early Christians for their faith — martyred by felines of a much larger variety. On another day I visited the ancient Christian catacombs, where the devout hid from the anti-Christian powers and where so many of their remains still rest. How eerie it was to walk stooped under low-ceiling tombs with hundreds of skulls lined up on shelves like books in a macabre library. I also visited the monument of another kind of martyr, the statue of Victor Bruno, who was burned at the stake for daring to suggest, among other things, that the Earth revolved around the sun. I wondered what sacrifices were in store for those who will fight our new world view — who challenge the orthodoxy of our own day and the inflexible powers of the New World Order.

While there I visited with the members of the Italian MSI (the Italian Social Movement) and was granted an audience with Signor Almirante, the leader of the party. I thought it gracious that he took some of his time to talk with a young college student about the issues of the day. He told me, using similar arguments to those of George Lincoln Rockwell, that fascism had much in common with the original government of the United States. He told me that other than the Stars and Stripes, no other symbol finds more association with early America than the fascist symbol, being found woven in the original rug of the U.S. Supreme Court and proudly displayed on the interior walls of the U.S. Congress. He gave me a present of a beautiful gold-edged book, *Jefferson and/or Mussolini*, written by America's greatest 20th-century poet, Ezra Pound. In Almirante I felt I had shaken a hand that still had within it the genes that built the greatness of Rome.

From Rome I went on to Munich. As I stepped off the tarmac, a blast of chilly late-September air made blood rush to my face. It was the first really cool air I had felt since the previous winter in Baton Rouge, and it was wonderful. It is true that sunshine and warmth easily seduce Europeans, probably because our forefathers battled for eons against the cold and wet of the Ice Ages, but nothing can animate and rekindle our spirits like cool temperatures. We do enjoy the brisk air.

It was the first time I had been back to Europe since my kindergarten days in Holland, so for me it was a homecoming. Since my racial awakening, returning to the homeland of our ancient racial ancestors had a special meaning for me. The soil of Europe is holy, consecrated by the thousands of generations who drew their sustenance from it and by those millions who defended and nourished it with their blood. The cleanliness of the villages and even the cities, the excellence of the schools, the cultured atmosphere, the magnificence of the Alps; no place on Earth is like Europe. I saw beautiful faces everywhere I went, and even the youngest of girls could walk late on the streets without fear. Yes, truly it is the land of my forefathers. Many of the villages had been a community since even before recorded history, and in spite of a minor language barrier, I felt part of that community, a traveler returned to his homeland after a long absence.

I also knew that this was what many parts of America were like before the advent of multiracialism and diversity. And I realized that when we win our revolution, America will someday be like this again.

I visited the concentration camp at Dachau, and I noted that the camp was in the process of important changes. I had read that the camp was an extermination camp containing chambers in which many thousands of Jews had been murdered. But placards had been changed. They now read that it once had a working gas chamber, but that it had "never been used." I recalled my reading of the Nuremberg War Crimes Trials' documents alleging the gassings at Dachau. Not all the exhibits had been changed at that time; some of them still suggested the mass murder of prisoners. In a restaurant near the camp, I spoke with an old man who told me that his brother, during the American occupation, had been one of the laborers who had put in the plumbing for the "gas chamber."

I also visited the historical landmarks of National Socialism. In Munich I went to the very spot where Hitler stood when he addressed his men at the Burger Brau Keller, the hall (since torn down) where the putsch of 1923 began. I visited Brannau and Bertesgarten, the indescribably beautiful city of Salzburg with its medieval castle overlooking it from the Monchsberg, a hill rising in the middle of the city.

From there I went on to West Berlin, and was amazed that so much destruction remained from the Second World War. In front of the ruins of the Reichstag, I talked to a German soldier who knew little of politics, and I felt as though I was talking to a Confederate War veteran during the time of Reconstruction. I told him that the allies had their share of war guilt, especially the Soviets, but the difference was that the Germans lost the war and history almost always vilifies the loser. He was amazed that an American would say these things, and he told me of the terrible loss of life in his own family. Among other relatives, he told me, he had lost three aunts and seven cousins who were burned to death in the bombing of Cologne. His father, he said, had died in a British POW camp almost a year after the war from the effects of malnutrition and resulting disease, and his mother had gone to the camp every day but had not been allowed to give him the food he needed to live. Even some of his civilian relatives had died from disease in the first few months of occupation when there was no food. "No one cries any tears for them," he said plaintively. "I have," I told him, "and for all the White men, women, and children who died in that terrible war."

Seeing the devastation in Berlin and the ugly monstrosity of the Berlin Wall, I grieved again for all of our folk who had died in that internecine war on both sides of the conflict. I bore no prejudice against the Germans, and I knew other nations bore equal if not greater guilt for the physical and genetic devastation of the war. But I felt Hitler had to bear an especially heavy burden. He had a lot more racial understanding than the other leaders. He should have realized the extreme lengths our traditional enemies would go to incite the war, and he had to know the incalculable damage that such a conflagration would do to our European genotype. He failed in his responsibility to more seriously prepare for possible conflict, and he could certainly have done far more to avoid it. Although the widened scope of the war was not his intention, as he did not expect the French and English to be drawn into the war with Poland, he had let himself be drawn into it by his own provincial dreams of German glory and *lebensraum*.

The war left Europe devastated and half of it enslaved. It meant the loss of the British Empire and with it the decline of the entire White world. Even more importantly, it secured an unchallenged Jewish supremacism throughout the European world. Stalingrad was the turning point not only for the Second World War, but also for the White race in the 20th century. More than any other factor, that horrendous war is why Europeans everywhere currently face the terrifying prospect of genetic and cultural genocide. As the century draws to a close, the evolutionary forces of White renewal and renaissance are still crippled by the legacy of the Second World War.

EUROPE AND HOME 549

After Berlin, I traveled to Great Britain and met with British activists, and then finally boarded the plane for New York, bound for New Orleans. On the plane, I considered the things that had occurred in just the past few weeks — my encounter with the starving Indian child, the close call in Israel, and the renewal of my spirit in Greece and later in the heart of Europe. I reviewed what I considered to be the headlong rush of our civilization to disaster and our race to genocide.

I thought about one of my last days spent in Germany. I traveled to Dortmund and visited the monument to Herman. His story has to be one of the most triumphant, and yet, one of the most personally tragic in all of history. It has pertinence for every person of European descent.

About the time of Christ, Rome decided to conquer northern Europe. Although it is often said that Rome controlled the entire known world, in reality there was one part of the world the Roman Caesars knew about, could not conquer. It was Germany beyond the Rhine. One of the largest armies in the history of the Roman Empire, three legions under the command of General Quintilius Varus, marched in 7 AD to conquer and garrison the territory. Rome would have succeeded except for the foresight and courage of one man: Herman, who the Romans called Arminius.

The statue of Herman near Dortmund.

Herman, chief of the Cherusci, a Teutonic tribe inhabiting parts of what is now Germany, was born about 18 BC and served with distinction as a colonel in the Roman army between 1 and 7 AD. He discovered in 6 AD that the Romans planned to conquer his homeland. After resigning his commission, he took it upon himself to organize the Germanic tribes to resist the Roman invasion. Through his commanding physical presence, and convincing intellect and spirit, Herman rallied the chronically feuding German kingdoms to band together and fight the invader.

In a brilliant tactical maneuver, he decided to attack the advancing Roman Legions, led by General Varus, in the thickly wooded area called the Teutoberger Wald. He knew that fighting the battle in the thick forest would bring out the superior individual fighting skills of the Germanic warriors and lessen the advantage of Roman tactical expertise. In a great battle lasting for days, the Roman legions were decimated. It was said that Caesar cried in the Roman Senate and plaintively demanded: "Varus, where are my legions? Give me my Legions." Tacitus described the great battle in his *Annals* of history about 100 years later.[961] It was one of the worst military defeats in the history of Rome and was so severe that although the Romans won some battles in the years following, they never were able to conquer the region.

Herman, though, suffered greatly. His pregnant wife's father was Segestes, who betrayed his homeland and his daughter by delivering her to the Romans as a hostage. Caesar paraded her in chains through the streets of Rome, and later mistreatment caused the death of the son she gave birth to in Roman captivity. Tacitus, in his *Annals*, quotes Herman's rousing speech to his fellow countryman:

> "Noble the father," he would say, "mighty the general, brave the army which, with such strength, has carried off one weak woman. Before me, three legions, three commanders have fallen. Not by treachery, not against pregnant women, but openly against armed men do I wage war.... Let Segestes dwell on the conquered bank... If you prefer your fatherland, your ancestors, your ancient life to Roman tyrants and their new colonies, follow me to glory and to freedom rather than Segestes to ignominious servitude."[962]

Standing before the huge statue of Herman, gazing at his heroic pose of sword pointed to heaven and cape clasped by the ancient symbol of the White race, the sunwheel, I felt again the call of my genes, and their demand for courage like his in the fateful days ahead for the White race. I also thought of an old poem that goes,

> **Herman was the first, He gathered the brave,**
> **The mark of the sunwheel, Odin then gave.**
> **Throw blinkerd and scabbard away out of sight,**
> **To Ragnarok sail the glorious fight.**[963]

I knew the conflict ahead would be for our very survival against the aliens who would wipe away our freedom and heritage. I knew that the decades ahead would be the most crucial in the long history of our race, and would demand the same love of freedom and honor that Herman had shown. I felt I just could not wait any longer, and that time was running out for our people. *Why finish school and get a college diploma?* I thought. It would not greatly affect my level of knowledge. It seemed time to begin my political work. It later turned out to be an error that made me more vulnerable to the powers of the establishment. It is my hope in relating my mistake, young Aryans reading this will finish their education before embarking full-time in their political work.

My girlfriend, Chloê, finished up her degree in Home Economics Education. She decided to move to New Orleans and teach there. Interestingly, she landed a job in an exclusive, college-preparatory Black Catholic school. I got busy and launched what I conceived as a modern kind of political Klan, the National Party, which had racial principles similar to those of the South African National Party. We adopted the Klan symbol of the crosswheel and laid out a racially-conscious political program for America that called for:

- **An end to Third World immigration**
- **A reduction of the welfare illegitimate birthrate**
- **The abolition of so-called affirmative-action programs**
- **The ending of forced integration in schools and neighborhoods**
- **The reduction of the size and influence of the government**
- **The breaking up of the Jewish media conglomerates**
- **An America-first trade and foreign policy**
- **More self-determination for both the Black and White race**

With little money, a hostile media, and determined opposition from the governmental establishment, we had, as one man remarked to me after a speech, "as much chance of success as a toothpick in Lake Ponchartrain." But I believed that the power of truth could overcome all odds. If just a handful of men would stand up and tell the truth — its power would attract more and more adherents until we would win elections and *become* the government. I had lots of ideas, a great deal of energy, and a heart that ached for victory.

I opened a small office for the National Party at 3214 Dumaine Street, in a racially mixed New Orleans neighborhood. It was a poor location and a dangerous one. Blacks jumped more than one of our youthful supporters as they walked the two blocks from the bus stop. We lived for days at a time on New Orleans-style red beans and rice — it was all we could afford — but slowly we got support from people in the community who became inspired by our activism and vision. I began hearing from White activists all over the nation who liked our fresh approach, and we became the largest local White-rights group anywhere in the nation, with hundreds of active members and with regular demonstrations and parades participated in by hundreds of people, most of them young. Many of them loved the way we went out and challenged the enemy on their own turf. One of our more exciting forays was against Jerry Rubin, the Yippie leader who was famous for the riots at the Democratic presidential convention in Chicago in 1968.

Rubin had a reputation as one of the most militant of all the Marxist anti-war advocates in the United States. He openly supported the Viet Cong and openly applauded their killing of American servicemen. Another one of his most well known lines, which he reiterated at every speech, was "Kill your parents." Perhaps he meant it rhetorically, but he said it as if he meant it literally. He railed against what he called "the system" and advocated violence against the government and against racists. He spoke in the Cotillion Ballroom at LSU accompanied by a cadre of beret-wearing Marxists. I attended the speech with a dozen of my friends. A question-and-answer period had been advertised, but when I showed up, the Marxists in charge quickly decided to cancel it.

As soon as the speech ended, my friends and I left angry that we had not gotten the opportunity to challenge Rubin. On our way out, we spotted him near the candy counter in the LSU Union foyer, where he was holding court with his followers. I decided on a strategy unusual for me, but very appropriate for *him*. I went straight through the crowd and right up to the diminutive Marxist. I put on a scowl, edged up to his face, and said, "You sounded real tough up on the lectern talking about killing your parents and smashing in the heads of racists. Well, let's see how tough you really are. I challenge you anyway you want, you Commie bastard — a debate or just you and me going at it with our fists. Let's see how tough you are. Right in front of you is what you call a racist and fascist, a live one right in front of you. Do have the nerve, or are you just a sniveling Jewish Commie coward?"

Rubin's face turned as white as the linoleum floor, and without so much as a word he swiveled around on the soles of his shoes and made a beeline for the back door of the Union. The Marxists who had been so impressed with him just 10 minutes before were crestfallen. I jumped up on a concrete planter and told the crowd, which had by now grown quite large, that we would hold an impromptu Free Speech Alley on the front steps of the Union. The crowd followed us outside, and I gave them an inspired speech for about half an hour, ridiculing and exposing Jerry Rubin. It was met with much laughter and much applause. I slept well that night.

Our activism brought down to New Orleans some fine patriots from around the nation. One of the first who relocated was Dennis Nix, a well-read and dedicated activist who was an excellent writer and cartoonist of professional caliber who moved from Missouri. Another young man was Hamilton Barrett, an idealist who brought along a whole series of well-written poems and pieces extolling our heritage and its struggle for survival. The youngest recruit from out of state was Lewis Darne, who came all the way from New York in the service of his race. No one was more devoted or more courageous to the cause than he. Dennis and I worked full time for bare subsistence. He slept on the couch in our 500-square-foot office. Hamilton and

Lewis worked at regular jobs, but sacrificed almost every cent other than their most immediate needs of food and shelter, on getting the organization going. Most of Chloê's teacher pay went into the work as well.

Most of our activists came from among high-school and college students as well as young working people, but we also had many supporters who were older, and even Jim Lindsay gave a hand when he was not working with his Klan organization. Dennis and I edited and published the *Nationalist* monthly magazine and frequently led activities in the streets. We helped organize the White students who proudly attended a high school named after Confederate General Francis T. Nichols. As the school's population became increasingly Black, White students suffered greatly from Black violence and criminality. They turned to our group to represent them at the school board meetings, where they aired their grievances. The school had a long history and proud tradition, and the students and parents became incensed at the effort of the Blacks to change the school's symbol from the Rebels. We picketed with the students on these issues and had a tremendous amount of support from them. We were able to hold off the name change until the school became almost entirely Black.

We also demanded more law enforcement to halt the rising Black crime rate in New Orleans. One of our demonstrations was a torchlight parade scheduled in remembrance of Cynthia LeBoef, a young White bride-to-be who was raped and murdered by a Black assailant.

A.I. Botnick, regional head of the ADL (the Jewish Anti-Defamation League of B'nai B'rith) had a close working relationship with the New Orleans Police Department. They were able to use the

554 MY AWAKENING

local Intelligence section of the police department as their own harassment squad against our organization. They, the FBI, and other plainclothes detectives began showing up at our meetings and taking flash pictures in the face of every person who would attend our public meetings. They tried to get us out of the building on zoning charges. They would look for the slightest infraction on anyone's automobile. They would stop and frisk young people on the street on the way to our headquarters and threaten them with jail for associating with us. They would go to hotels where we had meetings scheduled and pressure the management to cancel our room contracts. Even more intimidating, they would go to the places of work of our members, identify themselves as police, and tell the boss that our supporter was under suspicion for crimes and was being watched and urged them to report any suspicious behavior.

FBI Used Cash From Mississippi Jews
$36,500 Paid for Ambush
By Jack Nelson
© 1970, Los Angeles Times
MERIDIAN, Miss., Feb. 12— The FBI and the Meridian police, bankrolled by an alarmed Jewish community, paid $36,500 to...

killed and a liceman and wounded. T man receive sentence.

It might be hard for the reader to imagine these kinds of operations in a supposedly free nation, but such tactics were even admitted by federal authorities during the congressional Cointelpro (counter intelligence programs) investigations. Federal agents set up Cointelpro as a dirty tricks operation against those groups considered politically subversive of both the political right and left.[964] One of the more egregious examples of a Cointelpro-like activity was the planned ambush and murder of White activists in Meridian, Mississippi. Los Angeles Times columnist, Jack Anderson, exposed it in 1970.

A.I. Botnick provided over $37,000 dollars to police agencies to incite Klan activists to violence and then arranged to ambush them in a hail of automatic gunfire. A pretty, young White-activist teacher, Kathy Ainsworth, who was riding with the Klansmen, was killed in the ambush.[965] Jack Nelson, in a fine piece of investigative reporting, discovered that the event was essentially a murder-for-hire committed by the police and FBI for the ADL. Nelson quotes Kenneth Dean, a young

Kathy Ainsworth entering her classroom

civil-rights activist in Mississippi, saying that Botnick was asked to "make a contract somewhere in the north... to have two Klansmen liquidated." Dean then quotes Botnick as saying, "Those responsible for the trouble in Mississippi should be killed." Anderson goes on to report that, "Botnick told Dean that he could arrange for such a liquidation and that there would be no investigation." Police officers are quoted as saying that when they dragged a severely wounded Klansman, Tommy Tarrants, from the bushes, they intended to continue shooting him, but had to stop because a crowd of neighbors had gathered.

Even the liberal Los Angeles Times editorialized against the FBI and the ADL for attempting to act as, "Mrs. Ainsworth's judge, jury and executioner." It went on to say, "The authorities later discovered Kathy Ainsworth (the only one to die in the trap) was connected to the White Knights, but the police and the FBI have found no evidence linking her to any crime..." Even after learning that the murdered Mrs. Ainsworth was pregnant at the time, ADL leader A.I. Botnick told Nelson, "We were dealing with animals and I would do it again." Anderson was incredulous that a private organization could give money to a public police agency for the express purpose of eliminating an enemy.

In the government efforts against me, all of my lieutenants and I had clean records and had stressed nonviolence and legality at every opportunity. The same government that said it was opposed to violence would send in *agent provocateurs* to *encourage* violence. Police and FBI undercover operatives would infiltrate our organization and begin suggesting illegal activities. We would not stand for that talk, and we ferreted them out. I knew enough to keep stressing to all of our members that we had to be strictly legal, because the government was looking for any excuse to shut us down, lock us up and silence us.

The man who arranged for the ambush of Kathy Ainsworth, A.I. Botnick, was headquartered in New Orleans and worked closely with Freddie O'Sullivan, the Jewish head (with the Irish-sounding name) of New Orleans' Police Intelligence. They were determined to stop my growing organization at all costs.

In spite of all the harassment, we kept growing. Our demonstrations were becoming larger and more irritating to our opponents. The scheduled torchlight parade for Cynthia LeBoef was the biggest function we had yet planned. The Wednesday afternoon before the Friday-night march, a good supporter, Johnnie Schlosser, and I made kerosene lanterns for the parade using a method that the troops used for light in Vietnam and Laos. Kerosene was placed in a thick, 7 ounce, returnable coke bottle just as in a lantern and a cotton wick inserted in its mouth. A simple kerosene lantern such as this would provide light for hours. We had tested about three or four of them on the office's front stoop when a police car roared up and asked what we were doing. I told the officer how we were making lanterns for Friday night's parade. The officer said he saw nothing wrong, but he had orders to watch our office and report everything to the intelligence office. He asked to use our phone. We let him in, and after he told the chief what we were doing he was instructed to arrest us. The officer protested but was ordered to take us in. Johnnie and I were charged with filling a glass container with flammable liquid. Within minutes it was reported the radio news that we were making "Molotov cocktails."

We were arrested, handcuffed, and hauled down to police headquarters, mugged, sprayed down with insecticide, and separated. I was taken upstairs and put into a four-man holding cell with three Blacks. They intentionally locked me up with three members of the Black Panther Party in jail for attacking a White racist candidate for governor, Roswell Thompson, at the Robert E. Lee Monument circle on St. Charles Avenue.

The cell was isolated from any guards. Although, I had already talked to James Lindsay, and he was posting bail for me, I wondered what I would I do until that happened? I gave them a talk about Marcus Garvey and Black Nationalism. They were so stunned, that by the time they realized what was going on, I was released.

We went ahead and had the parade the next night and a good crowd of about 250 showed up on a rainy, cold night. I had to get a lawyer for the pending charges, which strained our already small budget. All the charges were dropped when the lab proved the liquid was kerosene, which was not a class-A flammable liquid as the law specified. I told the press that if I was to be arrested for this, then so should the mayor if he had a bottle of whiskey in his house. Of course, we had no resources to sue the city for false arrest, and the authorities saw the whole episode as a sign that they could do anything they wanted against us, knowing that we had little power to defend ourselves. In spite of continuing harassment, we stepped up our activism by becoming involved with the presidential campaign of George Wallace.

George Wallace was shot that spring while campaigning in the Maryland Democratic Primary. Although he was not as forthright as we wanted him to be on the race issue, he was the only national politician we could support. We hoped that he would, despite his injury, stay in the race and perhaps run as a third party candidate. His headquarters certainly kept its lights burning in Montgomery, and we kept our hopes alive. We worked as hard as we could in South Louisiana for George Wallace, and our shipments of materials came marked as the New Orleans' Wallace Campaign Headquarters. The national office was shipping us boxes of material every week and they in turn received a great deal of support from our area. Then, one very hot day in June, our world collapsed.

Chapter 33:

In the Belly of the Beast

As the summer of 1972 progressed, the National Party grew to hundreds of members, including at least 100 active high school and college students in the New Orleans area. We held parades, public meetings, and literature distributions. Our office on Dumaine Street became the makeshift headquarters for the New Orleans' George Wallace Campaign: recruiting young people, raising funds, and distributing Wallace literature and paraphernalia.

One afternoon in late June, police besieged our office. My girlfriend, Chloê Hardin, co-workers Hamilton Barrett and Lewis Darne, and I were arrested under the charge of theft for supposedly misrepresenting ourselves as Wallace campaigners. Handcuffed, the four of us watched as our files and personal possessions were rifled and trashed. Our membership records were seized, and our checkbook and much of our literature were boxed, sealed-up, and carted away. Even my private, personal correspondence with Chloê and with my parents was taken.

As I watched the agents tear apart my office, mouthing obscenities against me and my friends, I felt as if we had entered a Franz Kafka tale or perhaps a historical account of Communist KGB agents sacking the newspaper offices of dissidents of Eastern Europe. We were opposed to drugs, we didn't cheat in college,...we didn't even litter. But suddenly our freedom was being taken away, our personal possessions confiscated and our political organization smashed. All because we challenged the status quo.

Exhausted, demoralized and scared, I was fingerprinted, photographed front and side, and then locked in a small holding room perhaps seven feet by nine. A passed-out drunk and I were alone with a prisoner who loomed like a frightful dark apparition.

"Give me yo' money," the figure growled as soon as I was left alone with him. "Hand it over, *now!*" His blood-shot eyes resembled hot coals, and he stared at me with an intense focus that I pretended to ignore.

It was not bravery that made me refuse to hand over my last bits of change to the 250-pound, corn-rowed-haired Black who threatened me. I was just taking the course I felt I must to survive. I desperately needed my change to use the pay telephone and reach people who might be able to get my comrades and me out of jail.

The New Orleans Police Intelligence Division had been running a campaign of nonstop harassment against my fellow activists and me. Freddie O'Sullivan ran it, a former vice-squad cop who despite his seemingly Irish name, proved to be a Jewish member of Touro Synagogue. A huge picture of Communist revolutionary Leon Trotsky adorned a wall of his police headquarters. Whatever his attachments to the persona of Trotsky, he later turned out to be such a committed Zionist that he immigrated to Israel a few years later. O'Sullivan and his cohorts repeatedly showed up at our meetings, often sticking cameras in visitors' faces and obnoxiously using the flash. The agents would obtrusively take photos and make it clear that all visitors of our public meetings were under intense surveillance by police. These were clear violations of our civil rights, but even more damaging was their intimidation of our members at their workplace or school. Some lost their jobs. Many more lost heart.

Many local police departments had their own brand of dirty tricks — their own miniature versions of Cointelpro — to use on political troublemakers like us.

We had been fully authorized as a Wallace campaign headquarters by his national office in Montgomery, Alabama. We had sent the national office money and ordered extensive campaign supplies, and they had addressed all the packages and correspondence to us as the "New Orleans Wallace Campaign Headquarters" acknowledging us as the proper local representatives of the campaign.

O'Sullivan, however, had cleverly telephoned the Montgomery headquarters and asked the staff if David Duke, a Ku Klux Klan leader, was connected to the George Wallace for President Campaign. Fearing a scandal, the Wallace worker on the phone defensively said that Wallace had no connection to me.

On that pretext, O'Sullivan triumphantly dispatched a caravan of squad cars to arrest us for theft. Also, because we had many young people working in the campaign, they added the specious charge of "contributing to the delinquency of minors," an offense that would appear to most law-abiding people as some sort of sex-abuse charge.

My three comrades and I were idealistic and naive — easy prey for the corrupt and dirty world of the New Orleans ex-vice-squad agents. We found ourselves in a 95 percent Black jail. I only had $100 in the bank and no attorney. But my most immediate problem was this huge creature demanding the few nickels in my pocket.

I did not know it at that moment, but I later found out that the brute was a convicted murderer who had just been recaptured after an escape. Unfortunately, I was then under the delusion that one should always stand up to a bully. For most of my life, that principle had worked quite well, for even if I lost a fight, I was less likely to be picked on again. A code that had practicality in the schoolyard, however, was unrealistic in a contemporary American jail. Later I learned from more experienced White prisoners that sometimes one had to submit to a degree of petty theft, humiliation, and intimidation to survive, but that one still had to have a clear line of how far to go in accommodating the powers around you. Most Whites drew that line at the sexual advances of the Black prisoners.

There are at least half a million homosexual rapes in American jails each year. Black perpetrators commit a vast majority of them against White victims. It is a subject that is often joked about, but the high frequency of this bestial practice is certainly one of the most terrible symptoms of the barbarism to which our society has sunk. Obviously, severe punishment, including a much wider use of the death penalty is appropriate for violent criminals, but there can be no clearer example of constitutionally prohibited cruel and unusual punishment than the widespread homosexual rape plaguing our prisons. Its ubiquity is one more proof that the U.S. Constitution means little today to our rulers. Rather than upset politically correct notions of racial equality, young White men are forced to suffer the ultimate in personal torture and indignity. The media ignore this travesty and I, like most, had not thought much about the subject until my incarceration made me fear its ugly threat. My resolve was to fight to the death if need be to prevent such an act. If I were to be raped, I decided that my assailants would defile only my dead body.

The only other prisoner besides my tormentor in the tiny holding cell was White, but he was passed out, drooling on the wooden bench that lined one of the walls. The menacing Negro was unlike any of the friendlier Black souls I had known when, as a young man, I had worked at Gary's Garage. As the murderer approached me, I fully realized his immense size. He looked like a heavyweight boxer. Tall and stocky with a bull neck mounted on wide and powerful shoulders, he viewed my six-foot-two, thin, 175-pound, white-skinned frame with contempt. He took a boxer's stance and feigned a punch, to which I raised my fists.

He began to taunt me. "Yeah, you a prizefighter, huh, you a prizefighter."

Muttering incoherent strings of unintelligible words spiced with obscenities, he worked himself into frenzy, balling up his fists and contorting his face until it looked as though the veins in his neck would explode. I picked up my hands, put them in front of my chin, tightly closed my fists, and braced for the onslaught.

Suddenly, the jangling sound of keys broke the silence. A guard appeared, carrying a six-inch brass ring of keys. He opened the door and pushed five more prisoners into the crowded cell. Four of them were White. I felt like a prisoner on death row getting a last-second reprieve from the governor. The murderer just recoiled against the wall and stared silently at me. Finally, he spoke again, "I'll see you 'gin, you find out how it works in heah, You see me 'gin."

An hour later they moved me to the drunk tank. The cell was a 15-foot square, terrazzo-floored room with no benches or chairs. Its only adornment: a urinal on a red brick wall. It was a blazing hot late June, but this cell was air-conditioned and I felt freezing cold in my short-sleeved, thin cotton dress shirt. Vomit dripped off the edge of the urinal, and the stench was sickening, but I was so emotionally exhausted that nothing could keep me from stretching out, shivering, on the dirty stone floor. I laid my head on my forearm and quickly passed to a dream state, only to awake intermittently from my shivers and the commotion as prisoners were brought in and out.

A guard's thick hands shook me awake at six a.m. Soon I was reunited with my two friends, Hamilton and Lewis. We were transferred to two dirty, two-man cells in the central lockup, Lewis in one cell, Hamilton and I in the other. Each cell had a rusty upper and lower steel bunk with no mattress, and each was stifling hot in the steam-bath humidity of New Orleans. Because they had booked us so late, we could not be arraigned before a judge until the following morning. Given a chance to use the telephone down the hall, I called Jim Lindsay to arrange for a lawyer and was soon locked back with Hamilton in the closet-sized cell. We made up revolutionary songs, told jokes, and made imaginary revolutionary speeches through the bars. Then we both became silent, imagining ourselves being framed, convicted, and sentenced to years in prison.

I also thought about Chloê. I hated to picture her in this filthy and brutal place. I recalled cool spring nights when I lay next to her in the soft, moist grass around the lake at LSU. In that time and place, love was pure and it seemed that if our dreams were passionate enough, they might just come true. *In Sir Walter Scott's classics*, I thought, *right always triumphed in the end*. I had not anticipated then that standing up for the things I believed in could harm the most sincere and beautiful person I knew — the person I cared most about in the world.

Night fell, but the heat lingered and we soaked in our own hot sweat. After swapping small talk of our fears and our faith, Hamilton and I found sleep on the rust-coated bunks. But not for long. I awoke from a heavy sleep with a sensation of something stinging my face. I sat up, realizing in horror that it was a roach. I had felt the prickly sensation of this three-or-four-inch-long creature biting at my flesh.

In the dim light, we could make out a half dozen more of these prehistoric monsters, scrambling along the crevices in the wall or scuttling across the floor outside the bars. We could hear them as we tried to return to sleep, sounding more like buzzing machines than living things as they took flight. It was as if they were waiting for us to close our eyes before they began their air attack, pouncing on our bunks and us. When we could, we struck at the roaches with our shoes. Hamilton and I cynically tried to make a game of it, keeping count of the feral creatures we had killed. I knew that Chloê hated roaches even more than I did, and I worried about what she must be facing in the women's section. I prayed that she was better off than we were.

By morning we were exhausted. We reeked of sweat. Our clothes were crisscrossed with streaks of brown powder and spotted with tiny rust flakes. It was in this condition that we were sent to our arraignment.

Arraignment was to be held in the Orleans Parish Courthouse two blocks away. The courthouse was connected to the infamous Orleans Parish Prison, a place where the news reports frequently reported inspections that uncovered drugs and weapons. It also had more than a modest share of assaults, murders, and suicides. Handcuffed to a dozen other prisoners, Hamilton, Lewis, and I snaked through the hallways, down the stairs, into and out of a van and up a staircase to adjoining holding cells just outside the courtroom. My two comrades were with me in a cell holding perhaps 25 inmates, of whom perhaps nine or ten were White. In the cell directly across from us were about 30 Blacks. Their cell had a large Black Panther crudely sketched in charcoal on the wall, the capital letters BPP underneath; they had also crudely scrawled several misspelled Black power slogans on the gray painted brick. Open toilets, slopped with human waste, garnished both cells.

Women awaiting arraignment were held in the cell diagonal to ours. I caught sight of my beloved Chloê. She tried to put on a brave smile. My eyes began to glaze over, but I bit my lip and told myself that I had to be strong for her and my younger friends.

The Blacks in the crowded cell directly across from mine caught sight of Chloê in the women's cell. Her beauty had persevered through a difficult night, and she looked as though a ray of light illuminated her in comparison to the dark, rough-hewn, criminal elements surrounding her.

The Blacks began to taunt her, calling out and mocking the crude acts they wanted to do to her. It pains me just to remember the vicious, pornographic, sadistic things they told Chloê. Here was an American girl who came from a loving, Christian home, who now faced unspeakable filth, humiliation, and terror — simply for defending the beautiful heritage of our people and country . . . and for daring to love and believe in me.

Like we three men, Chloê tried to be strong. I got the impression that she was trying to be strong for me. She knew it made me suffer knowing that I was powerless to rescue her. As the obscene trash talk mounted, I could see tears glistening in her eyes and her lips beginning to quiver as she turned her face down into her hands. Jealous of all the attention given to Chloê, the Black women in her cell also turned on her with verbal abuse as she retreated to the back of the cell and sobbed.

Hatred welled up in me against the animals that would treat a woman so cruelly. Ridding the Earth of the filthy scum in that cell would have been an highly moral act. No doubt, my opponents will interpret these words as proof of my depravity. So be it. But I would hold that it is a depraved society that allows the highest and most beautiful creations of God to be defiled by such vile creatures.

I know that sustained hatred destroys the hater as much as the hated, and that the greatest works and treasures of man are truly built in the service of love and creation, not hatred and bitterness. Yet when we lose the capacity to hate evil or of those who inflict it on the innocent, we have lost a tool necessary for survival. At that point, we would become the perfect slaves, bereft of emotion, ready to endure any indignity, any wrong and any tyranny as long as the name of love is invoked. When the passion comes back to the hearts of our people, only then we shall triumph.

We were finally called into court. I brought up to the judge that all of us had clean records and pointed out to him that many of the violent criminals who preceded us were given release on their own recognizance. The prosecution argued we were such political radicals that the bond should be kept high. Our political incorrectness kept our bond higher than we could pay. As the guards led us to the lower floors of Parish Prison, Hamilton turned to me and said sarcastically, "I am so thankful that I live in America, where you can't be imprisoned for your political beliefs."

Once again we were chained to other prisoners in the box and marched out of the courtroom to face new perils. Chloê's eyes followed me all the way out of the courtroom, but in my own trepidation I could not decide whether her look was one of pain, or of disappointment in my failure to secure our freedom.

Hamilton, Lewis, and I had talked with a number of prisoners, and we knew that the worst was coming. Central Lockup, our previous jail, was luxurious compared to the bowels of Parish Prison. I kept my ears open and frequently asked questions of the prisoners who knew what was ahead so that I could find out how to better protect myself and my friends.

Guards first herded us into a room where they checked our valuables and money. Heeding the warnings of experienced prisoners; I checked every dollar I had, saving only a few nickels for the telephone. Most people entering jail for the first time think they should keep some money for personal needs like cigarettes, toiletries, and snacks. Not so in Parish Prison.

Most control over prisoners was by other prisoners called trustees. After formal check-in, as soon we entered the large open room in the basement of Parish Prison, Hamilton and Lewis were relieved of whatever money they kept with them. In fact, the Black trustees took Hamilton's wallet in addition to the cash in it. There was no possibility of resisting their demands because the basement area, called A-1 Receiving, housed about 60 criminal Blacks and only seven or eight Whites, and they were mostly worthless winos and bums picked up for vagrancy or other petty offenses.

In such a place, the Black-skinned man is king. Anybody who resisted Negro rule was likely to be beaten to a pulp, raped, or possibly killed. No one dared report acts of violence or larceny for fear of being labeled a "snitch" and suffering the ultimate punishment for the worst offense of the prisoner's moral code.

Before my time in jail, I had wondered how there could be so much drug use in prison considering its high cost. I learned firsthand that the drug dealers and users conduct regular shakedowns of other prisoners. There is so much cash in jail, in fact, that even a few guards are induced to sell drugs to prisoners. Inside the jail system, as on the outside, there is a vested economic interest in maintaining the status quo.

My introduction to the main prison reminded me of the Hollywood version of Nazi concentration camps. After surrendering all our clothes and valuables, showering, and being sprayed with insecticide to prevent diseases spread by fleas and lice, we changed into our jail house dungarees and walked into the main area of the large cell-block around 11 a.m. The A-1 holding area consisted of a large room divided by a corridor of iron bars. What I saw there was a nightmarish scene, only thing, it wasn't a nightmare a man could wake up from; it was real. I have never seen a movie portraying scenes as repulsive as what my friends and I saw in the Orleans Parish Prison.

There was a seatless, open toilet on a platform in the middle of one end of the larger room. It overflowed with human waste and vomit. Urine collected around the area like rain in street gutters after a thunderstorm. The stench permeated the entire cellblock. It was extremely hot, and in New Orleans — hot means much more than just high temperature; it was so oppressively humid that sometimes you had to force yourself to breathe. There just wasn't enough oxygen in the air. Everyone not sitting directly in front of the large belt-driven fan was drenched in sweat.

In addition to the redolence of human excrement and the worst body odors imaginable, there was also an odor in the air that at first I couldn't identify, and then I realized what it was: the musky scent of semen.

The Blacks and Whites segregated themselves. The one small group of Whites sat together in a section of rusty benches and tables that reminded me of wagons circled against the Indians on the American frontier. The ebony prisoners were loud and boisterous, often argumentative, and the room echoed with alternating shouts of anger and raucous laughter. The White minority was quiet and sullen, its conversation low-key and usually between two or three prisoners at a time. Whites avoided making eye-contact with the Black prisoners, and when Black trustees ordered some of the White prisoners to mop the floors or dispose of some trash, there was only quiet resignation as they did what they were told.

One prisoner among us had a glazed look in his eyes and sat motionless and mute. I discovered to my horror that the man had been raped a few days before. When he stood up, I noticed bloodstains on the seat of his trousers. I asked one of the prisoners about it, and he said that such was a common result of prison rapes. He then told me of a brutal practice sometimes-used in prison rape. Attackers will use a razor blade to split the sphincter muscle to mechanically facilitate homosexual rape. The inmate told us of this practice as casually as if he had been talking about the weather. I could not help but look at him in a mixture of macabre fascination and pity. He seemed to sense my gaze, and when he turned his eyes to mine, it was as if I looked into the portals of hell. They were eyes without any glint of life and hope, eyes staring out from a dead shell. Seeing such barbarism in that forlorn place struck me in the pit of my stomach, and for a while I wondered if I would retch and add to the stench of the place.

My friend Lewis was only 18, and he looked even younger, a handsome, young freckle-faced lad who looked more like 16 than his real age of 19. He had traveled to New Orleans from New York to work with me in the National Party. As soon as he had walked into the cell, the Black inmates made fun of this slight, innocent-looking, red-haired kid. Immediately they began to taunt him with sexual propositions and innuendo.

The Black ringleader was named Derrick. He was of medium height and fairly muscular build, but the source of his domination came not from his physical condition but from his swift talk and intimidating swagger. Approaching us, he looked Lewis over from head to toe. He smiled and said, "You be my bitch tonight, Cherry Top." Immediately, the other Blacks chimed in as well, calling him offensive names spelling out in disgusting detail their sordid plans for him.

Lewis just ignored them, but our apprehension mounted when Whites told us how the place got even worse once night fell. We saw a couple of Blacks across the room surreptitiously fondling what looked like a dagger or ice pick. On inquiry, our fellow prisoners told us that there were literally hundreds of knives and other weapons in the jail. It seems almost comical now to recount it, but in dead earnest we tried to sharpen our plastic toothbrush handles under the tabletop. We hoped that they could be our defensive weapons in case of attack.

It was still only midday. After a lunch of some Spam-type substance on mustard-garnished hard rolls that seemed more like paper than bread, a White teenager was added to our cell. His name was Tommy Brown, and he had long, straight blond hair that fell almost to his waist. He was a muscular, working kid with tattoos and a thick, brown leather wristband. I thought about how the Norse berserkers of the Middle Ages might have resembled him.

Tommy had been arrested after his friend (who was driving) failed to obey a stop sign. As the officers wrote the driver a ticket, they had noticed some tablets on the floor at the back seat. Although the driver insisted that they were his nephew's Sweet Tarts sugar candy (as tests later confirmed), Tommy and his friend were arrested on suspicion of drugs.

Upon seeing Tommy and his long blond tresses, Derrick and his cohorts went wild. "Dey done locked a White woman with us in here!"

"You goin' to be my honey tonight!"

"We goin' to grab you by yo' hair and make you suck!"

"I'll bent you over and have your white ass!"

Tommy ignored them. Derrick asked in a falsetto voice what his name was. "I'm Daaaaarrrreeeeek, 'ho are youuuu?" Returning the question with a piercing stare from his cold blue eyes, Tommy responded with powerful defiance, "My name's my own business."

Derrick shot him the finger and began cursing him. Red with anger, Tommy put up his fists. The two men began to circle one another, and the trustees moved quickly to herd the rest of us into an adjacent cell. Evidently, they were going to allow the fight, while the other prisoners were to be separated to prevent a race riot. As all the Whites, including me, were herded into the other cell, I realized too late, that there were still ten or 12 Blacks left in the cell with Tommy. My heart sank and my hands gripped the bars shaking in anger, as I saw a dozen Blacks surround Tommy. In a matter of seconds, they waded into him like a whirring machine, kicking, punching, tearing, and jabbing. Two of the assailants began cracking him over his head and hands with mop handles. Tommy could only try to cover his head and eyes as he slumped into a corner. The whole attack took only about 30 seconds. Then the cell doors were opened again and we were allowed back into the main room.

I rushed over to Tommy. He had a broken thumb and a concussion. His nose was bleeding. Dark blood trickled down from his left temple. As I helped him from the floor, Derrick began to threaten me, but I ignored him and guided Tommy over to the sink to clean his wounds. I felt guilty for stupidly leaving him alone with those animals, but I was surely not going to let any of them stop me from helping him. After a few minutes Tommy's hand, head and left eye were terribly swollen, and I was able to convince a trustee to take him to get first aid. Apparently the Blacks' bloodlust was satisfied for the moment, but Hamilton, Lewis, and I knew that our turn was coming.

We had friends on the outside working to find an honest judge who would sign a recognizance bond. If we could somehow survive the coming night, we thought we might be released the next day. Hamilton suggested that in the movies prisoners would sometimes deliberately strike guards so that they could be put in the "hole," meaning isolation or solitary. That idea became untenable when we discovered that the "hole" in this prison was a tiny cell inhabited by three or four of the worst Blacks in the jail.

Soon we overheard Derrick and the other Blacks arguing among themselves over which one would get the first chance to sodomize Lewis. Then we heard angry shouts from a group of Blacks who had been listening to the radio while playing cards in a corner of the room. WYLD, the Black music station, had announced that "David Duke" and three other "White supremacists" connected to the KKK had been arrested in New Orleans.

Even the dumbest of the Black jailbirds instantly understood who my friends and I were. For a moment the whole cellblock seemed to fall silent. At first, it seemed my media reputation intimidated them. The Klan had a reputation, although undeserved, like that of the mafia. Some of the Black inmates obviously thought that if they did anything to harm me, a "Godfather" type of character, they might soon end up with their feet in cement at the bottom of the Mississippi. Eventually, though, emboldened by each other's comments, their group hatred and anger overcame their individual fears. Whispers and furtive looks became evil stares and a hissing anger that boiled over into indecipherable gibberish and threats of torture and death toward the three of us. "Wait till tonight!" was their refrain.

By a fortunate circumstance, once a week, Orleans Parish Prison inmates were visited by young social workers from Tulane and other local colleges. By God's will, it seemed, this was that day. As the social worker, an overweight young man with a poor complexion and wire-rimmed spectacles, came in and set up a desk to interview prisoners, we decided to tell him our story in the hope that he could arrange for us to be temporarily segregated until our bond was secured. I related everything that had happened and the menace that we faced. To my dismay, when I finished my story he quickly informed me that even though he was well aware of the horrors of the jail, there was really nothing he could do. "After all," he said, "most of the others are in the same boat as you."

I returned to the small group of besieged White prisoners and I told Lewis and Hamilton what had happened. I had just finished when my comrades' faces froze. Towering behind me was the nameless prisoner who had confronted me two days before — the same recaptured murderer who was in my original holding cell. His size and reputation gave him instant command of the Blacks in A-1, and even smart-mouthed Derrick became his quiet supplicant.

With hatred again igniting his eyes, he stared in my eyes and said, " I told you I'd get you, tonight yo' ass is mine, mother-f ---er!"

At that point, we collectively decided that we had to devise a very intelligent and well-thought-out plan if we were to survive. We had no choice but to act immediately and take a big gamble.

I called the lawyer whose name Jim Lindsay had given me, but unable to reach him, I left a message on his answering service. Then I went back to the social worker and told him that I had informed my lawyer of the details of the situation and had given him the social worker's name. "If anything happens to us tonight," I said, "you will be the one held directly responsible."

Exasperated, the social worker told me that there was no guarantee the prison administration would move us, and that by telling my story to the guards and trustees we would put ourselves in the category of "snitches," a likely death sentence if they kept us in the general population. After a quick discussion, my friends and I agreed that we had no other choice, so I went ahead and told our story to the guard, who was right in front of the hostile prisoners. I demanded to see the warden. After a few minutes of arguing, the guard agreed to send me up to the administration offices.

A practically senile old man came down from the warden's office to escort me up. On the elevator, I told him the circumstances of our situation. Oblivious to reality, he suggested that we should just fight it out with them. I do not know how I found any humor left in me, but I responded, "Oh, we'd love to fight it out, the three of us against 30 vicious, hate-filled Black criminals — but don't you think we'd be taking unfair advantage of them?" A smile cracked the corner of his lips, and he said, "Oh, I guess I see your point."

I was able to convince the warden of our imminent peril, and he reluctantly agreed to move us — on the condition that I was certain bail would arrive the next day. He cautioned us that if we were not released then, we would have to go back to A1.

Uncomfortable, but safe for the moment, Hamilton, Lewis, and I stretched out on three tattered, stinking mattresses on the floor of the cell with the Black Panther drawn on the wall. Conversation eluded us and each retreated into his own thoughts. I said some prayers and hoped that the next day would restore us all to freedom.

I lay awake thinking for quite a while after Hamilton and Lewis had fallen asleep. Exhausted and anxious about the next day, I reviewed my life like a film editor reviews his footage. Things just were not working out the way I thought they would. To me the truth had always seemed like the ultimate weapon: No matter how unpopular or reviled, it is bound to prevail. But here I was in Parish Prison, facing an uncertain fate, aware that the truth of our cause offered no protection and no solace. That night I matured from the fantasies of youth to the hard realities of adulthood. Right is not always vindicated by power. Sometimes truth and life itself are crushed into the Earth. For truth to triumph, those who cherish it must give it more might than the lie.

My thoughts turned to Chloê and I imagined her angelically caressing my brow and visiting me with her sweet kiss. In the waning hours of the morning, sleep came to me cloaked in the ethereal visage of Chloê, who took me into her restful arms.

In the morning, only a couple of days before my 22nd birthday, I was out again — free to walk openly under the burning but welcome New Orleans summer sun. A Black judge, Israel Augustine, had signed my recognizance bond. How ironic — with an election drawing near, no White judge would dare sign our bond for fear of being labeled a racist. Judge Augustine was obviously immune to that charge, for he was also a hero of the civil-rights movement. Judge Augustine had been an ideological opponent, but he earned my respect that summer day. A free man, I was able to arrange for Lewis, Hamilton, and Chloê to be released as well.

That evening Chloê and I lay in each other's arms for hours under the rumbling drone of an old air conditioner. I was thankful to be alive; thankful that Chloê was now safe beside me and that we had all came through our ordeal unharmed. Over the next few days I re-examined my commitments. I resolved not to let the terrifying experience deter my mission. The conditions I had witnessed in jail only reinforced my views of race and the deplorable state of our civilization. Freddie O'Sullivan's corrupt and brutal attempt to suppress our movement and philosophy had left me even more convinced that my cause was right, and that my enemies represented an evil force upon the world. Only an evil system would ignore the barbaric rape of thousands of men. I remembered the quote that said that the best way to judge the level of civilization in a nation is by the conditions in its jails.

I understood too that no matter how terrible the experience seemed to me at the time, it had lasted only a few days. It was insignificant compared to what so many other patriots had suffered. In a historical context, many revolutionaries faced far worse incarceration, torture, and even death. No matter how difficult their imprisonment, though, most historical revolutionaries were locked up with their own comrades. In the America of the last days of the 20th century, the White dissident is likely to be locked in jails dominated by the living denizens of his worst nightmares.

Over the next couple of days, I re-read the wonderful letters written by St. Paul, some of which he had composed in the worst jails of the ancient world. My comrades and I would readily have traded the savage inmates of the modern American jail for the poor rations and lack of sanitation of those jails of Bible history. Both inside the jails and out, St. Paul kept his composure, and love of the Lord, and love of life. His example and inspiring words restored my strength and nourished my spirit.

Now that I was out of jail, I realized that O'Sullivan and his cronies probably knew from the beginning that we would not be convicted of any crime. By terrorizing us with imprisonment, damaging us financially with legal fees, and publicly discrediting us with negative news coverage, they had accomplished their objectives.

I had found out the hard way that the cause in which I invested myself was not a game. We were in a struggle of epic proportions against a vastly more organized and unscrupulous enemy. It was not enough to stand up on the street corner and tell the truth. It was about being able to defend your *right* to stand on that corner. Our enemies did not want us in the game at all, and were willing to go to almost any extreme to defeat us. They already tightly controlled information through the mass media. They had already put the politicians in debt to them for their favorable coverage and campaign donations. People like myself, who stepped out of the normal political boundaries, were a threat that they dealt with first by censorship, and then by character assassination. If those failed, they then utilize the same apparatus every tyranny in history has used to defend its supremacy: the law and its agents.

With my organization in tatters, my members and supporters intimidated, and my reputation sullied, I knew that I had to make some changes before politically organizing again. I needed credentials; otherwise, I would get no respect from the press, the police or the public. No matter how well read I might be or how articulate, I needed a college degree, the minimum that modern society demands for credibility. I resolved to go back and finish my final year of college and to continue preparing myself for the struggle ahead.

A week later, the George Wallace Campaign acknowledged quietly to the New Orleans district attorney that I had indeed been authorized by the campaign. All charges against my comrades and me were dropped. We never received any financial compensation for wrongful imprisonment, of course. But I was as determined as ever to find my compensation in victory over the powers that would commit such base acts. Later, perhaps as a small consolation for his campaign staff's cowardly betrayal, Governor Wallace appointed me to the honorary rank of lieutenant colonel in the Alabama State Militia.

The traumatic series of events also made me fully realize the wonderful and dedicated partner I had in Chloê, and we decided to marry.

CHAPTER 34:

THE KNIGHTS OF THE KU KLUX KLAN

Chloê and I put behind us the trauma of our time in jail and in the two months before our marriage, we were happier than we had ever been. I stored my files and papers at my family's house at the lakefront, sold my car, and we drove down together in Chloê's car to be married in West Palm Beach. My good friend Ray Leahart came down to our wedding in the West Palm Beach Presbyterian Church. Chloê sewed her own wedding dress and made a beautiful bride. It was a simple wedding with a nonalcoholic party afterward in the church reception hall.

Chloê and I decided that we needed to get as far away from minority-controlled New Orleans as we could, and decided to visit my sister for a while in the very European-American, Seattle area. We planned to stay with her a while, find work, and either complete my college education there, or go back to LSU. The drive to Seattle was to be our honeymoon. But we decided to spend the first day of our honeymoon near Key West, camping on one of the many small islands we could sail to on Chloê's small *sunfish* sailboat. The plan was that after a couple of days sailing and camping, we would return to Palm Beach, drop off the boat, and begin our long trip to Seattle. We'd travel from the very tip of the Southeastern-most point of the continental United States to nearly the Northwestern-most point.

We arrived near Key West in the late afternoon, loaded the sailboat, and headed out in the shallow lagoons looking for a hospitable sandy-beached island. After about three hours, and too far from our car to return that night, we still hadn't found a suitable spot. All the little islands shown on the marine maps turned out to be simply thick groves of mango vines coming directly out of the shallow water. We couldn't find a clear beach anywhere. Finally, we found a little island with no beach, but it did have an old dock with a small, doorless hut the size of an oversize telephone booth, occupied by an empty old wooden, cable spool, laying on its side and filling the enclosure.

The sun was low, so we decided to stay for the night on the old dock, which was only about two feet wide and about 15 feet long. We put out a blanket and quickly shed our clothes, anxious to get into the emerald water. We dove into the clear water and after a few minutes were reclining on the blanket watching a glowing orange sun merge with the ocean horizon, happy to be with each other. As the dusk faded, I kissed her. Suddenly she broke away from my lips and said, "ouch." Just as I was about to say what did I do? An "oww" blurted from my own throat. A bloodthirsty swarm of mosquitoes had descended on us, and I thought these beasts worse than any I had ever seen in Louisiana's darkest swamps. Luckily, we had some repellent, but the infernal creatures still managed to find an unprotected spot here and there, even if it meant penetrating some clothing.

After using about half of the bottle of repellent, we seemed to have the mosquito problem under control. But, just before the light was completely gone, Chloê motioned to me that there were eyes staring at us from the mangrove. I thought she must be imagining them, but when I turned to look, I could see little pairs of eyes catching the ambient light. They were the eyes of rats. Then we saw it. A rat the size of a dachshund crept up the dock toward us, showing no fear of us and no respect for us as a honeymoon couple. Others had congregated on the far end of the dock as if they were soldiers assembling for a military operation. I threw a few shells at them, and they scurried away. But they remained at the edge of the mangroves, waiting for their opportunity. We saw their eyes glowing like red coals until the dusk turned to an inky darkness that extinguished their color. I shined my flashlight up the dock, inspecting it plank by plank until I could see dozens of glowing eyes peering at us from the darkness.

So far our wedding night had been something less than blissful. Still, we made the best of it. We stayed alert, and I kept a supply of shells nearby to keep the rats at bay. At about 10 p.m. the wind picked up and a thunderstorm bubbled up out of the warm-watered Gulf side of the island. The dock had not been big enough for us to set up our pup tent, so when the bonechilling rain came, it soaked our bedding and clothes. Lightening came down streak after streak while we remained exposed at the end of the dock. Every bolt illuminated the rag-tag troop of rats that lurked at the dock's edge, looking for a meal. In the worst of the downpour, we grabbed our things and headed for the shack, rats or no rats.

We could have fit within the wooden rims of the empty spool turned on its side, and thus been sheltered completely from the rain, but we did not want to be down on the floor with the rats — which by that time had sought their own shelter there. A six-inch-diameter metal pipe ran from the hollow axis of the spool on the floor up through a hole in roof. We sat on top of the spool, still getting wet from the hole in the ceiling through which the metal pipe protruded well beyond the roofline. We huddled as close as we could, the rusty metal pipe between us — the rain dripping on our heads and the lightening crashing all around. It occurred to us that the metal pipe amounted to a lightening rod that would likely end our marriage before our honeymoon ended, but we resolved to stay where we were, come what may.

In the morning, worn out and sleepless, we saw that the bright sun had banished the rats and mosquitoes back into the mangroves, so we stretched out on the dock and dried out. Chloê scraped up some breakfast while I fished unsuccessfully, and then we decided to see if we could find a better island. If not, we would get back to the car and return to Palm Beach. We had had enough of that island paradise.

We found nothing suitable and sailed in the direction of highway 1, where we had parked the car. About 1 p.m. we found our small boat being escorted by two nice-size sharks, occasionally cutting the shallow, crystal-clear water with their oily-looking gray dorsals. We had difficulty maneuvering in the shallow reef water and had to raise the centerboard about halfway. Then, a really fierce afternoon thunderstorm approached us from the South. We had never seen a sky of exactly that color — a deep, deep purple. The wind and waves and rain buffeted us terribly as we lowered the sail and tried to keep the small boat into the wind the best we could. We couldn't lower the centerboard all the way because of the coral, and the boat was unstable in the wind and waves. In our frazzled state of mind we were sure that if we capsized the sharks would satisfy their appetites. Chloê began to cry, but we hung on until the storm had passed. Our boat, with its scarred centerboard and damaged sail, finally made it in. We wearily loaded it onto the trailer and headed for West Palm Beach. It had been a memorable 24-hour honeymoon.

We stayed another night in West Palm Beach, and with less than $200 we set off for Seattle. Of course, one could go a long way on $200 in a compact car when gasoline cost 35 cents a gallon. Still, to make it on that money we had to camp out all the way, sleep in our pup tent, and cook our food on a sterno. We visited Yellowstone and Glacier National Parks. In Yellowstone, in our small pup tent, we awoke shivering as a six-inch layer of snow had blanketed us. Our car had no heater; it was a south Florida car. Despite our limited budget, we went to the park cafeteria that morning and had our first restaurant meal on the trip — bowls of hot oatmeal, two cups of hot coffee, and a wonderful respite by the brick fireplace. We arrived at Glacier National Park right after they reopened the Going to the Sun highway following an early snowstorm. The mountains were beautiful in their early white dusting. I told Chloê that they had put on their white wedding dress just for us.

We finally arrived at my sister and brother-in-law's home in mid-September. We were broke, tired, and ready to find work. In less than a week we both found employment at the Sea-Tac Motor Inn in Federal Way, Washington, and we found a dingy rent-by-the-week room at a motel. I put in for a job at Boeing Aircraft as a painter, and we decided that if it came through, we would remain in the Northwest and I would complete my degree at the University of Washington. I did not get the job, so we decided to make as much money as possible at Sea-Tac and save every possible penny so I could attend LSU in the spring semester. To do that we had to work double shifts. I bell-hopped and bused tables, and Chloê waitressed for hotel functions. With Chloê's college degree in home economics education, she was soon managing the waitresses and setups for the scheduled events. Many days we worked 16 hours, but we knew we were working for the future. Even though I still read a number of books a week, the long mindless hours on the job gave me a chance to think about the cause and the best way to spread the truth. Jim Lindsay wrote me a few times from New Orleans and urged me to become active in the Klan again. He sent me some books on Nathan Bedford Forrest and some excellent material he had written about the original Klan being the first successful racial movement in history.

As for me, I had my racial worldview, but I needed guidance on the vehicle that could be built to take that ideology to victory. I concentrated my reading on the histories of revolutionary movements. I read books on the American and French revolutions. I also studied the Communist movement, Nazism, and the Fascist movements of Mussolini and Sir Oswald Mosely. I looked into the political movements of populists Huey Long of Louisiana and William Jennings Bryan. I also looked into the dynamics of religious movements and even the principles by which commercial enterprises are successfully organized. It seemed that all I thought about during my days at work and my reading at home was the creation of a movement that could wake up our people, and organize them for victory.

On a Friday in late October, I had worked a 16-hour double shift, during which time I turned over and over in my mind how I could best serve the Movement. That evening I fell into a restless sleep, Chloê by my side. At 6 a.m. I woke up completely alert and resolved. I knew exactly what I would do, my plan was laid out in my mind for the years ahead.

As of the fall of 1972, Klan groups around America had dwindled to shadows of what they once were. I contacted Jim Lindsay and proposed that we completely modernize the Klan. My concept did not mean that we would moderate its beliefs, but that we would deepen them with greater racial and scientific understanding. We would build upon its traditions to create a modern social movement. To me, that meant building the Klan into a political machine to change men's minds. It meant focusing on the young and the next generation while still venerating the old Klan traditions, and it meant the full rights of women to participate in the struggle for the survival of themselves and their children. It would be a literate Klan that would meet in the hotel conference rooms as well as in farmer's fields, the big cities as well as the villages, the colleges as well as the factories. The Klan had to be re-created like the original movement, led by knowledgeable and honorable men. This was my vision.

I called James Lindsay and asked him a simple question. Would he let me modernize the Klan from top to bottom? "Would I let you?" he responded. "I want you to do this more than anything in the world." In his typically dramatic way of saying things, he told me, "You know, it's your destiny to do this."

For the next few weeks, I worked days at the hotel and nights at the apartment completely rewriting the program and policies of the Knights of the Ku Klux Klan. I adopted the more modern version of the symbol and redesigned the publications, often conferring with Jim by telephone.

Chloê and I finally left Federal Way in November. We went straight down the West Coast to San Francisco. We drove around the University of California campus at Berkeley and were shocked by the brazenly Communist posters that seemed to have been posted on every telephone pole. The open promotion of homosexuality also surprised and disgusted us. We knew that the rest of the country was just a bit behind Berkeley. Was this what we could expect soon back home?

Then we set off to the redwoods of the Giant Forest, a place I had always wanted to visit again since I read the writings of Madison Grant, the White racialist who was the American most responsible for the preservation of these magnificent trees. It was interesting to me that I was drawn to his conservation work long before I knew of his devotion to also preserving the beauty of Western mankind. Walking beneath the redwood behemoths, one realizes how small and short-lived a single human being is in the natural scheme of things. It really brought home to me our subservience to Nature and her laws.

Our next stop was the Grand Canyon. We tied our sleeping bags to our backs, packed some food and began a hike down to the Colorado River. At the South rim the snow was two feet thick. Halfway down, the trail turned to mud, and the rest of the way the temperatures were mild and beautiful.

Over the years I have returned to the Canyon at least a dozen times. Every time I approach the South rim after a long absence, I am so overwhelmed by its beauty that I find it difficult to speak for a while. Seeing the carving of the river into the magnificent canyon is like opening a great encyclopedia of the Earth's history. To me such a place is more beautiful than any man-made temple and a more eloquent expression of God's word than any written form. We also stopped off in Flagstaff and paid homage to my aunt and uncle, Mildred and Wally Hatcher, at the memorial to those who died in the great air collision over the canyon.

The last important stop on our way back was at San Antonio. Seeing the Alamo for the first time since becoming racially aware had a powerful impact on both Chloê and me. The men who had fought and died there had their origins in almost every nation of Europe. They gave their lives so that people of our heritage could live in freedom across this entire continent. Their sacrifice not only inspired the Americans to victory against the Mexicans and Santa Anna at San Jacinto, but it should inspire every European for as long as our genotype lives.

To see prostitutes, drug dealers and other scum tolerated just outside the walls of this monument made us realize how tragically fast and far our people have descended. It made me anxious to begin again my political work, and I think I drove a bit faster than usual all the way back to Louisiana.

Chloê and I settled in Baton Rouge and I enrolled back in LSU. I was a ball of energy, filling my days and nights with study and activity. I began organizing and built the largest Klan unit in the nation in Baton Rouge and at LSU, and I established 22 other new Dens in Louisiana and Mississippi. Chloê and I also opened a successful day care center at Woodlawn Baptist Church in the eastern section of Baton Rouge. I took heavy academic loads of 18 to 21 semester hours, and I began traveling on weekends organizing the Klan. As my work for the Klan became more successful, Lindsay appointed me as Grand Dragon of Louisiana and also the National Information Director of the organization. The Klan began to rise again.

Chapter 35:
The Klan Rises

By the end of 1973, the Klan had dramatically grown. Not only were we reaching and recruiting many new people, most of them in their 20s or 30s, but we made sure that the quality of each new member was high. The media had carefully created an image of the Klan as violent, ignorant, and hateful. To overcome that image, we stressed to every member that he had to be "super-legal," that he had a responsibility to stay out of trouble, not only for the sake of his own well-being, but also for that of his Klan brothers. We viewed our organization as having a sacred mission to secure the survival and advancement of our racial heritage and rights. Our members knew that acts of violence against minorities were not only wrong, but also actually hurt our cause rather than helped it.

Any time White-on-Black violence occurred in America, it received national media coverage for days or weeks, while millions of White victims of Black violence received only brief local coverage from the media, if that. Thus the media made it appear that hatred and violence were intrinsic to the White rights movement, whereas the civil-rights movement was represented as a force for love and brotherhood. We were in the middle of a psychological war, and our enemies had a tremendous advantage through their media domination.

Many young Whites learned by experience how much damage integration did to their neighborhoods, schools, and communities. Its injustice became obvious to anyone who attended a heavily integrated school or who saw the decline in his neighborhood as it went Black or Mexican. Young White people were anxious to stand up for themselves, but they did not know how. The Hollywood portrayal of opponents of integration as violent or as "cross-burners" actually encouraged that kind of behavior among young Whites desperate for a way to defend themselves. In any social institution, young people were never permitted to have White-rights groups or exhibit any kind of White pride, while Black pride and solidarity were officially sanctioned and encouraged.

The only response depicted on television or in movies against integration was physical resistance. Some alienated Whites imitate the violent, anti-Black behavior they see on television. Such behavior only reinforces the image the media has created of hateful and violent White racists.

Of course, only a small fraction of cross-race crimes were White crimes against Blacks, and whenever a Black-White altercation ended with the White winning, the media depicted it as a racial incident. Any fight between Blacks and Whites in which the Blacks won simply resulted in a police report, and rare media coverage. If Blacks dragged a White child off his bicycle and beat him up, it was just kids fighting. But if White children did a similar thing to a Black child, and the Black child had to go to the hospital, it became a nationally spotlighted, "racial incident." Jesse Jackson and a few sports stars — along with a dozen news crews — were likely to show up at the hospital room for a photo opportunity and a round of anti-White propaganda.

That pattern still goes on today. On rare occasions, a criminal White person will hurt or kill a Black. Invariably, it will be on the news for days, accompanied by statements, by both White and Black political leaders, decrying White racism. Tearful interviews with family members and drawn-out coverage of their trials by a morally incensed media will follow. As shown in my race and society chapter, the reality is that acts of criminal violence by Whites against Blacks are extremely rare, while acts of Black brutality, rape and murder against Whites are commonplace.

As I began to receive publicity for my Klan stance, many children who attended integrated schools wrote to me, complaining bitterly of their experiences. From their letters, I could see that they had a right to be angry. Many had been intimidated and attacked by Blacks. They were forced into an environment of primitive behavior and criminality. They were taught in school that their ancestors were exploiters, while Blacks were taught pride for themselves and hatred for the White people. After appearing on national media programs, I began to receive dozens of letters a month from White students all over the nation, many of them writing about horrendous conditions and terrible incidents that people never hear about in the mass media. Over the years, the number of similar letters has increased to the point where I receive more today than at any time since the beginning of my public activism.

I explain to those who write to me, that they have the right to defend themselves if attacked, but that doing illegal things just makes matters a lot worse for themselves, their families, and their friends. I tell them that the last place they really want to be is in jail, outnumbered by the very worst of the Blacks. I also stress that our movement is not about hatred but about love for our traditions, heritage and freedoms. I knew then as I do now, that the only way we could build a lasting movement was not on hate, but upon a deep and abiding love of our people and their highest ideals.

As my notoriety grew, nothing bothered me more than being referred to as a "hater" or part of a "hate group." It is the integrationists and multiculturalists through their misguided programs, who are creating a climate of racial hatred. What do the liberals think that a chronic recital of White "evil" against Blacks does to Black attitudes toward Whites? The media dwell on historical enslavement of Blacks, discrimination against Blacks, lynching of Blacks, and the killing of Black civil-rights leaders. Blacks are being taught to hate Whites, a visceral hatred that is often expressed in their epidemic violence toward White people.

At the same time that Blacks are taught to hate Whites, Whites who simply want to preserve their *own* rights are called *haters*. Whites who want to live in a safe and decent neighborhood of their own heritage are called *haters*. Whites who want their children to attend academically excellent and safe schools are called *haters*. Even by simply discussing the realities of racial differences, we are called *haters*. Yet, it is a failure to recognize and deal with those racial differences that produce the climate of hatred in the first place. The kids who are most embittered and hateful are the ones forced into the integrated schools, and for *good reason*, because they have suffered unjustly. White children who are in all White schools have a lot less animosity, and often, very good feelings toward Blacks and other minorities. The Whitest areas of America have the most liberal attitudes toward Blacks and other racial minorities. If I had my way, I would stop these insane programs of forced integration and there would be a lot less hate.

If people truly want to end racial animosity and hatred, all they need do is recognize the differences that God and Nature made, and simply cherish and preserve those distinctions. Instead, they espouse an artificial equality that can only cause friction. Furthermore, by allowing massive non-White immigration and by encouraging the welfare breeding of vast numbers of more primitive and violence-prone people — we naturally create a society permeated with far more barbarism, crime and hatred.

I had a lot of debates at LSU and a number of professors invited me to visit some of their classes. One argument I heard repeatedly was that recognizing racial inequality leads to brutalities such as the Holocaust. I pointed out that most of our Founding Fathers did not believe in racial equality, and they built no gas chambers. I would also point out, that by almost any measure — far more people were murdered in the name of human equality than any other doctrine in history. In the name of equality, the Jacobeans of the French Revolution murdered tens-of-thousands of the finest and most cultured people of France. In Russia, China, the nations of Eastern Europe, Cambodia, Vietnam, and elsewhere — many tens of millions were killed in the name of equality. Equality is a religion of hatred and envy. When its false doctrine doesn't produce equal results, it enforces the "equality" of people by repression or even murder.

Jewish supremacist groups such as the ADL, the Anti-Defamation League of B'nai B'rith, are the most notorious users of the word *hate* to describe those of us who oppose their hypocrisy and misanthropy. They love to call us *White supremacists*. But what we really want is not to rule over any other race but to simply live in our own societies by our own values, oppressing no one. Racial separation makes racial oppression impossible, and racist hatred a lot more difficult.

On the other hand, Jewish ethnocentrism is truly supremacist in the classical sense, for they don't want to simply separate and have their own society in the way that we Whites almost always seek the company of our own kind. They don't want to be apart from us, they actively seek to rule us. As this volume has shown, Jewish supremacists hypocritically seek to weaken and degenerate the people among whom they dwell.

They requite us with the ultimate evil that they associate with the Holocaust: genocide. Yet, they seek to destroy our traditions, our history, our culture, and ultimately, even our genetic existence — which is certainly an accurate description of genocide. Their final solution is to destroy the racial heritage of the people that they believe have so wronged them, and the genocide of our race is happening as on a world-wide basis. They call us haters for exposing Jewish supremacism, but they are never called haters for their incessant accusations of Christian intolerance against Jews.

We are attacked for believing in White intellectual superiority over Blacks by the same Jewish-dominated media that unabashedly promotes the idea of Jewish intellectual and moral superiority over Gentiles.

They portray, as narrow-minded bigots, those Whites who oppose race-mixing between Blacks and Whites, while their own organizations run multimillion-dollar ad campaigns in Jewish publications against Jewish intermarriage.

We are morally chastised for wanting to control our borders from massive non-European, illegal immigration, while the Jewish media praises Israel, a nation that allows only their own race to immigrate.

Jews constantly cast guilt on Europeans and Christians for the Jewish Holocaust in the Second World War but call us haters for simply pointing out the leading role of Jews in the early days of the Communist regime in Russia that murdered tens of millions of Christians.

In the 1970s, the Jewish dominated media frequently talked about White terrorism, while the FBI reports showed that the leading terrorist group in America was the radical Jewish Defense League[966] (the JDL committed the most bombings of any group).

When I became active in the Klan again, I hoped that the fascinating character of the organization would be able to attract media coverage. Hollywood used the image of an evil KKK to further the objectives and image of the Civil-Rights movement, but in using that device it made the Klan fascinating and newsworthy. In January 1974, I made a media breakthrough on the nationally televised *Tomorrow Show* with Tom Snyder. From then on I found that many in media could not resist the ratings opportunities of having an outspoken Klan leader on their talk shows. Even some of my most dedicated ideological Jewish opponents simply could not resist both the challenge and the probability of higher ratings. Still today, a number of talk shows invite me specifically during their rating periods, so as to boost their audience numbers.

One of the most interesting shows I did after my *Tomorrow Show* appearance in 1974 was the *Stanley Siegel Show*, which was aired live in Nashville (he later moved to New York). Siegel had watched the *Tomorrow Show* and decided to take an approach unlike Tom Snyder's. If he couldn't argue with my facts, he would ridicule me. I knew he was a tough interviewer, and our Klan Den in Nashville kept a file of clippings on him. So I was ready with a good response to any personal attacks he might make. He kept trying to argue my points and kept losing, so near the end of the show he let loose what he thought would be his trump card.

"Mr. Duke," he said, "isn't it true that the reason why you and other Klansmen are so opposed to Blacks is because you White racists feel sexually inadequate to Black males? Aren't you just jealous of their sexual prowess?"

I stared him down and responded: "You know Stanley, only a sick person like yourself would even think in those terms. Let me ask you a couple of questions."

"You say I'm mentally ill, but isn't it true that you have been treated by a psychiatrist for ten years?"

"Isn't it also true that you once dove naked into a huge vat of Jell-O?"

"And, Stanley, speaking of feelings of inadequacy, why is it that you (pointing to his raised stool) have your stool raised up so you can look as tall as your guests? Are you feeling inadequate?"

"You know," I said, "Sexual inadequacy as compared to Negroes would never cross my mind, but I can understand why it crosses yours. You know, only a perverted little Jew like yourself could come up with something like that."

Siegel was so shattered he could barely finish the show, after which he immediately ran off to his dressing room, crying like a baby. I even felt a little sorry for him, but he really asked for it.

Those programs are satisfying on a number of levels. I reach millions of people with the truth about race. I break down old stereotypes about the Klan, and I must confess that I enjoy the challenge. When I was in the Klan it was great to walk into every show, every college speech, as a hated underdog and then turn the tables on my smug opponents. Most of these media people really believe their own propaganda. Because they have never really heard both sides of the racial issue and exposure of Jewish supremacism, they are simply not ready intellectually. Many of these hosts are masters of the spoken word, and they knew how to use humor, a turn of phrase, or even commercial breaks or the cameras to their advantage. But the basic truth of our position and the easily revealed hypocrisy of my opponents are an advantage that cannot be remedied despite their clever repartee.

I frequently also have a bit of fun, too. At a college speech at Vanderbilt University in Nashville, Tennessee, in the question-and-answer session, a loudmouthed White girl came to the microphone towing with her, by the hand, a Black man. While I was speaking, she rubbed her hands through his hair, put her arms around his neck, and kissed him repeatedly about the head and neck. When she finally came to the microphone, the audience grew completely silent. As she held his hand, she looked at me and said sarcastically, "Well, Mr. Duke, what do you have to say about this!"

I just ignored her, looked at the Black fellow, and said empathetically, "I'm really surprised to see a gentleman like you with such White trash." The audience laughed and roared for about three minutes until the woman had to sit down in shame.

More media presence also resulted in more college speaking invitations. At that time I received an honorarium of about $1,200 per speech, which really helped us get the equipment we needed for the movement. Starting from almost no funds, we had steadily built up our book stock and office material. We made every dollar go a very long way. I bought a used printing press and plate-maker and learned to print. Soon I printed, at very low cost, the thousands of leaflets we distributed as well as our monthly newsletter, then called *The Klan Action Report*, and later, *The Crusader*. At the same time, Chloê and I were the sole managers of the day-care center we had started at Woodlawn Baptist Church, but luckily she did almost everything that the center needed. Sometimes when she was overwhelmed or had to run errands, I would go to the center and fill in. I loved to sit at the church's piano and make up stories for the children about knights and dragons and damsels, complete with sound effects from the creaky old upright. My stories and fairy tales were anything but politically correct, and I think that's one reason the kids enjoyed them so much.

In my last semester in college, the spring of 1974, I had to earn 24 hours to graduate. To do it, I obtained permission from a professor and took a credit exam for a sociology course, which I passed easily. I also received permission from the dean to take more semester hours of course work than usually allowed. In spite of my Klan activity, I completed the full 21 hours that semester with an A or B in every subject. 1974 was a great year; I had worked hard and looked forward to the graduation ceremony. Finally, I would be able to pursue my life's work full-bore and full-time. Two weeks before graduation, I received an invitation and air ticket to a television talk show in Chicago that happened to fall on graduation day. I knew immediately which event I would attend. My whole college career was about furthering the cause of our heritage, and I knew that I would further it more in Chicago than by attending my commencement exercises.

That summer I crisscrossed America and spoke at two or three meetings every week. In September of that year, a United States Judge, Arthur Garrity, ordered the busing of thousands of White and Black students in Boston, Massachusetts. The working-class neighborhood of Southie found many of its sons and daughters ordered to attend school in Roxbury, a drug and crime-filled area similar to Harlem, while numbers of Blacks from Roxbury were to be bussed to Southie. Some of the leaders of the anti-busing resistance in Southie had seen me on a television program weighing in against busing, so they invited me to come up and help organize the people of Boston. I sent two of our organizers to organize the Klan in the area. Immediately I made a call in the press for Freedom Rides North, making a parody on the freedom rides that had descended on the South in the civil-rights days. I then flew up to Boston and was given a hero's welcome by the young men who were desperately fighting to save their neighborhood and the very lives of their children.

The people of Boston — once the very heart of the Abolitionist movement and the center from which the great attack was made on the South in the 1960s — now fought with all their might to resist integration. I saw the Boston resistance as the ultimate vindication of the South, and interestingly, the folks in Boston were on average a lot more radical than the ones in Louisiana and Mississippi. I had to continually explain to them that violence would only end up hurting their efforts. I told them how violence destroyed the resistance to integration in the South. Dr. Edward Fields,[967] who was active in Birmingham with the National States Rights Party at the time, told me how thousands of Whites had massed in the streets to oppose school integration. Then, in the aftermath of the church bombing in 1963, they were gone.

I stressed that Whites had to keep the moral imperative on our side. "The truth is," I told them, "it is the integrationists who are causing the loss of life, for they have already caused the loss of thousands of lives of Whites, and will cause the loss of many more thousands of European American lives in the cities of our nation. If we have our way, I told them, we will save the lives of both Whites and Blacks — and our civilization as well!"

At one point I joked about the radicalism of the Bostonians, saying to one of my organizers from Louisiana, "We've got to calm these people down. They want to kill all the Negroes, while we just want to get them safely back to Africa."

Back home I soon learned the news that Chloê was pregnant. It was a wonderful moment for both of us when we discovered that we would bring a new life into the world. The unbroken chain that had brought together our two families was to add another link from the past to the future. It was difficult for Chloê who had to contend with the day care center and the Klan office work while she was pregnant, but she never complained. She was ecstatic over the thought of our first child.

I began to be invited to increasing numbers of universities. I traveled to the University of North Carolina at Chapel Hill for a speech on April 4, 1975. The speech had been scheduled in an old auditorium with about 2000 seats. All were filled, and there were more than 500 students in an adjacent room hooked into a public-address system, and many others were outside the auditorium, crowded by the windows. Black students had picketed outside for about an hour before the speech. Just before the start of my scheduled speech, about a hundred militant Blacks forced their way into the hall and lined up between the audience seating and the stage. They were screaming, jiving, blowing whistles, throwing objects, and doing anything they could to stop the speech. Because they were between the audience and me, the crowd could not hear anything of my introduction or of my opening remarks. Ironically, the Blacks began to chant, "Free-dom! Free-dom! Free-dom!" They became more violent and unruly, until the dean called off the speech. That evening I wrote a long letter to the university newspaper decrying the loss of freedom of speech at UNC. I was also able to show how the primitive behavior of the Black students attempting to suppress freedom was reminiscent of the lack of freedom in Black Africa. I warned that as the racial composition of America continued to grow darker, that our freedoms would diminish further.

In June, James Lindsay, my friend and father figure since my high-school years, was killed. He was murdered the day before his divorce would become final, enabling his wife to inherit all his wealth. She was later charged with the homicide, but she had an excellent lawyer who won her an acquittal. News of his death struck me like a hammer, and I grieved hard for three days, hardly coming out of the house until I served as a pallbearer for his funeral in New Orleans. Chloê and I resolved to include his last name in the name of our first child.

In 1975 I decided to make my first race for public office: a run for the Louisiana State Senate. My opponent was Ken Osterberger, a very popular Republican incumbent who, like most Republicans, was a decent conservative and good family man, but he simply refused to address the critical issues facing the nation. I ran pledging to fight the

586 MY AWAKENING

forced busing of the federal government, promising to work for legislation to end the discrimination against Whites called affirmative action, reform the welfare system, and slow down the illegitimate welfare birthrate. As the youngest candidate in the state, I garnered 33 percent of the vote and greatly increased the public acceptability of the Klan.

A month before Election Day, something occurred of much

Kristin Duke and her year-older sister Erika

greater importance to Chloê and me than the election: the birth of our first child, my daughter Erika. Like many expectant fathers, I had initially hoped that my first child would be a son, and when the doctor said that it was a girl, a tinge of disappointment touched me for a moment. But when I looked at her and held her in my arms, I was just thankful to God to have her and pleased that she was so perfect. We named her Erika Lindsay Duke. Gazing into her bright eyes I saw the eyes of generations before me and the generations ahead. A year and one-half later, Chloê and I again were blessed with another beautiful and healthy daughter, Kristin Chloê Duke, and she would prove in later years to be just as dedicated to the cause as I am.

I thought about how ironic it is that some people will deny race when it is in the very look of our children and in their spirit as they grow. Race is simply an extension of the family, a vital extension that will affect virtually every part of our children's lives. It is true that everyone is an individual, but the racial makeup of a society has an obviously profound impact on one's life and one's family. Race is not just found in the form of a child's face; it is found in the form of a society. If my children were to grow up in a non-White land, their likely opportunities for achievement and quality of life would be greatly lessened. However, their genes would give them inherent advantages wherever they were. It seems so strange to me that some people cannot see the elemental realities of race. Perhaps, one of the factors that create such a divorce from reality comes from thousands of TV shows and movies that portray the only difference between the races as their skin color. People don't think about the fact that in those dramas, both the White and Black actors speak words almost always composed from the mind of a White person (the script writer). The Black actor simply parrots back through memory the feelings, values, and mores that come from a White writer. No wonder the media makes the races seem so much alike in their nature.

Although I made many radio and television appearances, a great many were canceled at the last moment because of pressure from the ADL and other groups, and some programs taped for later airing were canceled after the interviewer did not do as well against me as he had planned. One top-rated and very well spoken radio and television host in Los Angeles, the English-accented Jew, Michael Jackson, invited me on his TV program and even sent me a plane ticket. On the air, he said that I had "buried Tom Snyder," but he figured he could defeat me easily. First, we did the live radio show at midday, in which he did not fare too well, and then we went on to tape the TV show for its airing two days later. On the TV show he came on very belligerently and began accusing me of being "full of hate." He had used the "hate" argument earlier on the radio show, so I made some Xerox copies of some particularly hateful Talmudic quotations as well as some very anti-Gentile quotations from the Jewish press.

I told him, "I don't hate Blacks, I just want to live among my own people according to my own values, but if you want to hear some hate, I'll give you some examples of hate." I began to quote Talmudic writ such as the "best of the Gentiles should be killed" and "Gentiles are like unclean animals." "Imagine if I said similar things about Blacks and Jews." Jackson was speechless; dumbfounded that anyone would dare quote from the Talmud. He began stumbling over his words as the show ended.

He never allowed the program to be aired. Jackson had a no-lose proposition; if he had defeated me he would have been anxious to broadcast the show, but, because it was taped, he could avoid hurting his reputation by simply erasing the tape and airing another show.

In other appearances around the country, openly Communist-revolutionary organizations showed up and called for my death and urged physical attacks against me. Communist newspapers such as that of the progressive Labor Party sported headlines that said "Death to Duke." In one radio station in Chicago, Communists invaded with lead pipes, smashing the station and trying to strike me as I defended myself with a chair until the police finally expelled them from the facility. By 1977 I was speaking at about 100 meetings and doing 200 radio and TV talk shows a year. As our organization grew, the authorities became more brazen in their attempts to intimidate and disrupt our movement.

In 1975 we held a Klan convention in Metairie along with an International Anti-Communist conference; participants came from around the world. Plainclothes officers in the hotel parking lot made a point of photographing guests, sometimes blinding them with flashes just inches from their faces. I asked them to leave and went to get the management of the hotel.

During my absence, one of the delegates, a 78-year-old man, got into a scuffle with the police and was arrested. Some of the delegates berated and harangued the intelligence police, protesting the arrest. About eight hours after the incident, they decided to arrest me on a misdemeanor charge of incitement to riot. Along with Dr. James K. Warner[968], head of the New Christian Crusade Church, I was found guilty by a kangaroo court, but the verdicts were later thrown out on appeal. Then the state dropped one of the charges so I would not be entitled to a jury trial. Even though the evidence clearly exonerated me, Judge Thomas Wicker, in an incongruent verdict, found me guilty of inciting a riot, but officially noted for the record that the "riot" caused no injury and no property damage. Some riot. A couple of years later, Wicker's wife received an appointment to a Federal judgeship.

In the mid-'70s I actively sought ways to publicly expose the threat to the nation's racial and cultural integrity from the massive illegal immigration pouring over the border from Mexico. Our leaders decided that a novel way to capitalize on the Klan notoriety would be to increase public awareness of the problem. We decided to launch a Klan Border Watch — that is, to have our members, from California to Texas, patrol the Mexican-American border and report illegal-alien crossings to the undermanned U.S. Border Patrol.

We started things off with a tour of the San Yasidro Port of Entry at San Diego. The facility had given tours to the public at request, so I asked for one and, surprisingly, they accommodated me. The press was incensed that the leader of the KKK would be given a tour at a major government facility. The Communists went ballistic. They arrived with their Mestizo and Jewish minions to physically attack us. By the end of my tour, a sizable contingent of Marxists had launched a riot, attacking the Border Patrol and us. They rampaged through the facility throwing rocks and eggs. I remember that one projectile hit a well-dressed Mexican woman, who was coming through the customs checkpoint as a visitor. She lay on the ground as medics attended to her badly cut face. The police were able to end the melee, but it spawned many sensational newspaper stories and set the stage for our Klan Border Watch activity. Almost every newspaper in the United States, as well as every broadcasting network, covered the Klan Border Watch. In interviews, I stressed the alien threat to our American heritage. Many of the stories cast us in the worst possible light, some even suggesting that we would attack the Mexicans, but

590 MY AWAKENING

millions of Americans saw that at least a few people would stand up to the alien invasion, and that at least one organization saw the invasion as a crisis.

The U.S. Border Patrol agents loved the fact that our Border Watch focused attention on the massive alien influx and even issued a public statement after my announcement of the Klan Border Watch, saying that they would "welcome information from any citizen on illegal border crossings." One of the politicians who attacked me most was the mayor of San Diego at that time, Pete Wilson. Wilson sent a telegram to U.S. Attorney General Griffin Bell saying, "I profoundly disagree with the attitude implied by local [Border Patrol] officials, which seems to condone the assistance of the notoriously racist KKK." During that time Wilson consistently downplayed the dangers of immigration and discounted the nefarious nature of affirmative action. Years later, however, he adopted my positions and used those same issues to propel himself to the California governorship.

In an unexpected turn of events, we discovered that the Mexican newspapers and broadcast outlets had sensationalized our organization even more wildly than did the American press. Almost every Mexican newspaper ran front-page stories featuring the Klan Border Watch. Most of them boasted sinister-looking photographs of burning crosses and old, turn-of-the-century stock photos of lynched Negroes. Some of the papers even used old photographs of the Christian ascetics in Spain with their peaked hoods and candles — labeling them as Klansmen.

Coinciding with the lurid headlines in Mexico, U.S. Border Patrol estimates of crossings by illegal aliens dropped dramatically, as apparently the would-be illegal aliens believed that hooded Klansmen waited for them on the American side of the border, nooses in hand. The only thing our Klan Border Watch did was simply drive through the border areas and report locations of groups of illegal aliens heading north.

Because of the supposed Klan threat to Mexicans, the Mexican government ordered its troops to patrol their side of the border. And, to make sure no harm came to wetbacks on our side of the border, President Carter beefed up U.S. patrols. The Chronicle News Service reported, "The Border Patrol spokesman said the presence of troops must have accounted for decreased illegal alien activity during the weekend. He said only one illegal alien was encountered Saturday."

The overanxiousness of the press to paint us as dangerous people had inadvertently curtailed the alien flow for a few months. Another positive effect was that, because of the hype about the possible violence of Klan patrols, the State of California sent state police there and urged local policing of the border areas. So, in an effort to protect the aliens from the big bad Klan, the state actually ended up patrolling and protecting our American borders. I became well versed in using the vast power of the media against itself in a form of political jujitsu pioneered by George Lincoln Rockwell.

One of the most interesting and effective of my adventures during this period was a trip to Great Britain in 1978. Britain was experiencing massive third-world immigration, much like the United States, and British patriots thought that my presence there could raise British consciousness of immigration in the same way our Border Watch had in the United States. Similar to immigration history in the United States, Jewish organizations play a dominant role in promoting British non-White immigration, and during a critical period of immigration, they were able to block all proposed laws limiting the alien influx to the already densely populated island. By the time I had planned my trip to Britain, London was already beginning to experience a taste of the violent crime that plagues America's major cities, and the Black crime rate in Britain was strikingly similar in proportion to that found in the United States — about 10 times higher per capita than White crime.

Racially aware Britons had visited me in Louisiana and gone through the Klan ritual and returned home to set up Dens in England and Scotland. They urged me to come to Britain in early 1978. I also had a standing invitation from some of the professors at Oxford to come and lecture to their classes on our view of the Reconstruction period and the dynamics of racial politics in the South. Some media had also expressed interest in interviews. The time was certainly right for me to go, but the problem was that the British government had banned me as politically undesirable. Still, I was determined to get in.

I decided on a low-key strategy. After letting my beard grow for a couple of days, I flew to New York, and then flew standby on a flight to Britain on Laker Airlines. This way, the British government would have no warning of my arrival time. Seven hours later, I stood in front the passport queue at British customs, needing to make a decision. Five checkers were comparing the passport names against the proscribed list, before granting the visitors entry visas. Three of them were spiffy English types, and the other two were Black immigrants plainly from the former British colonies in the West Indies. I decided to go directly to one of the Black West Indians, thinking that they would likely be less conscientious. I immediately smiled and said, "How ya doin', Mon." He laughed and lackadaisically failed to look at the proscribed list when he stamped my passport.

Once my visa was stamped, I was in the country legally despite being on the banned list. I thought it apropos that I was able to be in the country to speak against immigration because of the incompetence of a non-White immigrant. I began meeting with our British Klan members as well as with activists in the British National Front. We knew that my presence in Britain would create a great story in the sensationalistic British press. We decided that we would use the publicity to stress the immigration issue. I met with two reporters and the photographer from one of the largest daily papers, the *Daily Mirror*.[969] I told them that I was "Paul Revere in reverse," that I had come to warn my British brothers and sisters about the dangers of multiculturalism and multiracialism. My late-hour, clarion call was, "The Third World is coming! The Third World is coming!" I pointed out that America is rife with racial problems, and that Britain had a chance to avoid these terrible problems, keep their peace, and preserve their way of life, but that she needed to act soon.

"Why is it?" I asked, "that Britain and Europe always seem to copy the worst aspects of America rather than the best? Must your cities and schools face the same ruin as ours, the same violence? Why must you repeat America's mistakes?"

Immediately the Home Secretary of the British government issued a deportation summons and issued my photograph to every policeman in the country. But through a series of intermediaries, I arranged interviews, radio programs, and appearances all over the country. Adding to the mystique of the affair, BBC television did an interview from the back seat of a moving automobile. I posed in Klan robes with a view of Parliament and Big Ben in the background. I also appeared on the most watched television show in Britain, the *Tonight Programme*. On the program, I recounted my Scottish and English heritage and made it plain how much I loved and respected the British homeland and my ancestors. I pointed out that the reason the government wanted to deport me was to keep me from telling the British people the truth about the failure of multiracialism in the United States.

"Why is your government trying to keep out a visitor of British descent who is simply suggesting that you should preserve your wonderful nation, while that same government lets in millions who hate Britain and everything she stands for — and allows them to live here?"

After the show I became instantly recognizable in London, and I did some "walkabouts" among the public. The British people treated me royally, almost everyone who recognized me had something complimentary to say. The respected British newspaper the *Daily Telegraph* reported my success on the *Tonight Programme* as follows: "Such was Mr. Duke's aplomb in handling the surly aggression of the *Tonight Programme* interviewer, millions of Britons may be forgiven for thinking that there is something to be said for the Ku Klux Klan after all."[970]

A real cat-and-mouse game developed between Scotland Yard and me. In the Cunard Hotel lobby, while in the midst of an interview with a reporter, I could see through the large hotel windows — the police storming through one of the doors. A jump ahead of them, as they came up the 50-foot escalator, I went down the other side, waving and smiling, and dashed into the street to a waiting car. The next day, newspaper headlines read, "Grand Wizard Does Vanishing Act," and "Bobbies in Keystone Kops Fiasco With Klan Leader."

Many of the papers dubbed me the Klan's "Scarlet Pimpernel," a positive reference to the legendary Englishman who rescued many of the French aristocracy from the terrors of the French Revolution. He was known for his disguises and elusiveness. I kept speaking and traveling for about two weeks, and avoided capture, despite front-page stories every day in almost all the major newspapers. It became a bigger story with each passing day.

The event began to capture the imagination of the British people, who, whether or not they agreed with me, rooted for me as they would a fox running from the hounds. The British people touched my heart as well, and I fully realized that they, as much as the American people, were overwhelmingly opposed to the Third World immigration. But the enemies of their heritage controlled both media and the politicians, so nothing was done to halt the onrushing catastrophe. Today, some parts of London resemble more the Mideastern region than the Britain of old. The British people, much like we Americans,

THE KLAN RISES 595

are now blessed by what the media call the joys of diversity. It is just hard to understand how escalating crime and drugs, overburdened welfare rolls, high taxes, and failed schools are joyful.

Even when addressing large crowds, the people would not give me up to the authorities. At Oxford University I lectured to 200 students and faculty and left shortly before the police arrived. A farmer named Beau Claire of the Red Ascot Farm hosted a cross-lighting ceremony for me in the countryside. A massive traffic jam occurred because of people trying to attend the rally in spite of the police roadblocks. I stayed away, but the next night I went to the Red Ascot Farm, and we held another one. I did a radio program at a studio in East London, and when the police arrived, I escaped through a side door. In response to these events, the headlines read, "Klansman Still Not Run to Ground." The newspapers also played on the Home Secretary's first name, Merlyn, and continually referred to "Merlyn and the Wizard." Many poems were written and published about the affair. Hundreds of political cartoons were published which were entertaining and sometimes quite effective for our issues. One cartoon, for instance, showed a line of immigrants at the welfare office and a robed Klansman talking with the officer, saying, "I have been here for so long, surely I'm entitled to something."

It was all great fun. The plaintive words of the lead editorial in the *Mirror* sum up the circus atmosphere of the affair: "Mr. Duke is a

There were literally hundreds of cartoons about my British visit. Below are pictured two of them that use my visit for good purposes. One uses my unauthorized entry to show the illegal alien Third World invasion (right), and the other mocks the welfare system. The Klansman is sitting in the welfare office and says, "I have been here so long, surely I'm entitled to something." (below)

smooth, plausible spokesman, the best imitation the Klan's ever had of a 'good guy.'"[971] The *New Statesman* ran a cartoon and a poem showing the carnival atmosphere of the cat and mouse game I played with the government:

Sing a song of watchdogs	*Nobody could trace him,*
Hoping for a fluke;	*Not for love or money;*
Twenty thousand policemen	*Jardine called it farcical*
Hunting David Duke.	*But no one found it funny.*
Katch a clever Klansman,	*Now that he's been cornered,*
Wrap him in a sheet;	*We praise our smart police;*
You'll find him in a public house	*But most of all the wizard's wand*
Or posing in the street.	*Should go to Merlyn Rees.* [972]

One afternoon, while all of Scotland Yard searched for me, I sat in the *ABC Evening News* -European office on Fleet Street (the media center) and did an interview with Peter Jennings for that evening's broadcast. Afterward, we had an excellent visit for an hour over tea and cakes. We had a frank discussion sympathetic to the plight of the Palestinians. Jennings was one of the few higher-ups in the media who understood the Zionist injustice in Palestine (he had been assigned once to the Mideast bureau for ABC). While on Fleet Street, I also met with an Associated Press reporter I had befriended. From his office I watched the photos he had taken of me in front of Big Ben go to the major cities and newspapers of the world — Moscow, New York, Prague, Peking, Buenos Aires, and even remote nations such as Nepal and Borneo. I knew that every bit of publicity would ultimately be more opportunity to get the truth of race to our people.

I kept on doing radio programs by phone from different locations, asking the British people why the government was so anxious to shut me up about the immigration issue. I emphasized that the real question was not really *my* right of free speech, but *their* right to hear a dissenting view on this vital question. To make light of the whole affair, while being hunted, I posed for photographs with the Beefeaters at the Tower of London and actually had a photo taken by my AP friend right beneath the revolving Scotland Yard sign in the street in front of their headquarters in London. I spoke at some British National Front meetings, and the reception to my speeches was ecstatic. The audiences were especially pleased that the British people were hearing from one American who didn't sing the praises of racial integration.

Government agents finally apprehended me through a treacherous reporter who sold me out for the big story. The authorities caught up with me in a pub appropriately named the *Fox and the Hounds*. Both the reporter and I had mustaches and, true to the bureaucratic incompetence existing in every nation, the agents mistook the reporter for me. The lead agent, as if reading from a script, said, "Well, Mr. Duke, you have led us on a merry chase, but now we have finally caught up with you," and then he handed the reporter the summons. In a poor imitation of a British accent, I mumbled something about filing the story, and actually made it out of the pub while the reporter comedically tried to tell the Home office undersecretary that they had the wrong man.

I started away in the darkness behind the pub, but they caught up to me only five doors from the safety of the home of a supporter. The papers reported that I appropriately had said "God save Britain and the Queen" upon their giving me the summons. My friends engaged a good solicitor, and I was able to stay a few more days and make a considerable number of appearances before I had to get back to pressing Klan business in the United States.

I viewed the British trip as successful because it made people confront the immigration issue. It even had an impact in America, because of dozens of national wire stories, many TV news stories, and a full-page article in *Newsweek*. Furthermore, it enhanced the Klan's image, for it became tough to portray the Klan as a band of ignorant Southerners, when its leader found so much popular support in Britain.

My Klan group began to make headway in other perceptions as well. Some in the media grudgingly noted that my group, the Knights of the Ku Klux Klan, was nonviolent and law-abiding; that our leadership was educated and articulate; that ours was the only Klan group in which women could fully participate; and that we were predominantly a movement of younger people.

Ben Bradlee, Jr. wrote an excellent series of articles on our organization for the Los Angeles Times called "The New Klan," one of the fairest pieces I had seen. The Klan was definitely bucking against the tide of the media, but we began to get some decent publicity from the honest reporters and editors left in the business.

We made significant headway, but as we continued to make breakthroughs, the ADL and the government became increasing worried. A Klan made up of a few "good ole boys" letting off steam on a Saturday night — they could handle that. But they certainly did not want to see the beginnings of a serious mass movement, a politically oriented Klan with an effective spokesman. That just wouldn't do.

The ADL began an extreme attack on my organization and me. They mailed poison pen "information packets" on me to every reporter, every editor possible in both print media and broadcasting. They warned about giving me publicity, and they subtly let media outlets know that anything less than caustically condemning me was practically equivalent to condoning the Holocaust. The press began to reach new levels of nastiness. In the late 1970s, one prominent Jewish journalist even wrote a novel based on my character called the Grand Dragon.

CHAPTER 36:

THE GRAND DRAGON AND THE JEWISH PSYCHE

I faced increasing attacks in the Jewish press. While some news reporters endeavored to treat me fairly, I increasingly encountered Jewish media and particular Jewish reporters who heaped abuse upon me. They showed no reluctance to use the dirtiest of tricks. Geraldo Rivera interviewed me at my headquarters in Metairie, Louisiana for ABC's *Good Morning America* television program. He interviewed me for more than two hours, and he wore his hatred for me as blatantly as the tattooed Star of David on his wrist. Half Puerto Rican and half Jewish, he identifies far more with his Jewish side. When the program aired, I discovered that he had edited the two hours to just about two minutes. That's okay by the constraints of TV news, but he diced up those two minutes in a way to completely convey me in a distorted and hateful way. Some of his cleverly edited clips only showed parts of my sentences — completely distorting my words and meanings.

As the ADL and the Jewish media attack intensified, rather than retreat before the onslaught, I began to bring up the Jewish issue even more frequently on radio and television programs and in the speeches on my college speaking tours. In response, the Jewish-dominated media became even more hysterical against me. One Jewish newsletter called me the most dangerous anti-Semite in the world. They even utilized fiction as a means to discredit me, for they knew that in fiction there are absolutely no constraints at all on authenticity: they could paint an emotional and evil portrait of me.

In 1975 an all-star cast including Richard Burton, Lee Marvin, Linda Evans, Lola Falana and O.J. Simpson, appeared in the film

THE GRAND DRAGON 599

called *The Klansman*.[973] An extreme anti-White hate film, the story line centers on a black man as falsely accused of raping a white woman -- her character played by Linda Evans. (one more film about an innocent Black being persecuted by evil Whites). Klansmen in the film are unspeakably vile degenerates who delight in raping an innocent and young Black woman. In a graphic scene, Three Klansmen viciously rape and beat Lola Falana. A heroic young Black man, O.J. Simpson, does the "right thing" and plots an assassination of the leader of the Klan. The Klansman is a young, well-spoken, intelligent, and seemingly pleasant young man who hides a heart of evil. On a series of TV talk shows, the producers said they modeled the Klan leader after "David Duke in Louisiana."

Melvin Belli, the famous trial attorney in San Francisco, became so incensed about what he referred to as "this blatant incitement to murder," that he invited me to his office in California to discuss a suit against Paramount. Nothing ever came of the suit, but after some legal posturing, the producers and actors stopped mentioning my name in their talk show appearances. Some of the executive producers of the movie included: Alvin Bojar, Jerry Levy, Michael Marcovsky, Howard Effron, Joe Ingber, Peter A. Rodis Bill Shiffrin, Daniel K. Sobol. The main screenwriter, Millard Kaufman, fronted for the Communist screenwriters during the McCarthy era. The message in the film was clear -- Klan leaders are so evil that Blacks are justified in killing them.

In early 1977, an American-born, Jewish reporter based in Britain came to Louisiana to do a cover story on the Klan for the prestigious *Telegraph Sunday Magazine*. Her name is Irma Kurtz, and she wrote a novel called the *Grand Dragon* based on her experience as a journalist interviewing leaders of the KKK for the *Telegraph*. Years later she penned a regular feature called "The Agony Column" in *Cosmopolitan*, and she subsequently became the magazine's editor. Her novel, *The Grand Dragon*,[974] is a vicious attack on me, but it is fascinating because it confirms everything I had learned about Jewish supremacism and hypocrisy.

In America's Jewish-dominated literary establishment, which writer Truman Capote once labeled the "Jewish literary mafia," racial hatred is a White Anglo-Saxon trait. In *The Grand Dragon*, Kurtz not only reveals deep-seated Jewish fear and hatred of Gentiles; she blatantly justifies and advocates it.

Her story is about an American Jewish woman journalist who, working in England for a British newspaper, travels back to the United States to do an assignment on the Ku Klux Klan. Once she is in the States, she visits her parents. Her father expresses his life-long, virulent hatred of Gentiles. Considering herself cosmopolitan and fully assimilated into Gentile society, the young reporter disputes and ridicules her father's hatred.

Visiting a couple of Northern Klan leaders, the Jewess finds them more pathetically ignorant and impotent than dangerous. She then visits the Deep South to interview a young Klan leader who is educated and speaks before colleges, and who does not fit the media stereotype of a Klansman. Kurtz bases the story in Natchez rather than New Orleans (although, interestingly, the book's proofreaders failed to catch an erroneous reference to New Orleans in the text). Kurtz loosely bases the story on real events, such as an interview over lunch when I first met her. Some of the lines came word for word from that first conversation with me. But, only a few snippets of truth emerge from her narration from that point on.

In Kurtz's novel, a Jewish heroine falls in love with the young Klansman and sexually gives herself to him. After a night of sexual bliss, she attends a Klan rally, where the erudite Klansman transforms into a crass and hateful creature who utters every conceivable racial obscenity — to the delight of his Gentile followers. After hearing his speech, the heroine feels defiled and ashamed and realizes that her father was right all along in saying that Gentiles are inherently evil. She embraces her Jewish heritage and decides to immigrate to Israel.

If a Gentile had written the *Grand Dragon*, no major publisher would have allowed it to be printed, for only Jews can write in their periodicals and books that which reveals the undercurrent of hatred that Irma Kurtz and many other Jews feel toward non-Jews. As is always the case with our biased media, whoever exposes Jewish intolerance is charged with intolerance. By exposing this book on numerous occasions, my reputation as an anti-Semite has become greatly enhanced.

Early in the book, Kurtz shows her father's hatred toward Gentiles:

"... and inside the goyim, every goy, is a Jew killer!"[975]

"They're cannibals. What's their wafer and their wine that they gobble on Sunday's? The flesh and blood of a Jew."[976]

"'Dangerous people. . . they hated Jews. They should all be dead! They should all be lined up against a wall and shot! They should all...' He paused, searching for the most terrible thing he could invent.[977]

One morning my father took me to one side and asked me how I could endure being touched by a Christian.[978]

Could the reader imagine a Gentile writer turning it around?

"And he asked me how I could endure being touched by a Jew."

Or

"Inside the Jews, every Jew is a Christ killer."

At first, Kurtz points out in the book that she disagreed with her father, she just did not believe that Gentiles could be *that* bad. But by the end of the novel she realizes that her father was right all along.

Kurtz's heroine states,

At last I understood my father's fear at coming out into the high grass of the Diaspora, where tigers lay in wait for Kosher meat. She continues, "Some of these people had never met a Jew or seen one, but anti-Semitism brooded inside them anyway, carried on the tip of the gentile sperm and born in their offspring. . . .[979]

If a Gentile novelist created a character who made similar remarks about Jews — sentiments defended in the end by the book's heroine — shrill charges of anti-Semitism would pour from the critics. Such remarks would certainly brand both character and its author as evil. Not surprisingly, the Jewish and Judeophile book reviewers saw nothing objectionable about such intolerance in the *Grand Dragon*.

The author suffered reproach from the media only on the literary quality of her work, not for her anti-Gentile hatred. Instead, she rose to the editorship of arguably the largest feminist magazine in the world.

A number of other things can be gleaned from her book, about both the Jewish psyche and Jewish tactics against their enemies. Had Irma Kurtz done a nonfiction narrative of her experiences with the Klan and me, rather than writing a work of fiction, she could not have so easily twisted the facts. To justify her vile depiction of me and to incite her reader's hatred, she invents a hideous speech for me near the end of the book in which I call for the murder of Jews and Blacks. At one point, my fictional character even compares the Jews to spiders who must be exterminated.

Her message to the readers of *Grand Dragon* is clear: I may sound logical and intelligent, even compassionate, so much so that even an educated Jewish woman might find sympathy with my arguments, but actually, I hide a heart of evil. As proof, she made up a completely bogus hate speech, an invention of her own prejudice.

Many parts of the book give perceptive insight into the Jewish mindset. At the same time that she ultimately embraces the idea that Gentiles are evil, blondness and the European aesthetic fascinate her — much like Phillip Roth in his novel, *Portnoy's Complaint*.[980] She also reveals how hostile many Jews are to our culture and values. She cites her flight over the Atlantic when she witnessed a Jewish father rip the movie headphones off his young boy's head because the child was enamored by the Blond, Gentile-looking hero of a cowboy film. Note her passages about the Klansman she meets.

> **. . ., for I knew a man of that golden American blend could not be for my breed, . . ., and find me in conversation with the hero of a western movie.**[981]
>
> **. . . His blond hair fell straight across his forehead, and he pushed it back with a gesture of impatience and vanity. Whatever his origin – Teutonic, I reckoned, or Viking – the Grand Dragon's virtuous health and ruthless good looks, were then being delivered by nature only to the American-born**[982]
>
> **. . .Hitler's grandfather, some said, had been a Jew, and all Adolf's excesses were only an attempt to hide the stain on his own soul' maybe all prejudice was an expression of self-loathing. But the Grand Dragon turned his head toward me again, and I knew there was no Jewish blood in him; no dark patriarch had broken his golden line. He was straight from the Norse God of mischief.**[983]

In the *Telegraph Sunday magazine*, Kurtz used the same kind of language: "Duke is slim, handsome, with hair in a shade of Teutonic cornsilk at a mod length that pleases the university audiences he frequently addresses."[984] Kurtz even admits that she thinks the Klansman is honest.

"I knew that any hypocrite could be destroyed by a revelation of the truth he was hiding, but a man who believed totally that he was telling the truth, and whose truth was dangerous, was impervious to anything but destiny or a bullet. I sensed that the Grand Dragon was such a man."[985]

> **But I looked at him, bristling with sincerity, brimming with it, shining with it, and I could only think again, He's dangerous, because I knew – I had known from his first words- that I was bound to be defeated in argument with this Klansman as he had probably defeated all his interviewers.**[986]
>
> **I realized then that they did exist, the golden goys, willing to die for a country that to me was a strange place. . .**[987]

A Jewish Psychiatrist could have a field day interpreting the psyche of Ms. Kurtz as she finds herself being attracted to the Klansman and his intellectual arguments. The purpose of the book is to condition the public and especially the press, that no matter how convincing I might seem to be, that underneath — there is a heart of evil. Ironically, while the book condemns the Klansman's efforts to preserve his own heritage, she dotes on the relief felt by her father's parents when they heard his new bride from the Midwest speak Yiddish. Before they knew the bride was Jewish, his parents, "were all set to cover the mirrors in mourning for the loss of a son, until mother said a few words in Yiddish that sent her new mother-in-law into tears of relief..."[988]

In an early part of the book, before she flashes back to her encounter with the Grand Dragon, her hatred bubbles forth:

> **I want the Grand Dragon to grow old, I thought, and I enjoyed the picture of him disappointed, feeling his hold on life loosen as each arthritic finger curled back into his palm. I wanted him to grow old alone in prison, in one locked cell, a fortress patrolled by dumb strangers until his body was ugly and empty and lay in six feet of prison yard.**[989]

Such a depth of hatred seems strange coming from the people who are presented as the people of tolerance and love. It is those of my persuasion who are supposed to be the ones filled with hate and thoughts of vengeance.

Imagine for a moment if I had written a novel about a young man whose parents hated Jews while he nobly refuses to accept their prejudice. Then he travels to interview a Jewish leader and learns that Jews have an inherent hatred toward Gentiles. Suppose my hero in the novel pronounces that anti-Christianism is carried in the "tip of the Jewish sperm, and born in their offspring," and then he finally comes to realize that his father — who has a murderous hatred for Jews — was right all along. And so he goes off to immigrate to an all-White and non-Jewish country. How would such a book be viewed?

There was not a peep of protest against the anti-Gentile racial hate that Kurtz spews forth in the book, and not a note of criticism of this still-prominent media personality. The major criticism connected to this book is criticism of me for pointing out its hatred. As I write these words, a pertinent passage in Kurtz's book is still inscribed in my mind:

> **He's honest I thought, and then I felt sorry for him, for honesty in my opinion is a vice of children, and a vice my kind never had. We were old liars.**[990]

The *Grand Dragon* illustrates that point very well.

Chapter 37:

Disillusionment and New Directions

In 1972, when I became active in the Klan again, it was a fading remnant of past glory. However, the intelligent leaders of the group, such as Don Black — my second in command, J. McArthur — our newspaper editor, and our other leaders across America had breathed life into it. The Klan then became a lot more attractive to the more educated and successful of our heritage. We preached legality and nonviolence and sought to educate and organize European-Americans for the preservation of our race, cultural heritage, and freedom.

Attracted by the radical image of the Klan name and its mystery, the media found the Klan irresistible — they simply *had* to cover it, even if just to put it down. Once I had the opportunity to speak, I always sought to tell the racial truth in an intelligent and reasonable way. In part, the interest in the Klan came from the media's sensationalistic coverage, and that in turn made the group fascinating to the public.

Many Klansmen in the 1960s alleged that agents of the federal government actually encouraged illegality and then, once they initiated violence, used the illegality to destroy the organizations. Cointelpro, the government's counterintelligence program, orchestrated a series of dirty tricks against Klansmen even to the extent of sending a phony love-letter to a Klan leader's wife suggesting infidelity, thus hoping to destroy their marriage and weaken the movement. They also had Klan leaders harassed by the IRS or arrested on trumped-up charges, or had FBI agents visit them on their jobs, causing some to be fired.

In a very anti-David Duke book called the *Rise of David Duke*, written by a journalistic character-assassin with the New Orleans *Times Picayune*, a police officer is quoted as saying that even though they knew it was not true, their agents would tell Klansmen that I was an FBI informant. They would go to any lengths to discredit and weaken my organization.

The undercover agents were under orders to try to undermine Duke's credibility by responding that Duke was actually a police informer. "We'd say, 'Hey, he's with us.' It wasn't true, but we hoped word would get out so he'd have less credibility [among his own supporters]," said Fred O'Sullivan, who headed the New Orleans police intelligence unit when Duke got his start in the Klan.[991]

Ultimately, they promoted a more radical and pro-violent competing Klan group to weaken my organization and to hurt the Klan image. A member of my organization, Bill Wilkinson, broke off from my group under the auspices of the FBI. Later discovery of FBI records by *The Nashville Tennessean* showed that he had regularly conferred with them only days after joining my Klan.[992] The interesting thing was that Wilkinson's group used inflammatory rhetoric and became involved in violence against minorities. He used the derogatory term "niggers," which I did not, and cultivated a Hollywood-styled version of the Klan as a violent and hate-motivated organization. When asked about the prominent display of weapons at his rallies, he'd tell reporters, "Shotguns are for 'killing people.'" Even though I couldn't prevent distortions by the press, I was always careful to present a good image of the Klan. Wilkinson understood that the media loved to give big publicity to anyone spouting hateful and violent rhetoric. Because there was no copyright on the KKK name, we could not keep him from presenting himself as a legitimate Klan leader. The public had difficulty understanding that the Klan groups were not all alike.

As the Klan I led grew dramatically, I did not realize at first that the excellent publicity I had cultivated would help, not just my own organization, but all the "Klan" groups, some of whom more reflected the Hollywood image of the Klan rather than its historical reality. More of these so-called Klan leaders began to appear on TV talk shows, sometimes representing just a handful of people, yet presented as "the Klan." One "Klansman" of this stripe did more damage to my work than a dozen anti-Klan programs or dramatic stories. It was one thing for the media to allege that the Klan was hateful and stupid, it was altogether worse for a "Klansman" to *behave* that way. Of course, this was a result of the unassailed power of the media, for obviously they could televise ignorant and hateful members of any group. This problem has continued on into the late 1990s, illustrated by a Klan "leader" from Louisiana featured a few times on the Jerry Springer TV show who was, in fact, living with a Black woman.

The government and the Jewish groups took a role in promoting such false Klan leaders and encouraging conflicts between the organizations. Those efforts hurt my carefully cultivated media approach and ultimately my credibility. When I went on a TV or radio show, I always pointed out that the Klan was a legal and law-abiding movement for the preservation of our European-American heritage, and that it was not about hatred of other races, but about simply the love of our own families and our people. All it took was for the host to play a tape of another "Klan leader" who talked about "killing the n------s and the Jews," to make me look untruthful. Hosts also loved to throw up a violent act committed by a "Klansman," even though I never had the slightest connection to the perpetrator or the organization he belonged to. A whole cadre of idiots came out of the woodwork who discovered they could get a lot of publicity, maybe even an all expense-paid trip to Los Angeles or New York City, by putting on a Klan costume and saying outlandish things. The media loved it. Since the Klan had no copyright, it was impossible to curtail such activities. It is not possible to expel people that do not even belong to our group in the first place.

It was a difficult period. The authorities informed us of serious assassination threats. I traveled most of the time, leaving little time for the needs of my family. We had little money and I continued struggling with the jealousies and rivalries between different Klan movements. By the late 1970s, I was frustrated by constantly having to deal with alleged statements of counterfeit Klans and having the allegations against other Klan's thrown in my face. It became harder to discuss the critical issues facing our race and nation.

Every aspect of my life seemed difficult and strained, including my marriage. I was certainly not the easiest person to live with at that time. Ultimately, Chloê and I separated and she returned to South Florida to live near her parents, although she was still as committed to the cause as I was. We stayed respectful of each other and faithfully committed to the well-being of our children. I remained in Louisiana and was at a turning point in my life.

I was proud of the historical Klan and of what we had accomplished in the 1970s, but it seemed we weren't moving toward the victory that motivated me. I knew that the important thing wasn't any particular organization, but the victory we had to win to preserve and advance our heritage. Although I still revered the honorable history and tradition of the original organization of Reconstruction and the good work of the Klan that I led, it became obvious to me that the movement had to take a new form if it was to succeed. The Klan is not an end in itself; it has meaning solely as an instrument for the survival and evolutionary advancement of our people. I believed, no matter how I much loved the symbols and heritage of the organization, that I had to take whatever path I believed to be the most effective for the sacred cause of our racial survival and upward evolution.

The form of the organization is not vital, its underlying principles and substance are what's sacred. I also felt that those who fulfilled the Hollywood image of the Klan, whether intentional or not, did the memory of the once noble organization a great wrong. But I did not want to say anything critical of those who sincerely were doing the best they knew how for their heritage.

I called a meeting of the important leaders in the organization, and we discussed a possible name change for the organization — one that would differentiate our group from the others, and enable us to register it and protect its reputation. We desired a name that could express our principles without any association to illegality, violence or racial hatred. We decided to start a new organization and let those who still wanted to take the Klan approach remain with the Klan group. My close friend and second in command, Don Black, succeeded me as Grand Wizard of the Ku Klux Klan, and I decided to develop an altogether new organization.

Over the years, many people had suggested to me the name National Association for the Advancement of White People. If there could be a National Association for the Advancement of Colored People, why couldn't we have a group dedicated to the rights and heritage of Whites? The concept grew on me, and I saw that simply using the name would expose the double standards of the media. Every one of our top leaders — Don Black, J. McArthur, and others — agreed with my plan to form the National Association for the Advancement of White People. Even those who said they would remain with the Knights of the Ku Klux Klan, understood my sentiments and endorsed my efforts with the NAAWP.

The NAAWP had a strong start. I was able to recruit two retired U.S. Navy admirals for our national board, Admiral John G. Crommelin, Ret., who was referred to as the "heart of the *U.S.S. Enterprise*" aircraft carrier during the Second World War, and Admiral Ira McMillan, Ret. I also had obtained the endorsement of the group from a courageous retired Marine officer, General Pedro Del Valle, Ret., who lived near Annapolis, Maryland. From the beginning, the

NAAWP approach was effective. Although it did not receive the same level of publicity that the Klan did, it was much better publicity. No allegations of illegality or violence could be cast against it. All of our spokesmen represented our views accurately, and only our designated leaders had our permission to officially speak for the organization. Over the next few years I traveled the nation, appearing on talk shows and doing speeches at our rallies and other movement functions.

The name of the organization worked well in exposing the hypocritical positions of the media. Why should standing up for White civil rights be considered reprehensible, when standing up for Black rights was laudable? I pointed out repeatedly that European-Americans must have the most basic civil right of all, the right to keep their heritage and culture alive. When the government tried to prevent our meetings in public facilities or when newspapers tried to refuse our advertising, everyone could quickly see the double standards. If the NAACP could use a public facility, why not the NAAWP? If the NAACP could promote a Miss Black America contest, why couldn't the NAAWP promote a White Miss America?

I worked hard promoting the principles of the NAAWP in my local area of Metairie, always ready to stand up for the rights of Whites in the schools, on the job, and also to expose the anti-White bias of the media. More and more people began to understand that I did not advocate violence or oppression, but represented a legal organization trying to stop the discrimination and coming oppression of our own heritage.

In the 1970s, I laid the foundations of a political apparatus, having hundreds of local people dedicated to our principles. In 1979, in Metairie, while still in the Klan, I ran against a strong incumbent, Joe Tieman, for the Louisiana State senate and received 26 percent of the vote, a good base from which to work. I promoted the NAAWP in the 80s and continued to travel the nation rallying our people to stand up for their rights and heritage. Then in 1988, I entered some Democratic primaries for President. I traveled America awakening White consciousness. I did a half-hour paid television show, which aired in markets around America as well as in New Orleans. I scored 26,000 votes in Louisiana, exceeding the totals of some of the main contenders for nomination for the Presidency of the United States. Later in the year, I won the nomination of the Populist Party for president and campaigned across America, receiving 150,000 votes on Election Day.

CHAPTER 38:

POLITICAL VICTORY

In 1988 I traveled the country, running in Democratic presidential primaries much like George Wallace once did. In the New Hampshire primary, I also campaigned for the Democratic Vice-Presidential nomination, and won the primary with 60 percent of the vote. Although not a strongly contested nomination, it proved that people would vote for my ideals if given the opportunity. I believed that the American people were so desperate for someone to stand up for them — that the media attacks on someone as a "racist" would backfire.

In the Louisiana Democratic presidential primary, I came in ahead of several of the major candidates. In some areas, I received vote totals exceeding those of mainstream Democratic candidates such as Al Gore, Gary Hart, Paul Simon and Dick Gephardt. *The Times-Picayune*, attempting to downplay my good showing, listed my vote totals as "other." For example, the vote totals in St. Bernard Parish, an adjacent parish east of New Orleans, had Gephardt 13 percent, Gore 6 percent, Simon 1 percent, Hart 7 percent, and "other" at 17 percent. The "other" vote category was almost entirely my votes. My campaign workers became angered that a candidate such as Senator Paul Simon of Illinois, with only 1- percent, was listed, but I, with 17 percent was designated as "other." Such blatant media distortion is used to keep people unaware that there are significant numbers of people who will support political candidates who stand up for the rights of European Americans.

The media operates by one of the oldest and most reliable advertising principles, namely, that the most important thing is not how good or bad your product is, but whether people think it's popular.

Below is chart the *Times Picayune* put in for the Presidential primary in 1988. The "Other" sizable vote total is my vote that they did not want to acknowledge.

parish area

Jefferson			St. John			Plaquemines			St. Bernard		
Democrats			Democrats			Democrats			Democrats		
262 of 264 precincts reporting (99%)			16 of 16 precincts reporting (100%)			19 of 19 precincts reporting (100%)			36 of 36 precincts reporting (100%)		
Dukakis	13,268	30%	Dukakis	1,502	17%	Dukakis	732	22%	Dukakis	4,753	35%
Gephardt	5,013	11%	Gephardt	734	8%	Gephardt	265	8%	Gephardt	1,782	13%
Jackson	9,300	21%	Jackson	4,112	45%	Jackson	1,264	37%	Jackson	2,817	21%
Gore	8,829	20%	Gore	1,232	14%	Gore	511	15%	Gore	859	6%
Simon	488	1%	Simon	66	1%	Simon	35	1%	Simon	127	1%
Hart	1,623	3%	Hart	431	5%	Hart	145	4%	Hart	970	7%
Other	4,994	14%	Other	977	11%	Other	420	13%	Other	2,343	17%

The press still does everything it can to portray me as unpopular, hoping that doing so will *make* me unpopular. One can see the same underlying principle at work in the schoolyard when children tend to like those that the popular kids do, and to dislike those the popular kids don't.

In 1988 I traveled to Cincinnati and sought the Populist nomination under the leadership of Willis Carto and Don Wassal. I won it over two major contenders: Democrat Congressman John Trafficant of Ohio and retired Colonel Bo Gritz. The next few months led me to many states where I used every opportunity to speak for the rights and heritage of the European American. In the end the Populist Party under my Presidential campaign won 150,000 votes nationwide, a total that far exceeded other third parties who had more campaign funds than our party.

The grueling travel and campaigning had tired me out, but I learned a lot. Talking with people the length and breadth of the nation, I knew that most European-Americans down deep believe in the same things I do. Every poll had shown that more than 80 percent of the people oppose affirmative action, forced busing for integration, and the Third World immigration invasion. It was true that many do not know the scientific facts of race, but the overwhelming majority clearly want to live among their kinsmen and live in a society representing the values and culture of Western mankind. European Americans make that clear by whom they choose to associate with. They also have a vision of America that is radically different from the multicultural nightmare promoted by the media. But, our people have simply not been given a voice.

What really holds back candidates who are openly pro-European-American is the media-instilled psychology of defeat. People are told it is useless to vote for a White-rights advocate because he has no chance to win. Basically Whites are told repeatedly that they are alone and unpopular in their beliefs. It became clear to me that the soft underbelly of American politics is on the local level, because on that level, through personal contact, a sincere candidate can overcome disproportionate campaign spending and media bias. If a candidate participates in debates and forums, and knocks on enough doors, his message can be powerful — as effective as he can present himself on a personal level. It became clear to me that once a candidate passes a visible threshold of support and people *believe* that his winning *is* possible, then it *becomes* possible.

I also learned that the psychology of victory becomes easier under the banner of a major party. Up until that year I had been a George Wallace-style Democrat, but the Democratic Party's Marxist and vocal minority elements made it impossible for me to remain in the

Democrat party any longer, even superficially. I could not remain in the party of Jesse Jackson and Michael Dukakis. I received the nomination and ran as the Populist Party candidate for President as a means of building the Populist movement and to increase the racial awareness of the American people. But the only real victory made possible by running in such a race is not the office itself, but the winning of the hearts and minds of millions of Americans.

To get elected, cognizant of the realities of American politics, it is necessary to go through one of the major parties. Although the Republican Party leadership has also sold out our European-American heritage, Whites have overwhelmingly shifted to Republican because the Democratic Party has become an even worse alternative. Millions of Whites have joined the Republican Party because they are under the impression that the Republicans will defend the traditional heritage of America.

Although Republican leaders don't want to admit it, racial issues propel the Republican Party in the South. For instance, the first great Southern breakthrough of the Republican Party in the '60s came with the candidacy of Senator Barry Goldwater, who had defiantly voted against the Civil Rights Act. Nixon and Reagan frequently talked about White issues such as forced busing, welfare abuse, crime and affirmative action — all of which had clear racial components. But once in office, the Republicans did not act on these issues, and, in fact, under both Nixon and Reagan — forced busing, welfare, minority crime and affirmative action — all increased dramatically.

In the end, many Whites migrated to the Republican party for the same reasons they had emigrated to the suburbs: They simply felt more comfortable among their own kind, and the Democratic Party had become a party of every conceivable racial minority, radical feminists, homosexuals, and far left weirdoes. The Democratic party isn't of "their own kind" and they see Republicans as the better of two evils.

No matter how one might wish it otherwise, the American political structure is organized on a two-party basis. There is not one member of the U.S. Senate in America who is not a member of one of the two main parties. Obviously, America has a wide range of political thought, however, the fact that only two parties control practically all the representation in government shows the built-in bias of the system. Almost all other democratic nations have multiparty systems with a much wider range of political thought.

The one redeeming factor of the two-party system is that because the parties are omnipresent, they are viewed as public entities that must allow anyone to participate. Anyone can run as a Democrat or Republican in most races for public office. It is a right that the parties find very uncomfortable. Even though I served as an elected Republican legislator, I was denied even the right to put my name on the ballot for the Republican presidential nomination in some states. I was able to prevail in the federal courts, but I did not win the decision until several months after the election. The old adage that in America anyone has the right to run for president is rapidly becoming obsolete.

Running under the banner of a major party gives one a lot more credibility than running as a third-party candidate, and thus is important for developing the all-important winning psychology. Everyone takes it for granted that only a Democrat or a Republican can win, so when someone runs as a Third Party candidate, it hurts the candidate's credibility. I believe that when a successful European-American third party does arise in America — which I think will occur in the first decades of the 21st century — it will emerge out of one of the major parties — likely the Republican Party. There is no barrier within the major parties that can prevent patriots from organizing within it, for example, as "America First" Republicans, and building a true grassroots movement inside the party apparatus. Even an official third-party movement and organization can get involved with a major party unofficially, and in it learn the mechanics of the election process.

Election Victory

In the fall of 1988, Chuck Cusimano, II, a member of the Louisiana House of Representatives from my home District 81 in Metairie, was elected to a judgeship, leaving his seat open. John Treen, chairman of the Republican Party in Jefferson Parish and the brother of a former Republican governor, Dave Treen, looked to go into the office easily. Even though Treen had the machinery of the Republican Party behind him, the open seat attracted a number of major local candidates, including school board member Delton Charles, who had the support of the most powerful politician in the parish, Lawrence Chehardy, the tax assessor. Another major candidate was Democrat D.J. (Bud) Olister who had the support of the popular Chinese-American sheriff of Jefferson, Harry Lee. Because of the frequent Black robberies occurring in White neighborhoods, Lee acquired a national "racist" reputation when he ordered his deputies to stop dilapidated old cars driven by Black teenagers in all-White neighborhoods. He was also in hot water with the press for trying to put up barricades on streets linking Black Orleans Parish and White Jefferson Parish.

After conferring with my long-time friend, Howie Farrell, and other friends and supporters, I registered Republican and decided to enter the election. A total of seven hard-working, full-time candidates campaigned for the seat.

POLITICAL VICTORY 613

I did not change my rhetoric from that of the NAAWP other than to emphasize those issues that were pertinent to the district's voters. I spoke forthrightly about affirmative action and the massive discrimination against Whites, the high illegitimate welfare birthrate that was destroying our economy and causing the productive to become outnumbered and outvoted. I dared to speak about the minority crime that was reducing our streets to barbarism, and the fact that we needed at least one man in the legislature who would forthrightly stand up for us, just as the Black legislators do for their own people. Only then could we change the direction of government.

I had limited funds, but as always, I made them go far, writing and composing my own campaign literature and even working with the printers to print, fold, and mail my own letters to the voters. I hit the streets from early morning until 10 or 11 at night. I attended every political forum and was well prepared and confident at each one. I won the overwhelming support of the crowds at the candidate debates. With each new forum, the psychology of my supporters began to change as they saw my broad-based support, and realized that they were not alone in backing me. The district had thousands of homes, making it impossible for me to knock on every door, so I decided to work first the homes and businesses on the main roads. Many residents gave me permission to put up campaign yard signs on their front lawns. As soon as I had enough sign commitments for a good showing, a dozen volunteers and I worked all night for three nights, putting up signs all over the district. When people awoke to a sea of

Don Black (on left) accompanied by long-time Duke supporters

blue and white Duke signs, not just on public property, but on voter's lawns, it had a dramatic effect on the psychology of the voters. Suddenly, it became fashionable to support me. Each new sign going up had a compound effect; it enabled others who secretly supported me to become braver and begin talking to their friends about me or order a sign themselves. Soon we had more signs in people's yards than all the other candidates combined.

A large amount of visible support was critically important to my campaign. People needed the reinforcement. Howie Farrell had suggested I use just a plain blue sign with reversed out letters in white with a small-lettered DAVID, a big-lettered DUKE, and a small-lettered STATE REPRESENTATIVE. My signs stood out and their location on the main thoroughfares made them seem even more numerous. It took large sums of money and a lot of time to keep the signs up. Our enemies would often tear them down the same night that we erected them. We lost thousands of signs, but we also discovered that many were taken by supporters who wanted them for their own yards or by teenagers wanting them for their rooms. Hundreds of DUKE signs even began appearing in yards far from the district.

On Election Day of the first primary (with the top two vote getters going to a run-off), I received 33 percent of the vote. The next closest candidate was John Treen, with 19 percent. When I ran first, the last barrier of defeatism that held me back, evaporated. Many of the people in my district realized that for the first time in their voting life they could actually vote for someone who represented their own viewpoint. For the first time someone was saying outloud what people say in the privacy of their homes or among their friends. People got excited. Many middle-aged people told me that they believed their vote for me was the most important one they had ever cast.

Our main campaign photo (Dist. 81)

POLITICAL VICTORY 615

The *Times-Picayune* also finally realized that I had a real chance to win. They couldn't label my first-place victory in the primary as "other" this time. The newspaper and the power structure went into a frenzy. Their treatment of me went from the silent treatment to an all-out personal assault.

Pictures of me at age 19 picketing William Kunstler and photographs of me in Klan robes flooded every home of the district by direct mail, and were shown repeatedly in the media. Tens-of-thousands of Jewish dollars poured into the Treen campaign, and the *Times Picayune* went into a tirade against me (which still recurrently flares up to this day).

A radical Jew from New York, Mordechai Levy of the Jewish Defense Organization, came down to New Orleans to hold rallies against me. He upset the local Jewish leaders because they knew that the people of my district were not well disposed to New York Jews coming into Metairie to tell them how to vote. Certainly, the local left wing Jewish groups wanted to tell them how to vote, but not so overtly. Levy promised that the Jews would stop me and destroy my campaign by any means necessary, even if it took "bloodshed."[993] In a satellite hookup from New York, the New Orleans ABC affiliate, WVUE-TV, interviewed Levy by a live hookup on the 6 o'clock news. When Levy thought the live interview was over and the microphone was turned off, he told the reporter that the people of Metairie were "asshole-idiot White devils." By a fortuitous technical glitch, the feed was still live on the air when he said it, and the people of Metairie heard loud and clear what my Jewish antagonists really thought of them. The good people of my district were appalled. Advertisements attacking me as a Nazi, a Klansman, a racist, and an anti-Semite saturated TV, radio and newspapers. Jewish organizations making sensational charges against me filled the local newscasts. Jewish money poured into Treen's war chest, and dozens of Jewish students from Tulane knocked on the doors of my district tearfully telling the voters that electing me would be equivalent to another Holocaust. The Jews leaned on practically every elected official in Louisiana, whether Republican or Democrat, to denounce me and endorse John Treen. Jewish leaders became so desperate that they

With patriot and friend Howie Farrell.

put out the damnable lie that I was somehow anti-Christian and anti-Catholic (my district was 65 percent Catholic). To me, that was the ultimate hypocrisy — the most dedicated anti-Christian group since the time of Christ had the chutzpah to viciously smear me as anti-Christian — they had no shame!

They even put pressure on the very respected Catholic archbishop of New Orleans, Phillip Hannan, to write a statement to be read in the mass of every Catholic Church in the district. It read, "The election will determine the convictions of the voters of the district about the basic dignity of persons, recognition of human rights of every person, and the equality of races made by divine providence."

The church's reading the statement during the Lenten season, the holiest time of year for Catholics, was expected to make a great impact. But, courageously, a number of brave Catholics arose from their pews and protested the reading, saying it was wrong to bring politics into the church. Catholics who supported me became so upset that the Archbishop ultimately backtracked a bit and issued a statement reading, "At no time have I stated either verbally or in writing that I support either of the candidates." Howie Farrell, my campaign manager, and a devout Catholic, pointed out in a letter to the archbishop that not a single anti-Catholic writing or utterance by me had ever been produced by my detractors. As the election neared, my enemies knew, just as I did, that victory in this one small race would have ramifications far beyond District 81. White people would be emboldened to speak out across America, maybe even around the world.

As the stakes got bigger, the traditional enemy pulled out all stops. They had President George Bush write a letter to the district voters discussing the crucial importance of the election. (Of course, the reason that a small House race in Louisiana became crucial to the president of the United States was because it was seen as critically important by the Jewish power.) Ronald Reagan did radio commercials telling people to vote for "his friend" John Treen.[994] Under intense pressure — almost every state representative came out against me; every state senator; every U.S. congressman and U.S. senator in Louisiana and from many neighboring states; the Governor and Lieutenant governor; the heads of the Chamber of Commerce; the archbishop; many Protestant ministers; as well as coaches, sports heroes, Hollywood actors, and the president of the United States, vice-president of the United States and a number of former Presidents of the United States. I frequently said in my speeches, "The only one who didn't show up to oppose me was the Ayatollah Khomeini. And the only reason he didn't was because he was dead."

On Election Day, thousands of people came out on the streets to demonstrate for me. People spontaneously decorated their cars in support of my campaign and paraded around all day long by the hundreds, flashing their lights and blowing horns. ABC news correspondent Mike Von Fremd expressed amazement to me as he watched this show of incredible support. He said, "You know you could win an election for the U.S. Senate if it were not for your Klan background." After watching the euphoria for another few minutes he added, "No, I think you could win anyway." [995]

The turnout was 78 percent of the registered voters, which is about every voter in the district (who had not moved away, or died). It was the highest turnout in Louisiana history for a House race.

Howie Farrell and I went to the First Parish Courthouse in Metairie for the tabulation. It was back and forth through the evening, until finally I pulled ahead and won with 8,459 to Treen's 8,232.

Howie was jubilant, and I just sat there in disbelief for a moment. I went to a pay phone and called Father and then Mother. I was never more proud in my life than at the moment I gave them the news. On the way over to the election party, everyone in the car listened to the election coverage and cheered or booed the commentators' remarks. I thought about all the abuse I had taken over the years for my beliefs. In that one moment of victory, all of it was worth it. It was a breakthrough that I know could inspire many more across America, perhaps even for years to come. If I could win such a race in the highest educated district of Louisiana with my opponents showing a picture of me from my youth with a swastika, and from more recent years in Klan robes — if I could overcome what many would say was the political kiss of death, then great opportunities existed for others who simply espoused my beliefs without having my controversial past.

Of course, the fact that my past was controversial propelled the election and made me the most well-known state legislator in America. I proved that it is possible to overcome great odds when one has the power of the truth and faith in its power. The truth can be held down for a while, but it will find victory some way, somehow, if only we will relentlessly stand up for it.

A forest of satellite dishes and blinding lights greeted Howie and me at the victory party at the Lion's Club on Metairie Road. Hundreds of cheering supporters waited outside in the chilly night, and, inside, the small hall was jammed wall-to-wall with ecstatic people. I mounted the podium and gave a short speech that I could hardly finish for the roars of the crowd. Then I went out into the cold to greet the people who couldn't fit into the hall. I climbed onto the trunk of a car and spoke to them:

> **I had to come out here to be with you too, out in the cold, for this is what this campaign has been all about — the fact that the founding elements of this country, many of the men and women**

whose ancestors built America, are now out in the cold of affirmative action. Many are out in the cold by not being able to send their children to the very schools paid for by their own taxes.

We are braving the cold tonight because we have a vision for America — a vision of being able to walk on our own streets without fear, being able to use our schools, and having equal rights for all in America, not special privilege for a few. We share a vision of truly helping the poor by reforming the welfare system that has only fueled illegitimacy and increased drugs, poverty, and crime.

We demand an America based on merit. We are dedicated to our children striving toward excellence in a society based on the best of our heritage. And, my friends, we will not let our heritage be sacrificed on the altar of multiculturalism.

You great people — will not be in the cold too long. Next time we meet, we'll exchange greetings in the great warm House that Huey [Long] built, the state House of Representatives in Baton Rouge.

Representative Duke

The next few days alternated between heaven and hell. We had heard that our opponents were determined to take away illegally what they could not accomplish in the election. An attempt was made to challenge the length of time that I had lived in the district and thus invalidate my candidacy and void the election. The Clerk of Court had already certified the election, and after a court battle, a judge had validated my victory. But still my opponents decided to challenge it in the legislature itself, to try to have a "special investigation" prevent me from being sworn into office.

The law on residency was very specific. It gave those who contested a candidate's qualifications for office a specific length of time to file a complaint. Once the deadline expired, there was no opportunity for challenge. Of course, the law did not stop my opponents, who had no qualms about holding me to a different standard than every other elected official in the state. The legislature finally put the challenge to a vote, and I prevailed. When I was sworn in, the world watched it live on CNN.

Even though George Bush, Vice-president Dan Quayle, and Lee Atwater, national chairman of the Republican Party denounced me, I was treated quite well by the Republican delegation in the Louisiana House of Representatives. I was accepted as a full member of the delegation, and my name was included on the masthead of the monthly delegation newsletter. Members of the delegation supported all of my proposed legislation, just as I supported theirs. Over the next three years I amassed a perfect Republican voting record, and I was still an official member of the Republican delegation when George Bush endorsed the liberal democrat candidate J. Bennett Johnston for U.S. Senate. Later, he endorsed the flamboyantly corrupt liberal democrat Edwin Edwards, against me for the governorship. Not only did Bush betray me as a fellow Republican, but by hurting me, he also hurt the political chances of all the Republican candidates statewide.

As a freshman representative, I offered a series of groundbreaking pieces of legislation. Among a number of issues, I authored legislation that proposed:

1) The outlawing of affirmative action by forbidding any affirmative action program that discriminated against better-qualified Whites in jobs, promotions, scholarships, college admissions, or the awarding of contracts.

2) The mandatory use of birth control such as Norplant by welfare mothers as a condition of welfare assistance. They had the freedom to have all the illegitimate children they wanted, they just did not have the right to make the taxpayer pay for them.

3) The mandatory drug testing of welfare recipients and residents of public housing, and their removal from welfare rolls if they tested positive. If we could drug-test people who work for a living and pay taxes, why not require welfare recipients to stay off drugs.

I also co-authored bills for Workfare instead of welfare, stronger penalties for rape and murder, and greater protections of Louisiana's wetlands and environment. Although it was hard to get these bills through committee, my vote and speeches on many bills and amendments had an impact on a great deal of legislation. And the Republican delegation did support me on my specific bills. Also, my presence made other Republicans mimic my legislative proposals. For instance, Republican Senator Ben Bagert, who planned to run for the U.S. Senate (against me) proposed a comprehensive welfare-Workfare bill that I co-authored which the House passed — one of the first welfare reform bills passed in the nation. The governor, a conservative Democrat named Buddy Roemer, ran on a no-tax increase program, saying that if any tax increase raised its ugly head, he would chop it off. Just as George Bush's "Read my lips, no new taxes," quote on the national level, Roemer now proposed the most massive tax increase in the history of the state of Louisiana. The increased tax was one of the reasons why Roemer had supported my opponent, John Treen, who had promised to go along with his proposed tax increase. Because the tax amendment was constitutional in scope, it had to win both the majority of the voters as well as two-thirds of the legislature. Not only was the bill an anathema to me for tax reasons, it also included a minority set-aside provision (anti-White discrimination) included to garner the support of the legislature's Black Caucus. The amendment passed the legislature easily, and the polls looked as though it would easily win approval in the election. I met with Assessor Lawrence Chehardy of Jefferson Parish, and we publicly joined forces in opposing the bill

620 MY AWAKENING

throughout the state. With his power in Jefferson and my support throughout north Louisiana, we set out to defeat the tax bill.

I traveled the state day and night for the three weeks leading up to

In my legislative seat going over the tax proposal with the fiscal officer.

the vote. The proponents of the tax, mostly big business, were spending millions, while the small and medium-sized businessmen of the state and the working people had only had a tiny media budget. The core of our effort was my statewide effort of public speeches and news interviews against the proposal. As the governor and I crisscrossed the state opposing the tax issue, we knew our paths would cross again in the future politically. In Shreveport and elsewhere across the state, I drew much larger crowds than Roemer. In his hometown of Shreveport, I spoke to students and working people, drawing cheers at the university while Roemer talked to the fat cats across town. The *Shreveport Journal* headlined, "Duke outdraws Roemer." All Roemer could say was, "I don't care what David Duke and the American Nazi Party have to say about the tax election!"

On election night at the Electrical Union Hall in Metairie, with 300 supporters, a keg of beer, and no band, we waited for the results. It was quite a contrast to the proponents' champagne parties in the swankiest hotels of the state. But when the returns came in, after challenging the governor and the big money head on, we had won. The voters overwhelmingly rejected the measure. Reporters crowded around as I said that the voters had spoken clearly. "They reject any new taxes! And they reject the anti-White racism called set-asides!"

The Senate Race

In early 1990 the time seemed right to press our advantage. Senator J. Bennett Johnston was up for re-election. An 18-year incumbent, Johnston was the epitome of the career politician. When it had been politically smart to do so in the South, he opposed integration and even filed suit in opposition to it. But, as the climate changed and the media power became clear, he went along with the entire liberal program. Hypocritically, in spite of his segregationist past, he criticized me for my "racist and bigoted past." Although he had an image of a conservative Democrat, he had a voting record that Ted Kennedy would have been proud of. In fact, in some senatorial surveys, only Kennedy out of the entire U.S. Senate had a more liberal record. He had betrayed the South and the European majority countless times in everything from affirmative action to subservience to Israel. I believed he was vulnerable even though the first major poll for the Baton Rouge *Morning Advocate* showed him defeating me 60 to 23 percent.[996] I knew that I had to run now and run hard, because the powerful forces in the media and the government establishment would eventually wear down some of my public support.

State Senator Ben Bagert garnered the Republican nomination as a foregone conclusion because of the structure of the Republican convention, which was heavily weighted by the insiders. But Louisiana has an open primary system, which means that anyone of either party could run in the first primary, and if no one had a majority, the top two vote getters would then be in the runoff for the Senate. It was a good situation for me, because I was confident that I could significantly out-poll Bagert, and Johnston would then be forced into a runoff. Once any incumbent senator is in a runoff, he is vulnerable to defeat, as the challenger has a strong psychological edge.

As I traveled the state, my campaign drew tremendous support. People came out and supported me even though the newspapers had hammered at me for more than a year. The media accused me of being un-American, bigoted, unprincipled, anti-Christian, anti-Semitic, hateful, and financially corrupt. They evoked about any personal attack that could have been imagined and they did it day after day. But the people knew that I really wanted the same things they did. In promoting multiracialism, the media created a false version of the world. To make multiculturalism more fashionable, they pretend everybody is for it. In reality, European-Americans are dissatisfied about the direction of the country. But, they desperately need those who will stand up and tell them the truth. They must know they are not alone. I stood up and said in public what most people had already said in their private conversations. The media repeatedly told them that my sentiments were unpopular, held by only a few backward and bigoted people, but when people came to my rallies or saw them on TV, they realized that thousands of others shared their own views. They discovered that most of their friends and relatives believe just as *they* do — and just as *I* do.

We raised about $2.4 million in the race and were outspent about 3 to 1 by Bennett Johnston and other anti-Duke forces. Also, because we had to raise our money in small amounts in the mail and by expensively advertised rallies, it cost us far more to raise our money than the cost-free donations of the big PACs. So we could spend only a tiny fraction of what our opponent spent in vital campaigning activities such as media advertisements.

Unlike the Johnston campaign, mine had extremely few large contributors. I had to use mass mailings and public meetings. If it cost my campaign $50,000 to do a mailing in postage and preparation fees, I might get only $75,000 back in contributions, sometimes even less. So although I raised $75,000 in funds, only $25,000 was available for use for signs, advertising, and other means to solicit voters. The same principle held true on the public meetings. In order to hold one we had to rent the facility, hire a band, pay for catering and do extensive advertising. We were lucky if the event broke even. Our supporters could not afford $1,000, and most not even $100-per-plate dinners. Instead, we had free events, and if we had a dinner, it was more likely of the $20 red-beans-and-rice variety. If I spent $3,000 for an event, the event would certainly raise the total of my campaign funds, but it would often cost more to put on the event than the money I raised from it. Of course, the functions were great for inspiring and organizing our people, but they raised little money for television advertising.

As for the news coverage, every major daily in the state came out for Johnston and frequently ran extremely biased articles against my candidacy. Every article carefully repeated my Klan past like it was part of my given name, even though not a person in Louisiana was unaware of it. Almost every article introduced me as "ex-Ku Klux Klansman David Duke" and most of those I read left out any mention my official title as a state representative!

I attracted 10 times the number of contributors than the 18-year incumbent I challenged, but the contributions from my many middle-class supporters were small, while his contributions from his few moneyed-supporters were large. My small contributions came from the middle class; his large contributions came from the special interests looking to get back a good return for their investment.

Additionally, my Jewish antagonists formed several groups against me, such as the Coalition against Racism and Nazism and the Louisiana Coalition (more than 90 percent financed by Jews). Every time the media covered an event, their slander squad members were there to give extensive interviews. Whereas most candidate's speeches and campaign stops Johnston made were simply reported in the media, almost every report of my stops centered about charges made by the radicals following me around. The media was happy to oblige them with lavish publicity. Often one or two Jewish opponents who came to my rallies were given more airtime than my speech and the hundreds of supporters in attendance.

The most effective of my opponent's tactics was economic blackmail: "Even if you like Duke and agree with him," the argument went, "you can't vote for him because if you do you won't be able to feed your family." They threatened the people of my state with predictions that the Pentagon would close the state's army and air force military bases, such as the Air Force Base in Alexandria, Louisiana. Also, they asserted that our state would lose important federal projects such as the proposed super-collider project, as well as U.S. Navy shipbuilding contracts at Avondale Shipyards.

I used what little advertising money I had on producing and promoting a 30 minute campaign television program in which I asked people to call in a pledge for my campaign. The programs were a great success, people loved hearing someone talk openly about the issues they truly cared about, issues no other candidate would raise.

Despite the economic blackmail and the media's intense character assassination, it looked certain that we were heading for a runoff with Bennett Johnston. Then a bombshell exploded. With only a week left until Election Day, the official Republican-endorsed candidate, Ben Bagert, dropped out of the race and endorsed Johnston — an unprincipled act of betrayal to the people of my state and even his own voters. He withdrew so close to Election Day that his name could not be removed from the ballots, and all those who had voted for him absentee, (who would have probably become my voters) lost their votes. Bagert's withdrawal assured Johnston of victory in the first primary.

When Johnston's entourage heard the news of Bagert's withdrawal, they stopped their Winnebago caravan on the shoulder of a north Louisiana highway — broke out champagne and danced with joy.[997]

Johnston and the media predicted a landslide victory for Bennett Johnston. Lance Hill, the former pro-Viet Cong seditionist who was head of the Committee against Nazism and Racism, predicted my smashing defeat. Instead, I garnered 44 percent of the vote to Johnston's 54 percent. Only Bagert's withdrawal prevented a runoff election and thus a good chance that I would have won a U.S. Senate seat. Hill said, "The election was a referendum on hate, and hate won."[998]

In a way, Hill was right. The media and the powerful Jewish minority that so hated me and the American way of life that I stand for, had won. I had lost along with my voters — the best-educated, hardest-working people in the state. I received over 60 percent of the White vote statewide. The overwhelming majority of welfare recipients, drug addicts, criminals, and illiterates voted for my opponent, yet the media prattled how that the good people of the state prevailed in the race. On the positive side, the vote I received sent a message that reverberated across America. Hundreds of candidates from coast to coast said to themselves, "If David Duke can receive that kind of support because of his stand for the European American, — despite his controversial background — and despite media opposition and being dramatically outspent, maybe I can use his issues effectively" The next year, Senator Jesse Helms, for the first time in any of his campaigns, used opposition to anti-White affirmative action to win reelection in a tightly-contested North Carolina race.

After the race, many people began to talk to me about the race for governor that was coming up the following year. The enemies of our heritage now knew I was stronger than ever and that I posed the most serious political threat to them in decades. They were determined to use every resource at their disposal to end that threat.

Trials and Tribulations

As soon as I was elected to the state House of Representatives, I read Jewish publications referring to me as a "budding Hitler" and as "the most dangerous threat to Jewish interests in the world." I began to feel the harsh effects of Jewish power more than ever. This volume is not a refutation of the many allegations of my enemies against me. To properly refute all the false smears would take an entire volume by itself. This book is about what I believe and how I came to believe it. But, at the same time, it is vital for the reader to understand how our traditional enemy uses character assassination against all effective leaders for our cause.

Soon after my election to the House, I honored a previous speaking engagement for the Populist Party in Chicago. In the reception area after the speech, a man I did not know and had never met before, innocently approached me, greeted me, and shook my hand. Suddenly a half-dozen photographer's flashbulbs popped off, and I was informed that the man was the flamboyant head of the Nazi Party in Chicago. It was just what the media wanted, and they reprinted the photo all over the nation and, of course, blanketed the state of Louisiana with it. It is almost impossible to defend oneself against that kind of smear. "See there," the argument went, "Duke is a Nazi, here he is meeting and greeting the head of the American Nazi Party!" After the incident, one veteran legislator told me that when I was first elected I could have been elected to any office in Louisiana, but after that, I might not.

My opponents began to run repeated exposés on me. Jewish groups even had a Holocaust exhibit brought into the lobby of the state capitol and put not far from my desk — to combat what they alleged was the growing racial hatred in the state since my election. They sent elderly Jewish women, with news cameramen in tow, to cry in anger for my insensitivity to the Holocaust. I had a bookstore in Metairie for years, and my enemies visited the NAAWP headquarters and obtained some old books exposing Jewish supremacism from one of my volunteers, and then announced that I was selling anti-Semitic books from my legislative office. They tried to imply that I had inappropriately used my state-financed office to sell books, and anti-Semitic books at that. In fact, Louisiana gives only a small stipend for an office, and expects almost every legislator's office to be located in his normal business offices or connected to them.

My opponents showed up at every function to dog me and counter every word that I said to the press. *The Times-Picayune* employed a sleazy journalistic character assassin, Tyler Bridges, who would ingratiate himself with my supporters and then selectively use whatever they had to say to make my supporters and me look bad. His nearly full-time assignment was to dig up any dirt he could on my associates or me. He later wrote a book after interviewing hundreds of people, but interestingly enough, although I received over 60 percent of the White vote, he somehow could not find anyone of stature that had much good to say about me. His later marriage to his Black girlfriend might suggest the temper of his bias against me.

Practically every story the *Times-Picayune* paper ran about me — and there were many dozens during those years — intentionally put some sort of slant on the article to make me look stupid, inept, corrupt, sinister, or deceitful. During one campaign they ran an utterly false, hearsay story that I had used cocaine once in Colorado. Another time, again with not a shred of corroborating evidence,

Bridges repeated a tabloid press allegation from a prostitute who claimed that I had a liaison with her years before. Not surprisingly, he failed to mention in his book that she had also alleged that the CIA had planted transmitters in her head and that space aliens had abducted her.

Another story implied that I had never held a job, knowing full well how I have worked hard all my life. They implied that I was a womanizer, although at another time they wrote about an ad placed for my organization in a homosexual publication (which my group did not place or authorize) — implying that I could be homosexual. In my television broadcast I pointed out jokingly that if I am both a homosexual and a womanizer that "I must be very busy!" They implied I was draft dodger, when they knew how much I wanted a military career in the U.S. Army and was the "Outstanding ROTC cadet at LSU." Unlike Bill Clinton who went to Britain and supported America's Communist enemies, I had supported the American war effort as a teacher in Laos during the conflict.

They assembled every quotation, accurate or not, from my past that made me look hateful or unintelligent and kept repeating them to the public. The fact that I repaired my nose that had been severely broken on several occasions, became a "face lift" and "plastic surgery" to "make me look more Aryan." They suggested I was getting rich from my election campaigns, but knew full well that I came out of every election in personal debt.

With Kristin and Erika after winning election for state representative.

Three days before the Governors election day, on November 13, 1991 the *Times-Picayune*, a thoroughly anti-Christian, Jewish-owned newspaper, ran a story headlined across the top of the front page: "Religious leaders doubt Duke's Christianity" written by Mr. Schleifstein.[999] The charges were vicious and never-ending. Most often, the public would never even hear my answers to the incessant charges. *The Times-Picayune* published only four of my letters in response to many dozens of unprincipled attacks against me. One leftist reporter, Jason Berry, went so low in a column as to allege that I had once tried "to set my mother on fire." It was a story based on a tale told by a Black housekeeper (long after Pinky)who had worked for our family a short while until Mother fired her for stealing (a tale told only after I became famous).

No charge, no allegation, no smear was too low for my opponents. What frustrated me was that the media could say the most terrible things about me to thousands of people — who were unlikely to ever hear my side of the story. One day, as an experiment, I had a secretary blot out my name in a long smear article against me, and I pretended that I was an uninformed reader. By the time I finished the piece, I thought to myself, *This guy is a real jerk!* And the story was about me. The experience made me much more forgiving of people who believed only the worst about me.

Sometimes, people would ask me, "If the stories are not true, why don't you sue?" Those people are completely unaware how the libel laws in America allow the press to say practically anything they want about a public figure, correct or not, with little recourse. Plus, it is practically impossible for a middle-income, public figure to successfully sue the major media entities with their million-dollar legal staffs. A person alleged to be a "White racist" would have little luck anyway, given the minority makeup of so many of our courts.

Even though I had to learn to accept smears as simply facts of life, they still sometimes took their toll. Some personal attacks, of course, also have a bit of truth in them. There have certainly been times when I have spoken intemperately, or made a mistake in judgment. There have certainly been times when I have failed someone whom I loved.

But, when one dares to challenge those that Christ called the "fathers of the lie," every human failing whether real or imagined will be magnified a hundredfold. Over the years, I have come to expect such attacks, and borne them with the knowledge that I must endure them — far more because of my virtues, than because of my faults. The intensity of the personal attacks that the alien, media masters levy on an Aryan activist directly corresponds with how much they fear his effectiveness.

In addition to yellow journalism, the establishment has many other means to harass its opponents than simply the press. When I was elected to the House of Representatives, Dan Quayle announced that "We have ways of taking care of David Duke." Within months of my election, I received notice of my first extensive IRS audit. My attorney inquired as to the source of the request for an audit, and they admitted that it came from outside the agency itself.

While I was in office, fighting the governor's tax amendment and getting ready to run for the U.S. Senate, I suddenly faced an exhaustive, every-scrap-of-documentation audit. Because I knew the government was anxious to discredit and perhaps even jail me if it could, I had to engage expensive and competent legal council and accountants, which posed a terrible financial burden. After years of audits and procedures, the auditors found no criminal wrongdoing, but by disallowing a small deduction from six years earlier, with penalty and interest, they came up with a tax bill of over $40,000. At the time, even with my legislative salary, I made far less than that a year. By the time I had completed the governor's race, various government agencies had me enmeshed in seven separate audits. Four years of personal tax-return audits, one by the Federal Elections Commission for the Senate Campaign, one by the state for the governor's race, and one for my home parish for the governor's race.

No criminal violations were found — in any of the audits. The federal government found only 15 minor errors out of almost 50,000 individual contributions in my campaign for the U.S. Senate. The 15 donors had contributed slightly more than allowed. For instance some had simply failed to note that the contribution was from both husband and wife which would have made the amount acceptable. For these errors, made by our staff while I was out campaigning, they personally fined me $20,000. More importantly, they tied up hundreds of hours of my time and practically bankrupted me in the process. I completed dealing with my personal audits in 1997. Despite these efforts directed against me, I just plowed on ahead during my campaigns, but the public never knew of the difficulties I faced behind the scenes. As is true in my whole political life, the unfair tactics against me only stiffened my resolve. My personality is much like that of a child who becomes more defiant the more you strike him.

I am aware that my authorship of this book will cause an extreme reaction around the world by the mortal enemies of our people. If not for my many good friends and supporters, I would find it hard to face the difficulties that I know are ahead.

The Governor's Race

The next year's race for governor found my campaign more organized than we had been for U.S. Senate. We now had a statewide organization in place. I had beaten the incumbent governor in the tax-amendment referendum, and had come close to beating an 18-year incumbent U.S. Senator.

The field was crowded with six, full-time, hard-working and well-financed candidates. Unlike the Senate campaign, there were a number of televised debates that aired statewide. In spite of the character assassination I continued to endure from the press, my support had never been stronger. When the election night voting returns came in for the first primary, former governor Edwards led slightly, with 34 percent of the vote. I was only 1 percent behind him at 33, and Governor Roemer trailed badly behind me at only 27 percent. Governor Roemer had switched to the Republican Party a few months before, trying to head off my candidacy. But I defeated the sitting governor as well as the official Republican Party nominee, Congressman Clyde Holloway, and became the Republican candidate in the runoff against the archenemy of the party in Louisiana: the very liberal and corrupt Democrat, Edwin Edwards.

The same *Times-Picayune* that repeatedly railed against Edwards' corruption in his last term as governor suddenly did an about-face, and told the people of Louisiana that he had changed and now simply wanted to be elected so he could redeem his sullied reputation. Corruption in the Governor's chair meant little to the *Times-Picayune* compared to the ethnic interests of its owners. When it became obvious that most people did not believe in Edwards' miraculous change, Edwards supporters printed thousands of bumper stickers reading simply, "Vote for the Crook, it's Important."

My opponents mobilized to defeat me, as they never have in any other American election. The Jewish-financed groups spent millions of dollars from Zionist fat cats — while my campaign had limited donations. As long as they spent ostensibly against a candidate rather than for one, they were technically not beholden to the same campaign laws that I was. Edwards raised many millions of dollars and even spent $1,500,000 on Election Day alone in a vote-buying program called "voter hauling." In other strange procedures, the Registrar of Voters in some parishes actually went into the jails to register prisoners to vote and in the final days even allowed them to vote in the election absentee.

The Times-Picayune ran front-page editorials against me, many days running, called: "The Choice of Our Lives." Supposed news articles read like editorials against me in all the major papers of the state. The head of the Louisiana National Guard went on television commercials *in uniform* to denounce me and urge people to vote against me, as well as sending a political letter opposing me to all the members of the Louisiana National Guard. Anti-David Duke TV and radio commercials were on at a ratio of at least 50 to 1 against me. Media advertising guru Raymond Strother said at the time, "It has to be the largest single advertising buy ever in American politics against one man."[1000] But even after all that deluge of the best propaganda money could buy — and some that money could not buy — the election was still neck and neck.

After the senate campaign, the Jewish political experts finally figured out the only way they could beat me: economic blackmail. Jew-

630 MY AWAKENING

ish officers of national conventions such as that of the American Medical Association wrote letters to public officials saying they would cancel their Louisiana conventions — at the cost of millions in Louisiana tourist and tax revenue — if I were elected. The major newspapers did not simply report the blackmail tactics; they printed photocopies of the letters on their front pages in colorful, graphic advertisements. Workers at plants got notices with their paychecks that if I were elected, the company would move from Louisiana and they would lose their jobs. Coaches of major sports team, including LSU's popular basketball coach, Dale Brown, warned that my election would damage their recruitment programs and damage all the university sports' programs. It was said that a scheduled Super Bowl would not come to New Orleans.

After the all-out assault on my character didn't work well enough, the Jews then made direct threats against the citizens of the state effectively telling them that if Louisiana voted for me, they would ruin Louisiana and everyone in it. No major papers or media outlets in Louisiana even dared to criticize this orchestrated use of naked coercion and intimidation to control the outcome of an election.

Seeking to find out how effective the blackmail campaign was going, I talked to friends at the United Cab Company, which at that time had only White drivers and who had lost two drivers who were murdered by Black criminals in recent years. An earlier survey showed that 90 percent voted for me in the U.S. Senate race and in the first primary. After the blackmail campaign had reached a crescendo, we found that now only 60 percent planned on voting for me. A few Cab drivers told me that they had no choice but to vote for Edwards or lose their livelihood. Understanding that they were under that kind of pressure, I felt thankful and gratified that 60 percent voted for me in spite of the fact that they believed it would lead to financial hardship for their families.

When the returns came in, even with the largest Black turnout in the state's history at more than 30 percent of the total votes, I still received almost 40 percent of the vote against Edwards. That meant that

I had received about 60 percent of the White vote. In spite of the personal smears; having only a tiny fraction of the campaign advertisements; having all the newspapers and media against me — and even with the threat of economic ruin against them, White people voted for me in a landslide. Without the economic blackmail, I am confident that I would have easily won the additional 15 percent of the White vote I needed to win.

I stayed with my supporters late into the campaign night. The hotel where we had an election-night party had given me the presidential suite. At about midnight I slipped into a steaming-hot tub, too tired to feel much of anything after campaigning for 17 hours or better every day for almost nine months. I shook at least 75,000 hands, gave a thousand talks, wrote almost all the campaign literature, arranged for the advertising and the mailings. I was so exhausted, I fell asleep in the bubbling water and when I awoke, the water was cold. I headed for the starched sheets and their cool escape from defeat.

The next day, my friend Howie Farrell pointed out to me how ironic it is that Whites, who are 70 percent of the state did not get their overwhelming choice as governor of Louisiana, while Blacks at only 30% got theirs. The Jewish media gloated that "Black voters had saved White voters from themselves." Because the governor's race and legislative races are held at the same time, I could not run for reelection and governor at the same time. I served out my term in the legislature until the newly elected representatives took their seats in January.

Not holding any current seat, I was free to take the message that I had successfully spread in Louisiana to the rest of the nation. My last two races showed that I had good support among the White voters, not only in Louisiana, but also across America. Even though I was a long shot for the nomination, I decided to enter some of the Republican presidential primaries. Every public appearance gave me an opportunity to awaken more European Americans.

I announced my candidacy at the National Press Club in Washington, D.C., but decided to pass up the New Hampshire Primary and concentrate on some of the Southern primaries. One side effect of my entry into the race was to give Pat Buchanan some much-needed breathing room. As much as the Jewish-dominated media distrusted Buchanan — in comparison to me, he seemed downright moderate. Fearing a nationwide repeat of what I accomplished in Louisiana, they saved most of their venom for me, and laid off him for awhile. Then, when Buchanan scored well against George Bush in New Hampshire, it propelled his candidacy past mine. I cannot overemphasize that voters are equally concerned with a candidate's issues *and* his prospect of winning. Voters will more often than not vote for their second choice if they think that their first choice has little chance.

For most people politics is the art of the possible, not a pure expression of their preferences.

I received respectable vote totals in a number of states, more votes, even with Patrick Buchanan in the race, than some candidates who were sitting senators and congressmen. But Buchanan's New Hampshire showing had shifted too much of my vote in subsequent primaries to him. I bowed out early, leaving the right wing of the party completely open to him, and, despite his unkind remarks about me, I helped him as much as I could. After Buchanan negated my threat to the establishment, the Jewish press then descended on him with the fury they had previously focused on me. In the 1996 primaries, a number of my supporters helped the Buchanan candidacy. In South Carolina, my South Carolina campaign coordinator in 1992, Dr. William Carter, became an officer in Buchanan's campaign. The media lambasted Buchanan for daring to have former Duke supporters in his campaign. In an ill-advised move, Buchanan kicked out every Duke supporter the press could find in his camp. The action weakened him among the ranks of many of his best supporters. He should have just responded to the press that to be elected President of the United States, you shouldn't be in the habit of telling people not to vote for you.

In spite of Buchanan's disparagement of me, I still helped him in the Louisiana Republican Caucuses, and my dedicated supporters around the state were the major reason he won the Louisiana Republican primary. Although Buchanan leaves much to be desired, he was certainly the best candidate with a chance to win in 1996. I have always believed that we must put aside our own personal considerations and do what is best for our race and nation. Even though, in an attempt to deflect press criticism, he said some nasty things about me, I still supported him.

In the Louisiana Senate race of 1997, I entered a crowded field of six major Republican candidates and two major Democrats and came in second among the Republicans, behind Representative Woody Jenkins, who, much like Buchanan, got the jump on me early. The polls indicated that he had the best chance to avoid an all-Democratic runoff. I still ran strongly, with 12 percent of the vote in the crowded field even though I was outspent dramatically by all of the other major candidates.

All my electoral successes came from a team effort of capable individuals such as my brilliant, right-hand man for many years, Glenn R. Montecino, and many others who gave unselfishly of their time in countless hours of work: The Farrell family, Kenny Knight, Dr. Shubert, Laura Otillio, the Jeffuses, the Donahues, Raymond Scalco, Mark Ellis, the Touchstones, Dan Murphy, and many other wonderful supporters. I could never hope to name all those who deserve mention.

POLITICAL VICTORY 633

I was elected to the Political Executive Committee of the St. Tammany Parish Republican Party in 1996, then eight months later in a unanimous vote, the committee elected me as its chairman. During my tenure as head of the Republican Party in St. Tammany Parish, it became the first Louisiana parish to have more registered Republicans than Democrats and it has the largest number of Republicans of any parish in the state. I serve as PEC Chairman until the year 2000. As the only elected official in entire United States who dares to tell the truth of race and Jewish supremacism, I continue to travel across America and around the world — going wherever there are European peoples to speak about the issues of vital importance to the survival and advancement of our heritage. The establishment's battle to suppress the truth goes on, but I find individual European Americans are more receptive than ever before to our message of heritage, rights, and renewal.

At Radio-Free South Africa

I traveled to South Africa and participated in broadcasts on "Radio Free South Africa," encouraging the Europeans to stand fast in the defense of the nation they built. In Russia, I met with many nationalist leaders including Aleksandr Solzhenitsyn and Vladimir Zhironovsky.

With Vladimir Zhironovsky at his party's headquarters at the Duma

In Red Square on a cold day.

I met with the Russian political leader in the Party's offices in the Russian Parliament.

One of the most unsettling aspects of contemporary times is an increasing tendency for both government and media to endorse and use methods of political suppression. On May 5, 1997, I had a speech scheduled in Tampa, Florida. Six meeting halls, including some public venues, were canceled after intimidation and threats of violence. The location where I finally spoke had to be kept secret until the very last possible moment. In my talk, I noted that if I were a Black elected official denied use of a public facility, there would have been a FBI civil-rights investigation. The government would have used every resource at its disposal to prosecute and imprison those who used threats of violence to deny my civil-rights. The supposed great defenders of the rights of freedom of speech: the press — did not defend my right to free speech. In fact, the largest and most prestigious paper in the area, the *Tampa Tribune*, actually applauded the fact that my supporters and I were denied our civil rights. An editorial stated: "It is a sign of progress that six meeting halls turned down Duke...When they tried to rent space for his speech."[1001]

The federal government never prosecutes Marxists who have repeatedly attempted to deny my civil rights through violence and intimidation. In 1996, when I participated in the most-covered public debate during the anti-affirmative — proposition 209 election, the Communists rioted in an attempt to keep me from appearing. No one was charged with conspiracy to deny my civil-rights. In Cleveland, in 1997, my supporters rented the Lithuanian Hall for me to give a speech. Marxists descended on the facility, assaulted anyone daring to enter the hall, and then attacked the police for simply keeping the door clear. They threw chunks of concrete at us and broke in the large glass door to the facility. The city police in the melee arrested a number of Communists.

The next day the local newspaper headline read: "Duke Sparks Riot." Anyone of my political persuasion who would have gone to a Black Civil Rights meeting and physically assaulted the participants and violently damaged the facility, would

POLITICAL VICTORY 635

have been charged with federal "conspiracy to deny civil rights." Of course, none of the Communists faced even a federal investigation. Efforts to restrict freedom of speech and thought also continue in the increasing passage of so-called hate laws where punishment is meted out according to the supposed thoughts in the mind of the offender. Reminiscent of what George Orwell's classic book *1984*,[1002] referred to as thought crimes have become a reality at the end of this century in America and in practically every European nation. The idea that one should be punished more severely because one does not like someone because of sexual orientation, or race, as opposed to the limitless other motives for a crime, is ludicrous. When government decrees that one thought in some one's mind at the time of a crime is more punishable than another, that is the first step toward outlawing those thoughts and expressions of them altogether. In Canada, Australia, England, France, Germany and most Western nations, such repression has already happened. In France a citizen can go to jail for telling a friend in your living room that the convictions at the Nuremberg Trials were unjust. Publishing a newsletter in England that dares to blame increased crime on Third World immigration can land one in prison. In Switzerland or Germany, simply telling the truth that the gas chambers shown tourists at Auschwitz are fakes, is punishable by imprisonment. I shall repeat this once more so no one can mistake what is happening.

Men are in jail at this moment in a number of so-called free European nations for simply questioning the Jewish interpretation of history. On the very morning that I write these lines, the *Times-Picayune* has an article reporting that states that a Swiss author and his publisher were sentenced to over a year in prison for simply publishing a book which alleged that the gas chambers shown to tourists at Auschwitz are fakes built after the war. (supported by videotaped comments by the chief curator of the camp, historian Dr. Francizek Piper).[1003] Whether or not one believes the author and his publisher are correct in their conclusions, it must be admitted that a truly free society does not imprison a man for stating an opinion about a his-

---

Denying Holocaust nets prison terms

BADEN, Switzerland — A Swiss author who wrote books denying the existence of Nazi gas chambers and a publisher who printed them were sentenced to prison terms Tuesday by a Swiss court. Writer Juergen Graf and his publisher, Gerhard Foerster, a former officer in Hitler's army, were convicted of breaking Switzerland's law against racial discrimination. Graf, 47, was sentenced to 15 months and Foerster, 78, received one year. Graf stood by his views, claiming the Holocaust is an exaggeration and the Nazis never used gas chambers to kill Jews. "I'm very happy with everything I have achieved," said Graf, who has been writing revisionist books since 1993.

torical event. Imprisoning these two men for expressing an unpopular opinion goes against the very basis of the United Nations Covenant of Human Rights, the Helsinki Accords, and every principle of freedom of speech and press that the media and the civilized nations of the world supposedly uphold. Is not one of the proofs the media uses to prove the evil of Nazism is that they burned books? If such is proof of evil and tyranny then what exactly is it when nations not only outlaw politically incorrect books, but also imprison their writers and even their publishers?

An example of how crazy it has become in Western nations can be seen in another recent act by Swiss authorities. Jews around the world have organized a vicious campaign against the Swiss in order to extort billions. Unless the Swiss banks capitulate, the Jews have threatened to use their influence to close down Swiss banking and business affairs in nations all over the world, including the United States. A patriotic Swiss gentleman suggested that if the Jews boycott Switzerland, that in self-defense the Swiss should boycott the Jewish commercial concerns and not vacation in Israel. He was convicted of fomenting racial hatred for advocating the same thing that the Jews are currently doing against the Swiss on a world scale!

It's a neat trick — extorting a billion dollars from a nation and getting a law passed requiring that anyone who complains about it is thrown into prison.

In America, "hate crimes laws" are the first steps toward similar draconian methods to prevent the truth from reaching the American people. Simon Wiesenthal, the ADL and others have begun a campaign to keep web sites off the Internet that simply expose Jewish supremacism, Israeli suppression of Palestinians, or the scientific facts of racial differences. They have already succeeded in outlawing such sites in Germany, France, Switzerland and a number of other European nations. They have been behind software filters that block sites in schools, libraries and homes that simply defend European-American rights and heritage. In some public libraries, if someone types in my Web site address: www.duke.org — the inquiry is routed to a notice that my site is a "hate site" and then the visitor is routed to an ADL homepage attacking me and others who dare to expose Jewish supremacism.

I can completely understand the Jewish efforts to suppress freedom of speech, for suppression is the only way to prevent exposure of lies. The revolution that will flow from the truth is the only thing that can upset messianic dreams of dominion and the genocidal, final solution planned for our people. The truth, though, shall prevail only if we dare to speak it, defend it and fight for it with intelligence and courage.

Chapter 39:
An Aryan Vision

If by some calamity almost all the Golden Labrador Retrievers were killed leaving only a small number of that admirable breed in the world, it would certainly be viewed as tragic if they were not preserved. It seems very strange that some people care more about preserving a unique breed of dog than about continuing our unique and beautiful breed of humanity.

Imagine if the government began a program to kill off the smartest, most accomplished, educated, and talented people. What if it confiscated the money of the intelligent, hardworking, responsible and productive people — reducing their birthrates, and used it to financially encourage high birthrates among the least intelligent, least successful, and most criminally active people in the nation?

Those are precisely the policies of every government of the West. Our government does not line up the most intelligent and productive against a wall and shoot them, but every Western society exterminates their precious genes over time by promoting the factors that lower their birthrates. In every civilized society, the least capable, least responsible, and least intelligent, as well as the alien flood of nonwhite immigrants, invariably have the greatest numbers of children. Most Western governments, through welfare programs, actually give economic incentives to the underclass to create more like themselves.

In the Race History chapter I discussed the paradox of civilization. With the passage of time civilization rises, building upon its great art and architecture, experience and learning, technological and cultural achievements and then — invariably — it declines, often far more rapidly than it rose. The brilliant philosopher of history, Oswald Spengler, in his magisterial work of history, *Decline of the West*,[1004] surveyed ancient civilizations and offered the thesis that they were organic in nature. He suggested that each had remarkably similar stages that could be contrasted with a human's life having a period of gestation, birth, growth, decay, and death. He viewed these passages of civilization as inevitable life stages similar to the life cycle of a person. His pessimistic view of the West's decline seemed to come true in his realized predictions of Germany's devastation in Second World War and the accelerating decline of Western Civilization as the century ran its course.

Spengler was certainly right about civilization seeming to have an organic life of its own. But when one understands race, it becomes apparent that civilization is just an external manifestation of something much deeper. The real essence of civilization, underneath the shiny exterior of its art and architecture, science and technology — is the genetic quality of its people. When early civilizations arose out of nothing, they were outward manifestations of the genetics of an evolutionarily advanced people. Biologists call the resulting outward appearance or expression of the interaction of the genotype with the environment the *phenotype*.[1005] Our Caucasian ancestors created a written language in a world of no writing. Where there was no wheel, he invented one. Where there were no buildings, save of sticks and mud, he constructed great edifices that required the skills of higher mathematics and engineering. He created from nothing what the African has never even successfully copied. If poor environments keep people down, then our forefathers would have never arisen from the mud at the edge of the ice fields of ancient Europe.

In truth, an incredibly harsh environment over many thousands of years is precisely what made our people what we are. Before civilization, Nature pitilessly killed those individuals and groups who did not have the genetic fitness to survive. Over thousands of generations Nature gradually elevated Western man until he finally broke the bounds of his environment and literally created a new one called civilization. Its creation brought about both his greatness as expressed in its organization, form, and beauty, but also the seeds of his downfall, for civilization begins a process that chips away at the best genes.

The bounty created by civilization made survival far less dependent on intelligence, foresight, self-discipline and courage. The rabble could live on the garbage scraps of the great, or submit to another's generosity for their daily bread. The group altruism that arose in the ice ages, which enabled our people to help each other survive through the centuries of brutal ice and snow, found expression once civilization arrived, through indiscriminate welfare and an understandable pity for the unfortunate.

While the genetic elite found their greatest satisfaction in achievement and the luxuries of wealth and power, the lowly found it almost exclusively in sex. And while the brave and fittest went off to war to bleed, the cowardly and incompetent stayed home to breed. Finally, when civilized nations conquered lesser peoples, they brought their captives home as slaves with whom they gradually interbred. Ultimately, their slave's strands of DNA became entwined with that of their masters. All these factors destroyed the genetic vitality of the civilization.

Spengler failed to see that it is not civilization that is the living organism, but the genotype beneath it. Great genes give it birth, then as cultural and scientific achievements accumulate, and dysgenic policies take their toll, the genetic quality of the people degenerates until the shell of civilization collapses on the rotted core.

Every civilization has failed, but Nature has not. A chain of life arose on this planet from the lowest amino acids to the highest forms of consciousness and evolution. If we just continue the genetic progress of our kind, civilization can continue to evolve to higher forms, the same way that evolution has succeeded in progressing life from the its simplest form to the most advanced creations of God.

It is now time for a new civilization, and a new creed, one that recognizes the Laws of the Natural Order. We do not have to follow the letter of the Natural Law as expressed in Nature's capriciousness, only its spirit. We have the capacity to act on her laws with love and compassion, rather than with the brutality and indifference of the law of tooth and claw.

What I came to realize was that maintaining the genetic strength of our civilization would prevent the decline that seemed inevitable from history. Further, I saw that with our technology and culture paired with genetic advancement, new heights could be scaled that are scarcely conceivable today.

For almost his entire history, man has concentrated his genius primarily on his education, his tools, his machines and his ideas, rather than on improving his own inner quality. Through the practice of medicine our kind attempts to cure the vagaries of illness, and many wise men have formulated prescriptions for the healthy life. But these efforts are akin to a mechanic keeping an engine running on an old Model T, and repairing an occasional breakdown rather than designing an altogether more advanced engine.

Modern efforts at education and training are similar to trying to make the Model T automobile engine capable of going 200 miles per hour just by feeding it a better grade of motor oil and higher octane gasoline. It could be said that civilization actually wears down the engine, and as parts become worn out they are replaced by less sturdy metal until finally the engine fails to run at all and the society falls to barbarism. Now, science is beginning to learn how to make changes

640 My Awakening

in the genetic structure to cure the biologic breakdowns of disease and impairment.

Someday, we shall harness the power of the genes not simply to repair the failures of an old engine, but to create an infinitely more powerful engine that will cure the endemic social ills that plague us, and speed us to higher levels of beauty and accomplishment.

Count Arthur de Gobineau began to understand these concepts midway through the 19th century. Coinciding with Gobineau's study of the immediate role of the effect of races on civilizations, Charles Darwin, in his study of the changing and evolving character of all life forms, demonstrated that principles of heredity combined with what he called, *Natural Selection*, had developed the exceptional abilities of mankind itself. His masterpiece, *The Origin of Species* has a subtitle that expresses his whole idea in a nutshell: *The Preservation of Favoured Races in the Struggle for Life.*

As observant and perceptive minds began to understand the role of heredity in intelligence and other character traits, a whole new science came about, Eugenics.

Sir Francis Galton, the pioneer researcher of human heredity coined the term eugenics from the Greek *eugênes* meaning well-born. He describes eugenics as "that science that deals with all influences that improve the inborn qualities of a race; also with those that develop them to utmost advantage."[1006] From the very beginning, Eugenicists had the highest humanitarian motives. Galton wrote the following in his *Memories of My Life*:

Man is gifted with pity and other kindly feelings; he has also the power of preventing many kinds of suffering. I conceive it to fall well within his province to replace Natural Selection by other processes that are more merciful and not less effective.[1007]

The idea began to grow that through the improvement of mankind itself, tremendous suffering could be lessened and the opportunities of mankind vastly improved. Darwin himself, after reading Galton's masterpiece wrote him and told him that he completely supported his point of view.[1008]

By the early years of the 20th century, the eugenic idea and ideal had the endorsement of many of the leading lights of Western Civilization — scientists such as Julian Huxley and Sir Arthur Keith, playwrights and writers such as George Bernard Shaw, H.G. Wells and Charles Dickens. It also had the endorsement of other outstanding personalities such as J. Maynard Keynes, the young Winston Churchill, Arthur James Balfour (British Prime Minister), and the President of the United States, Teddy Roosevelt.

ARYAN VISION 641

In his classic play, *Man and Superman*, George Bernard Shaw noted that "being cowards, we defeat Natural Selection under cover of philanthropy."[1009]

Eugenic concern is good for every race and every nation. Dysgenic (or genetic degeneration) trends should be just as important a concern for Black people as they are for White people. For instance, Black rural farmwomen near the bottom of the socioeconomic ladder have an incredibly high average birthrate of 5.4, while Black women college graduates have an average rate of 1.9, less than needed to maintain their numbers.[1010] Such dysgenic trends mean that Black problems will only intensify in years ahead.

Two schools of eugenic thought arose: positive eugenics and negative eugenics. What is called positive eugenics is simply encouraging the best to procreate. Teddy Roosevelt was its most well-known advocate. It could be characterized by generous tax breaks for children as taxpayers are generally more competent than those who do not pay taxes. It means letting those of achievement know that no matter how impressive their work, nothing exceeds the importance of passing down their inherent abilities and talents to the next generation. It means when a spouse is infertile and the couple opts for artificial insemination or *in vitro* fertilization, that they should select from the most genetically gifted of donors. Positive eugenics can mean finding a way to let a career woman have children without penalizing her, professionally or economically.

Negative eugenics means no longer financing welfare illegitimacy, and encouraging recipients' responsibility not to bring unwanted children into the world. It means encouraging those with serious genetic defects to adopt or utilize artificial or *in vitro* fertilization. It means protecting our borders from Third Worlders and stopping foreign aid to the Third World that says in effect — the more you breed, the more we feed. In doing these things we are greatly lessening future human suffering, we are helping to preserve the Earth's ecosystem — as well as helping those nations create higher standards for their own people.

One of my interviewers, Evelyn Rich, once told me an amusing story about her mother in Scotland. It seems that whenever her mom gets an appeal for a donation to feed the starving of some Third World country, she simply places a condom in the return envelope and mails it back; enough said.

When I served as a representative, I consistently voted for programs to help the gifted, and at the same time I supported programs to assist the disabled and the mentally and physically impaired. I supported and sponsored with my fellow legislators, events such as the Special Olympics. As I watched the extraordinary children compete in the many events of the Special Olympics in New Orleans, I felt a joy for those children who were accomplishing what were, for them, Herculean feats. However, the joy became mixed with the sorrow of seeing their pain to attain physical standards that do not even approach what we all take for granted.

I pinned a blue winner's ribbon on a little 12 year old girl named Lola who sprinted 40 yards on her wobbly, deformed legs. When she crossed the finish line I could see her crying both from the physical pain and from the joy of her accomplishment. She hugged and kissed me and her tears moistened my cheeks.

After witnessing a number of Special Olympics, I understood how the adoption of good eugenic policies not only made good sense, but was the only way mankind could someday see the day when no child is born congenitally blind, or deaf, or deformed, or suffering in searing pain.

Both the positive and negative variety of eugenics are keys to not only advancing the health, intellectual capacities and desirable characteristics of mankind; they are truly the way to achieve the lessening of human pain and suffering. Not only will our future generations be born with fewer hereditary defects and diseases, but we can also have more productive and creative people from whom everyone benefits. That fewer children will have to endure mental retardation is a truly humanitarian cause. And when fewer are born that way, more monies and resources are available for better care of those who do bear infirmities.

The standards of assistance to the mentally retarded and the physically impaired should be far greater than they are now, but it must be remembered, that helping the impaired only helps *them*, while helping those of exceptionally high ability helps *everyone*, including the impaired. Children of genius are far more likely to one day devise effective technologies, treatments and medicines, as they are to produce societal wealth that enables the less fortunate to receive the costly care they need. Society should make at least as much effort to develop the innate talents of the gifted as it does to maintain the impaired. In doing so, a better life can be created for all.

After one of the events at a Special Olympics, a woman who obviously knew little about my record supporting special children, rushed up to me and hatefully asked, "Why are you here at the Special Olympics? With your views you have no right to be here." She had heard the vicious and untrue allegation that I endorsed the killing of the mentally and physically handicapped.

I calmly pointed out that it was the 5th function for special kids that other legislators and I had helped sponsor. "But you want to eliminate them!" she protested.

"Not them," I answered, "I want to eliminate *the genes* that give them their debilitation and their pain. I want to see to it that someday no other child ever has to endure what they do." She looked puzzled after my comment and I offered to send her my complete position on the issue. We exchanged cards, and she melted into the crowd.

A few days later, a letter waited for me at my legislative desk accompanied by a single, beautiful red rose. In her note, the lady who had verbally accosted me, apologized and wrote: " I hated you before I really knew what you stood for, and I am ashamed of that. I read your paper and thank you for your intelligent and compassionate proposals for both making our impaired loved ones have better lives, and greatly reducing the suffering of future generations."

I am determined that the day will come when almost no child is born in pain and disfigurement; when every child has a chance for the beauty and promise that life has to offer, as full human beings with all the precious capabilities that human beings are meant to have — to walk, and run, and see and hear, and taste and smell and feel, and think and love, and gaze upon the heavens with hope and wonder.

And the other side of that vision is a humanity that goes beyond what we are today to a higher level of evolution tomorrow. My vision is to see the foundations of a society in which the quality and abilities of people grow with each generation. We have it within our grasp to foster Human beings with healthier, longer lives, with more intelligence, more powers of memory and more noble characters.

I can envision a future society with few criminals and thus only little need for restrictive laws or police or jails, and therefore a society with far more freedom. I can picture a future nation where a mother can raise her small children at home, if she so chooses, with no financial worry — where the finest education is based solely on the student's abilities and not his parent's bank account — where the best student and the impaired child get precisely the education forms they need to nurture their highest abilities. I can see a society in which the media teaches honesty, and honor, courage, accomplishment, rather than degeneracy and dissolution of the human spirit. I can see a society where each person finds a far greater personal joy in their own healthy body engaged in athletic activity and in the beauty of Nature — rather than as spectators of others. I envision a political system that elevates men to office by the quality of their character and their ideas — rather than the special interest money that they can muster.

I can see a healthy economy based on free enterprise, ingenuity, and competition, but one also based on honor and honesty rather than greed. I can see a medical profession oriented toward keeping people healthy rather than repairing the damage of unhealthy living. I can see a time when genetic research will cure cancer and diabetes and other diseases that ravage mankind. I can envision an Earth of clean air and clean water, uncrowded and uncorrupted.

I can see an artistic renaissance of Western man, love of beauty and form replaces today's alien cult of ugliness. I can see painting and sculpture that represent an idealization of mankind, not the misshapen images of a debauched world.

I see a nation of one people, one heritage, a society where each citizen shares a great community of love and concern for each other, a nation that protects and nurtures the most precious treasure of our people: the children.

There can never be a perfect society, and there will always be challenges for mankind, but only a more highly evolved mankind will be able to meet the unforeseen tasks ahead. There are many places on Earth where one can see a slight glimmer of the coming Natural Order of the 21st Century. In those regions that are today populated almost exclusively by our race, we can find communities of good schools, clean streets, low crime, and feelings of brotherhood. Many of our communities are essentially healthy in spite of alien media promotion of so much which is degenerate and destructive, and despite school curricula often damaging to our spirit. When our whole nation becomes a White community again, and when the media and our schools are a reflection of the highest of our Aryan ideals, the new millennium will truly arrive, and the Natural Order will commence.

Aryans seek far more than mere survival. We strive toward God. We fight for a new vision and New World. We fight to fulfill our destiny on Earth and in the stars. Once this vision becomes strong enough in our hearts and our minds, nothing can stop us from winning its victory.

Uncontrolled alien immigration and low White birthrates have created growing non-White percentages in formerly White nations, and will lead to Whites becoming a minority if left unchecked. Once that occurs, Whites will completely lose political and cultural control in their own societies.

Social integration of the races, accompanied by aggressive media promotion of race-mixing has produced higher rates of racial intermarriage — further diminishing White numbers, and lessening White allegiance in those families.

The inescapable fact is that unless there is a dramatic awakening of our people, and a dedicated and well-organized resistance, our race faces a true biological waterloo: the annihilation of our genotype.

In addition to the catastrophic genetic losses of this century, there has been an accompanying degeneration of the cultural and social institutions of Western mankind.

What We Want

We Aryans want the same kind of society for our children that our forefathers envisioned and created for us. We want an appreciation of Western art and music; we want a populace self-disciplined and self-reliant, healthy in body and spirit. We want a sense of brotherhood that we know is only possible in a more racially homogeneous society. We want good schools, clean and safe streets and neighborhoods, and a chance for advancement based on merit and hard work. We want an honest system free from corruption and rip-offs. We want our children to learn pride in our people and hope for the future. We want a society where we feel bonded to each other, rather than alienated and deracinated. We want to be part of a great people aspiring toward great accomplishments, getting better with every generation, striving toward God.

We know who we are. We are Aryans — racially conscious White men and women who are dedicated to the survival and evolutionary development of our people.

We shall achieve the following:

First, we Aryans shall survive. The most fundamental urge in all life forms is self-preservation. We shall see to it that our genotype lives and goes on, just as we desire the preservation of other species and subspecies in the natural world. To us, there is no more sacred task than to preserve our race as a unique and evolutionarily advanced creation of Nature. Our race has created magnificent paintings, sculpture, music, architecture, philosophy, literature, poetry, government, scientific achievement and religious expressions. Yet, in the final analysis, we don't have to justify ourselves to anyone but ourselves. We will obey the first law of life itself, self-preservation.

Second, we shall have our own society created in our own image, and populated by our own people, united in their common heritage, culture and a shared faith for the future. We desire to live in our own neighborhoods, go to our own schools, work in our own cities and towns, and ultimately live as one extended family in our own nation. We shall end the racial genocide of integration. We shall work for the eventual establishment of a separate homeland for African Americans, so each race will be free to pursue its own destiny without racial conflicts and ill will.

Third, we shall be free. We shall determine for ourselves, our own destiny. Government must be of our people and for our people. It must not serve any other race or foreign power, but us and us alone. Only we know what's best for ourselves, our families, our nation, our race. Just as any good father and mother will put their own child's well-being first, our leaders must put our welfare *first*. America must again become synonymous with ourselves and *our* posterity. We don't seek to suppress anyone else. Nor do we seek supremacy over any other nations. But we know what's best for us, just as other races understand what's best for them. We shall have a government oriented to our basic interests and values; committed to our people's independence, freedom and well-being, a government that puts America first.

Fourth, we shall have a free press. We know that in the age of modern media, what is called democracy is really rule by an oligarchy, because only an unelected, tiny few wield the great powers of the mass media — which in truth exceed that of a king or a president. The mass media must be free of alien domination, and they must become instruments that ennoble and strengthen our highest values, not debase them. Media power must serve our ideals, not cater to our weaknesses. Freedom of speech must be a sacred right for all our citizens, and at the same time the great media powers must be in our people's own hands and in the service of our evolutionary destiny.

Fifth, we want an advanced educational system that educates every person to the full measure of his ability and seeks out and nurtures those exceptionally gifted who will lead us into the future of science, the arts, and government. We want a system that teaches the fundamentals of life and language and science, but even more importantly trains the noble character. The first obligation of education toward every child is to teach him honor, duty, honesty, respect, brotherhood, unselfishness, courage, self-discipline, and self-reliance. The next is to foster an appreciation of his heritage, and how he is a part of a never-ending, upward chain of life, destined to live in a healthy and beautiful nation, and on a renewed Earth. We must consciously cultivate nobility among our people in both the spirit and the flesh and make ready for the next evolutionary step to a higher mankind.

Sixth, we want a healthy and organic society based on Natural Order. We see man's purpose realized in understanding and applying the natural laws of life. We state those as:

1) ***Racial Integrity*** **- the preservation of our racial genotype**
2) ***Natural Hierarchy*** **of individuals based on ability and contribution to society.**
3) ***Leadership by the Best***, **a political system that elevates those of best character and ability to leadership on every level.**
4) ***Territoriality***, **through recognition of the sovereignty of nations and cultures, and private property among individuals.**
5) ***Family and Motherhood***, **the enabling of healthy families and an economic structure that creates the financial ability and time necessary for mothers and fathers to give their children the guidance they need.**

6) *Respect for the Earth*, that the ecology of our planet be protected and replenished.

7) *Eugenic and Cultural Evolution*, Our first concern must be that each generation takes another step up the evolutionary ladder. We must consciously promote the advancement of our science and the arts, while continuing to promote the genetic improvement of future generations.

A Visionary Fashions a Weapon for Truth

In October, 1965, I first heard of Dr. William Shockley. I was an avid reader of *U.S. News and World Report*, which at that time was certainly the most conservative of the big three newsmagazines, the others being *Newsweek* and *Time*. I read an article entitled "Quality of U.S. Population Declining" — a long interview with Dr. William Shockley.[1011] In it, he dared to speak about racial differences in intelligence and about the declining genetic quality of mankind.

Shockley must be included in any list of the dozen most eminent scientists during the 20th century. Shockley led the three-man team at Bell Laboratories that invented the point contact transistor, and he invented by himself the junction transistor, the analog and the junction field-effect transistor. The transistor ushered in the modern electronic age and the computer age. For their major scientific breakthrough he and his colleagues were awarded the Nobel Prize for physics in 1956. Even before he won the Nobel Prize, during the Second World War he was director for research for the U.S. Navy Anti-submarine Warfare Operations Research Group, and in recognition of his work received the Medal of Merit from President Truman.

Shockley went on to found the Shockley Semiconductor Laboratories, the company which formed the basis for the computer industry's famous Silicon Valley. His invention of the transistor was the essential breakthrough that made possible the computer revolution. He sold his company and accepted a prestigious chair at Stanford University where he continued to conduct research and lecture after 1963.

Dr. Shockley wasn't the type merely to rest on his laurels. His brilliant mind found itself drawn to a new and far more important scientific inquiry; the genetic quality of mankind itself. A pure scientist, with little concern for fashion or popularity, but a great love for truth, he became convinced that human genetic quality was in jeopardy. In recognition of the crisis that faced our genotype — at the pinnacle of his career, he put aside his love of physics and devoted himself almost wholly to his crusade to rescue our people.

His concern for race and genetics had begun years earlier, when he did research during the Second World War with the Army Air Corps B29 group in India. While in India, he became interested in the problems of overpopulation because of the human misery he witnessed. In experiences similar to my own, he arrived at an understanding of the racial demise of the once great Indian Civilization. Shockley's analytical mind quickly led him to see that not only did the quantity of human beings greatly affect a nation's well-being, but also their quality.

In 1968 he was invited to lecture at the Brooklyn Polytechnic Institute, but found himself drowned out by Marxist militants. At Dartmouth in 1969, Marxist demonstrators rioted and stopped his speech. In 1971 at Sacramento State College, militants again staged a violent disruption.[1012] At Staten Island Community College he was to be part of a "controversial speaker" program that included Black Panther Bobby Seale. Shockley was canceled by the college administration; Seale was not. Even Harvard canceled his appearance scheduled for April, 1972, after a leftist disruption. Then, in 1973, Harvard Law School again prohibited his appearance. The *Harvard Crimson* newspaper quoted a Law School memo, which stated: "The realities and exigencies of a less than a free intellectual climate outbalanced the desirability of our making a stand for freedom of speech." [1013]

If one of America's most important Nobel-prize winning scientists can't make a speech about an important scientific subject at a major university because of threats of violence and terrorism, then what exactly is meant when someone asserts that America has "freedom of speech?" Not only did Shockley face the violence of intolerant egalitarians and Marxists; he also faced the calumny of the press. A man who was vital to the American war effort against the Nazis in directing anti-submarine research and development was dubbed a "Nazi" simply for telling the truth of race.

If Shockley deserved that label, then the press may as well go ahead and denote Washington, Jefferson, Lincoln and Teddy Roosevelt as "Nazis" too. (They will probably get around to that, eventually). The media also consistently lied about the facts of the whole racial controversy in the largest and most influential magazines of the day. For instance, in discussing Shockley's ideas, *Time* magazine wrote that "Virtually all scientists reject these views, of course, arguing that there is no sound evidence of intellectual differences based on race or of intellectual decline based on genetics."[1014] The truth is that most psychologists recognize the fact that Blacks have a lower average intelligence, and at least half of all the experts in the field believe that the racial differences in intelligence are at least partially genetic.

In spite of all the hatred and wrath he endured, Shockley kept on entering the lion's den. He would not relent, recant, or retreat. His patents provided him all the money he would ever need to live a very comfortable life, but he still chose to take the hard and honest road for no other reason than the fact that he loved his heritage and he loved the truth. He was a true Aryan.

When I was 16, Shockley was my idol: a bespectacled, slight man, standing up to the assassination threats and physical intimidation to speak the truths crucial to our survival and evolutionary progress. His example influenced me to devote my life to the same ideals. In the mid-60s, though, my reverence for him came almost entirely from his racial writings and his courage in carrying them to the public. It wasn't until two decades later that I truly began to understand his millennial significance. History will someday record Shockley as not only a great scientist who courageously fought in the public arena for the racial and eugenic truth; it shall someday also recognize him as the genius who created the tools vital for our eventual victory. In the '60s, solid state electronics was just coming into its own, and the personal computer was only science fiction fantasy. But from the transistor and the silicon chip transistor that Shockley created, a whole New World came to be. From his work came the modern communications revolution that included greatly expanded personal communication: affordable electronics, inexpensive long distance communication and ultimately — the Internet. In the last decade of the 20th century, information now flows farther, faster and better than ever before in history. Computers also make possible modern robotics that will have tremendously powerful social implications in the next century.

Robotics has already changed the face of American manufacturing and productivity. Robotics enable a relatively small workforce to produce a prodigious amount of goods. They also put a high premium on intelligence, for if the machines do most of the manual labor, then the jobs left are the ones that design the computers and the machines to do the labor and keep these highly technical creations going. Computer-driven societies are rapidly becoming more and more dependent on intelligent populations. European-descended populations which have largely engineered the computer/robotics revolution, have low birthrates. Concurrent with the phasing out of some forms of manual labor by machines, the population explosion, as it exists in Western nations, is mostly composed of the non-White elements most suited to manual labor. Computer programming and technology demands mathematical capability beyond the ability of many Whites and practically all Blacks. As these highly paid positions proliferate, proportionately fewer Blacks will be able to fill them. A computer driven society tends to clearly mark racial lines. A fundamental economic, political and social clash approaches born from this racial difference.

650 MY AWAKENING

Under a democracy, when the underclass becomes a majority, the productive elite can expect massive expropriation, political corruption and repression. There may be shiny, technologically advanced computers in the corridors of the federal government in Washington, D.C., but the city elected a semi-literate, crack-smoking whoremonger as its mayor. After serving time in jail, those same inept voters reelected him. .Such racial demarcation will become even clearer in the 21st century as robotics evolve in their capabilities to perform more jobs that are now filled by low-skilled labor. It will not be too long until advanced robots can take orders, flip hamburgers and give them to the customer; wash and wax a floor; iron clothes; cut a yard and trim a hedge; or wash a sink full of dishes. Most McDonald's restaurants will choose to employ a robot that never misses work, never asks for a raise, never steals and never requires Social Security payments.

It has been incorrectly stated that the cotton gin made Negro slaves obsolete. In reality, the cotton gin enabled the quick and easy processing of great amounts of cotton, fueling a demand for raw cotton and the continued use of slavery. What the cotton gin did not do, the computer revolution and robotics are doing, on a worldwide basis. As my chapters on Black-White IQ differences showed, many Blacks are even at present, unemployable. The percentage of Blacks in that category can only increase as the technological revolution continues.

Another interesting aspect of the computer revolution is that it will enable a nation with a small population but a high IQ tremendously disproportionate power. Robots can be programmed to make other robots, and those can make still more. Theoretically, a very small, but intelligently populated nation could have the capacity to produce as many televisions or automobiles or for that matter, ballistic missiles, as one of today's superpowers. Therefore, even if the White population becomes dangerously low, it will still be possible for Whites somewhere in the world to build a powerful society of immense defensive capability. The computer revolution has made this and many other things that we haven't dreamt of yet, possible.

The Democratization of Information

In the early part of the 20th century, the Jews moved to greatly expand their influence in the traditional communication media of newspapers, books, and magazines. They also quickly cornered the movie and broadcasting industries, which they have predominated ever since. The newness and the power of film and television made the format irresistible and authoritarian. When Edward R. Murrow or Walter Cronkite appeared on their television screens, for many of the undiscerning, it was almost as if God were talking to them. These figures seemed bigger than life, and when the talking heads spoke it seemed almost sacrilegious to contradict them. People found themselves transported to a magical world where it seemed anything; even the most improbable or impossible could occur.

The old adage *seeing is believing* translated into the most powerful form of propaganda the world had ever seen. The movie hero could jump from one flying jet to another jet's wing and make it look believable, or the good guy would escape being hit by a hundred machine guns firing at him at close range. Slowly though, people became a bit suspicious of the media, and they began to realize that it could be very deceptive. But unless they had personal and direct knowledge of a person or an event, they still had a difficult time discerning the truth, for the media were in the hands of a chosen few.

But with the advent of the transistor, silicon chip and the modern computer, that began to change. Instead of the easily-controlled "few-to-many" model of information flow, epitomized by the TV networks, we are now moving to a "many-to-many" paradigm. An intelligent person can now publish with a voice potentially as loud as the *New York Times* or CBS.

The rise of the Internet makes it possible for any capable person to make a print-audio-visual presentation qualitatively as good as that of a multi-billion dollar corporation. Suddenly, information and ideas are no longer controlled by a monopoly of the rich, powerful and connected. A web site designer with a limited budget but good skills can make an Internet page just as colorful, entertaining, and interesting as Michael Eisner's Walt Disney page or a printed page out of Gerald Levin's *Time* magazine. And more importantly, a person can see the page instantly and at no cost, from almost anywhere in the world.

The Internet has led to a great democratization of information allowing individuals to be at the cutting edge of communication for the first time since information was spread by a speech in the Town Square. It is still a big advantage for the big media powers such as the television networks to promote their own or other "approved" web sites, but not an insurmountable one. It is also true that once huge numbers of people begin to access a web page there will be high costs for bandwidth (use of the expensive transmission lines needed to carry large amounts of data). But proportionally, the Internet is by far the cheapest and fastest form of mass communication in the world.

When I opened my page at www.duke.org, almost immediately people began to visit my site and see and hear for themselves what I stood for rather than what the media says I believe in. The way the Internet has caused a revolution in accessing information can be illustrated in the way thousands of students do school reports on me each year. Until the advent of the Internet, if they wanted to learn about me, they had to go to their libraries and look up the *Guide to Periodical Literature* and find articles about David Duke in newspapers, magazines and journals. More often than not, the articles written about me are from Jewish owned, liberal newspapers and magazines — and even if the writer is not himself Jewish, he is often ideologically and morally opposed to me. Even a writer who is personally neutral on my issues knows what his Jewish or liberal employers expect of him in regard to coverage of David Duke. Often, the press distorts my positions and beliefs, quotes me out of context, and plays up whatever they think will discredit me or plays down anything about me that people might interpret as positive. In short, what people read about me in the major media is not what I say, but what the media says I say.

The Internet changes all of that. Now when a high school or college student does a report about me, the typical way is for them to go on the web and use a search engine to find pages with the name "David Duke." They will immediately find pages which attack me, which is fine by me because they also will find my own page — where with just a click of their mouse they can read for themselves what I believe in and what I stand for—in my *own* words. I can use as much space as I deem necessary to explain my ideas, and I can provide the documentation that backs them up. They can even hear me give a talk in my own voice, without the editing of a hostile media hack.

With Internet radio, anyone with a computer who is hooked up to the Internet anywhere in the world can hear my radio programs, on demand, 24 hours a day! There are no studio costs, no huge expenditures for technical equipment and there are no transmitter costs for a radio station that can broadcast all over the world around the clock. My only cost is the modest price I pay for the bandwidth used by those who are accessing my broadcast.

Suddenly the playing field is leveling. Ideas can now compete on their own merit, rather than simply because people have the media power to promote them. The Internet serves the truth like no other medium in the history of the world. People can judge for themselves what makes sense and what doesn't, as well as who is being hypocritical and deceitful. The Internet allows cross-examination on every issue!

I have no fear of free speech because I truly believe my position is consistent, factual and defensible. Of course, Simon Wiesenthal and others are trying to limit freedom of speech on the Internet. They are like witnesses who cannot stand the exposure of cross-examination.

What's more, the Internet is expanding at a tremendous pace and within a decade, most people of European descent will be connected. Internet speeds and technology are improving rapidly — enabling in the near future, the transmission of high quality digitized audio and video. This will give any computer the potential power of a TV station that can broadcast quality video programming anywhere in the world. Perhaps you can understand why the Anti-Defamation League and the likes of Simon Wiesenthal are getting so nervous that they are hysterically advocating new "hate laws" to block freedom of speech on the Internet. They know that when people have the opportunity to see and hear the other side of the Israeli-Palestinian question that they will learn the naked truth of Jewish supremacism. They know that when people learn of the Jewish-Soviet murder of tens of millions of Christians, they will see the hypocrisy of the never-ending hype of the Jewish Holocaust.

Doctor Shockley's invention of the transistor also makes it now possible for a person with a $500 camera and a $1000 computer to make a video documentary of very high quality, dependent only on an individual's creative ability. And it will not be long before the video can be sent as easily as one sends an email today. (For those not familiar with email, those on the Internet around the world can send up to thousands of pages of text and graphics in a matter of minutes, to anywhere in the world, at no cost other than the small monthly access fee to an Internet provider. The first years of the 21st century will also make it possible to send video in the same way.)

People of European descent the world over will be the most Internet and email connected people on the globe. The potential for awakening our people is tremendous. In Iran, the Ayatollah Khomeini undermined a powerful and strongly entrenched regime with simple audiocassettes. We can make a revolution in thought and action with video and audio, and written material that can be transmitted on the Internet to millions in a matter of minutes.

In the future, almost every European will be connected to email and the Internet. Most will keep their address book on the Internet, and because of the inexpensive cost of disk storage space, most people will keep an electronic address book that will continue to grow their whole lives. Those who keep email addresses can send a particular letter to their entire address book by a simple command taking but a few seconds. Suppose someone with a personal address book of 1000 people, received a particularly thought-provoking article on the race issue from a friend. He could forward it immediately to all 1000 people in his address file. The same could be done with an audio recording or even a powerful and entertaining video documentary on Jewish supremacism. Even if the item only impresses a few of his friends and family, those who find it interesting will forward it to their own address books. The material can reach millions in only a matter of days.

When I first started speaking out publicly at LSU, I believed the truth would set us free, but at that time I just did not have the means to reach the masses of people with my ideas fully expressed. Now, all that has changed almost in the blink of an eye, or perhaps I should say, the twinkle of the eyes of Dr. William Shockley.

I had the privilege to speak with Dr. Shockley a number of times over the telephone from the early 1970s all the way to shortly before his death in 1989. While he lived, I never mentioned that I knew him publicly because I knew that media association with me could only cause him more grief from the press. He always had a kind word of encouragement, and told me that if he were but 30 years younger and healthier, he would campaign for me. He was hard man, undiplomatic on a personal level and unforgiving of error. He lived a life as stringent outside the laboratory as he did inside it.

About the time he died, the Internet revolution was just getting underway, and people began to see how it would change the world. I read some papers on the possibilities of cheap and easy mass communication, and it dawned on me that Dr. Shockley was not only a courageous advocate of my core beliefs, but that he has given me and all the Aryans on Earth the ultimate weapon in the struggle for our survival and evolutionary advancement. He has given us the means to allow the truth to stand on an equal footing with the powerful purveyors of the lie.

Our last talk occured during the hurricane season in Louisiana. In a conversation with him in the fall of 1988, not long before his death, he was uncharacteristically emotional. He told me that his invention of the transistor had no meaning unless our European genotype survived. "Our unique genotype," he told me, "is worth infinitely more than every invention in the history of the world. Our genes are the mother of invention, and the source of our every hope for the future." We discussed a beautiful and seemingly intelligent blonde actress in the news who had married a Black actor. With a passion I was not used to from his usually dispassionate, scientific persona, he said, "The loss of her genes from our gene pool of our people is a tragedy beyond any we can imagine. For her loss is tragic to all the generations that came before her and to all the generations that would have carried her genes on in the future."

"I would surrender the Nobel Prize, he pleaded, "even the achievement of the transistor, just to have prevented that sacrilege. You see, her Genome is infinitely more magnificent than any transistor or computer chip in the world, and the loss of it is incalculable."

He told me of his feeling of apprehension for our heritage and the terrible times ahead of us. I was aware of the fact that he was ill, and I told him that when a man is in the eye of the hurricane, he doesn't feel its power. It seems that the great men who change the world seldom understand the ultimate power unleashed by their own creation. I shared with him my belief that he had succeeded in his struggle for our genetic heritage more than he ever knew, because he, more than any other man on Earth, put into motion the computer and communication revolution that would turn the tide of our racial struggle for survival. I told him that he had given us the most powerful weapon the world has ever seen: the power of the truth unleashed. A power that would take us from devolution and destruction — to evolution and creation.

He died the year that I was elected to public office, and though I missed the man I so admired, his spirit stayed with me, urging me on, even to this very moment. But even more importantly, each day through the electronic revolution that he helped make possible, he empowers our revolution, Dr. Shockley forged for the truth, an electronic Excalibur that we shall wield unto victory!

The Ethnic War: A Short History

At the turn of the century, the leaders of the world Jewish community had but a whisper of the power they would acquire by its end. They had only a slightly disproportionate impact in the primary forms of mass communication, which were then the printed media of newspaper, magazine, and book publishing. Their power in academia and government in the Western world had definite limits set by both law and custom, and in most Western societies they had only limited social intercourse with the Gentile elite. In that period, their greatest power came from their wealth, as they had considerable presence in international banking and trade and among them were some of the world's richest financiers. Nations could rise or fall by what Theodore Herzl called "their terrible power of the purse."

Then through a series of cataclysmic events, they made a rapid climb to world power that has been, perhaps, the most amazing in all of history. As much as the 20th century has been catastrophic for the White race, the century has been incredibly empowering for the Jewish people — their social and political power reaching undreamed of heights by its close.

It seems apropos that a Jewish assassin (Prinzip) sparked the flames of the First World War by his murder of Austrian Archduke Francis Ferdinand in Sarajevo, for the act began the first of two world wars that dramatically augmented Jewish power.

The First World War procreated the Jewish-led Soviet state, and the murder of a much-hated enemy, the ruling Christian Czar of Russia. It also directly laid the foundation of the Zionist State in Palestine. The British government made a deal with the House of Rothschild to issue the Balfour Declaration, and promised Palestine to the Jews in return for bringing America into the war. Establishment of the Zionist State, though, had to wait until the end of the next great war.

The Second World War, like the first, had significant Jewish involvement from 1933 onward, when world Jewry formally declared war on Germany.[1015] Their power of the press created a demonized perception of Germany in Western nations, and they skillfully used their considerable political influence behind the scenes to agitate for war. By the time shots were fired in Poland in 1939, the allies had been psychologically prepared for war.

Although the Holocaust is seen as the great tragedy of the Jewish people, and certainly constituted a grievous loss of life, the worldwide Jewish community emerged from the Second World War more powerful than ever before in their long history. The Holocaust story itself became a pivotal weapon in their postwar ascension to power. Although at war's end there were far fewer Jews in central Europe due to displacement and war casualties, as world power shifted to the United States, so too, did Jewish power. It became concentrated in our geo-political, postwar ascendancy. From the nexus of the government bureaucracy and their media, they rose vis-à-vis the United States — to world hegemony.

Jewish media influence rapidly grew from the time of their purchase, near the turn of the century, of America's most famous newspaper: *The New York Times*. Over the next decades they greatly widened their presence in print media, and then turned their attention on the enormously powerful forms of mass communication: radio, films, and television. An effective team effort squeezed out the Gentile inventors and innovators of the motion picture industry. Men such as Thomas Edison and D.W. Griffith were elbowed aside by the Goldwyns, Mayers and Selznicks, and the Chosen reigned as sovereign rulers over what Jewish film critic, Neil Gabler, aptly describes as *An Empire Of Their Own*.[1016]

Correctly perceiving the immense power of radio and television broadcasting to advance their political and social objectives, David Sarnoff, William Paley, and Leonard Goldenson, (the prime movers of NBC, CBS, and ABC) moved swiftly to dominate and consolidate broadcasting. These three warm Jews[1017] whose families fled from the Russian Czars, effectively used the news and entertainment media to advance Jewish objectives.

At the beginning of the 20th century, Jewish financial power was mostly limited to their most famous profession, moneylending. However, in the first two decades they also gained strategic positions in the political and economic sectors of the World, using their wealth to barter their way into the council of presidents and premiers. They dominated international banking and trade. Jewish financiers such as Jacob Schiff and Bernard Baruch controlled billions of dollars in the international financial houses and stock exchanges.

Schiff was able to assemble the financing of the successful Japanese war against the Russians, which weakened the Czar and paved the way for Bolshevism. Jewish financiers jumped at the chance to finance all the antagonists of the First World War. In the desperation of that war, International Jewish financiers become indispensable to men such as the American President Woodrow Wilson, British Prime Minister Lloyd George, French Premier Georges Clemenceau and the German Kaiser. In contrast, their financial boycott of the Imperial Russia wrote the death warrant for the Czar and his family.

In America, Bernard Baruch, Jacob Schiff, and a host of others consolidated their power over the American banking system with the passage of the Federal Reserve Act. Since its passage in 1913, the Federal Reserve Corporation, a private concern that ostensibly has its top posts appointed by the President of the United States, has been greatly influenced by Jewish bankers and economists right up to the current chairman, Alan Greenspan.

In the political realm they established themselves as the chief fund-raisers and contributors in both political parties in America. So much so that the Clinton White House became an exclusive hotel for the richest and most powerful of Jewish moneymen. They also influenced many key parties in Europe and insinuated themselves into the highest echelons of government on both sides of the Atlantic.

By the 1930s they had amassed great power in newspapers, radio, theater, movies, and book publishing. Combining their media power with their governmental influence, the Jews fomented the fratricide of the Second World War. They had to destroy the one great remaining threat to them on a global scale: National Socialist Germany. After the war began, they also sought to protect their Soviet creation from German conquest.

Their accumulation of extensive government and media power by the end of the Second World War led to the achievement of their messianic dream. For two thousand years "next year in Jerusalem" was their daily prayer, and now next year had arrived. The Jewish-supremacist, Zionist State came into being, built through the military conquest and dispossession of the Palestinians. Israel was not a nation established to gather all the Jews of the world, but as an inviolable center from which to coordinate their new world power.

At the same time that they displaced the Palestinians, they accelerated their efforts to demonize, criminalize, and marginalize all who would resist their supremacism. They consolidated their power in media and their power behind the scenes in government and finance. Skillfully, they launched a well-organized attack against every aspect of the traditional White establishment:

- **They taught egalitarianism in academia and the media, to destroy White racial consciousness and solidarity.**
- **They spearheaded the effort to open the borders of America and other Western nations to the Third World.**
- **They taught guilt and supplication among Whites for slavery, Third World exploitation and the Holocaust.**

- **They instilled resentment and hatred in growing non-White racial minorities.**
- **They led the legal and government assault on White schools and neighborhoods.**
- **They helped to undermine the family through feminism, lower moral standards, and economic restructuring.**

After the passage of two thousand years they could now act in earnest against their many enemies who defeated and dispersed them. They would finally have their revenge against the Gens (the Roman ruling families from which comes the name Gentiles). The descendants of Esau would finally get to feel the wrath of Jacob.

By the end of the Second World War, they had the power to do it — more than enough power. The West was exhausted from the fratricidal conflict. The partisans of the New World Order knew that if they could control the media and the politicians, no one could stand in their way. Knowing that this ethnic war is one fought on the quiet battlefields of political and economic power, they understand that it is primarily a psychological war. To win it they must make an intensive team effort while at the same time they must destroy the spirit of their competitors. In every war there are accusations against the enemy of atrocities and mass murder, and this war is no different. They realized that they could disguise their own supremacism and at the same time lessen Gentile solidarity by intensifying, long after the war, the war propaganda against the Germans. After successfully creating postwar German guilt for the Holocaust, they saw the opportunity to do the same to all Gentiles worldwide. By ingraining the horrors of the Holocaust on every racial European, they could insulate themselves from criticism and take away the moral justification for European ethnic self-defense.

Ultimately, using their power in mass media, they even succeeded in displacing the Second World War as the central event of the 20th century. Ian J. Kagedan, director of government regulations, B'nai B'rith stated that "The Holocaust stands as Western Civilization's greatest failure...Achieving our quest of a 'new world order' depends on our learning the Holocaust's lessons."[1018]

The Holocaust became the most written about, spoken about, and cried about event in the history of the world. The war itself simply became the Holocaust's context. Never mind the other 40 million casualties of the war. Jewish suffering became the central issue of the conflict. A temple to commemorate the holy Holocaust was consecrated in Washington, D.C. amongst the most sacred of American government monuments, long before there was any move to build a major memorial to commemorate the American sacrifices in the Second World War.

Not only were Jewish school children taught a fresh story of Haman in the personage of Hitler, but we and our children have been subjected to a non-stop, decades-long lecture decrying the ultimate guilt of the entire Gentile world. They successfully expanded the responsibility for the evil far beyond the Germans. It grew to include the Poles, Slovaks, Ukranians, French — even the Americans and British bore guilt for not doing enough to prevent the calamity and for denying entrance to refugees. Finally, even traditional European Christianity itself was blamed for laying the groundwork for genocide.

Through the powerful modern media of film and television, every Jew learns of the evil and murderous nature of the Gentiles, and the need for solidarity and sacrifice for the Jewish people. Jewish supremacism soars to new heights. Gentiles also learn their lesson that any resistance against Jewish domination is morally equivalent to the horrors of the Holocaust. Even to criticize Jews for tens-of-thousands of civilian deaths in Palestine and for their wholesale denial of human rights — is equated with anti-Semitism and thus is morally similar to the Holocaust.

Through the power of their media, the most racist people on Earth successfully present themselves as victims of racism. Anyone who exposes Jewish hatreds of their ethnic enemies becomes accused of hate. The people who present themselves as a morally and intellectually superior people, supposedly chosen by God, hypocritically characterize Gentiles who dare to oppose *Jewish* supremacism as hateful anti-Semites. Only through their domination of the media could such an inversion of reality be foisted upon the public.

Every leading Gentile public figure learns to beg for the forgiveness and blessings of the Chosen people and to prostrate himself before them. And every young Gentile learns that those who dare to oppose the Chosen people are the epitome of evil.

The way became clear for our traditional enemy. They expanded their control of the media, and they are still tying up the loose ends. Every politician in America learns that it is possible to oppose the NRA and tobacco lobby, but opposing the Jewish lobby is political suicide.

No government of the West will dare oppose them, including, as much as it pains me to say it, the government of my own beloved nation, the United States of America. As I showed in my chapter on ZOG, even their own pundits in the Israel press boast that America no longer has a government of Gentiles. We are now in an occupied land, and we can see ZOG's handiwork across the breadth of it. Now in the final stages of conquest and consolidation, they have even begun to destroy centuries-old Western traditions of free thought and speech.

The former Jewish head of the European Parliament, Simone Veil, promotes imprisonment for anyone who dares to even question the Jewish interpretation of history.

Blinded by the false glow of the controlled media, we allow our hard-won freedoms to be taken away with hardly a peep of protest. For daring to contradict Jewish views, men are at this moment in jail in Germany, France, England, Italy, and Canada.

- **If a man points out Jewish hatred of Gentiles, he is called a hate criminal; it is now called a hate crime to expose hate!**
- **To seek the same rights for our own people that Jews seek for themselves is called hate!**
- **To seek the preservation of our own way of life and our own standards of art and beauty is called hate!**
- **To have a different opinion of historical events than the Jewish approved version is called hate!**
- **Freedom of speech is called hate!**
- **Freedom of thought is called hate!**
- **To defend freedom of speech is a hate crime!**

After centuries, the Jews are now finally free to exact their revenge for actions of Pharaoh, Haman, Caesar, and Hitler. They revel in our dispossession and our degeneration.

- **They set loose Sigmund Freud's sexual degeneracy and the modern feminism of Bella Abzug, Betty Friedan, and Gloria Steinem to break the bonds of our families.**
- **They set loose the egalitarianism of Franz Boas, Ashley Montagu, and Stephen J. Gould to destroy our understanding of race.**
- **They set loose the alienism of Emma Lazarus, Emanuel Cellar and Jacob Javits to break down our borders and flood our nation with millions of non-Whites.**
- **They set loose the forces of Kivie Kaplan and Jake Greenberg of the NAACP to destroy our schools and our cities with integration and Black crime.**
- **They set loose the hideous sub-art of Jacob Epstein and Jacques Lipchitz, the scatological scribbling of Norman Mailer, and the perversion of Allen Ginsberg to poison our spirits.**
- **They set loose Michael Milken, Ivan Boesky and Meyer Lansky to defraud us.**
- **They set loose filmmaker Stanley Kramer to tell us to give our daughters to Negroes, and Steven Spielberg to tell us to give our souls to the Jews.**
- **They set loose the zero-population preacher Paul Ehrlich to tell us to have no more children, and teachers like Doctor Spock to tell us not to discipline and strengthen the ones we do have.**
- **They have set loose Simon Wiesenthal and Abraham Foxman to take away even our right to free speech.**

The 20th century has been the century of Jewish power and the most devastating and dangerous hundred years in the long history of the White race. Our political sovereignty has been supplanted in our own nations and now, even our very existence is threatened in our own homelands. America, Canada, England, France, Australia, Italy, even the sparsely populated Scandinavian nations of Norway and Sweden have rapidly growing non-European minorities. In the most powerful Western nation, America, and our sister nation Canada, Whites are only a few short years away from becoming a minority. Now is the time for us to create and enact our own evolutionary strategy, our own blueprint for our race's survival and the continuation of our evolutionary advancement.

A White Evolutionary Strategy

In this volume, I have written much about the disastrous effects of Jewish power in the Western world. It is true that their power could not have been achieved without their deceit, but it must be admitted that neither could it have been accomplished without their considerable abilities and a number of admirable traits. Their survival in a multicultural world could not have been possible otherwise.

Jews developed ideologies that support the preservation of their genotype. At its core, Judaism is an evolutionary strategy for the preservation and advancement of the Jewish genetic and cultural heritage. Their scriptures express their religion's relationship with God not in a spiritual afterlife, but in promises of power for the Jewish people here on Earth if they obey his laws. Central to these laws is preservation of their genetic heritage. Ultimately, Judaism has even cast the Jewish people as being greater than even God. Only within the Jewish religion could their most holy writ describe incidents where rabbis defeat God in argument and prove God wrong, or scriptures in which rabbis dispute His existence or mock Him. For Jews, God has become in many ways synonymous with themselves. ("...hitting a Jew is the same as hitting God.").[1019] Zionism became a secularized version of this supremacism, which symbiotically (as per secular Israel) permits Judaism to remain in place as a eugenic mechanism and guardian of the Jewish genotype. In deference to the racial principle, even Jews who reject religion support the religious-racial superstructure of their people. Other Jewish strategies can be summarized as follows:

- **They have stressed education and prized scholarship.**
- **They have actively encouraged the most intelligent and successful of their race to have the largest families.**
- **They have kept alive their history, traditions, culture, and values.**

- **While they have worked together as a team for their objectives in the Gentile community, they have stressed individual responsibility.**
- **They have stressed the importance of the family unit.**
- **They speak against intermarriage and elevate genetic purity as one of their highest values (members of the Jewish Priest class are only the purest of Jews, i.e. they are forbidden to marry converts or their descendants).**
- **Successful and powerful Jews are extremely generous to Jewish causes and never reluctant to use their power on behalf of their own people.**

All these traits are admirable, and in the multicultural societies we live in we can learn from these successful moral strategies. Of course, the reason why a Jewish problem exists comes from the fact that they inflict on their host peoples an opposite morality to their own. If their host peoples would have practiced values similar to that of Jews, the Jews could never have accrued power in Gentile societies. Therefore, they learned to survive by stoking their own ethnocentrism, while at the same time they intentionally weakened their host's well-being, solidarity and self-esteem. Such a goal is perfectly realized in Spielberg's *Schindler's List*, a film that increases Jewish solidarity and distrust of Gentiles while at the same time decreases Gentile resistance against Jewish power. Such an attitude explains the almost universal Jewish effort against the European eugenic movement during the 20th century, while Jews have solemnly promoted eugenic practices among themselves for thousands of years.[1020] It explains why they encourage racial intermarriage for Gentiles, while opposing intermarriage for Jews — why they support group loyalty and solidarity among Jews, but individualism and universalism among Gentiles — and why they orchestrate open immigration into Western nations, but rigidly restrict immigration to Israel only to Jews.

If we are to survive, Aryans must adopt a similar strategy, but without the Jewish hypocrisy.

- **Aryans must have a movement and ideology that defines the preservation of our racial heritage as the highest act of morality and the destruction of it as the greatest crime.**
- **Aryans must adopt a team strategy and solidarity.**
- **Aryans must support education, scholarship, and economic self-sufficiency among our ranks.**
- **Aryans must be racially altruistic and financially supportive of the movement for our racial survival, now more than ever.**
- **Aryans must be intensively supportive of the family and look at the well-being, education, and training of our children as a holy obligation.**

While these values are similar to that of Jews, we must at the same time recognize that our genotype is fundamentally different from theirs. Our racial patriotism does not aspire to supremacy over other races, but simply sovereignty in our own societies. We envision ourselves as an organic and evolving genotype, celebrating our European values, and reaching for the stars. And we understand and support the natural right and impulse of all races to pursue those same ideals on behalf of their own genotype.

We seek not to rule over or exploit other races; we want only to create our own society structured on our own culture and dedicated to promoting our most noble attributes. We wish the same kind of fulfillment for the other races of mankind in the distinct societies that will reflect their own natural traits and character. Unlike Jewish supremacists, we don't preach one morality for us and another for the other peoples of the world. We are consistent, and act with a clear conscience and good spirit, and we respect those of other races who seek their own ideals.

Unlike the Jews, we Aryans refuse to wallow in mournful mythologies of past persecutions, but instead shall focus on and celebrate our sagas of triumph. We will not dwell on past suffering, but seek heroic lives in the present, and never-ending future glories. We want a future society not based on chronic recitals of the evils of our historic enemies, but one that celebrates the spirit and beauty of our heroes and heroines.

White Strategy for Victory

The antagonistic Jewish minority in the West relies on deception to maintain and augment their power, deception made possible by their domination of the mass media and their undue influence in government. They have for generations been bred for that duplicity, while we were bred in our European homelands to put honesty and honor as high virtues. Our instincts compel us to the virtues of truthfulness and courage. Only through our virtues we can prevail, not our sins. We cannot sneak-up on our enemies in the shadows, for they are the rulers of the night while we, of light. Our battlefield must be bathed in the light of day. Today, the field of engagement is the debating hall, the political campaign, the family gathering, or just the simple conversation — wherever our kind gathers and however we communicate. Our weapons are books, video documentaries, and all forms of the written and spoken word; and today: email, web sites and chat rooms.

Every awakened White person becomes an Aryan:, a racially conscious White person dedicated to our survival and evolutionary advancement. As Aryan numbers grow, we will form a bond as powerful for our race as Judaism has been for Jews. Our real strength can only come from our utter dedication to the truth, the whole truth, and nothing but the truth. That truth can be hard, it can be costly, it can generate our persecution from those who cannot stand its light, but truth, utter truth, is the only possible path to our eventual victory.

Europeans have never chosen to be the enemy of the Jews, our ancestors tried to assimilate its Jewish interlopers for 2,000 years as full beneficiaries of our culture, religion, and societies, if just they would respect our ways and our God. Nevertheless, while the Jews enjoyed all of the benefits of living in our advanced societies rather than the squalid realms from whence they came, they only seemed to become more jealous of us. Every open hand and every open church door was met with more defiance and ethnocentrism. They chose to destroy the very societies that gave them refuge; they chose ethnic war. Our people have long tried to avoid the conflict. We have tried to ignore it, to pretend it didn't exist and vainly hope it would go away. No longer. We now know that we cannot ignore the assaults of those who at this moment plan our genocide. If we are to perish, we shall go to our fate as Aryan warriors, not as whimpering dogs licking the hand of the master who whips them.

Every White person must realize that there is no easy way to win this struggle for our survival. Our champions, if they are true, will feel the wrath of our enemies, for we cannot win our war for survival unless we name the group that has chosen to be our enemy. We must defend our cultural, political, and genetic ramparts. Our race cannot survive unless we acknowledge that the races of man *do exist*, and that *our* race is in mortal danger. We must make all of our kinsmen understand what is at stake: our very *survival*. And, we can never have a real and permanent victory unless we understand what true victory is: a revolution of thought and action that will preserve our genotype and move our people toward a higher evolutionary destiny.

Furthermore, there is no way to stop a worldwide coordinated effort against our folk without a corresponding universal effort. Although our philosophy recognizes the right of each nation and heritage within the West to maintain its ethnic, cultural and political distinctiveness, all Aryans worldwide must be united in our racial defense. Whether we are English or Irish, Teutonic or Slav, Scandinavian or Italian, Basque or Spaniard, Croat or Serb, our slogan is simple: White Pride — Worldwide. We are one greater blood, one faith, one folk; and we all have one overriding quest — that of the survival and evolutionary advancement of our people. Wherever we live on the Earth, we shall share the same vision, the same sense of beauty, the same courage and sense of duty and honor. We shall triumph together.

Practicalities

Although we must name the enemy and state with conviction what we fight for, we still know that this is an ethnic war that must be strategically fought on all fronts. As in all wars, we must fight intelligently and sometimes covertly. Not every Aryan need shout from the rooftops his creed, but every Aryan must act to support the leaders who *do*. Some Aryans can best help by supplying the real ammunition of the fight: *money*, and others with *influence*, and others with simply their tireless *work*. Some will fight politically, some socially, some religiously, some financially and some even physically before the victory is won; but every Aryan must fight in the way that he can contribute the most.

Aryans should not retreat from the institutions of society, but remain in them and transform them into our own instruments. And we must strive to bring all the Europeans in those institutions — to Aryan awareness. Aryan political leaders must not and will not remain silent in military service, government, business, high school or Sunday school. On campuses, Aryans will spread our message of racial survival, freedom, life and evolution. We will do whatever we must do so that our people shall live. Some of our ranks will quietly go their way building our base, increasing our power, widening our influence, turning the wheels of revolution from within the system. Others will be on the table tops and the rooftops shouting our truths.

At the same time that we work to transform the institutions of our society, we must create a parallel Aryan community where we gather together for fellowship and direction, inspiration and education. An Aryan community can be as small as a handful of students in a high school sharing their Aryan brotherhood, or a whole city, county or state led by Aryan activists. And so it must be until our awakened ones lead our nation and every nation of the Western World.

Women and the Revolution

In an ideal world, women would not have to go to war, but there have been times in our history when women have had to pick up the pitchfork or the rifle to protect kith and kin. We are now in a struggle for the very survival of our race on this planet. Women are full participants in our revolution and in the Natural Order ahead, for although the sexes are profoundly different, we are made so that these differences harmonize with each other to forge the genetic soul of our race. In this worldwide racial emergency, women's participation in our cause is vital. Jewish feminism has tried to drive men and women apart, it is our sacred task to come together as a team in this struggle for our survival.

Gifted women naturally must have the right to pursue careers in any area of professional expertise. Hopefully, though, they will make marriage and children a vital concern, not just for the nation, but also for their own well-being. When having beautiful and intelligent children becomes as fashionable for those exceptional women as having the best designer clothes, magnificent homes, sleek cars, and career success, we will be moving toward the Natural Order with all deliberate speed.

A Message to the Young

It must also be understood that an Aryan is not simply one who *believes*, but one who is dedicated and thus *acts* on behalf of our people. The original meaning of the word "Aryan" in Sanskrit is "noble one," and every Aryan must know that he advances our cause not only by what he believes and his activism for the cause, but also by how nobly he lives his life. The ultimate proof of being an Aryan is the exemplary life he lives. Our people need leaders by example — the way an Aryan activist lives, is just as important as the truth that he tells. The more accomplished, successful and honorable the Aryan, the more he can do for our cause.

In 1998 I received an email from a young man named Ben Smith. He told me that he was 15 years old, that he believed deeply in our cause, and that he wanted to become and Aryan. Here is how I answered him in an email:

> **Dear Ben,**
> **It is great to hear that you are dedicated to your people. We are in a fight for our freedom and heritage even more important than the American Revolution or the ideals of the Alamo.**
>
> **You want to be an Aryan. The first thing you must know is that there is a great difference between wanting and achieving. Being Aryan is all about achieving, not wanting.**
>
> **You are in the formative stages of your life, so your first task for the cause is to make yourself grow stronger: physically, mentally, emotionally. You must evolve to a higher level the same way you want our race to go upward. If you really believe in our cause and want to be a true Aryan warrior, you must become a leader among your fellow European Americans.**
>
> **Study hard, and discipline yourself to learning, for knowledge is power. In everything you do, be an example of excellence and achievement.**
>
> **Let your conduct exemplify the ideals that you believe in. That means being honest, honorable and noble.**
>
> **Keep your body healthy. Exercise and unleash the strength that is coiled in your genes. The leaders of our race need to be strong and attractive in the Greek ideal of body, mind, and spirit. Become a man that other men admire and women desire. Only if you are strong can you make our race strong as well.**

Reject the Jewish degeneracy sponsored by the mass media, and stay away from smoking, drugs, and refrain from irresponsible behavior with alcohol or sex.

Force yourself to study and concentrate in class, and achieve true accomplishment and success in your career and life. If you find little discipline at school or home, then discipline and steel yourself by the power of your own will!

Become an example of what an Aryan is. For an Aryan is not simply a White person — an Aryan is a racially conscious White person dedicated to the evolutionary survival and advancement of our people. You prove that by your bearing and your actions.

It also means staying legal and law-abiding. If someday the time comes for physical self-defense and revolution, you must be ready for it, but now our movement can only succeed through the power of the word, not the sword. If a spiritual revolution does not sweep our people, a physical and political one can never come.

In addition to what you learn in school, you must learn the scientific facts of race, and expand your knowledge until you can win every debate. Not only must you learn the basis of your beliefs but also how to present them effectively.

I know that some of things I am telling you may sound difficult. Sometimes you cannot help but fall short of your ideals, but it is in the relentless striving that makes you a true Aryan, in the same way the striving of our race will lead to higher man.

The next few decades will be the most exciting and important in the long history of our people, and you will have the chance to be in the midst of the most important revolution in the history of mankind. You will accomplish great things in your life if you just dare to have great dreams and then act upon them with discipline.

So, if you really want to be a true Aryan, your task at 15 is to reach down into the depths of your soul, and find what is noble in your genes and then — give that nobility expression in your life.

Sculpture a strong, healthy body, educate your mind, nourish your spirit and steel your will — become an Aryan — and help usher in the Natural Order of the coming age.

It is your destiny, my friend.

David Duke

Chapter 40:

What We Must Do Now

ARYAN: **A RACIALLY AWARE WHITE PERSON DEDICATED TO THE SURVIVAL AND EVOLUTIONARY ADVANCEMENT OF HIS PEOPLE.**

Knowing the truth is both exciting and burdensome. When we of good blood learn of the crisis of our people, we know that we cannot turn away from the struggle. It suddenly becomes the most important thing in our lives, for we understand that we owe our genetic forebears everything, for our traits and our talents, our loving families, even for our existence itself. If we of the best blood fail our people now, then all the sacrifices and genius, work and struggle, beauty and love of countless generations will be lost. Even more importantly, we will not realize the evolutionary promise for which we have long prepared.

It is my belief that we will not fail. Consider the millions of men and women of genius in our race who, racially unaware, have devoted their talents and their money exclusively to their businesses, homes, hobbies, jobs, and other mundane pursuits. As we touch them with our truth, their genes will answer the call to life and freedom, and they will use their talents on behalf of our survival. They will create a force unequaled in history. Our people still have tremendous power and vast wealth. We are like a blindfolded tiger tormented by a mouse. This book removes the blindfold. What has kept our people down is only their lack of knowledge. When they learn the truth they will find the courage to act upon it.

The Task of the Aryan

There are those reading these lines who could, by their own financial means, dramatically advance our movement. They need to realize that their money can help change the world. No one is asking the wealthy to be reduced to poverty, for Aryans recognize private property and revere accomplishment. However, all Aryans should give generously, even sacrificially, during this period of racial crisis. The next few decades will decide whether our kind will live or die. Every Aryan should designate pro-White individuals and organizations as beneficiaries in insurance and wills. Supporting our cause is the surest way to leave a legacy for the generations to come. Indeed, the generosity of a few may well make the difference between racial extinction and a racial renewal. A friend put it this way, "If we lose, you will not be remembered. If we win, you will be remembered as one who did his duty."[1021]

Far more important than the gift of the Aryan upon his death, is the activism of the Aryan in his life. Only when millions of our people find in this sacred cause their highest motivation and meaning can we achieve our visionary agenda. We must view every person of European descent as a kinsmen whom we must help find his way back to the bosom of his people. In the awakening of our people, one-by-one, our race shall stir from its long sleep.

Every Aryan should become computer literate, become connected to the Internet, and learn how to use it to spread our truth and awaken our race. Internet proficiency is as important to our cause as was learning to use a sword in the Middle Ages, or a long rifle in the American Revolution.

Every Aryan must come to realize that truly hateful rhetoric or terrorism only fulfills the false, Jewish-created, media image of what we are and what we stand for. Those who embarrass us with the language or behavior of hatred work against our victory more than the worst Jewish supremacist.

Those who pick up a gun in a moment of anger, or commit terrorist acts, undermine our cause. They alienate the very people we must win for our movement. In addition, the perpetrator of such an act can do little for our cause in jail or dead. If our race is to survive, our people must *live* for our cause, rather than *die* for it. They must do the hard, and at times, unrewarding work necessary to wake up our kinsmen, rather than follow a visceral impulse. Before the battle is over, many of us will find a heroic death, but far more important to victory will be those who lead a heroic life. Heroic lives do not come from a moment of intemperance, but from hard, relentless, untiring work and activism for the cause.

A physical revolution may be required someday to free our people and secure our survival, and such is justified by the highest laws of Nature and God. But no revolution, whether physical or political, can ever succeed without first winning the hearts and minds of the people. It is this task that is our *first* task.

Many in our movement need to take the political path. But there must be caution here, for politics has a way of muting a revolution. Political tactics and programs must be flexible, but the foundations of our Natural Order must be like steel. Our race cannot survive with anything less than a government and a mass media composed of our own people, dedicated to the new ideals we share.

There is Only One Issue

I am an elected official of the Republican Party in Louisiana. On many issues I could be classified as a Conservative. For instance I support the Constitution of the United States, and less government. If I had the power, I would dismantle the IRS and abolish the income tax. I would take control of the Federal Reserve from the bankers. I believe in the inviolate right to keep and bear arms. I support neighborhood schools. I oppose affirmative action. I believe in an America First foreign policy. I oppose illegal immigration and support severely restricting legal immigration. I could go on and on, but I don't need to, for there is only one issue that is vital to every other one: *race*.

A Newt Gingrich advocating statehood for Puerto Rico or mixed-race adoptions makes him and other Republicans like him, just as much our enemy as the Bill Clintons or the Ted Kennedys of the world. Perhaps he is even worse than those destroyers because he is in the ranks of the majority. He undermines our own people more than any racial outsider ever could.

Conservative politicians have been losing on these issues for decades and they face obliteration on these issues as racial demographics change. If Black and Mexican voters had their way, the President of the United States would be Jesse Jackson, a man who went to Communist Cuba and exhorted the Marxist minions: "Viva La Castro, Viva la Revolución." On American soil he has chanted, "Hey Ho, Hey Ho, Western Culture has to Go!" There can be no victory on any of the critical issues facing America if we become a minority in the nation that our own forefathers carved from the wilderness. And, there can be no real victory on any critical issue until the media is again in the hands of the American people, rather than in the hands of aliens who lie to us and poison our minds and our spirits.

Fighting small battles such as wrangling over the capital gains tax, or whether or not President Clinton had his pants down with a Jewish princess in the Oval Office — are like arguing over a Shuffleboard point on the deck of the Titanic. Aryans should devote their money and their time *only* to organizations that are openly working for the survival of the White race and/or the exposure of Jewish supremacism. Either we will win victory for everything in which we believe, or we will win nothing. In fact, if we lose the struggle coming in the first few decades of the 21st century, it will not only mean loss of economic well-being and the tyranny of the New World Order, but the extinction of our kind.

672 My Awakening

Ironically, those of liberal persuasion should be just as concerned about Jewish supremacism and the racial destruction of America as conservatives are. Ecologists should only have to look at the population explosion and environmental devastation of the Third World to know what is in store for America's and the World's ecosystems if the unbridled masses of the Third World overrun us.

Feminists should consider the fate of women's rights if the Western World becomes subsumed by the Third World — societies where women's rights are non-existent and millions of young girls are enslaved, circumcised and mutilated.

Civil libertarians must realize that the epidemic criminal behavior of non-Whites directly results in draconian laws and the destruction of civil liberties for all. Believers in compassion, charity, brotherhood and love must understand that these attributes are most possible and most practiced and appreciated in Western monoracial communities, not multiracial ones. Acquiescence to Jewish supremacism violates every moral principle that liberals claim to profess.

The issue is *race*. It is expressed in the wealth and poverty of nations, the scepter of power or the cry of the powerless, the pulse of history, and in the laws of evolution and life itself. Now, our people must take up the cause of our own right to life and the preservation of the sacred cultural forms that only we can create. Every healthy form of life on this planet has an instinct for self-preservation, it is time that we find ours and nurture it.

The startling facts contained in this book need no longer be known only by a few. They can, and they must — be known to everyone.

The essential facts have been laid out clearly in this volume:

- **The vital role of heredity in intelligence and character.**
- **The scientific facts that expose the new religion of racial equality as a fraud.**
- **The inherent differences between the races that so powerfully affect society, and ultimately history.**
- **Our natural right to preserve our own genetic and cultural heritage.**
- **The racial crisis looming in almost every Western nation.**
- **The anti-Western character of the Jewish race and Jewish supremacist doctrine that has so plagued every nation in which it has have thrived.**
- **The Jewish efforts to preserve their own genetic integrity as they attempt to destroy ours.**
- **The paramount Jewish role in the Soviet Revolution and the greatest killing machine in human history, International Communism.**

- **The theft of Palestine and the establishment of their nakedly supremacist, Israeli state.**
- **The Jewish infiltration and control of the media and government of the United States and other Western nations.**
- **The shameless use of the tragedy of the Holocaust as a tool to both heighten their own ethnocentrism and weaken our own ethnic defenses.**
- **The efforts of organized Jewry to destroy freedom of speech and press around the world.**

It's all here. I have documented the realities of the world, compiled in my 30-plus years of reading, listening, analyzing and activism. Now, all we must do is disseminate it. The truth is powerful — more powerful than the might of presidents and prime ministers; parliaments and congresses. In the end, the truth is ultimately even more powerful than are marching armies; for armies are led by men and men are susceptible to the truth.

The truth, if disseminated, is far more convincing than the easily disproven lies of the Jewish media. That's why the forces of organized Jewry are working so hard to pass so-called "hate laws" and are endeavoring to jail dissident voices and filter and censor the Internet. They know that free speech will expose their hypocrisy, and that they have no choice but to try to nakedly suppress the truth and imprison the truth tellers.

As other books that have exposed Jewish Supremacism, this book will be banned in many nations. The ultimate racists will call it racist. The haters will call it a book of hate. It will be burned by censors and suppressors. The great masters of the lie may attack and suppress it, but it will be read, simply because of the power of the truth that is in it. Everyone of our heritage who is awakened by it will go out of their way to obtain and disseminate more copies to their family and friends. Thousands of awakened Aryans will include selected chapters of this volume on their websites and links so the public will find it and read it.

Tens of thousands will email these truths to hundreds of their friends, and millions in turn will spread the word. Many of the newly awakened Aryans will support a fund to get this volume into every public and school library, and also place it in the hands of every European American politician, scientist, actor, singer, businessman, journalist, and opinion leader in America and across the Western World. Once in their hands, my notoriety gives this book a good chance to be read!

We are in a battle for men's minds, a battle that will determine whether our heritage will survive or be driven to extinction.

To the best of my ability, I have told the truth. I have surveyed the natural forces that make us as we are, both as individuals and races —

and I've also revealed powerful forces in the modern world that are far different than commonly perceived.

Our revolution is not just about prevailing over those who would destroy us. It is far more than simply our longing for freedom and our determination to live in a society that expresses the deepest desires of our soul. It is about the essence of life itself. Our revolution will not just be political, social and cultural. It finds its most fundamental expression in the DNA spiral — upward to a higher mankind. It is a path to a renewed Earth and a stairway to the stars — an evolutionary path our people are destined to take in their Aryan awakening. The path to our destiny begins with the *truth* and with *you*

We speak the truth because it is in our genes to do so.

We speak the truth for our survival. For our freedom. For our way to the heavens.

As George Orwell said, *In a world of deceit, telling the truth is a revolutionary act.*

Let the revolution begin.

END.

ENDNOTES

[1] Mason, David P. (1975). *Massacre at Fort Mims: Red Eagle Was There*. Mobile, Alabama: Greenbeery.
[2] Halbert, H. S. & Ball, T. H. (1995). *The Creek War of 1813 and 1814*. Originally published in 1895. Birmingham: University of Alabama Press.
[3] Carson, Rachel. (1962). *Silent Spring*. Greenwich, Connecticut: Fawcett.
[4] Montagu, Ashley. (1945). *Man's Most Dangerous Myth: The Fallacy Of Race*. New York: Columbia University Press.
[5] Griffin, John Howard. (1961). *Black Like Me*. Boston: Houghton Mifflin.
[6] Lee, Harper. (1960). *To Kill a Mockingbird*. Philadelphia: Lippincott.
[7] Shuey, A. M. (1958/1966). *The Testing Of Negro Intelligence*. Lynchburg, Virginia: Bell Edition, New York: Social Science Press.
[8] Roosevelt, Theodore. (1996). *Theodore Roosevelt on Race, Riots, Immigration, and Crime*. Washington, DC: Scott-Townsend. (PO Box 34070, NW Washington, DC 20043.
[9] Putnam, C. (1961). *Race And Reason: A Yankee View*. Washington: Public Affairs Press.
[10] Jefferson, Thomas. (1829). *Autobiography*, First published in 1829 and later by an Act of Congress in 1853. p.1.
[11] Orwell, G. (1982). *1984*. New York: Harcourt Brace Jovanovich.
[12] Lincoln, A. (1953-55). *Collected Works*. The Abraham Lincoln Assoc. Springfield, Illinois. Roy P.Basler, Editor; Marion New Brunswick, N.J.: Rutgers University Press. Contents: Vol. 1. 1824-1848.--2. 1848-1858.--3. 1858-1860.--4. 1860-1861.--5. 1861-1862.--6. 1862-1863.--7. 1863-1864.--8. 1864-1865. — Index.
[13] Lincoln, A. (1953-55). *Collected Works*.
[14] Lincoln, A. (1953-55). *Collected Works*.
[15] From the Proclamation Issued from President Lincoln On Sept. 22, 1862, attested by William H. Seward, Secretary Of State (U.S. Statutes At Large, Vol 12, 36th Congress. p.267).
[16] Lincoln, A. (1953-55). *Collected Works*.
[17] Lincoln, A. (1953-55). *Collected Works*.
[18] Bilbo, Sen. Theodore G. *Take Your Choice*. Poplarville, Mississippi: Dream House Publishing Co. p.72. Quoting The Peace Movement of Ethiopia.
[19] Putnam, Carleton (1967). *Race and Reason*.
[20] *Random House Websters Unabridged Electronic Dictionary*. (1996). New York: Random House.
[21] Boring, E. G. (1923). Intelligence As The Tests Test It. *The New Republic*. June 6. p.35-37.
[22] Jensen, A. R. (1980). *Bias In Mental Testing*. New York: Free Press.
[23] Neisser, Ulrich. (1996). Intelligence: Knowns And Unknowns. Report By The American Psychological Association Committee. *American Psychologist*. Vol. 51. p.7-101.
[24] Jensen, A. (1998). *The "g "Factor: The Science Of Mental Ability*. Connecticut: Praeger, Westport. p.77.
[25] Duncan, O., Featherman, D. & Duncan, B. (1979). *Socio-Economic Background and Achievement*. New York: Seminar Press.
[26] McCall, R. M. (1977). Childhood Predictors of Adult Educational and Occupational Status. *Science*. Vol. 197. p.14.
[27] Herrnstein, R. & Murray, C. (1994). *The Bell Curve: Intelligence And Class Structure In American Life*. New York: Simon & Schuster.

[28] Jencks, C. (1979). *Who Gets Ahead? The Determinants Of Economic Success In America*. New York: Basic Books.
[29] Hunter, J. E. (1986). Cognitive Ability, Cognitive Aptitudes, Job Knowledge, And Job Performance. *Journal Of Vocational Behavior*. December. p.40-362.
[30] Dawis, R. V. (1996). Vocational Psychology, Vocational Adjustment, And The Workforce: Some Familiar And Unanticipated Consequences. *Psychology, Public Policy, And Law*. Vol. 2. p.229-248.
[31] Gordon, R. A. (1997). Everyday Life As An Intelligence Test: Effects Of Intelligence And Intelligence Context. *Intelligence*. Vol. 24. p.3-320.
[32] Gottfredson, L. S. (1997). Why *g* Matters: The Complexity Of Everyday Life. *Intelligence*. Vol. 24. p.79-132.
[33] Murray, C. (1998). *Income Inequality And IQ*. Washington, DC: The AEI Press.
[34] Gottfredson, L. S. (1997). Why g Matters: The Complexity Of Everyday Life. *Intelligence*. Vol. 24. p.90, 79-132.
[35] U.S. Department Of Defense, Office Of The Assistant Secretary (Force Management And Personnel).(1989). Joint-Service Efforts To Link Enlistment Standards To Job Performance: Recruit Quality And Military Readiness. Report To The House Committee On Appropriations.
[36] O'Toole, B.J. (1990). Intelligence and Behavior and Motor Vehicle Accident Mortality. *Accident Analysis And Prevention*. Vol. 22. p.11-221.
[37] O'Toole, B.J. (1990). Intelligence And Behavior And Motor Vehicle Accident Mortality. p.220.
[38] *The Odyssey (IV, 60)*.
[39] Bennett, Jonathan Francis. (1971). *Locke, Berkeley, Hume: Central Themes*. Oxford: Clarendon Press.
[40] Galton, F. (1869). *Hereditary Genius*. London: Macmillan.
[41] *Buck vs. Bell*. (1927). 274 U.S. p.201-208.
[42] Berg, R.L. (1988). *Acquired Traits: Memoirs Of A Geneticist From The Soviet Union*. D. Lowe, trans. New York: Viking Penguin.
[43] Medvedev, Z. A. (1971). *The Rise And Fall Of T. D. Lysenko*. I. M. Lerner, trans. Garden City, New York: Anchor-Doubleday.
[44] Soyfer, V N. (1994). *Lysenko And The Tragedy Of Soviet Science*. L. Gruliow & R. Gruliow, trans. New Brunswick, New Jersey: Rutgers University Press.
[45] Whitney, G. (1998). The Vernalization Of Hillary's America. *Chronicles*. Vol. 22, #2. p.6-47.
[46] Farber, S. (1981). *Identical Twins Reared Apart: A Reanalysis*. New York: Basic Books.
[47] Bouchard, T. (1981). Familial Studies Of Intelligence: A Review. *Science* Vol. 212. p.55-1059.
[48] Snyderman, M. & Rothman, S. (1988). *The IQ Controversy: The Media And Public Policy*. New Brunswick, New Jersey: Transaction Books.
[49] Jensen, A. R. (1998). *The g Factor: The Science Of Mental Ability*. Westport, Connecticut: Praeger.
[50] Avery, R. D. *Et. Al*.(With 51 co-authors). (1994). Mainstream Science On Intelligence. *The Wall Street Journal*. December 13. p.A-18.
[51] Gottfredson, L. S. (1997). Editorial: Mainstream Science On Intelligence: An Editorial With 52 Signatories, History, and Bibliography. *Intelligence*. Vol. 24. p.3-23.
[52] Coren, S. (1994). *The Intelligence Of Dogs*. New York: Free Press.
[53] Glees, P.(1988). *The Human Brain*. Cambridge University Press.
[54] Gould, S. J. (1996). The Mismeasure Of Man. *Journal Of Personality and Individual Differences*. Vol. 23. p.69-180.
[55] Rushton, J. P.(1997). Special Review: Race, Intelligence, and the Brain: The Errors And Omissions Of The 'Revised' Ad. Of S. J. Gould's, The Mismeasure Of Man. *Journal Of Personality And Individual Differences*. p.69-180

56 Willerman, Et Al. *In Vivo* Brain Size And Intelligence. (1991). *Intelligence*. Vol. 15. p.23-228.
57 Chorney, M.J., Chorney, K., Seese, N., Owen, M.J., Daniels, J., McGuffin, P., Thompson, L.A., Detterman, D.K., Benbow, C., Lubinski, D., Eley, T., & Plomin, R. (1998). A Quantitative Trait Locus Associated With Cognitive Ability In Children. *Psychological Science*. Vol 9. p. 59-166.
58 Chorney, M.J., *Psychological Science*. Vol 9. p. 59-166.
59 Shuey, A. M. (1958/1966). *The Testing Of Negro Intelligence*. Lynchburg, Virginia: Bell Edition, New York: Social Science Press.
60 Shuey, A. (1966). The Testing Of Negro Intelligence. New York; Social Science Press.
61 *Larry P. v. Wilson Riles* (1979). No. C-71-2270 Rfp.United States District Court For The Northern District Of California., October 16. 495 F. Supp. 26.
62 Jensen, A. R. (1998). *The g Factor: The Science Of Mental Ability*. Westport, Connecticut: Praeger.
63 Gottfredson, L. S. (1997). Why *g* Matters: The Complexity Of Everyday Life. *Intelligence*. Vol. 24, #1. p.9-132.
64 Herrnstein, R. J. & Murray, C. (1994). *The Bell Curve*. New York: Free Press.
65 Jensen, A. R. (1998). *The g Factor: The Science Of Mental Ability*. Westport Connecticut: Praeger.
66 Levin, M. (1997). *Why Race Matters: Race Differences and What They Mean*. Westport Connecticut: Praeger.
67 Herrnstein, R. J. & Murray, C. (1994). *The Bell Curve*. New York: Free Press.
68 *Newsweek*. (1994). IQ: Is It Destiny? October 24. p.4.
69 Jensen, A. R. (1985). The Nature Of The Black-White Difference on Various Psychometric Tests: Spearman's Hypothesis. *Behavioral And Brain Sciences*. Vol. 8 p.193-219.
70 Jensen, A. R. (1987). Further Evidence for Spearman's Hypothesis Concerning the Black-White Differences on Psychometric Tests. *Behavioral And Brain Sciences*. Vol. 10. p.12-519.
71 Jensen, A. R. (1992). Spearman's Hypothesis: Methodology And Evidence. *Multivariate Behavioral Research*. Vol. 27. p.25-234.
72 Jensen, A. R. (1998). *The G Factor: The Science Of Mental Ability*. Westport Connecticut: Praeger.
73 Jensen (1980). *Straight Talk About Mental Tests And Bias In Mental Testing*. New York: Free Press. p.470.
74 Jensen, A. R. (1980). *Bias In Mental Testing*. New York: Free Press.
75 Jensen, A.R. (1993). Spearman's Hypothesis Tested with Chronometric Information Processing Tasks. *Intelligence*. Vol. 17. p.7-77.
76 Jensen, A.R. & Whang, P.A. (1993). Reaction Times and Intelligence. *Journal Of Biosocial Science*. Vol. 25. p.97-410.
77 Wigdor & Garner, eds. (1982). *Ability Testing: Uses, Consequences, And Controversies*. Washington, DC: National Academy Press. p.7.
78 Scarr, S. & Weinberg, R. A. (1976). IQ Test Performance of Black Children Adopted By White Families.
79 College Board. (1992). *Profile of SAT and Achievement Test Takers*. New York.
80 Seligman, D. (1992). *A Question Of Intelligence: The IQ Debate In America*. New York: Carol Publishing. p.60
81 Jensen, A. R. (1980). *Bias In Mental Testing*. New York: Free Press.
82 Jensen, A. R.. (1998). *The g Factor: The Science Of Mental Ability*. Westport Connecticut: Praeger.
83 Palmquist, Matt. (1998). *University Wire*. May 5.
84 Spilka, S. (1996). Letter Of May 9 from Wiley Manager of Corporate Communications.
85 Spitz, H. (1986). *The Raising Of Intelligence*. Hillsdale, NJ: Erlbaum.
86 Currie J. & Thomas D. (1995). Does Head Start Make a Difference? *American Economic Review*. June. p.41-364.

[87] Ferguson, Jr., G. O. (1916). The Psychology Of The Negro. *Archives Of Psychology*. No. 36. April.

[88] Scarr, S. & Weinberg R. A. (1976). IQ Test Performance of Black Children Adopted By White Families. *American Psychologist*. Vol. 31. p.26-739.

[89] Weinberg, R. A., Scarr, S., & Waldman, I. D. (1992). The Minnesota Transracial Adoption Study: A Follow-Up of IQ Test Performance at Adolescence. *Intelligence*. Vol. 16. p.17-135.

[90] Lynn, R. (1994). Reinterpretations Of The Minnesota Transracial Adoption Study. *Intelligence* Vol. 19. p.1-27.

[91] Levin, M. (1994). Comment on The Minnesota Transracial Adoption Study. *Intelligence*. Vol. 19. p.3-20.

[92] Reed, T. E. (1969). Caucasian Genes in American Negroes. *Science*. Vol. 165. p.62-768.

[93] Reed, T.E. Letters. *Science*. Vol. 165. p.353.

[94] Lynn, R. (1991). Race Differences in Intelligence. *Mankind Quarterly*. Vol. 31. p54-296.

[95] Zindi. (1994). Differences In Psychometric Performance. *The Psychologist*. Vol. 7. p.49-552.

[96] Owen. (1992). The Suitability of Raven Standard Progressive Matrices for Various Groups in South Africa: *Personality and Individual Differences*. Vol. 13. p.49-159.

[97] Lynn R. (1991). Race Differences In Intelligence: A Global Perspective. *Mankind Quarterly*. Vol. 31. p.55-296.

[98] Owen, K (1992). The Suitability of Raven's Standard Progressive Matrices for Various Groups in South Africa. Personality And Individual Differences. Vol. 13. p.49-159.

[99] Zindi, F. (1994). Differences In Performance. *The Psychologist*. Vol 7. p.49-552.

[100] Lynn, R. (1994). The Intelligence of Ethiopian Immigrant and Israeli Adolescents. *International Journal Of Psychology*. Vol. 29. p.5-56.

[101] *The New York Times*. (1972). July 17. p.4.

[102] Garber, H. L. (1988). *The Milwaukee Project: Preventing Mental Retardation In Children At Risk*.

[103] Jensen, A. R. (1989). Washington DC: American Association on Mental Retardation. Raising IQ Without Increasing G? A Review Of *The Milwaukee Project: Preventing Mental Retardation In Children At Risk* By H. L. Garber. *Developmental Review*. 9. p. 34-258.

[104] Spitz, H. H. (1986). *The Raising of Intelligence: A Selected History of Attempts to Raise Retarded Intelligence*. Hillsdale, New Jersey: Erlbaum.

[105] Soyfer, V. N. (1994). *Lysenko and the Tragedy of Soviet Science* (L. Gruliow & R. Gruliow, trans.). New Brunswick, New Jersey: Rutgers University Press.

[106] Whitney, G. (1998). The Vernalization Of Hillary's America. *Chronicles*. Vol. 22, #2, p.6-47.

[107] Spitz, H. H. (1989). Raising Of Intelligence. Also See: *Chicago Tribune*.(1989). Chicago Schools Get an Education in Muckraking. May 8.

[108] Seligman, D. (1992). *A Question Of Intelligence: The IQ Debate In America*. p.51

[109] Putnam, Carleton (1967). *Race and Reason*. Howard Allen edition (1980). (PO Box 76, Cape Canaveral, FL 32929)

[110] Random House Webster's Electronic Dictionary (1992). (College Edition). New York: Random House.

[111] Putnam, Carleton (1967). *Race and Reason*. Howard Allen edition (1980). (PO Box 76, Cape Canaveral, FL 32929)

[112] Furedy, J. J. (1997). The Decline of the *Eppur Si Muove* Spirit in North American Science: Professional Organizations and PC Pressures. *The Mankind Quarterly*. Vol. 38. p.5-66.

[113] Pearson, R. (1997). *Race, Intelligence And Bias In Academe*. 2nd Ed. Washington, DC: Scott-Townsend.

Endnotes 679

114 Rushton, J. P.(1994). The Equalitarian Dogma Revisited. *Intelligence*. Vol. 19. p.63-280.
115 Whitney, G. (1995). Ideology And Censorship In Behavior Genetics. *The Mankind Quarterly*. Vol. 35. p.327-342.
116 Whitney, G. (1997). Raymond B. Cattell And The Fourth Inquisition. *The Mankind Quarterly*. Vol. 38. p.9-125.
117 *Racism*. Random House Webster's Electronic Dictionary. (1992). (College Edition.). New York: Random House.
118 Snyderman, M. & Rothman, S. (1988). *The IQ Controversy: The Media And Public Policy*. New Brunswick, New Jersey: Transaction Books.
119 Jensen, A. R. (1998). *The g Factor: The Science Of Mental Ability*. Westport Connecticut: Praeger.
120 Avery, R. D. *Et. Al.*(With 51 co-authors). (1994). Mainstream Science On Intelligence. *The Wall Street Journal*. December 13. p.A-18.
121 Gottfredson, L. S. (1997). Editorial: Mainstream Science On Intelligence: An Editorial With 52 Signatories, History, And Bibliography. *Intelligence*. Vol. 24. p.3-23.
122 Herrnstein, R. J. & Murray, C. (1994). *The Bell Curve: Intelligence And Class Structure In American Life*. New York: Free Press.
123 Jensen, A. R. (1998). *The g Factor: The Science Of Mental Ability*. Westport, Connecticut: Praeger.
124 Levin, M. (1997). *Why Race Matters: Race Differences And What They Mean*. Westport Connecticut: Praeger.
125 Rowe, D. C. (1994). *The Limits of Family Influence*. New York: Guilford Press.
126 Rowe, D. C. & Cleveland, H. H. (1996). Academic Achievement In Blacks And Whites: Are The Developmental Processes Similar? *Intelligence*. Vol. 23. p.5-228.
127 Rushton, J. P.(1995). *Race, Evolution, and Behavior*. New Brunswick, New Jersey: Transaction.
128 Shuey, A. M. (1966). *The Testing Of Negro Intelligence* (2nd Ed.). New York: Social Science Press.
129 Rushton, J. P.(1995). *Race, Evolution, And Behavior*. New Brunswick, New Jersey: Transaction.
130 Gould, Stephen Jay. (1981). *The Mismeasure of Man*. New York: Norton
131 Rushton, J. P.(1997). Special Review: Race, Intelligence, and the Brain: The Errors and Omissions of The "Revised" Edition Of S. J. Gould's *The Mismeasure Of Man* (1996).
132 *Personality And Individual Differences*. Vol. 23. p.169-180.
133 Carothers, J. C. (1972). The Mind of Man in Africa. London: Tom Stacey Ltd.
134 Ho, K.C., Roessmann, U., Hause, L., And Monroe, G. (1981). Newborn Brain Weight In Relation To Maturity, Sex, And Race. *Annals Of Neurology*. Vol. 10. p.43-246.
135 Broman, S. H., Nichols, P.L., Shaughnessy, P., & Kennedy, W. (1987). *Retardation In Young Children*. Hillsdale, New Jersey: Erlbaum.
136 Rushton, J. P.& Osborne, R. T. (1995). Genetic and Environmental Contributions to Cranial Capacity Estimated in Black and White Adolescents. *Intelligence*. Vol. 20. p.13.
137 Darwin, C. (1874). *The Descent Of Man*, 2nd Edition. London: John Murray. p.1-82.
138 Whitney, G. (1996). The Return of Racial Science. *Contemporary Psychology*. Vol. 41. p.189-1191.
139 Rushton, J. P.& Ankney, C. D. (1996). Brain Size and Cognitive Ability: Correlations with Age, Sex, Social Class and Race. *Psychonomic Bulletin And Review*. Vol. 3. p.21-36.
140 Jensen, A. & Johnson, F. (1994). Race and Sex Differences in Head Size And IQ. *Intelligence*. p.9-333.
141 Connolly, C.J. (1950). *The External Morphology of The Primate Brain*. Springfield, Illinois.
142 *One Flew Over The Cuckoo's Nest* (1975). Milos Forman. United Artists Cinema.

[143] *Frances* (1982). Graeme Clifford. Brooks Films.
[144] Halstead, Ward C. (1947). *Brains And Intelligence.* Chicago. p.49.
[145] Connolly, C.J. (1950). *The External Morphology of The Primate Brain.*
[146] Plomin, R., Defries, J. C., McClearn, G. E., & Rutter, M. (1997). *Behavioral Genetics (3rd. Ed.).* New York: W. H. Freeman.
[147] Sherman, S. L., Defries, J. C., Gottesman, I. I., Loehlin, J. C., Meyer, J. M., Pelias, M. Z., Rice, J., & Waldman, I. (1997). Behavioral Genetics '97: ASHG Statement. Recent Developments In Human Behavioral Genetics: Past Accomplishments And Future Directions. *American Journal Of Human Genetics.* p.60. p.265-1275.
[148] Rector, R. (1991). Food Fight. *Policy Review* Vol. 58. p.1-46
[149] Banfield E. (1974). *The Unheavenly City Revisited.* Boston, Massachusetts: Little Brown.
[150] Rector R. & McLaughlin M. N.D. (1992). *A Conservative's Guide To State Level Welfare Reform.* Washington, DC: The Heritage Foundation.
[151] Banfield, E. (1974). *The Unheavenly City Revisited.* Boston: Little Brown.
[152] Bayley, N. (1995). Comparisons Of Mental And Motor Test Scores For Ages 1-15 Months By Sex, Birth Order, Race, Geographical Location, and Education Of Parents." *Child Development.* Vol. 36. p.379-477.
[153] Rushton, J. P.(1995). *Race And Crime: An International Dilemma. Society.* p.2, 37-41.
[154] Raine, Adrian. (1993). *The Psychopathology of Crime: Criminal Behavior as a Clinical Disorder.* San Diego: Academic Press.
[155] Raine, Adrian, Editor (1997). *Biosocial Bases of Violence.* New York: Plenum Press.
[156] Raine, A., Bushbaum, M.,& LaCasse, L. (1997). *Journal Of Biological Psychiatry* Vol. 42. September 15. p.95-508
[157] Hamilton, W. D. (1964). The Genetical Theory of Social Behaviour, I, Ii. *Journal Of Theoretical Biology* 7:1. p.2.
[158] Plomin, R. Lichtenstein, P., Pedersen, N. McCleran, G. E., & Nesselroade, J.R. (1990). *Behavioral Genetics: A Primer* (2nd ed.). San Francisco: Freeman.
[159] Rushton, P.P., Fulker, D.W., Neale, M.C., Nias, D.K.B., & Eysenek, H.J. (1986). Altruism and Aggression: The heritability of individual differences. *Journal of Personality and Social Psychology.* 50. p. 1192-98.
[160] Tellegen, A., Lykken, D.T., Bouchard, T.J., Jr. Wilcox, K.J., Segal, N.L., &Rich, S. (1988). Personality Differences of Twins Reared Apart and Together. *Journal of Personality and Social Psychology,* 54. p. 1031-039
[161] Floderus-Mnyrhed, B., Pederson, & Rasmuson,J. (1980). Assessment of Heritibility for Personality Based on a Short Form of the Eysenek Personality Inventory: A Study of 12,898 Twin Pairs. *Behavioral Genetics,* 10, p. 153-63.
[162] Keller, L.M., Bouchard, T.J.,Fr., Arvey, R.D., Segal, N.L. & Dawis R.V. (1992). Work Values: Benetic and Environmental Influences. *Journal of Applied Psychology.* 77. p. 79.-88.
[163] Bouchard, T.J., Jr., (1984). *Twins Reared Together and Apart: What They Tell Us about Human Diversity* in S.W. Fox (Ed.), Individuality and Determinism. New York: Plenum.
[164] Dreger R. & Miller, K. (1960). Comparative Psychological Studies of Negroes and Whites in the United States. *Psychological Bulletin* Vol. 57. p.61-402.
[165] Kochman, T. (1983). *Black And White Styles In Conflict.* Chicago: University Of Chicago Press. p.1-34, 106-110.
[166] Gynther M. (1972). White Norms And Black MMPI's: A Prescription For Discrimination. *Psychological Bulletin* Vol. 78. p.86-402.
[167] Mischel, W. (1961). Preference for Delayed Reinforcement: An Experimental Study of Cultural Observation. *Journal Of Abnormal And Social Psychology* Vol. 62:1. p.7.
[168] Banfield, E. (1970). *The Unheavenly City: The Nature And Future Of Our Urban Crisis.* Boston: Little Brown.

Endnotes 681

[169] Banfield, E. (1974). *The Unheavenly City Revisited. Inability To Defer Gratification, Extreme Present Orientation.* Boston, Little Brown.
[170] Ross, R., Bernstein, L. Judd, H. Hanish, R. Pike, M. And Henderson, B. (1986). Serum Testosterone Levels In Healthy Young Black And White Men. *Journal Of The National Cancer Institute.* Vol. 76. p.5-48.
[171] Rushton, J. Philippe. (1995). Race And Crime: An International Dilemma. *Society.* 32. p.7-41
[172] Draper, P. (1989). African Marriage Systems: Perspectives From Evolutionary Ecology. *Ethology And Sociobiology.* 10. p.45-169.
[173] Montagu, Ashley. (1945). *Man's Most Dangerous Myth: The Fallacy Of Race.* New York: Columbia University Press.
[174] Diamond, J. (1994). Race Without Color. *Discover Mag.* November.
[175] Cavalli-Sforza L., Menozzi, P. & Piazza (1994). *The History And Geography Of Human Genes.* Princeton, NJ: Princeton University Press.
[176] Caccone, A. & Powell, J. (1989). DNA Divergence Among Hominoids. *Evolution* 43. p. 25-942.
[177] Gibbons A. (1990). Our Chimp Cousins Get That Much Closer. *Science.* 250. p. 76.
[178] Gibbons, A. (1995). Out Of Africa At Last? *Science.* 267. p. 272-1273.
[179] J. Phillippe Rushton, (1996). *Race Is A Biological Concept.*
[180] J. Phillippe Rushton, (1996). *Race Is A Biological Concept.*
[181] Lynn, R. (1991). The Evolution Of Racial Differences In Intelligence. *Mankind Quarterly.* 31. p. 9-121.
[182] Krantz, G. S. (1980). *Climatic Races And Descent Groups.* North Quincy: Christopher Publishing House.
[183] Baker, J. R. (1974). *Race.* Oxford: Oxford University Press.
[184] Robins, A. H. (1991). *Biological Perspectives On Human Pigmentation.* Cambridge: Cambridge University Press.
[185] Coon, C. S. (1965). *The Living Races Of Man.* New York: Alfred A. Knopf.
[186] Coon, C. S. (1967). *Story Of Man.* Harmondsworth: Penguin.
[187] Coon, C. S. (1962). *Origin Of The Races.* Knopf.
[188] Coon, C. S. (1972). *The Races Of Europe.* Westport, CT: Greenwood Press.
[189] Coon, C. S. (1971). *The Hunting Peoples.* Boston: Little Brown.
[190] Coon, C. S. (1982). *Racial Adaptation.* Chicago: Nelson-Hall.
[191] Lee, R.B. & DeVore, I.. (1968). *Man The Hunter,* Chicago: Aldine.
[192] Nelson, R.K (1969). *Hunters Of The Northern Ice.* Chicago: University Of Chicago Press.
[193] Miller, E. (1994). Paternal Provisioning Versus Mate Seeking In Human Populations. *Personality And Individual Differences.* 17:2. p. 27-255.
[194] Alexander, R.D., Hoogland, J.L. (1979). Sexual Dimorphism And Breeding Systems In Pinnipeds, Ungulates, Primates, And Humans. Chagnon, N. & Irons, W., editors. *Evolutionary Biology And Human Social Behavior.* North Scituate, MA: Duxbury Press. p. 02-532.
[195] Miller, E. (1993). Could "R" Selection Account For The African Personality And Life Cycle? *Personality And Individual Differences.* Dec. 15:6, p. 65-676.
[196] Baker, J. (1974). *Race.* New York: Oxford University Press.
[197] Ama, Simonau, Boulay, Serrese, Theriault & Bouchard (1986). Skeletal Muscle Characteristics In Sedentary Black And Caucasian Males. *Journal Of Applied Physiology.* 61.
[198] Malina R. M. (1988). Racial/Ethnic Variation In The Motor Development And Performance Of American Children. *Canadian Journal Of Sports Science.* 13. p. 36-143.
[199] Trivers, Robert (1986). *Social Evolution.* Benjamin.
[200] Buss, David (1992). *The Evolution Of Desire.* Basic.
[201] Symons, Donald (1979). *The Evolution Of Human Sexuality.* Oxford.

[202] Detroit News Wire Service (1991). U.S. Syphilis Cases At Highest Level Since '49. *Detroit News*. May 17.
[203] Reid, Alexander (1990). Rate Of Illness From Sex Rises In Teenagers. *Boston Globe*. April 11. p. .
[204] Stolberg, Sheryl Gay (1998). Epidemic Of Silence: A Special Report. Eyes Shut, Black America Is Being Ravaged By Aids. *New York Times*. June 29. p.
[205] Koh, Eun Lee (1998). Survey Says Hispanics See Aids As Major Threat To Public Health. *San Antonio Express-News*. May 2. 10A.
[206] Stolberg, Sheryl Gay (1998). Epidemic Of Silence: A Special Report. Eyes Shut, Black America Is Being Ravaged By Aids.
[207] Miller, E. (1995). Environmental Variability Selects For Large Families Only In Special Circumstances: Another Objection To Differential K Theory. *Personality And Individual Differences*. Dec. 19:6. p. 03-918.
[208] Miller, E. (1991). Climate And Intelligence, *Mankind Quarterly*. Fall/Winter. Vol. XXXII No. 1-2, p. 27-132. .
[209] Carruth, W.H. *Each In His Own Tongue*.
[210] Jerison, Herold. (1973). *Evolution Of The Brain And Intelligence*. Academic Press.
[211] Brooke, James. (1994). Romantic Rio Has Become The Sickest City In Brazil. *New York Times News Service* published in the New Orleans *Times-Picayune* Oct.30 A-27.
[212] Pendell, E. (1967). *Sex Versus Civilization*. Los Angeles: Noontide Press.
[213] Pendell, E. (1977). Why Civilizations Self-Destruct. Cape Canaveral, FL: Howard Allen.
[214] Hart, M. (1992). *The 100: A Ranking Of The Most Influential Persons In History*. New York: Citadel.
[215] Asimov, I. (1989). *Chronicle Of Science And Discovery*. London, Grafton Books.
[216] Herrnstein, R. & Murray, C. (1994). *The Bell Curve*. Simon & Schuster.
[217] Darnton, J. (1994). A Lost Decade Drains Africa's Vitality. *New York Times*. Jun. 20. p.A1-A9.
[218] *Human Events*. May 26. 1995. p. 8.
[219] Diamond, Jared (1998). Guns, Germs, And Steel. Norton.
[220] Wells, H. G. (1971). *The Outline Of History. Being A Plain History Of Life And Mankind*. Garden City, .NY: Doubleday.
[221] De Gobineau. (1967). *Inequality Of The Races*. Los Angeles, California. The Noontide Press.
[222] Darwin, C. (1859/1972). *The Origin Of Species By Means Of Natural Selection, Or The Preservation Of Favored Races In The Struggle For Life*. New York: E.P. Dutton.
[223] Prichard, H. (1971). *Where Black Rules White: A Journey Across And About Hayti*. Free Port, New York: Books For Libraries Press.
[224] Snyderman, M. & Rothman, S. (1988). *The IQ Controversy: The Media And Public Policy*. New Brunswick, NJ: Transaction Books.
[225] Putnam, C. (1967). *Race And Reality*.
[226] Roger Pearson (1992). *Schockley On Eugenics and Race*. Washington, DC: Scott-Townsend Publishers.
[227] Jensen, A. (1980). *Straight Talk About Mental Tests*. New York: Free Press.
[228] Ed. Dudley Randall. (1988). *The Black Poets* p. 26. (Quoted In *The Other Side Of Racism*. Anne Wortham. Columbus, OH: Ohio University Press, 1981, p. 57.)
[229] Herrnstein, Richard J. & Murray, Charles (1994). *The Bell Curve: Intelligence And Class Structure In American Life*. New York: Free Press.
[230] Jaynes, G. & Williams, R. (1989). *A Common Destiny: Blacks In American Society*. Washington, DC: National Academy Press. p. 92, 278.
[231] Hacker, A. (1992). *Two Nations*. New York: Scribners and Sons. p. 72.
[232] Rubinstein, D. (1994). Cut Cultural Root Of Rising Crime. *Insight*. Aug. 8. p. 8-20.

ENDNOTES 683

[233] Jaynes, G. & Williams, R. (1989). *A Common Destiny: Blacks In American Society.* 295.
[234] Rushton J. P.(1988). Race Differences In Behavior: A Review And Evolutionary Analysis. *Personality And Individual Differences.* 9. p. 009-1024.
[235] Hacker A. (1992). *Two Nations.* Scribners and Sons.
[236] Gest, T. (1995). A Shocking Look At Blacks And Crime. *U.S. News And World Report.* Oct 16. p. 3-54.
[237] Journal Of The American Medical Association Issue On Firearms And Violence. (1996). Jun. 12.
[238] Levin, M. (1998). *Why Race Matters.* Westport, CT: Praeger.
[239] Rushton, J. P.(1995). Race And Crime: An International Dilemma. *Society.* 32. p. 7-41.
[240] August 26, (1997). *Washington Post.*
[241] Adam Walinsky in the July 1995 issue of *Atlantic Monthly.*
[242] Richter, L & Lichter, R. (1983). *Prime Time Crime.* Washington, DC: The Media Institute. p. 3.
[243] Whittaker, K. (1990). *Black Victims.* Washington, DC: Bureau Of Justice Statistics, Office Of Justice Programs, Department Of Justice. Tables 1, 16.
[244] FBI Oct. (1993). *Uniform Crime Reports.*
[245] *American Enterprise.* (1995). Crime And Race. May/June. Compiled from Justice Department data from 1991.
[246] *American Enterprise.* (1995). Crime And Race May/June Issue.
[247] U.S. Department Of Justice, *Sourcebook Of Criminal Justice Statistics 1991* (1992). Washington, DC: U.S. Government Printing Office.
[248] Lafree, G. D. (1982). Male Power And Female Victimization: Toward A Theory Of Interracial Rape. *American Journal Of Sociology.* Vol. 88, No.2. Sept.
[249] Wilbanks, W. (1990). Frequency And Nature Of Interracial Crimes. *Justice Professional.* Nov. 7 Data From The Department Of Justice, Criminal Victimization In The United States.
[250] FBI Oct. (1993). *Uniform Crime Reports.*
[251] Hacker, A. (1992). *Two Nations.* Scribners And Sons. p. 81.
[252] Wilson, J. & Herrnstein, R. (1985). *Crime And Human Nature.* New York: Simon And Schuster. p. 62.
[253] Thompson, T. (1989). Blacks Sent To Jail More Than Whites For The Same Crime. *Atlanta Journal And Constitution.* Apr. 30. p. A.
[254] Levin, M. (1998). *Why Race Matters.* Westport, CT: Praeger. 247.
[255] Reynolds, G. Ed. (1996). *Race And The Criminal Justice System.* Washington, DC: Center For Equal Opportunity Press. "When Race Trumps Truth In The Courtroom." By M. Weiss And K. Zinmeister. p. 7-64.
[256] Cleaver, E. (1967). *Soul On Ice.* New York: McGraw-Hill. p. 1.
[257] Cleaver, E. (1967). *Soul On Ice.*
[258] *New York Times Book Review.* Quoted from the jacket of published edition.
[259] Paul Sheehan (1995). The Race War Of Black Against White. *Sydney Morning Herald.* May 20
[260] Harry Ploski And James Williams, Eds.(1983). *Negro Almanac.* Bronxville, .NY: Bellwether Publishing 348).
[261] Wilbanks, W. (1987). *The Myth Of A Racist Criminal Justice System.* Monterey, CA: Brooks/Cole Publishing Company. p. 35.
[262] Silberman, C. (1978). *Criminal Violence, Criminal Justice.* New York: Random House. p. 78,118.
[263] Associated Press (1989). School Costs Up But Not Grades, Report Laments. *Omaha World Herald.* Aug. 24. p. 6.
[264] *The Economist* (1989). Willingly To School. Oct. 7.
[265] Sanchez, R. (1989). D.C. Dropouts Quit Even Earlier, Study Finds. *Washington Post.* Jan. 12.

266 Feder, D. (1991). Schools Have Flunked Out. *Orange County Register*. Sept. 9. p.B9.
267 Hood, J. (1990). Money Isn't Everything. *The Wall Street Journal*. Feb. 9. p.A10.
268 *Chronicles*. (1990). Restoring Family Autonomy In Education. Oct. p. 7.
269 Zinsmeister, K. (1990). Growing Up Scared. *The Atlantic*. Jun. p. 1.
270 Hartocollis, A. (1992). School Violence Felt Nationwide. *Newsday*. New York. Feb. 28. p. 7.
271 *New York Times*. (1991). Crime Draws Some Of The Lines In Blueprints For Schools. Mar. 6. p.B8.
272 *The Economist*. (1990). Pick Your Number. Feb. 17. p. 7.
273 Feder, D. (1991). Schools Have Flunked Out. *Orange County Register*. Sept. 9. p.B9.
274 Hood, J. (1990). Money Isn't Everything. *Wall Street Journal*. Feb. 9. A10.
275 West, E. (1990). Restoring Family Autonomy In Education. *Chronicles*. Oct. Edition. p. 7.
276 *Detroit News*. (1992). Aids, Homicides Increase Gap In Black White Life Expectancy. Jan. 8. p. A.
277 Stout, H. (1991). Life Expectancy Of U.S. Blacks Declined In 1988. *Wall Street Journal*. April 9. p.B1.
278 *Detroit News Wire Service*. (1991). U.S. Syphilis Cases At Highest Level Since '49. *Detroit News*. May 17.
279 *Rocky Mountain News*. (1997). Dick Feagler. Scripps Howard News Service. p. 1-20.
280 Levin, Michael. (1997). *Why Race Matters*. Westport: CT: Praeger. p. 09.
281 Morgan, J. (1991). Co-Op Sanctioned For Ads Without Blacks. *Newsday*. Nov. 21.
282 Pogrebin, R. (1991). Suit Against The Times: A Model Dilemma. *New York Observer*. Feb. 11. p. .
283 Rosen, D. (1991). Poverty Rate For Hispanic Children Rises 29% In 1980's. *Orange County (Calif.). Register*. Aug. 27. p.A15.
284 *Monthly Vital Statistics Report* (1991). National Center For Health Statistics. 40:8(S). Dec. 12.
285 Fogel, Robert W. & Engerman, Stanley (1974). *Time On The Cross: The Economics Of American Negro Slavery*. Boston: Little, Brown
286 McAlister, B. (1989). To Be Young Black And Male. *Washington Post*. Dec.28. p. A.
287 Section 703(J) Of Title VII Of The Civil Rights Act.
288 Snow, E. (1988). The Grove City Horror Show. *Chronicles*. Nov. p. 1.
289 Detlefsen, R. (1991). *Civil Rights Under Reagan*. San Francisco: ICS Press.
290 Taylor, J. (1992). *Paved With Good Intentions*. New York: Carroll & Graf. p. 38
291 Freeman, R. (1976). *Black Elite*. New York: McGraw-Hill. Chap. .
292 National Research Council. *A Common Destiny*. p. 47.
293 *Time* (1995). Domestic Crime. Cops And Robbers. A Shocking Murder Highlights The Corruption Among New Orleans' Underpaid. March 20. Volume 145, No. 11.
294 Lincoln, A. (1953-55). *Collected Works*. The Abraham Lincoln Assoc. Springfield, Illinois. Roy P.Basler, Editor; Marion New Brunswick, N.J: Rutgers University Press. Contents: Vol. 1. 1824-1848.--2. 1848-1858.--3. 1858-1860.--4. 1860-1861.--5. 1861-1862.--6. 1862-1863.--7. 1863-1864.--8. 1864-1865. — Index. *The Collected Works Of Abraham Lincoln*, Edited By Roy P. Basler, Rutgers University Press, 1953. September 1859 (Vol. III. p. 99).
295 *Amsterdam News*. (1994). Khalid Muhammad Reiterates Call For Black South Africans To Kill. Nov. 19.
296 Stoddard, L. (1969). *The Rising Tide Of Color*. New York: Scribners & Sons.
297 Grant, Madison. (1970). *The Passing Of The Great Race*. New York: Arno Press.
298 Senate Committee On Government Affairs, Permanent Subcommittee On Investigations. Investigations Of The INS Criminal Alien Program, Minority Staff Statement (1993). Nov. 10.

Endnotes 685

299 Simcox, D. (1993). Senior Fellow At The Center For Immigration Studies. *Social Contract Magazine.* Spring.
300 *The New York Times* (1994). April 5.
301 Huddle, D. (1996). *The Net Costs Of Immigration: The Facts, The Trends, And The Critics.* Department Of Economics, Rice University, Oct. 22.
302 *American Demographics*, Oct. 1991.
303 Weisberger, B. (1994). A Nation Of Immigrants. *American Heritage.* Feb.-Mar. p. 5.
304 Jay, J. (1901). *The Federalist: A Collection Of Essays.* New York: The Colonial Press.
305 Paine, T. (1803). *Common Sense.* Boston, J. M. Dunham.
306 Brimelow, P.(1995). *Alien Nation: Common Sense About America's Immigration Disaster.* New York: Random House.
307 *NAAWP News* (1988). #48. p. . quotes from the New Orleans *Times-Picayune.*
308 *NAAWP News* (1988). #48. p. .
309 Ehrlich, P.(1968). *The Population Bomb.* New York: Valentine Books.
310 Friedan, Betty Naomi Goldstein. (1984). *The Feminine Mystique* (reissue edition). New York: Dell Publishing. p.22.
311 Moir, Anne and Jessel, David. (1989). *Brain Sex*. New York: Dell Publishing. p.127.
312 *U.S. News & World Report.* (1995). His Brain, Her Brain. February 27. p.27.
313 Flor, Henry P. (1979).Gender, Hemispheric Specialization and Psychopathology. *Social Science and Medicine.* 12b. p.155-62.
314 LIFE. (1998). *Were you BORN that Way?* April. p.39.
315 Moir, Anne and Jessel, David. (1989). *Brain Sex*. New York: Dell Publishing. p.42.
316 Inglis, J. and Lawson, S. (1981). Sex differences in the effects of unilateral brain damage on intelligence. *Science.* Vol. 212. p.693-95.
317 Witleson, S. F. (1985). The Brain Connection: The Corpus Callosum is Larger in Left Handers. *Science.* Vol. 229. p.65-68.
318 De Lacoste-Utamsing, C. and Holloway, R.L. (1982). Sexual dimorphism in the human corpus callosum. *Science.* Vol. 216 p.1431-32.
319 Moir and Jessel. p. 47-49.
320 Jensen, Arthur R. (1980). *Bias in Mental Testing.* New York: The Free Press. p.625-627.
321 Benbow, C.P., and Benbow, R.M. (1984). Biological correlates of high mathematical reasoning ability. *Progress in Brain Research.* Vol. 61. De Vries, G.J. et al. (eds.). Elsevier, Amsterdam. p. 469-90.
322 Moir and Jessel. p. 47-49.
323 Maccoby, E. and Jacklyn, N. (1975). *The Psychology of Sex Differences.* Stanford University Press.
324 Moir and Jessel. p.17.
325 McGuiness, D. (1985). *When Children Don't Learn.* Basic Books: New York.
326 Benbow, C.P. and Benbow, R.M. (1984). Biological correlates of high mathematical reasoning ability. *Progress in Brain Research.* Vol. 61. De Vries, G.J. et al. (eds.). Elsevier: Amsterdam.
327 American Health. (1993). *The Gay Debate: Is homosexuality a matter of choice or chance?* March. p.70.
328 Archer, J. (1976). Biological explanations of psychological sex differences. *Exploring Sex Differences.* Lloyd, B. and Archer, J. (eds.). Academic Press: London. p.241-65.
329 Wilson, Glenn. (1992). *The Great Sex Divide.* Washington, DC: Scott-Townsend. p.26-7, 73-6.
330 Durden-Smith, J. and De Simone, D. (1983). Birth of your Sexual Identity. *Science Digest.* September. p.86-88.
331 Moir and Jessel. p.24-25.
332 Wilson. p. 32.

333 Gorski, R. A. (1987). Sex differences in the rodent brain: their nature and origin. *Masculinity and Femininity*. Reinisch, J.M., et al. (eds.). Oxford University Press. p.37-67.
334 Leiberburg, I., et al. (1979). Sex differences in serum testosterone and in exchangeable brain cell nuclear estradiol during the neonatal period in rats *Brain research*. Vol. 178. p.207-12.
335 Goy, R.W. and McEwen, B.S. (1980). *Sexual Differentation of the Brain*, Massachusetts Institute of Technology Press: Cambridge, Massachusetts.
336 Ehrhardt, A.A. and Baker, S. (1974). Fetal androgens, human central nervous system differentiation, and behaviour sex differences. *Sex Differences in Behaviour*. Friedman, R.C. et al (eds.). John Wiley & Sons: New York. p.33-51.
337 Ehrhardt, A. A. and Meyer-Bahlburg, H.F.L. (1979). Prenatal sex hormones and the developing brain. *Annual Review Med*. Vol. 30. p.417-30.
338 Money, J. et al. (1955). *An Examination of Some Basic Sexual Concepts: The Evidence of Human Hermaphroditism*. John Hopkins Hospital: Baltimore, m. Vol. 97 p.301-19.
339 *New York Times*. (1997). *Defying an Intervention, Sexual Identity Prevails* March 14.
340 *New York Times*. (1997). *Defying an Intervention, Sexual Identity Prevails*.
341 *New York Times*. (1997). *Defying an Intervention, Sexual Identity Prevails*
342 Berg, I. et al. (1963). Change of assigned sex at puberty. *Lancet*. 7 December. p.1216-18.
343 *New York Times*. (1997). *Defying an Intervention, Sexual Identity Prevails* March 14.
344 Dörner G. (1985). Sex-specific Gonadotrophin Secretion, Sexual Orientation and Gender Role Behavior, *Endocrinologie*, 86 August 00 1-6)
345 Dörner, G. (1979). Hormones and Sexual Differentiation of the Brain. *Sex, Hormones and Behavior*. CIBA Foundation Symposium 62. Excerpta Medica: Amsterdam.
346 Moir, Anne and Jessel, David. (1989). *Brain Sex*. New York: Dell Publishing. Cited within.
347 Ward, I.L. (1974). Sexual Behaviour Differentiation: prenatal hormonal and environmental control. *Sex Differences in Behavior*. Friedman, R.C. et al. (eds.). John Wiley & Sons, New York. p.3-17.
348 Atlantic Monthly. (1993). *Homosexuality and Biology*. March.
349 The Washington Blade.(1993). *X Marks the Spot?* July 16. p.1.
350 *Insight*. (1994). Family Research Council: Taxpayer Funded Gay-Science or Legitimate Cancer Research? February.
351 Socarides , Charles W. (1995). *Homosexuality: A Freedom Too Far*. Phoenix: Adam Margrave Books.
352 American Psychiatric Association. (1994). *Fact Sheet*. September.
353 Frank, Barney. (1996). Why Party Politics Matters. *The Harvard Gay & Lesbian Review*. Spring.
354 *Dallas Morning News*. (1995). Studying sexes' brain differences a sensitive area. March 5. p.12A.
355 Wilson. (1992). p.101-111.
356 Moyer, K. E. (1987). *Violence and Aggression: A Physiological Perspective*. Paragon House: New York.
357 Langevin, R. (ed.). (1985). *Erotic Preference, Gender Identity, and Aggression in Men: New Research Studies*. Lawrence Erlbaum Associates: New Jersey.
358 Comfort, A. (1987). Deviation and Variation. *Variant Sexuality: Research and Theory*. Wilson, G. (ed.). Croom Helm: London. p.1-20.
359 McGuiness, D. (1976). Sex Differences in Organization, Perception, and Cognition. *Exploring Sex Differences*. Lloyd, B. and Archer, J. (eds.). Academic Press: London. p. 123-55.

ENDNOTES 687

360 Hutt, C. (1975). Neuroendocrinological, behavioural and intellectual differentiation in human development. *Gender Differences: Their Ontogeny and Significance.* Ousted, C. and Taylor, D. (eds.). Churchill Livingstione: London. p.73-121.
361 Garai, J. E., and Scheinfeld, A. (1968). Sex differences in mental and behavioural traits. *Genetic Psychology Monographs.* Vol.77. p.169-299.
362 Gaulin, S.J.C. et al. (1986). Sex differences in spatial ability: An evolutionary hypothesis and test. *The American Naturalist.* Vol. 127, No. 1. January. p.74-88.
363 Hoyenga, K.B. and Hoyenga, K. (1980). *Sex Differences.* Little, Brown and Company: Boston.
364 Prince, Melissa Weaver. (1988). The Fate of European Women. A popular Monograph circulated on the Internet.
365 United Nations International Report on Female Circumcism. United Nations: New York.
366 *New York Times.* (1997). March 14.
367 Cancian, F.M. (1985). Gender politics: Love and power in the private and public spheres. *Gender and the Life Course.* Rossi, A.S. (ed.). New York: Aldine. p.235-64.
368 Symons, D. (1979). *The Evolution of Human Sexuality.* Oxford University Press.
369 Reinisch, J. M. et. al. (eds.). (1987). *Masculinity and Femininity.* The Kinsey Institute Series. Oxford University Press.
370 Wilson, G.D. and Nias, D.K.B. (1976). *Loves Mysteries: the Psychology of Sexual Attraction.* Open Books: London. p.131.
371 Wilson, Glenn. (1992). *The Great Sex Divide.* Washington, DC: Scott-Townsend.
372 Pendell, Elmer.(1967). *Sex Versus Civilization.* Los Angeles: Noontide Press. p.171.
373 McGill, Bryant, H. (1997). *Equality of the Sexes.* Monograph.
374 Ford, Henry, (1920-1922). The International Jew: the World's Foremost Problem. *Dearborn Independent.* Dearborn, Michigan.: The Dearborn Independent.
375 Irving, David. (1994). *Action Report.* Special Edition.
376 Goldhagen, D. (1996). *Hitler's Willing Executioners: Ordinary Germans And The Holocaust.* New York: Knopf, Random House.
377 *Who's Who In World Jewry.* (1965). New York : Pitman Publishing. Corp.
378 *Who's Who In American Jewry.* (1927-). New York : The Jewish Biographical Bureau, Inc.
379 Goldwater, B. M. (1960). *The Conscience Of A Conservative.* Shepherdsville, Kentucky: Victor Publishing Co.
380 Stormer, J. (1964). *None Dare Call It Treason.* Florissant, Missouri: Liberty Bell Press.
381 Schwarz, F. C. (1960). *You Can Trust The Communists.* Englewood Cliffs, New Jersey: Prentice-Hall.
382 Churchill, W. (1920). Zionism versus Bolshevism: A Struggle for the Soul of the Jewish People. *Illustrated Sunday Herald.* February 8.
383 Churchill, W. (1920). Zionism versus Bolshevism: A Struggle for the Soul of the Jewish People.
384 U.S. National Archives. (1919). Record Group 120: Records of the American Expeditionary Forces, June 9.
385 Wilton, R. (1920). *Last Days of the Romanovs.* New York: George H. Doran Co. p.148.
386 U.S. National Archives. (1919). Record Group 120: Records of the American Expeditionary Forces, June 9.
387 Francis, D. R. (1921). *Russia From the American Embassy.* New York: C. Scribner's & Sons. p.214.
388 National Archives, Dept. of State Decimal File, 1910-1929, file 861.00/5067
389 Nettl, J. P. (1967). *The Soviet Achievement.* New York: Harcourt, Brace & World.
390 *Encyclopedia Judaica.* p.791-792.
391 Trotsky, L. (1968). *Stalin: An Appraisal of the Man and His Influence.* ed. trans. Charles Malamuth. London, MacGibbon & Kee.

688 MY AWAKENING

392 Shub, David. (1961). *Novyi Zhurnal* no. 63.
393 Shub, D. (1966). *Lenin: a Biography*. Harmondsworth, Penguin.
394 *Review de Fonds Social Juif*. (1970). no. 161.
395 Ben-Shlomo, B. Z. (1991). Reporting on Lenin's Jewish Roots. *Jewish Chronicle*. July 26. p.2.
396 Hoffman, Michael. (1997). Campaign for Radical Truth in History. P.O. Box 849. Coeur d' Alene, ID 83816. Ehrenburg won the Order of Lenin and the Stalin Prize and willed his papers to the Israeli Yad Vashem Holocaust Museum.
397 Goldberg, Anatol. (1984). *Ilya Ehrenburg : Revolutionary, novelist, poet, war correspondent, propagandist : the extraordinary epic of a Russian survivor*. New York : Viking.
398 Solzhenitsyn, A. (1974). *The Gulag Archipelago, 1918-1956 : An Experiment in Literary investigation*, I-II. Tran. Thomas P. Whitney. London : Collins: Harvill Press. p.79.
399 Aronson, G. (1949). *Soviet Russia and the Jews*. New York: American Jewish League Against Communism.
400 *The Jewish Voice*. (1942). New York. January.
401 *The Congress Bulletin*. (1940).(New York). American Jewish Congress, January 5.
402 George Bernard Shaw, quoted in *The Jewish Guardian* (1931). said: "I have seen the statement which Stalin gave recently to the Jewish Telegraphic Agency on anti-Semitism and in which the Soviet leader said that under the Soviet laws militant anti-Semitism is punishable by death."
403 Joseph Stalin (Note to the Jewish Telegraphic Agency). 12th January 1931, Collected Works, vol. 13.
404 Gregor Aronson. (1949). *Soviet Russia and the Jews*. New York: American Jewish League Against Communism.
405 *Encyclopaedia Britannica*. (1947). Vol. 2. p.76.
406 Latimer, E.W. (1895). *Russia and Turkey in the 19th Century*. A. C. McLury & Co. p. 332.
407 *Jewish Communal Register of New York City*. (1918). p.1018-1019
408 *New York Journal American* (1949). February 3.
409 Andelman, M.S. (1974). *To Eliminate the Opiate*. New York-Tel Aviv: Zahavia. Ltd. 26
410 Nedava, J. (1971). Trotsky and the Jews. Philadelphia. Jewish Publication Society.
411 Marx, Karl, (1936). *Das Kapital*. English. New York: The Modern library
412 Marx, Karl, (1932). *Capital, the Communist manifesto and other writings*. New York: The Modern library.
413 *Chicago Jewish Sentinel*. (1975). Inside Judaica. October 30.
414 *The Encyclopedia of Zionism in Israel*. (1971). New York: Herzl Press/McGraw-Hill. p.496-497.
415 Wilton, R. (1920). *Last Days of the Romanovs*. New York: George H. Doran Co. 148.
416 Rapoport, Louis. (1990). *Stalin's War Against The Jews*. Free Press/Simon & Schuster.
417 Curtis, William Elroy. (1907). *National Geographic Magazine*. The Revolution in Russia. May. p.313.
418 Orwell, George. (1948). 1984.
419 Exodus (1960). dir. Otto Preminger United Artists.
420 Kurtzman, Daniel. (1995). Ousted House Historian Seeks Restitution and a Straight Record. *Jewish Telegraphic Agency*. October 31.
421 Bible. King James Version. Ezra chapter 9.
422 KJV Numbers 33:55
423 KJV Joshua 6:21
424 KJV Joshua 10:32-34
425 KJV Joshua 10:37
426 KJV Isaiah 34:2-3

427 RSV Deuteronomy 20:16
428 KJV Deuteronomy 7:2-3
429 KJV Deuteronomy 7:6
430 KJV Ezra 9:12
431 Maimonides, *Mishneh Torah. Laws On Murderers* 2,4,11.
432 KJV Galatians 3:26-29
433 *The Winds of War, War and Remembrance,* and others.
434 *New York Herald Tribune.* (1959). Nov. 17.
435 Dilling, E. (1980). *The Jewish Religion.* Los Angeles: CDL Report (Renamed From The Plot Against Christianity)
436 Talmud, Sanhedrin. (1935). Soncino Edition. p.400.
437 Simon, M. Trans. (1936). 57a Gittin. London. Soncino Press. p.261
438 *Jewish Encyclopedia.* (1907). Balaam. p.469.
439 Talmud, Sanhedrin. (1935). Soncino Edition. 5th footnote on p. 388.
440 *Funk And Wagnalls Jewish Encyclopedia.* (1905). Min. p.594.
441 Talmud. (1935). Soncino Edition.
442 Talmud, Sanhedrin (1935). Soncino Edition. p.388.
443 *Funk And Wagnalls Jewish Encyclopedia.* (1907). Gentile. New York. p.617.
444 Talmud. (1935). Baba Mezia. Soncino Edition. 114a-114b.
445 *Funk And Wagnalls Jewish Encyclopedia.* (1907). Gentile. New York. p.621.
446 Talmud, Sanhedrin (1935). Soncino Edition. 58b. p.398.
447 Talmud, Baba Kamma. (1935). Soncino Edition. p.211.
448 Talmud, Baba Kamma. (1935). Soncino Edition. p.666.
449 Talmud, Sanhedrin. (1935). Soncino Edition. 76a. p.470.
450 Talmud, Sanhedrin. (1935). Soncino Edition. 57a. p.388.
451 Talmud, Baba Kamma. (1935). Soncino Edition. 37b.
452 Talmud, Baba Kamma. (1935). Soncino Edition. p.664-665.
453 Talmud, Yebamoth. (1936). Soncino Edition. 98a.
454 Talmud, Abodah Zarah. (1935). Soncino Edition. 22a-b.
455 Talmud, Abodah Zarah. (1935). Soncino Edition. 67b.
456 *Funk And Wagnalls Jewish Encyclopedia.* (1907). Gentile: Discrimination Against Gentiles. p.617-621.
457 *Funk And Wagnalls Jewish Encyclopedia.* (1907). Gentile. New York. p.617.
458 Talmud, Sanhedrin (1935). Soncino Edition. 105a-b. p.717.
459 Talmud, Sanhedrin (1935). Soncino Edition. 105a-b. p.726.
460 RSV John 8:13T
461 Luther, M. L. (1962).*The Jews And Their Lies.* Chicago. Christian Press Translated From The Erlangen And Weimar German Editions. (1483-1546). Works. 1883 D. Martin Luthers Werke; Kritische Gesammtausgabe. Weimar, H. Böhlau, (1883-1985).
462 *Random House Websters Unabridged Electronic Dictionary.* (1996). "Purim."
463 Holiday Observances (1997). *Jewish Art In Context.*
464 Goldwasser, Phillip. (1998). *Bon Appetit.* Hosted by the Jewish Communication Network on the Internet.
465 Hess, Moses, (1958). 1812-1875. *Rome And Jerusalem.* Translated By Maurice J. Bloom. New York: Philosophical Library.
466 Dubnow, S. (1906). *Foundation Of National Judaism.* Translated From Die Grundlagen Des Nationaljudentums. S.M. Dubnow. Berlin : Jüdischer Verlag.
467 Menuhin, Moshe. (1965). *The Decadence Of Judaism In Our Time.* New York: Exposition Press
468 Menuhin, Moshe. (1965). *The Decadence Of Judaism In Our Time.* 482-483.
469 *Attack.* (1976). Goldmann quoted in Zionism I: Theory. no.42. (Hillsboro. WV. www.natvan.com).
470 Brandies, L. at a speech before the Menorah Society at Columbia University.

690 MY AWAKENING

471 Herzl, T. (1967). *The Jewish State: An Attempt At A Modern Solution Of The Jewish Question*. London, Pordes.
472 Wyman, David S. (1985). *The Abandonment Of The Jews: America And The Holocaust,* 1941-1945. Pantheon.
473 Lazare, Bernard. (1967). *Antisemitism: Its History And Causes*; Translated From The French. London, Britons Publishing Co.
474 Encyclopaedia Judaica. (1994). Decennial Book, 1983-1992 Events Of 1982-1992 Jerusalem : Encyclopaedia Judaica.
475 De Mille, C. B. (1956). *The Ten Commandments*. Hollywood. Paramount.
476 Spielberg, S. (1993). *Schindler's List*. Hollywood. Universal.
477 *Jewish Press*. Brooklyn, NY.
478 *The Jewish Press*. (1988). Feb. 19. 10A.
479 *The Jewish Press*. (1988). Feb. 19. 8C.
480 Bermant, C. (1991). Some Carefully And Carelessly Chosen Words, *Jewish Chronicle*. May 17.
481 *New Republic*. (1992). May.
482 *Who's Who In World Jewry*. (1965). New York : Pitman Pub. Corp.
483 Who's Who In American Jewry. (1927-). New York : The Jewish Biographical Bureau,
484 Putnam, C. (1961). *Race and reason: A Yankee View*. Public Affairs Press.
485 RSV Acts 17:26
486 RSV Acts 17:26.
487 RSV Joshua 6:21
488 KJV Joshua 10:39
489 RSV Deuteronomy 20:10-18
490 KJV Leviticus 19:18
491 KJV Exodus 20:13, 15, and 17
492 RSV Leviticus 19:18
493 TANAKH. (1985). A New Translation of The Holy Scriptures according to the Traditional Hebrew Text. Philadelphia. The Jewish Publication Society.
494 Talmud - Baba Kamma (1935). 113b. p.666. Soncino Edition.
495 *Funk and Wagnalls Jewish Encyclopedia*. (1905). Gentile. p.620.
496 Hartung, John. (1995). Love Thy Neighbor: The Evolution of In-Group Morality. *Skeptic*, Vol. 3. No. 4.
497 KJV Leviticus 25:44-46.
498 KJV Deuteronomy 7:2-6.
499 KJV Deuteronomy 7:4.
500 RSV Ezra 9:1.
501 KJV Ezra 9:2.
502 KJV Leviticus 20:24.
503 KJV Nehemiah 13:3.
504 KJV Galatians 3:26-29.
505 RSV Ephesians 6:5.
506 RSV 1 Timothy 6:2.
507 RSV Titus 2:9-10.
508 RSV 1 Peter 2:18 .
509 RSV Leviticus 25:44-46.
510 RSV Luke 7:9.
511 KJV Luke 22:36 .
512 KJV John 2:15.
513 Schonfield, H. J. (1965). *The Passover plot; new light on the history of Jesus*. New York: B. Geis Associates. Random House.
514 KJV Hebrews 8:9.
515 "Judaism." *Encyclopedia Judaica,* p. 396.
516 "Conservative Judaism," Enc. *Encyclopedia Judaica,* p. 906.
517 *Universal Jewish Encyclopedia*, "Authority" p. 637.

518 Talmud, Sanhedrin (1935). Soncino Edition. 105a-b. p.717.
519 Simon, M. Trans. (1936). 57a Gittin. London. Soncino Press. p.261.
520 Talmud, Sanhedrin (1935). Soncino Edition. 105a-b. p.726.
521 Talmud, Sanhedrin (1935). Soncino Edition. 52b. p.356.
522 Talmud, Sanhedrin (1935). Soncino Edition. 105a-b. p.726.
523 Shahak, I. (1994). *Jewish History, Jewish Religion*. Boulder, Colorado. Pluto Press.
524 Shahak, I. (1994). *Jewish History, Jewish Religion*. 97-98.
525 Shahak, I. (1994). *Jewish History, Jewish Religion*. p.21.
526 Shahak, I. (1994). Jewish History, Jewish Religion. 23 & 93.
527 "Goy" *Talmudic Encyclopedia* as quoted by Shahak.
528 Shahak, I. (1994). *Jewish History, Jewish Religion*. 87.
529 Shahak, I. (1994). *Jewish History, Jewish Religion*. p.23.
530 Luther, M. L. (1962). *The Jews And Their Lies*. Chicago. Christian Press Translated From The Erlangen And Weimar German Editions. 1483-1546. Works. 1883 D. Martin Luthers Werke; Kritische Gesammtausgabe. Weimar, H. Böhlau, 1883- <1985.
531 RSV Deuteronomy 7:6-12.
532 RSV Romans 9:1–3, 6–8, 24–26.
533 KJV Hebrews 8:6–7, 9–10, and 13.
534 KJV Matthew 21:43-45.
535 KJV John 8:42-48.
536 KJV John 1:47.
537 RSV 1 Thessalonians 2:14-16.
538 RSV Titus1:13–14.
539 Solzhenitsyn, A. (1974). *The Gulag archipelago, 1918-1956 : an experiment in literary investigation, I-II.* Tran. Thomas P. Whitney. London : Collins : Harvill Press. p.79.
540 RSV John 7:13.
541 KJV Hebrews 8:9.
542 Koestler, A. (1976). *The Thirteenth Tribe*. New York: Random House.
543 Chase, G. A., & V. A. McKusick (1972). Founder Effect In Tay-Sachs Disease. *American Journal Of Human Genetics*. 25:p.339-352.
544 *The Encyclopedia of Zionism in Israel*. (1971). New York: Herzl Press/McGraw-Hill.
545 Glazer, Nathan. (1970). *Remembering the Answers: Essays on the American student revolt*. New York: Basic Books
546 Britton, F. (1979). *Behind Communism*. Noontide Press.
547 Cohen, Jacob. (1993). The Rosenberg File. *National Review*. July 19.: p.48-52
548 Neville, John F. (1997). *The Press, the Rosenbergs, and the Cold War*. London: Praeger.
549 Strom, Kevin. (1998). *We Are All Prejudiced*. Internet Article. April 13.
550 Boas, F. (1911). Rev. Ed., (1938). *The Mind of Primitive Man*. New York.
551 Herskovits, Melville J. (1953). *Franz Boas; the science of man in the making*. Clifton, NJ: A. M. Kelley, p. 65.
552 Mead, Margaret. (1961). *Coming of age in Samoa; a psychological study of primitive youth for Western civilization*. Foreword by Franz Boas. New York: Morrow.
553 Freeman, D. (1983). *Margaret Mead and Samoa: The Making and Unmaking of an Anthropological Myth*. Cambridge University Press.
554 Freeman, D. (1990). *The Samoan Reader: Anthropologists Take Stock*. Lanham, Maryland: University Press of America.
555 Freeman, D. (1991). On Franz Boas and the Samoan Researches of Margaret Mead. *Current Anthropology*. p.32, 322-330.
556 Montagu, Ashley. (1945). *Man's Most Dangerous Myth: The Fallacy of Race*. New York: Columbia University press

557 Pearson, R. (1996). Heredity and Humanity: Race Eugenics and Modern Science.. Washington, DC: Scott-Townsend Publishers.
558 Gelya, F. (1997). Jews, Multiculturalism, And Boasian Anthropology. *The American Anthropologist.* Vol. 99. #4. p.731-745.
559 Yerushalmi, Y. H. (1991). *Freud's Moses: Judaism Terminable and Interminable.* New Haven: Yale University Press. p.98.
560 Gay, P. (1988). *Freud: A Life For Our Time.* New York: W. W. Norton.
561 Freud, S. (1939). *Moses and Monotheism.* New York: Vintage.
562 Freud, S. (1938). *Totem and Taboo; Resemblances Between the Psychic Lives of Savages and Neurotics.* Harmondsworth, Middlesex: Penguin Books.
563 MacDonald, K. (1996). *A People That Shall Dwell Apart.* Westport, Connecticut: Praeger.
564 Freud, S. (1969). *The Interpretation of Dreams.* Trans. J. Strachey. New York.
565 Yerushalmi, Y. H. (1991). *Freud's Moses: Judaism Terminable and Interminable.* New Haven: Yale University Press. p.45.
566 Yerushalmi, Y. H. (1991). *Freud's Moses: Judaism Terminable and Interminable.* New Haven: Yale University Press. p.45.
567 Freud, S. (1939). *Moses and Monotheism.* Trans. by K. Jones. New York: Vintage. .p.114-117.
568 Mannoni, O. (1971). *Freud.* Trans. R. Belice. New York. p.168.
569 Friedman, Murray. *What Went Wrong.* (1995). New York: Free Press.
570 Garrow, David.(1983). *The FBI and Martin Luther King.* Penguin Books, New York.
571 Strom, Kevin Alfred. (1994). *The Beast as Saint.* Radio broadcast. Printed transcript available from National Vanguard Books, Box 330, Hillsboro, WV 24946.
572 Pappas, T. (1992). A Houdini of Time. *Chronicles.* November 26-30.
573 Abernathy, R. (1989). *And the Walls Came Tumbling Down.* New York: Harper & Row.
574 *Newsweek.* (1998). Books: The Middle of the Journey, Taylor Branch's Grand Civil-Rights History Rolls On. January19. p.62. Quoting from *Pillar of Fire: America in the King Years 1963-65.* Taylor Branch. Simon and Schuster.
575 Kaye, Evelyn. (1987). *A Hole in the Sheet: a Modern Woman Looks at Orthodox and Hasidic Judaism.* Secaucus, New Jersey: L. Stuart.
576 Kaye, Evelyn. (1987). A Hole in the Sheet.
577 *Jewish Encyclopedia.* (1905). Talmudic prayer. p.617.
578 Talmud. (1936). Kethuboth. Soncino Edition. Kethuboth 11b. p.58.
579 Talmud. (1935). Sanhedrin. 69b. p.469.
580 Talmud. (1936). Yebamoth. Soncino Edition. 57b. p.386
581 Walt, Vivienne. (1998). Backlash In Africa Against a Major Ritual. *The Sacramento Bee.* July 12.
582 *New York Times.* (1992). December 9.
583 *Network.* (1976). Director: Sidney Lumet. Producer: Howard Gottfried. Screenwriter: Paddy Chayevsky. Editor: Alan Heim. United Artists-MGM.
584 Thunderbolt. P. O. Box 1211 Marietta, GA 30061.
585 *Schindler's List.* (1993). Universal. Director: Steven Spielberg. Producers: Gerald R. Molen, Steven Spielberg. Screenwriters: Kurt Luedtke, Steve Zaillian. Cinematographer: Janusz Kaminski. Editor: Ewa Braun.
586 Gabler, N. (1988). *An Empire of Their Own : How the Jews Invented Hollywood.* New York: Crown Publishers.
587 Stein, B. (1979.). *The View From Sunset Boulevard.* New York: Basic Books.
588 Stein, Ben. (1997). Do Jews Run the Media: You Bet they Do — And What of it? *E! online Internet Magazine.*
589 National Vanguard Books, P. O. Box 330 Hillsboro, WV 24946. Or <http://www.natvan.com>
590 *Time.* (1962). The Newspaper Collector. July 27. p.56.

ENDNOTES 693

591 Robertson, W. (1981). *The Dispossessed Majority*. Cape Canaveral, Florida. Howard Allen Enterprises, Inc. (PO Box 76, Cape Canaveral, FL 32920).
592 Pierce, Dr. William. (1998). National Vanguard Books. P.O. Box 330, Hillsboro, WV. 24946. Or www.natvan.com. Edited By Brett Anderson.
593 *Birth Of A Nation*. (1915). Director, Composer: D.W. Griffith. Screenwriter: Frank E. Woods, D.W. Griffith. Producer: Frank E. Woods. Cinematographer: Billy Bitzer. Editor: James Smith.
594 *Gone with the Wind*. (1939). Editor: Hal Kern. Producer, Screenwriter: David O. Selznick
595 Dixon, T. (1905). *The Clansman: An Historical Romance Of The Ku Klux Klan*. New York: Grosset & Dunlap,.
596 Shakespeare, W. (1600). *The Excellent History Of The Merchant Of Venice*: With the extreme cruelty of Shylock the Jew towards the saide merchant, in cutting a just pound of his flesh and the obtaining of Portia by the choyse of three caskets. London: J. Roberts.
597 *Canadian Jewish News*. (1991). January 31. p.33.
598 Mitchell, M. (1936). *Gone with the Wind*. New York: Macmillan.
599 *Guess Who's Coming To Dinner*. Columbia. (1967). Director, Producer: Stanley Kramer. Screenwriter: William Rose. Cinematographer: Sam Leavitt.
600 *Newsweek*. (1991). June 10.
601 *Roots*. (1977). Wolper Productions. Directors: Marvin Chomsky, John Erman, David Greene, and Gilbert Moses. Producer: David Wolper.
602 *The Holocaust*. (1978). Titus Productions. Director: Marvin Chomsky. Producers: Robert Berger and Herbert Brodkin. Screenplay: Gerald Green. Music: Morton Gould. Producer: Robert Berger.
603 Haley, A. (1976). *Roots*. Garden City, New York: Doubleday.
604 Courlander, H. (1967). *The African*. New York: Crown Publishers.
605 *Freedom Road* (1979). Zev Braun Productions, Freedom Road Films. Director: J'an K'adir. Producer: Zev Braun. Writer: Howard Fast. Editor: Anne Goursaud.
606 Fast, H. (1990). *Being Red*. Boston. Houghton Mifflin.
607 *Farewell Uncle Tom*.[1972] Cannon Releasing Corporation.
608 Medved, M. (1996). Jews Run Hollywood, So What? *Moment*. August.
609 *Priest*. (1994). Miramax Films.
610 *The Crying Game*. (1992). Miramax Films.
611 *Seven Years In Tibet*. (1997). Sony Pictures Entertainment, TriStar Pictures, Mandalay Entertainment, Reperage & Vanguard Films, Applecross.
612 *Larry King Live*. (1996). Guest: Marlon Brando. Friday, April 5.
613 Bar-Yosef, Avinoam. (1994). The Jews Who Run Clinton's Court. *Maariv*. September 2.
614 Fulbright, Sen. William. (1973). *Face the Nation*. CBS: New York. April 15.
615 Buckley, William F. (1970). *McCarthy and His Enemies; The Record and Its Meaning*. New Rochelle, New York: Arlington House.
616 *Wall Street Journal*. (1978). American Jews and Jimmy Carter. March 2. p.18.
617 Getler, Michael. (1974). Pentagon Chief Suggests Israel Lobby Has Too Much Influence. *Los Angeles Times*.
618 *San Francisco Chronicle*. (1968). November 23. p.9.
619 Bar-Yosef, Avinoam. (1994). *The Jews Who Run Clinton's Court*. Maariv.
620 Bar-Yosef, Avinoam. (1994). *The Jews Who Run Clinton's Court*. Maariv.
621 Bar-Yosef, Avinoam. (1994). *The Jews Who Run Clinton's Court*. Maariv.
622 Jonathan Broder. (1997). *Salon*. February 17.
623 *The New York Times News Service*. (1997). Albright Upbraids Stubborn Balkan Leaders: Refugees.... June 1.
624 *Jewish Week*. (1997). March 3.
625 *Jewish Week*. (1997). January 24
626 *New York Times*. (1997). October 4.

627 *The Times-Picayune.* (1998). Swiss banks, Holocaust survivors settle war claims. August 13. p.A-13.
628 Findley, Paul. (1989). *They Dare to Speak Out: People and Institutions Confront Israel's Lobby.* Chicago, Illinois: Lawrence Hill Books.
629 Bar-Yosef, Avinoam. (1994). *The Jews Who Run Clinton's Court.* Maariv.
630 *Network* (1976). Director: Sidney Lumet. Producer: Howard Gottfried. Screenwriter: Paddy Chayevsky. Editor: Alan Heim. United Artists-MGM.
631 Kornberg, R. (1993). Theodore Herzl: From Assimilation to Zionism. Bloomington: Indiana University Press. inner quote from Herzl diary, 161.
632 *Microsoft Encarta 96 Encyclopedia.* (1993-1995). "Anti-Semitism." Microsoft Corporation. Funk & Wagnalls Corporation.
633 *Grolier's Encyclopedia.* Anti-Semitism.
634 Heschel, Susannah. (1993). *Anti-Semites Against Anti-Semitism.* Tikkun, November/December. p.52.
635 Todd Endelman, (1979). *The Jews of Georgian England, 1714-1830.* Philadelphia. p.95.
636 Wisse, Ruth. (1991). The Twentieth Century's Most Successful Ideology. *Commentary.* Vol. 91, #2. February. p.33.
637 *Jerusalem Post.* (1990). Editorial.). September 15. p.24.
638 Hertzberg, A. (1993). *Is Anti-Semitism Dying Out?* New York Review of Books, XL (12), p.51-57.
639 Lewis, N. and Reinhold, M. (1955). *Roman Civilization: Sourcebook II: The Empire.* Harper Torchbooks: New York.
640 Bishop, John. (1964). *Nero: the Man and the Legend.* Robert Hale Limited: London.
641 *The Times-Picayune.* (1998). Study Affirms Genetic Link in Jewish Priestly Class. July 9. p.A11
642 Twain, M. (1899). Concerning the Jews. *Harper's Monthly Magazine.* September.
643 Rose, P. L. (1990). *Revolutionary Antisemitism in Germany, from Kant to Wagner.* Princeton, New Jersey: Princeton University Press. p.7.
644 KJV. Deut. 23:20.
645 KJV. Deut. 23:21.
646 *The Code of Maimonides,* ed. L. Nemoy. (1965). Yale Judaica Series. New Haven, Connecticut: Yale University Press.
647 Roth, C. (1978). *A History of the Jews in England,* 3rd edition. Oxford: The Clarendon Press.
648 Chazan, R. (1973). *Medieval Jewry in Northern France: A Political and Social History.* Baltimore: The Johns Hopkins University Press.
649 Weinryb, B. D. (1972). *The Jews of Poland: A Social and Economic History of the Jewish Community in Poland from 1100 to 1800.* Philadelphia: The Jewish Publication Society of America.
650 Neuman, A. A. (1969). *The Jews in Spain: Their Political and Cultural Life During the Middle Ages*; Vols. I & II. New York: Octagon Books. (Originally published in 1942.)
651 Baldwin, J. W. (1986). *The Government of Philip Augustus: Foundations of French Royal Power in the Middle Ages.* Berkeley: University of California Press.
652 Rabinowitz, L. (1938). *The Social Life of the Jews of Northern France in the XII-XIV Centuries as Reflected in the Rabbinical Literature of the Period.* London: Edward Goldston Ltd.
653 Luchaire, A. (1912). *Social France at the Time of Philip Augustus.* New York: Frederick Ungar.
654 *Encyclopedia Britannica* (1952).Vol. 13. Jews. p.57.
655 Davidson, N. (1987). The Inquisition and the Italian Jews. *Inquisition and Society in Early Modern Europe.* Totowa, New Jersey: Barnes & Noble.
656 Haliczer, S. (1987). *Inquisition and Society in Early Modern Europe* Trans. S. Haliczer. Totowa, New Jersey: Barnes & Noble.

Endnotes 695

[657] Pullan, B. (1983). *The Jews of Europe and the Inquisition of Venice, 1550-1670.* London: Basil Blackwell. p.159.
[658] Kornberg, R. (1993). *Theodore Herzl: From Assimilation to Zionism.* Inner quote from Herzl diary. Bloomington, Indiana: Indiana University Press. p.183.
[659] Kornberg, R. (1993). *Theodore Herzl: From Assimilation to Zionism.* p.161-162.
[660] Kornberg, R. (1993). *Theodore Herzl: From Assimilation to Zionism.* p.183.
[661] Aquinas, Thomas. *On the Governance of the Jews.*
[662] Finkelstein, L. (1924). *Jewish Self-Government in the Middle Ages.* Westport, Connecticut: Greenwood Press. p.280.
[663] Katz, J. (1961). *Tradition and Crisis: Jewish Society at the End of the Middle Ages.* New York. The Free Press of Glencoe. p.24.
[664] KJV. Lev. 25:14.
[665] *The Code of Maimonides.*(1965). ed. L. Nemoy. Yale Judaica Series, New Haven, Connecticut: Yale University Press. Ch. XII:1. p.47.
[666] Katz, J. (1961). *Tradition and Crisis: Jewish Society at the End of the Middle Ages.* New York: The Free Press of Glencoe. p.61.
[667] Roth, C. (1974). *A History of the Marranos,* 4th ed. New York: Schocken Books.
[668] Random House Unabridged Webster's Electronic Dictionary. Marrano.
[669] Shaw, S. J. (1991). *The Jews of the Ottoman Empire and the Turkish Republic.* New York: New York University Press.
[670] Hundert, G. D. (1992). *The Jews in a Polish Private Town: The Case of Opatow in the Eighteenth Century.* Baltimore: Johns Hopkins University Press..
[671] Hundert, G. D. (1992). p.54.
[672] Hundert, G. D. (1992). p.57.
[673] Liebman, A. (1979). *Jews and the Left.* New York: John Wiley & Sons. p.267-268.
[674] *Encyclopaedia Britannica.* (1947). Vol. 2. p.76.
[675] Mosse, W. E. (1987). *Jews in the German Economy: The German-Jewish Economic Élite 1820-1935.* Oxford, U.K.: The Clarendon Press.
[676] Gordon, S. (1984). *Hitler, Germans, and the "Jewish Question."* Princeton, New Jersey: Princeton University Press.
[677] Birmingham, Stephen (1967). *Our Crowd: The Great Jewish Families of New York.* New York: Harper & Row.
[678] Ehrlich, J. and Rehfeld B. (1989). *New Crowd: Changing of the Jewish Guard on Wall Street.* Boston: Little, Brown & Company.
[679] Schwartz, M. (1987). Irangate and Boesky Affair Worrisome to Jews. *Palm Beach Jewish World.* January 30.
[680] *Newsweek.* (1971). November 17.
[681] Anderson, J. (1971). Israel is Crook's Promised Land. Washington Post. December 19.
[682] Messick, H. (1971). *Lansky.* New York: Putnam. p.276-277.
[683] *Bugsy.* (1991). Director: Levinson, B. Screenwriter: Toback,J. Tristar.
[684] Messick, H. (1971). *Lansky.* New York: Putnam. p.8-10.
[685] Brokhin, Y. (1975). *Hustling on Gorky Street.* Dial Press.
[686] Simis, K. (1982). *USSR: The Corrupt Society.* Simon and Schuster.
[687] Friedman, R.R. (1998). The Most Dangerous Mobster in the World. *Village Voice.* May 26.
[688] Ibid.
[689] Luther, M. (1974). Quoted by Leon Poliakov. *The History of Anti-Semitism.* New York. p.233, note 10.
[690] RSV. Lev. 25:44.
[691] Marcus, J. (1952). Jews. *Encyclopaedia Britannica.* Vol. 13. p.57.
[692] Grayzel, S. (1948). *A History of the Jew: From Babylonian Exile to the End of World War II.* Philadelphia Jewish Publication Society of America. p.312.
[693] White, W. (1966). *Who Brought the Slaves to America?* White Publishing.

696 MY AWAKENING

⁶⁹⁴ Raphael, Marc. (1983). *Jews and Judaism in the United States: A Documentary History*. New York: Behrman House, Inc. Vol. 14. Raphael is the editor of *American Jewish History*, the journal of the American Jewish Historical Society at Brandeis University in Massachusetts.

⁶⁹⁵ Platt, Virginia B. (1975). *And Don't Forget the Guinea Voyage: The Slave Trade of Aaron Lopez of Newport*. William and Mary Quarterly. Vol. 32,# 4.

⁶⁹⁶ Marcus, J. (1970). *The Colonial American Jew: 1492-1776*. Detroit, Michigan: Wayne State University Press.

⁶⁹⁷ Marcus, J. (1974). *The Jew and the American Revolution*. Cincinnati, American Jewish Archives. 3[3

⁶⁹⁸ Liebman S. B. (1982). *New World Jewry 1493-1825: Requiem for the Forgotten*. KTAV, New York, p.170, 183. [Liebman is an attorney; LL.B., St. Lawrence University, 1929; M.A. (Latin American history), Mexico City College, 1963; Florida chapter American Jewish Historical Society, 1956-58; Friends of Hebrew University, 1958-59; American Historical Society Contributor to scholarly journals on Jewish history.

⁶⁹⁹ Wiznitzer, A. (1960). *Jews in Colonial Brazil* .p. 72-3 [Note: Wiznitzer, Arnold Aharon, educator; Born in Austria, December 20, 1899; Ph.D., University of Vienna, 1920; Doctor of Hebrew Literature, Jewish Theological Seminary of America; Emeritus research professor, University of Judaism, Los Angeles; Contributor to historical journals in the United States and Brazil including the Journal of Jewish Social Studies and the Publications of the American Jewish Historical Society. Former president, Brazilian-Jewish Institute of Historical Research.]

⁷⁰⁰ Marcus, J. (1989 *United States Jewry). 1776-1985*. Detroit: Wayne State University Press, p.586.

⁷⁰¹ *The Secret Relationship between Blacks and Jews*. (1991). Prepared by the Historical Research Department of the Nation of Islam. Chicago, Illinois: Latimer Associates.

⁷⁰² Spielberg, S. (1997). *Amistad*. Los Angeles: Dreamworks.

⁷⁰³ Raphael, Marc. (1983). *Jews and Judaism in the United States: A Documentary History*. New York: Behrman House,

⁷⁰⁴ Bristow, E. J. (1983). *Prostitution and Prejudice*. New York: Shocken books.

⁷⁰⁵ Bristow, E. (1986). *Studies in Contemporary Jewry, II*. Bloomington, Indiana: Indiana University Press. p.310.

⁷⁰⁶ Specter, M (1998). Slave-traders Lure Slavic Women. *Times-Picayune*. New York Times News Service. January 11.

⁷⁰⁷ Specter, M (1998).[or]Ibid

⁷⁰⁸ Specter, M (1998).[or]Ibid

⁷⁰⁹ Katz, Samuel M. (1998). Hookers in the Holy Land. *Moment*. April. p.45-78.

⁷¹⁰ Katz, Samuel M. (1998). Hookers in the Holy Land. p.47.

⁷¹¹ Katz, Samuel M. (1998). Hookers in the Holy Land. p.48.

⁷¹² Katz, Samuel M. (1998). Hookers in the Holy Land. p.49.

⁷¹³ Josephus, F. (1989). *The Works of Josephus, Antiquities of the Jews*. Complete and unabridged, trans., W. Whiston. Peabody, Massachusetts: Hendrickson Publishers. (12:224).

⁷¹⁴ Josephus, F. (1989). *The Works of Josephus, Antiquities of the Jews*. (12:224)

⁷¹⁵ Alon, G. (1989). *The Jews on Their Land in the Talmudic Age* (70-640 C. E.). Trans. G. Levi from Hebrew. Cambridge: Harvard University Press (Originally published in 1980, 1984 by the Magnes Press, Hebrew University, Jerusalem) p.16.

⁷¹⁶ Avi-Yonah, M. (1976). *The Jews under Roman and Byzantine Rule: A Political History of Palestine from the Bar Kokhba War to the Arab Conquest*. Jerusalem: The Magnes Press, reprinted 1984. p.261.

⁷¹⁷ Parkes, J. (1934). *The Conflict of the Church and the Synagogue: A Study of the Origins of Antisemitism*. London: The Soncino Press. p.263, 257-258.

[718] Grant, M. (1973). *The Jews in the Roman World.* New York: Charles Scribner's Sons. p.288.
[719] Ibid. p.289.
[720] Jones, A. H. M. (1964). *The Later Roman Empire 284-602: A Social Economic and Administrative Survey,* 2 vols. Norman, Oklahoma: University of Oklahoma Press. p.950.
[721] Shaw, S. J. (1991). *The Jews of the Ottoman Empire and the Turkish Republic.* New York: New York University Press. p. 25.
[722] Ibid. p.26.
[723] Shaw, S. J. (1991). *The Jews of the Ottoman Empire and the Turkish Republic.* New York: New York University Press. p.77.
[724] Amador de los Rios, R. (1875-1876). *Historia Social, Politica y religiousa de los Judios de España y Portugal.* Madrid. Vol. I.
[725] Ballesteros y Beretta, A. (1918-1936). *Historia de España y Su Influencia en la Historia Universal.* Barcelona. Vol. II.
[726] Castro, A. (1954). *The Structure of Spanish history.* Trans. E. L. King. Princeton, New Jersey: Princeton University Press.
[727] Stillman, N. A. (1979). *The Jews of Arab Lands: A History and Source Book.* Philadelphia: The Jewish Publication Society of America.
[728] Irving, D. (1981). *Uprising!* London: Hodder and Stoughton.
[729] RSV. Genesis 37:6,7.
[730] RSV. Genesis 37:26
[731] RSV. Genesis 39:7-23
[732] RSV. Genesis 41:33.
[733] RSV. Genesis 47:14.
[734] RJV. for all of above quotes.
[735] Weizmann, C. (1949). *Trial and Error: The Autobiography of Chaim Weizmann.* New York: Harper and Brothers. p.90.
[736] KJV. Genesis 25:23-33
[737] KJV. Genesis: 27: 19-39
[738] Patai, R. (1977). *The Jewish Mind.* New York: Scribners. p.234.
[739] Aleichem, S. (1937). *Funem Yarid.* New York.
[740] Hook, S. (1989). On Being a Jew. *Commentary.* Vol. 88, # 4. October 29.
[741] Spitz, L. (1946). Sermon by rabbi Leon Spitz. *American Hebrew.* March1.
[742] Truman, Harry S. (1945). As quoted from the diaries of Henry A. Wallace from his papers at the University of Iowa. Included in Victory Lasky's book, *It Didn't Start Watergate.*
[743] Halkin, Hillel. (1998). Here to stay: An Unrepentant Zionist Reflects on his Aliyah. *Moment.* p.5.
[744] Menuhin, Moshe. (1965). *The Decadence of Judaism in Our Time.* New York: Exposition Press, Inc. p.159.
[745] Menuhin, Moshe. (1965). *The Decadence of Judaism in Our Time.* New York: Exposition Press, Inc. p.397.
[746] *Encarta Encyclopedia.* (1996). Funk and Wagnalls.
[747] Brenner, Lenni. (1984). *The Iron Wall : Zionist Revisionism from Jabotinsky to Shamir.* Totowa, New Jersey. : Biblio Distribution Center
[748] Jabotinsky, V. (1923). *The Iron Wall: We And The Arabs.*
[749] U.N. Archives. (1948). A. 648. September 16. p.14.
[750] U.N. Archives. (1948). A. 648. September 16. p.14.
[751] KJV. Joshua 23:12-13.
[752] *Exodus* (1960). Director & Producer: Otto Preminger. United Artists.
[753] De Reynier, J. (1950). Chief Representative Of The International Committee Of The Red Cross In Jerusalem. (A Jerusalem Un Drapeau Flottait Sur La Ligne De Feu', Geneva.
[754] Yediot Ahronot. (1972). April 4.

755 Ankori, Zvi (1982). Davar. April 9.
756 Begin, M. (1964). *The Revolt: The Story Of The Irgun.* Tel-Aviv: Hadar Pub. p.162.
757 Haber, E. (1979). *Menachem Begin, The Man And The Legend.* New York: Delle Book. p385.
758 Erlich, G. (1992). Not Only Deir Yassin. *Hebrew Daily Ha'ir.* May 6.
759 Rokach, L. (1980). *Israel's Sacred Terrorism.* Bellmont, Mass: Assoc. Arab American University Grads.
760 Ibid.
761 Ibid.
762 Fisk, R. (1996). Massacre In Sanctuary: Eyewitness. *The Independent.* April 19. p.1.
763 Le Monde. (1993). September 12. p.118.
764 *Look Magazine.* (1962). January 16.
765 Encarta. Balfour Declaration.
766 George, D. L. *Memoirs Of The Peace Conference.* p.726.
767 Landman, S. (1936). *Great Britain, Great Britain:] The Jews And Palestine.* London: New Zionist Press. p.3-6.
768 Grose, P. (1984). *Israel In The Mind Of America.* New York: Knopf. p.64.
769 Encarta. Balfour Declaration.
770 Trial Of The Major War Criminals Before The International Military Court. Nuremberg : November 14th 1945 Oct. 1 1946. Official French Text. 26th April 1946. Debates, Tome XII. D 321.
771 *Daily Express.* (1933). Judea Declares War on Germany. March 24. p.1.
772 Dawidowicz, L. (1976). Memo Of June 21, 1933, In: *A Holocaust Reader.* New York: Behrman. p.150-155.
773 Nicosia, F. R. (1985). *The Third Reich And The Palestine Question.* Austin: University Of Texas. p.42.
774 Niewyk, D. L. (1980). *The Jews In Weimar Germany.* Baton Rouge. p.94-95,126-131,140-143.
775 Nicosia, F. (1985). *Third Reich.* p.1-15.
776 Prinz, J. (1934). *We Jews. [Wir Juden.]* Berlin: Erich Reiss.
777 Hohne, H. (1971). *The Order Of The Death's Head.* Ballantine. p.376.
778 Herzl, T. (1970). *Jewish State.* New York: Herzl Press. p.33, 35, 36.
779 Weckert, I. (1981). *Feuerzeichen: Die Reichskristallnacht.* TüBingen: Grabert. p.212.
780 Black, E. (1984). *The Transfer Agreement.* New York: MacMillan. p.73.
781 Herzl, T. (1897). *Der Kongress.* Welt. June 4. Reprinted In: Theodor Herzls *Zionistische Schriften* (Leon Kellner, Ed.), Erster Teil, Berlin: Jüdisher Verlag, 1920, p. 190 (And p. 139).
782 Rundschau. (1935). September 17. Quoted In: Yitzhak Arad, With Y. Gutman and A. Margaliot, Eds. Documents On The Holocaust (Jerusalem: Yad Vashem. (1981). p.82-83.
783 Kern, E. (1935). *Verheimlichte Dokumente. Der Angriff.* Munich. (1988). December 23. p.148.
784 Nicosia, F. (1985). *Third Reich.* p.56.
785 Brenner, L. (1983). *Zionism In The Age Of The Dictators.* p.138.
786 Margaliot, A. (1977). The Reaction.... *Yad Vashem Studies* Jerusalem. Vol. 12. p.90-91.
787 Levine, H. (1975). A Jewish Collaborator In Nazi Germany. *Central European History.* Atlanta. September. p.251-281.
788 Wise (1938). Dr. Wise Urges Jews To Declare Selves As Such. *New York Herald Tribune.* June 13. p.12.
789 Nicosia, F. (1935). *Das Schwarze Korps.* September 26. Quoted In: *The Third Reich And The Palestine Question* (1985), p.56-57.
790 Nicosia, F. (1985). *Third Reich.* p.63-64, 105, 219-220.
791 Nicosia, F. (1985). *Third Reich.* p.141-144.

ENDNOTES 699

[792] Wistrich, R. (1985). *On Hitler's Critical View Of Zionism In Mein Kampf.* See Vol. 1, Chap. 11. Quoted In: *Hitler's Apocalypse.* p.155.
[793] Nicosia, F. (1985). *Third Reich.* p.26-28.
[794] Kotze, H. V. (1974). *Heeresadjutant Bei Hitler.* Stuttgart. p.65, 95.
[795] Arad, Y. (1981). *Documents On The Holocaust.* p.155.
[796] Feilchenfeld, W. (1972). *Haavara-Transfer Nach Palüstina.* Tübingen: Mohr/Siebeck.
[797] Yisraeli, David (1971). *The Third Reich And The Transfer Agreement, Journal Of Contemporary History.* London. No. 2. p.129-148.
[798] Encyclopaedia Judaica. (1971). Haavara. Vol. 7. p. 1012-1013.
[799] Nicosia, F. (1985). *The Third Reich.* p.44-49.[consistency!]
[800] Hilberg, R. (1985). *The Destruction Of The European Jews.* New York: Holmes & Meier, p.140-141.
[801] Levy, R. S. (1984). Commentary, Sept. 68-71.32.
[802] Original Document In German Auswurtiges Amt Archiv, Bestand 47-59, E 224152 And E 234155-58.
[803] Yisraeli, D. (1974). *The Palestine Problem In German Politics 1889-1945.* Israel. p.315-317.
[804] Polkhen, K. (1976). The Secret Contacts. *Journal Of Palestine Studies.* Spring-Summer. p.78-80.
[805] Yoar-Gelber. (1939-1942).Zionist Policy And The Fate Of European Jewry. *Yad Vashem Studies.* Vol. XII. p.199.
[806] Rosenblum, H. (1958). Yediot Aahronot. *Jewish Newsletter.* New York. November.
[807] Bar Zohar. (1966). *Le Prophète Armé — : Ben Gourion.* Fayard. Paris. p.146.
[808] United Nations General Assembly. (1965). The International Convention on the Elimination of All Forms of Racial Discrimination.
[809] Shahak, I.. *The Racism Of The State Of Israel.* p.57.
[810] Badi, J. (1960). *Fundamental Laws Of The State Of Israel.* New York. p.156.
[811] Ennes, J. (1979). *Assault On The Liberty.* New York: Random House.
[812] Gross, F. B. (1975). Faces of Death. MPI Home.
[813] Irving, D. (1964). *Destruction of Dresden.* New York: Holt, Rinehart and Winston.
[814] Bacque, J. (1989). *Other Losses.* Canada: Stoddart Publishing.
[815] Kaufman, Theodore N. (1941). *Germany must Perish!* New York: Gordon Press.
[816] Frank, Anne. (1952). *Diary of a Young Girl.* Translated from the Dutch by B. M. Mooyaart-Doubleday, with an introduction by Eleanor Roosevelt. Garden City, New York: Doubleday.
[817] Ibid.
[818] Wiesel, E. (1969). *Night.* New York: Avon Books. p.41-44, 79, 93.
[819] D. Calder. (1987). *The Sunday Sun.* [Toronto, Canada. May 31. p.C4.
[820] Wiesenthal, S. (1967). *The Murderers Among Us.* New York: McGraw-Hill
[821] Encyclopaedia Britannica (1952).
[822] Encyclopaedia Britannica (1947),(1952). & (1956).
[823] Encyclopaedia Britannica. (1967).
[824] Paroles d'étranger (1982). Editions du Seuil. 86.
[825] Kennedy, J. F. (1963). *Profiles in Courage.* New York: Pocket Books.
[826] Ibid.
[827] Ibid.
[828] Ibid.
[829] *Washington Daily News.* (1949). January 9.
[830] *Sunday Pictorial.* (1949). January 23. London.
[831] *Chicago Daily Tribune.* (1948). February 23.
[832] Blumenson, M. (1972). *The Patton Papers.* Boston: Houghton Mifflin.
[833] Sack, J. (1993). *An Eye For An Eye.* New York: Basic Books.
[834] Bacque, James (1997). *Crimes and Mercies : The Fate of German Civilians Under Allied Occupation, 1944-1950.* Toronto: Little, Brown and Company, Canada.

700 MY AWAKENING

835 *Holocaust Revisionism Source Book.* (1994). Quote from Vanity Fair. pg.1.
836 Butler, R. (1983). *Legions of Death*. England. p.235-237.
837 Nuremberg exhibit, U.S.S.R. p.197.
838 Porter, Carlos. (1988). Made in Russia. Facsimile reprint from (IMT (Blue Series) vol.1. p.252.). p.159.
839 Wiesenthal, S. (1946). *Die Neue Weg.* 17/18 p.4-5
840 Shirer, W. L. (1960). *The Rise and Fall of the Third Reich : A History of Nazi Germany.* New York. p.971
841 Laqueur, W. (1981). *The Terrible Secret : Suppression of the Truth About Hitler's "Final Solution."* Boston: Little, Brown and Company.
842 Sereny, Gitta. (1974). *Into That Darkness: From Mercy Killing to Mass Murder.* New York: McGraw-Hill. p.141.
843 *Los Angeles Times.* (1981).Nazi Soap Rumor During World War II. May 16. p.II/2.
844 *Toronto Globe & Mail.* (1990). April 25.
845 Weber, Mark. (1991). Jewish Soap. *Journal for Historical Review.* Vol. 2. p.224.
846 Hugo, R. (1983). *The Hitler Diaries.* New York: Morrow.
847 After much intimidation Cole later repudiated his revisionist viewpoints, but the tape of Franciszek Piper remains.
848 Van Pelt, R. J. & Dwork, D. (1996). *Auschwitz: 1270 to Present.* New Haven and London: W.W. Norton & Company. p.363-364.
849 Hinsley, F. H. (1984). *British Intelligence in the Second World War: Its Influence on Strategy and Operations.* New York: Cambridge University Press.
850 Pressac, J. C. (1989). *Auschwitz: Techniques and Operation of the Gas Chambers.* New York: Beate Klarsfeld Foundation.
851 Mayer, A. J. (1988). *Why Did The Heavens Not Darken?: The "Final Solution" In History.* New York: Pantheon Books. p.365
852 Ibid.]p.362.
853 Compton's Multimedia Encyclopedia. (1991). Miriam Webster.
854 Ibid.
855 Hilberg, R. (1961). *The Destruction of the European Jews.* New York: Harper & Row.
856 The Revised Hilberg. (1986). *Simon Wiesenthal Annual.* Vol. 3. 294.
857 Kelley, J., Eisler, P., Kelly K. (1997). Silent Witness. *USA Today.* May 2. FINAL Page 13A.
858 Kennedy, J.F. *Profiles in Courage.*
859 Mason, A. T. (1956). Harlan Fiske Stone: Pillar of the Law. Viking Press. p.746.
860 Hilberg, R. (1996). *Holocaust.* Encarta Encyclopedia.
861 Goldmann, N. (1978). *The Jewish Paradox.* New York: Grosset & Dunlap.
862 Ibid. p.122-123.
863 Wiesel, E. (1982). *Legends of Our Time.* (chapter 12: Appointment with Hate.) New York: Shocken Books. p.142.
864 Dina Kyriakidou. (1996). *Le Pen Fights Fine.* Reuters Wire Service. June 21.
865 Churchill, Winston, Sir. (1989). *The Second World War.* Norwalk, Connecticut: Easton Press. Indexes: 1. Gathering storm -- 2. Their finest hour -- 3. Grand Alliance -- 4. Hinge of fate -- 5. Closing the ring -- 6. Triumph and tragedy.
866 Eisenhower, Dwight D. (1997). *Crusade in Europe.* Baltimore, London: Johns Hopkins University Press.
867 Wiesenthal Center Press Release (1997). December 8.
868 *Daily Express.* (1933). Judea Declares War on Germany. March 24. p.1.
869 Smith, Drew L. (1971). *The Legacy Of The Melting Pot.* North Quincy, Massachusetts. Christopher Publishing House
870 Congressional Record, April 12, 1924. 6,265-6,266.
871 Ross, E. A. (1914). *The Old World And The New: The Significance Of Past And Present Immigration To The American People.* New York: The Century Co. p.144..
872 Congressional Record, April 12, 1924. 6,272.
873 Congressional Record, April 23, 1952. 2,285.

[874] Joint Hearings Before The Subcommittees Of The Committees On The Judiciary, 82nd Congress, First Session, On S. 716, H. R. 2379, And H. R. 2816. March 6- April 9, 1951. 563
[875] Congressional Record, April 23, 1952. 4,320.
[876] Javits, J. (1951). Let's Open Our Gates. *New York Times Magazine*. July 8. p.8, 33.
[877] *Congress Weekly*. (1956). Editorial of February 20. p.3
[878] Cohen, N. W. (1972). *Not Free To Desist: The American Jewish Committee 1906-1966*. Philadelphia: The Jewish Publication Society Of America.
[879] Ibid. p.342.
[880] Sachar, H. (1992). *A History Of Jews In America*. New York: Alfred A. Knopf.
[881] Ibid. p.427.
[882] MacDonald, K. B. (1994). *A People That Shall Dwell Alone: Judaism As A Group Evolutionary Strategy*. Westport, Connecticut: Praeger.
[883] MacDonald, K. B. (1998). *Separation And Its Discontents: Toward An Evolutionary Theory Of Anti-Semitism*. Westport, Connecticut: Praeger.
[884] Silberman, C. E. (1985). *A Certain people: American Jews and Their Lives Today*. New York: Summit Books.
[885] Higham, J. (1984). *Send These To Me: Immigrants In Urban America*. Baltimore: Johns Hopkins University Press.
[886] Bennett, M. T. (1963). American Immigration Policies: A History. Washington, DC: Public Affairs Press. p.181.
[887] A. M. Rosenthal. (1992). New York Times. December 9.
[888] A. M. Rosenthal. (1992). .New York Times. December 9.
[889] Jewish Bulletin. (1993). July. 23.
[890] Jewish Bulletin. (1993). Feb. 19.
[891] Weyl, N. & Possony, S. (1963). *Geography Of Intellect*. Chicago: H. Regnery Co.
[892] Van den Haag, E. *The Jewish Mystique*. New York, Stein and Day.
[893] *Pittsburgh Post Gazette*. (1969). Apr. 1. p.26.
[894] Darwin, C. (1892). *The Origin Of Species By Means Of Natural Selection, Or The Preservation Of Favored Races In The Struggle For Life*. New York, D. Appleton And Company.
[895] Keith, Arthur, Sir, (1949). *A New Theory of Human Evolution*. New York. Philosophical Library
[896] Hamilton, W. D. (1964). *The Genetical Theory Of Social Behaviour* .Vols. I, II. Journal Of Theoretical Biology. 7:p.1-52.
[897] Wilson, E. (1975). *Sociobiology: A New Synthesis*. Cambridge: Harvard U. Press.
[898] *Grolier's Electronic Encyclopedia*. (1994)."Dog"
[899] Frank, Gelya. (1997). Jews, Multiculturalism, And Boasian Anthropology. *The American Anthropologist*. (99 (4) 731-745.
[900] Frank, Geyla (1997).
[901] Meyerhoff, B. (1978). *Number Our Days*. E. P. Hutton.
[902] Chase, G. A., & V. A. McKusick (1972). Founder Effect In Tay-Sachs Disease. *American Journal Of Human Genetics*. 25:339-352.
[903] Fraikor, A. L. (1977). Tay-Sachs Disease: Genetic Drift Among The Ashkenazi Jews. *Social Biology*. 24:117-134.
[904] Sachs, L., & M. Bat-Miriam (1957). The Genetics Of Jewish Populations. *American Journal Of Human Genetics*. 9:117-126.
[905] Mourant, A. E., A. C. Kopec, & K. Domaniewska-Sobczak (1978). *The Genetics of the Jews*. Oxford, England: Clarendon Press.
[906] Mourant, A. E., Kopec, A. C. & Domaniewska-Sobczak D. (1978). *The Genetics Of The Jews*. Oxford, England: Clarendon Press.
[907] Bonné-Tamir, B., Ashbel, S., & Kenett, R. (1977). *Genetic Markers: Benign And Normal Traits Of Ashkenazi Jews In Genetic Diseases Among Ashkenazi Jews*. Ed. R. M. Goodman & A. G. Motulsky. New York: Raven Press.

702 My Awakening

908 Karlin, S., R. Kenett & Bonné-Tamir, B. (1979). Analysis Of Biochemical Genetic Data On Jewish Populations II. Results And Interpretations Of Heterogeneity Indices And Distance Measures With Respect To Standards. *American Journal Of Human Genetics.* 31:341-365.

909 Mille, S. & Kobyliansky, E. (1985). Dermatoglyphic Distances Between Israeli Jewish Population Groups Of Different Geographic Extraction. *Human Biology.* 57: 97-111.

910 Kobyliansky, E. & Livshits, G. A. (1985). Morphological Approach To The Problem Of The Biological Similarity Of Jewish And Non-Jewish Populations. *Annals Of Human Biology.* 12:203-212.

911 Sofaer, J. A., Smith, P. & Kaye, E. (1986). Affinities Between Contemporary And Skeletal Jewish And Non-Jewish Groups Based On Tooth Morphology. *American Journal Of Physical Anthropology.* 70:265-275.

912 Lenz, F. (1931). *The Inheritance Of Intellectual Gifts In Human Heredity,* Trans. E. Paul & C. Paul, Ed. E. Baur, E. Fischer, & F. Lenz. New York: Macmillan.

913 Patai, R., & Patai, J. (1989). *The Myth Of The Jewish Race.* Detroit, Wayne State University Press.

914 Cohen, Steven M. (1986). *Vitality And Resilience In The American Jewish Family.* In S. M. Cohen & P. E. Hyman (Eds.), The Jewish Family: Myths And Reality. New York Holmes & Meier. 228.

915 Stolper, P. (1984). *Jewish Alternatives In Love, Dating, And Marriage.* NCSY/Orthodox Union/University Press Of America. 64.

916 Landau, D. (1993). *Piety And Power: The World Of Jewish Fundamentalism.* New York: Hill And Wang. 300.

917 Shaffir, W. (1986). *Persistence And Change In The Hasidic Family.* In *The Jewish Family: Myths And Reality.* Ed. S. M. Cohen & P. E. Hyman. New York: Holmes & Meier. p.190.

918 Ellman, Y. (1987). Intermarriage In The United States: A Comparative Study Of Jews And Other Ethnic And Religious Groups. *Jewish Social Studies.* Vol. 49. p.1-26.

919 Kosmin, B. A., Goldstein, S., Waksberg, J., Lerer, N., Keysar, A., & Scheckner, J. (1991). *Highlights Of The CJF 1990 National Jewish Population Survey.* New York: Council Of Jewish Federations.

920 Meyer, M. A. (1988). *Response To Modernity: A History Of The Reform Movement In Judaism.* New York: Oxford University Press.

921 Waxman, C. (1989). *The Emancipation, The Enlightenment, And The Demography Of American Jewry. Judaism.* Vol. 38. p.488-501.

922 Elazar, D. J. (1980). *Community And Polity: Organizational Dynamics Of American Jewry,* First Published In 1976. Philadelphia: The Jewish Publication Society Of America.

923 Ibid

924 Zborowski, M., & Herzog, E. (1952). *Life Is With People: The Jewish Little-Town Of Eastern Europe.* New York: International Universities Press.

925 Lieberman, S. & Weinfeld. (1978). Demographic Trends And Jewish Survival. *Midstream.* November.

926 Jeremias, J. (1969). *Jerusalem In The Time Of Jesus: An Investigation Into Economic And Social Conditions During The New Testament Period.* Trans. F. H. Cave & C. H. Cave (Based On An Earlier Draft Of A Translation By M. E. Dahl). Philadelphia: Fortress Press. p.311.

927 Shahak, I. (1994). *Jewish History, Jewish Religion.*

928 Rushton, J. Philippe. (1995). Race, Evolution, and Behavior : A Life History Perspective. New Brunswick, New Jersey. Transaction Publishers.

929 Churchill, W.I. (1920). Illustrated *Sunday Herald.* February 8.

930 Levinson, B.M. (1960). A Comparative Study Of The Verbal And Performance Ability Of Monolingual And Bilingual Native Born Jewish Preschool Children Of Traditional Parentage. *Journal Of Genetic Psychology.* Vol. 97. p.93-112.

931 Brown, F. (1944). A Comparative Study Of The Intelligence Of Jewish And Scandinavian Kindergarten Children. Vol. 64.p.67-92.
932 Backman, M. E. (1972). Patterns Of Mental Abilities: Ethnic, Socio-Economic, And Sex Differences. *American Educational Research Journal*. Vol. 9.p.1-12.
933 Levinson, B. M. (1957). The Intelligence Of Applicants For Admission To Jewish Day Schools. *Jewish Social Studies*. Vol. 19 p.29-140.
934 *Journal Of Genetic Psychology* (1958). Cultural Pressure And WAIS Scatter In A Traditional Jewish Setting. Vol. 93.p.277-286.
935 *Journal Of Genetic Psychology*. (1960). A Comparative Study Of The Verbal And Performance Ability Of Monolingual And Bilingual Native Born Jewish Preschool Children Of Traditional Parentage. Vol. 97.p.93-112.
936 *Journal Of Genetic Psychology*. (1962). Jewish Subculture And WAIS Performance Among Jewish Aged. Vol. 100. p.55-68.
937 Mosse, W. E. (1987). *Jews In The German Economy: The German-Jewish Economic Élite 1820-1935*. Oxford, England: Clarendon Press. p.166.
938 Swartzbaugh, Richard. (1973). *The Mediator; His Strategy for Power*. Cape Canaveral, Florida: Howard Allen.
939 Lynn, R. (1987). The Intelligence Of The Mongoloids: A Psychometric, Evolutionary And Neurological Theory. *Personality And Individual Differences*. Vol. 8.p.813-844.
940 Rushton, J. P. (1991). Race Differences In Intelligence: A Global Perspective. *Mankind Quarterly*. Vol. 31. p.255-296.
941 J. Lynch, C Ed. (1992). Intelligence: Ethnicity And Culture. In *Cultural Diversity And The Schools*. Ed.. S. Modgil. London and Washington, D.C.: Falmer Press.
942 Hertzberg, A. & Hirt-Manheimer, A. (1998). Relax. It's Okay to be the Chosen People. *Reform Judaism*. May.
943 Yockey, Francis P. (1963). *Imperium : The Philosophy of History and Politics*. Sausalito, California: Noontide Press.
944 U.S. Bureau of Census. (1996). Projections for the 21st Century.
945 Smith, Drew L. (1971). *The Legacy Of The Melting Pot*. North Quincy, Massachusetts. Christopher Publishing House.
946 Plessy v. Ferguson (1896). U.S. Supreme Court. Citation:163 U.S. 537
947 Wilson, Woodrow. (1902). *A history of the American people*. New York: Harper and Brothers.
948 Griffith, D.W. (1914). Birth of a Nation. Included in the film as a faceplate.
949 *Encyclopaedia Britannica*. (1910). p. 942-43.
950 Churchill, Ward. (1990). *The Cointelpro Papers : Documents From The FBI's Secret Wars Against Domestic Dissent*. Boston, Massachusetts : South End Press.
951 Perkus, Cathy. (1975). *Cointelpro : The FBI's Secret War On Political Freedom*. New York : Monad Press.
952 Hill, Napoleon. (1965). *The Master-Key To Riches*. New York: Ballantine Books.
953 Creedence Clearwater Revival. (1969). *Bayou Country*. Born on the Bayou
954 *Discover* (1994). Riddle of the Chinese Mummies: What are 4,000-Year-Old Caucasians doing in Xinjiang. April (cover story).
955 Polosmak, Natalya. (1994). Mummies Unearthed from the Pastures of Heaven. *National Geographic*. October. p. 80-103.
956 In Louisiana a Creole is one who has French and Spanish ancestry.
957 The Bhagavad Gita (1984). translated by Winthrop Sargeant. Albany, NY : State University of New York Press
958 Hamilton, Edith. (1963). D.A. Thompson from the *Legacy of Greece* quoted in *The Greek Way*. New York: Time, Inc.
959 Hamilton, Edith. (1963). *The Greek Way* New York: Time, Inc.
960 Hamilton, Edith. (1963). *The Greek Way*.
961 Tacitus, P. Cornelius. (109 AD). *The Annals*. 13. ch. 57.
962 Tacitus, P. Cornelius. (109 AD). *The Annals*. BOOK I, A.D. 14, 15.
963 Hoskins, Richard Kelly. (1961). Quoted from, *Our Nordic Race*. Savannah, GA:

704 MY AWAKENING

964 Churchill, Ward. (1990). *The Cointelpro Papers.*
965 Nelson, Jack. (1993). *Terror in the Night: The Klan's Campaign Against the Jews.* New York: Simon & Schuster.
966 Federal Bureau of Investigation. (1980s). Annual (ODEH) reports of terrorist bombing during the 1980s) Washington, DC.
967 Fields, Edward. R. *The Truth At Last.* P.O. Box 1211. Marietta, GA 30061.
968 Warner, James K. Christian Defense League. Arabi, Louisiana.
969 *The Daily Mirror* (1978). March 3.
970 *The Daily Telegraph.* (1978). 135 Fleet St., London. March 9.
971 *The Mirror.* (1978). Mirror Editorial Comment. March.
972 *New Statesman.* (1978). April.
973 *The Klansman.* (1974). Screenplay by Millard Kaufman and Samuel Fuller. Hollywood: Paramount.
974 Kurtz, Irma. (1979). *The Grand Dragon.* New York: E.P. Dutton.
975 Kurtz, Irma. (1979). *The Grand Dragon.* p.47.
976 Kurtz, Irma. (1979). *The Grand Dragon.* p.49.
977 Kurtz, Irma. (1979). *The Grand Dragon.* p.45.
978 Kurtz, Irma. (1979). *The Grand Dragon.* p.80.
979 Kurtz, Irma. (1979). *The Grand Dragon.* p.214.
980 Roth, Philip. (1969). *Portnoy's Complaint.* New York: Random House.
981 Kurtz, Irma. (1979). *The Grand Dragon.* p.133.
982 Kurtz, Irma. (1979). *The Grand Dragon.* p.134.
983 Kurtz, Irma. (1979). *The Grand Dragon.* p.158.
984 Kurtz, Irma. (1977). The Klan Rises Again: Will it Come to Britain?. *Telegraph Sunday Magazine.* April 24.
985 Kurtz, Irma. (1979). *The Grand Dragon.* p.139.
986 Kurtz, Irma. (1979). *The Grand Dragon.* p.139.
987 Kurtz, Irma. (1979). *The Grand Dragon.* p.172.
988 Kurtz, Irma. (1979). *The Grand Dragon.* p.153.
989 Kurtz, Irma. (1979). *The Grand Dragon.* p.5.
990 Kurtz, Irma. (1979). *The Grand Dragon.* p.135.
991 Bridges, Tyler. (1994). *The Rise of David Duke.* Jackson, Mississippi: University Press of Mississippi. p.51.
992 Thompson, Jerry. (1982). *My Life in the Klan.* New York: Putnam.
993 Zatarain, Michael. (1990). *David Duke: Evolution of a Klansman.* Gretna, Louisiana: Pelican p.37
994 *Times-Picayune.* (1989). Bush, Reagan Endorse Treen in Race. Feb. 16. p.A1.
995 Zatarain, Michael. (1990). *David Duke: Evolution of a Klansman.* Gretna, Louisiana: Pelican p.46.
996 McMahon, Bill. (1990). Johnston Would Defeat Duke, Poll Says. *Morning Advocate.* January 9. p.6A.
997 *Times-Picayune* (1990). Bagert Quits to Keep Duke Out of Runoff. Oct. 5. p.A1.
998 Bridges, Tyler. (1994). *The Rise of David Duke.* Jackson, Mississippi: University Press of Mississippi.
999 Schleifsten, Mark, & Grissett, Sheila. (1991). Religious Leaders Doubt Duke's Christianity. *Times-Picayune.* November 13. p.1A.
1000 Bridges, Tyler. (1994). *The Rise of David Duke.* p.232.
1001 *Tampa Tribune* (1997). Editorial Page. May 10.
1002 Orwell, George. (1984). *Nineteen Eighty-Four.* New York, NY : New American Library.
1003 Cole, David.
1004 Spengler, Oswald. (1962). *The Decline of the West.* New York: Knopf.
1005 *Random House Websters Unabridged Electronic Dictionary* (1996). "phenotype."
1006 Galton, Sir Francis. (1909). *Essays in Eugenics.* Eugenics Education Society. London. p.35.

ENDNOTES 705

[1007] Galton, Sir Francis. (1908). *Memories of My Life*. New York. Dutton. p.322

[1008] Pearson, R. (1996). *Heredity and Humanity: Race Eugenics and Modern Science*. Washington, DC: Scott-Townsend Publishers (Quotes Darwin letter of December 3, 1869 to Galton.). p.20.

[1009] Shaw, G. B. (1965). *The Complete Works of George Bernard Shaw*. London: Paul Hamlyn. p.159.

[1010] Pearson, Roger. (1992). *Shockley on Eugenics and Race*. Washington, DC: Scott-Townsend Publishers. p.19.

[1011] *U.S. News and World Report*. (1965). Quality of U.S. Population Declining — An Interview With Dr. William Shockley. October.

[1012] *Sacramento Journal*. (1971). June 1.

[1013] *Harvard Crimson* (1973). October 24.

[1014] *Time* (1977). December 19.

[1015] *London Daily Express*. (1933). Judea Declares War on Germany." March 24. p.1.

[1016] Gabler, Neal. (1988). *An Empire of their Own: How the Jews Invented Hollywood*. New York : Crown Publishers.

[1017] Bar-Yosef, Avinoam. (1994). "Warm Jews" is the term used by the Israeli newspaper *Maariv* to describe Jews who are loyal to Jewish interests The Jews Who Run Clinton's Court. September 2.

[1018] Kagedan, Ian J. (1991). Memory of Holocaust Central to New World Order. *Toronto Star*. Nov. 26.

[1019] Talmud. (1936). London. Soncino Press. Sanhedrin 58b.

[1020] Weyl, N. & Possony, S. (1963). *Geography Of Intellect*. Chicago : H. Regnery Co.

[1021] Strom, Kevin Alfred. (1988). In personal conversation with author.

Index

The 100: A Ranking of the Most Influential Persons in History, 113
A Certain People: American Jews and Their Lives Today, 445
A Hole in the Sheet, 286
A New Theory of Human Evolution, 451
A People That Shall Dwell Alone, 445, 281
ABC, 294, 301, 302, 304
ABC Evening News, 596
Abzug, Bella, 286
Achaeans, 536
ADL (Anti-Defamation League of B'nai B'rith), 219, 238, 266, 351, 352, 430, 443, 448, 486, 553-555, 580, 587, 597, 598, 636
Adler, 298
Aesop's Fables, 5
affirmative action, 63, 161, 163, 164, 165, 168, 586, 590, 610, 611, 613, 618, 619, 621, 624, 671
Africa, 19, 27, 39, 40, 42, 57, 65, 74, 84, 85, 90-100, 112-116, 124, 128, 136, 160, 195, 507, 540, 584, 585
African-American teachers organizations, 169
Africans, 42, 66, 89, 93, 96, 100, 104, 114, 129, 155, 186
Afternoon Press, 297
agent provocateurs, 485, 555
Agra, 516, 517, 521
Aid to Families with Dependent Children (AFDC), 159
AIDS, 96, 126, 147, 149, 151, 152, 183, 203-206
  HIV- positive, 178
Aiken family, 174
Ainsworth, Kathy, 554, 555
Air America, 512
Air Force, United States, 421
Alabama, 297, 485, 558, 570
  Birmingham, 30, 143
Al-Aqsa Mosque Massacre, 372
Albright, Madeline, 318, 319, 320, 321
Alexander the Great, 121
Alexander, Richard, 451
Alger, Horatio, 51
Ali, Mohammed, 97, 308
Allies, 379, 380, 381, 401, 408, 409, 410, 412, 415, 428, 429, 430, 434
All-Movie Guidebook, 308

Almirante, Signor, 546
Almog, Shmuel, 328
Alps, 187, 473, 547
Al-Sammou' Massacre, 372
Amalakites, 258, 265
Amazon, 19, 131, 187
Ambrose, Stephen, 418
American Association of Physical Anthropologists, 67, 92, 279, 453
American Civil Liberties Union (ACLU), 322
American Colonization Society, 41
American Hebrew, 364
American Heritage Dictionary, 241, 264
American Indians, 9, 18, 38, 61, 116, 128, 129, 166
  Battle at Wounded Knee, 9
  Ft. Mims Massacre, 9
American Jewish Historical Society, 352
American Language School, 505, 529
American Medical Association (AMA), 322
American Nazi Party, 487, 621, 625
American Psychiatric Association, 202
American Psychological Association, 47, 67
American Revolution, 493, 667, 670
Amistad, 352
Amschel, Mayer, 339
An Empire of Their Own, 295
Anderson, Jack, 554, 555
Andersonville Prison Camp, 410
Anglo-Saxon, 142, 173, 184, 485, 600
Ankori, Zvi, 371
Annals, 550
Anne Frank - Diary of a Young Girl, 218
Anti-Defamation League of B'nai B'rith (ADL), 219, 238, 265, 306, 327, 430, 448, 527, 533, 534, 553, 580, 653
Antiquities of the Jews, 356
Aphrodite, 131
Appomaddox, 23
Aptheker, Herbert, 220, 253
Aquinas, Saint Thomas, 335
Arabs, 218, 328, 355, 356, 367, 368, 369, 370, 383, 387, 390, 391, 400, 433, 446, 448, 455
  Palestinians, 218, 318, 319, 329, 355, 365, 368, 370, 374, 375, 377, 378, 388-390, 394, 397, 433, 440
Arad, 389
Arendt, Hannah, 328
Arens, Richard, 446
Argentina, 118
Aristotle, 535, 542, 544
Arkansas, 314
Armed Forces Qualification Test (AFQT), 48, 49, 61
Army Reserves, 403
Army, United States, 480, 493, 528, 626, 648
Arndt, Ernst, 129
Arts & Entertainment (A&E), 302, 312
Aryan, 121, 124, 281, 366, 448, 465, 517, 518, 522-525, 536, 538, 540, 542, 545, 627, 637, 644, 649, 665-670, 674
Ashbel, 454
Ashkenazim, 271, 454
Asimov, Isaac, 113
Assault on the Liberty, 393
Assyrians, 118, 258
Athenia, 535
Athens, 533, 534, 535, 539
Atwater, Lee, 618
Augustine, Israel, 568
Auschwitz, 353, 404, 406, 410, 418-428
Australia, 635, 662
Austria, 6, 7, 138, 280, 312, 328, 361, 386, 418
  Vienna, 6
Avon Books, 418
Baba Kamma, 242, 243, 259
Babi Yar, 406
Babylon, 240, 290, 291
Babylonian, 241, 242, 260, 264, 271, 348, 366, 460
Backman, 465
Bagert, Ben, 619, 621, 623, 624
Balaam (Jesus Christ), 242
Balfour, Arthur, 380, 641, 656
Ban Houi Sai, 512
Banfield, Edward, 84
Bangkok, 506, 508, 509
Barrett, Hamilton, 552, 557
Barry, Marion, 151, 168, 176
Baruch, 657, 658
Baruch, Bernard, 316, 379, 381

INDEX 707

Bar-Yosef, 317
Bass, Harry, 306
Battle of Shiloh, 482
Bauer, Professor Yuhuda, 416
Beale, Howard, 293, 294, 295, 326
Beavis and Butthead, 303
Beethoven, 124
Begin, Menachem, 329, 369, 371, 372, 388, 466
Behind Communism, 276
Bein, Alex, 327
Being Red, 309
Beirut, 373, 374
Belgium, 324, 361, 432
The Bell Curve, 47, 59, 113
Bell, Lieutenant, 474, 475
Bellarmino, Cardinal, 68
Belli, Marvin, 599
Belth, Nathan C., 327
Benbow, Dr. Camilla, 195
Benedict XIII, 245
Benedict, Ruth, 278
Bengal Raiders Special Forces ROTC training organization, 503
Ben-Gurion, David, 369, 372, 373, 376, 377, 388, 467
Berger, Robert, 309
Berger, Sandy, 317, 318
Berman, E.F., 316
Bernadotte, Count Folke, 369
Bernstein, Richard, 301
Berry, Jason, 627
Bertesgarten, 547
Bhagavad Gita, 525
Bible
    New Testament, 238-240, 245, 261-270, 378
    Old Testament, 219, 237-240, 258-262, 264, 271, 378, 460
Big Ben, 594, 596
Bilbo, Theodore, 128
Binet, Alfred, 45, 46, 47, 67
Birth of a Nation, 305, 312, 480, 482
Black Nurses Association, 169
Black Panthers, 489
Black Perspectives on the News, 306, 351, 355
Black Police Officers Association, 169
Black, Don, 604, 607
Blockbuster Video, 303
Boas, Franz, 277, 278, 279, 465, 467
Boesky, Ivan, 340, 341, 342, 661
Bolshevik, 226, 231, 235, 365, 379, 398, 399, 438
Bombay, 521
Bonné, 454
Book of Civil Laws, 333, 334

Boone, Daniel, 10
Border Patrol, United States, 589, 590, 591
Boring, Dr. Edward, 46
Born on the Bayou, 509
Borneo, 596
Bornstein, Steven, 302
Bosnians, 189
Bosporus Peninsula, 533
Boston, 583
Boston University, 284
Botnick, A.I., 553, 554, 555
Bouchard Jr., Dr. Thomas J., 52
boxing, 97, 124, 191
Bradford, William, 4, 5
Bradlee Jr., Ben, 597
Brahmin, 518, 524
Brandeis, Judge Louis, 250, 316, 328, 381
Brando, Marlon, 313
Brannau, 547
Braun, Ewa, 295
Braun, Zev, 309
Brazil, 117, 118, 187
Bristow, Edward, 353
Britain, 116, 128, 138, 139, 190, 279, 339, 350, 369, 379-381-387, 425, 441
Broder, Jonathan, 318
Brodkin, Herbert, 309
Brokhin, Yuri, 345
Bronfman, Edgar, 304, 324, 325
Brookings Institution, 318
Brothman, Abraham, 276
Brown vs Board of Education, 43, 149
Brown, George S., 316
Brown, Julia, 494
Brown, Tommy, 494, 555, 565, 566, 630
Browning, Christopher, 410, 428
Bryan, William Jennings, 574
Buchanan, Patrick, 631, 632
Buck vs. Bell, 51
Buckley, William, 487
Buena Vista Television, 302
Buenos Aires, 596
Bugsy, 343, 344
Bull Run, 23
Bumpers, Dale, 314
Burger Brau Keller, 547
Bush, President George, 316, 616-619, 632
Butler, Rupert, 411
Byrd, Robert, 1
Café du' Monde, 171
Calcutta, 521
Calhoun, John C., 23
California, 10, 14, 15, 46, 58, 63, 138, 163, 180, 182, 190

Cambodia, 217, 397, 398, 399, 436, 580
Campanis, Al, 79
Canaanites, 238, 258
Canada, 116, 139, 176, 190, 276, 323, 418, 436, 441, 446, 463, 635, 661, 662
Canadian Jewish News, 306
Cannanites, 258
Capital Cities/ABC, 302
Capitalists, 108
Capone, Al, 343
Capote, Truman, 600
Caravan Pictures, 302
Cardella, George, 115
Caribbean, 116, 117, 125
Carmel, 389
Carrollton Avenue Church of Christ, 256
Carter, President Jimmy, 315, 316, 459, 591
Carto, Willis, 474, 610
Caruthers, John C., 74
Casanova, 499
Catechism for the Teutonic Armyman, 129
Caucasian, 83, 89, 90, 112, 124, 139
Cavalli-Sforza, 85
CBS, 294, 301-304, 314, 342, 652, 657
Celler, Emanuel, 442-444
Census Bureau, United States, 478
Chamberlain, Neville, 438
Chandler, Raymond, 435, 499
Chaney, 283
Charles, Delton, 612
Chayefsky, Paddy, 293, 295, 296
Chehard, Lawrence, 612, 620
Chein, Isador, 278
Cheka, 228, 231, 235
Chernin, Peter, 304
Cherusci, 549
Chicago Jewish Sentinel, 233
Chile, 118
Chimpanzees, 85, 104
China, 108, 217, 398, 399
Chitterlings Explanation, 60
Chomsky, Marvin, 266, 308, 309
Christianity, 8, 9, 27, 102, 144, 160
Christian, 481-487, 518, 546, 562, 580, 590, 601, 616, 622, 656
    Bible, 219, 237, 238, 244, 256-260, 262, 264, 271, 272, 358, 363, 366, 377, 378, 459, 486, 532, 569
    Catholic Church, 246, 251, 253, 256, 267,

268, 281, 307, 450, 483, 484, 551, 616
Christ, 8, 24, 25, 101, 102, 169, 183, 211
Church of Christ, 256
Jesus Christ, 25, 102, 219, 239-248, 254, 256, 260-273, 328, 330, 331, 348, 351, 367, 378, 462
Methodist, 219, 253, 256, 257
New Christian Crusade Church, 589
Presbyterianism, 256
West Palm Beach Presbyterian Church, 571
Woodlawn Baptist Church, 576, 583
Christmas, 247, 263, 272, 274, 275, 289, 365, 388
Chronicle of Science and Discovery, 113
Churchill, Winston, 223, 226, 232, 284, 437, 463, 488, 641
Cicero, Marcus, 347
Cincinnati, 610
Citizens Council, 31, 32, 220, 221, 234-236, 241, 274, 409, 441, 473, 479, 485
Civil Rights, 40, 143, 152, 157, 161-163, 213
Clark, K.B., 278
Clark, Kenneth, 43
Clarke, 411
Clay, Henry, 41 *The Clansman*, 305
Clement VIII, 246
Cleopatra, 113, 120, 124, 349
Clifton L. Ganus Junior High school, 101, 256
Clinton, President Bill, 178, 182, 316-322, 374, 626, 658, 671
The Collected Works of Abraham Lincoln, 40
The Conscience of a Conservative, 222
CNN, 618
Coalition against Racism and Nazism, 623
Cochran, Johnny, 166
Code of Maimonides, 336
Cohen, Mark, 244
Cohen, Rabbi Simcha, 252
Cohen, Steve, 456
Cohen, Wilbur, 316
Cointelpro, 485, 554, 558, 604
Colisseum, 546
Collins, Marva, 67
Cologne, 548
Colonies, American, 23, 116
Colorado River, 575

Common Pleas Court, Philadelphia, 306
Common Sense, 220, 221, 222, 223, 224
Communist Manifesto, 233
Communist Party, United States, 54
Community and Polity: Organizational Dynamics in American Jewry, 458
Confederacy, 22, 23, 26, 480, 482, 547, 553
Congress of Racial Equality (CORE), 283
Congress, United States, 42, 173, 483, 485, 546
Constitution, United States, 22, 23, 27, 117, 142, 183, 184, 486, 671
Coon, Dr. Carleton, 67, 68, 92
Cooper, Gary, 98
Copernicus, 68
Coplin, Judith, 276
Cosby, Bill, 346
Cosmopolitan, 599
Cossacks, 218
Costa Rica, 117
Courlander, Harold, 308
Craig, Gordon, 418
Creedence Clearwater Revival, 509
Crick, Madeline, 12
Crick, Thomas, 12
Criminal Justice, 147
Croatia, 319
Croats, 189
Crockett, Davy, 8, 10, 28
Cro-Magnon man, 109
Crommelin, Admiral John G., Ret., 607
Cronkite, Walter, 651
The Crusader, 583
The Crying Game, 302, 312, 468
Cuba, 323, 399
Cunard Hotel, 594
Currie, J., 64
Curtis, Michael, 328
Cusimano, Chuck, 612
Cyclades, 536
Da Costa, Isaac, 349
Dachau, 408, 412, 413, 422, 547
Daily Telegraph, 527, 594
Dale, Colonel Joseph, 503, 630
Damascus, 264
Danzig, 415, 438
Darne, Lewis, 552, 557
Darwin, Charles, 55, 119, 185, 450, 640
Das Kapital, 233
The Das Schwarze Korps, 385
Davidow, Jeffrey, 323
Davidson, 335

Davilia, Diego Arias, 338
Davis, Jefferson, 10, 22, 23
Dayan, Moshe, 373
De Gobineau, 119, 120
Dead Man's Road, 18, 19
Dean, Kenneth, 554
Death Register, 421
The Decadence of Judaism, 249
Deckert, Gunter, 425
Declaration of Independence, 27, 28, 37, 38, 42, 120, 171, 183
Decline of the West, 533, 637
Defoe, Daniel, 347
Del Valle, General Pedro, Ret., 607
DeMille, Cecil B., 219
Demjanjuk, John, 426, 427
Democrats, 108
Den Hague, 5
Denmark, 80
Denver, 141
Department of Agriculture, United States, 77
Department of Energy, United States, 490
Department of Housing and Urban Development (HUD), 157
Derrick, 565, 566, 567
Der Angriff, 385
Der Neue Weg, 415
Der Stürmer, 382
Deuteronomy, 239, 258, 260, 268
Devil, the, 26, 68, 70
Dewey, Thomas, 342
Diamond, Jared, 85, 115, 199
Diaspora, 250, 333, 357, 367, 457
Dickens, 332, 347
Dickens, Charles, 640
Dickstein, Samuel, 442
Dilling, Elizabeth, 241, 265
Dillinger, John, 178, 343
Discover, 85, 133, 280
The Dispossessed Majority, 301
Dismukes, Mrs., 30, 31
Disney World, 302
Disney, Walt, 8, 652
Disneyland, 302
Disraeli, Benjamin, 382
Dixon, Thomas, 305
DNA (deoxyribonucleic acid), 76, 86-91, 103, 104, 131, 197, 639, 674
Domaniewska-Sobczak, 454
Dorians, 536
Dortmund, 549
Dostoevsky, 54, 332
Doubleday, 31
DreamWorks SKG, 304

Index 709

Dreger, 83
Dresden, 400, 401, 436
Dubnow, Simon, 249
Dubois, W. E. B., 221, 282
Dukakis, Michael, 611
Duke, Chloé Hardin, 502, 508, 528, 550, 552, 557, 560, 561, 562, 568, 570-576, 583-585, 587, 606
Duke, Dotti, 2, 14, 15, 20, 21, 25
Duke, Erika Lindsay, 587
Duke, Ernest M., 13, 490
Duke, Kristin Chloé 587
Dumaine Street, 557
Durant, 119
Dutch (language), 5, 6, 7
Dwork, Deborah, 420
E!-online, 295
East Prussia, 409
Easter, 247
Eastwood, Clint, 98
Ebonics, 60
Edison, Thomas, 305, 312
Edwards, Edwin, 619, 629, 630, 631
Egypt, 109, 112, 120-123, 173, 247, 269, 270, 324, 330, 332, 358-360, 378, 386, 390, 391, 460
Egyptians, 238, 258, 265, 359, 360, 370, 391, 392, 394
Ehrenberg, Israel (Ashley Montagu), 279
Ehrlich, Judith, 340, 448
Ehrlich, Paul, 185, 662
Eisenhower, President Dwight D., 148, 173
Eisler, Gerhart, 276
Eisner, Michael, 302, 304, 312, 468, 652
Elazar, Daniel, 458
Elliot Halpern & Simcha Jacobvici Productions, 312
Ellman, 457
Elysian Fields Methodist Church, 256
Emancipation Proclamation, 23, 40, 41
Emerson, Ralph Waldo, 115, 332
Emory University, 416
The Emperor's New Clothes, 79
The Encyclopedia of Zionism in Israel, 234
Encyclopaedia Britannica, 230, 334, 348, 405, 406, 483
Encyclopedia Judaica, 227, 251, 264, 405
Engerman, Stanley, 160
England, 526, 592, 600, 635, 661, 662

English Channel, 339
Ennes, Lieutenant James, 391, 393, 394
Epcot Center, 302
Erman, John, 308
Esau, 362, 363, 364, 365, 366
ESPN, 302
Euripides, 535, 542, 544
Euro Disney, 302
Europe, 6, 7, 77, 90-101, 105, 116, 117, 124, 136, 138, 158, 177, 179, 187, 196, 208, 211
evolution, 79, 90, 92, 97, 101-111, 195
Exodus, 237, 238, 258, 358, 360, 368, 370
The Faces of Death, 397
Farewell Uncle Tom, 310, 311
Farmer, Frances, 75
Farrell, Howie, 612, 614, 616, 617, 631
Fast, Howard, 309
Federal Bureau of Investigation (FBI), 137, 140, 141, 144, 284, 320, 346
Federal Elections Commission, 628
Federal Reserve Board, 316, 319, 320
Federal Reserve Corporation, 658
Fields, Dr. Edward, 294, 321 584
Fighters for the Freedom of Israel, 386
Findley, Paul, 325
First Amendment Coalition, 306
Florida, 475, 503, 573, 606, 634
  Miami Beach, 187
  West Palm Beach, 503, 571, 573
Florida International University, 141
Fogelman, Robert, 160
Food and Drug Administration (FDA), 319, 320
Footlik, Jay, 320, 321
Ford, 475
Ford, Gerald, 316
Ford, Henry, 217
Forrest, Nathan Bedford, 482, 574
Fort Hood, 510
Fort Knox, 510
Fortune, 303, 341
Foundation of National Judaism, 249
Founding Fathers, 37, 38, 42, 44, 45, 170, 182, 183, 273
Fox and the Hounds, 596
Fox Television Network, 304

Foxman, Abraham, 662
France, 116, 118, 125, 128, 138, 139, 176, 190, 249, 251, 324, 328, 334, 339, 342, 361, 381, 403, 404, 417-419, 426, 438, 441, 442, 455, 580, 635, 636, 661, 662
  government, 46
  Paris, 127
Frances, 75
Frank, Anne, 218, 401, 402, 404, 405, 435
Frank, Antoinette, 165
Frank, Gelya, 279, 453
Frankel, Max, 299
Franks, David, 349
Free Speech Alley, 495, 496, 498, 501, 552
Freedman, Robert, 346
Freedom Rides North, 583
Freedom Road, 308, 309
Freeman, Derek, 278
French Revolution, 125, 129
Freud, Sigmund, 280-286, 352, 464-469, 494, 661
Freudianism, 468
Friedan, Betty, 286
Friskey, 14, 19, 20
From Assimilation to Zionism, 335
Fryday, Mr., 499
Ft. Sumpter, 22
Fuchs, Klaus, 276
Fuchs-Gold ring, 276
Fulbright, William, 314, 315, 325
Funk and Wagnall's Encyclopedia, 327
Furet, Francois, 328
The g Factor, 47
Günther, Hans, 129
Gabler, Neal, 295, 296, 312
Galileo, 68, 70
Galton, Sir Francis, 50, 51, 57, 640
Ganus Junior High School, 30
Garber, Howard L., 67
Garment, Leonard, 316
Garrity, Judge Arthur, 583
Garvey, Marcus, 42, 171, 277, 556
Gary's Garage, 135
Gary's Super Service, 29
Gaza Strip, 391
Geffen, David, 304
Geller, Rabbi Laura, 286
General Electric, 304
Genesis, 70, 358, 359, 360, 362
The Genetics of the Jews, 454
Gens, 546, 659
Gentilly Woods, 1, 7, 11, 23, 28, 174, 175, 191, 493

710 MY AWAKENING

Geography of Intellect, 450
Georgia, 473, 474, 528
　Atlanta, 22, 142, 530
　Gainesville, 475
Gephardt, Dick, 609
Gerber, David A., 328
Germany, 108, 138, 178, 190, 201, 223, 228, 277-280, 324, 328, 339, 375, 379, 381-388, 402, 408, 409, 412, 418, 423-428, 432-441, 446, 447, 454, 455, 465, 466, 512, 526, 531, 549, 635-661
Berlin, 108, 324, 340, 385, 548
　Berlin Wall, 548
　West Berlin, 547
Germany Must Perish, 401
Ghana, 115, 221, 282
ghettos, 154
Gingrich, Newt, 238
Ginsberg, 306, 321, 322
Gittin, 242, 265
Glacier National Park, 573
Glatzer, Nahum Norbert, 327, 329
Glatzner, 329, 330
Glazer, Nathan, 275
Glees, Paul, 55
Glickman, Dan, 319, 320
Gobineau, 640
Godchauxs, 298
Goethe, 332
Gold, Harry, 276
Goldberg, Arthur, 316
Goldberg, Danny, 302
Golden Age, 537, 538
Goldenson, Leonard, 294, 302, 657
Goldmann, Nahum, 250, 433, 434
Goldwater, Barry, 161, 162, 222, 482, 611
Goloshekin, 234
Gone with the Wind, 26, 305, 307, 480
Good Morning America, 304, 598
Goodman, 283
Gorbachev, Mikhail, 421
Gordis, David, 342
Gore, Al, 321, 609
Gottfredson, Linda, 48
Gottfried, Howard, 296
Gould, 280, 467
Gould, Morton, 309
Gould, Stephen Jay, 54, 55, 74, 132, 279
Graham, Katherine Meyer, 300, 322
Gralnick, Jeff, 304
Grand Canyon, 12, 13, 26, 575
Grand Dragon, 576, 597, 599, 600, 601, 602, 603

Grand Wizard, 482, 594, 607
Grant, Madison, 173, 575
Great Britain, 548, 591, 592, 593, 594, 597, 599, 626
Great Depression, 280
Great Paradox, 109, 110
Great Society, 51, 158
Greece, 121, 475, 526, 534, 535, 536, 537, 538, 539, 540, 541, 542, 543, 544, 545, 549
Greek empire, 50, 113, 121, 122
The Greek Way, 543
Greeks, 113, 118, 121, 122, 261, 468
Green, Gerald, 309
Greenberg, Judge Stanley, 306
Greene, David, 308
Greenglass, David, 276
Greenspan, Alan, 316, 319, 320, 658
Gregory IX, 245
Gregory XIII, 246
Gregory, Dick, 499
Griffin, Gordon, 323
Griffith, D.W., 305, 312
Gritz, Colonel Bo, Ret., 610
Grolier's Encyclopedia, 328, 451
Gross Glockner, 6
Grosset & Dunlap, 433
Guess Who's Coming to Dinner, 308
Guide to Periodical Literature, 652
Gusinsky, Vladimir, 345
Haass, Richard, 318
Ha'avara, 386
Habad-Lubavitch, 252
Haber, Rick, 66, 67
Haganah, 371, 372, 375, 385, 388
Haiti, 125, 126, 127, 175, 176
　Port - au - Prince, 126
Haley, Alex, 308
Halstead, Ward C., 76
Haman, 247, 248
Hamilton, Edith, 542, 543
Hamilton, William, 81
Hannan, Archbishop Phillip, 616
Hannibal, 124
Hanukkah, 247, 460
Hardin, Jim and Eleanor, 503
Harper's, 332
Hart, Gary, 609
Hart, Michael, 113
Hartung, Dr. John, 259
Harvard Crimson, 649
Harvard University, 46, 52, 132
Hassidim, 252
Hatcher, Mildred and Wally, 12, 576

Hatzor, 389
Haul, Keel, 409
Hawaii, 506
Head Start, 64, 77, 149
Health, Education, and Welfare Department, 316
Hebrew Union College, 450
Hedger, Florence, 13
Heidelberg University, 425
Heim, Alan, 296
Helen of Troy, 535
Helladic, 536
Hellenes, 535, 536, 538, 543
Hellespont Strait, 539
Helms, Jesse, 624
Hepburn, Katherine, 308
Herald-Journal, 297
Herbert, Congressman F. Edward, 504
Herman, 549, 550
Herodotus, 535, 538, 541
Herrnstein, Richard J., 47, 137
Hersh, Stuart, 302
Herskovits, Melville, 278
Hertzberg, 330, 467
Herzl, Theodor, 250, 255, 275, 289, 290, 327, 335, 384
Herzog, Elizabeth, 458
Hess, Moses, 234, 249, 274, 411
Higham, John, 446
Highlights of the CJF 1990 National Jewish Population Survey, 457
Hilberg, Raul, 410, 421, 428, 432
Hill, Lance, 624
Hill, Napoleon, 490
Hindu, 517, 518
Hinsley, Sir Frank H., 422
Hintze, James, 494
Hirt-Manheimer, 467
Hispanics, 96, 138, 140, 168, 177
Hiss, Alger, 276
The History and Geography of Human Genes, 85
History of the American People, 483
Hitler, Adolf, 68, 218, 249, 337, 368, 383-388, 418, 428, 435, 457, 547, 548, 602, 660, 661
Hitler's Willing Executioners, 220
Ho Chi Minh Trail, 514
Hoess, 410, 411
Hoffman, Abbie, 276, 314, 357
Holland, 6, 25, 116, 547
Hollander, Xaviera, 352
Holloway, Clyde, 629
Hollywood, 218, 219, 263, 294, 295, 308, 310, 311,

INDEX 711

312, 313, 344, 349, 368, 436
Hollywood Pictures, 302
Hollywood Ten Case, 276
Holmes Jr., Chief Justice Oliver Wendell, 51
Holocaust survivors, 266, 403, 404, 464
Holocaust (miniseries), 218
Holocaust Denier, 417
Homer, 535
homosexuality, 76, 81, 147, 195, 200, 201, 202, 203, 204, 205, 206
Hong Kong, 506, 507, 508
Hook, Sidney, 363
The House Committee on Un-American Activities, 276
House of Representatives, 21, 174
Houston, 302
Huckleberry Finn, 8
The Human Brain, 55
Human Genome Project, 81
Hungary, 223, 324, 328, 357, 361
Hunter, John E., 48
Hunters of the Northern Ice, 92
Hussein, Saddam, 293, 294, 324, 325, 375
Hustling on Gorky Street, 345
Huxley, Julian, 640
Ibrahimi Mosque Massacre, 372
Ice Age, 525, 547
Iceland, 125, 127
Iliad, 535, 536
illegitimacy, 27, 48, 84, 149, 158, 159, 160
Illinois
  Chicago, 22, 67, 76, 150, 233, 276, 302, 340, 488, 551, 583, 588, 625
Illith, 389
Illustrated Sunday Herald, 488
Immigration Act of 1965, 168, 171, 172, 478
Imperium, 474
India, 83, 121, 173, 514, 515, 517, 518, 519, 520, 521, 522, 524, 525, 526, 527, 538, 648
Inequality of the Races, 119
Innocent IV, 246
INS (Immigration and Naturalization Service), 203
International Relations at Cambridge University, 422
Internet, 636, 650, 652, 653, 654, 655, 670, 673
INTERPOL, 139
Into That Darkness, 416
Ionians, 536

Iowa, 177
The IQ Controversy: The Media and Public Policy, 70
Iraq, 356, 375, 454, 455, 463
Iron Age, 536
Irving, David, 217, 343, 357, 398, 400, 418, 419, 420
Israeli Ministry of Religions, 267
Israel's Sacred Terrorism, 373
Italian MSI, 546
Italy, 117, 123, 124, 187, 190, 280, 361, 418, 441, 545, 661, 662
  Florence, 13, 124
  Padua, 124
  Rome, 122, 123, 124, 128
  Venice, 124
Jabalia Massacre, 372
Jabotinsky, Vladimir, 369
Jackson, Andrew, 41
Jackson, Jesse, 120, 146, 182, 578, 611, 671
Jackson, Michael, 587
Jacobites, 238, 258
Jamestown, 116
Japan, 85, 108, 506, 507
  Japanese Tower, 507
  Tokugawa Shogun period, 507
  Tokyo, 108, 506, 507, 508
Japanese, 104, 105, 179
Javits, Jacob, 442-444
Jeff, Morris, 184
Jefferson and/or Mussolini, 546
Jefferson Memorial, 28, 38, 39
Jefferson, Thomas, 10, 22, 23, 27, 28, 38, 39, 40, 41, 44, 57, 169, 171, 542, 612, 620, 649
Jeffrey, Christina, 238
Jensen, Dr. Arthur, 47, 60, 61, 70, 75, 132, 133
Jerusalem Report, 318 *The Jewish Encyclopedia*, 242, 259, 265, 271
The Jewish Family: Myths and Reality, 456
The Jewish Mind, 363
The Jewish Mystique, 450
The Jewish Paradox, 433, 434
The Jewish Religion- Its Influence Today, 241, 265
Jewish and Female, 286
Jewish Art in Context, 248
Jewish Chronicle, 228, 252
Jewish Encyclopedia, 226, 242, 243, 264, 265, 271, 405
Jewish History, Jewish Religion, 266, 279, 327
Jewish Social Studies, 457
Jewish Week, 305, 321, 322

461, 462, 463, 464, 465, 466, 467, 468, 469 *The Jews and Their Lies*, 246
The Jews of the Ottoman Empire and the Turkish Republic, 338
Jews and Judaism in the United States: A Documentary History, 349
Jim Crow, 30, 167
Jimmy the Greek, 79
John F. Kennedy (school), 476
John XXII, 246
Johnson, President Lyndon, 158, 162, 173, 316, 392, 393
Johnson, Rodney, 516, 518, 519, 522
Johnston, J. Bennett, 619, 621, 622, 623, 624
Jones, George, 299
Jones, LeRoi, 134, 143
Jordan, 324
Josephus, 356
Journal of Biological Psychiatry, 80
Judgment at Nuremberg, 407
Judische Rundschau, 385
Julius III, 246
Justice Department, United States, 158, 163, 166
K'adir, J'an, 309
Kafr Qasem Massacre, 372
Kahn, Michael, 295
Kamin, Leon, 54, 132, 279, 280, 467
Kaminski, Janusz, 295
Kann, Peter R., 300
Kansas, 4, 5, 12, 13, 14, 92
The Kansas City Star, 13
Kant, Immanual, 332
Kaplan, Kivie, 221, 282
Kaplan, Rick, 304
Kareski, Georg, 385
Karlin, 454
Katz, Jacob, 328, 336, 337
Katzenberg, Jeffrey, 304, 312
Kaufman, Millard, 599
Kaye, Evelyn, 286, 287, 455
Kayemet, 389
Keats, John, 542
Keith, Sir Arthur, 640
Kemp, Jack, 157, 181
Kenett, 454
Kennedy, John, 283
Kennedy, Robert, 283
Kentucky, 10
Kessler, Robert, 319
Key, Francis Scott, 41
Keynes, J. Maynard, 640
KGB, 228, 357, 408, 411, 421, 427
Khaddafi, Muammar, 324
Khazar (Chazar), 271

Khomeini, Ayatollah, 616, 654
kibbutz, 385, 386
Kibya Massacre, 372
Kids, 302
King Antiochus IV, 247
King Darius, 538
King Faysal, 356
King Jr., Martin Luther, 169
King, Larry, 313
King, Martin Luther (Michael King), 248, 283, 284
Kirshmans, 298
Kissinger, Henry, 316, 318, 504, 508
Klain, Ron, 320, 321
The Klan Action Report, 583
Klan Border Watch, 589
Klan of the Reconstruction South, 479
The Klansman, 599
Klatzkin, Jakob, 249
Klineberg, Otto, 278
Kochman, Thomas, 83, 99
Koestler, Arthur, 271
Kohlmeyer & Company, 340
Kopec, 454
Kornberg, Arthur, 327, 335
Kornblum, John C., 324
Kosmin, 457
Kowloon, 507, 508
Kozak, Michael, 324
Krakowski, Shmuel, 416
Kramer, Stanley, 308, 661
Kreplach, 248
Krisis und Entscheidung (Crisis and Decision), 249
Ku Klux Klan, 1, 305, 307-309, 479, 480-488, 492, 496, 501, 551, 553-555, 558, 566, 571, 574-578, 581-584, 586, 588-, 597, 599, 600-608, 615, 617, 622, 623
Kunin, Madeline, 324
Kunstler, William, 488, 489, 615
Kurtz, Irma, 599-603
La Raza Unida, 184
Lack, Andrew, 304
Lake Garda, 187
Lamarck, Jean, 51
Landau, 457
Landsell, Herbert, 194
Lange, Jessica, 75
Lansing, Sherry, 303
Lansky, Meyer, 342, 343, 345, 661
Laos, 504-515, 526, 529, 555, 626
   Luang Prubang, 505
   Vientiane, 505, 506, 509, 511
Laqueur, Walter, 416
Larry P. vs. Wilson Riles, 58

The Last Days of the Romanovs, 234
Law School Admissions Test (LSAT), 163
Lazarus, Emma, 440, 441, 442
Le Monde, 375
Leahart, Ray, 488, 502, 571
Leave it to Beaver, 7
Leavitt, Rep., 442
Lebanon, 368, 372, 373, 393, 397
Lebensraum, 375, 438
LeBoef, Cynthia, 553, 555
Lee, Harry, 612
Lee, Robert E., 10, 22, 556
Legacy of the Melting Pot, 172 441
Lehman, Herbert, 442, 443
Lelyveld, Joseph, 299
Lemurs, 104
Lenin, 220, 225, 227, 232, 234, 235, 379, 398
Leonidas, 535, 538, 539, 540
Leuchter, Fred, 423, 424, 425, 426
Leutheusser-Schnarrenberger, 425
Levi, Edward, 316
Levin, Gerald, 300, 301, 302
Levin, Michael, 65, 156
Levine, Alan J., 304
Levinson, Barry, 344
Levinson, Stanley, 283, 284
Leviticus, 258, 259, 260, 262, 348
Levitts, 298
Levy, Mordechai, 599, 615
Lewis, Bernard, 328
Lewontin, Richard, 132 54 279, 280, 467
Liberia, 41, 42
   Monrovia, 42
Liberty, 390, 391, 392, 393, 394, 395, 441, 442
Lieberman, 320, 459
Lifetime Television, 302
Lilienthal, 266, 464
Lincoln, Abraham, 22, 28, 37, 40, 41, 43, 170
   as "The Great Emancipator", 37
   Gettysburg Address, 28
Lindbergh, Charles, 403
Lindsay, James, 485, 486, 487, 553, 556, 560, 567, 574, 575, 576, 585
Lipshutz, Robert, 459
Lipstadt, Deborah, 416
Litani River, 373
The Living Races of Man, 92 376
The London Times, London, 526, 591, 594, 595, 596
London Daily Mirror, 592

Long, Huey, 574
Lopez, 349
Lopez, Aaron, 349
Los Angeles, 302, 346
Louisiana
   Baton Rouge, 491, 495, 499, 547, 576, 618, 621
   Lake Ponchartrain, 16, 17, 476, 477, 551
   Metairie, 588, 598, 608, 612, 615, 617, 621, 625
   New Orleans, 1, 4, 7, 12-22, 25, 29-32, 94, 101, 135, 136, 144, 153, 154, 164, 165, 171, 184, 220, 256, 295-298, 310, 353, 391, 441, 473-478, 485, 490, 491, 508, 548-560, 564, 566-571, 574, 585, 600, 604-609, 615, 616, 630, 642
      Benjamin Franklin High School, 153
      Carondolet Street, 32, 33
      Claiborne Avenue, 25
      French Quarter, 144
      New Orleans Police Intelligence, 555, 558
   Plaquemines Parish, 32
   Slidell, 17
   St. Bernard parish, 487, 609
   St. Tammany parish, 487, 633
Louisiana State University (LSU), 83, 310, 311, 434, 489-498, 501, 503, 504, 511, 552, 560, 571, 574, 576, 579, 630, 654
Luchaire, Achille, 334
Luedtke, Kurt, 295
Lumet, Sidney, 296
Lustig, Branko, 295
Luther, Martin, 246, 267, 283, 347
Lynn, Richard, 65
Lysenko, T. D., 51
Maariv, 314, 317, 325
MacDonald, Kevin, 281, 445, 451
Madison, James, 41
The Madonna and Child, 468
Maimonides, 240, 333, 334, 337
Maine, 432
Man and Superman, 641
Man the Hunter, 92

Man's Most Dangerous Myth: The Fallacy of Race. See Montagu, Ashley
Mankiewicz, Frank, 316
Marathon, 538
Marcus, Jacob, 334, 348, 350, 405
Marines, United States, 126
Marion, David, 306
Markhasev, Mikail, 346
Markton family, 174
Marx, Karl, 223, 232, 233, 234, 249, 465, 467, 530
Maryland, 149, 155, 194, 556, 608
Massachusetts, 583
　Boston, 22
The Master Key to Riches, 490
Mauritania, 115
Mayer, Arno J., 426
Mayer, Gus, 298
Mayer, Louis, 307
MCA, 304
McArthur, James, 604, 607
McCall, R.B., 47
McCarthy, Senator Joseph, 300, 315
McCormick, Colonel Robert, 300
McGonagle, William, 393
McGovern, George, 508
McMillan, Admiral Ira, Ret., 607
McPherson, Jim, 88
McVeigh, Timothy, 401
McWilliams, Louis, 488
Mead, Margaret, 278
The Mediator, 466
Mediterranean, 533, 538, 542
Medved, Michael, 311, 312
Mein Kampf, 245
Mekong River, 509
Melville, 278, 332
Memories of My Life, 640
Menuhin, Moshe, 249
Merchant of Venice, 305, 306, 333, 364
　Shylock, 305, 333, 364
Merinid, 356
Mesopotamian, 366
Mestizo, 448
Mexicans, 63, 121, 138, 140, 154, 169, 173, 179, 183
Mexico, 116, 117, 125, 175-177, 184, 276, 323, 381
Meyerhoff, Barbara, 453
Michaelangelo, 124, 545
Michigan, 48
　Detroit, 156, 177
　Kalamazoo, 48
Microsoft Encarta, 327, 328, 330, 367, 368, 380, 421, 432
Middle Ages, 68, 542, 565, 670

Mideast, 218, 314, 318, 327, 367, 368, 373, 379, 388, 499, 500, 512, 596
military, United States, 14, 22, 48, 119, 126

The Mismeasure of Man, 55, 74
Milken, Michael, 340, 341, 661
Milky Way, 474
Miller, 83, 101
Miller, Edward, 94, 451
Milton, 332
Milwaukee Project, The, 66
Minchuck, Peter, 306
The Mind of Man in Africa, 74
The Mind of Primitive Man, 277
Minhinnette, Babs, 494
Minhinnette, Virgil, 494
Miramax Films, 302
Mischel, Walter, 83, 84
Mississippi, 32, 128, 171, 283, 309, 444, 485, 554, 566, 576, 584
Missouri, 4, 5, 12, 552
Mitchell, Margaret, 307
Mitzphen-Ramen, 389
Mogilevich, Semion, 346
Mohammed, Khalid, 171
Molen, Jerry, 295
Money, Dr. John, 199
Mongol, 356
Mongoloid, 87, 90
Monroe, James, 41, 42
Montagu, Ashley (Israel Ehrenberg), 30, 84, 85, 279
Moors, 116
Morning Herald, 144
Morning Register, 297
Morocco, 356, 455
Moscow, 361, 412, 421
Mosely, Sir Oswald, 574
Moses, 228, 234, 238, 249, 258, 259, 274, 282, 343, 382
Moses and Monotheism, 280, 282
Moses, Gilbert, 308
Moskowitz, Miriam, 276
Mossad, 527, 532, 533, 534
Mossad le-Aliya Bet, 386
Mount Everest, 103
Mourant, 454
Movement to Opportunity, 149, 157
Mozart, 98, 131
Mt. Hood, 21
MTV, 303
mulattos, 89
Muller, Dr., 425
multiculturalism, 8, 43, 155, 171, 181, 182, 189, 190
Multi-Regional Hypothesis, 90

Munich, 526, 546, 547
Murdoch, Rupert, 304
Murray, Charles, 47
Muslim, 522
Muslims, 128
Mussolini, 574
Mycenaean, 366
The Myth of the Jewish Race, 456
Napoleon, 339, 347, 413
Nashville, 581, 582
National Academy of Sciences, 62
National Alliance, 295
National Archives, United States, 488
National Association for the advancement of colored people (NAACP), 184, 220, 221, 222, 282, 283
National Association for the Advancement of White People (NAAWP), 607, 608, 613, 625
National Basketball Association (NBA), 78, 157
National Collaborative Perinatal Project, 75
National Convention, Democratic and Republican, 38
National Enquirer, 220
National Football League (NFL), 78
National Geographic, 16, 235
National Organization of Women (NOW), 289
National Security Council, 316, 317, 318, 320, 345, 394
National Socialism, 383, 387
National Vanguard, 295
Native Americans. *See* American Indians
Natural History, 280
Natural Selection, 640, 641
Nature, 280, 469, 475, 575, 638, 639
Navy, United States, 391, 392, 393, 485, 487, 607, 623, 647
Nazareth, 389
NBC, 294, 301, 304, 307
Nelson, Jack, 554, 555
Nepal, 596
Nero, 269, 331
Netherlands, 5
Network, 293, 295, 302, 326
Neufeld, Victor S., 304
New Delhi, 515, 517, 520, 521, 533
New World, 84, 116
New World Entertainment, 304
New World Jewry, 1492-1776, 350

714 MY AWAKENING

New World Order, 285, 439, 463
New York, 1, 67, 122, 138, 143, 157, 165, 178, 231, 234, 264, 291-302, 305, 314, 322-325, 329, 340, 342, 353, 371, 381, 385, 389, 402, 434, 442, 446, 447, 474, 528, 548, 552, 564, 581, 592, 596, 606, 657
New York City, 231, 305, 325, 342, 381, 389
The New York Times, 67, 143, 157, 291, 294, 295, 296, 298, 299, 314, 322, 329, 353, 371, 446 299, 324, 402, 446, 447
New Zealand, 189
Newhouse, 476
Newmann, 340, 341, 342
Newport, 349, 352
Newsweek, 59, 280, 294, 299, 300, 308, 343, 352, 597, 647
"Next Year in Jerusalem", 249
Nichols, General Francis T., 553
Nickelodeon, 303
Nigeria, 179
Night, 404
1965 Immigration Act, 440, 444
1984, 40
Nix, Dennis, 552
Nixon, President Richard, 295, 299, 316, 318, 504, 508, 511, 611
Nixon, Richard, 162
NKVD, 228, 285
Nobel Prize, 647, 655
None Dare Call It Treason, 222
North America, 115, 116
North Carolina, 584, 624
Northern Hemisphere, 92
Northern Ireland, 189
Norway, 324, 662
Number Our Days, 453
Nuremberg, 361, 382, 385, 390, 400, 405, 407-410, 412, 414, 415, 419, 423, 431, 434, 438, 531, 547, 635
O'Dell, Jack, 284
O'Sullivan, Freddie, 555, 558, 605
O'Toole, Brian, 49
Ober, Eric, 304
Ochs, Adolph, 299
Odyssey, 535, 536
Oklahoma City bombing, 373, 401

One Flew Over the Cuckoo's Nest, 75
Origin of Species, 119, 451 450, 640
Origin of the Races, 92
Orleans Parish Prison, 561, 562, 563, 567, 568
Orlet, Dr., 425
Orwell, George, 39, 235, 635, 674
Oschner Hospital, 477
O'Toole, Brian, 49
Ottoman, 338, 356, 357
Our Crowd, 340
Ovitz, Michael, 312
Oyon Qara Massacre, 372
Padua, 508
Paine, Thomas, 220, 543
Pakistan, 526, 527
Paley, William, 294, 302, 657
Paramount Pictures, 303
Pariahs, 518, 524
Paris, 318, 324, 381, 419
The Parthenon, 113, 535
Passover, 247, 460
Passover Plot, 263
Patai, Ralph and Jennifer, 456
Patai, Raphael, 363
Paternal Provisioning versus Mate Seeking in Human Populations, 94
Pathet Laos, 505
patricians, 122, 123
Patton, General George S., 403, 409
Paul (Apostle), 240
Paul IV, 246
Paved With Good Intentions, 162
Pearlstine, Norman, 303
Peking, 596
Peloponnesus, 536
Pendell, Elmer, 109
Pentagon, 623
People Magazine, 303
People's Canal, 11
Percy, Charles, 325
Perelman, Ronald, 304
Perez, Judge Leander, 32
Perlman, 442
Perry, James M., 315
Persia, 538
Pharisees, 240, 245, 248, 263, 269
Phelps, Ashton, 298
Philadelphia, 232, 283, 302, 306, 349
Philistines, 238, 258
Phoenicians, 543
Pierce, Dr. William L., 295, 302, 304
Pinky, 2, 25, 26, 32, 33, 135, 170, 627

Piper, Dr. Franciszek, 411, 418, 420
Pius IV, 246
Pius V, 246
Plataea, 539
Plato, 67, 535, 543
Playboy, 396
Pledge of Allegiance, 23
Plessy v. Ferguson, 482
Plymouth, 4, 5, 116
Podhoretz, Norman, 285
Poitier, Sidney, 308
Poland, 324, 334, 338, 353, 405, 411, 419, 427, 438, 444, 454, 455, 548, 657
Poliakov, Leon, 328
Polish Communist, 420
Pollard, Johnathan, 317, 357
Poppaea Sabina, 270, 331
Popular Mechanics, 16
Portnoy's Complaint, 602
Portugal, 116
Possony, Stephan, 450
Post Herald, 297
Post-Standard, 297
Potiphar, 358
Potomac River, 28
Pound, Ezra, 546
Prague, 596
Prentice Hall, 303
Priests, 302
Prince, Melissa Weaver, 207
Princeton University, 426
Prinz, Joachim, 384
Pritchard, Hesketh, 126
Profiles in Courage, 407
promiscuity, 84, 159, 209, 212
Prostitution and Prejudice, 353
The Population Bomb, 185
Prynne, William, 347
Psychological Bulletin, 83
Ptolemies, 356
Public Broadcasting System (PBS), 305, 306, 351, 355
Publisher's Weekly, 301
Puerto Ricans, 138
Pulitzer Prize, 407
Pullen, Brian, 335
Purim (Feast of Lots), 247, 248, 364, 460
Putnam, Carleton, 32, 42, 45, 70, 132, 133, 167, 174
Pyramids, 113
Pythagorean Theorem, 113, 495
Qana, 373, 374
Quayle, Dan, 618, 627
Queen Isabella, 116
R.M.S. Queen Mary, 7
Raab, Earl, 447, 448
Rabinowitz, 334
Race: Man's Most Dangerous Myth, 279

Race and Reason, 32, 33, 37, 67, 69, 135, 256
Race, Evolution, and Behavior, 461
Race, Riots, and Revolution, 32
racism, 27, 30, 37, 43, 70, 115, 135, 136, 137, 139, 148, 157, 158, 159, 169, 175, 181
  racist, 1, 28, 58, 59, 68, 113, 115, 137, 140, 141, 142, 144, 145, 146, 156
The Racialist, 496, 498
Random House, 247, 301, 333, 424
Random House Dictionary of the English Language, 247
Rankin, John, 444
Raphael, Mark, 349
Rapoport, Louis, 234
Rassinier, Paul, 403
rats, white, 71, 72, 197, 198, 200, 201
Raven Progressive Matrices, 66
Raymond, Henry, 299
Reagan, President Ronald, 316, 616
Rebecca, 362, 366
Reconstruction, 479, 480, 482, 483, 484, 548, 592, 607
Reconstruction era, 305, 308, 309, 389, 480
Rector, Robert, 77
Red Chinese, 376, 511
Red Sea, 370
Redstone, Sumner, 301, 303
Reed, Cindy, 1
Rehfeld, Barry, 340
Reich, Robert, 317, 319
Reichbloom, Bob, 304
Reichstag, 547
Reinharz, Jehuda, 328
Religiosity of the Indo-Europeans, 129
Renaissance, the, 117, 123, 124, 545
repatriation movement, 40, 41, 42
Republican, 294, 297, 315, 318, 319, 407
Revlon, 304
The Revolt-The Story of the Irgun, 371
Reynier, Jacques de, 371
Rhine river, 549
Rhode Island, 349, 352
Rich, Evelyn, 641
Rifkind, Judge Simon, 443
Rig Veta, 518
Rio De Janeiro, 108
Rio Grande, 116

Rise and Fall of the Third Reich, 415
The Rise of David Duke, 604
Rivera, Geraldo, 598
Riverside Military Academy, 473, 474
RJF, 416
Robertson, Wilmot, 301
Rockwell, George Lincoln, 487, 488, 489, 546, 591
Rocky, 97
Roemer, Buddy, 619, 620, 621, 629
Rohatyn, Felix, 324, 342
Romania, 324
Romanian, 415
Romans, 118, 122, 123, 124, 265, 266, 268, 363, 377
Rome, 526, 544, 545, 546, 549, 550
Rome and Jerusalem, 249
Roosevelt, President Franklin Delano, 251
Roosevelt, Theodore, 10, 19, 28, 32, 641, 649
Roots, 308, 309, 376
Roper, Trevor, 418
Rose, 280
Rose, Stephen, 54
Rosen, Sal, 306
Rosenberg, Ethel and Julius, 276
Rosenthal, A.M., 291, 329, 446, 447
Rosenthal, Erich, 328
Ross, Dennis, 317, 318, 320
Ross, Edward A., 317, 320, 443
Rostow, Walt, 316
ROTC, 493, 503
Roth, Joe, 302, 312
Roth, Phillip, 602
Rothschild, 230, 232, 233, 339, 340, 341
Rothschild, Baron, 232
Rothstein, Murray, 301, 303
Roxbury, 583
Royal Geographic Society, 126
Royal Laotian forces, 505
Rubin, Jerry, 275, 311, 314
segregation, 25, 27, 43, 145, 158, 170, 189
S: The Secret Relationship Between Blacks and Jews, 351
Selznick, David O., 307
Send These to Me: Immigrants in Urban America, 446
Seneca, Lucius, 347
Serbs, 189
Sereny, Gitta, 416
Sermon on the Mount, 545
Seven Years in Tibet, 312
Sex Versus Civilization, 109

sexually transmitted diseases, 96
  syphilis, 96, 151
Shahak, Dr. Israel, 255, 266, 267, 389, 464
Shakespeare, William, 67, 202, 305, 332, 364, 468
Shamir, Yitshak, 369
Sharafat Massacre, 372
Sharett, Moshe, 373
Sharon, Ariel, 373
Shatila, 372, 373, 397
Shaw, George Bernard, 640, 641
Shawcross, Sir Hartley, 415
Sheehan, Patrick, 144
sheigetz, 252
Shell Oil Company, 5, 7, 13, 15
Shephardim, 271, 454
Sherman, 320, 410
shiksa, 252
shikselke, 252
Shirer, William, 415
Shockley Semiconductor Laboratories, 647
Shockley, William, 57, 70, 132, 133, 647, 648, 649, 650, 654, 655
Shuey, Audrey, 32, 58
Siegel, Martin, 315, 341, 344
Silberman, Charles, 147, 445
Silicon Valley, 647
Simis, Konstantin, 345
Simon, Paul, 609
Simon, Theodore, 46
Simpson, O. J., 87, 142, 166, 171
Simpson, O.J., 288
Single Origin Hypothesis, 90
Sistine Chapel, 106, 124, 272, 468
Slack, Alfred, 276
slaves, 23, 38, 41, 42, 109, 116, 120, 187
smallpox, 113, 203
Smirnov, L.N., 414
Smith, Drew, 172, 441, 478
Smith, Mattie, 220, 232, 236, 275
Smith, Richard, 11
Smithsonian, 218, 280
Smithsonian Institution, 218
Snow, C.P., 450
Snyder, Tom, 307, 581, 587
Sobell, Morton, 276
The Social Life of the Jews, 334
Sociobiology- A New Synthesis, 451
Socrates, 535, 536, 542
Solomon, 366
Solzhenitsyn, Aleksandr, 270
Soncino (translation of Talmud), 242, 244, 265

Sony Corporation, 304
Sophocles, 541
South African National Party, 551
South America, 115, 116, 150
Southeast Asia, 490, 504, 505, 510
Southie, 583
Soviet Gulags, 217
Soviet Union, 51, 229, 230, 236, 270, 285, 345, 356, 377, 383, 399, 409, 438, 511
Spain, 482, 590
Spanish Inquisition, 219
Spanner, Dr. Rudolf, 415
Sparta, 535
Spartans, 539
Spearman, Charles Edward, 46
Special Olympics, 642
Spengler, 119
Spengler, Oswald, 533, 637
Spielberg, Steven, 295, 304, 352, 661, 663
Spitz, Herman, 67
Spitz, Rabbi Leon, 364
Spock, Dr. Benjamin, 499, 500, 662
Sports Illustrated, 303
Springer, Jerry, 606
St. John's College, 422
Stalin, 225, 227, 229, 234, 285, 398, 435
Stalin's War Against the Jews, 234
Stalingrad, 540, 548
Stanley Siegel Show, 581
Starski, Allan, 295
State Department, United States, 490, 505, 528, 529
Stein, Ben, 295
Steinem, Gloria, 286
Stern Gang, 375, 386, 400
Stern, Wilhelm, 46
Stoddard, Lothrop, 173
Stolper, 456
Stormer, John A., 222
The Story of Man, 92
Streicher, Julius, 382
Strole, Zena, 7
Strother, Raymond, 629
Student Government Association, LSU, 499
The Student Non-Violent Coordinating Committee (SNCC), 283
Students for a Democratic Society (SDS), 498
Sudan, 114, 115, 128
  Nuba Mountains, 115
Sulzberger, 299, 322
Sunday Pictorial, 408
Supreme Court, United States, 30, 43, 51, 152, 162, 163

Sverdlov, 227, 228, 234
Swaggart, Jimmy, 271
Swartzbaugh, Richard, 466
Sweden, 324, 662
Swiss Family Robinson, 16
Switzerland, 6, 138, 150, 324, 463
Syria, 247, 356, 392
Syromolotov, 234
Tacitus, 347, 550
Taft, Robert, 403, 407, 431
Taj Mahal, 516, 520, 521, 522
The Tales of Uncle Remus, 29
Talmudic Omissions, 267
Tamir, 454
Tarrants, Tommy, 555
Taylor, A.J.P., 418
Taylor, Jared, 162
Tay-Sachs disease, 272, 454
Tecumseh, William, 410
Tel Aviv, 354, 400, 527, 529, 530, 531
Telegraph Sunday Magazine, 599
The Ten Commandments, 219, 251
Tennessee, 481, 485, 582
  Pulaski, 481, 482
Terman, Lewis, 46
The Testing of Negro Intelligence, 32, 58
testosterone, 84, 96, 100, 136, 152, 197, 205
Teutonic, 540, 549, 602, 665
Texas, 154, 485, 589
Thailand, 509, 515
Thanksgiving, 8
Thatcher, Becky, 175
Present Immigration to the American People, 443
Themistocles, 539
Thermopylae, 535, 538, 539, 540
Thessalian, 539
The Terrible Secret, 416
Thessaly, 536
They Dare to Speak Out, 325
Third World, 134, 149, 177-187, 207, 484, 485, 511, 512, 524, 525, 551, 593, 594, 610, 635, 641, 659, 671, 672
Thirteenth Tribe, 271
Thomas, D., 64
Thompson, Roswell, 542, 556
Thucydides, 541
Thunderbolt, 294
Time, 280, 294, 298, 300, 301, 302, 303, 352, 402, 473, 647, 649, 652
Time on the Cross, 160
Time Warner, 301, 302, 303
Time Warner Trade Group, 301
Times-Herald, 300, 337

Times-Picayune, 31, 88, 135, 217, 295-298, 325, 353, 355, 396, 476, 609, 615, 625, 627, 629, 635
Tisch, Laurence, 303, 304, 342
Titanic, 171
Toback, James, 344
Today, 279, 304, 306, 329, 335, 351, 401, 412, 432, 444
Tokyo Disneyland, 302
Tolstoy, Leo, 67, 230, 332
Tom Sawyer, 8, 175
Tomorrow Show, 307, 581
Tonight Programme, 594
The Toronto Globe & Mail, 418
The Unheavenly City Revisited, 84
Totalitarians, 108
Totem and Taboo, 281
Touchstone Pictures, 302
Touchstone Television, 302
Touro Synagogue, 558
Toynbee, 113, 119
Tracy, Spencer, 308
Trafficant, John, 610
Trebisch, Lincoln, 178
Treen, David, 612
Treen, John, 612, 614-616, 619
Trinidad, 83
Trotsky, Leon (Lev Bronstein), 220, 223, 225, 227, 232, 233, 253, 285, 379, 435, 530, 558
Truman, President Harry S., 173
Truth at Last, 321
Tulane University, 488, 489, 567, 615
Turner Broadcasting System (TBS), 303
TV Guide, 309
Twain, Mark, 237, 332
20th Century Fox Films, 304
3214 Dumaine Street, 551
U.S. Agency for International Development, 473
U.S. National Archives, 418
U.S. Naval Hospital, 534
U.S. News and World Report, 294, 300, 647
U.S.A. Today, 429
U.S.S. Liberty, 391, 393
U.S.S. Stark, 393
UCLA, Berkeley, 575
Union (United States), 22, 23, 67
United Cab Company, 630
United Nations (UN), 126
Universal Pictures, 304
University of California, Berkeley, 46, 50, 182

INDEX 717

University of Chicago, 76
University of Kansas, Lawrence, 13
University of Minnesota, 52
University of North Carolina, Chapel Hill, 584
University of Texas, 55, 163
University of Washington, 574
University of Western Ontario, 139
Uprising, 357
Uruguay, 118
USAID, 490, 505, 509
USSR: The Corrupt Society, 345
Van Den Haag, Ernest, 450
Van Houten, 474
Van Pelt, Robert Jan, 420
Vanderbilt University, 582
Varna, 518, 523
Varus, General Quintilius, 549, 550
Vashem, Yad, 416
Viacom, Inc., 301, 303, 304
Vidal, Gore, 266
Vienna
    Russian Zone, 6
Viet Cong, 318, 357, 489, 551, 624
Vietnam, 285, 314, 318, 357, 399, 432, 473, 477, 489, 493, 499-509, 514, 555, 580
Vietnam War Moratorium Committee, 504
Vietnam Era, 54, 144
The View from Sunset Boulevard, 295
The Village Voice, 346
Viking Press, 418
Virgin Mary, 244, 246, 265
Virginia, 1, 22, 64, 149
Voikov, 234
Voltaire, 328, 332
Von Fremd, Mike, 617
Waldman, I.D., 64
The Wall Street Journal, 294, 295, 299, 300 300, 315
Wallace, George, 556, 557, 558, 570, 609, 610
Walt Disney Company, 302, 304, 312, 468
Walt Disney Picture Group, 302
Walt Disney Television, 302
Walter-McCarran act of 1952, 443, 446
War Between the States (The War for Southern

Independence, The Civil War), 238, 305, 410, 412
Warner Books, 301
Warner Brothers Studio, 303
Warner Music, 302, 303
Warner, Dr. James K., 589
Warren Commission, 436
Washington Daily News, 408
Washington Post, 66, 294, 295, 299, 300, 314, 322, 344, 393
Washington, D.C., 28, 38, 40, 41, 139, 143, 148, 149, 155-157, 176, 218, 292, 322, 325, 337, 340, 368, 436, 437, 631, 650, 660
Washington, George, 10, 154, 169, 504
Wassal, Don, 610
Waterloo, 339, 340
Wayne, John, 8, 98
Weaver Prince, Melissa, 207
Weber vs. Kaiser Aluminum, 162
Weber, Mark, 416
Webster, Daniel, 41
Wefald, Knud, 443
Weinbaum, Sidney, 276
Weinberg, Richard, 64, 65
Weinfeld, 459
Weinstein, 302
Weir, Mrs., 117
Weizmann, Chaim, 361
welfare, 48, 52, 99, 109, 131, 134, 151, 158, 159-161, 172, 174, 177-181, 183, 184, 186, 207
Wells, H.G., 118, 640
Weltfish, Gene, 278
Wepner, Chuck, 97
Western Destiny, 474
Western Hemisphere, 116, 118, 125
Westinghouse Electric Corporation, 304
Weyl, Nathaniel, 450
White Youth Alliance, 496, 499, 502
White, Ed, 485
White, Walter, 349
Who Brought the Slaves to America?, 349
Who's Who in American Jewry, 221, 253
Who's Who in World Jewry, 220, 253

Why Did the Heavens Not Darken?: The "Final Solution" in History, 426
Why Race Matters, 156
Wicker, Judge Thomas, 589
Wiesel, Elie, 404-406, 435
Wiesenthal, Simon, 313, 404, 412, 415, 418, 437, 636, 653, 654, 662
Wilbanks, Dr. William, 141
Wilkins, Roy, 222, 282
Wilkinson, Bill, 605
William C. Claiborne school, 7
Williams, G.C., 451
Williams, Ronald, 165
Wilson, D. S., 451
Wilson, Dr. Edward O., 2, 58, 132, 451
Wilson, Edward, 451
Wilson, Woodrow, 305, 316, 381, 482, 658
Wilton, Robert, 225, 234
Wolper, David, 308
World Jewish Congress, 304, 324, 383, 385, 433, 434, 439
World News Tonight, 304
World War II, 219, 227, 348, 356, 403, 427, 429, 430, 445, 448
World Zionist Organization, 250, 386
Xerxes, 538, 539
Yad Le'akhim, 267
Yassin, Deir, 371, 372, 400
Yediot Ahronot, 371
Yellowstone National Park, 573
YMCA, 515, 522
Yockey, Francis Parker, 474
Young Americans for Freedom, 494, 502
Yurvsky, 234
Zaillian, Steve, 295
Zaire, 114, 189
Zalman, Rabbi Shneur, 252, 253
Zborowski, Mark, 458
Zimbabwe, 66
Zindi, Fred, 66
Zionist Occupational Government (ZOG), 323, 325, 466
Zucker, Jeff, 304
Zuckerman, Mortimer B., 300
Zundel, Ernst, 423
Zyklon B, 412, 422, 423, 424, 425

THE AWAKENING PROJECT

Has the powerful message of *My Awakening* moved you? Many of its readers are committed to its widespread dissemination throughout the United States and the world. A fund has begun for that purpose. The project seeks to place the book in school and public libraries and to present it to leading personalities. The Awakening Project seeks to deliver this vital book to every major author, entrepreneur, scientist, educator, clergyman, entertainer and elected official in the Western World. Your Generous donation to the Awakening Project is much appreciated. We are convinced that when this book becomes widely read — it will change the course of history.

THE AWAKENING PROJECT
CARE/OF
BOX 88
COVINGTON, LA 70434